BEHAVIOR IN ORGANIZATIONS: A SYSTEMS APPROACH TO MANAGING

BEHAVIOR IN ORGANIZATIONS: A SYSTEMS APPROACH TO MANAGING

Second Edition

EDGAR F. HUSE
JAMES L. BOWDITCH

Boston College

ADDISON-WESLEY PUBLISHING COMPANY
Reading, Massachusetts
Menlo Park, California • London • Amsterdam • Don Mills, Ontario • Sydney

HD
58.7
.H87
1977
X

ISBN 0-201-02965-0
  DEFGHIJ-MA-79

PREFACE

The thrust of this book is to develop an understanding of behavior in organizations. It is *people* who make an organization succeed or fail, regardless of the type of organization. The X-ray machines, the computers, the welfare programs, the mortgage loans, the lathes, the "signing on" procedures, the planning and organizing that go into making an organization work—all involve people.

But human behavior does not occur in isolation. Behavior in organizations can be understood only in context. In other words, human behavior is highly influenced by the design of the organization and the nature and way in which information and work flow through the organization. Therefore, behavior in organizations can be understood only by also understanding the entire organization as a complex system composed of interrelated subsystems.

Our purpose is to help you become more effective as an individual in coping with organizational life—both today and in the future. Why is this important? It is important because so much of a person's waking time is spent in contact with various organizations. Most people were born in an organization—a hospital. Students have contact with educational organizations. Citizens are affected by municipal, state, and federal governments. As participants, people belong to such formal and informal organizations as the Girl Scouts, Little League, Sierra Club, bowling team, tennis club, high school "group," college fraternity or sorority, and bridge or poker clubs. Most adults hold jobs in organizations—law firms, dental clinics, travel bureaus, hospitals, universities, or industrial companies. Generally, people spend at least eight hours a day in such formal organizations, followed by the time spent in clubs, political activities, or social events. Even when watching television or driving down a street, a person is involved with or affected by organizations; for example, stopping for a traffic light is a consequence of an organizational decision. Organizations cannot be avoided.

This book is also concerned with the impact of rapidly accelerating change—on individuals, organizations, and the culture within which both exist—and how to deal effectively with change. Just as organizations are inevitable, so too is change. Exhibit 1 gives an example of such change. Can you imagine such rules being applied today? People would regard the rules as ridiculous. Yet those rules *were* taken seriously less than a hundred years ago.

Therefore, organizations must be considered in contact with their environ-

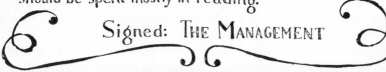

Rules To Employees
CARSON, PIRIE, SCOTT CO., CHICAGO ~ 1856

1. Store must be open from 6 a.m. to 9 p.m.

2. Store must be swept, counters and base shelves dusted, lamps trimmed filled and chimneys cleaned, a pail of water, also a bucket of coal brought in before breakfast, and attend to customers who will call.

3. Store must not be open on the Sabbath Day unless necessary and then only for a few minutes.

4. The employee, who is in the habit of smoking Spanish cigars, being shaved at the barber shop, going to dances and other places of amusement, will surely give his employer reason to be suspicious of his honesty and integrity.

5. Each employee must not pay less than $5 per year to the church and must attend Sunday School regularly.

6. Men employees are given one evening a week for courting and two if they go to prayer meeting.

7. After 14 hours of work in the store, the leisure time should be spent mostly in reading.

Signed: THE MANAGEMENT

Exhibit 1 Work rules at Carson Pirie Scott & Co., 1882.

ment, including the impact of new technologies and knowledge on organizations and the way they operate. For example, in the future, hospitals, as organizatizons, will be run much differently from the way they are today. Similarly, the appearance and activities of tomorrow's business organization may well be quite different from what they are today. We cannot accurately predict what those changes will be. But we can say flatly that change will occur at an increasing pace. The more successful manager will be more adept at *managing* change rather than only reacting to change.

Our *point* is that in this culture, we are continuously in contact and interaction with organizations. Our *emphasis* and *thrust* are primarily on behavior in work organizations. Our *belief* is that organizations in the future will change even more rapidly than they have in the past. Our *concern* is that you understand such change and become adept at dealing with and controlling change, especially on the job. If change did not occur, we would not have needed to write a second edition of this book. There have been extensive additions to our knowledge about behavior in organizations since the first edition, and we have reflected such changes in this edition.

Before discussing the book itself, we would like to share with you some of our thoughts about the term "theory." We will be dealing with theories throughout the book. Building a theory occurs in much the same way as did the early settlement of America. A small clearing was hacked out of the forest by a pioneer. Other pioneers made their own clearings and built their separate cabins. Later, when cabins were closer together, footpaths began to emerge and eventually became roads.

The evolution of management thought has occurred in much the same fashion. In one part of the "forest" someone developed a "clearing" (theory) while someone else was developing another theory, quite independently. Now, the theories are interconnected by conceptual pathways and roads. Yet theories of organizational behavior and administrative science are continually being revised. In the same way, the Apollo and Viking missions have brought about revisions in theories of both the moon and Mars, based on landings (clearings) in different spots. Throughout the book, we will show how new developments are occurring in the behavioral and related sciences, together with their links to the past.

This is not a "how to" book in the sense of providing "off the shelf" answers to specific problems. Rather, we have attempted to provide relevant theory instead of specific techniques. Relevant theory can show how to analyze an organization or a specific organizational problem so that the individual can then make judicious selections of specific techniques. There do exist appropriate techniques for solving specific problems, but the most important problem is to define the goals and the source of the difficulty. Here, relevant theory is essential. Throughout the book, we provide concrete illustrations and examples of problems in organizations so that you can become more analytical in defining problems and selecting better techniques to solve problems. In addition, the learning objectives, cases, exercises, and questions at the end of the chapters are designed to help you apply what you have learned to real-life situations or to classroom simulations.

Finally, writing, reviewing, editing, and producing a book is a complex process. Although only two names appear as authors, a number of people made significant contributions to the publication of this book. A number of reviewers made valuable comments, recommendations, and suggestions about the content, structure, and style of the first edition. Specifically, we would like to thank the following: Jon H. Barrett (University of Texas at Austin), Wilmar F. Bernthal (University of Colorado), Frederic Finch (University of Massachusetts), Bernard L. Hinton (Indiana University), Thomas A. Kayser, David A. Kolb (Massachusetts Institute of Technology), Gerald C. Leader (Tulane University), Leon C. Megginson (Louisiana State University), John W. Newstrom (Arizona State University), Walter Nord (Washington University), Benson Rosen (University of North Carolina), Peter B. Vaill (University of Connecticut), and Arthur Walker (Northeastern University).

Of particular help in making this second edition possible were Joseph Nowlin (University of Delaware), Fredrick Wickert (Michigan State), David Ford (University of Texas at Dallas), Bernard L. Hinton (Indiana University), and Halsey Jones (University of Texas at Permian Basin). Our special thanks are extended to the large number of users of the first edition who were willing to spend their time on the telephone giving us helpful information and recommendations for improvement.

We would like to thank the following people at Boston College for their comments and suggestions: Dalmar Fisher, John W. Lewis, III, Vivian Nossiter, and Jack Rosin; Pearl Alberts, reference librarian, who can find the most obscure references; Dwight Adams, who gave us case-writing assistance; Cynthia Isaacson and Gerald Russo, our assistants, who cheerfully took on every assignment given them; and Beth Bridges McLeish and Anne Shenkman, who gave us secretarial support. We also thank the Reverends J. Donald Monan, S.J., and Charles Donovan, S.J., for their encouragement and Dean Albert J. Kelley for arranging for secretarial support.

We would also like to express our appreciation to the staff at Addison-Wesley for their help and encouragement in our undertaking. Last, but certainly not least, we extend our thanks and appreciation to our wives, Mary Huse and Felicity Bowditch, whose patience, understanding, encouragement, and occasional harrassment made this book possible.

Chestnut Hill, Massachusetts   E. F. H.
January 1977   J. L. B.

CONTENTS

PART I SETTING THE STAGE

1 Introduction   3

Introduction   6
A structural-design perspective of management   10
A work-flow perspective of management   19
A human perspective of management   22
An integrated perspective of management   25
Summary   29

2 The Organization as a System   33

Introduction   36
General systems theory   36
Advantages and disadvantages of the systems approach   39
Characteristics of human organizations   44
Differing perspectives of organizations as social systems   55
The need for a more integrated approach   60
Summary   62

PART II INTRAORGANIZATIONAL BEHAVIOR: THE MICRO VIEW

3 The Individual in the Organization   69

Introduction   72
Motivation and performance   74
The individual in interaction with the organization
—the psychological contract   76
Static-content models of motivational systems   80
Dynamic-expectancy models of motivational systems 100
Relationship between satisfaction and productivity 105
Toward a situational model of motivation 105
Implications for the manager 106
Summary 109

4 Interpersonal Perception and Communication   115

Introduction 118
Perception 119

Communications 128
Transactional analysis 141
Conclusions and implications for the manager 149

5 The Group in the Organization   **155**

Introduction 158
The group as a system 159
Why and how groups are formed 161
The internal operation of groups 168
Group task, building, and maintenance activities 176
Observing group process 180
Temporary groups 183
Group outputs—productivity and satisfaction 187
Implications for the manager 189
Conclusion 191

6 Groups in Interaction   **195**

Introduction 198
Intergroup relationships 198
The functions and types of conflict 202
Effects of intergroup conflict 207
Reducing intergroup conflict and competition 210
Summary 213

7 Influence, Power, and Leadership   **217**

Introduction 220
Influence and power 220
Leadership 224
Summary and conclusion 245

8 The Manager in the Organization   **251**

Introduction 254
What is a manager? 254
Managerial functions 262
Management by objectives 266
Exploded myths of management 271
Summary 273

PART III   ORGANIZATIONAL BEHAVIOR: THE MACRO VIEW

9   Climate, Environment, and Organizational Planning   283

Introduction 286
Research findings on climate 288
The environment 292
Organizational planning and objectives 309
Summary 320

10   Organizational Improvement—Structural-Design Perspective   325

Introduction 328
Traditional organizational theory 330
The individual organization approach 332
Organizational design as a dependent variable 333
A contingency theory of organizational improvement 341
Conclusions 350

11   Organizational Improvement—Work-Flow Perspective   353

Introduction 356
Models and model building 356
Management information systems 365
Integration through the informal organization 367
More formalized integrative approaches—sociotechnical systems .. 369
Conclusion 378

12   Organization Development—Human Perspective   383

Introduction 386
Change, planned change, and action research 387
Approaches to OD interventions 395
Selected organization development interventions 400
Problems with organization development 414
Conclusions 417

13   Toward an Integrated Systems Theory
of Organization Development   423

Introduction 426
The competent organization 426
Dealing with organizational change 428
Using systems theory to provide an integrated approach to
organization development 433

Application of the systems approach to organization development 442
Conclusion 455

14   An Integrated Study of Organization Development   459

The approach to change 462
Results of the program 464
Summary and conclusion 486

15   Conclusion   487

The micro approach 488
The macro approach 489
The manager of the future 492

Appendix: Case Studies

Changing Work Procedures A–2
Cleaning the Tank A–5
Exercise Career Values A–7
An Exercise in Rating Supervisory Behavior A–12
The Experimental Program A–13
Group Conflict A–18
The Howard Company A–19
International Systems Corporation—Ajax Plant A–22
NASA Moon Survival Task A–33
The New Product Meeting A–40
Participative Decision Making A–44
The Provincetown Advocate A–46
The Road to Hell A–50
State of Vermont, Welfare Commission, Oldcity District A–57
Survival Training A–69
Technology, Incorporated A–70

Index I–1

PART I

SETTING THE STAGE

1

INTRODUCTION

History is bunk.

HENRY FORD

LEARNING
OBJECTIVES

When you have finished reading and studying this chapter, you should be able to:

1. Differentiate between the micro and macro approaches to organizational behavior.

2. Explain why the material in this text progresses from individual to group to organizational issues.

3. Describe the three-perspective, or viewpoint, format of the book and explain how these viewpoints came about.

4. Outline in the most general terms the progression of the field of organizational behavior and where the field seems to be going.

You will be expected to define and use the following concepts:

Structural-design perspective

Work-flow perspective

Human perspective

Universal principles of management school

Structuralists

Scientific management

Bureaucracy

Time-and-motion study

Operations research

Human relations school

Organization development school

Styles of leadership:
  authoritarian
  democratic
  laissez-faire

T-group

Hawthorne effect

Macro approach to organizational behavior

Micro approach to organizational behavior

Management style

Productivity and satisfaction

Environment and change

THOUGHT
STARTERS

1. What does the term "organization" mean to you?
2. How many different organizations have you been involved with during your lifetime?
3. Does a change in culture affect organizations?
4. How many different ways might you look at organizations?
5. How would a banker and a salesman describe an organization?
6. Is a family an organization? Explain.

I. INTRODUCTION

This is a book about organizations and the people in them. Because a substantial amount has been written on this topic, we decided to provide a *structure* and describe a *process* that will help you organize your thoughts. This structural aid is an examination of an organization from three different viewpoints or perspectives. We look at the organization from a static-photographic viewpoint in terms of who does what. That is, our first viewpoint, or perspective, is a *structural-design* viewpoint. The second, dynamic perspective focuses on what happens to orders, information, rumors, and the like when they come to an organization; it is a *work-flow* perspective. The third viewpoint, the major focus of this text, deals with what people perceive, what they say, and how they operate in groups—as leaders and as members of the total group—in organizations. We call this a *human* perspective.

You will read about these three perspectives in the rest of this chapter, and you will discover that each perspective in and of itself is incomplete. Organizational behavior is really an integrated phenomenon; thus the end of the chapter completes the structural stage-setting by pulling it all together into an integrated perspective (see Fig. 1.1).

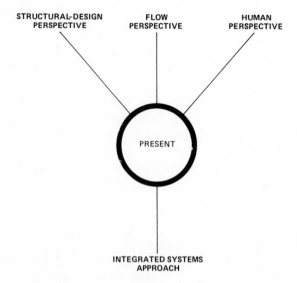

Fig. 1.1 Outline of the three perspectives used in this book.

The *process* that we use to describe the operations of individuals, groups, and organizations is the *systems* approach. An organization is very similar to a biological system; each exists in its own environment, affecting and being affected by that environment. The major difference is that people within an organization are able to modify their environment in a way that organisms within a biological system are unable to do. Chapter 2 is a detailed examination of what is meant by the concept *system* and how we view the organization as a system.

Two more characteristics of this book should be noted. We progress from topics pertaining to the individual, to those dealing with the group—how certain individual functions relate to group activities (leadership)—and finally to topics about the organization. In other words, we start with the small units, doing microanalysis, proceed through the intermediate units, and finally get to the larger units and their interaction with the environment (macroanalysis). Thus we progress from a micro to a macro treatment of organizational behavior.

The second characteristic is almost demanded of us by recent research that tells us in no uncertain terms that there is no one best way to approach anything, be it motivating people, leading people, or designing an organization. This is not to say that it does not matter how these activities are accomplished. Rather, in order to be effective, one must know the dimensions that determine the most effective way to motivate people, lead them, or design an organization. Because some of the research is so new, some of the topics have more certain answers than others. Yet it seems clear that the contingency, or situational, approach is here to stay. As time goes on, advice given in this edition of *Behavior in Organizations* will become outdated; newer findings will have challenged older principles. This book is written for *now* in Western culture.

The book is divided into three parts. We have already described Part I (Chapters 1 and 2). Part II examines four micro areas: motivation, perception and communication, group and intergroup activities, and leadership and the manager. Part III takes a micro and macro look at the environment, and a macro view of the organization from our three perspectives. Finally, there is a concluding chapter, which you may find useful to read before going on to Chapter 2.

The Building Blocks

In Part II we discuss the things that affect the individual, the group, and more specifically the manager and other leaders in the organization. Most of us, without thinking about it too much, would probably say that money motivates people in a working situation. But of course there are other influences as well, and we look at the conditions under which these other factors act as motivators. We divide motivational models into two classes: the static-content and the dynamic expectancy. Each of these two classes is conceptualized differently.

Following the discussion on motivation, we examine perception and communication. Humans retrieve information in a variety of ways. They see, hear, and feel, and the way in which they interpret or process what they see, hear, and feel is what we call perception. Closely linked to perception is the most basic group phenomenon—two-person communication. We note the variety of ways in which people communicate—verbally, "with daggers in their eyes," by shifting uncomfortably in a chair. A person communicates as an authority, as someone subservient—"yes, sir"—or on a rational, adult level. All of these variations in communication are discussed in Chapter 4.

After looking at the individual as a discrete system, with unique motivators and ways of perceiving and communicating, we move to the next larger unit of analysis, the group. Treating the group from our three perspectives, we look at the internal operations of groups, why the group's early experience is important, and why developed ways of doing things (norms) help us to understand the group. We then break down group activities into three types —task activities, building activities, and self-serving activities—and examine group outputs (productivity), what the group does, how it feels (satisfaction) about what it does, and what this all means to the manager.

Chapter 6 focuses on group climate and interaction. One of the most motivating factors of group phenomena is the feeling one gets as part of a group or organization. If that feeling is stifling, one outcome will result; if it is open and free, another comes about. Group conflict affects and is affected by climate. You have undoubtedly noticed the difference in what happens when your team wins and loses. The conflict situation is explored, as are the benefits and problems it provides. One of management's most troubling problems is how to properly manage conflict, and we list some of the ways this can be done.

Chapters 7 and 8 can really be considered together. Chapter 7 treats the more research-oriented side of leadership—what some of the great theorists have found about leadership. Martin Luther King, John F. Kennedy, Indira Ghandi—each of these leaders exemplifies a particular kind of power and leadership base. After looking at these differences, we turn to recent research, which suggests that there is no one best way of leadership. At certain specified times, one leadership style is effective; at other times, another. We also point out that contrary to "common sense," there is a *difference* between a "leader" and a "manager." We conclude Chapter 7 by presenting a new way of looking at leadership—by examining the leader's goals first. Much of the recent leadership research has treated leadership in this situational manner. This area is less certain, although more researched, than other topics in this book.

Chapter 8 deals with the manager and management functions. One well-known managerial technique (management by objectives) is described, and a number of pervasive myths about management are examined. A manager's job is not simply compartmentalized by a job description; rather, a manager takes orders from many people and spends a great deal of time in and is influenced by lateral contacts as opposed to superior-subordinate contacts.

The Transition

All organizations exist in an environment, and that environment both impacts on and is impacted by the organization. Think for a moment about the recent emphasis on cleaning up streams and the air to rid our environment of various forms of pollution. In simple terms the organization caused the pollution by dumping raw wastes into the environment (though this may have been caused by people in the environment who wanted goods at the lowest possible cost, thus fostering the pollution). At the same time, when pollution became so great, another sector of the environment reacted and affected the organization by putting pressure on it through government and other channels to clean up the pollution. We look at the environment by first noting the cultural environment, which is characterized by an accelerating pace of change. We then compare some of the macro and micro issues in the environment, and finish by treating the most pervasive "environmental" issue of today, social responsibility.

Having treated the various "micro" issues and the environment, which has its micro and macro sides, we can now talk about the total organization from our three perspectives.

A Systems Approach to Organizational Improvement

Following our discussion of the environment, in Part III we present three models for improving an organization. To attain optimal effectiveness in an organization, one needs to be aware of organizational structure, flow, and human behavior. We look at the organization from each of these three viewpoints, realizing that they are incomplete by themselves. The case study we provide illustrates each of the three perspectives. Finally, we treat the organization as an integrated system from a totally holistic, macro, approach. It may be useful to read Chapter 14, on the integrated approach, after Chapter 1, so that you will see where we are headed.

II. A STRUCTURAL-DESIGN PERSPECTIVE OF MANAGEMENT

Within this perspective three different views of management have developed historically, each of which has its slightly modified counterpart today. These three views do not exhaust structural-design schools; instead, they are simply representative of this viewpoint. These three schools are the universal principles of management school, the structuralist school, and the scientific management school.

A. Universal Principles of Management School

The principles of management regarded as the foundation of this viewpoint were seen as common to state, church, military, and industrial organizations. Mooney and Reiley, for example, cite the efficiency of the Roman Catholic church and the military and their management of people.[1] They trace the history of management from the government of ancient Greece to recent industrial organizations. More than half of their book gives the historical background and principles upon which they believe all management depends. Taking an authoritarian, one-best-way approach to all problems, these theorists treat workers as extensions of machines and derive their principles from a logical approach.

The traditional, classical theorists were concerned with a variety of concepts—the structure of the organization, distinctions between line and staff, the division of labor, and managerial functions. Fayol lists 14 principles of management (see Table 1.1) useful for all organizations, although he does note that these principles must be flexible rather than absolute.[2]

On the basis of Fayol's work, other theorists distilled and grouped these 14 principles into five descriptive categories. These five categories represent the essence of this school's axioms.

1. Structure This term refers to the way in which an organization is formally designed in order to insure orderly specialization among its subsystems. Early theorists were fairly adamant about the fact that there was one best way to organize. Fayol, for example, says that "the same framework is appropriate for all individual concerns of whatever kind, employing the same number of people," although he also states that the same general appearance does not require exactly the same detailed structure and that implicit in this concept is the difficulty of "how to find essential personnel and put each where he can be of most service."[3]

Implicit to the notion of structure is the distinction made between line and staff, a distinction borrowed from military organizations. The line organization is the primary chain of command which comes directly from essential

Table 1.1   An outline of Fayol's principles of management

---

1. Division of work—the specialization of workers, including management, to improve efficiency and increase output.

2. Authority and responsibility—"the right to give orders, and power to exact obedience" (p. 21). Responsibility occurs as a direct result of authority.

3. Discipline—in essence, "obedience, application, energy, behavior" (p. 22) given to the organization, and it depends on the worthiness of the leaders.

4. Unity of command—the principle that no one should have more than one boss.

5. Unity of direction—there should be only one plan for accomplishing goals (related to 4).

6. Subordination of individual interest to general interest—the organization's concerns should be placed ahead of the individual's concerns.

7. Remuneration (pay) of personnel—specifies fair pay arrangements, satisfactory to all, whereby competence is rewarded, but not overrewarded.

8. Centralization—consolidation of the management function should be done according to the circumstances surrounding the organization.

9. Scalar chain—the chain of command, which can sometimes have several tracks. Persons at parallel levels down the tracks may be authorized to solve problems with each other, laterally, with the superior's knowledge.

10. Order—the principle that everyone has a position and should operate only from that position; similarly, all materials should have, and be in, a certain place.

11. Equity—loyalty should be encouraged by kindliness and justice, but equity does not exclude sternness and forcefulness when needed.

12. Stability of tenure of personnel—high turnover of personnel both causes and is the result of inefficiency; better organizations have stable managerial personnel.

13. Initiative—the necessity for "thinking out a plan and ensuring its success" (p. 39). Fayol sees this as strength for businesses, particularly during hard times.

14. Esprit de corps—morale and team feeling are enhanced by keeping teams together and having good face-to-face communication.

Adapted from H. Fayol, *General and Industrial Management*, trans. C. Storrs (London: Sir Isaac Pitman and Sons, 1949).

functions, or subsystems, of the organization, e.g., manufacturing, finance, and distribution. Staff activities are purely advisory to line functions. Definitions of line-staff relationships are, however, varied and have changed throughout the years. For example, early definitions made it clear that a line officer exercises *authority* over the entire organization and that "staff" activities are purely *advisory*. According to Mooney and Reiley, "It is the function of the staff merely to counsel; that of the line, and the line only, to command," although they do point out that this is oversimplified, since the line "represents the authority of man; the staff, the authority of ideas."[4] This concept has undergone considerable change, as is demonstrated by Fisch's conclusion that the changing mix of organizations may well make the line-staff concept obsolete. "Research, development and engineering can surely no longer be considered as staff departments . . . they are of equal importance and hence require equal authority with manufacturing and sales."[5]

2. Division of labor Obviously, work must be divided into different segments, or components; otherwise, every job would be so broad and inclusive that effective performance would be impossible. Accordingly, structural-

One of the first applications of the moving assembly line was this magneto operation at a Ford plant in 1913. Magnetos were pushed from one workman to the next, thereby reducing production time by half. (Photograph courtesy Ford Motor Company)

design theorists have been concerned about such topics as whether an organization should be centralized or decentralized, set up by product or function, etc. Since the concept of division of labor extends from the top to the bottom of the organization, it may appear to be overly "formalistic" to spell out exact job descriptions and positional interrelationships, but as Mooney and Reiley state, it is necessary for total efficiency.[6]

3. The coordinative principle   Since division of labor is essential to the proper functioning of a large, complex organization, unity of action for achieving organization goals can be achieved only through proper coordination. Initially, it was assumed that each superior was in charge of coordinating the work of his or her subordinates. Presently, high-technology organizations are characterized by a great deal of lateral coordination, sometimes without the benefit of the supervisor.

Although he recognized the need for contact and communication across the formal hierarchy, Fayol stressed that informal communication was helpful so long as there was no conflict.

So long that F and P [two subordinates reporting to different managers] remain in agreement, and so long as their actions are approved by their immediate superiors, direct contact may be maintained but from the instant that agreement ceases or there is no approval from the supervisors direct contact comes [immediately] to an end and the scalar chain [vertical chain of command] is straightaway resumed.[7]

In other words, conflict is resolved, in theory at least, only at the top.

4. The scalar principle   This concept prescribes a hierarchical chain of superior-subordinate relationships such that each subordinate has only one superior. According to Mooney and Reiley, "Wherever we find an organization even of two people, related as superior and subordinate, we have the scalar principle. This chain constitutes the universal process of coordination, through which the supreme coordinating authority becomes effective throughout the entire structure"[8] What follow from this, of course, are the principles of leadership, delegation (of authority), and functional definition, which refers to the superior's definition of a subordinate's function in the organization.

5. The functional principle   In contrast to the scalar principle, the functional principle refers to the differentiation of duties on a nonhierarchical basis. The vice-presidents for finance and marketing may be on the same level on the organization chart, for example, but they have different functions within the organization.

B. The Structuralist School

The structuralists' approach to the problem of management is very different from that of the classical theorists. The classicists used deductive reasoning to prescribe a conceptually clean organizational design and description of how each person within the organization *should* behave. The structuralists, on the other hand, examined existing organizations and used inductive reasoning to generalize about the true nature of organizations. Their descriptive approach focused on what organizations are *really* like rather than on what they *should* be like.

One of the best-known early structuralists, Max Weber, characterized organizational rules in terms of an "ideal" bureaucracy. (However, as Etzioni notes, the degree of an organization's bureaucratism may change in accor-

Bureaucracy in a post office. (H. Armstrong Roberts/E. P. Jones)

dance with the times.)[9] Weber notes that the ideal type of bureaucratic organization has the following characteristics:[10]

1. "A continuous organization of official functions bound by rules."

2. "A specified sphere of competence." This means that bureaucrats have highly differentiated functions and the necessary authority to carry them out.

3. "The organization of offices follows the principle of hierarchy." This concept is similar to the scalar principle, i.e., no office is left to "drift" in an organization, and each office reports directly and solely to a higher-level office.

4. "The rules which regulate the conduct of any office may be technical rules or norms." In an editorial comment, one of Weber's translators notes that the "rules" deal with constraints that promote efficiency in an organization, whereas "norms" in Weber's thinking define the conduct on grounds other than efficiency. However, it is important to note that Weber emphasized prescribed rules in bureaucracies.

5. Ownership of an organization and the administrative and production functions should be separated. In other words, the administrators in a bureaucracy do not own the equipment needed for production or administration, e.g., a clergyman does not own the church he serves, and a governor does not own the state of which he or she is chief executive.

6. An incumbent must not be allowed to control either positions or trappings of office. Such a rule preserves the independence and freedom of an organization from the particular incumbent.

7. "Administrative acts, decisions and rules are formulated and recorded in writing, even in cases where oral discussion is the rule or is even mandatory." This, of course, is to stress the impersonal nature of a bureaucracy and insures that the rules will be applied consistently in all situations.

To summarize, it is interesting to note that there are many features common to both the structuralist and classical approaches, particularly those related to the scalar principle. The major difference appears to be the way in which the concepts were obtained.

Another of Weber's contributions is the distinction he made between illegitimate and legitimate power.[11] Weber postulated that the exercise of raw illegitimate power alienates the worker, but that the exercise of legitimate power, which conforms with worker norms, results in the worker's internalizing the rules. Weber also said that having the organization, rather than its clients, pay workers' wages would insure worker loyalty, as would promotions and organizational career planning. Finally, Weber saw the need for continued protection of the bureaucratic organization.

In examining Weber's model, Etzioni notes that many organizations have mixed modes of authority—partly traditional, charismatic, and bureaucratic.[12] In short, a pure bureaucracy is hard to find; moreover, it may not remain "pure" for long.

C. Scientific Management School

The scientific management school emphasizes the measurement of work rather than the nature of the organization or its principles of organization. Nevertheless, this school had a major effect on the ways in which tasks were combined into jobs and organizations were put together. As in the other two schools of thought, the scientific management theorists assumed that a person

Mass production in an automobile assembly plant about 1913. (Photograph courtesy Ford Motor Company)

is machinelike—that a worker's feelings, personality, and work group are relatively unimportant. This view seems quite naive today, but at the time, operating under these assumptions was effective, given the largely immigrant labor force and the large number of tasks requiring mainly unskilled labor.

Frederick W. Taylor, the founder of this school, started his work around the turn of the twentieth century.[13] He is best known for his work in determining how much pig iron a laborer should be able to carry between two points. By studying workers' bodily motions and the time required to complete them, Talyor concluded that a laborer could carry 47.5 rather than 12–15 long tons per day if he took lighter loads each time and had scheduled rest periods. Taylor also developed different sized shovels to provide a 21-pound load for any given kind of material, the optimal amount for long-term work. Formerly, steel workers had been using the same shovel for rice coal and the heavier iron ore.

It is important to stress that although Taylor was interested in the application of science and the search for the one best way, he also assumed a commonality of interest between workers and management. This latter concern, however, was largely ignored by the "efficiency experts" of the 1920s and later.

One of Taylor's associates, Frank Gilbreth, continued to develop time-and-motion studies for industry showing the most efficient physical motions for accomplishing particular tasks. Again, the emphasis was on the worker as an extension of a machine. Time-and-motion studies continue to this day, as inputs into job design.

Since it focuses on the components of task performance rather than on broad principles of management theory, scientific management is more inductive and data-based than the universal principles of management school and therefore does not fit entirely within a structural-design perspective. Nor does it explicitly identify a systems approach to work, as does a work-flow perspective. Scientific management has as its focus the shop level; it does not extend into the whole organization.

D. Evolving Concepts of a Structural-Design Perspective

Early theorists examined organizations as they knew them from a limited background of research. Current concepts of organization improvement have been heavily influenced by expanding knowledge about human behavior, organizational design (including the concepts of formal and informal organization), and the human relations movement. Research and theory in this area have led current theorists away from a "one-best-way" approach and toward a contingency theory of organizational design.

Koontz and O'Donnell give an excellent review of organizational thought and history and show how research has heavily influenced current thinking about organizational improvement.[14] Another excellent presentation of organizational thought and history is given by Scott. He traces the underpinnings of the classical theorists, briefly describes the division of labor, the scalar and functional processes, structure, and the span of control, under the rubric of "The Classical Doctrine." He then describes what he calls the "Neoclassical Theory of Organization," which accepted the classical theory, but superimposed "modifications resulting from individual behavior, and the influence of the informal group" and introduced the concepts of the social being and the informal organization, which had been largely ignored by the classicists.[15]

Worthy studied span of control (the number of people reporting to one boss) in two different types of Sears Roebuck stores.[16] Both types of stores had approximately 150 to 175 employees, but one type was organized along conventional lines—store managers, section managers, and approximately 30 department heads. The other type of store had a much flatter structure with a much wider span of control—approximately 30 department heads reported directly to the store manager. In terms of such criteria as profitability, promotability of department heads, and overall employee morale, stores with the "flat" structure were superior.

Unfortunately, Worthy's findings were reported anecdotally and were generalized well beyond the scope of the original study of a single organization. In a compilation of a number of studies across organizations regarding correlates of organizational structure, Porter and Lawler found no evidence to indicate that a flat organization improves both attitudes and performance on the job.[17] Rather, they found that a flat structure in smaller organizations appears to enhance employee satisfaction and productivity. From their review of the research, Porter and Lawler conclude that the advantages of having a flat organizational structure decrease, and even become a liability, as the organization becomes larger.

Porter and Lawler also found that upper-level managers were more satisfied than lower-level managers with the nature of their jobs. Additionally, insofar as it is possible to distinguish between line and staff jobs, line personnel felt better about their jobs, there was a much higher turnover of staff jobs, and line personnel were better informed about what was going on in the organization.

Porter and Lawler found that the size of subunits within the organization appears to be related to satisfaction; satisfaction and morale appear to be greater in small subunits, there is less absenteeism, and turnover is lower. Moreover, the larger the subunit, the greater the likelihood of labor disputes. Their findings about productivity, however, were equivocal; they were cautious about commenting on the relationship between an organization's total size and workers' attitudes and behavior. Similarly, there were no clear-cut findings about the efficacy of a centralized or decentralized organization.

One of the interesting features about the work by Porter and Lawler is that even though their starting point was the structural-design perspective emphasis on structure, they took an inductive, research view of the correlates of structure and many of the findings deal with the performance and feelings of individuals on the job. Their work exemplifies the blurring of the lines between the structural-design and human perspectives. Perhaps the classical managerial theorists could argue that what was happening in the organizations studied should not have happened according to their principles, but the important thing to remember is that although prescriptions for behavior may be unrealistic, the data collected about the behavior do not lie.

In another evolutionary study, Hall found some confirmation of his hypothesis that organizational divisions or hierarchical levels with nonroutinized jobs are significantly less bureaucratic than those levels at which more routine activities take place.[18] Organizational flexibility and instability are thus negatively related to the rules of a bureaucracy as Weber envisioned them.

III. A WORK-FLOW PERSPECTIVE OF MANAGEMENT

Many management theories in this category are concerned primarily with information flow, which has become synonymous with the "mathematically quantifiable" nature of computer usage and simulation. Work-flow theories developed from operations research during World War II, but as new approaches to management emerged from these beginnings, the boundaries of work-flow theories have become blurred, just as they did with structural-design theories.

A. Operations Research

As was true for most of the other schools of management thought, operations research (OR) came into being to fulfill specific organizational needs. Initially, OR was considered an integration of the behavioral, social, and physical sciences. However, since mathematicians predominate in the area, OR has not lived up to its original idea. As Churchman notes, the earliest use of OR, the "*systems* or *overall* approach to problems," was to bring about an organized approach to military strategy.[19] In her chapter on the history of OR, Trefethen indicates that its roots may be found as far back as the third century B.C., when the King of Syracuse asked the mathematician-philosopher Archimedes to create a way for him to break the Roman siege of his city.[20]

In World War I there were attempts at mathematical analysis of military operations, and by World War II there were organizations with the title "operational research" in Great Britain. OR was slower to take hold in the United States, but by the early 1950s it had become established, and since then it has been increasingly influential.

One of the early problems solved by OR specialists during World War II was determining how to allocate reconnaisance aircraft to detect enemy ship convoys. By figuring out the patterns and speeds of enemy ships and the ability of aircraft to cover a given amount of space in a certain time, Allied commanders were able to significantly reduce the number of reconnaisance aircraft needed and to increase the effectiveness of their surveillance of enemy sea routes.

One of the distinguishing characteristics of OR is its use of a mathematical model to systematize the particular problem, thus allowing for an optimum solution to any given situation. Another unique characteristic is that differences in *performance* between individuals or groups in various situations are usually excluded from the model, although their *capabilities* are taken into account.

Churchman takes a systems approach within a framework of easily quantifiable factors to describe the phases of OR:

1. formulating the problem
2. constructing a mathematical model to represent the system under study
3. deriving a solution from the model
4. testing the model and the solution derived from it
5. establishing controls over the solution
6. putting the solution to work—implementation.[21]

The overall approach is to take account of as many variables as possible, so that the result should be reasonable, workable alternative courses of action. The basic form of the model is that the effectiveness of the system (E) is a function of those variables (x) which are subject to control and those variables (y) which are not subject to control. The solution that is derived may be either deductive (analytic) or inductive (numerical). Since no model is anything more than a "representation of reality," controls or guidelines to the solution must be set before the model can be tried out. If any of the variables vary beyond certain prescribed limits, a new model or new relationship will have to be determined. Finally, the solution is attempted. Should some significant new and different variables appear, a new solution must be found.

Newer considerations   A more recent mathematical model, closely linked to operations research, is Forrester's "system dynamics," an attempt to describe the interaction of an organization's behavior and the external environment.[22] Forrester develops methods for organizational improvement by taking account of six "quantifiable" subsystems in his model: (1) orders (from buyers), (2) materials (raw and premanufactured), (3) money, (4) personnel, (5) capital equipment, all of which are interconnected by (6) information flow. This relatively small number of variables is considered by some to be an oversimplified view of reality. In addition, the large amounts of data that are "plugged" in to the model require large computing facilities, thus making it difficult to use.

Another, more recent, contributor to this area is Emshoff, who in a very lucid fashion distinguishes between behavioral (human) and mechanistic (non-human) problems.[23] Emshoff differentiates between an *output* and an *input* model representing reality. The output model uses empirical data which do not include causal and other antecedent factors in behavior. One example of output data for humans might be that the elderly tend to die before the young. This is a mechanistic factor requiring little understanding of human life. On the other hand, if some effort were made to determine whether blacks, whites, or Asians die earlier, it would help to have input data such as diet, sanitation, work habits, etc., or *antecedent* variables perhaps causally related to death. Emshoff states in effect that input-oriented rather than output-oriented research is needed for behavioral systems.

Still another approach which has been gaining use recently is the management information systems approach which, with the help of computers, speeds information across the organization so that orders can be filled rapidly, production can be scheduled, purchasing requirements can be forecasted, customers can be billed, etc. Diebold notes that in order for this system to be effective, the traditional departments in organizations must be less compartmentalized within the organization.[24]

A final set of concepts is embodied in the research on sociotechnical systems, which is discussed in more detail in Chapter 11. The important point of the research is that one must integrate new technology into an industry, with an awareness of the culture and what will be acceptable to that culture. Thus an automobile company may set up a production line in its United States plant, but do away with the production line in a plant making the same models in Europe.

Clearly, the newer work-flow theorists are aware of the importance of the human component. The fact that both Emshoff and Forrester are concerned with the human variable is an indication of its recognition by the quantitatively oriented theorists.

IV. A HUMAN PERSPECTIVE OF MANAGEMENT

Management theories in this category are oriented toward the work group. Early forerunners of the human-perspective viewpoint were Alfred Binet, who in his early work attempted to test for individual differences in intelligence, and Hugo Munsterberg, who set up training programs for persons running trolley cars on the Boston Elevated Railroad. Yet there was another factor that had even more impact, namely, the effect of the work group on organizational goals. Only then was the importance of the worker's needs, desires, and feelings recognized.

A. Humans Relations School

The human relations school in management became identified as a separate tradition as a result of five closely related studies done at the Hawthorne plant of the Western Electric Company near Chicago. In 1924 Western Electric, together with the National Research Council of the National Academy of Sciences, set out to examine the relationship between illumination level and productivity in simple, repetitive tasks—inspecting small parts, assembling relays, and winding coils.[25]

The initial findings were that productivity rose almost identically in both the experimental and control groups, even though the timing of increases in light intensity differed and the tasks differed slightly. In addition, productivity did not decrease when light levels decreased from 44 foot candles to 3 foot candles. Moreover, when two women volunteered for a separate study of production (splitting mica) under lighting equal to that of a full moon, production did not decrease.

In the second Hawthorne study, the length and timing of rest periods were varied. A special production room was created, and two female volunteers recruited three others. The room's temperature and humidity were recorded hourly, and the assemblers underwent physical examinations every six weeks. During the three-year period of the study, these five individuals became a cohesive group and appeared to enjoy the periodic changes in their rest periods. The women socialized off the job and seemed to appreciate the friendlier climate in their production room. To the reseachers, it appeared at this point that employee attitudes might impact on performance, and this led to the third study, a mass-interviewing program.

The mass-interviewing program began in a 1600-member inspection branch. The researchers wanted to find out what constituted effective supervisory practices and the relationship between morale and productivity. (Incidentally, research is still being conducted in these two areas elsewhere.) This was the first study of the series to focus on individuals and their interpersonal relationships rather than on working conditions. One of the findings was that people reacted differently to similar surroundings, thus confirming psychological theories about individual differences. Wages, hours of work, and the physical setting had heavy social importance to the workers as members of a work group. From this study, the researchers concluded that not only individual attitudes were important, but also that group dynamics and norms appeared to be in some way related to leadership and productivity. These findings and questions led to the fourth study, the Bank Wiring Observation Room study.

The Bank Wiring Observation Room study was in some ways a replication of the first study. There was a fairly small group (14 men divided into three semiautonomous work groups). It was relatively easy to separate out a group for intensive study, and output could be easily measured. However, unlike the first study, management had elsewhere tested a complicated wage-incentive plan and was interested in studying its effects. This fourth study seemed to indicate that the group had a norm for production levels. Men who exceeded the norm were called "slaves" or "speed kings"; men who did not come up to the norm were called "chiselers." Workers were hit on the top of their forearms, a practice called "binging," as a means of enforcing the group's production norm. One of the findings from this study was that the group's production norm was more important than wage incentives in affecting output.

The final Hawthorne study, an intensive personnel-counseling program, was started four years after the end of the Bank Wiring Observation Room study. In the intervening years the world had gone through an economic depression, during which formal research at Hawthorne had been suspended. The goals of the fifth study were to: (1) interview employees and then assess their problems, and (2) improve communication within the company. Counselors involved in the program helped supervisors to be more understanding and helped workers to adjust better. Overall, the study helped management to better understand the workers and their feelings.

What can be concluded from these Hawthorne studies? First, formal and informal work groups are important, even if they exist in isolation or lack a common purpose. People's behavior may differ, depending on whether they are acting as group members or as individuals. Second, people's behavior may change if they know that they are being watched by persons who are interested in their behavior patterns. This change occurs because workers assume that the watchers are interested in their activity. Finally, the research itself was allowed to determine the next phase of the study. The research was not heavily structured in advance, and there were no predetermined conclusions.

One of the lasting outcomes from these studies was the term "the Hawthorne effect." A work situation is said to involve "the Hawthorne effect" when the workers' behavior changes because they are aware that persons important in their lives are taking an interest in them.

After the Hawthorne studies, researchers became interested in worker attitudes, morale, and group effects. This in turn led to interest in supervisory styles, a move away from classical, prescriptive management thought. (This interest in supervisory styles and the relationship between morale and productivity will be taken up in more detail later.) The post-World War II studies done at the University of Michigan and Ohio State University indicated that "people oriented" leadership was more effective than "production oriented" leadership.[26] From this school emanated human relations training, which was designed to make "nice guys" out of foremen who heretofore had been trained to be authoritarian and strict. Inasmuch as the reinforcement structure of the work situation was not changed, however, foremen coming back from human relations training, or "charm school," were frequently ridiculed to such an extent that it did not take long for them to fall back into their old behavioral patterns and leadership styles. In some circles human relations has been described as "warm feeling" training and consists primarily of company picnics, getting the wives together, and company-sponsored athletics. But this is a distortion of the research findings provided by the original human relations studies.

Closely related to the human relations school, but with one very important difference, has been the attempt to integrate interpersonal and intergroup relationships with systems theory. In their book *Organizations*, written in the late 1950s, March and Simon put the available human research into systems terms.[27] The interesting feature about this work is that its essentially human-perspective data are put into the methodological framework of work flow.

B. Organization Development School

The origin of the organization development school of theorists is difficult to pinpoint, since it is really an extension of the human relations school. Perhaps as much as anyone, Kurt Lewin and his associates, and Coch and French are regarded as the founding fathers of the organization development school. In a post-World War II study entitled "Overcoming Resistance to Change," Coch and French show that when the workers in a pajama factory helped plan production changes, the "lag time" for production to return to a normal rate was far less than when the changes were imposed on the workers by an authoritarian management style.[28]

Just prior to World War II, Lippitt and White (1939), two of Lewin's disciples, found that the leadership style in children's clubs affects the group process and output.[29] Children in groups with authoritarian leaders produced more articles but of lower quality than did the groups led by democratic leaders. In addition, the authoritarian groups fell apart when the leader left the room, whereas the democratic groups continued to produce. As might be expected, satisfaction was higher in the democratic groups. The third style of group leadership, *laissez-faire* ("to leave alone"), was less successful on all counts than was either of the other two kinds of groups. This group of studies is relevant here because it focuses on problems with which the researchers have continued to be concerned—effectiveness within groups.

In 1946 Lewin and his associates met to develop action frameworks in social psychology. Out of this came the forerunner of sensitivity training, or T-groups. Many T-groups are agendaless meetings lasting one day to two weeks or longer and are designed to make the participants more aware of their personal strengths and weaknesses, how they communicate to others, and how to change their behavior (Chapter 12). At this point, we can say that the T-group and its variations have become a standard tool of organization development practitioners, but recently have been a source of controversy.

Since the early stages of organization development, many other techniques have come to the forefront as methods and devices specifically designed or adapted for use in organizations. These will be considered in detail in Chapter 12, "Organization Development."

V. AN INTEGRATED PERSPECTIVE OF MANAGEMENT

Each of the various perspectives on management is important in the functioning of organizations. Each developed in a historical and cultural context which met a need at a particular time. To criticize these viewpoints now as naive is missing the point. We all see things more clearly with hindsight.

What will be described in this section are the more recent, current efforts to integrate the management research and theories coming from more than a single perspective. Perrow, in a recent history of organizational theory, noted that an organization's environment, perhaps the major determinant of its behavior, is likely to be more influential than any internal factor.[30] One part of the organization's environment is technology. Perrow notes that the relative importance of the functional areas (marketing, production, development, etc.) depends on the situation, as does leadership style (authoritarian, democratic, *laissez-faire*).

Perrow argues that selectivity is the key concept in the application of various organization development techniques, such as job enrichment, T-groups, and the like, and that none of these techniques is a panacea for all types of organizations. His review of the literature suggests that structural rearrangement of organizations is probably the most effective and simplest way of problem solving, but that it must be used in conjunction with an examination of the following issues: (1) where authority lies; (2) how tasks are assembled into jobs; (3) how information gets from one place to another; (4) how rewards are structured; and (5) the nature of employee and management expectations. He suggests that the variables thought important should be manipulated and that the O.D. specialist should then wait for a few months for the manipulation or change to take hold. This procedure is not dramatic, but it is based on organization theory and research and is probably more effective than some of the simplistic approaches currently popular.

Today the evolution of management thought has come to an approach which, although lacking scientific parsimony and simplicity, appears to be a summary of organizational problem solving. The rest of this section is devoted to a brief discussion of how we got to that point. Keep in mind, however, that in 10–20 years, additional research and theorizing will have outdated what we have proposed as the latest work.

Attacking the problems of organization from a multidimensional structural perspective is Woodward, who studied a large number of firms in a relatively small geographic area in England.[31] Using a sample of 100 firms which varied considerably in size and type, she and her associates found a wide range of organizational structures among successful firms in different industries with different technologies. For example, she found that the most successful firms and industries using unit- or batch-production technology had considerably wider spans of supervisory control with fewer levels of hierarchy than did successful firms with more stable, continuous-process technologies.

Building on Woodward's work, Burns and Stalker closely examined some 20 different organizations covering a wide variety of products and applications and found two basic types of organizational structures—"mechanistic" and "organic."[32] The mechanistic system, used in organizations operating under relatively stable external conditions, emphasizes well-defined rules, procedures, and functional roles. Since only those at the top of the organization have access to the overall knowledge and since the command hierarchy is well defined, interaction within the organization is vertical rather than horizontal. The "organic" system, on the other hand, operates in uncertain and changing environments, e.g., the electronics industry. Jobs are less clearly defined, and interaction tends to be lateral rather than vertical. Much more knowledge (and the power to make decisions) is contained at lower levels in the management hierarchy.

In the early 1960s Likert proposed his linking-pin theory, which is transitional because it takes both a structural and humanistic view of the organization.[33] However, even though it is based on substantive research, Likert's

assumption is that there is *one best approach* to management of an organization. Likert notes that a superior in one work group is a subordinate in the
next higher work group (Fig. 1.2). Thus although a foreman supervises a
work group, he or she is a subordinate of the supervisor of foremen. In
Likert's linking-pin approach, each work group has a head, or chief, who is
tied in with the next higher group. The "linking-pin" is the chief who has
contact with both groups.

One of Likert's key concepts is that of supportive relationships. He notes
that a worker must feel wanted, needed, and important. The superior must
understand the subordinate's expectations, and the superior must know how
he or she is perceived by the subordinate. The feeling of support is the key to
high motivation within a work group. A corollary concept is the key role of
the work group. Likert states that since people want to achieve a feeling of
value and personal worth, the supportive work group is *the* way to achieve
this and that an organization will function best when workers function "not
as individuals but as members of highly effective work groups with high performance goals."[34]

One of the interesting features of Likert's theory is that it integrates the
structural and human approaches to management. However, since it ignores
the informal group and does not take account of extreme situations, the
theory's usefulness is somewhat limited.

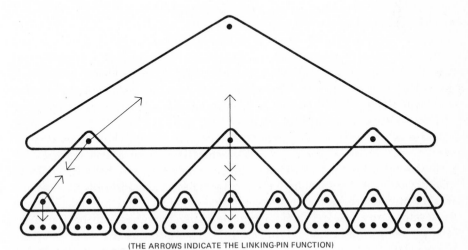

(THE ARROWS INDICATE THE LINKING-PIN FUNCTION)

Fig. 1.2 Likert's linking-pin theory. (From *New Patterns of Management* by R.
Likert, p. 103. Copyright 1961 by McGraw-Hill. Used with permission of McGraw-
Hill Book Company.)

The new contingency theory, developed from the work of Fred Fiedler and discussed in Chapter 7, is a model based on three variables: (1) leader-member relationships; (2) task structure or definition; and (3) position power of the leader.[35] Through extensive research, Fiedler found that when the work situation is either very favorable or very unfavorable for the leader, an authoritarian approach is warranted. When the situation is of intermediate favorableness, a democratic, or egalitarian, approach is justified.

This early example of a contingency, or situational, approach to management was later expanded by Lawrence and Lorsch, who applied it to the organizational structure and to the roles to be maintained by individuals in the organization.[36] However, the contingency approach does not ignore the human component; rather, it suggests that perhaps organizational structure should be *situationally* determined, depending on such variables as the rate of technological advance in the given industry. The Lawrence and Lorsch research is of further interest because in order to arrive at their principles, they had to empirically examine successful and unsuccessful organizations in different industries to determine the most successful structure for a given industry.

Perrow has taken the work of such researchers as Woodward, Lawrence and Lorsch, and others and considerably expanded upon it in stressing the need for a proper "fit" between the organization and the environment.[37] Perrow reports evidence that the proper design and management of organizational structure is the key to changing both human behavior within the organization and organizational competency. He developed an elaborate, fourfold typology of organizations—craft, nonroutine, engineering, and routine—and concluded that each type of organization needs to be designed differently. He points out that it is essential to carefully analyze technology and structure in light of the organizational environment—that a style of management which is successful in one situation may well be dysfunctional in another situation unless it is considerably modified.

One of the early attempts at integrating all three perspectives was by March and Simon, who approached organizations from a systems point of view, taking account of structure, information flow, and behavior.[38] Their quantification of relationships between variables in the form of propositions was an attempt to systematize complicated organizational interrelationships as developed by research and to provide many hypotheses to be tested by later research. More recently, the late J. D. Thompson used a more "macro," or sociological, approach than did March and Simon to continue developing integrated propositions about organizations. Although March and Simon treat the organization as a system, it is a closed system that does not take into account the environment in which the organization finds itself. Thompson, on the other hand, treats the organization as both a closed and an open system in continuous interaction with the environment, thus protecting itself so that it can survive and grow.[39]

A. Current Situation in Organization Theory and Practice

Presently a number of approaches to the study of organizations appear to be converging. The micro theorists, frequently with a background in psychology, start with the individual and move toward the organization. The macro theorists, with their sociological approaches, start with the organization's relationship with the environment and move toward some of the managerial or interpersonal issues. It is clear that *the appropriateness of alterable interpersonal or organizational attributes depends on the situation.* "The situation" includes external and internal environmental factors, time, the organization's purpose, extrinsic and intrinsic motivation, and the like. All of the organizational variables are not only interrelated, but also interdependent. Organizational research that manipulates one variable creates a ripple effect throughout the organization and the environment.

No one style of leadership is *always* appropriate; in fact, one theorist (Perrow) doubts that one can determine *when* a particular leadership style will be effective.[40] Additionally, different things motivate different people, and various organizational structures are appropriate at various times. The emphasis now in organizational problem solving should not be on the *prescription*, but on the diagnosis—a theme increasing in importance. One author has listed the various information-gathering techniques, the structurally oriented approaches to change, and the process-oriented approaches to change in organizations.[41] As one might expect, their effective use is situationally determined.

In brief, there is no one best approach to managing all organizations. Organizational design is situational, it must be created for each company. Situational management, though it needs much refinement, does provide a relative novel and realistic approach for understanding and designing effective management strategy.

VI. SUMMARY

In this chapter we set the stage in a number of ways. First, we provided an outline of the book from the more micro to the more macro issues. We introduced three viewpoints of management and discussed the history of their development, along with a fourth, integrated perspective—the systems approach, which is developed in Chapter 2. The distinctions raised here are continued

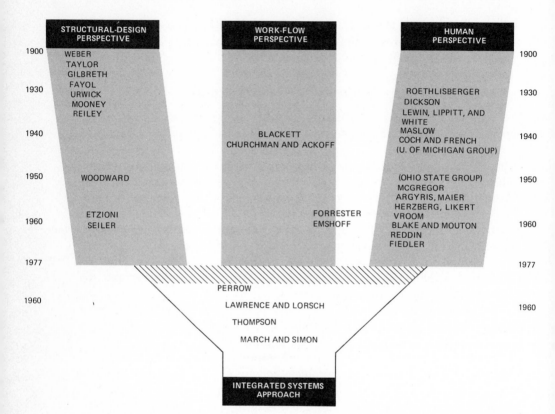

Fig. 1.3 Names and dates of major theorists in organizational behavior.

throughout the book. The universals of management theorists, the scientific management proponents, and the structuralists all fall into a structural-design perspective. The operations researchers and the management scientists represent the beginnings of a work-flow perspective. Finally, the human relations group and the organization development theorists come within the framework of a human perspective.

An expanded version of Fig. 1.1 is given in Fig. 1.3. We have added some of the key names and groups of researchers. Placing them in a framework should be helpful as you read through this book.

REVIEW

1. What are the differences and similarities between the universal principles of management school and the structuralist school? How appropriate are these schools currently?

2. Operations research attempts to solve a problem by putting all dimensions of an organizational situation into quantifiable terms. How does this approach differ from those allied with a human perspective?

3. What influence does the "Hawthorne effect" have on structural-management approaches?

4. "Those who do not understand history are doomed to repeat it." What does this mean in the context of the evolution of management thought?

REFERENCES

1. J. D. Mooney and A. C. Reiley, *The Principles of Organization*, rev. ed., New York: Harper and Brothers, 1947.

2. H. Fayol, *General and Industrial Management*, trans. C. Storrs, London: Pitman, 1949.

3. *Ibid.*, pp. 57, 58.

4. Mooney and Reiley, *op. cit.*, p. 33.

5. G. G. Fisch, "Line/Staff is Obsolete," *Harvard Business Review* **39,** 5 (Sept.–Oct. 1961), p. 80.

6. Mooney and Reiley, *op. cit.*

7. Fayol, *op. cit.*, p. 35. Reprinted by permission.

8. Mooney and Reiley, *op. cit.*, pp. 14–15.

9. A. Etzioni, *Modern Organizations*, Englewood Cliffs, N.J.: Prentice-Hall, 1964.

10. M. Weber, *The Theory of Social and Economic Organization*, trans. A. M. Henderson and T. Parsons, ed. T. Parsons, New York: Oxford University Press, 1947, pp. 329–340.

11. *Ibid.*

12. Etzioni, *op. cit.*

13. F. W. Taylor, *Scientific Management*, New York: Harper & Row, 1911.

14. H. Koontz and C. O'Donnell, *Principles of Management*, New York: McGraw-Hill, 1968, pp. 231–403.

15. W. G. Scott, "Organizational Theory: An Overview and an Appraisal," *Journal of the Academy of Management* **4,** 1 (April 1961): 7–26.

16. J. V. Worthy, "Organizational Structure and Employee Morale," *American Sociological Review* **15,** 2 (April 1950): 169–170.

17. L. W. Porter and E. E. Lawler, "Properties of Organization Structure in Relation to Job Attitudes and Job Behavior," *Psychological Bulletin* **64,** 1 (July 1965): 23–51.

18. R. H. Hall, "Intraorganizational Structural Variation: Application of the Bureaucratic Model," *Administrative Science Quarterly* **7,** 3 (September 1962): 295–308.

19. C. W. Churchman, R. L. Ackoff, and E. L. Arnoff, *Introduction to Operations Research*, New York: Wiley, 1957.

20. F. N. Trefethen, "A History of Operations Research," in *Operations Research for Management*, ed. J. F. McCloskey and F. N. Trefethen, Baltimore: Johns Hopkins Press, 1954.

21. Churchman, Ackoff, and Arnoff, *op. cit.*, p. 13.

22. J. W. Forrester, "Counterintuitive Behavior of Social Systems," *Technology Review* **73**, 3 (Jan. 1971) Alumni Association of the Massachusetts Institute of Technology, pp. 52–68.

23. J. R. Emshoff, *Analysis of Behavioral Systems*, New York: Macmillan, 1971.

24. J. Diebold, "APD—the Still-Sleeping Giant, *Harvard Business Review* **42**, 5 Sept.–Oct. 1964): 60–65.

25. F. J. Roethlisberger and W. J. Dickson, *Management and the Worker—an Account of a Research Program Conducted by the Western Electric Co., Hawthorne Works, Chicago*, Cambridge, Mass.: Harvard University Press, 1939.

26. E. A. Fleishman, E. F. Harris, and R. D. Burtt, "Leadership and Supervision in Industry," *Ohio State Business Education Reserve Monograph* **33** (1955).

27. J. G. March and H. A. Simon, *Organizations*, New York: Wiley, 1958.

28. L. Coch and J. R. P. French, "Overcoming Resistance to Change," *Human Relations* **1** (1948): 512–532.

29. R. Lippitt and R. K. White, "An Experimental Study of Leadership and Group Life," in *Readings in Social Psychology*, ed. T. M. Newcomb and E. L. Hartley, New York: Holt, Rinehart and Winston, 1947.

30. C. Perrow, "The Short and Glorious History of Organizational Theory," *Organizational Dynamics* **2**, 1 (Summer 1973): 2–15.

31. J. Woodward, *Management and Technology*, London: Her Majesty's Printing Office, 1958.

32. T. Burns and G. Stalker, *The Management of Innovation*, New York: Barnes & Noble, Social Science Paperbacks, 1961.

33. R. Likert, *New Patterns of Management*, New York: McGraw-Hill, 1961.

34. *Ibid.*, p. 105.

35. F. Fiedler, *A Theory of Leadership Effectiveness*, New York: McGraw-Hill, 1967.

36. P. Lawrence and J. Lorsch, *Organization and Environment: Managing Differentiation and Integration*, Boston: Harvard University Graduate School of Business Administration, Division of Research, 1967.

37. C. Perrow, *Organizational Analysis: A Sociological View*, Belmont, Cal.: Wadsworth, 1970.

38. March and Simon, *op. cit.*

39. J. D. Thompson, *Organizations in Action*, New York: McGraw-Hill, 1967.

40. Perrow, "The Short and Glorious History of Organizational Theory," *op. cit.*

41. Y. K. Shetty, "Contingency Management: Current Perspective for Managing Organizations," *Management International Review* **14**, 6 (1974): 27–35.

2

THE ORGANIZATION
AS A
SYSTEM

For want of a nail the shoe is lost,
For want of a shoe the horse is lost,
For want of a horse the rider is lost.

GEORGE HERBERT

LEARNING
OBJECTIVES

When you have finished reading and studying this chapter, you should be able to:

1. Differentiate between the idea of a system as an analytical concept and as an evaluative (right or wrong) one.
2. Describe a system in terms of inputs, transformations or operations, and outputs.
3. Explain what is meant by system complexity, interdependence, and open versus closed systems.
4. Use force-field analysis in analyzing changing a system.
5. Use the complexity and interdependence of systems as analytical tools.

You will be expected to define and use the following concepts:

System	Balance
Subsystem	Interdependence
Levels	Open versus closed systems
Boundary	Physical versus social systems
Environment	Contrived systems
Input	Complexity
Transformation	Interdependence
Output	Feedback
Force-field analysis	Deviance reducing
Different systems perspectives	Deviance amplifying

THOUGHT STARTERS

1. How do you personally define the term "systems"?
2. What are several ways in which people use the term "system"?
3. In what sense can a small group of people working together be considered a system? What are some possible subsystems of that small group?
4. What happens when a system is characterized as "good" or "bad," "functional" or "dysfunctional"?

I. INTRODUCTION

If you step on my toe, you hurt me. If the battery is dead, the car won't start. If the electric power goes off, the furnace doesn't operate. If the planes are grounded at Airport X, passengers may not make their scheduled flight from Airport Y. The American-Russian spacecraft link above the earth in 1975 required major modifications in both the Apollo and Soyuz spacecraft, and a 10 ft by 5 ft airlock was necessary because of the different atmospheric pressure in the two spacecraft.

These examples show the interrelationships among the parts in a system. The concept of "system"—the interstate highway system or the educational system—is one with which we are all familiar, perhaps too familiar, since the meaning of the term has become blurred. One way of looking at organizations is by the systems approach, which is a frame of reference or a categorizing scheme for explaining, predicting, and controlling complex phenomena. In this chapter, we first describe the modern organization in systems terms. We start with a brief description of general systems theory and identify various levels of systems. The rest of the chapter focuses on management or organizational systems theory, which is a subset, or a part, of general systems theory. After examining some advantages and disadvantages of the systems approach, we consider the organization as a "social system" with interdependent and interrelated parts. Such a system is dynamic and continually changing, yet usually manages to achieve an internal "balance" as it interacts with itself as well as with its environment. Finally, we describe three different perspectives of social organizations to help you gain a better understanding of how organizations can be improved and made more effective, yet still allow the employees to better reach their own personal goals and objectives.

Knowledge of the characteristics of systems, especially social systems, is becoming essential for understanding organizations—small or large. A humanly contrived social system usually has an existence beyond that of the human beings in it; people may come and go, but the social system lives on.

II. GENERAL SYSTEMS THEORY

The word "system" is not a new one. The concept can be traced back to Aristotle, who suggested that the whole is greater than the sum of its parts. Today, the term is widely used and just as widely misunderstood. We read newspaper stories about weapons systems, early-warning systems, communications systems, and records systems. Astronomy brings to mind the solar system; physiology, the digestive system, the nervous system, and the circulatory system; economics, the monetary system; physics, the atomic system. The word "system" is used so widely that it has become almost meaningless.

Underlying the concept of "general systems theory" is the assumption that general laws and concepts form the foundation of such diverse fields as biology and physiology in the physical sciences and economics and psychology in the social sciences. The examination and identification of these laws or principles can be used to unify science. Thus the basic concept is that things do not just happen, but rather that they evolve from multiple causes and multiple effects.

The founder of general systems theory was a biologist, von Bertalanffy, who began writing about general systems theory about 1920 and continued doing so until his death in 1972. He suggested that understanding the parts

This is how many people view "the system." (Harold M. Lambert/E. P. Jones)

was not enough, that it was also important to understand relationships among the parts. For him, "General Systems Theory is a logico-mathematical field whose task is the formulation and derivation of those general principles that are applicable to 'systems' in general."[1] One of the authors who in the 1930s described the concept of general systems was Henderson, who pointed out that "the interdependence of the variables in a system is one of the widest inductions (inferences) from experience that we possess; or we may alternatively regard it as the definition of a system."[2]

At this stage, we can define a system as a series of interrelated and interdependent parts, such that the interaction or interplay of any of the subsystems (parts) affects the whole. In fact, if we use the systems approach, the interactions and interdependencies among the subsystems are at least as important as the individual components. For example, the automobile is a total system, consisting of a number of subsystems—ignition, fuel, steering, engine, and drive-train. If all the subsystems are working well, so does the car. But malfunction of one subsystem affects the performance of the entire system, the car.

Boulding has pointed out that there are at least nine different levels of systems, ranging from static structures (the simplest) to cybernetic structures (such as a thermostat) to human and social systems (the most complex).[3] Each succeeding level is more complex and more difficult to conceptualize (see Table 2.1). These nine levels of systems are arranged in ascending order of both complexity and openness to change and modification *from the outside*. The higher the level, the more likely the system is to be influenced and affected by outside events or phenomena.

Boulding believes that these nine levels serve a useful function by indicating where there are serious gaps in our knowledge. He believes that our knowledge is generally inadequate to build mathematical or other models beyond the level of the dynamic structure (level 2). However, strides are being made at the upper levels, especially with the cybernetic system and the self-maintaining system, though we still know very little about the process of self-maintenance. Boulding also believes that we have not yet discovered the rudiments of theoretical models beyond the fourth level. For example, he points out that economic theorists still use concepts drawn primarily from levels 2 and 3, although the material and subject matter being studied is at level 8.

As a practical matter, he warns that although a great deal of work has been done at levels 7 and 8, our ability to build actual theoretical, systematic models is far in the future and that we still have a tremendous amount to learn before we can capture and identify the variables sufficiently to build an adequate model. Nevertheless, the most important concept to keep in mind is the need to *think* in systems terms. This thought process overrides the importance of attempting to *measure* each variable.

Table 2.1 Levels of systems

1. Static structure—the ordering of planets in the solar system
2. Simple, dynamic system—most machines and most of Newtonian physics
3. Cybernetics system—control mechanisms, such as the thermostat
4. Open system—the self-perpetuating structure, such as the single cell
5. Genetic-societal system—division of labor, including subsystems, such as a plant
6. Animal system—includes self-awareness and mobility, as well as specialized subsystems for receiving and processing information from the outside world
7. Human system—includes the capacity for self-consciousness, self-awareness, and the use of symbolism to communicate ideas
8. Social organizations—humans as subsystems within the larger organization, or system
9. Transcendental systems—alternatives and unknowables which are yet to be discovered

Adapted from K. Boulding, "General Systems Theory: The Skeleton of Science," *Management Science* **2**, 3 (April 1956): 197–208.

III. ADVANTAGES AND DISADVANTAGES OF THE SYSTEMS APPROACH

In analyzing the organization as a social system, we need to reiterate that the systems approach to looking at organizations (and the individuals within them) is only one approach. The systems approach is a frame of reference, a categorizing scheme by which we can explain, predict, and influence a complex phenomenon. The advantages and disadvantages of this approach will be described in some detail.

A. Advantages of the Systems Approach

1. Open versus closed systems In simplistic terms, a system is closed if no energy enters the system boundaries; a system is open if energy enters from the outside. There are relatively few closed systems in real life, of course. However, the concept is a useful one, since we can agree that there are *degrees* of openness. A thermostat, responding only to temperature variation, is more of a closed system than is the student who is actively taking notes or asking the instructor a question. The student may be responding to a number of inputs.

The concept of open versus closed system is useful for analyzing organizations. For example, we may want to create a "closed system" in order to conduct an experiment in which we manipulate one variable and try to hold all the others constant. In addition, it may be important for an organization to maintain some subsystems in a relatively closed position.

For example, in reviewing the concept of open versus closed systems, Thompson notes that two basic but different models of organizations have emerged.[4] Under the terms of the first, or *rational* model, the emphasis is on control and the elimination of uncertainty—a *closed-system strategy*. The *open-system strategy*, by contrast, assumes much more uncertainty; since the system has more input from outside, fewer of the variables can be predicted and controlled. Thompson believes that it is not accidental that the concepts of *planning* and *controlling* are heavily stressed by the closed-system strategists, whereas such concepts are given little weight by those using the open-system strategy.

He also notes that the logics associated with the two approaches seem, at first glance, to be incompatible; the one avoids uncertainty, whereas the other assumes uncertainty and variability. However, he suggests that on closer examination, the two logics are *not* incompatible: "We will conceive of complex organizations as open systems, hence indeterminate and faced with uncertainty, but at the same time as subject to criteria of rationality and hence needing determinateness and uncertainty."[5] Thompson resolves the previous dilemma by suggesting that organizations attempt to operate their technical cores as closed systems, operating under norms of rationality and certainty by providing the central core with buffers from external, environmental influences. He uses the example of manufacturing, which has inventories at both the input and output ends. Buffering in a hospital, by contrast, might consist of establishing priorities for nonemergency admissions.

Further, organizations set up special units to deal with environmental uncertainty away from their technological core. For example, hospitals establish emergency rooms away from the central core; airlines and hotel chains set up reservations systems, and universities generally admit more students than they anticipate will actually accept. In other words, the more central a unit is, the more it is treated as a closed system; the closer to the environment a unit is, the more it is treated as an open system.

The idea of a closed system also helps with analysis. As we discuss motivation, group dynamics, and leadership, for example, we will be treating these variables primarily in isolation as closed systems; doing so provides ease and clarity in teaching.

2. Choosing the level of analysis The concept of "system" allows us to choose a particular level of analysis of an organization while still keeping in mind that we are dealing with a total system. For example, we can take the macro approach and study the organization in relationship to its environment. Or we can take the micro approach and analyze an individual, a group, or a particular unit of an organization while still keeping in mind that the focus of our study is a *subsystem* within the total system and that the organization as a total system can also be considered as a subsystem within the larger environment. Indeed, according to one author, "If you want to improve organizational theory, quit studying organizations."[6] He suggests that the large, complex organization forces the analyst to lower his sights because of the very complexity of the analysis and that anything that happens in the organization also happens in more visible form elsewhere.

Lundberg has suggested the matrix shown in Fig. 2.1 to help one choose the appropriate level of system or subsystem for analysis.[7] The matrix has three levels of complexity: the individual, or personal, system; the group, or interpersonal, system; and the multigroup, or organizational, system. Lundberg notes that additional levels could be added, such as the community and the society as a whole. At the least complex level, we can focus on the motives, goals, and wants of the individual. At the group level, we can focus on such variables as communications, group cohesiveness, group tasks and norms, and leadership. At the third level, we can focus on such issues as profits, goals, and organizational competence; the design of the system; and such issues as power and authority.

In addition to analyzing by level of complexity, we can also look at the relationships between or within systems existing at the same or different levels. The cells on the diagonal (A-A', B-B', and C-C') represent the relation-

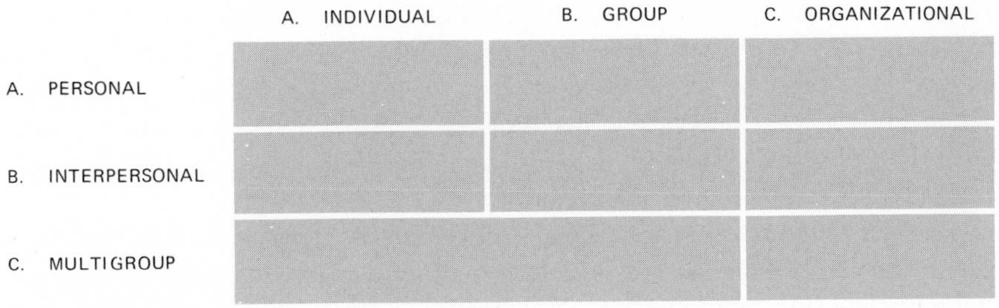

Fig. 2.1 Different levels of interrelated systems. (Adapted from C. Lundberg, "Toward Understanding Behavioral Science by Administrators," *California Management Review* **6**, 1, Fall 1963, p. 49.)

ships between two systems at the same level. We can also use the matrix to visualize the way in which a broader system can include subsystems.

3. Structure versus process When we are dealing with relatively simple systems, such as a thermostat, we can focus primarily on *structure*. We can also focus on structure when dealing with complex organizations. When you read Chapter 3, on motivation, you will find that early, "rational" models of human motivation assumed that an individual would "fit" neatly into the structural hierarchy and follow orders. Newer approaches to motivation are less concerned with such static models and are more concerned with the process by which a person becomes motivated.

One of the advantages of systems theory is that it also *forces* us to be concerned with, and analyze, the concept of process—the interaction within and between subsystems. The higher the level of the system, the more important the process becomes rather than the structure as such. " 'Process,' then, points to the actions and interactions of the components of an ongoing system, in which varying degrees of structuring arise, persist, dissolve or change."[8] We will pick up this point again when we discuss one of the disadvantages of the system concept—the idea that a social organization is a "contrived" system.

B. Disadvantages of the Systems Approach

1. Physical versus social systems General systems theory grew out of biology and was then extended to other areas, including mechanical systems and social systems. However, it is important to distinguish between the physical and social models. Katz and Kahn warn that "there has been no more pervasive, persistent and futile fallacy handicapping the social sciences than the use of the physical model for the understanding of social structures."[9]

One of the characteristics of a machine, an organism, or an organ, e.g., the heart, is that each part has definite functions which are well known and can be identified. The overall structure has a high degree of permanence unless changed or *modified from the outside;* for example, we can graft a new branch onto a tree, redesign a machine, or conduct a heart or kidney transplant. The physical model, in general, requires that a change in structure be imposed *on* the system.

Social systems do exist in nature, such as the complex ant colony. However, these social systems are based on instinct or early learning and are relatively unchanging. Human social systems, on the other hand, differ from biological machine or instinct models of systems in that they can be restructured or redesigned from the outside. "The fact that social organizations are contrived by human beings suggests that they can be established for an infinite variety of purposes and do not follow the same life-cycle patterns of birth, growth, maturity and death as biological systems."[10] In the same fashion, machines may slowly wear out unless they are given external maintenance. With the development of artificial intelligence, cybernetics, and similar advances, the distinction between physical and social systems may lessen, but we need to be careful to avoid applying the findings of general systems theory too literally to social systems as a subset of the larger approach. Rather, we need to recognize the utility of systems theory as applied to social organizations, but bear in mind that organizations are held together with psychological rather than biological cement.[11]

2. Difficulties in measurement In the mid-1950s Boulding suggested that we know relatively little about defining and measuring systems concepts, especially at the seventh level, that of the human system.[12] Although great strides have been made in recent years, we still do not have good ways of defining and measuring the myriad of system variables involved. As a result, we frequently need to use an intuitive, or "best guess," approach. One of the difficulties with the systems concept is that the cybernetic approach is misleading, particularly the well-worn example of the thermostat. In this orderly world, the furnace is either on or off, and the thermostat is either off or on. However, the social system is different; psychological states are not necessarily mutually exclusive (off or on), but may coexist and be multivalued at the same time. "The possibility that multiple states exist simultaneously for a single psychological variable is plausible because actors remember, perceive, and anticipate. These three processes can generate different states for a single variable at a single moment in time."[13]

Nevertheless, the attempt to expand the mathematics of the model continue. A computer model has been used to simulate the interaction of organizational structure and technology. In this case, the researchers attempted to build a model based on a theoretical structure and to determine how it applied to the actual structure of a bomber wing in the Air Force, consisting of flight and maintenance crews. In this case, the model was used as a way of building explanatory theory.[14]

3. The need to be more precise in terminology As noted at the beginning of this chapter, the widespread use of the word "system" has made it almost meaningless. As Weick points out, "People working in the field of organization theory are currently being victimized by two nouns, organization and systems."[15] He suggests that the use of these two nouns has seduced people into talking about *things* rather than relationships (and relationships are at the core of systems theory). Weick postulates that to assume that an organization is an "open system" does not specify the conditions under which an organization really is an open system.

Further, we need to be more precise when we move from closed-system to open-system thinking; when we move from subsystem to total-system thinking; when we do not properly delineate levels; when we do not accurately describe systems boundaries. "For example, when we use the term 'organizational behavior' are we talking about the way the organization behaves as a system or are we talking about the behavior of the individual participants? By goals, do we mean the goals of the organization or the goals of the individuals within the organization?"[16]

These are some of the problems with systems theory. On balance, however, the attempt to use the systems approach is fruitful, even though the state of the art is not yet complete enough to solve all of the problems associated with it. Although we cannot yet be *mathematical* in our approach (and perhaps should not be), we can at least attempt to be *systematic* in our use of systems theory.

IV. CHARACTERISTICS OF HUMAN ORGANIZATIONS

The primary advantage of using the systems approach is that it provides us with a conceptual model, or mental image, of an organization. This abstract model makes use of particular concepts or relationships to represent "the real thing." Our primary concern in this book is with systems levels 7 and 8 of Boulding's classification (the human system, or model, and the social system, or model). One way to develop a human model would be to use the biological approach, according to which a human being comprises a number of subsystems—nervous, circulatory, digestive, reproductive, etc.—each of which can be considered as a system in its own right. Each of these individual systems is a subsystem of the total system, and all of them are interrelated and interdependent, i.e., a change in one of the subsystems affects the other subsystems. If an individual becomes excited, for example, his or her glandular system pumps more adrenalin into the blood stream, the circulatory system speeds up, the stomach lining turns red as excess acid is poured into the stomach (which may produce ulcers), and under extreme stress, the functioning of the nervous system may be impaired. However, since there are limitations to using the biological model, it may be more appropriate to look at the human system from a psychological perspective.

In a psychological perspective, the important variables are one's attitudes, motives, feelings, values, and norms of behavior, and they all interact with and are affected by the others. Throughout the text, we use the psychological perspective to study the human being as a complete system and also as a subsystem of the social organization (level 8 of Boulding's classification system) and society as a whole.

Researchers are now examining social organizations—schools and other educational systems, governmental bodies, business, industry, etc.—from a systems point of view. Although our knowledge is still inadequate for building mathematical models, it is possible to discuss in systems terms what appear to be some common characteristics of social organizations. Thus we can describe social organizations (systems) by their complexity, degree of interdependence of their subsystems, openness, balance, and multiplicity of purposes, functions, and objectives.

A. Complexity and Interdependence of Social Systems

Any social system, or human organization, consists of a number of individuals, groups, or departments, each of which is a subsystem within the total system. For example, the subsystems of a university include the different colleges, the various departments within the colleges, and such support functions as purchasing, security, and janitorial service. A manufacturing company's subsystems include the purchasing, finance, accounting, and marketing functions. A bank may have such subsystems as commercial deposits, loan, and investment departments.

The existence of subsystems causes the social organization to be complex. But even more important to management theory is the interdependence among the subsystems. Sayles and Chandler provide a dramatic illustration of the interdependence of subsystems. In the NASA biosatellite program, researchers found that an artificial bladder designed to handle the waste products of the monkey passenger was incapable of doing so. "A '2 bladder' replacement system cost half a million dollars and created enormous design problems."[17]

Figure 2.2(a) is an oversimplified diagram of a hypothetical organization of three members, A, B, and C. The square around A, B, and C represents the closed boundary of the organization, and the elastic bonds of the interdependence of A, B, and C to one another and to the organization are shown by the various two-way arrows. The system is in "static" equilibrium—a steady state, or balance. If organization member C moves to a new position, as shown in Fig. 2.2(b), all three members of the organization will be affected, and the original state of static equilibrium, or balance, will be dynamically altered to reflect the change that has occurred, thus establishing a new state of equilibrium.

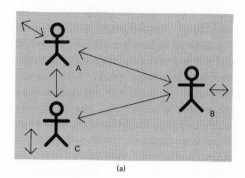

(a)

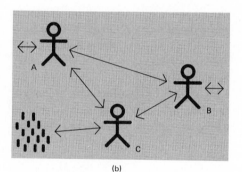

(b)

Fig. 2.2 A closed system.

B. The Social System as an Open System

Although Fig. 2.2 depicts a self-contained organization, most systems are open —they are continually interacting with the outside environment. A human organization is open in that it exists in a wider environment of many other larger or smaller organizations, or systems. Thus since any particular system (human organization) is itself a subsystem in interaction with other subsystems in the environment, we cannot understand the functioning of an organization without taking into consideration the influence of other subsystems and the environment. For example, the behavior of a business organization cannot be fully understood without knowing something about its market, suppliers, the public, and the governmental rules and regulations affecting it.

Figure 2.3 shows typical patterns of interpersonal interaction. The system created by interaction at a party, for example, is also in dynamic interaction with the environment, e.g., governmental officials (represented by the mailman in the foreground) and other systems (shown by the painter).

OTHER SYSTEMS
(ORGANIZATIONS)

Fig. 2.3   An open system.

One of the important concepts of an open system is "input," or something that enters the system from the environment. For example, the input for a computer subsystem is data, without which this subsystem cannot operate. In the human system, the input of information from the outside world comes from the five senses.

Obviously, the complexity and variety of the input increase with the complexity of the system. The input for a social system, or organization, is highly complex—information, people, energy, materials. Similarly, each type of input is also highly complex and varied.

Once an input enters the system, it undergoes "transformation," or "operation." A manufacturing company, for example, has elaborate mechanisms for transforming incoming raw materials into finished goods. Once these inputs have been transformed, they represent "output" and are ready to leave the system as finished goods. In other words, a system's "output" is the result of the operation, or transformation, process. An automobile manufacturer, for example, "exports" finished goods (cars) to dealers who in turn "export"

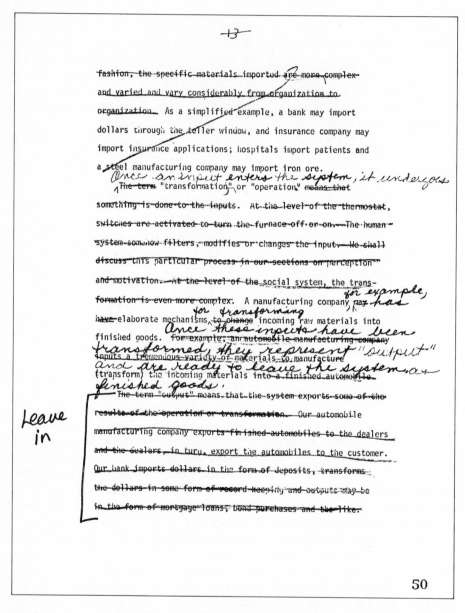

Fig. 2.4 An author receives feedback in the form of an editor's markings on the manuscript; the editor, in turn, gets feedback from the author, e.g., "leave in."

cars to customers. Or, a bank "imports" dollars (deposits), "transforms" them (record keeping), and "exports" the money to customers (mortgage loans, bond purchases, etc.). Figure 2.4 illustrates the transformation process that occurs on an author's manuscript.

The term "feedback" originated from studies on cybernetics conducted by Norbert Wiener to better understand the processes of control and communication.[18] For Wiener, the key explanatory mechanism for communication and control is the feedback loop, which carries a continuous flow of information between the system, its parts, and the environment. In other words, a portion of a system's or subsystem's output is fed back to the inputs in order to affect succeeding inputs. Since open systems are never completely closed off from the outside world, they are affected by the environment and in turn have an effect on the environment through output information, which is fed back into the system as an input to guide and control the operation of the system. Figure 2.5 shows that feedback comes from not only the environment, but also the various subsystems of a social organization.

Fig. 2.5 The feedback concept.

Several examples may help here. At the lowest cybernetic level, the input from the outside environment causes a thermostat to turn the furnace on; as the thermostat gets feedback about the house temperature, it turns the furnace off at the appropriate point. A simple experiment illustrates feedback at the physiological level. Place a coin or pencil on your desk. Then close your eyes and pick it up. This is quite easy to do, because the nerves in your hand send "feedback" information which enables you to pick up the object. Finally, the information about sales relayed back to a company by a salesman (feedback) may be used as new input by the organization in determining its future production activities.

Another concept of an open system is that of "boundaries." In real life, there are few truly closed systems with impenetrable, impermeable physical boundaries. Rather, almost all systems require, as a minimum, energy from the outside to maintain the system. It is difficult, however, to define the boundaries of social systems, since there is a continuous inflow and outflow of energy through the boundaries of the system.

A boundary exists when there is less interchange of inputs across the line than within the system. However, this definition of the boundary is somewhat arbitrary, since a social system has multiple subsystems, and the boundary line for one subsystem may not coincide with that for a different subsystem. Nonetheless, we may need to assign arbitrary boundaries to a social organization, depending on the variables we wish to stress. The boundaries used for studying or analyzing leadership, for example, may be quite different from those used for assessing marketing strategy.

In addition, the permeability of boundaries varies considerably in social organizations. For example, the boundaries of a community's police force are probably far more rigid and sharply defined than those of the political parties in the same community.

C. Balance and the Social System

In any social system there are two conflicting forces—one directed toward maintaining the "status quo" and the other directed toward change and growth. Although such terms as "equilibrium," "entropy," and "homeostasis" are often used to describe the relationship between these forces, we prefer to use the term "balance." "Balance" does not imply a static, unchanging organization, because the organization can reach and maintain a balance at different places along a continuum—the balance point may change.

In discussing balance, one must distinguish between "fixed-point" balance and "steady-state" balance. For example, a person's body temperature is usually a fixed point (98.6°F), and the body will resist attempts to raise or lower this temperature. The term "steady state" describes a balance that is not dependent on such a fixed point, or level. Although many managers strive for a "fixed-point" balance in the hope that things will "settle down," their efforts are meaningless, because social organizations are highly dynamic. Although many of the forces within a social system—the individual, the subsystems of which the manager is a part, the managerial hierarchy, and inputs from the outside environment—seek a balance within the organization, many of them also continually disturb the "steady state" of the organization. To see these opposing forces at work, one need only attend the meetings of a university academic senate comprising students, faculty, and administrators.

Change by itself is neither good nor bad. An organization must be able to change and modify itself to meet changing conditions. At the same time, it needs to avoid both unnecessary, dysfunctional change and wild, erratic swings. Therefore, organizations need to have two types of feedback loops (see Fig. 2.6). The concept of "deviation-reducing, negative" feedback loop(s) describes the forces working against change and is used to collect and transmit information to keep the system directed toward a preset goal or objective. In an industrial organization, for example, deviation-reducing, negative feedback is used to ensure that production plans and schedules are being met. "Deviation-amplifying, positive feedback," on the other hand, is used to change the course or direction of the organization—it upsets the organization's existing balance. Examples are a salesperson in the field reporting that sales are not going well and insisting on a change, or a market research group recommending that a new product be developed and put on the market. The recent upswing in medical malpractice suits has forced some state governments to change by providing pooled malpractice insurance.

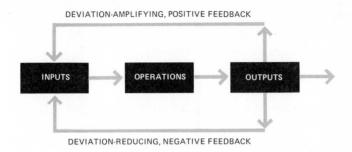

Fig. 2.6 Two types of feedback loops.

Now let's take a closer look at how the feedback loops might work in an organization. An organization is moving from A to B, as shown in Fig. 2.7. If it moves in a perfectly straight line, there is no oscillation. Oscillations are caused by both deviation-reducing and deviation-amplifying forces. Deviation amplifies as the organization moves away from a projected path and decreases as it moves back toward its original path. If a system is to change direction (toward C, for example), some deviation-amplifying forces and intervention are necessary.

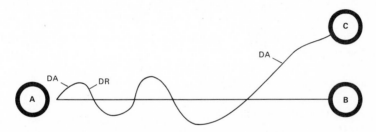

Fig. 2.7 Deviation-amplifying and deviation-reducing forces at work.

Lewin has developed a method called a "force-field analysis" for analyzing these opposing forces.[19] Figure 2.8 shows this process. The arrows represent forces, or vectors, applied to the body at rest. The length of a vector is equivalent to its strength. If the algebraic sum of the vectors is equal, the body will remain at rest, but if the strength of the vectors on either side changes, the balance point changes until the sum of the vectors is again equal. In other words, one can either increase the force on one side or decrease the force on the other side.

The same concept can be applied to social organizations. The organization can reach a new balance point if one set of vectors is either increased or decreased. However, the forces exerted on social organizations—feelings, attitudes, and emotions—cannot be quantified. For example, a supervisor's demand for greater productivity (increased vector) is likely to be met by in-

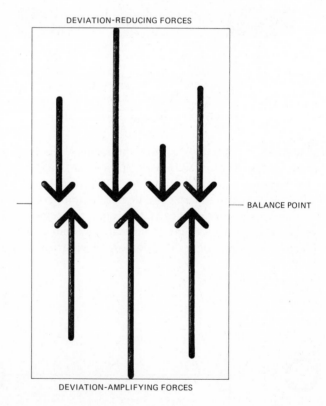

Fig. 2.8 Force-field diagram (length of each vector—arrow—is equal to amount or strength of force).

creased resistance, distrust, and hostility on the part of the workers; a person who is "pushed" is likely to "push" back. For example, a group of high school boys were working as dishwashers and general kitchen help in a nursing home. When a new man was put in charge of the kitchen, he reduced lunch breaks, eliminated coffee breaks, and pushed hard for increased work in an effort to increase the workers' productivity. As a result, the boys slowed down their work and took even longer to accomplish their tasks than they had in the past. In this case, the equilibrium of productivity actually moved downward as a direct result of the pressure to move productivity upward. In other words, a simple, mechanistic model cannot be applied to the social organization, because increased pressure from one direction may result in increased counterpressure from the other direction.

Organizational equilibrium can be altered by either *increasing* the set of forces in the desired direction or *reducing* the set of opposing vectors. Table 2.2 shows some of the forces that affect the present balance of the social organization, e.g., the accelerated rate of knowledge expansion and product obsolescence, the changing values of the work force, and increased public

Table 2.2 Forces affecting organizational balance

Deviation-amplifying forces	Deviation-reducing forces
Increasing rate of change, e.g., product obsolescence, etc.	Rigidity of bureaucratic approaches
Increased pressure from public sector	Failure to use systems approach
Changing values of the work force, including managers	Overemphasis on single perspective
More laws and regulations	Obsolete managerial concepts
Increasing knowledge in behavioral and quantitative sciences	Need for stable manufacturing schedule
	Managerial myopia— clinging to outmoded concepts
	Fear and distrust of change
	Organizational inertia
	Conflicting objectives

pressure for cleaner air and water and greater social responsibility by business. Deviation-reducing forces may take the form of top management's refusing to seize an opportunity because of the inherent personal risks involved. Or, a manager may exert a reactive pressure by ignoring improvements that threaten his or her deeply held assumptions.

Argyris believes that the strongest reactive forces lie not only within the managers, but also in the other individuals within the social organization.[20] He believes that most individuals are "systematically blind" to their behavior and are therefore "culturally programmed" to behave in ways that reduce the probability of change. The strength of these reactive forces cannot be lessened simply by increasing the amount and degree of the deviation-amplifying forces. Rather, a much more effective approach is to reduce the amount and degree of the resistance to change by reducing the strength of the deviation-reducing forces.

D. Multiplicity of Purposes, Functions, and Objectives

Most social organizations have a multiplicity of subsystems, each of which is in dynamic interaction with the others. However, we do not always need to look at the entire system—we can focus on specific parts, or subsystems, for study and enlarge our analysis from the micro to the macro level. For example, an individual is a subsystem and thus has certain needs, goals, and expectations. Not all of these goals and objectives will coincide with those of the organization, and we could therefore expand our study to examine the stresses and strains resulting from the discrepancy between individual and organization goals.

At another level of complexity, we may consider the individual as a member of a group which in turn has its own set of goals and expectations. For example, a group may establish work norms inconsistent with those of top management.

At the highest level of complexity is the system in interaction with other systems in the outside environment. Here, we can consider a particular organization as either a system in its own right or a subsystem within a supersystem. As in lower levels, the supersystem may have goals and expectations which differ considerably from those of the social organization under consideration. The current emphasis on ecology—including air, water, and thermal pollution—is one example of such diversity of goals. A particular industrial organization, striving for survival, may regard enforcement of pollution laws as threatening its own survival.

In short, the complexity of internal and external forces acting on the social organization makes it difficult for the organization to either arrive at a steady-state balance or have only one objective. This multiplicity of forces also makes it impossible to maintain what Seiler calls "the single cause habit of thinking" —the assumption that events have a simple, single cause. Since the variables affecting an event are so highly interrelated and interdependent, we must recognize a multiplicity of causes. Nonetheless, one can still "isolate" the number and range of phenomena to be studied, thus dealing with one level of complexity at a time.

Seiler makes an important point when he discusses the tendency of the system to seek equilibrium, or balance. He makes a strong distinction between the tendency to seek equilibrium and the need for a more optimal equilibrium.

The tendency toward equilibrium is a fact. The tendency toward optimal balance is not. The administrator's challenge is to find ways, through his understanding and imagination, to uncork more effective balances between systems. It is not humanistic values but a considerable body of clinical observation and methodical research which leads us to the conclusion that the work group hostile to management is not experiencing the only viable balance between itself and other systems. While conflict between systems is inevitable by the definitional difference between systems, there is no evidence to support the idea that conflict is inevitably nonproductive.[21]

We can now revise our definition of an organization as a social system, as follows:

1. An organization (firm, company) is composed of a number of subsystems, all of which are interdependent and interrelated.

2. An organization (system) is open and dynamic, having inputs, outputs, operations, feedback, and boundaries.

3. An organization (system) strives for balance through both deviation-amplifying and deviation-reducing feedback.

4. An organization (system) has a multiplicity of purposes, functions, and objectives, some of which are in conflict. The purpose of the administrator is to strive for an optimal balance among the subsystems.

V. DIFFERING PERSPECTIVES OF ORGANIZATIONS AS SOCIAL SYSTEMS

There are several different perspectives, or viewpoints, from which we can look at organizations as total, open systems. First, we must differentiate between formal and informal systems within organizations. The formal organization, run according to prescribed rules, policies, and procedures, is best depicted by the organization chart, the officially prescribed structure, or framework, of the organization as a formal system. Koontz and O'Donnell point out that the structure of an organization involves not only the departmental framework, but also the procedures for assigning formal activities to these departmental units.[22]

The informal organization, or system, evolves from the ways in which the employees (at all levels) interact and work with one another. Many of these activities and interactions are not prescribed by the organization and are much more informal in nature.

Bakke stresses the importance of both formal and informal systems: "As factors influencing human behavior, the formal and informal systems are not separable. . . . The social system to which participants in an organization reach and which is an effective determinant of their behavior, is a synthesis of both formal and informal elements."[23] Or as Katz puts it, "The organization that depends solely upon its blueprints of prescribed behavior is a very fragile social system."[24]

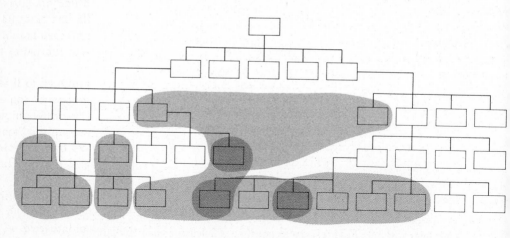

Fig. 2.9 The interaction between formal and informal systems.

Figure 2.9 shows a typical organization chart. The solid lines represent the lines of authority, and the boxes show who reports to whom. The shaded areas represent areas of interaction which are not prescribed by the formal organization and which cut across organizational lines. We are all familiar with the difference between the two—there is always somebody in an organization who can circumvent the "red tape" and get something done quickly. If you know the mechanic at the local gasoline station, you may get work done faster than someone else. The student whose girlfriend works in the registrar's office may get information about his grades long before the official grade notification is sent out.

The concept of the formal/informal structure is implicit in all three perspectives of organizational systems outlined in the previous chapter: a formal, structural-design perspective; a work-flow perspective; and a human perspective. In other words, both formal and informal structures exist simultaneously in organizations within each perspective, and each perspective represents a different way of looking at the organization as a system.

A. A Structural-Design Perspective

The most usual way of looking at organizations is from a somewhat depersonalized point of view. This perspective of the organization as a total system emphasizes formal structure and predetermined lines of authority and responsibility. For example, if we look at an industrial organization from this perspective, its most salient characteristics are the formal subdivisions, or subsystems, formed on the principles of specialization and the division of work tasks. This view of the organization as a system is essentially vertical.

1. Marketing department The function of this subsystem is to carry out market research, advertising, and other activities to sell the outputs of the total system.

2. Manufacturing department This subsystem is concerned primarily with "operation," or the transformation of goods from raw materials to finished goods, or output, to be handled by the marketing department.

3. Finance and accounting department This subsystem deals mainly with inputs (in the form of money) and operation (in the form of internal feedback through accounting records, etc.).

4. The organization as a whole Here, we can view the organization as a total, formal, departmentalized system consisting, minimally, of the three subsystems just mentioned, as well as such others as personnel and research and development.

B. A Work-Flow Perspective

This perspective of subsystems within the total organization is essentially horizontal, as it focuses on the ways by which work flows through an organization. As organizations continue to increase in size and complexity, as the boundaries between organizations and their outside environment become more vague and diffuse, as organizations increase the diversity of their products, and as the importance of computers and management information systems becomes greater, we must give more attention to the way in which work flows through an organization. For example, Jasinski stresses the importance of increasing organizational effectiveness through more direct consideration of work flow. He points out that the normal, vertical approach causes problems by not giving adequate consideration to this factor, and he states that techniques must be developed to ensure that greater time and attention are given to this concept.[25] Jasinski comments that he knows of companies which studied the work-flow process in anticipation of installing data-processing equipment. However, when they realized that merely studying the process could save them money, they decided they didn't need the equipment after all. The increasing use in both management practice and the literature of such terms as "project manager," "program manager," and "integrator" attests to the need for greater attention to the way in which work flows through an organization.

As J. W. Forrester points out, there are at least five interacting subsystems, which are interconnected primarily by information flows and a decision-making network, which need to be considered in the work-flow process:[26]

1. Information flow The flow of ideas and information from the environment in to and out of an organization influences its present and future decisions.

2. Material flow This process deals with the input of raw materials from outside the organization, the transformation of these raw materials into

Incoming natural gas from various sources is processed through automation for distribution to many plants. (Photograph courtesy W. R. Grace & Co.)

finished goods, and the output, or exportation, of finished goods to the environment. The process of material flow includes such areas of the organization as purchasing, manufacturing, accounting and finance, and marketing.

3. Money flow The flow of money throughout the entire system involves the same departments as those concerned with the flow of materials.

4. Order flow Any complex system requires extensive paperwork to follow the flow of orders into the organization (one type of input) through the final stage when shipping orders and bills of lading are made out (one type of output).

5. Capital equipment generation and usage Forrester views this subsystem as a process to determine whether capital equipment is needed, to order and purchase such equipment, and to determine the proper usage of such equipment.

A number of other authors have also discussed the importance of the work-flow concept. For example, Sayles points out that the manager's primary role is not to deal with subordinates, but rather "to maintain the regularity or the sequential pattern of one or more of the (work) flow processes."[27] Diebold indicates that one reason for the inefficient use of the computer is that there is no place for it in the traditional business structure. "The new technology makes it imperative that we build information systems which break through the compartmentalized structure of the traditional business organization."[28]

If an organization were run according to the horizontal work-flow concepts, there would be a manager of information flow, another manager of materials flow, etc. In such an organization, the roles and responsibilities of the various managers are vastly different from those of managers in other types of organizations. Although at present few organizations fall into a work-flow category, the increased use of the computer and the emphasis on integrated management information systems (information flow) make work-flow concepts and practices ever more important.

C. A Human Perspective

The primary concern in this perspective is with human beings and the ways in which they interact in the total organization.

1. The individual The individual is both an entire system and a subsystem within the organization. As such, she or he has motives, needs, and desires. The person also belongs to groups (larger subsystems) within the total system and has an impact on those groups and on the organization as a whole.

2. The group Since groups (subsystems) are composed of individuals, a group is obviously at a higher level of complexity than the individual. In addition, a group facilitates several types of interaction (either formal or informal): among individuals, an individual on the group, or vice versa. Finally, the group has an impact on the total organization.

3. The organization Finally, we can look at the organization as a total human system composed of subsystems of individuals and groups, each of which affects the others and the organization. In other words, the various subsystems and the total, human organization are interdependent.

4. The environment This refers to the process by which human beings come out of and go back into the organization's environment.

VI. THE NEED FOR A MORE INTEGRATED APPROACH

Although the structural-design approach to organizations will probably always exist, recent advances in knowledge of human beings and group dynamics, the advent of the computer, the attempts at integrated management information systems, and the espousal of such concepts as program management are forcing us to rethink and reconsider our ideas about organizations as large, complex systems. We can understand an organization better and help it to be more effective if we consider the concepts of all three perspectives, and this task is made easier by clearly delineating the differences among the three approaches.

The study and understanding of an organization's interrelated, interdependent subsystems are just beginning. In the past this lack of understanding caused many problems. For example, in many manufacturing organizations there is often conflict between the manufacturing department, which is charged with making and assembling goods, and the quality control department, which is charged with inspection. Manufacturing believes that quality control is out to "trap" them; quality control feels that the shop is out to "put something over" on them.

In the same vein, the finance department, concerned with cash flow, tends to keep the inventory low. Manufacturing, on the other hand, likes to maintain a high inventory of parts. Marketing likes to have many different products with a high inventory so that they will never be out of stock and lose a sale.

These conflicts, which are not "caused" by people, are built into the organization, because organizations have not really been designed to maximize the concept that the various subsystems are interrelated and interdependent. Thus differing segments of the same organization may well have quite different overall goals and objectives.

In the past, this was not too important, since products changed slowly and organizations were relatively stable. Further, the built-in conflict was not too damaging, since formal departments could function semi-independently of one another. Now, however, the amount, degree, and rate of change are increasing so rapidly that organizations need to remain flexible.

For example, one company attempted for two years to install a computer-based, complete management information system. The project finally failed after several million dollars had been spent. The computer programs were well written. But,

with the advent of mechanized programs, work groups that in the past have been quite independent become much more interdependent. The walls between groups, units, and sections begin to crumble as the programs and information flow out, across and through them. Currently, the possibility of losing "control" of one's own operation and being dependent on other areas is quite threatening, especially to the manager of what has been an autonomous area.[29]

Another example of the difficulty in keeping up with the change process has been the development, especially since World War II, of the "project," or "matrix," organization. According to Gaddis:

A project is [defined as] *an organization unit dedicated to the attainment of a goal—generally, the successful completion of a developmental product on time, within the budget, and in conformance with predetermined performance specifications.*[30]

Gaddis notes that many projects have a manager whose task is to coordinate the project across the traditional, departmental lines. The need for the project approach arises primarily in the more modern, advanced technology industries where change is the norm. Further, it is in these industries—electronics, astronautics, nucleonics—that complex products are designed, developed, and manufactured according to predetermined performance specifications and due-dates. Implicit in the use of the project-manager approach in such industries is the admission that traditional managerial and organizational concepts have not worked. The project approach has been, in essence, "grafted on" to the existing, and largely obsolete, concepts of traditional organizations.

Forrester has dramatically pointed out the tremendous impact on the organization of poorly designed information flow.[31] In one of his models, for example, he shows how relatively small changes in retail sales can lead to large swings in factory production and how a factory manager may find it impossible to fill orders even though it is always possible to produce more goods or materials than are being sold to consumers (Fig. 2.10). Similarly,

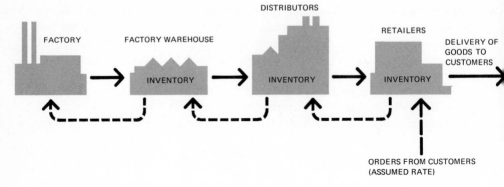

Fig. 2.10 Organization of production-distribution systems. (Adapted from J. W. Forrester, *Industrial Dynamics,* Cambridge, Mass.: M.I.T. Press, 1961, p. 22.)

Lawrence and Lorsch have shown that the organization must be designed to fit its particular environment and that proper design of the organizational structure can make major impacts on the profitability of the organization.[32]

VII. SUMMARY

In this chapter, we traced the evolution of systems theory and discussed some of the advantages and disadvantages of the systems approach. Although it is necessary at times to consider the organization as a closed system, one must also regard it as an open system that affects and is affected by its environment. Further, the interdependencies among the subsystems are as important as, if not more so, than the individual subsystems. Although organizations strive to achieve a balance among their subparts, this balance is continually changing in response to a nonstable environment and the interdependence of the parts of the social organization.

Social organizations may be seen from several different perspectives, or camera angles: the structural-design perspective, the work-flow perspective, and the human perspective. It is not enough to study organizations from just one perspective; for a complete understanding, one must use an integrated approach.

REVIEW

1. How do you distinguish between the "formal" and "informal" organization? Discuss.

2. Are there times when resistance to change may be valuable for an organization? Discuss.

3. What impact does the installation of a computer have on an organization? Short-term? Long-term?

4. From your own past experience in organizations, describe instances in which the "informal" organization was (a) helpful in assisting the formal organization and (b) harmful to the formal organization. What were the reasons underlying these results?

5. The next time you go to a cafeteria, note what the employees and customers are doing. How would you describe a cafeteria as a system?

6. What basic relationships must exist to make a concept of systems workable?

REFERENCES

1. L. Bertalanffy, "The History and Status of General Systems Theory," *Academy of Management Journal* **15,** 4 (December 1972): 411.

2. L. Henderson, *Pareto's General Sociology,* Cambridge, Mass.: Harvard University Press, 1936, p. 80.

3. K. Boulding, "General Systems Theory: The Skeleton of Science," *Management Science* **2,** 3 (April 1956): 197–208.

4. J. Thompson, *Organizations in Action,* New York: McGraw-Hill, 1967.

5. *Ibid.,* p. 10.

6. K. Weick, "Amendments to Organizational Theorizing," *Academy of Management Journal* **17,** 3 (Sept. 1974): 487.

7. C. Lundberg, "Toward Understanding Behavioral Science by Administrators," *California Management Review* **6,** 1 (Fall 1963) 43–52.

8. W. Buckley, ed., *Modern Systems Research for the Behavioral Scientist,* Chicago: Aldine, 1959, p. 497.

9. D. Katz and R. Kahn, *The Social Psychology of Organizations,* New York, Wiley, 1966, p. 31.

10. F. Kast and J. Rosenzweig, "General Systems Theory: Applications for Organization and Management," *Academy of Management Journal* **15,** 4 (December 1972): 455.

11. Katz and Kahn, *op. cit.,* p. 33.

12. Boulding, *op. cit.*

13. K. Weick, "Middle Range Theories of Social Systems," *Behavioral Science* **19,** 6 (Nov. 1974): 361.

14. D. Gerwin and W. Christoffel, "Organizational Structure and Technology: A Computer Model Approach," *Management Science* **20,** 12 (August 1974): 1531–1542.

15. Weick, "Middle Range Theories of Social Systems," *op. cit.,* p. 361.

16. Kast and Rosenzweig, *op. cit.*, p. 455.

17. L. Sayles and M. Chandler, *Managing Large Systems—Organizations for the Future*, New York: Harper & Row, 1971, p. 10.

18. N. Wiener, *The Human Use of Human Beings: Cybernetics and Society*, Garden City, N.Y.: Doubleday/Anchor, 1954.

19. K. Lewin, *Field Theory in Social Science*, New York: Harper & Row, 1951.

20. C. Argyris, *Management and Organizational Development*, New York: McGraw-Hill, 1971.

21. J. Seiler, *Systems Analysis in Organizational Behavior*, Homewood, Ill.: Richard D. Irwin and Dorsey Press, 1967, p. 15. Reprinted by permission.

22. H. Koontz and C. O'Donnell, *Principles of Management: An Analysis of Managerial Functions*, 4th ed., New York: McGraw-Hill, 1968.

23. E. Bakke, *Bonds of Organization*, New York: Harper & Row, 1957, p. 191.

24. D. Katz, "The Motivational Basis of Organizational Behavior," *Behavioral Science* **9**, 2 (April 1964): 132.

25. F. J. Jasinski, "Adapting Organizations to New Technology," *Harvard Business Review* **37**, 1 (Jan.–Feb. 1959): 79–86.

26. J. W. Forrester, *Industrial Dynamics*, Cambridge, Mass.: M.I.T. Press, 1968.

27. L. Sayles, *Managerial Behavior*, New York: McGraw-Hill, 1964.

28. J. Diebold, "ADP—the Still-Sleeping Giant," *Harvard Business Review* **42**, 5 (Sept.–Oct. 1964): 60–65.

29. E. Huse, "The Impact of Computerized Programs on Managers and Organizations: A Case Study in an Integrated Manufacturing Company, in *The Impact of Computers on Management*, ed. C. Myers, Cambridge, Mass.: M.I.T. Press, 1967, pp. 290–291. Reprinted by permission.

30. P. Gaddis, "The Project Manager," *Harvard Business Review* **37**, 3 (May–June 1959): 89.

31. Forrester, *op. cit.*

32. P. Lawrence and J. Lorsch, *Organization and Environment: Managing Integration Differentiation*, Boston: Harvard University Graduate School of Business Administration, Division of Research, 1967.

PART II

INTRAORGANIZATIONAL BEHAVIOR: THE MICRO VIEW

In Chapters 1 and 2 we provided an overview of the book. We said that we would use a building-block approach, proceeding from the smaller subsystems (such as individuals) up through the organization as a total system (or as a subsystem in the larger environment or culture). One of the advantages of a systems approach is that a particular level of systems analysis can be chosen deliberately. At the same time, we can be aware that we are dealing with a particular system level but that one subsystem interacts with other subsystems and with the larger whole.

Part II focuses on the behavioral building blocks. Individual motivation is one such concept. The idea that individuals work in groups and that groups affect behavior is another such concept. Managers must continually deal with the influence that groups have on one another. Leadership and its effectiveness must be clearly understood by the effective manager. We have separated leadership from managing as such because of the clear distinction between "leader" and "manager." Many people use these terms interchangeably, but to do so is to fail to understand and fully deal with the richness of organizational life.

THE INDIVIDUAL IN THE ORGANIZATION (CHAPTER 3)

Knowledge of individual motivation allows one to better understand oneself and the other person. Chapter 3 focuses on the individual as a subsystem in his or her own right. The study of motivation is divided into two different but related approaches. One is the static "content" model of motivation. The other, which is attracting increasing attention, is the dynamic "expectancy" model. We then move on to study the individual subsystem in interaction with the larger system. Here, the focus is on the process of social exchange, or the "psychological contract," whereby an individual contracts to give something to, in exchange for something from, the organization. An important issue here is the way in which an individual's needs and motivations do or do not get get satisfied on the job. The individual will "give" to the organization only to the extent and degree that the exchange is seen as being relatively equal. Should the person see the exchange as being unequal (for example, giving more than getting), then the person must decide whether to leave the organization for one that offers possibilities of getting a better break or to remain and adjust the level of work output to achieve a "proper" balance or exchange.

PERCEPTION AND COMMUNICATION (CHAPTER 4)

This chapter deals with the ways in which the person sees, or "perceives," the world. Perception is highly affected by the individual's internal motivational state. The perceptual process is highly important, because it gives major clues about why people behave as they do. Each of us behaves in ways "that make sense to us as we see the world." In addition to explaining and describing perception, we show how perception can be improved.

Closely linked to the perceptual process is the problem of communication —the clear, accurate transmitting and receiving of information. Thus we move from the individual as a subsystem to people in contact with one another. We describe the communication process and give you some insights and ideas for improving communications.

THE GROUP IN THE ORGANIZATION (CHAPTER 5)

At a higher level of complexity is the person as a member of a group. Most of us have and will continue to work with many different groups in our lifetimes. In Chapter 5 we examine the individual's influence on the group and the influence of the group on the person. We discuss the process of group formation and examine how the group works as a subsystem within the more complex system, the organization. Groups have strong influence on their members and on the organization as a whole, and we describe a number of ways to better understand and diagnose group effectiveness. We also suggest some methods for increasing not only your own effectiveness within a group, but also the effectiveness of the group as a whole.

GROUPS IN INTERACTION (CHAPTER 6)

People interact with and influence one another. So also do groups. The way in which groups interact can be either helpful or harmful to the organization. Chapter 6 describes and explains some of the ways in which groups work together. The chapter also examines some of the advantages and disadvantages of intergroup conflict and tension. Sometimes such tension is helpful; at other times it is not. The chapter also suggests how such tension can be constructively managed.

INFLUENCE, POWER, AND LEADERSHIP (CHAPTER 7)

The term "leadership" usually brings to mind formal leadership, that is, a boss with formal authority and responsibility. If we think of an organization as a system with interdependent and interrelated subsystems, the issue of influence, power, and leadership becomes much broader. Chapter 6 deals with several types of both formal and informal power and influence. Influence, for example, is a complex, two-way process which can, but does not always, involve the manager. After considering power and influence, we describe several current theories of formal leadership. The chapter is also written to give you insight into the effectiveness of different influence styles on human behavior. Understanding this chapter will help you to understand the dynamics of influence at all levels of an organization.

THE MANAGER IN THE ORGANIZATION (CHAPTER 8)

The manager's job is becoming more important and more complex. There is growing awareness that many different organizations, including hospitals, universities, and governmental units, need to be managed. A conductor of a symphony orchestra is a manager, as is a head nurse in a hospital. The manager is heavily involved with other subsystems and groups, primarily at the lateral, work-flow level. Thus the manager's function is much broader than just a formal leader of subordinates. Since organizations have changed greatly in recent years, the manager's duties and functions must be reexamined. For example, today's effective manager spends more time in the lateral, work-flow process than does the less effective manager, who spends more time in vertical relationships with subordinates and supervisors. Chapter 8 describes methods for improving the work of subordinates through Management by Objectives (MBO) and then critically examines some myths about managerial jobs. We conclude our examination of the manager's job by describing it as a highly important, shifting set of relationships requiring the continual making and renegotiating of decisions. To be successful, the manager must be able to interact with a large number of people at variety of levels, both inside and outside the organization.

To summarize, Part II of this text covers the micro building blocks of behavior in organizations. We begin at the level of the individual in the organization, examining the problems of motivation, perception, and communication. We then discuss the concepts of group formation and effectiveness, as well as relationships between groups. We then distinguish among different types of power and influence, examine the nature and functions of leadership, and provide insights into the manager's job in today's complex organization.

3

THE INDIVIDUAL
IN THE
ORGANIZATION

All the world's a stage,
And all the men and women merely players:
They have their exits and their entrances;
And one man in his time plays many parts.

SHAKESPEARE

LEARNING
OBJECTIVES

When you have finished reading and studying this chapter, you should be able to:

1. Define the concept of motivation within the framework of a total system.
2. Trace the evolution of thought about individual motivation.
3. Distinguish among conditions that lead to satisfaction but not to higher performance and among those that lead to satisfaction and higher performance.
4. Define each of the following and state the differences between it and each of the other terms in this list: force-coercion, economic/machine, growth and open systems, achievement, and dynamic-expectancy models of motivation.
5. Provide at least three hints for managers (and others) in working with people.

You will be expected to define and use the following concepts:

Motivation	Need hierarchy
Individual goals	Need for achievement
Performance	Growth/hygiene
Exchange	ERG theory
Psychological contract	Valence
Models of motivation	Instrumentality
Force and coercion	Expectancy
Economic/machine	Intrinsic rewards
Affective/affiliation	Extrinsic rewards

THOUGHT STARTERS

1. What motivates or "turns you on" in a work situation?
2. Under what circumstances is a happy person a productive one?
3. Give several examples of motivational models changing as the culture changes.
4. Explain this statement: "You can't really motivate someone else, even though common-sense, everyday language uses this expression."

I. INTRODUCTION

Our primary concern in this chapter is why people work and behave as they do in formal work organizations. We first describe a basic performance model in which motivation plays a significant part. After examining the individual in interaction with the organization, we consider two categories of motivational models: (1) the static-content and (2) the dynamic-expectancy models of motivation. As you read about these models, keep in mind that like Lawler, we are assuming that:

1. *People have many conscious, often complex and competing goals.*
2. *Most behavior is consciously goal directed.*
3. *People have affective reactions to the outcomes they obtain as a result of their behavior.*[1]

Most people spend one-third of their adult years on jobs. There are several compelling, common-sense reasons for working. First, people need jobs in order to earn a living—to survive. In the early days of our society, John Smith coined the phrase, "He who does not work does not eat." In all races and all cultures, people work. In primitive cultures in some of the rural and decaying urban areas of the United States, survival is perhaps the most important reason for working.

Another major reason why we work is that society expects it of us. Ours is a work-oriented society, and even those whose survival does not depend on their earning a living usually hold some sort of job. By complying with society's expectations, we acknowledge that the opinions of "others" are important to us. Wealthy Texas oilmen and Greek shipping magnates are two examples of such cases. However, society may be gradually shifting to a less work-oriented ethic.

In addition, work can also be fun, challenging, and exciting. Although Webster defines work as "bodily or mental effort exerted to do or make something; purposeful activity; labor; toil," such efforts can also be pleasurable, and frequently that is sufficient reason for working. Small children build a snowman; the amateur artist paints a picture; the skier goes down the mountain; the machinist makes a highly complex part; the advertising executive develops a new campaign for a client—all of these people are probably enjoying their work. But even enjoyable work has its troublesome moments: children have to repair the snowman; the artist cannot get the colors right; the skier makes a *sitzmark;* and the client rejects the proposed advertising campaign.

Many people have the impression that "work" is a hardship that must be endured until they get home from the job and can begin their leisure-time "play." But this is a false distinction, for to a great extent, play is work and work is play. To be sure, many people have jobs they do not enjoy, and many jobs are only minimally rewarding. Yet there is a great deal of potential satisfaction and enjoyment that can be obtained from work—whether it be on or off the job.

"Work is play; play is work." These men are enjoying the challenge of the annual 26-mile Boston Marathon race. (The Christian Science Monitor)

II. MOTIVATION AND PERFORMANCE

An individual may be thought of as a system, and one can examine variables that affect the quantity and quality of that person's work performance. After defining the concepts of motivation and attitudes, we analyze their influence on behavior.

Earlier, we said that social systems are characterized by their complexity, openness, striving for balance, and their multiplicity of purposes and objectives. The same can be said of individuals. They are complex, consisting of a multitude of subsystems; they are open, acting on inputs received from the outside world; they seek a balance between their desire for consistency and stability and their need for growth and change; and they have a multiplicity of objectives, some of which conflict with one another. For example, a woman may find that her need to work outside her home conflicts with her desire to be at home with her young children. Or, the need of a college student to go to a movie may conflict directly with the need to study for an examination being held the next morning.

As Vinake has shown, a number of variables affect the quantity or quality of an individual's work performance: intelligence, ability, muscular coordination, past experience, practice in the task, and motivation.[2] Figure 3.1 shows the relationship of these variables to the individual's output, or performance.

Motivation can be defined as "the conditions responsible for variation in the intensity, quality, and direction of ongoing behavior."[3] The "conditions" are both *extrinsic* and *intrinsic* to the individual. Most, if not all, behavior is

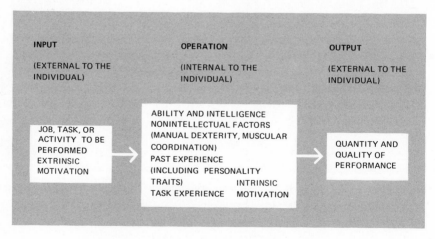

Fig. 3.1 Variables influencing performance.

caused by the individual's attempts to satisfy his or her needs. Similarly, the individual avoids activities that do not provide rewards or reinforcement or that would result in punishment, a negative kind of need satisfaction.

The human motivational system is highly complex, and the individual may have a number of highly interrelated and sometimes contradictory motives. Therefore, the motivation system requires a steering function. Such guidance may be in the form of the individual's values, sentiments, habits, and defense mechanisms, all of which are included in the term "attitude" used by Vinake. As he points out, attitudes are developed over time, are relatively permanent, and are cognitive structures which determine, or "steer," the individual's behavior.

Because there are both positive and negative consequences to behavior, any specific behavior is a complex interrelation of the individual's perceptions of both the goal and his or her own performance, the outside situation, and the task—its importance, the extent to which it will satisfy motivations and needs, and its difficulty. The individual may be highly motivated to achieve, but may not even try if the task seems too difficult or unrewarding.

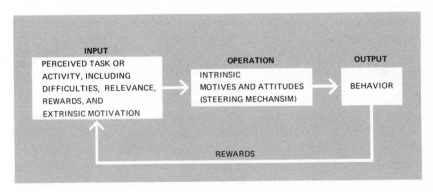

Fig. 3.2 Human motivational system.

Figure 3.2 shows that behavior is a direct function of both the perceived task or activity, including the possible rewards or reinforcement for task accomplishment, and the current motivational state and attitudes of the individual. In other words, the person is always asking, "What's in it for me?" The particular behavior that occurs in a given situation is a direct result of the answer to that question.

III. THE INDIVIDUAL IN INTERACTION WITH THE ORGANIZATION—THE PSYCHOLOGICAL CONTRACT

Behavior is caused; people work to satisfy needs. In this sense people are *always* motivated either extrinsically or intrinsically. Thus the individual comes to the organization with a set of needs; if the organization provides a climate conducive to the satisfaction of those needs, the individual will work. If, however, the larger system does not provide these opportunities for need satisfaction, the individual will subordinate the organization's goals to the satisfaction of his or her own needs.

For example, there is the well-known story of the man who bought a new car that rattled. He took the car back to the dealer several times, but the rattle persisted. Finally, the mechanic conducted a thorough search to locate the source of the rattle and found a bottle suspended from a piece of string inside the right front door. The note attached to the bottle was, "Noisy, ain't it?" The "saboteur" had certainly been motivated, but in a form obviously contrary to the goals of the manufacturer. This story illustrates that fact that it is easier to change the situation to allow people to satisfy their needs on the job than to try to change the people.

As the individual interacts with the organization, two key elements emerge.

1. Interaction is always a two-way process of exchange. Unless both parties benefit from the exchange, the interaction will be reduced or halted by the one dissatisfied. As Homans states:

Social behavior is an exchange of goods, material goods, but also non-material ones, such as the symbols of approval or prestige. Persons that give much to others try to get much from them, and persons that get much from others are under pressure to give much to them. This process of influence tends to work out at equilibrium to a balance in the exchanges. For a person engaged in exchange what he gives may be a cost to him, just as what he gets may be a reward . . . Not only does he seek a maximum for himself, but he tries to see to it that no one in his group makes more profits than he does. The cost and value of what he gives and what he gets vary with the quantity of what he gives and what he gets.[4]

Thus motivation is a balance—motivation equals reward minus cost $(M = R - C)$. There are personal costs to remaining in an organization; the individual may have to give up some autonomy and independence in order to have a steady, secure job, but for doing so expects something from the organization in return.

In a laboratory study, Adams and Rosenbaum found that an individual's productivity is considerably greater when he believes his pay is too high.[5] However, some doubt was cast on this *wage inequity theory* by Valenzi, who found that differential effects on productivity may be caused by the worker's attempt to protect his self-esteem rather than by his perception of pay inequity.[6] Whatever the interpretation of the research, however, it is clear that interaction is an exchange, whether it be money for productivity or self-esteem for productivity.

2. Interaction always involves a sense of mutual obligation. If either person in an interaction fails the other, the relationship will probably be discontinued. In an organization, of course, this process of mutual obligation, or interdependence, is of critical importance in maintaining the stability of the organization.

One of the most important concepts in organizational behavior is the implied individual-organization relationship, usually called the *psychological contract*. We define "psychological contract" as the mutual exchange and reciprocation between the individual and the organization. This includes the influence process for mediating conflict between the goals of the organization (larger system) and those of the employee (subsystem). This psychological contract stipulates that material wages and "psychological income" be given to the individual, who in turn makes a commitment to work toward the goals of the organization. In other words, the psychological contract constitutes the sum total of the expectancies perceived by *both* the individual and the organization about their relationship. The organization expects the employee to be at work, to work hard, and to obey its authority, and it uses its authority to enforce these expectations. The employee expects payment for work and fair and just treatment from the organization. If the organization fails to live up to these expectations, the employee is likely to withhold his or her involvement or to become alienated and apathetic.

Etzioni has developed a typology for classifying different types of organizations according to the types of power they exercise and the types of involvement and expectations of the employee.[7]

1. If the organization exercises primarily coercive power and authority, as do jails, penal institutions, concentration camps, and slave labor camps, the worker is likely to become *alienated* and to withdraw psychologically from the organization of which she or he is coerced to remain a member.

2. The second type of organization exerts primarily rational/legal authority and uses economic rewards in exchange for membership and performance.

At the highly automated automobile plant in Lordstown, Ohio, workers' reaction may be primarily *calculative*. (Photograph courtesy *The Warren Tribune Chronicle*)

The member's reaction is primarily *calculative*—"a fair day's work for a fair day's pay."

3. Hospitals, colleges and universities, professional associations, and religious institutions exemplify organizations that stress *normative* rewards; membership in the organization or the opportunity to perform a task or function has intrinsic value. The member of this type of organization regards involvement with the organization as having intrinsic value rewards and performs his or her function primarily because of this value. In addition, the individual is frequently willing to accept the lower economic rewards provided by this type of organization.

Table 3.1 shows the nine types of organization relationships which Etzioni's typology produces. Etzioni stresses that the type of "psychological contract" depends heavily on the kind of power or authority used by the organization. Schein states that the types of organizations that fall along the diagonal seem to have workable and "just" psychological contracts. The kind of involvement obtained is consonant with the kinds of rewards given by the organization and the kind of authority exercised.[8] If a manufacturing concern

Table 3.1 Types of involvement versus types of power:
the psychological contract

Type of involvement	Type of power		
	Coercive	Utilitarian	Normative
Alienative	X		
Calculative		X	
Moral			X

Adapted from A. Etzioni, *A Comparative Analysis of Complex Organizations*, Glencoe, Ill.: Free Press, 1961.

uses primarily "scientific management," economic rewards, and rational/legal authority, for example, it should expect a calculative type of involvement from its members. If it expects its members to be "loyal," to enjoy their work, and to be morally involved, it may be asking its workers to give more than they are receiving in return.

The importance and influence of the psychological contract on members of the organization cannot be overestimated. In his review of the literature on labor turnover among life insurance salesmen, industrial employees, nurses, and supermarket employees, Scott found a number of studies which clearly showed that new employees often quit their jobs because they had no opportunity to "achieve what they expected when they were hired."[9] Scott strongly recommends that prospective employees be given a much clearer picture of their jobs and the organization's expectations of them so that they can make a better choice. In one industrial firm, "30% of prospective employees decided not to sign up after a tour of the plant."

Perrow reports the change in attitudes and behavior of workers in a juvenile correctional institution, which was basically an alienative organization.[10] Applicants for low-level supervisory positions in the organization were asked to complete a questionnaire about their opinions on delinquency and differences between delinquents and nondelinquents. The responses indicated that the applicants were enlightened and permissive. After the applicants had been employed by the institution and had gained experience, the questionnaire was readministered to them and to all of the other personnel of the institution. The opinions of the new supervisors had changed radically to conform with the attitudes of the other personnel in the correctional institution; they had become much less permissive and were taking a punitive approach. In other words, the new supervisors had adjusted to the implicit "psychological contract" prevailing in the institution and had changed their opinions and attitudes to conform to the behavior that was expected of them.

In an article about the assembly line, which is perhaps the best example of Etzioni's utilitarian (economic/machine) model, Serrin quotes a supervisor describing the assembly-line worker, "You don't think . . . You're just an automated puppet." A worker said, "That's all I'm working for—my paycheck and retirement." The article also describes the case of an employee who began shooting "at everybody in white shirts" with an M-1 carbine. In several minutes three men were dead. At the trial, the worker was found innocent because of temporary insanity resulting from his early life in the South as a sharecropper and the impact of factory life. As one juror was heard to remark, "Working there would drive anyone crazy."[11]

In recent years the nature of the psychological contract has slowly changed from coercive/utilitarian to utilitarian/normative, particularly in R&D organizations. As organizations increasingly expect their members to become committed to organizational goals and to value their work, management must change its part of the psychological contract to give workers more opportunity for personal involvement, decision making, and growth. For example, Volvo and Saab-Scania are using a team-production method whereby semiautonomous groups of four to seven workers assemble truck and auto components.[12] Female assembly workers at Volvo spend one day every two weeks performing office jobs. The Swedish automakers report other experiments and indicate that they are getting improved production quality and lower employee absenteeism rates. (In the United States, by contrast, the absenteeism rates in the auto industry rose from 2.8% in 1960 to 5.3% in 1970, both times of relatively full employment.

Thus as we move toward discussion of motivational models, think about the assumptions, feelings, and involvement a worker is likely to make about coercive, utilitarian, normative, and mixed types of power situations in organizations. Also consider the converse: What kinds of assumptions is the manager likely to make of the worker in each of the power situations? Each motivational model is based on different assumptions about human characteristics, which in turn are reflected in the nature of the psychological contract.

IV. STATIC-CONTENT MODELS OF MOTIVATIONAL SYSTEMS

A "model" is a representation of reality. However, since "reality" differs for each person, more than one model is required. First, it is difficult to find out what really makes another individual "tick," since sometimes the individual does not know this. The second reason for using several models is that as research expands the field of motivational theory, new models are needed to reflect the new findings.

Throughout history, there have been a number of different assumptions, or "models," which have attempted to explain why people work and behave as they do. Today, none of these models appears in a completely pure state. Rather, they form a continuum along which workers' behavior and the ideas guiding the actions of supervisors can be placed.

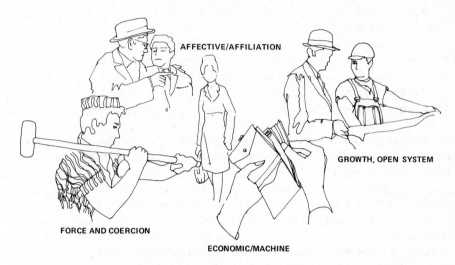

Fig. 3.3 Models of motivation.

Four major points, or models, along this continuum are shown in Fig. 3.3. The use of only four models is a vast oversimplification of the complex area of motivation, but it illustrates the lack of sharp demarcations between the models. Each of these models is in use today, although the emphasis in the literature has shifted heavily toward the right-hand side of the continuum. Prisons, for example, are run on force-and-coercion principles of motivation. Business organizations rely heavily on economic factors to motivate their members; clubs rely on social concerns to motivate people. Although educational systems strive to promote "growth," their emphasis on grades sometimes overshadows their efforts to promote learning as an end in itself.

A. Force and Coercion Model

Many of the early models depended on coercion and force as "motivators." Perhaps one of the earliest recorded descriptions of such an "incentive system" is given in the Book of Exodus. Since the Pharoah felt that the Israelites were not being worked hard enough, he gave orders that their task (making bricks) be made more difficult. No longer would they be given the straw with which to make the bricks; rather, they would also have to collect the straw, while still maintaining their previous quota of bricks. When the quota was not met, "the children of Israel were scourged" as an incentive to meet the quota.

Prior to the French Revolution, serfdom was a form of coercive motivation as was slavery in the United States. Indeed, coercive authority was widely used in England in industrial organizations immediately after the Industrial Revolution. However, there is evidence that slavery and feudalism were not economically viable. For example, in order to avoid the corrupting influence of wealth, the Cistercian order of monks during the Middle Ages deliberately built their abbeys in wastelands far from towns and were not allowed to have serfs. They did the work themselves and were embarrassed to find that this method of operation was far more profitable, since the "old-fashioned great estate, cultivated by servile labor, was not a very profitable property for its owner."[13]

Reliance on coercion caused problems in more modern times, too. Coercion used by the Nazis during World War II resulted in high sabotage rates in war plants. In the post-Stalin era, Soviet leaders have failed to maintain a coercive state, and their more "enlightened" methods of motivation have caused a considerable relaxing of state rules and regulations, with an accompanying "decentralization" of decision making.

In summary, the basic assumption behind this model is that people work best when they are forced into a situation in which they must produce or be punished. The problem with this assumption is that coercion at best produces alienation and withdrawal—either actual or psychological—from the task. When physical withdrawal is not possible, sabotage, uprisings, and other forms of rebellion may occur.

B. Economic/Machine Model

The two branches of this model are conceptually related, but may also be considered separately (Fig. 3.4). The first branch is the economic model, which stresses economic rewards. The second branch uses methods of "conditioning" to achieve the desired behavior.

1. Economic model The so-called economic theory of motivation replaced the coercive model of human behavior long before Adam Smith formulated his assumptions about economics in 1776. The coercive and economic models were used conjointly for a long time, perhaps most clearly in the world's

FORCE AND COERCION   ECONOMIC/MACHINE   AFFECTIVE/AFFILIATION   GROWTH, OPEN SYSTEM

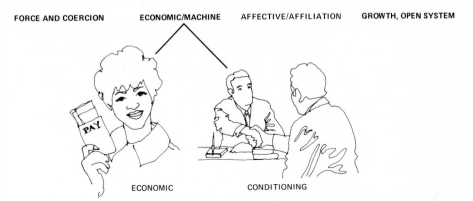

ECONOMIC   CONDITIONING

Fig. 3.4 The economic/machine model of motivation.

navies at about the time of the Revolutionary War. Sailors were often flogged (coerced), and prize money was used as an economic motivation.

It was Adam Smith who did the best job of conceptualizing the economic basis of human motivation. According to this model, people work primarily for money. They are like a machine in that they are unconcerned about social feelings, do not need other rewards such as feelings of accomplishment and achievement, and are motivated to do only that which provides them with the greatest immediate economic reward.

The concept of rational-economic human behavior was popularized by Taylor and more particularly by the "efficiency experts" who followed his lead in the 1920s and 1930s. This model makes many of the same assumptions about human nature as does the coercive model—workers are motivated primarily by money; they are inherently shiftless and lazy; they will respond only when "bribed" by financial rewards; work needs to be planned out for them in great detail; and the manager needs to tightly supervise and control the workers' activities if work is to be performed properly.

In Chapter 1 we described how Taylor used scientific methods to increase the amount of pig iron carried by a laborer between two points. Taylor describes the set of formal instructions that he gave to Schmidt, his experimental worker. First, Taylor asked Schmidt whether he was a high-priced man, which in Taylor's terms was the difference between $1.15 and $1.85 per day. When Schmidt admitted that he was a high-priced man, Taylor stressed the importance of Schmidt's following instructions without ever questioning the correctness of the instructions. As Taylor put it, "Now, a high-priced man does just what he's told to do, and no back talk."[14]

According to Weber, the ideal human organization is highly standardized, and everyone knows his or her duties and follows them to the letter. The individual's needs and wants are subordinated to the requirements of the institution, and the individual's formal economic rewards are based on performance.[15] Obviously, then, the primary incentive in the economic model is financial reward, usually based on the rate of the worker's output.

The importance of pay as a motivator has been discussed widely. In general, managers and economists have tended to considerably overrate the importance of pay, whereas psychologists and sociologists have tended to underemphasize the importance of economic rewards. All too often, theorists regard pay as *either* "financial" *or* "psychological" income. In fact, however, pay serves both functions; some sort of an income is necessary to satisfy lower-level "existence" needs.

In addition, money serves as a tangible sign of recognition and achievement, thereby satisfying the individual's social, ego, and other higher-level needs. Although a large portion of a top executive's pay increase may be lost through higher taxes, it may still provide a great deal of inner satisfaction.

Because money is precise and easily measurable, it is an excellent yardstick for measuring comparative success, recognition, accomplishment, and achievement. In this context, research has amply demonstrated that the *relative* amount of pay is far more important than the *absolute* amount of pay. In other words, many people are not bothered by knowing that they could leave their place of work and go somewhere else for more money. However, they are troubled by knowing that a co-worker is making more money than they are. On the other hand, money can act as a bribe to keep people in jobs they dislike.

Success can also be measured, symbolically, by the *method* of payment, i.e., wage or salary. In recent research, five companies using salaries for all personnel reported positive results following a period when employees tested the sincerity of management. In conjunction with other forward-looking personnel practices, the use of straight salary probably gives employees a greater sense of security and increases their sense of personal worth and responsibility. At the same time, such measures are a shift from the economic model toward the growth model, to be described later.[16]

2. Operant conditioning model The second branch of the economic/machine model is best described by Skinner, who believes that human behavior depends on operant conditioning and is, therefore, shaped largely by the environment.[17] Operant conditioning theory postulates that a person responds to rewards; behavior that is reinforced by rewards will continue, whereas behavior that is not reinforced by rewards will cease. All that is necessary for an "operant response" (behavior) is that the behavior be "reinforced" by some type of reward. As Nord states, "If the outcome is pleasing to the individual, the probability of his repeating his response is apt to be increased."[18] Of course, the converse is also true.

Operant conditioning is one of the major attractions of slot machines. The gambler never knows when the machine will yield "a killing." (Photograph by Felicity S. Bowditch)

In his tightly reasoned article, Nord makes the strong point that although operant conditioning is applicable to a wide variety of situations, it has not been given enough consideration by theorists interested in human motivation. He points out that one of the most crucial factors in operant conditioning is the pattern of frequency by which a particular behavior is rewarded. One pattern is the continuous schedule, in which the reinforcement, or reward, follows the response every time the response occurs. He also describes several patterns of "partial reinforcement" and shows that a schedule of variable or random reinforcement leads to more durable, long-lasting response patterns than do either fixed or continuous schedules. Sport fishing is an excellent ex-

By permission of John Hart and Field Enterprises, Inc.

ample of a variable-reinforcement schedule; the fisherman never knows when he is going to "get a strike," or catch a fish.

Skinner has trained pigeons to peck thousands of times at a target without reinforcement—the pigeon does not know when it will get a food pellet. For humans, conditioning acts at a subverbal level. Ask a touch-typist where the letter "a" is on the keyboard; that person is more likely to wiggle the little finger on his or her left hand than to give you a verbal description.

A well-known example of positive reinforcement in industry was reported at Emery Air Freight, where loaders were encouraged by positive reinforcement (PR) techniques to use larger containers for shipping purposes. With PR techniques the utilization rate went from 45% to 90% and resulted in an estimated savings of $52,000 a year.[19]

Perrow describes two cases in which operant conditioning was used to train pigeons to inspect drug capsules and small electronic parts called diodes. In both cases, the pigeons' accuracy of inspection surpassed that of human inspectors. In the diode-inspection case, one pigeon had an error rate of one percent while inspecting 1000 pieces per hour for extremely minute defects. When two pigeons inspected the same pieces, the error rate was infinitesimal. However, top management killed the project, primarily because of cultural reasons and the possible adverse reaction of organized labor. As the chairman of the board of the drug company said, "Who would trust medicine inspected by pigeons?"[20]

There appears to be a current interest in behavioral modification in industry. Behavioral modification is the application of rewards by operant-conditioning techniques. One recent review article notes that most of the interest in behavior modification is in educational and mental health care rather than in industrial applications, but recently there has been more activity in industrial settings.[21] For example, two studies used behavioral modification to reduce absenteeism. In one case the setting was a hardware company; in the other, a manufacturing distribution facility. In both situations there was a statistically significant decrease in absenteeism,[22] although in one case the difference was operationally not very meaningful.[23]

In a third study, behavioral modification was used in a tree planting section of a lumber, pulp, and paper company.[24] Contrary to many of the findings from laboratory studies, a continuous-reinforcement schedule (reinforcement after every planting of a bag of 1000 seedlings) was more successful than any of the partial-reinforcement schedules. Part of the problem seemed to be that the partial-reinforcement techniques allowed workers to participate in a lottery after planting 1000 seedlings. This appeared to be nothing more than gambling, which was offensive to some of the workers and supervisors. Another problem was that the "continuous" reinforcement procedure was in reality a fixed-ratio reinforcement of once every 1000 trees. Finally, the whole procedure complicated the tax paperwork and was overlaid onto a basic salary, thus highlighting some of the difficulties of doing this kind of research in industry.

In spite of the difficulty of applying a behavioral-modification technique to many industrial settings, the more popular, less research-oriented journals still carry articles promoting behavioral modification as an effective management tool.[25] Behavioral modification is one way to develop an interactive program, since the technique necessarily involves the organization, supervisors, and workers.

C. Affective/Affiliation Model

Both the coercion and economic/machine models assume that people are controlled primarily by their environment. The affective/affiliation model assumes that many people at various times have high social needs and that being with other people is important. This need first became apparent during the Hawthorne studies. In mid-1940s studies at the Harwood pajama factory, Ohio State University, and the University of Michigan, researchers found that interpersonal consideration and considerate behavior toward the work group were important. In England Trist and Bamforth demonstrated that breaking up a work group in order to introduce allegedly more efficient coal-getting procedures and equipment actually reduced the amount of coal that was mined as the group was splintered.[26]

In two developmental-motivational theories to be discussed more completely in the next section (Maslow's need hierarchy and Alderfer's existence-relatedness-growth—ERG—theory), there is a stage of development that takes account of affective/affiliation needs. Furthermore, in his studies of need for achievement and need for affiliation, McClelland notes that some persons have high needs for affiliation.

D. Growth-Open System Model

According to this model of motivation, each individual:

1. Is a decision-maker
2. Is purposive and has individualized goals
3. Follows only those orders that are compatible with his or her own needs and values
4. Has motives that are far more complex and interrelated than those in the force-coercion, economic/machine, and affective/affiliation models.
5. Strives for growth, responsibility, and achievement when conditions for growth are present.

Theorists have used these assumptions to go in three interrelated directions—the human self-actualizing theories of Maslow, the need-for-achievement model of McClelland, and the motivation/hygiene theories of Herzberg and his associates (see Fig. 3.5). Although all three models are currently popular, they have yet to be proved viable in terms of solid research.

1. Human self-actualizing model The economic/machine model of motivation was discredited by the Hawthorne studies (discussed in Chapter 1), which showed that physiological factors are less important than psychological factors on the job and that social pressures from peers have a greater impact on productivity than do purely economic incentives. The enthusiasm and cooperation of the group of workers being studied was highly related to the interest the supervisors and researchers showed in the work group, the lack

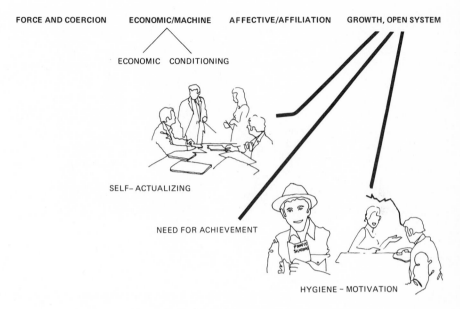

FORCE AND COERCION   ECONOMIC/MACHINE   AFFECTIVE/AFFILIATION   GROWTH, OPEN SYSTEM

ECONOMIC   CONDITIONING

SELF–ACTUALIZING

NEED FOR ACHIEVEMENT

HYGIENE – MOTIVATION

Fig. 3.5   The growth-open system model of motivation.

of coercion on the group, and the participation that allowed the workers to become involved in changes that would affect them.

As a result of the valid questions about the economic/machine model, researchers began placing more emphasis on the study of groups and group behavior. These studies laid the foundation for a rather uncritical acceptance of Maslow's theory of human self-actualizing. According to Maslow:

1. Motives in the adult are highly complex, and no single motive affects behavior. Rather, a number of motives may be in operation at the same time.

2. There exists a hierarchy of needs so that in general, lower-level needs must be at least partially satisfied before a higher-level need is satisfied.

3. A satisfied need is not a motivator. In other words, when a need is satisfied, another emerges to take its place so that in a sense, an individual always remains a wanting being.

4. The higher-level needs can be satisfied in many more different ways than can the lower-level needs.[27]

Maslow also identified five levels of needs: physiological, safety, social, ego, and self-actualization, or developmental (see Fig. 3.6).

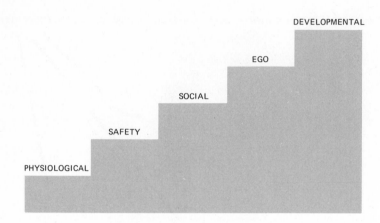

Fig. 3.6 Hierarchy of needs.

1. The lowest level of the need hierarchy comprises the universal physiological needs for food, clothing, and shelter. People generally tend to concentrate on meeting these needs before concerning themselves with higher-level needs. When an individual has at least partially satisfied this level of need, other needs emerge.

2. The second level of need is for safety and security. Although Maslow defined "safety" as freedom from physical harm, more recent writers include freedom from job layoff, loss of income, etc. Most people in the United States, except for minority-group members and people in economically depressed areas, are able to satisfy their needs at these two levels. The importance of these needs can be seen in the widespread emphasis on some form of job tenure and protection, various types of insurance, and savings accounts. However, when these needs are threatened, behavior changes, e.g., people may trample one another in trying to escape from a fire.

3. At the third—social, or belonging—level in Maslow's hierarchy, people are concerned about their social relationships. They want to belong, to be loved, and to be accepted by others. This need begins within the primary human group, the family, and expands to include one's social and work groups. Some groups are, of course, far more important to the individual than others. The importance of social groups is perhaps most striking in the adolescent, whose peer group may become far more important than his or her family.

4. At the fourth level are esteem, or ego, needs. A person needs to have a firm, stable, and usually high self-evaluation. It is not enough to merely be-

long to a group; a person also needs and wants the respect and esteem of those group members. In other words, the ego level has both internal and external aspects. The internal aspect is represented by the individual's self-perceptions; the external aspect is the desire to appear competent to one's peers, to be accepted, and to be recognized as capable in one's job, family, and social life. The person needs *deserved* respect from others.

This ego level of need differs from the social level, in which an individual wants only to be accepted as a person; at the ego level, she or he wants to be seen as competent and capable. At this higher level, people are concerned about *earned* promotion, achievement, accomplishment, prestige, and status. Failure to satisfy these needs can lead to feelings of inferiority, helplessness, and weakness, which in turn may give rise to either compensatory or neurotic trends or to feelings of discouragement, passivity, and apathy.

5. The highest-level needs—for development and self-actualization—are satisfied only after needs at the four lower levels have been met. At this fifth level, the individual is concerned with the development of his or her full potential, which requires psychological health. The few people who reach this stage have a better perception of reality, accept themselves and others, are more creative, and are, in a sense, better able to become completely human in the realization and development of their full potential.

The model of human self-development and self-actualization is based on the assumption that an individual has innate needs to grow and mature and feels a sense of meaning and accomplishment in both life and work. As lower-level needs are satisfied, the higher-level needs are activated.

Since Maslow's hierarchy covers a wide span and several levels may be in operation at any one time, e.g., security, social, and ego needs, not all needs may be satisfied at one place and at one time. Some aspects of the job may be more satisfying than others; some motives may be involved only in job behavior, whereas others are reserved for behavior away from the job.

In applying Maslow's need hierarchy to management personnel, Lyman Porter investigated perceived need-fulfillment deficiencies of nearly 2000 managers in numerous companies.[28] The questionnaire he constructed was divided into five need categories: security, social, esteem, autonomy, and self-actualization. Responses were grouped according to managerial levels: presidential, vice-presidential, upper-middle, lower-middle, and lower.

Porter found that managers at all levels had similar security and social needs. However, satisfaction of the three higher-level needs varied greatly with managerial rank; the lower the manager's level, the less likely it was that these needs would be satisfied. Nonetheless, satisfaction of esteem, autonomy, and self-actualization needs seemed to be critically deficient at all levels of management, with the possible exception of the top managerial level, as McClelland would have predicted. Porter concluded that top management may have to be as concerned with the satisfactions and motivations of their lower-level managers as they are with the motivations of their blue-collar workers.

Vroom provides a review of similar studies that have been conducted by other researchers.[29] However, the studies conducted by Porter and others can be criticized for being cross-sectional rather than longitudinal. In other words, situational, selection, or cultural factors, rather than growth factors, may have determined the results. To test this hypothesis, several researchers conducted longitudinal studies of Maslow's need hierarchy. Lawler and Suttle, for example, collected longitudinal data in questionnaire form from 187 managers in two different organizations in order to test the validity of Maslow's concept of the need hierarchy.[30] One group completed the questionnaire twice in six months; data for the other group were collected over a period of one year. There was little evidence to support Maslow's theory that human needs exist in a hierarchy of levels. However, six months is a relatively short period of time.

The authors suggest a two-level theory, with the basic biological needs at one level and all of the other needs at the second level. They predicted that needs at the higher levels would emerge only after those at the lower level and been satisfied. On the basis of the results, Lawler and Suttle could make no prediction as to which of the higher-level needs would emerge at any given time. For some people, it might be social needs; for others, self-actualization needs.

In another longitudinal study of Maslow's need hierarchy, Hall and Nougaim interviewed a group of managers over a period of five years.[31] The researchers did not find strong evidence for the hierarchy; rather, they found that as managers advance, their needs for safety tend to decrease, and their needs for affiliation, achievement, esteem, and self-actualization increase. Hall and Nougaim argue that these changes result from sequential career stages rather than from lower-order need gratification.

Building on the Hall-Nougaim study, Alderfer, like Lawler and Suttle, has proposed modifying Maslow's need hierarchy by reducing the number of categories.[32] As shown in Fig. 3.7, Alderfer has combined the Maslow categories into three groups of core needs: maintenance of material existence, maintenance of interpersonal relationships with people who are significant to the individual, and the need to find opportunities for growth and personal development.

Alderfer's first level of needs—*existence*—includes Maslow's physiological (survival) and safety categories, including pay, fringe benefits, and work-

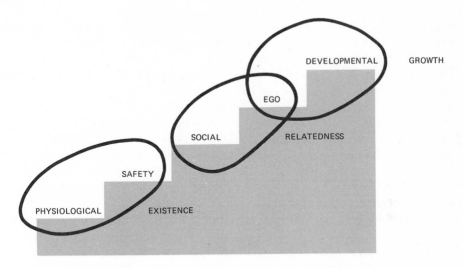

Fig. 3.7   Alderfer's modification of Maslow's hierarchy of needs.

ing conditions. Alderfer's second level—*relatedness*—encompasses Maslow's
social and esteem levels and includes such significant persons as family members, co-workers, subordinates, superiors, enemies, and friends. Alderfer indicates that the basic ingredient of this need is sharing, or mutuality. He believes
that relatedness needs are distinguished from existence needs in that "the
process of satisfaction for existence needs prohibits mutuality." According to
Schein, this model of "social man" provides evidence which "lends support
to the assumptions that man is essentially socially motivated in his organizational life."[33]

As Fig. 3.7 shows, there is an overlap between Maslow's ego category and
Alderfer's *relatedness* and *growth* categories. Whereas Maslow combined the
external and internal aspects of ego needs, Alderfer has separated these two
factors. To Alderfer, growth includes the individual's desire to be self-confi-
dent, creative, and productive—to engage in problems or tasks that require
full utilization of capacities, as well as to develop additional capabilities or
skills.

In modifying Maslow's need hierarchy, Alderfer's existence-relatedness-
growth (ERG) model does not assume that lower-level needs must be satisfied
before higher-order needs can emerge. He also feels that his modification
conforms to a later distinction Maslow made between deficit and growth motivators.[34]

2. Achievement motivation   For a number of years, McClelland[35] and others
have been studying the achievement motive, especially with regard to en-

trepreneurship and the development of the achievement motive (n Ach), which is clearly similar to growth seeking or self-actualization. McClelland's research suggests that most people can be divided into two broad psychological groups. People in the smaller of the two groups are challenged by opportunity and are willing to work hard to achieve something. People in the other group are not so highly challenged, because they have less n Ach.

One way that McClelland measures n Ach is by asking his subjects to write a story about a set of relatively ambiguous pictures. This so-called projective technique forces the subjects to reveal, or "project," themselves in their writing. Thus in examining the subjects' stories, the researcher scores them on the basis of the revealed desire to be successful in competitive situations or to perform up to a particular standard of excellence.

McClelland believes that the amount of n Ach that the person exhibits is a function of a number of different causes. For example, it is possible that people with high n Ach were as children expected to meet high standards for performance and independence and that their mothers were especially important in judging their accomplishments favorably or unfavorably.

Much of the research that has been conducted to date concerning managers indicates that n Ach is higher in middle-level executives than in either lower- or higher-level executives. In other words, n Ach helps propel an individual upward into middle management; in large organizations, top-level executives have already satisfied this need.

A concept related to n Ach is that "achieving societies" can be differentiated from "nonachieving societies" by examining the books that children read in different societies. The more achievement-oriented the society is, the more the number of achievement-oriented stories. Thus, for example, Chinese textbooks contain a great deal of n Ach, whereas children's books in India show much less n Ach. Similarly, Britain (around 1925) was ranked fifth among 25 different countries on n Ach in children's readers, but by 1950 the British level of n Ach had dropped to 27th of 39 countries, with correspondingly severe economic and related losses in the spirit of enterprise.

A second major theme is that to some extent, n Ach can be taught to adults and children. McClelland and his associates have been developing techniques to develop n Ach, particularly among business leaders whose work would benefit from increased n Ach. Such training programs have four major goals: (1) to teach participants how to act, talk, and think like people who already have n Ach; (2) to provide the participants with methods for setting higher but planned and realistic goals for themselves for a two-year period; (3) to provide the participants with greater feedback and knowledge about themselves and the difference between improving performance and just making a good impression or making more friends; (4) to establish a group *esprit de corps* through group interaction and the sharing of such experiences as success and failures, hopes, and fears.

The courses have been held in such diverse areas as the United States, Mexico, and India. Except for Mexico, statistical results were developed showing that after two years, the persons taking the course had been more successful (in terms of expanding their businesses, getting promoted, or making more money) than comparable individuals who had not taken the course. For example, in two comparable cities in India, about 20 percent of those studied showed *n Ach*. After the program, given in one city, about 50 percent of the participants showed an unusual amount of *n Ach*. However, McClelland points out that such programs do not seem to work well among low-income groups. In one case, for example, boys from a lower-class income group showed initial improvement, but later dropped back, perhaps because the environment did not encourage either upward mobility or achievement.

According to follow-on studies, there appears to be a close relationship between *n Ach* and successful entrepreneurial activities. One such study involved 51 small, technically based companies in the Boston area. All were between four and ten years old when the study was conducted, and all were "spin-offs" from either the Massachusetts Institute of Technology research laboratories or from industrial laboratories around the Boston area. The success of the company, as determined by growth rate in terms of sales, was found to be closely related to the degree of *n Ach* that the company president had.[36]

Most of the research on achievement motivation indicates that an individual is most likely to be motivated when he or she has an opportunity to perform moderately challenging tasks in competitive situations in which performance depends on an important skill and feedback is given regarding performance. The evidence also suggests that those who have high *n Ach* tend to find situations in which they have the opportunity to achieve and to enjoy the opportunity for successful performance. Those who are high on achievement motivation tend to approach and persist in achievement-related activities, perhaps because they tend to see success and failure as more directly related to their own efforts and thereby experience greater internal rewards and punishments than do those without high *n Ach*.[37]

Because it is so narrowly based, the achievement motive can be seen as a special case of the need hierarchy, particularly in the areas of esteem and/or growth.

3. Motivation-hygiene model This third branch of the growth-open system model is closely related to Maslow's need-hierarchy model with its subsequent alterations. The motivation-hygiene theory emerged from two studies, published in the 1950s, which had a profound impact on motivational research. These reviews, by Brayfield and Crockett and Herzberg *et al.,* demonstrated that there is little or no relationship between productivity and morale.[38] The results of these two comprehensive reviews came as a great shock to other researchers and practitioners in the field who had always assumed that these two factors are closely linked. Subsequently, there has been more research on motivation and morale, reviewed in Chapter 9.

To study the relationship between productivity and morale more closely, Herzberg and his associates used semistructured interviews to elicit from accountants and engineers events that made them like or dislike their work.[39] The five areas of critical incidents cited most frequently by those who liked their work were: achievement, recognition, nature of the work, responsibility, and advancement—all of which pertain to job *content* and are growth, or motivating, factors. Workers who were dissatisfied with their jobs, on the other hand, cited critical incidents related to the job *context.* The most important of these dissatisfiers, or hygiene factors, was company policy and administration (ineffective, deleterious, or unfair). Other dimensions were supervisors' lack of competence in carrying out their functions (poor technical qualifications or poor interpersonal relations) and poor working conditions (Fig. 3.8).

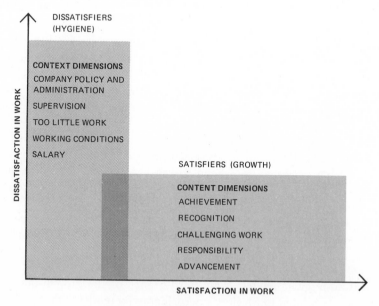

Fig. 3.8 Hygiene versus growth factors.

The findings can be summarized as follows. Herzberg would call the content dimensions to the right of the overlap area growth, or motivating, factors. The context dimensions to the left of the overlap area are dissatisfiers, or "hygiene" factors. In effect, he is saying that improvement of the hygiene factors is a little like vaccination—it can keep one from getting sick, but it doesn't make the person well.

One of the unique aspects of the Herzberg study is the finding that different dimensions account for satisfaction and dissatisfaction. Herzberg and his associates believe that earlier studies could find no consistent link between morale and productivity because investigators were tapping attitudes found in both the satisfier and the dissatisfier dimensions.

According to the Herzberg findings, at least half of the long-range dissatisfier incidents resulted in physical or psychological withdrawal from the job. Half of the satisfier incidents reported improved the individual's attitude toward the company, whereas only one-fourth of the dissatisfier incidents resulted in more negative attitudes. One-fourth of the dissatisfiers adversely affected mental health, but only one-eighth of the satisfiers improved mental health (sleeping better, better frame of mind, etc.). One-fourth of all satisfier and dissatisfier incidents affected home life, but satisfied persons were more more likely to say home life would affect their job attitudes.

One of the many early criticisms of the Herzberg study was that since only engineers and accountants were interviewed, the results may not be applicable to other occupational groups. A later, and potentially more serious, criticism was that Herzberg allowed his methodology to determine his results. Since people usually attribute good results to their own efforts and blame others for bad results, it is possible that this human tendency predetermined Herzberg's findings. After reviewing more than 20 studies, Hinton concluded that "in general, the more the methodology varies from the methodology used in the 1959 Herzberg study, the more likely are the conclusions to vary also."[40]

One of the follow-on studies stemming from Herzberg's pioneering work was conducted by Myers, who used Herzberg's dimensions with various types of workers—supervisors, technicians, and female assembly workers.[41] Myers found that the variables affecting motivation may have quite different effects on productivity. Factors having a positive effect on productivity, growth factors, challenge and stimulate employees to work effectively. Factors that reduce productivity are "hygiene" factors.

As Myers points out, however, the motivating and dissatisfying factors vary with the individual's personality and type of job. For example, people who seek motivation, or "growth seekers," look for opportunities for achievement and responsibility, have positive feelings toward work and life in general, and derive a great deal of satisfaction from work accomplishment. Since these people strive for quality and are motivated primarily by the nature of the task itself and the desire to get the job done right, they are relatively unconcerned about poor environmental factors and, indeed, have a high tolerance for them.

"Maintenance seekers," on the other hand, tend to avoid looking for motivational opportunities, are more passive and cynical about their jobs, and distrust the positive values of work and life in general. Their dissatisfaction is expressed in their concern with the maintenance factors surrounding the job —pay, fringe benefits, job security, supervision, working conditions, fellow employees, and company policy and administration. These people seem to be more dependent on external conditions and are less inner-directed and self-sufficient than are growth seekers.

When growth seekers are treated like maintenance seekers, however, they tend to behave like maintenance seekers; in the absence of growth opportunities, they become more concerned with the environmental factors. Similarly, when maintenance seekers are treated like growth seekers, they tend to adopt the latter role and to acquire the behavior and value patterns of growth seekers.

Another set of findings based on Herzberg's interviewing methodology suggests that when content and context issues are further broken down into the actual events (task activity, amount of work, responsibility, etc.) and into the agents producing the event (organization, persons), one could not differentiate job context from job content events in terms of the dissatisfaction-satisfaction continuum. Both context and content events produced satisfaction *and* dissatisfaction. The agents were differentiated, however, such that persons attributed satisfying events to themselves and dissatisfying events to external agents.[42] (This tendency is sometimes referred to as the ego-defense hypothesis.) These findings were consistent with other research that used a questionnaire to assess occupational values and that similarly found that job context and content could not be differentiated on the dissatisfaction-satisfaction continuum, but that workers attributed pleasant experiences to the self and unpleasant experience to others.[43]

Thus in the past few years, Herzberg's findings have been challenged by more precise data-gathering and analysis techniques. Although his research broke through the unidimensional theorizing about motivation and was helpful in establishing the basis for job enrichment (to be discussed later), it cannot be considered rigorous research. It persists, however, because it has common-sense and face validity—it looks impressive—to some managers and practitioners in the organizational world.

E. Comparison of the Theories

Although the various theories of motivation differ and the research does not solidly support any one theory, there are areas of common agreement, and the various models and theories are interrelated. If we use Alderfer's basic core needs of existence, relatedness, and growth, perhaps we can put the state of the current motivational art into better perspective (see Fig. 3.9).

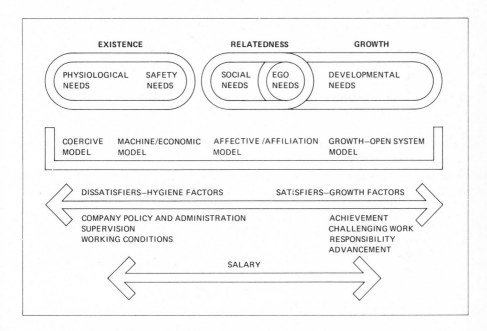

Fig. 3.9 Interrelationships of the content models and theories of motivation.

Existence includes the coercive model, since people do strive for existence and survival, as well as parts of the economic/machine model, since money and economic rewards are necessary for survival. Existence also incorporates many of Herzberg's dissatisfiers; if such aspects of the surrounding environment as working conditions, company policy and administration, and salary are unsatisfactory, workers will be less motivated.

The core need for *relatedness* is consistent with Maslow's social and ego categories and can also include Herzberg's supervision and recognition factors as being either satisfiers or dissatisfiers. Finally, the core need for *growth* fits the growth-open system model, since it includes both Maslow's developmental category and Herzberg's satisfier factors of achievement, challenging work, responsibility, and advancement.

Nord feels that all three core needs can be satisfied through operant conditioning. He discusses the need for exchange of both economic and social reinforcers and points out that the process of social exchange depends on the set of rewards which follow behavior, stressing that "the operant approach focuses attention on these exchange processes."[44]

F. Limitations of the Static-Content Models of Motivational Systems

The major problem with the bulk of the preceding theorizing and research is that it looks at motivation at only one or at most three or four periods of time. In a way, it is similar to a snapshot or at best a number of snapshots as to what may be motivating a person at a particular time. This has been either present-time-oriented (as for research emanating from Maslow's need hierarchy and Alderfer's ERG theory) or past-time-oriented (as for Herzberg's two-factor theory). What may be called for is a model similar to a movie picture as opposed to a snapshot, such that the *process* of how people are motivated is as much a focus as is the *content* of what motivates people. In this way, one can observe the process of motivation, and with refinement of measures, make predictions as to what will motivate people. It is this particular problem to which valence-instrumentality-expectancy theory (VIE theory) is addressed.

V. DYNAMIC-EXPECTANCY MODELS OF MOTIVATIONAL SYSTEMS

A. Description and Research

Three important terms in the discussion of this model are *valence, instrumentality,* and *expectancy. Valence* refers to the relative importance a goal has for an individual and is expressed as either a positive or a negative number. A goal that has no importance to an individual therefore has no valence. *Instrumentality* refers to the subjective probability, ranging from $+1.00$ to -1.00, that an individual will estimate that a first-level outcome will lead to a second-level outcome, e.g., good grades lead to the person's admittance to graduate school. Finally, *expectancy* is the probability that an individual's effort will be associated with a first-level outcome. In short, then, instrumentality refers to outcome-outcome relationships; expectancy, to effort-outcome relationships.

One of the problems with the static-content theories is that several needs may be operating simultaneously, and sorting out which behavior is associated with what need can be exasperating. Another approach is to examine the goals—material, social, growth, security, etc.—people wish to attain (or avoid) to establish preferences. By examining these goals, one can establish relative preferences for these goals. If a goal is highly sought after, it has high positive *valence*. If an outcome is undesirable for a person, it has high negative valence; finally, if a goal is neither desirable nor undesirable, it has no valence. Valence can be considered to be the positive or negative importance a person attaches to an outcome.

In our discussion of VIE theory, we will be making two distinctions. First, there are intermediate goals, which intervene between an action or effort and a final goal. We will consider intermediate goals as first-level goals; final goals, as second-level ones. Each goal, be it first- or second-level, has valence attached to it. Second, two major classes of outcome relate to individual motivation—*extrinsic* and *intrinsic* outcomes. Extrinsic outcomes are externally derived, such as good grades, wages, appreciative friends, etc. Intrinsic outcomes are internally derived, such as personal satisfaction for working hard, knowing that you are trying to help friends, etc.

The second feature of VIE theory is that people have in their own minds subjective probabilities that their goals may be reached (or avoided) by certain behavior. This behavior is perceived to be more or less instrumental in achieving or avoiding a second-level goal, and its probability of being attained is referred to as an *instrumentality*. In much of the theorizing, the numerical value of an instrumentality ranges from -1 (perceived as having *not* led to a second-level goal) to $+1$ (always leading to a second-level goal). In most cases an instrumentality is derived from an intermediate or first-level outcome, or goal, which leads to the second-level goal. Examples of first-level outcomes are high performance (instrumentally related to gaining a promotion), good grades (instrumentally related to getting into graduate school), and love and concern for a member of the opposite sex (instrumentally related to finding a marriage partner).

The final component of VIE theory is *expectancy*—the likelihood or probability an individual's action will lead to a first-level outcome which has instrumentality needed for the final goal. Studying hard usually, but not always, produces good grades. Your personal concept of working hard usually, but not always, is interpreted as high performance. Sending flowers to your loved one may or may not be interpreted as loving concern. In any event, the *expectancy* that any of these actions may lead to a first-level outcome is something less than a certainty. Thus the expectancy that studying hard will lead to good grades is fairly high to someone who usually gets good grades, because the relationship is fairly well established. The good grades are a first-level outcome and have differing instrumentalities for getting into graduate school or obtaining a good job. The difference between an *expectancy* and an *instrumentality* is not always made clear by theorists, but for our purposes we can think of expectancy as being slightly more tentative and instrumentality as being more established.

Figure 3.10 represents an example of some of the expectancies, valences, and instrumentalities associated with the behavior or effort of studying hard. On the plus side is the common expectancy that studying hard will result in good grades—a desired first-level outcome. It is even more likely to result

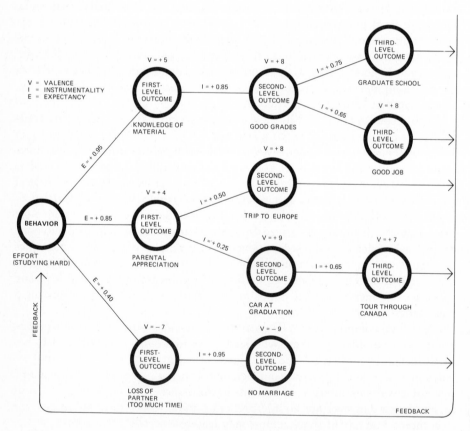

Fig. 3.10 Expectancy motivation model.

in parental appreciation; even if you don't get good grades, your parents will be pleased that you are making the effort. On the other hand, there may be a slight though significant expectancy that your studying hard will take up so much time as to wreak havoc with your social life. You might lose your steady date, an undesired outcome, since having one is instrumentally necessary to marriage.

In 1964 Vroom developed the two basic components of VIE theory as applied to organizations.[45] The first component was a way of predicting valence, or the positive or negative importance of an outcome to a person; the second, a method of predicting the force on the person to perform or act in such a way as to lead to a high-valence outcome. More recent derivations have included a distinction between intrinsic and extrinsic task goals and expectancy I and II, which differentiates between reaching initial task goals and more ultimate rewards.[46]

What have been the research findings with regard to VIE theory? In one summary article the author points out that most of the tests on the valence component of the model produced strong, significant findings.[47] Thus the writer feels that the model has fairly convincing predictive value. As for results on the force component of the model, the findings have predictive utility, but are not as strong as in the valence model. In part this is caused by the differences in methodology between studies and in part by the fact that thus far, researchers have had to restrict tests of the original models because of measurement difficulties.

Another exhaustive review of VIE theory notes that the most successful tests of the valence component of the theory have been in the prediction of the valence of pay, an extrinsic reward.[48] The authors point out that any complete formulation of a VIE theory must include the intrinsic valence of extrinsic outcomes.

B. Limitations of the VIE Model

A more negative view of VIE theory outlines the mathematical-logical assumptions on which expectancy theory rests and concludes that although VIE theory can explain some of the variance in work effort, it explains much less than is currently attributed to it.[49] These researchers take particular issue with the interactions between the sum of expectancies and valences, which they regard as causally complex and not well understood.

Another problem inherent in VIE theory is that a situation might arise in which negative instrumentalities and negative valences would predict the same outcome as positive instrumentalities and positive valences. Since the

Decisions, decisions. Which path has more instrumentality to get to the more important goal? (A. Devaney, Inc./E. P. Jones)

valence-instrumentality (VI) relationship is multiplicative, the theory would predict a similar outcome, but that aspect has yet to be tested. In addition, scaling and measurement procedures have not been sufficiently refined to explore the complexities of the model. Finally, although the theory makes predictions about within-person outcomes, virtually all of the studies to date have been on between-person outcomes.[50]

Clearly, more research is needed to find out both the long-term potential and the limits of the model's usefulness. It does seem fair to say that based on current journal accounts, VIE theory is attracting more research interest than are other areas in motivation.

VI. RELATIONSHIP BETWEEN SATISFACTION AND PRODUCTIVITY

The relationship between satisfaction and productivity is an issue that still arouses research interest. A comprehensive review of the literature concluded that there is no consistent relationship between satisfaction on the job and productivity.[51] More recent studies, aided by more sophisticated methodology and the distinction between extrinsic and intrinsic satisfaction, have shown that performance is related to intrinsic satisfaction, but that extrinsic rewards lead to performance level.[52] In other words, paying someone well to do work would increase his or her performance level, which in turn would increase intrinsic satisfaction. Although this finding is consistent with the wage-inequity theory advanced by Adams and Rosenbaum, the satisfaction-productivity relationship needs further research.

These results, coupled with the findings that those with higher intrinsic motivation also have higher motivation for performance-contingent extrinsic rewards, show that this field continues to provoke research interest and that in time, it should provide useful information to the manager.[53]

VII. TOWARD A SITUATIONAL MODEL OF MOTIVATION

Having reviewed the static-content and the dynamic-expectancy models of motivational systems, we might consider what is likely to happen to the field of motivation. Are the two types of theories compatible, or are they contradictory? Adopting Lawler's three criteria discussed earlier in this chapter, we can say that the former set of models dwells on the content of needs within people at any given point in time, whereas the latter, VIE, theory is more concerned with the process of predicting outcomes based on goals. The content theories can be helpful in identifying classes of needs, but they will not be precise in predicting behavioral outcomes. VIE models are, from the content standpoint, theoretical. They do not, for instance, say there are three primary drives (as one form of learning theory does) or three basic interrelated needs (as Alderfer does); instead, they focus on the preferences, subjective probabilities, and behavioral outcomes that are *for whatever reason* within us all. It is too early to fully develop an integrated situational model of motivation, but it is certain that behavioral outcomes may have valence because they meet certain categories of established needs. At the same time, these categories of needs, although explaining behavior in a reasonable sort of way, do not predict behavior with the accuracy of even the crudely developed VIE models presently available. In the next few years, one might expect prediction to assist in explanation; thus a number of integrated motivational models are likely to be tested.

VIII. IMPLICATIONS FOR THE MANAGER

Given the present state of research on motivation, what should the manager do? First, people differ according to their needs at any given time. Whatever typology is used, various things will motivate people at various times. Thus the manager should be aware that some people are maintenance seekers in some situations and growth seekers in other situations. Second, with the separation of intrinsic and extrinsic satisfaction, it is beginning to appear that high performance causes intrinsic satisfaction, but that extrinsic rewards cause high performance. Thus satisfiers and dissatisfiers are highly interrelated; often one and the same factor may have similar motivational affects on people. Pay is an extrinsic motivator that has been heavily researched and as such is very important.

The manner in which an employer or leader "motivates" others depends largely on: (1) that person's own motivation; (2) the accuracy of his or her perceptions of workers' needs; (3) the psychological contract with subordinates; and (4) the effectiveness of the communication process. As Kolb says, "We do not see people as they are, we see them for what they mean to us."[54] Therefore, the extent to which a leader understands his or her own motivational structure and applies this understanding in dealings with subordinates is one determinant of managerial success. Although never able be totally objective in perceiving another individual or situation, the successful manager must have the sensitivity and ability to diagnose, sense, and appreciate the differences among subordinates in order to take appropriate action.[55] Logically, then, initiating a proper psychological contract, the leader or manager will be that much better able to properly "motivate" his or her subordinates. In order to do this, the leader must calculate subordinates' expectations in relation to their abilities and motives.

Additionally, a manager apparently can train people to have high needs for achievement, as McClelland's research has indicated. At the same time, a caution is in order. An organization made up of nothing but growth seekers or persons with high needs for achievement is sure to be chaotic.

Finally, the manager should find out what people *say* motivates them. Much of the research on VIE theory is based on individuals' self-reports of goals important to them; thus a self-report can be a reasonable way of assessing motivation. However, most managers just *assume* that they know what motivates people. Their lists might well be different if they actually asked people and *listened* to the responses.

Another important motivational tool available to the manager is effective communication, which will be accepted more willingly and used more constructively by subordinates "when it is presented in a manner that [the worker] regards as objective, that is, without personal bias."[56] The sensitive and diagnostic manager will, therefore, have to understand his or her own assets and limitations in communicating to others.

The letter that follows is a humorous, if all too typical, example of what can occur when the processes of need fulfillment, motivation, and communication go awry.

Dear Boss,

I hereby give notice of my formal resignation, effective two weeks from today.

I've been a designer with the Gargantuan Grimble Group, Incorporated (G Cubed) ever since I finished college. My work here has been very educational, although I do confess to occasional bewilderment regarding big business management. This example should illustrate what I mean: Once at a gripe session the director of manufacturing responded to a question of mine by telling a story about the "mushroom" theory of management. He said that you should always keep your employees in the dark, feed them lots of horse manure, and, when they grow up, cut them off at the ankles and can them. Everybody thought it was a funny story; but by the time the meeting was over I still didn't have an answer to my question.

However, I'm not writing this letter to complain. I'd like to take this opportunity to thank you and the company for all you have done for me.

That $100 bonus I got last Christmas in exchange for patent rights on my 14th invention was a welcome addition to my son's college fund. And I get a real kick out of seeing the production department turning out thousands of my gadgets every day, even if my name isn't on the label. I only regret that I had to spend two years and write three fat proposals persuading you and the division manager that it was a good product in the first place.

In case you think that my decision to leave has anything to do with the layoff of Larry Longtimer last week, I want to put your mind at ease. I had been wondering why Larry was still on the payroll. His enthusiasm and drive really went to hell after he was promoted to vice president of historical planning. I just didn't feel he was doing the company any good in that new position. Confidentially, though, something has been puzzling me. Why did the top brass transfer him out of the Stockholder's Delight Division he started 12 years ago, especially right after it racked up its tenth straight record year? The new manager, Mr. Presidentson, isn't doing nearly as well.

At Larry's farewell luncheon last Friday, I was really moved by the company's generosity in giving him a solid-gold 25-year service pin with a real diamond in it. It's too bad Larry couldn't hold out until he was eligible for retirement next year, though. I guess it couldn't be helped, what with the big losses this year in the Stockholder's Delight Division. Anyway, that check for two weeks' severance pay should tide him over until he qualifies for unemployment compensation. I understand you can get as much as $75 per week nowadays.

I'd also like to say that my resignation is in no way related to my having to terminate those summer-hire students last year just two weeks after they started working. I guess the company's sudden realization that it was in a cash bind and required immediate layoffs couldn't be helped. I sure had a tough time explaining to those students, though. They went away grumbling some terrible things about their first introduction to big business.

Boss, I remember your explaining that the last 6 percent raise you gave me was the largest in the whole department, that I'm the youngest guy in the company's history to have the responsibilities I hold, and that my salary is the highest in the company for my job classification. I also recall that to be eligible for my next promotion to novice manager, I have to put in at least two more years with the company.

Boss, you've gotta understand! Each month, I get a copy of the *Alumni Review* from my alma mater. My wife reads me the class news at bedtime every evening after that damn thing comes in the mail. You wouldn't believe the jerks I used to have for classmates and lab partners who have started businesses of their own and are making out pretty well. One has launched a successful magazine with international circulation; another has his own real estate development corporation. Still another has a computer peripheral company with 500 people on the payroll that grossed $10 million last year, and our "most likely to fail" classmate is a bona fide magnate in the alfalfa exporting business. Phil Anthrope, my former class president, just made a $100,000 Alumni Fund donation to establish a perpetual scholarship bearing his name. With competition like this, you can understand why I was too ashamed of my career progress to go to last year's reunion. I know I'm at least as good as most of these guys, and I've got to prove it to my wife, my friends, and most of all, to myself. G Cubed timetables just don't hack it!

By now, I'll bet you're wondering what my plans are. I want you to know that I am not going to work for a competitor. You remember that new electromechanator Willie Whizbanger recently finished an 18-month development program on? You know, the one you circulated a memo about, saying the company was going to abandon it because there was no market for it? (You even let Willie buy the sole patent rights for $1.) Guess what? The vice president of corporate development at Upward Spiral Industries read Willie's recent *IEEE Transactions* article about it and called our Marketing Department to see if he could buy some electromechanators from G Cubed. When he learned we weren't going to make any here, the Upward Spiral man asked if they might buy the patent rights. That's when Marketing referred the call to Willie.

Later that evening Willie telephoned me at home to say that if I wanted to start a company with him to make electromechanators, Upward Spiral had indicated they would be our first customer. Willie said that the man at Upward Spiral even told him that he would help us get some venture capital if we would prepare a business proposal. He mentioned the possibility of our being a subsidiary or some such thing, but Willie and I are going to get more details after we finish working on our business plan. Incidentally, we will probably be calling our new company Nimble Whizbanger Laboratories. I'll be president and Willie will be vice president of engineering.

The main reason Willie and I feel so confident about our prospects for success is the way Fred Faithless and his group made out when they spun off to start Levitation Laboratories two years ago. They were just acquired last month by Colossal Conglomerate in a stock swap deal, and we understand that Fred has now retired to a cattle ranch in the Canadian Rockies at the tender age of 37.

Of the seven or eight companies started by former G Cubed staff members, the only one we know of that has failed was started by Stanley Spleen and Gilbert Gall. As near as we can reckon, their difficulties were basically due to walnut paneling, palace revolts, and their 35-hour work week.

Willie and I have built a new prototype of our electromechanator at my uncle's auto repair shop, using parts we bought at the Spleen and Gall bankruptcy sale. We have also gone to one of these new seminars on how to get started. Willie and I have talked to our wives about this, and last night we came to our final decision. Boss, it has been a pleasure working for you, and if you decide you might like to join us in about six months, we'd be glad to talk it over.

Sincerely,
Jack B. Nimble[57]

IX. SUMMARY

In this chapter we looked at some commonly held beliefs about why people work. We traced the history of motivational theory from the various static-content models, which assume that particular forces or needs motivate people at particular times, to the currently more prevalent view that people are complex and have multiple needs operating simultaneously. These latter models suggest that the best way to find what motivates people is to look at their goals from a dynamic-expectancy viewpoint.

We examined some of the important research bearing on all of these models. We concluded that neither the static nor the dynamic models in and of themselves are likely to be considered adequate over time and that a situational viewpoint will most likely emerge.

As we illustrate in a later chapter, behavior is a process of social exchange; the individual acts in ways that satisfy his or her own unique needs. A closely related concept is the psychological contract. According to Etzioni, social exchange within the organization is based on the notion that organizations must provide their workers with opportunities for need satisfaction—by changing job situations, if necessary.

REVIEW

1. Interview a worker and a manager about the unwritten expectations (psychological contract) they have of the organization and the organization has of them. What influence does this seem to have on their behavior?

2. Why were the authors motivated to write this book? What needs might have been satisfied?

3. Discuss the implications of the psychological contract. Describe from your own experience what effect the psychological contract has had in either the classroom or a job you have held or are now holding.

4. Discuss the implications of the statement "I can't influence you unless I allow you to influence me."

5. Discuss the reasons why there seems to be little consistent measured relationship between morale and productivity. How important is the presence of "good morale"?

6. Interview several different people—a manager, a worker, a labor leader— to get their ideas on why people work. Do their concepts agree? How do their ideas tie in to this text?

7. Discuss the statement "You cannot motivate someone else." What does it mean? Do you agree with it? What are the implications of the statement?

8. What is the psychological contract in this class as you perceive it? What are some of the ways it can be changed? Modified? Improved?

9. Compare Maslow's need hierarchy model with Herzberg's motivator-hygiene model. What are the similarities? Differences?

REFERENCES

1. E. E. Lawler, *Motivation in Work Organizations*, Monterey, Calif.: Brooks Cole, 1973, p. 5.

2. W. E. Vinake, "Motivation as a Complex Problem," in *Nebraska Symposium on Motivation*, ed. M. R. Jones, Lincoln: University of Nebraska Press, 1962, pp. 1–49.

3. *Ibid.*, p, 3.

4. G. Homans, "Social Behaviors as Exchange," *American Journal of Sociology* **63,** 6 (May 1958): 597–606. Reprinted by permission.

5. J. S. Adams and W. E. Rosenbaum, "The Relationship of Worker Productivity to Cognitive Dissonance about Wage Inequities," *Journal of Applied Psychology* 55, 1 (Feb. 1971): 161–164.

6. E. R. Valenzi and I. R. Andrews, "Effect of Hourly Overpay and Underpay Inequity when Tested with a New Induction Procedure," *Journal of Applied Psychology* **55,** 1 (Feb. 1971): 22–27.

7. A. Etzioni, *A Comparative Analysis of Complex Organizations,* Glencoe, Ill.: Free Press, 1961.

8. E. Schein, *Organizational Psychology,* 2d ed., Englewood Cliffs, N.J.: Prentice-Hall, 1970, p. 58 ff.

9. R. Scott, "Job Expectancy—An Important Factor in Labor Turnover," *Personnel Journal* **55,** 5 (May 1972): 360–363.

10. C. Perrow, "Reality Adjustment: A Young Institution Settles for Humane Care," *Social Problems* **14,** 1 (Summer 1966): 69–79.

11. W. Serrin, "The Assembly Line," *Atlantic Monthly* **227,** 10 (Oct. 1971): 62–68.

12. "Disassembling the Line," *Time Magazine,* Jan. 17, 1972.

13. J. R. Strayer, H. Mumo, and C. Dana, *The Middle Ages, 359–1500,* 4th ed., New York: Appleton-Century-Crofts, 1969, p. 248.

14. F. W. Taylor, *Scientific Management,* New York: Harper & Row, 1911, p. 46.

15. M. Weber, *Essays in Sociology,* trans. H. Gerth and C. W. Mills, New York: Oxford University Press, 1946.

16. R. D. Hulme and R. V. Bevan, "The Blue-Collar Worker goes on Salary," *Harvard Business Review* **53,** 2 (March–April 1975): 104–112.

17. B. F. Skinner, *Science and Human Behavior,* New York: Macmillan, 1954.

18. W. R. Nord, "Beyond the Teaching Machine: The Neglected Area of Operant Conditioning in the Theory and Practice of Management," *Organizational Behavior and Human Performance* **4,** 4 (Nov. 1969): 375–401.

19. "Where Skinner's Theories Work," *Business Week,* Dec. 2, 1972, pp. 64–65; E. J. Feeney, "At Emery Air Freight: Positive Reinforcement Boosts Performance," *Organizational Dynamics* **1,** 3 (Winter 1973): 41–50.

20. C. Perrow, *Organizational Analysis: A Sociological View,* Belmont, Cal.: Wadsworth, 1970, pp. 118–120.

21. C. Schneier, "Behavior Modification in Management: A Review and Critique," *Academy of Management Journal* **17,** 3 (Sept. 1974): 528–548.

22. Nord, *op. cit.*

23. E. Pedalino and V. U. Gamboa, "Behavior Modification and Absenteeism: Intervention in One Industrial Setting," *Journal of Applied Psychology* **59,** 6 (Dec. 1974): 694–698.

24. G. A. Yukl and G. P. Latham, "Consequences of Reinforcement Schedules and Incentive Magnitudes for Employee Performance: Problems Encountered in a Industrial Setting," *Journal of Applied Psychology* **60**, 3 (June 1975): 294–298

25. C. R. Gullett, and R. Reisen, "Behavior Modification: A Contingency Approach to Employee Performance," *Personnel Journal* **54**, 4 (April 1975): 206–210; R Beatty and C. Schneier, "A Case for Positive Reinforcement," *Business Horizon* **18**, 2 (April 1975): 57–66.

26. E. L. Trist and K. Bamforth, "Some Social and Psychological Consequences of the Longwall Method of Coal-Getting," *Human Relations* **4**, 1 (Feb. 1951): 4–38

27. A. Maslow, *Motivation and Personality*, New York: Harper and Brothers, 1954 p. 13.

28. L. M. Porter, "Job Attitudes in Management: I. Perceived Deficiencies in Need Fulfillment as a Function of Job Level," *Journal of Applied Psychology* **46**, 6 (Dec. 1962): 375–387.

29. V. Vroom, *Work and Motivation*, New York: Wiley, 1964.

30. E. Lawler, III, and J. Suttle, "A Causal Correlational Test of the Need-Hierarchy Concept," *Organizational Behavior and Human Performance* **7**, 2 (April 1972): 265–287.

31. D. T. Hall and K. Nougaim, "An Examination of Maslow's Need Hierarchy in an Organizational Setting," *Organizational Behavior and Human Performance* **3**, 1 (Feb. 1968): 12–35.

32. C. P. Alderfer, "An Empirical Test of a New Theory of Human Needs," *Organizational Behavior and Human Performance* **4**, 2 (May 1969): 142–175.

33. E. Schein, *Organizational Psychology*, 2d ed., Englewood Cliffs, N.J.: Prentice-Hall, 1970, p. 58 ff.

34. A. Maslow, *Toward a Psychology of Being*, Princeton, N.J.: Van Nostrand, 1962.

35. D. McClelland, *The Achieving Society*, Princeton, N.J.: Van Nostrand, 1961; "Business Drive and National Achievement," *Harvard Business Review* **40**, 4 (July-Aug. 1962): 99–112; "That Urge to Achieve," *Think*, International Business Machines, 1966.

36. H. Wainer and I. Rubin, "Motivation of Research and Development Entrepreneurs: Determinants of Company Success," *Journal of Applied Psychology* **53**, 3 (June 1969): 178–184.

37. B. Weiner and A. Kukla, "An Attributional Analysis of Achievement Motivation," *Journal of Personality and Social Psychology* **15**, (May 1970): 1–20.

38. A. Brayfield and W. Crockett, "Employee Attitudes and Employee Performance," *Psychological Bulletin* **52**, 5 (Nov. 1955): 396–424; F. Herzberg, B. Mausner, R. Peterson, and D. Capwell, *Job Attitudes: Review of Research and Opinion*, Pittsburgh: Psychological Services of Pittsburgh, 1957.

39. F. Herzberg, B. Mausner, and B. Snyderman, *The Motivation to Work*, New York: Wiley, 1959.

40. B. L. Hinton, "An Empirical Investigation of the Herzberg Methodology and Two-Factor Theory," *Organizational Behavior and Human Performance* **3**, 3 (August 1968): 286–309.

41. M. S. Myers, "Who Are Your Motivated Workers?" *Harvard Business Review* **42**, 1 (Jan.-Feb. 1964): 73–88.

42. E. A. Locke, "Satisfiers and Dissatisfiers Among White-Collar and Blue-Collar Employees," *Journal of Applied Psychology* **58**, 1 (Feb. 1973): 67–76.

43. Nord, *op. cit.*

44. D. A. Ondrack, "Defense Mechanisms and the Herzberg Theory: An Alternate Test," *Academy of Management Journal* **17**, 1 (March 1974): 79–89.

45. V. H. Vroom, *Work and Motivation*, New York: Wiley, 1964.

46. J. P. Campbell, M. D. Dunnette, E. E. Lawler, and K. E. Weick, Jr., *Managerial Behavior, Performance and Effectiveness*, New York: McGraw-Hill, 1970.

47. T. R. Mitchell, "Expectancy Model of Job Satisfaction, Occupational Preference and Effort: A Theoretical, Methodological and Empirical Appraisal," *Psychological Bulletin* **81**, 12 (Dec. 1974): 1053–1077.

48. M. A. Wahba and R. J. House, "Expectancy Theory in Work and Motivation: Some Logical and Methodological Issues," *Human Relations* **27**, 2 (April 1974): 121–147.

49. O. Behling and F. A. Starke, "The Postulates of Expectancy Theory," *Academy of Management Journal* **16**, 3 (Sept. 1973): 373–388.

50. Mitchell, *op. cit.*

51. Brayfield and Crockett, *op. cit.*

52. J. P. Wanous, "A Causal-Correctional Analysis of the Job Satisfaction and Performance Relationship," *Journal of Applied Psychology* **59**, 2 (April 1974): 139–144.

53. J. Dermer, "The Interrelationship of Intrinsic and Extrinsic Motivation," *Academy of Management Journal* **18**, 1 (March 1975): 125–129.

54. D. A. Kolb, I. M. Rubin, and J. McIntyre, *Organizational Psychology: An Experiential Approach*, Englewood Cliffs, N.J.: Prentice-Hall, 1971, p. 204.

55. Schein, *op. cit.*

56. R. M. Anthony, *Management Accounting: Text and Cases*, Homewood, Ill.: Richard D. Irwin, 1970, p. 418.

57. D. Dible, "Dear Boss: Why I'm Quitting . . . ," *IEEE Spectrum* **9**, 5 (May 1972): 63–64. This material has been adapted and exerpted from *Up Your OWN Organization! A Handbook for the Employed, the Unemployed, and the Self-Employed on How to Start and Finance a New Business*, Donald M. Dible, Santa Clara, Cal.: The Entrepreneur Press, 1971. Reprinted by permission.

4

INTERPERSONAL
PERCEPTION
AND
COMMUNICATION

O wad some power the giftie gie us
To see ourselves as ithers see us!

ROBERT BURNS

LEARNING OBJECTIVES

When you have finished reading and studying this chapter, you should be able to:

1. Differentiate between sensation and perception in systems terms.
2. Determine whether perception is an internal or external phenomenon.
3. Describe several specific determinants of perception.
4. Offer at least four reasons why we study perception.
5. Explain why people always act in ways that make sense to them *as they perceive the world*.
6. Differentiate between using the "communications" as a normative (good or bad) term and as an analytical tool.

You will be expected to define and use the following concepts:

Sensation	Filters
Perception	Manifest versus latent content
Perceptual set	Supportive climate
Expectancy	Defensive climate
Perceptual variation	Nonverbal communication
Stereotyping	Ameslan
Halo effect	Transactional analysis
Projection	Ego state
Expectancy	Stroking
Selective perception	Time structuring
Encoding	Game
Decoding	

THOUGHT
STARTERS

1. What do we mean when we say, "That person is acting in a way which makes no sense at all"?
2. What do we mean when we say, "Communications in this department are bad"?
3. What communications difficulties have you had with others in the past at work, at home, and where you live away from home? What are several ways in which you could communicate more effectively in each of these situations?
4. What difference is there between clarity and effectiveness of communications? Give an example or two.

I. INTRODUCTION

The processes of perception and communication form a system: communication depends on perception, and perception, in turn, depends on two classes of antecedents—internal states and external, or environmental, states. Most of the internal states depend on learning and include values, goals, beliefs, perceptions, (perceived) relations between actions and their outcomes, and the expected consequences of these actions.[1] The external states are totally environmental and include such things as upbringing, reading habits, and hobbies or other leisure-time activities. Obviously, the two states are closely related.

These two states determine our perceptual biases—the "rose-colored glasses" through which we see the world. Because of these two antecedents, we cannot be truly objective about anything. At best, we can only know what some of our prejudices are. The *perceptual set*, or outcome of the internal and external conditioning, determines what we communicate to others, our perception of what other persons hear, as well as what we hear from others (Fig. 4.1).

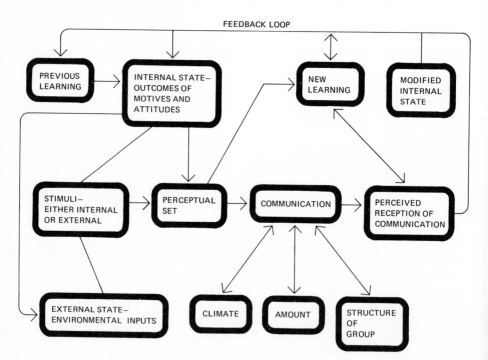

Fig. 4.1 Systems model of perception and communication. (Adapted from J. G. March and H. A. Simon, *Organizations*, New York: Wiley, 1958, p. 11.)

Perception and communication are the foundations of interpersonal behavior and have important implications for the four types of models discussed in Chapter 3. For example, a supervisor acting primarily according to assumptions of the economic/machine model is less likely to treat subordinates as "humanely" as if he or she were following the relatedness model. Similarly, a supervisor who believes that money is the sole motivator is unlikely to provide subordinates with opportunities for intellectual growth and achievement.

After discussing perception, we examine some of the reasons for both perceptual variation and the use of perceptual manipulating devices.

In the section on communications, we look at several factors that affect the communication process—the nature and amount of information received; how it is processed, condensed, and used; group factors in communication; and the "climate" of the situation. Finally, we review some specific techniques for improving the communication process.

II. PERCEPTION

A. Introduction

Such phrases as "That's not what I meant" or "That isn't what it means to me" are familiar expressions indicating that people see the world somewhat differently. Thus although two people may receive the same visual and aural stimuli, they may perceive these stimuli differently. In other words, *sensations* are the inputs to the sensory system, and *perception* is the process whereby these incoming data are organized.

The organization of sensations through the perceptual process serves a very useful and essential function. For example, it enables us to "screen out" the myriad sound waves continuously hitting our ear drums and thereby pay attention to only certain, selected sounds. This organizing process, or perception, is learned over time. A vivid example occurs when a person who is hard of hearing first begins to wear a hearing aid; it is virtually impossible to "screen out" all the sounds that the hearing aid picks up. Until the wearer has learned to readjust, the device will be more of a distraction than a help.

Not only does the perceptual process help us screen out unwanted stimuli, but it is also of great value in helping us organize what we see and hear into something that is meaningful to us. This enables us to view the outside world as something consistent, something with which we can cope. We can use a minimum of cues to help us understand what is going on in the world around us. We can make almost instant order out of what would otherwise be chaos. We can predict how people will behave, and we can understand situations better.

The perceptual process enables us to "straighten out" this distortion of the United Nations building caused by rain falling against the window. (The Christian Science Monitor)

Fig. 4.2   Perception as expectancy.

For example, look at the seven dots in Fig. 4.2. According to Gestalt psychologists, most people "see" a triangle and a rectangle. The perceptual process by which such ambiguous sensations are organized into patterns meaningful to the individual is called *expectancy*. In other words, we tend to see what we expect or wish to see. For example, we *know* from past experience that most rooms have walls and ceilings that meet at right angles. As a result, when we look at a room, we *see* the walls and ceiling in terms of right angles, even though optically, they are actually at odd angles to us from our position in the room.

Similarly, managers with different backgrounds will see different problems in a set of data. A large inventory welcomed by an auto salesman may be decried by the production manager. If different managers are given the same case to study or are asked to give their opinions about a company crisis, the manufacturing manager is more likely to see the problem as a need for more efficient production, whereas the financial manager is more likely to see the problem as the need to maintain a good financial picture for the company.

In the same way, management consultants with dissimilar backgrounds are quite likely to see very different solutions to any given problem. The consultant with a structural-design orientation may tend to see corporate inefficiency as resulting from poorly defined job descriptions, lack of centralized authority, too loose cost controls, poor industrial engineering, etc. The workflow consultant is more likely to see the problem as underutilization or misuse of the computer or the lack of appropriate mathematical models. The human-perspective consultant may well see the problem as a "people" problem and therefore recommend using better motivational techniques and pushing decision making to lower levels.

In summary, the manner in which we organize incoming sensations has two aspects.

1. Aspects of sensations that we have in common with others are called facts. An automobile accident witnessed by several persons is a fact, although they may not agree on the cause or details of the accident.

2. Sensations are organized in ways that are unique to us. This aspect of the perceptual process depends on biological mechanisms, past experience, and present assumptions, all of which stem from our own needs, experiences, values, and sentiments.

B. Internal and External Reasons for Perceptual Variation

Perceptual variation results from the fact that each person is different, with a different personality, background, and set of experiences. Therefore, several factors influence the development of the individual's perceptions.

1. Physiology A person's perceptions of the world are affected by his or her physiological condition. A glorious sunset, for example, may just look like so many shades of gray to someone who is color blind. Or, a loud passage from Stravinsky's *Firebird Suite* may not be very impressive to a person who is hard of hearing or tone deaf.

2. Family The strongest influence on a child is his or her family. Since the parents have already developed characteristic ways of seeing the world, they pass on many of their attitudes and perceptions to their children. It is no accident that most Catholics come from Catholic families and Lutherans from Lutheran families. A child whose father is a strong believer in trade unions is much more likely to grow up with similar attitudes and values. The attitudes and values provided by the family are, therefore, of primary importance.

3. Culture The culture and society in which one lives have a strong effect on the person's attitudes, values, and way of perceiving the world. In 1947 Bruner and Goodman conducted a social-psychological study in which they asked poor children and wealthy children to draw a quarter.[2] As might be expected, the poor children drew significantly larger quarters than did the wealthy children. Obviously, a quarter was more significant to a poor child than to a wealthy child. Another cultural variation is that people in some parts of the world consider dogs, cats, ants, snakes, and sheep's eyes to be delicious. The average American does not regard eating pork in the same way as does a devout Muslim and finds it difficult to understand why many Indians regard cows as sacred. In addition, any culture has subcultures, which may have greater influence on members than does the larger culture. Rock music, for example, is essential to one subculture but repugnant to members of other subcultures.

C. Devices for Manipulating Perceptual Data

An individual uses several devices to reduce the amount of data needed to work with, to avoid data that might otherwise tend to lower his or her self-esteem, and to try and keep combinations of events conceptually simple. The use of these devices, sometimes called a perceptual set, usually produces a tendency to behave in particular, predictable ways. Some of these devices are stereotyping, the halo effect, projection, perceptual defense, expectancy, and selective perception.

1. Stereotyping This phrase, originally coined by Walter Lippmann, refers to generalizations used to classify groups of people. "Blondes have more fun," and "Germans are methodical but unimaginative" are examples of stereotypes. Although stereotyping is frequently useful, it can also lead to highly inaccurate results. In 1950 Haire and Grunes examined what happened when people were confronted with information that did not fit a cultural stereotype, i.e., they were asked to justify the word "intelligent" in conjunction with the words "works in a factory."[3] Some subjects denied the incongruity. Others rendered the word "intelligent" meaningless by saying, "He was intelligent in the way he screwed the nut onto the bolt." Still others, recognizing the difficulty, used the discrepant information to make a real change in their previous stereotype.

We have used this exercise with our own students, using two lists—one containing the word "intelligent" and the other with the word left out. Our findings were essentially the same as those reported in the original study. Students using the list with "intelligent" left out always came up with much more uniform descriptions of the individual than did the groups of students using the list containing the term "intelligent."

2. The halo effect This is the process of using one particularly favorable or unfavorable trait to color everything else we know about a person. For example, we generally assume that an ambitious person is also energetic, aggressive, and punctual (because that person is so ambitious, she or he always seems to be around). If an "intelligent" person makes a mistake, our reaction might well be, "Anybody can make a mistake." On the other hand, if a "stupid" person who is a poor worker makes the same mistake as the "intelligent" individual, our reaction is quite likely to be, "What else could you expect?"

3. Projection Here, we attribute our own feelings or characteristics to someone else. In 1933 Murray studied this phenomenon by dividing children into two groups, one of which played a game called "Murder."[4] Both groups were then asked to judge some photographs. The children who had played the game "saw" much more malice and violence in the photographs than the control group did. A similar reaction occurs in labor relations; each group—the union and management—attributes its own malice and distrust to the other.

4. Perceptual defense Once we have established characteristic ways of seeing the world, we tend to have difficulty "letting go" of them. Perceptions are

"What makes you think I'm upset?"

useful in that they help us classify and organize the world in ways that make sense to us. However, these perceptions can also reduce our ability to fully understand another person in a given situation, i.e., that person may sometimes seem to act "out of character." Perceptual defense may also include such other perceptual devices as stereotyping, denial, and projection.

5. Expectancy In addition to visual perceptual expectancy, there are other types as well. Sometimes called the *self-fulfilling prophecy*, expectancy is the process whereby the person makes happen what he or she wishes to have happen. In his classic 1964 experiment, Rosenthal, for example, told some students that he had bred one group of laboratory rats for their intelligence and another for their stupidity.[5] He then asked the students to perform an experiment to see whether the rats could be differentiated according to their ability to learn a particular task. Sure enough, the smart rats did better than the stupid rats. However, Rosenthal had not been truthful with the students; in fact, there was *no* consistent difference between the two groups of rats. The students had seen what they expected to see.

Rosenthal conducted a similar study with teachers and children.[6] After intelligence tests had been administered to the students, the teachers were told that some of their pupils were much more intelligent than others. In actuality, however, the researcher had randomized the group; both groups represented the same level of intelligence. Nevertheless, those children the teachers *thought* were more intelligent received considerably better grades than those whom the teachers *thought* were less intelligent.

6. Selective perception   Another manipulative device is for the perceiver to draw unwarranted conclusions from an ambiguous situation. For example, a stockholder looking at a financial report may be so alarmed at noting that the company will not pay dividends this year that she or he completely overlooks the information that four highly salable new products will be introduced. In their 1965 study of selective perception, Dornbusch *et al.* noted that when children at a summer camp were asked to describe other children, the messages about *different* children from the *same* perceiver were more similar than descriptions of one child written by several others.[7]

These are only some of the processes that affect behavior. However, our purpose here is not to give a complete catalog of perceptual processes or devices, but rather to give example of the types of processes that operate in *any* perceptual situation.

D. Organizational Research Studies

In the "real world," of course, perceptual processes and devices do not occur in isolation. Rather, as the following studies show, they usually occur in combinations.

As Table 4.1 shows, there is considerable disagreement among workers, foremen, and general foremen about why people work. For example, managers believe that wages are much more important to subordinates than subordinates

Table 4.1   Perceptual differences about reasons for work

	Workers' self-ratings	Foremen's ratings for workers	Foremen's self-ratings	General foremen's ratings for foremen	General foremen's self-ratings
High wages	28%	61%	17%	58%	11%
Getting along well with people I work with	36%	17%	39%	22%	43%
Good chance to do interesting work	22%	12%	38%	14%	43%

Adapted from R. Likert, *New Patterns of Management*, New York: McGraw-Hill, 1961, p. 50.

do. Getting along with people is perceived as far more important by subordinates than by their managers. The same is true with the opportunity to do interesting work.

Table 4.2 Perceptual agreement and disagreement between supervisors and subordinates about their communications

	Workers see themselves	Foremen say about the workers	Foremen see themselves	Top management say about foremen
1. Feel very free to discuss important things about the job with the boss	51%	85%	67%	90%
2. Always or nearly always tell subordinates about changes affecting them or their work	47%	92%	63%	100%
3. Always or almost always get subordinates' ideas	16%	73%	52%	70%
4. Very often get a "pat on the back" for good work	13%	82%		

Data summarized and adapted from R. Likert, *New Patterns of Management*, New York: McGraw-Hill, 1961, pp. 47–53. Much of these data are from unpublished studies by F. C. Mann.

Table 4.2 shows Mann's findings that higher-level supervisors and their subordinates have widely divergent views about the subordinates' "freedom" to discuss important things about the job. Although 85% of the supervisors believe their subordinates feel free to talk about the job with the boss, only half of the subordinates share this belief. More than 90% of the foremen and 100% of the top management feel that they always or nearly always tell subordinates about changes affecting them or their work. Only about half of the subordinates feel the same way. Item 4 shows one of the major discrepancies—82% of the foremen say that they frequently give the man a pat on the back for good work, but only 13% of the men agree. There have been many studies like these, and the findings are always similar—there are major perceptual differences between bosses and their subordinates.

Even at a lower level, there is serious disagreement. Studying clerical jobs, O'Reilly found agreement on job content in only 67% of the jobs.[8] Job content differed by at least four tasks in about 32% of the disagreements. More than half of the cases showed disagreement on skill requirements of the job.

In summary, each individual is an open system, receiving information inputs, transforming them from sensations to perceptions, which then become modified outputs. These outputs may be modified still further as a result of the feedback loop. This perceptual process is shown in Fig. 4.3.

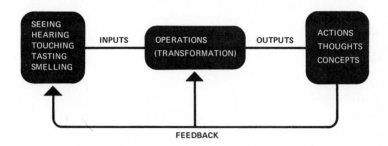

Fig. 4.3   The perceptual process.

The complexity of the operations, or transformation, process is highly dependent on the situation. For example, little perceptual bias or distortion occurs when one touches a hot stove; through the feedback process, the person recognizes what is happening and pulls his or her hand away almost instantly. In a highly complex social situation, however, many more factors are involved, including stereotyping and the halo effect. In general, perceptual biases and distortions are more likely to occur as (1) the information input becomes more central and more important to the individual and (2) the input diverges from deeply held beliefs. For example, a truly suspicious or paranoid person may perceive very innocent acts of other people as being extremely threatening. Here, the feedback process may be entirely internal in that the paranoid's suspicions may not be translated into direct action.

E. Summary

At the end of Chapter 3 we said that social behavior is an exchange; there is mutual interdependence and sense of obligation between people, and a person behaves in order to get something from the situation, the "psychological contract." However, because of the unique ways in which people see the world, one's attempts to influence others may be highly inaccurate because of inaccurate perceptions. We need to improve the accuracy of the perceptual process before we can increase the accuracy of our communications. This means that we must continually check our perceptions and assumptions and get feedback.

In addition to checking ourselves, we must also check the other person. In short, every individual behaves in ways that make sense to him or her. Each of us *always* acts in ways that are meaningful to us in terms of our perceptions of the world. Therefore, in order to better understand both how someone else feels about the world (communications) and that person's logic, we have to better understand both ourselves and others.

III. COMMUNICATIONS

A. Introduction

It has been suggested that about 70% of an active human being's life on the job is spent communicating, with a greater proportion (about 90%) of a typical manager's time at work being spent in the communications process. Earlier, we suggested that sensation consists of inputs to the sensory system and that perception is the process whereby these incoming data are organized. Communications consist of the ways incoming data from another person(s) are *interpreted*. It is the process of sending and receiving messages, and accurate communications do not take place unless the sender sends properly and the receiver receives the message in an undistorted form. However, there are a number of possible blocks, or filters, in the communications channel which may affect the interpretation. Figure 4.4 shows that communication requires encoding and decoding. The sender encodes a message into a suitable form and transmits the message, whereupon the receiver decodes it.

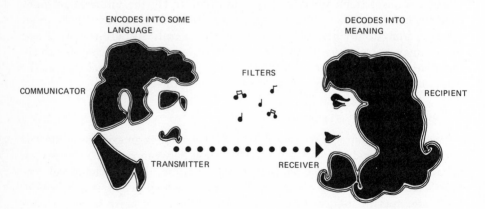

Fig. 4.4 The communications process.

Ambiguous messages block effective communications. (Photograph by Edgar F. Huse)

However, perceptual sets and/or "noise" in the line can reduce the clarity and accuracy of the information sent. For example, perceptual variation by both the sender and receiver is one of the biggest blocks to effective communications. Or, the sender's message may lack clarity, use the wrong transmission channels (perhaps a face-to-face meeting would be better than sending a memorandum), or be too complex. Similarly, the receiver may be preoccupied with other things, hear only what is expected, and ignore conflicting information, e.g., material that is contrary to "the facts" or to the receiver's feelings about the other person.

In addition, many people are apprehensive about their ability to communicate, which further increases the problem. For example, there is evidence that about 40% of college students are sufficiently concerned about their ability to communicate that that ability is impaired to some extent.[9]

B. Factors Affecting Communication

Although "open communication" is generally regarded as a desirable goal, perceptual factors greatly affect what is communicated. In this section, we examine some other variables relating to the communication process: (1) the manifest versus latent content of the message; (2) verbal versus nonverbal communication; (3) the nature of the information; (4) influences of the group structure; and (5) the effects of "climate" on communication.

1. Manifest versus latent content   When two people are communicating, "*it is the situation and not the words that we want to understand.*"[10] The situation is composed of both the setting and the people involved. For example, the situation of a college student talking with his or her professor is very different from that of two college students talking to each other at a bull session. Throughout their lives, people adapt their behavior to this fact; the situation has a tremendous impact on what people say and how they say it.

As a result, the words spoken have both an overt, or manifest, meaning and one that can be developed and understood only by understanding the situation. The same words may have very different meanings in different situations. For example, two men who have not seen each other for years meet at a college reunion. The obscenities they use while hugging and pounding each other on the back show a great deal of affection. However, those same words, when spoken by strangers in a bar, would cause a fight. The words are identical in these two contexts, but the emotions or sentiments behind the words are vastly different. As a result, the words themselves carry one meaning—the manifest one—but the sentiments convey another, or latent, meaning.

In the same vein, interpreters of diplomatic correspondence between two countries look closely for shades of meaning and nuances, which sometimes "tell" much more than the written words. Very often what is *not* said is just as important as what *is* said.

In short, words communicate not only information, but also sentiments. The receivers of organizational messages also have sentiments and emotions which will vary with the situation and the receiver's age, sex, official position, and informal position in the organization. Some terms, highly emotional for the listener, may have little emotional loading for the speaker. For example, a speaker at a luncheon meeting made the unfortunate mistake of using the term "girls" in referring to a work team of women employees. As a result, two women became angry and walked out of the audience, to the speaker's shock and dismay.

This same difference is operative in the following illustration. A young executive complains about the size of her desk. One method of answering her complaint would be to conduct an analysis of the number of papers she handles, the amount of area of the desk she uses, and the like. This is responding to the manifest complaint that the desk is too small for her to accomplish her work. The latent content of the message may be very different.

The complaint may arise because the individual wants more prestige and status in the organization. She has noticed that some executives have larger desks; *ergo,* she wants a larger desk.

In an actual incident, one company had just constructed a new corporate building. In furnishing the building, walnut desks were "collected" from local divisions so that the new office building would have a uniform style of furniture. The walnut desks in the other divisions were replaced with new steel desks, and soon numerous complaints were made about the steel desks being less effective than the older, walnut desks. The latent message was that moving to the new corporate offices was seen as a measure of status, and the steel desks only reinforced the complainers' feelings of lower status.

Meanwhile, in a geographically separate division, an engineering laboratory had just established a new research group. Most of the members of the group, including the director, were recently hired engineers. They had just received new steel desks; the older research groups had walnut desks. In this division, the steel desks were seen as a sign of prestige and status. In one part of the corporation, people were complaining that they did *not* have steel desks while in another part, people were complaining because they did. The situation was different, and the latent emotions and sentiments were also different.

Personal factors in the situation also affect both the manifest and the latent communications. For example, the more insecure a subordinate is, the more likely that person is to distort communications upward to the boss.[11]

In a classic article, Rogers and Roethlisberger suggested some barriers and gateways to improved communications.[12] The chief barrier to communication is the all too frequent tendency to be evaluative and judgmental, to approve and/or to disapprove statements coming from the other person or group, especially when the emotions are heightened. The chief gateway to communications is listening with understanding. The recipient needs to make a strong attempt to understand the manifest and latent communications from the other person's point of view, or frame of reference, understanding the situation as well as the individual.

To understand how difficult it is to actually listen with understanding, try this exercise, which we have used in classrooms and training programs. First, initiate discussion of a rather controversial topic and then establish a deceptively simple ground rule for discussing the topic—one person cannot present his or her ideas until repeating back what the other person has said and getting that person's verification. We find that this is a very difficult process for people to go through. Most of us, in a discussion or argument, are not really *listening* to what the other person is saying. Rather, we are waiting, more or less impatiently, to "get our oar in" as soon as possible. Thus we are "playing to the music in our own head" rather than hearing the other person's comments. One of the clearest signs of this occurs in meetings. One person will ask a question of another. The second person will give an elaborate and complete answer, *but to a different, unasked question.* The second person has become so involved that he or she has not actually heard the first person's question.

2. Nonverbal communication Nonverbal communication, or body language as it is sometimes called, is also an important aspect of the latent content of the communications process. In accentuating certain words, raising our eyebrows, or gesturing in certain ways, we are communicating nonverbally. A person whose head is tilted toward a speaker is expressing interest in what is being said; a subordinate whose eyes widen and narrow when listening to the boss is said to be reacting with interest. The pupils of a poker player's eyes may dilate involuntarily upon receiving a straight flush. The rise of a person's voice at the end of a sentence indicates a question; a drop in a person's voice at the end of a sentence may indicate a statement rather than a question.

An observer attending a press conference in Sweden did not understand the language, but it was easy for him to tell a factual question from a "loaded" one. The factual questions were shorter and delivered in a flatter tone of voice. The "loaded" questions were much longer, and the speaker's voice pitch was much higher. When one particularly loaded question was asked, two members of the panel leaned forward, their right shoulders extended further than their left, as though they were literally "blocking" the question. Disinterest was shown by one panel member, who talked to another while a third panel member was speaking. The chairman of the panel signified the close of the meeting by glancing repeatedly at his watch and "stacking" his papers in a neat pile. In short, it was possible to learn a great deal about the press conference from nonverbal signals alone, without being able to understand a word.

Frequently, the strictly verbal message is altered because of the nonverbal element. One manager is famous in a particular organization for flushing a bright red, pounding the table and saying, "What do you mean, I'm angry? I'm as cool as a cucumber." Under no circumstances will this man admit that he has lost his temper, although his body language clearly shows differently.

Birdwhistell developed a system for recording nonverbal factors. When he analyzed the body movements of an adolescent group's leader (who was not very articulate), he found that the leader's body movements were quite "mature," with little foot shuffling or other signs of lack of confidence. The leader's body movements indicated that he was receptive and that he was a good listener.[13]

During the last decade, serious research on nonverbal communication has emerged, especially in the fields of sociology, psychology, and anthropology.[14] Among the topics of study are voice tones, facial expressions, eye movements, and hand and body movements. For example, the usual nonverbal sign of agreement is a nod of the head. However, although a boss may regard it as such, subordinates may use that same gesture as a way of *avoiding* verbal agreement to something with which they disagree.

Subcultural groups may develop their own forms of nonverbal communication. For example, a college student who normally comes to class in blue jeans and open shirt is exhibiting nonverbal behavior when he dons a tie and jacket to go to an employment interview. For many people, the long hair prevalent in the late 1960s was a nonverbal sign of opposition to parental or societal codes.

Additionally, we know that there are common nonverbal "phrases" that are used in everyday life. For instance, a long exhalation may indicate satisfaction, whereas a short one may indicate a certain boredom. Still other common nonverbal phrases are hand gestures, open arms, and a greeting gesture to indicate a certain warmth. However, some gestures are characteristic of particular ethnic groups. For example, Fast reports that Jews in Nazi Germany were frequently identified by certain gestures not used by non-Jews.[15] Although people were apparently able to change their living arrangements, occupations, and appearance, they could not change their gestures, which were thus a complete giveaway.

The concept of body language, or nonverbal behavior, is popular, and a number of different books on the topic have sold millions of copies.[16] Although the research is growing, most of the books are popularized and vastly overstate the case.

However, one excellent piece of research is being conducted by teaching chimpanzees Ameslan, a sign language that is the primary means of communication for deaf people in North America.[17] Most of the work has been done with a chimp named Washoe, who in 1967 asked her "foster parents" to give her a piece of candy. Since then she has developed the ability to have increasingly complicated conversations. At first, Washoe had to be laboriously taught specific signs. Later, she began picking up new signs spontaneously by watching others and was also able to spontaneously use them in new combinations. Similar work has been conducted with dolphins.

Research of this kind is exciting, since it can tell us more about the communication process and can also begin to allow us to be more precise as to what is unique about human language.

3. Nature of the information Earlier, we discussed the concept of selective perception. The nature of the incoming information is affected by the kind of

The grimace is the message. (Underwood and Underwood/E. P. Jones)

information received, the quantity in which it is received, the individual from whom it is perceived, and the feedback process.

a) Kind of information received. Information that fits our preconceived stereotypes and biases is received and believed much more readily than that which contradicts what we already "know." In the next chapter, we will describe how three different presidents and their close advisers were able to distort or screen out accurate intelligence information that could have prevented three fiascoes: the Cuban Bay of Pigs, the war with China in Korea, and the Vietnam war. This phenomenon of selective attention to information is common to all of us, especially since we let our sentiments or our emotions override our better judgment based on logic.

b) *Overload.* One of the factors directly related to the nature of the incoming information is "overload." There are seven types of reaction to information overload.[18] Some are helpful; some reduce our capacity for action. Some of the more positive approaches are delegating the problem to someone else, establishing priorities, and delaying. During rush times, such as exam periods, we adopt the motto "Put off until tomorrow anything not due today, and put off forever anything possible."

Some reactions, however, are not so helpful. We may forget or ignore vital information, such as forgetting an important meeting. Another negative reaction to information overload is the deliberate avoidance of the information or the situation—the head-in-sand approach. Thus, for example, the student who is not doing well in a course may begin to cut classes more and more, avoiding seeing the professor to discuss the problem.

c) *The nature of the source.* Some people are more credible than others, and we tend to believe what they say and to discount information received from others. An expression frequently heard is "I wouldn't believe him if he swore it on a stack of Bibles." Some of the best evidence as to the kinds of people whose information is received, valued, and accepted comes from studies of informal helpers in the work relationship.[19] The effective helper is emotionally warm, accepts the ideas of others, is perceptive and a good listener, is patient and relaxed, has self-confidence, and is poised, articulate, and not self-conscious. The ineffective helper, one whose information is rejected, is emotionally cold, abrasive, timid, and inflexible.

d) *Feedback.* In considering the meaning of what is said, we must examine what was intended, as well as how it was interpreted. The concept of feedback, defined in Chapter 2, is one way of testing how well a communication is understood. Feedback, or "reality testing," is the process of reporting what was said or intended to the sender to "test" it for validity.

In an early study demonstrating the effects of feedback, Leavitt and Mueller note that although feedback improves the accuracy of task performance, it slows the process down.[20] A class of students was asked to draw a series of rectangles in various relationships to one another. In one experiment, no feedback was allowed, i.e., the instructor was not told when the students were having difficulty following instructions. In another experiment, free feedback was allowed—students could ask questions. The results confirmed the obvious. The "no feedback" condition was faster, because the instructor did not know how well the students had understood his directions. However, the "feedback" condition led to much greater accuracy, and the situation was perceived as such even prior to knowledge of the results.

The practical implications of this study are clear. Feedback can have either positive or negative results, depending on whether the goal is accuracy or speed. However, emphasis on speed (no feedback) can result in frustration for both the sender and receiver of the message. Providing for feedback, on the other hand, alleviates these frustrations. Therefore, although "efficiency" may be a goal of the formal, structural-design outlook, this goal may be thwarted without a consideration of worker morale. In the long run, it may be unwise for an organization to stress "efficiency" at the expense of morale. (Feedback will be discussed in detail in the next chapter.)

e) *Physical location.* Studies have been done on the effect of communication on status and prestige, who sits where, the effects of round versus square or rectangular tables, and the like. Relatively little work has been done on the effect of distance as such, but in one illuminating study, researchers found that the proportion of people with whom a person communicates, called the probability of communication, *decreases with the square of the distance between them.*[21] The curve of communication frequency begins to level out at about 25 yards. Corners, indirect paths, and particularly stairs have a negative effect on the communication probability.

4. Influences of group structure on communication   Table 4.3 shows the various ways in which information processes may be affected by group structure. The diagrams in the table show hypothetical situations, of course, since groups seldom have such clearly defined structures. However, they do help to explain some of the communication phenomena in groups. Some patterns of communication are linear, or unidimensional, flowing between a leader and each subordinate; others are circular—communication occurs only between adjacent positions on the circle; and others form a starlike pattern superimposed on a circle—characteristic of all-channel communication patterns. In a circular type of communication network, typified by a carefully defined gossip pattern, information processing is slow, and the accuracy is poor. The gossip simply proceeds from one person to the next, until it gets back to the originator. Obviously, there is a wide margin for error or distortion in this type of pattern, since at no point is there cross-checking or validation of the "facts." In organizations that adhere to this pattern of information flow, there is no clearly defined leader, or central processing agent, for the information. As a result, the organization is unstable, but morale tends to be very high. By contrast, in a unidimensional type of communication, characterized by a strong leader, information flow is fast, the accuracy is high, and because there is a

Table 4.3 Group structure and information

Speed	Slow	Fast	Fast
Accuracy	Poor	Good	Good
Organization	No stable form of organization	Slowly emerging but stable organization	Almost immediate and stable organization
Emergence of leader	None	Marked	Very pronounced
Morale	Very good	Poor	Very poor

A. Bavelas and D. Barrett, "An Experimental Approach to Organizational Communication," *Personnel* **27**, 5 (1951): 366–371. Reprinted by permission of the publisher. © 1951 by the American Management Association, Inc.

key person, the organization is stable. Curiously, however, the morale is poor.

The practical implications of this research are that if one is interested in group consensus on a project, one might strive for a leaderless group situation in which everything is discussed by everyone. On the other hand, if efficiency is of paramount importance, there should be a leader and well-defined, controlled communication channels. However, research such as this is artificially structured. Seldom do groups operate in these ways, for these models do not take into account informal groups, which in fact cut across all parts of an organization.

One study that does consider "real-life" communication patterns in organizations was conducted by Davis, who found that although the prescribed norm was communication down the chain of command, a great deal of communication took place across departmental lines, along the "grapevine," informal communication that is passed along very quickly.[22] In the industrial organization Davis studied, a company picnic was being planned for half of the executives (roughly 60 persons). Only two members who were *not* to be invited knew about it beforehand; all the invitees knew about it before they actually received their invitations.

This type of informal network, in addition to processing information quickly, also tends to remain "relevant"; that is, it is rarely carried over to the home or "off-campus" club. A third characteristic is that its relationship to the formal communication network is highly correlated; when there is an increase in formal communication, there is also an increase in informal communications. Thus one can use this close relationship to create a more open communication network simply by tying in some parts of the informal network with the formal network.

Davis suggests that one must increase the number of liaison persons between key organization members if communications are to improve. A communication network should depend much more on staff executives than on line executives for the spreading of information. In addition, the organization should develop a horizontal type of communication network across departments in conjunction with the vertical "chain-of-command" type of communication network and develop methods for bringing the more isolated groups into the communication network. This, in effect, may capitalize on the informal group by formalizing communication links across equivalent levels of the organization.

5. Effects of "climate" on communications In addition to informal group and horizontal communication links, both organizational climate and personal receptiveness affect how well communications are heard or received. If an organization insists on using the chain of command for all communications and if the climate is repressive or coercive, certain important communications may not be received.

As shown in Table 4.4, Gibb has outlined two basic types of climate: one that threatens or puts the receiver on the defensive, and one that is supportive.[23] Each threatening communication, however, can be made supportive, or at least nonjudgmental. For instance, the statement "The cafeteria provides horrible food" is threatening to someone connected with the cafeteria, whereas a descriptive remark such as "Last week, three out of the five dinner menus at the cafeteria featured some form of chicken" is factual and nonevaluative. Similarly, a question of control can be made less threatening by shifting the emphasis to a problem orientation. The recipient may feel threatened by perceiving "strategy" or artificial neutrality (or "clinical detachment," as Gibb says). The supportive equivalents to these types of perceived communications are spontaneity (no particular strategy) and empathy (an open concern for the receiver). A superior air is threatening, and equality is supportive; the former tends to either shut off communication or make it argumentative, thereby shutting off effective communication, whereas equality implies "no judgment" and openness.

Gibb's two final types of communication are "certainty" versus "provisionalism," the former creating a threatening, closed climate, and the latter creating a supportive climate. To illustrate the difference between these two types of

Table 4.4 Communication effectiveness

Supportive climate	Interference	Defensive climate
Description	Defensiveness increased by speech or other behavior which appears evaluative or judgmental.	Evaluation
Problem orientation	Resistance increased by speech or other behavior used to control the listener.	Control
Spontaneity	When the sender is seen as having ambiguous, multiple motivations or a "hidden agenda," the receiver becomes defensive.	Strategy
Empathy	When neutrality in speech appears to indicate a lack of concern for the listener's welfare, the receiver becomes defensive and resistant.	Neutrality
Equality	A sender who communicates feeling superior in power, position, intellectual ability, or other ways arouses defensiveness in the receiver.	Superiority
Provisionalism	People who are dogmatic, seem to know all the answers, or seem to require no data tend to elicit creative defensiveness and to put others on their guard.	Certainty

communication, suppose that an observer said to the individual running a meeting, "You have a real problem because you continually interrupt others." This exemplifies "certainty." However, the observer could have created a non-threatening, supportive climate by saying, "It is interesting to note that in the first hour of the meeting, only one other person was able to 'hold the floor' for as long as 24 seconds."

Carl Rogers, the nondirective psychotherapist, helps to pinpoint these issues in different terms.[24] Like Gibbs, he notes that one of the strong barriers to effective communication is a person's tendency to evaluate someone else's communication. If two or more people get into an argument, one may scream, "You're wrong!" or "That's a bunch of bull!" or "How silly can you be?" Such statements add only heat, not light, to the subject. People arguing from different perceptual sets tend to make highly evaluative, judgmental remarks, a situation Rogers regards as a major stumbling block to effective interpersonal communication.

How would you describe the climate of this communication? (Ewing Galloway/
E. P. Jones)

Another obstacle to listening, he reports, is heightened emotions. We all
know this. If we feel very strongly about a particular viewpoint, we find it
very difficult to listen. A third obstacle may be the size of the group, because
most people become defensive in large gatherings. A large group may inhibit
communication by intimidating the person from asking questions or stating a
position, particularly if he or she is uncertain how the group will react or is
certain that the group will respond with some sort of disapproval.

The solution to these problems, says Rogers, is to listen with interest,
which is much easier said than done. Listening with interest permits persuasion to occur; however, if one's mind is made up, one merely evaluates and
does not listen. Rogers notes that listening with understanding and interest
takes courage, for it requires an open mind. Listening with understanding can

be fostered by having an influential person listen empathically, trying to understand both the content of and frame of reference for what is being said. When the tone is thus set, listening will be much easier.

IV. TRANSACTIONAL ANALYSIS

Although it is too early to determine whether or not it is a fad, transactional analysis (TA) may be emerging as a new way of improving communications by developing some specific ways of analyzing the communications process. The concepts of transactional analysis stem from two sources: Gestalt therapy and the analysis of transactions as developed by Berne.[25]

Transactional analysis focuses on four areas: (1) the structure of the personality (structural analysis); (2) the way in which people interact (transactional analysis); (3) the ways in which people structure their time (time structuring); and (4) the roles that people learn to play in life (life scripts). Here we will focus primarily on the first three, those most important for communications purposes. Further information on all four can be found in much greater detail in several recent books.[26]

A. Structural Analysis

Each individual's personality is made up of three different ego states.[27] An ego state is "a consistent pattern of feeling and experience directly related to a corresponding consistent pattern of behavior."[28] The ego states themselves cannot be directly observed, but the behavior of the individual can tell us which of the three ego states is in operation at the moment. The three ego states can be likened to three different sets of tapes, since "the brain functions like a tape recorder to preserve complete experiences in serial sequence, in a form recognizable as 'ego states' "[29] One set of tapes is the Parent ego state; another is the Adult ego state; and the third is the Child ego state. The capital "P" is used to distinguish the ego state from the actual, biological parent. The same is true for the other two ego states. The ego states are realities rather than abstract concepts; "Parent, Adult, and Child represent real people who either now exist or who once existed, who have legal names and civic identities."[30]

The Parent ego state is the set of "tapes" or recordings that were developed by our parents or other powerful, influential forces in our early childhood. The "natural" impulses and attitudes learned from childhood experiences make up the Child ego state. Unlike the Parent or Child ego state, the Adult ego state is objective and dispassionate. The emotionality we have is contained in the Parent and Child ego states. When we are in our Parent ego state, we talk, act, or think as our parents did. When we are in our Child ego state, we talk, think or act as we did when we were children. When we are in our Adult ego state, we are objective—seeking, giving, and evaluating information and examining and weighing alternatives.

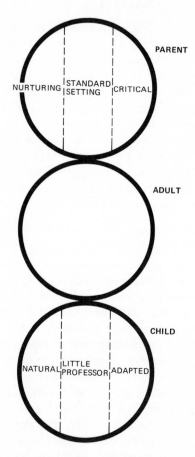

Fig. 4.5 Structural analysis.

As shown in Fig. 4.5, both the Child and Parent ego states can be differentiated. The Parent can be critical, as real parents sometimes are; the Parent can also be warm, loving, and nurturing; or the Parent can set standards, as real parents do in teaching their children how to get along in society or as a supervisor does in providing the rules and norms of behavior to a new employee. The dotted lines in Fig. 4.5 show that the boundaries are open—the standard-setting parent may also be a highly critical parent, for example.

The Child ego state is also subdivided. The Natural Child is joyful, rebellious, uninhibited, free, and spontaneous. The Little Professor, the precursor of the Adult ego state, mediates between the wishes of the Natural Child and the Adapted Child, which has fully conformed to parental desires and wishes.

For the fully developed personality, all three ego states are necessary, and none is better than the others. A person who behaves primarily from one ego state would be highly neurotic, if not psychotic.

We can move easily and quickly from one ego state to another. For example, one man visited a private school where he was considering entering his son. He reported that the school encouraged creativity and that the teaching was informal. While he was relating his experiences, three different reactions were clearly observable. Scowling, he said, " 'I can't see how anyone could learn anything at that school. There's dirt on the floor!' Leaning back in his chair, his forehead smoothed out as he reflected, 'Before I decide, I think I should check with the school's scholastic rating and talk to some of the parents.' The next minute, a broad grin crossed his face, and he said, 'Gee, I'd love to have gone to a school like that!' "[31]

When asked about his comment, the individual was able to clearly see that his first comment came from his Parent ego state; it was the kind of comment his own father would have made. The second comment came from his Adult ego state; it sought more information. The third comment came from his Child ego state; he remembered his unhappy experiences in school and thought of the fun he could have had at the school he had just visited. The man followed up on his Adult questions before making a final decision. His son is attending the school, achieving well, and is also enjoying himself.

B. Transactional Analysis

"Anything that happens between people will involve a transaction between their ego states. When one person sends a message to another, he expects a response. All transactions can be classified as (1) complementary, (2) crossed, or (3) ulterior."[32] A complementary transaction occurs when a message sent from one ego state receives the anticipated answer from the appropriate ego state in the other person. The message can be from Parent to Parent, from Child to Parent, Adult to Adult, and so on. For example, a man at work receives a telephone call that his wife has been hit by a car and is in the hospital. His fright and concern come from his Child. The most appropriate response of the man's boss would be to suggest that the employee go immediately to the hospital, a response from the Nurturing Parent (see Fig. 4.6).

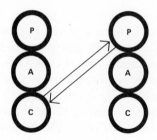

Fig. 4.6 Complementary transaction.

A crossed transaction occurs when a message sent from one ego state is responded to from an inappropriate ego state (Fig. 4.7). In our example above, the transaction would be crossed if the supervisor were to respond from his Child ego state by saying, "Don't bother me, I've got a lot of worries. It's been a bad day for me, too." Crossed transactions usually result in feelings of anger, hurt, or pain for the people involved in the transaction.

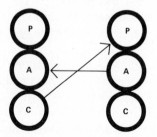

Fig. 4.7 Crossed transaction.

In both complementary and crossed transactions, the individual is acting from only one ego state. By contrast, ulterior transactions involve two ego states. The manifest meaning of a message may come from one ego state, but the latent intent of the words may mean something quite different, as Fig. 4.8 shows. The old cliche, "Would you like to come up and see my etchings?" is an example of an ulterior transaction.

Ulterior transactions also occur in the work setting. Suppose that a manager is working with a consultant once a week on correcting actions resulting from an attitude survey. The previous week, participative management had been discussed, as well as a problem of concern to the manager. The manager had indicated that he was trying participative management by having a group

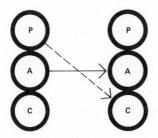

Fig. 4.8 Ulterior transaction.

work on the problem. The consultant asked, "What answer will they come up with?" The manager responded, "There's only one possible answer." The very different solution proposed by the group was unacceptable to the manager, partially because he had consciously or unconsciously withheld some vital information from the group. The manifest message that the manager was sending to the group was Adult-Adult (develop your own solution); the latent, ulterior message was Parent-Child (so long as it is *my* way).

"Stroking" is an important aspect of transactions. Everyone needs to be recognized as an individual in his or her own right, to be in contact with other people. This is as true for the adult as it is for the infant. The term "stroking" comes from the practice of picking up and fondling an infant, but it also includes any type of visual, physical, or oral recognition of one person by another. Transactional analysts often say, "If the infant is not stroked, his spinal cord shrivels up."[33] There is an actual case of a 22-month-old infant who received no love or attention by either parent.[34] When abandoned at a hospital, she had the average height of a ten-month-old baby and weighed only 15 pounds (the normal body weight of a five-month-old baby). The baby could neither speak nor crawl. A volunteer substitute mother spent six hours a day, five days a week with the baby. Within two months, the baby had grown two inches and had gained six pounds.

Although we have a hard time being articulate about it, adults also need strokes, even though they are only surface ones, such as "Good morning, how are you?" Positive strokes are usually appropriate, direct, and complementary transactions that give information to the individual about his or her competency or positive worth. Strokes are needed so badly that a person who does not get positive strokes will seek negative ones, especially if this pattern was learned in childhood. The person who has learned to seek negative strokes tends to "discount," or diminish, positive strokes as an adult. For example, an individual brings a report to a supervisor. The supervisor gives a positive stroke by saying, "This is a good report, Jim." Jim promptly discounts the positive stroke by replying, "I wish I could have gotten it in two days ago." Accepting the positive stroke could bring the reply, "Thanks, I hope it helps us get the contract." In everyday life, one frequently hears someone say, "Gee, I really like your dress (tie, jacket, scarf)." The immediate discounted answer is frequently, "This old rag? I bought it at a sale years ago."

Positive and negative reinforcement and positive and negative stroking and discounting are very closely related. However, our culture tends to inhibit us from giving or receiving positive strokes, although they are vitally necessary. In discussing the need for positive strokes, one first-line manufacturing foreman said, "Why should I? They're being paid to do a good job."

To get a "feel" for the difficulty in giving and receiving positive strokes, count the number that you give and receive in the next 24 hours. How many people do you discount?

C. Time Structuring

A third major focus of TA is the way in which people structure their time. Time structuring is a basic human "hunger," much as stroking is. There are six basic ways of structuring time: withdrawal, rituals, pastimes, activities, games, and authenticity. The "game" is the only one that will be described in any detail here, since games prevent people from being authentic with one another.

The term "game" in TA does not refer to such activities as football, basketball, tennis, checkers, and the like. Instead, it is a psychological game. A TA game must have three specific elements: (1) complementary transactions that have at least the appearance of being socially acceptable; (2) one or more ulterior transactions; and (3) a negative putdown or payoff that is predictable and is the real *purpose* of the game.[35] The game begins at an unconscious level; the participants are *not* aware that it *is* a game, but the negative putdown leaves one of the participants hurt, unhappy, and angry.

People play games in order to fill time, but the more basic purpose is to avoid authenticity or intimacy. Since excellent descriptions of games are given in the books already cited, we will describe only a few of them here. Psychological games have two basic variations: in the first, the game is started so that the other person gets the kick or the putdown; in the second, the game is set up so that the individual beginning the game gets the putdown.

In the game of *Yes, But*, for example, the boss asks subordinates for suggestions and then follows up each suggestion with a "Yes, but . . . ," comment; the boss maintains the power position, and the subordinate gets put down. This game is also frequently played at cocktail parties.

In the game of *Blemish*, a subordinate brings in a report to the boss, who quickly skims it. Although the report is a good one, the boss does not praise it, but instead finds one or two "blemishes"—a typographical error, perhaps—and points these out to the subordinate.

One of the best-known games is *NIGYSOB* ("Now I've Got You, You SOB). Here, the individual carefully waits until the other person has made an error and then, symbolically, pulls the trap door. The "payoff" or putdown can sometimes be delayed for years. For example, two young brothers had a model train set. One day, one of them put an obstacle on the track. The older brother tried in vain to get the younger brother to remove it, but finally had to leave the controls and do it himself. He told his brother, "I'm going to get you for this." As the two grew older and got married, relationships between the two were friendly, with each helping the other out with house repairs and the like. One night, however, the younger brother ran out of gas late at night when most stations were closed. When he called his brother for help, his brother answered, "Do you remember when you blocked the tracks? I told you I would get you for that. Find your own gas!"[36]

Some games are played so that the individual beginning the game gets the putdown. A favorite of people who have learned to get attention through negative strokes is the game of *Kick Me*. In this game, the individual does something that on the surface level seems acceptable; the ulterior transaction, however, is "Kick Me, I've Been Bad." For example, a woman may come to work late every morning. She always has a plausible excuse—heavy traffic, car trouble, a doctor's appointment. She eventually gets her payoff when she is fired for her habitual tardiness.

D. Use of TA in Communications

There are two basic ways in which TA can be used to improve communications and understanding. First, TA enables people to understand the ego state that they or others are using and to determine whether or not that ego state is the most appropriate. Second, the use of TA reduces the amount of wasted time and harm to individuals that come from playing games.

Transactional analysis is a way of understanding and charting the relationships (communications) between people in a systematic manner. Earlier, we suggested that critical, judgmental evaluation is one of the major barriers to communications. The critical, judgmental aspect of behavior comes primarily from the Parent ego state, and the most complementary return transaction is that of the Child. As a result, in many organizations the primary supervisor-subordinate relationship is Parent-Child, even though in many circumstances Adult-Adult relationships and communications might be more appropriate. It is the Adult that collects and keeps current on incoming data, that allows for change and modification. The rapidity of data development in many areas makes it very difficult for the Adult to keep up with incoming data, particularly if the individuals are "hooked" in a Parent-Child relationship. In other circumstances, the Little Professor in one person may be used to assist problem solving. In other words, it is important that individuals interact from ego states that are appropriate to the given situation.

Games are destructive and harmful to people. They waste time and keep people from being open and authentic.

Games can be recognized, because like an old and broken record, the groove keeps repeating. The words may differ slightly at times, but the tune is the same. Parents and children play games; husbands and wives play games; people at work play games. Frequently, it is the same game.

The most important aspect to stopping a game is to analyze the transactions and to recognize that they form a game. Usually, the game is repeated several times before it can be recognized. Once the game has been recognized, the participant can stop the game by refusing to respond in the old way. For example, one man and his daughter were "fond" of playing a game called *Uproar*. One day, the father came home and became angry because his daughter had not yet made lunch for him. The daughter had taken transactional analysis in high school and recognized the game beginning. Rather than pick up her "cue," she crossed the transaction and said mildly, "You seem awfully upset." The father stopped his tirade and blurted out, "You're not supposed to say *that!*"[37]

In another instance, a supervisor was playing *Yes, But*. Recognizing the game, the subordinate said mildly, "I wonder if you really want my ideas, or is your mind made up?" Here again, the refusal to play the game and the unexpected, crossed transaction led the supervisor to seriously question what had gone on.

In another situation, a subordinate was playing *Kick Me*. Recognizing this, the supervisor went out of his way on several occasions to give positive strokes before the subordinate could come in for negative ones. This reduced the incidence of the game playing, but did not eliminate it. When the subordinate came in with his Child ego state, asking for the Parent to provide the kick, the supervisor invariably responded from his Adult ego state, refusing to give the kick. However, this does not always work. In one situation, when the subordinate did not get enough negative strokes, he finally quit for another job.

Transactional analysis also points up the need for positive strokes in communication to reduce defensiveness. Rewards are important, and positive stroking is one of the most important of rewards.

V. CONCLUSIONS AND IMPLICATIONS FOR THE MANAGER

Perhaps as many as 40%–50% of college graduates have a great deal of unease in communicating and trying to sell ideas to others. Yet the evidence is also clear that one of the most important tasks, not only for college graduates but also for managers, is selling ideas and concepts to others at a variety of levels. Accomplishments on the job are highly contingent on excellent communication skills.

There are a number of ways to improve communications. One is to thoroughly understand the nature of the perceptual process. Each of us perceives the world differently, and each of us behaves in ways that make sense to us. The communication, then, comes from different perceptual "sets." Understanding that we may have stereotypes about certain facts or individuals is helpful in understanding communications. We frequently tend to reject "facts" because we dislike the information or because we distrust the sender of the message.

It is also important to make a distinction between the manifest and latent contents of the message. Communications do not take place in a vacuum. Rather, they take place in a total situation. The situation establishes the emotions and sentiments, the latent part of the message. Part of the latent content can be picked up through a better understanding of nonverbal signals, such as the tone of voice, bodily postures, and gestures.

Listening with understanding rather than being judgmental is highly helpful. There is no question that at times we must be judgmental, but not always. The essential aspect of most successful psychotherapy, for example, is its focus on listening with understanding. One part of listening with understanding is the use of transactional analysis to better analyze and describe what is going on in the series of transactions, particularly when "games" are being played. Another part of listening with understanding is feedback to the individual about the message or the way the person "comes across." (This will be discussed in greater detail in the next chapter.)

Davis has outlined several procedures for managers to follow to enhance their communications with workers.[38] One method is for the manager to adopt an open-door policy, although this policy may be difficult to implement if the manager is unreceptive, shy, or otherwise awkward about communicating with workers. Davis also suggests that social gatherings at which the families of workers and managers are present can aid communications. At such times, the worker and his or her boss see each other in a different, more relaxed setting, and this more "human" atmosphere can be translated into more effective communication on the job. Finally, the manager can encourage use of the "suggestion box." This technique, however, requires extensive feedback in order to be successful. Unless changes resulting from such suggestions are well publicized, the suggestion box is likely to remain empty.

Communications in a number of organizations have improved greatly from a "coffee with the boss" program, whereby the manager holds weekly meetings with randomized samples of employees. There is no agenda as such, but over time the employees become more comfortable in giving and receiving information.

Increasing external social pressures and internal humanistic pressures are forcing managers to operate much less by fiat and much more by persuasion.[39] Therefore, they have to improve their behavioral science and communications skills in order to work better with their peers and subordinates. One of the problems with improving communication skills, however, is the sheer number of meanings inherent in any communication; the dictionary lists 14,000 meanings for the 500 most used words, an average of 28 meanings per word! Or, as Mark Twain said, "The difference between the right word and the almost right word is the difference between lightning and a lightning bug." Another person suggested that the world is held together by the phrase "you know what I mean" (when we really don't).

After Watergate, we almost hesitate to make this final suggestion, yet it can be very helpful. As the small cassette tape recorder becomes financially available to almost everyone, it emerges as a powerful learning and development tool. Taping a meeting and then listening to the tapes can be a very enlightening, and sometimes chastening, experience. After listening to the tapes, one usually reacts by thinking, "Did I actually say *that?*" Of course, the taping should be done only with full permission and knowledge of those involved. Some feel that taping a meeting will reduce the openness of the conversation. This does not happen when the reasons for the tapes are understood by the participants.

REVIEW

1. Ask a number of different people how they interpret a particular controversial statement in a newspaper or magazine. How often and in what ways do these interpretations differ from the "sender's" intended meaning?

2. Which of your own attitudes or beliefs have never been exposed to a conflicting point of view in an argument? Explain how this can occur.

3. In a class discussion or elsewhere, try the following experiment. Establish the rule that each person must repeat the words or intent of the previous

speaker before he or she can begin speaking. Do this for 20 minutes. What effect does this have on communication? How do you feel about discussions handled in this manner?

4. Table 4.2 showed significant perceptual discrepancies between supervisors and subordinates about their communication patterns with each other. What is the impact of such perceptual differences on the people involved? How can such discrepancies be minimized?

5. With two or three others, observe people talking in a closed telephone booth. Without attempting to listen in on the conversation, draw your own conclusions about the content of the conversation from the speaker's body movements and gesticulations. Share your perceptions with the others in your group. Did everyone see the same things? Did everyone draw the same inferences from what was observed?

6. Describe what you perceive to be an individual's perceptual defense. When might such a perceptual defense be useful? Discuss.

7. Find an example of a "mixed message" and describe the situation.

8. Diagram an interchange of transactions between two people. How much Parent is involved? Adult? Child? Are the transactions appropriate?

9. Look for times when people discount positive strokes. What are some different ways they discount the strokes?

REFERENCES

1. J. G. March and H. A. Simon, *Organizations*, New York: Wiley, 1958.

2. J. S. Bruner and C. C. Goodman, "Value and Need as Organizing Factors in Perception," *Journal of Abnormal and Social Psychology* **42**, 1 (Jan. 1947): 33–34.

3. M. Haire and W. F. Grunes, "Perceptual Defenses: Processes Protecting an Organized Perception of Another Personality," *Human Relations* **3** (June 1950): 403–412.

4. H. A. Murray, "The Effect of Fear Upon Estimates of the Maliciousness of Other Personalities," *Journal of Social Psychology* **4** (August 1933): 310–329.

5. R. Rosenthal and R. Lawson, "A Longitudinal Study of Effects of Experimenter Bias on the Operant Learning of Laboratory Rats," *Journal of Psychiatric Research* **2** (June 1964): 61–72.

6. R. Rosenthal, *Experimenter Effects in Behavioral Research*, New York: Appleton-Century-Crofts, 1966.

7. S. M. Dornbusch, A. H. Hastorf, S. A. Richardson, R. E. Muzzy, and R. S. Vreeland, "The Perceiver and the Perceived: Their Relative Influence on the

Categories of Interpersonal Cognition," *Journal of Personality and Social Psychology* 1 (Jan. 1965): 434–440.

8. A. O'Reilly, "Skill Requirements: Supervisor-Subordinate Conflict," *Personnel Psychology* 26, 1 (Spring 1973): 75–80.

9. J. McCroskey, "The Implementation of a Large-Scale Program for Systematic Desensitization for Communication Apprehension," *Speech Teacher* 21, 4 (Nov. 1972): 255–264.

10. F. Roethlisberger, "Social Behavior and the Use of Words in Formal Organizations," in A. Turner and G. Lombard, eds., *Interpersonal Behavior and Administration*, New York: The Free Press, 1969, p. 71.

11. J. Athanassiades, "The Distortion of Upward Communication in Hierarchical Organizations," *Academy of Management Journal* 16, 2 (June 1973): 207–226.

12. C. Rogers and F. Roethlisberger, "Barriers and Gateways to Communication," *Harvard Business Review* 30, 4 (July–August 1953): 28–34.

13. R. Birdwhistell, "Kinesics and Communication," in *Explorations in Communication*, ed. E. Carpenter and M. McLuhan, Boston: Beacon Press, 1960), pp. 54–66.

14. J. Koivumaki, "Body Language Taught Here," *Journal of Communication* 25, 1 (Winter 1975): 26–30.

15. J. Fast, *Body Language*, Philadelphia: Lippincott, M. Evans, 1970.

16. *Ibid.*; M. Poiret, *Body Talk: The Science of Kinesics*, New York: Award Books, 1970; G. Nierenberg and H. Calero, *How to Read a Person Like a Book*, New York: Pocket Books, 1973; F. Davis, *Inside Intuition: What We Know about Nonverbal Communication*, New York: McGraw-Hill, 1973,

17. E. Linden, *Apes, Men and Language*, New York: Saturday Review Press, Dutton, 1974.

18. G. Miller, "The Magical Number 7, Plus or Minus Two: Some Limits on our Capacity for Processing Information," *Psychological Review* 63, 1 (Jan. 1956): 81–97.

19. H. Burke and T. Weir, "Helper Perceptions of Effective, Ineffective and Nonhelpers." Paper presented at the thirty-fifth annual meeting of the Academy of Management, New Orleans, August 10–13, 1975.

20. H. J. Leavitt and R. A. H. Mueller, "Some Effects of Feedback on Communication," *Human Relations* 4 (Dec. 1951): 401–410.

21. J. Allen, "Communication Networks in R&D Laboratories," *R&D Management* 1, 1 (Oct. 1970): 14–21.

22. K. Davis, "Management Communication and the Grapevine," *Harvard Business Review* 31, 5 (July–Aug. 1953): 44–49.

23. J. R. Gibb, "Defensive Communication," *Journal of Communication* 11, 3 (Summer 1961): 141–148.

24. Rogers and Roethlisberger, *op. cit.*

25. E. Berne, *Games People Play,* New York: Grove Press, 1964; F. Perls, R. Heffer-line, and P. Goodman, *Gestalt Therapy,* New York: Dell, 1965 (paperback reprint of 1951 edition published by Julian Press).

26. E. Berne, *What Do You Do After You Say Hello?* New York: Grosset and Dunlap, 1973; M. James and D. Jongeward, *Born to Win: Transactional Analysis with Gestalt Experiments,* Reading, Mass.: Addison-Wesley, 1971; D. Jongeward and Contributors, *Everybody Wins: Transactional Analysis Applied to Organizations,* Reading, Mass.: Addison-Wesley, 1973.

27. E. Berne, *Principles of Group Treatment,* New York: Oxford University Press, 1964, p. 364.

28. *Ibid.*

29. *Ibid.,* p. 281.

30. E. Berne, *Transactional Analysis in Psychotherapy,* New York: Grove Press, 1961, p. 32.

31. James and Jongeward, *op, cit.,* p. 19.

32. *Ibid.,* p. 24.

33. Eric Berne, *The Structure and Dynamics of Organizations and Groups,* Philadelphia: Lippincott, 1963, p. 157.

34. Cited in James and Jongeward, *op. cit,* p. 45.

35. *Ibid.,* p. 32,

36. *Ibid.,* p. 196.

37. *Ibid.,* p. 208.

38. K. Davis, *The Dynamics of Organizational Behavior,* New York: McGraw-Hill, 1967.

5

THE GROUP
IN THE
ORGANIZATION

We few, we happy few, we band of brothers.

SHAKESPEARE

LEARNING OBJECTIVES

When you have finished reading and studying this chapter, you should be able to:

1. Identify how and why a group operates as a system.

2. Describe the actions and behaviors of individuals as subsystems within the larger system of the group.

3. First decide *how* groups form and then state several reasons *why* groups form.

4. Define the term "cohesion" as a moderator between the concepts of "a group" and "its behavior."

5. Describe at least one cause and its effect of high group cohesion that is beneficial to the organization and then at least one that is harmful to the organization.

6. Differentiate between two group outputs—productivity and satisfaction —of concern to work organizations.

7. Identify leadership attempts within a group.

You will be expected to define and use the following concepts:

Group	Group-building activities
Formal group	Self-serving activities
Task	Johari window
Social group	Feedback
Sociotechnical systems	Temporary groups
Autonomy	Matrix organization
Internal structure	Task force
Leadership	Collateral organization
Cohesion	Productivity
Temporary groups	Satisfaction
Content	Delphi technique
Process	Nominal group
Task activities	Interacting group

THOUGHT STARTERS

1. How old were you when you first became a member of a group?
2. List at least five *different* groups you currently belong to.
3. How do you behave differently in each of these five groups?
4. How many different "leaders" may a group have? Have you ever "led" a group? In what sense were you a leader? What were the results for the group? Yourself? The other members and leaders of the group?

I. INTRODUCTION

In Chapter 3, we first considered the individual as a system, concentrating heavily on motivation and behavior in work settings. We also examined the individual as a subsystem in interaction with other subsystems (individuals perceiving and communicating with other individuals). Now we turn to groups, *which are central to all concepts of organizational behavior.* With a knowledge of group dynamics, members of groups and committees can become more productive. The group acts as a buffer between the individual and the organization.

According to Cartwright and Lippitt, groups do exist, they are omnipresent, group forces have extremely important effects on the individual, and the consequences of group behavior (from an organizational point of view) can be either good or bad.[1] Therefore, knowledge and understanding of group dynamics can be used to improve the consequences of group actions.

It is obvious that knowledge about group dynamics, especially group behavior, is tremendously important to the manager who wants to run an effective organization. The effective manager knows when to make unilateral decisions and when to use groups, including meetings and committees. For example, a new manager in a textile plant found the chief union executive and in no uncertain terms told him that when he ran a plant, he *ran it*, whereupon the union representative waved his hand. Recognizing this signal, the workers stopped work, and immediately the looms were shut down. The union representative said to the new manager, "O.K., now go ahead and run it."

For a long time, management literature did not discuss, understand, or recognize groups that were not "subordinate," i.e., did not report to a single manager. Although good managers have always been far ahead of the management literature, it was not until the Hawthorne studies in the late 1920s and early 1930s that management writers began to recognize that behavior is affected not only by formally defined relationships, but also by more informal relationships. Subsequent research and observation have made it abundantly clear that within the formal structure there exists a pattern of *social* relationships, or informal groups. These groups do not appear on the organization chart and may not be formally or even informally recognized by the organization. However, there is ample evidence to prove that these patterns of informal social relationships have a great deal of influence on employees' behavior. As we have noted elsewhere, informal groups can either restrict or enhance productivity. Similarly, the informal group can speed up or slow down information flow. Likert postulates that unless an organization is created and sustained through participative groups, the informal organization is likely to be at odds with, or at least not fully supportive of, the goals of the formal organization.[2]

When the organization is created and supported by participative groups, the formal and informal organizations will be undifferentiated.

In this chapter we examine the role of the group as a subsystem within the larger system, the organization. We also look at the group as a social system, the reasons and methods for group formation, the internal structure of groups, groups in interaction, and techniques for observing and diagnosing meetings.

II. THE GROUP AS A SYSTEM

A tremendous amount of work has been done on the concept of small groups. A 1968 bibliography listed more than 5000 articles and studies, and more work has been done since then.[3] One reason for the intensive study of groups is that they have a great deal of influence on the behavior of individual members. Another, eminently practical reason is that knowledge of group dynamics can help the group and its members be more effective. For example, in one organization sales districts were divided into the top fourth (measured by total sales) and the bottom fourth. It was estimated that the less effective sales teams cost the organization from $80,000 to $100,000 in profits each year as compared with the high-performing districts. Only two variables caused the difference between the high-performing and the low-performing sales teams —"team cohesion" and "leadership."[4]

It seems self-evident that a random collection of people—in a restaurant or on a bus—is not a group. However, if something happens to change this pattern so that they have a common purpose, the collection of people will have become a group. If, for example, people standing in a line band together to keep someone from crashing the line, they have transformed themselves from a collection of people to a group with a common purpose.

One way of looking at a group is as a subsystem within a larger system—the organization. Earlier, we characterized a system as: complex, with interdependent parts; open, consisting of inputs, transformations, outputs, feedback, and boundaries; in balance, resulting from positive and negative feedback; and having a multiplicity of purposes and objectives.

Figure 5.1 shows a social group from a systems point of view. As a system, a group has: inputs, including expectations from within and outside the boundaries of the system; operations, or transformations, including group structure, interactions, and leadership; and outputs, including productivity (whether helpful or harmful to the organization) and satisfaction. In addition, it has both positive and negative feedback, by which it attempts to achieve changes and maintain balance, respectively.

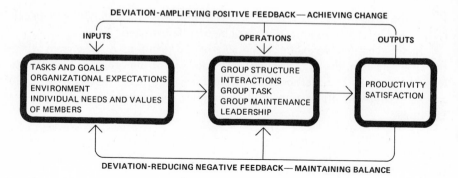

Fig. 5.1 The social group in systems terms.

In simpler language, a group, in the psychological sense, is any number of people who: (1) have a common purpose or objective, (2) interact with one another to accomplish their objective, (3) are aware of one another, and (4) perceive themselves to be part of a group. As a system, this group may be either closed (with only internal interaction) or open (processing much information coming from the outside).

The purpose of a particular group may or may not be well defined. The purpose of the group may be primarily social, highly work-oriented, or not even well understood. For example, teenagers who band together to "protect" themselves from their parents may be unaware of this fact. The interaction may be face to face, conducted by mail, or carried on over the telephone. The interaction may be either permanent or transitory, thus determining the length of the group's duration.

However, it is psychological awareness that differentiates a "group" from an "aggregation of people." Unless people are aware of one another and the fact that they are a group, they remain a collection, or aggregate, of people, rather than a group in our definition. They must perceive themselves to be a group in order to interact with one another to accomplish their common objectives. For example, the various tenants in a large apartment building constitute an aggregation of people, even though they have similar complaints about their landlord. If, however, they band together and "speak with one voice" to the landlord, they become a "group." They have a common purpose (getting the landlord to make repairs); they interact (organize) in order to accomplish this objective; are aware of one another (the result of their interaction); and most important, these tenants consider themselves to be part of a cohesive group (and so does the landlord).

A random collection of people banded together in an informal group to help turn around a San Francisco cable car. (Photograph by Edgar F. Huse)

III. WHY AND HOW GROUPS ARE FORMED

A group formed through and by the formal organizational structure is called a *formal* group; one formed to accomplish tasks on the job is a *work*, or *task*, group; one formed within the structure, but without official sanction, of the organization is an *informal* group; and a group formed for purely social reasons is a *social* group. In addition, there are such other types of groups as *family* and *interest* groups. Of course, there may be a great deal of overlap; a task group (group of managers) may also be a social group (golf foursome). A work group may be either formal or informal, depending on whether it is officially recognized and/or supported by the formal organization. For example, it is reported by several knowledgeable people that top management of a

This pit crew exemplifies a formal, cohesive work group. (Stephen J. Potter/Stock, Boston)

large computer manufacturing company gave an order to stop work on a particular product which did not seem to be worth the time and effort. A group of engineers from different units continued to work on the project under "bootleg" conditions. Within a few months they developed random-access memory, the core of the modern, third-generation computer that operates "on-line in real-time."

The type of group formed and the reason for its formation in work settings depend in large measure on the context in which it exists. Thus groups formed from a structural-design viewpoint will differ from those emerging from an "information flow" viewpoint. And groups formed on the basis of "human" needs will differ from those found in either of the other two types of perspectives.

A. Groups from a Structural-Design Viewpoint

The formal group, found primarily in structural-design contexts, exists to achieve organizational goals and is therefore established, maintained, and supported by the organization. The tasks or objectives of the formal group are usually well defined, and members are assigned to the group with little regard for either their personal wishes or ability to work together. In short, the formal group exists because of the *demands* of the organization.

A formal group consisting of a manager and subordinates may be relatively permanent, even though the group's membership may change. If, on the other hand, the formal group is established to attain a specific objective, it will probably be disbanded once its objective has been met. The use of such "temporary" groups is increasing rapidly, giving rise to such common terms as project manager or program director.

B. Groups from a Work-Flow Perspective

Since the formal organization sometimes cuts *across* the work-flow process, informal groups tend to form spontaneously, as the result of people interacting at work. It was only after the Hawthorne studies that the existence of informal groups was discussed in management literature, and only in the past 20 years have we begun to study and understand the operation of informal groupings within the formal social organization.

Informal groups, which are not sponsored, recognized, or perhaps even approved by the formal organization, exist primarily to expedite and improve the flow processes of information and communication. People whose work is interdependent and interrelated develop informal groups in order to get the job done better and more quickly. In addition, workers may find informal groups more rewarding than formal groups.

Whyte questions the wisdom of making a dichotomy between the formal and informal organizational structures; he feels that except at the opposite ends of a continuum (e.g., a supervisor giving a subordinate a direct order or a group of employees discussing a sports event during a coffee break), the two are inextricably mixed.[5] We will consider this intermingling of the formal and informal system in much more detail in Chapter 8, in which we show that managers spend the majority of their time in the lateral work-flow processes of trading, interacting, and negotiating.

Nevertheless, if we look at the organization as a work-flow process, interaction in an informal group is most likely to occur among persons whose work is interdependent and interrelated. In most organizations there exists an informal network of people who "get the job done" by avoiding the "red

This task group will be disbanded when the drilling is completed. (H. Armstrong Roberts/E. P. Jones)

tape" of formal communication channels. In their study of lateral work-flow relationships, for example, Walton *et al.* found that cooperative and harmonious relationships between departments were accompanied by informal exchanges that were more frequent and positive and that resulted in greater payoffs; departments with less harmonious relationships had greater adherence to formal rules and more formal interaction with fewer people.[6]

Farris confirms the Walton findings, noting that the informal organization "ticking along under the surface" can help an organization become much more effective and innovative.[7] He believes that the proper approach is to find the key people in the informal organization and to facilitate their informal interactions, even if they will thereby spend less time in their formal positions or jobs. This approach, he contends, is even more necessary in research-and-development groups, which need to be creative, than it is in other areas of an organization.

Stemming originally from the work of the Tavistock Institute in London, the concept of "sociotechnical systems" has elicited a great deal of attention. This attention has been directed toward modifying the work-flow process to take into account both the work that needs to be done and the way in which it may be redesigned so as to capitalize on both flow and human perspectives. Recent work in job redesign in Scandinavia, including the Saab and Volvo organizations, shows the importance of such concepts.

Rice suggests that a "task system" consists of a set of activities with both the human and physical resources that are required to perform the set of activities.[8] As a result, each subsystem or component activity of the system is interdependent with some of the other activities going on in the larger systems. All of the subsystems have inputs, etc., but they can be identified by the concept of "boundary." Under the sociotechnical approach, the concept of boundary is determined more by the necessities of the work flow than by the more formal, structural design of the organization. In other words, the flow of work establishes the boundaries of the subsystem. We will return to this concept in Chapter 11, when we discuss organizational improvement from the work-flow perspective.

A more theoretical note is sounded by Bucklow, who did an extensive literature review.[9] She notes that long-term studies have tended to question early assumptions that a work group's tasks provide a primary source of individual motivation. Not only the work group itself, but also the organizational climate and technological, economic, and sociopsychological considerations must be brought to bear in the integrating concept—the primary task the group has to perform. As a result, Bucklow suggests that major theoretical importance should be given to the concept of responsible autonomy in work groups and to the design of individual jobs.

To do so involves transferring power and control *to the group* for the operation and completion of the primary task. The work group itself should be given the central role in the task rather than the peripheral, supporting role given many work groups. Another advantage of transferring power and control to the group to perform the operation is that doing so creates an upward pressure so that all levels in the hierarchy have *more* opportunity to perform managerial tasks in a broader way. Coming to much the same conclusion, Taylor asserts that if handled properly, advanced and more sophisticated technology is an opportunity for the development of autonomous work groups.[10] In such a work group, the responsibility for the task rests with the group itself, and the immediate supervisor shifts to other areas, such as liaison and representation.

The concept of autonomous work groups has been put into practice in much of Europe, particularly in Scandinavia. For example, in one organization in Norway, autonomous work groups were begun as an experiment in 1965, and the entire plant converted within several years. In 1975 the manager commented that he would not go back to the old system: "The old way is all right for people with their heads cut off." Interviews with union workers involved in the original experiment indicated that they did not want to return to the old system either.

This concept of giving more responsibility to the work group may give some strong clues as to the success of the informal group, whose members have relatively equal power and authority. It may also give some clues as to why such areas as job enrichment seem to be effective. When properly installed, such programs may provide not only the individual but also the work group with greater autonomy, variety, task identification, and feedback.

In addition, this concept may suggest why group behavior may have functional or dysfunctional effects on the organization. The group as such is essentially neutral. Depending on some of the variables we have already described, the formal or informal work group may work for or against the larger system, as many studies have shown. Roy, for example, has shown that both formal and informal groups can work against the stated objectives and goals of the enterprise through informal quotas or quota restrictions.[11] He found that since they did not trust management, workers developed specific quotas; these quotas helped to protect the group members from what they saw as management's hostility.

C. Groups from a Human Perspective

In addition to being formed because of organizational demands or the requirements of the work-flow process, groups may arise because they meet certain personal needs, such as those described in Chapter 3. Since many of these needs cannot be satisfied by the individual alone, they must be satisfied by others, usually in groups.

The human animal is a social being. Belonging to groups satisfies needs that one cannot satisfy in isolation. According to Homan's exchange theory, therefore, every social activity or group represents a reward by meeting specific needs of the individual.[12] For example, one of the chief causes of casualties among troops in a battle is "bunching up." Men who are in danger need to be physically close to one another, even though they know that this increases their collective danger. As Stouffer's studies indicate, a soldier's need for contact with his buddies is considerably more important in determining his behavior as a soldier than are the orders he receives from his military supervisors.[13]

Since certain needs can be satisfied most effectively by the group, people turn to the group in order to satisfy those needs. Furthermore, by providing feedback, the group can help the individual meet his or her highest, self-actualization needs.

The need satisfaction obtained from group membership is highly complex; no single group can satisfy all of a person's needs, any or all of which may contribute to one's reasons for belonging to a particular group at a particular period of time. A person's change in needs is reflected in a change in group affiliations, both on and off the job. Group membership is maintained only so long as the needs being satisfied by that group are more important than the work or expenditure of effort necessary to remain within the group. When the group no longer satisfies the person's needs or when the energy level required becomes higher than the rewards obtained by the group, he or she drops out of that particular group.

As we have looked at groups in social organizations, one common theme in the "how" of group formation is the concept of interaction. Anything that causes people to interact with one another, whether at work or at home, increases the odds that they will form a group. It is a truism to say that if people do not know one another and have never met, they cannot comprise a group as we have defined it.

The simple matter of geography, then, has much to do with the formation of groups. One is much more likely to form a social group with his or her immediate neighbors than with people in the next block. For example, an individual has lived for several years in a house which has a high fence and a lot of shrubbery along the back end of the lot. The person does not know the names of the two "neighbors" on the other side of the fence. Similarly, individuals living near the main entrance of an apartment house are much more likely to know the other tenants than if they live on the top floor to the rear of the building. The same is true for people attending the same church, the same school, or working in the same company. Within an organization, people working in the same building or geographical area are much more likely to form groups with one another than they are with people working in a different building.

Although interaction can facilitate the development of a group, it is not the only factor in group formation. As we have seen, unless a group can satisfy the needs of its members, it will either cease to exist or individual members will drop out, although the group itself may remain as an entity. Common values or shared interests are thus a powerful factor in determining why groups form. People with shared interests, whether task-related or hobbies such as stamp collecting, golf, sailing, or photography, are more likely to gather together in groups than are those with dissimilar work interests or hobbies.

IV. THE INTERNAL OPERATION OF GROUPS

The clearly distinguishable internal structure of a group emerges over time. The extent to which this internal structure is effective determines, in large measure, the degree to which the operating group is successful in meeting its purpose, in reaching its objectives and, just as importantly, in satisfying the needs of its members. To understand the internal operation of groups, we need to explore such concepts as group leadership, group norms and standards of behavior, group cohesion and solidarity, and the group's decision-making process.

A. Group Leadership

The term "leader" usually connotes someone with formal authority, the "boss" of a formal task group. But since the "official" leader may be only a figurehead, we cannot use the term "leader" synonymously with "boss" or "manager." Rather, a leader is anyone who takes on group task, group-building, or self-serving roles. Therefore, a group may have, over time, many different leaders, some more effective than others. In other words, leadership is not a function or trait of a single individual, but is distributed throughout the entire group, and any group member may be a leader at any particular point in time.

This is not to deny that one or more individuals may be more influential than others in the group (e.g., the "boss" may well have more power and influence in a work group than any other single member). It is, however, essential to point out that leadership, in terms of power and influence, is *distributed*

lēad'er *n.* a person who makes an important decision,

then sits back,

and answers stupid questions for the rest of his life.

By permission of John Hart and Field Enterprises, Inc.

at various times in the lifetime of the group. In fact, groups frequently have at least two commonly recognized leaders—one who most frequently takes on the job of moving the group toward task accomplishment, and another who most frequently takes on the group-maintenance role. A person who frequently adopts a self-serving role may serve as a disruptive "leader," i.e., one who is influential in impeding the group from reaching its objective. (Leadership is discussed more fully in the next chapter.)

B. Group History

The historical background of a group influences the way in which the group members interact and do their work. Thus we need to differentiate between "ad hoc" groups—generally formed quickly, on the "spur of the moment," and whose members have had little or no previous interaction with one another—and "established" groups, whose members have worked together in the past. Their common history has enabled the members to acquire a knowledge of the strengths and weakness and many of the idiosyncrasies of the other members.

There has been relatively little research done on the relationship of the life span of the group and its impact on various measures of group performance and members' attitudes. Further, the research has shown mixed and inconclusive results.[14]

There has, however, been a fair amount of work on the way a group develops over time. An extensive review of the literature suggests that groups go through a four-stage process: forming, storming, norming, and performing.[15] If the group is an "ad hoc" one, the four-stage process requires very little time, since the relatively short life of the group makes it imperative that the problem-solving stage be reached quickly. These time constraints are not so important to a group that will be working together for a longer time period, and the group can go through the four-stage process in a longer time frame.

1. Forming   In its initial stage, the group is concerned with orientation, which is accomplished primarily through testing the boundaries of both interpersonal and task behaviors, determining the relationship with the leader, and the like.

2. Storming   The second stage is characterized by polarization and conflict about both interpersonal and task issues. The individuals in the group appear to resist group influence and task requirements.

3. Norming   In the third stage, resistance is overcome, intergroup cohesiveness develops, standards are evolved, and roles become more firmly established.

4. Performing   In the final stage, the group is ready to settle down to accomplish its task. Group energy can be channeled into the task, since the structural issues have been largely resolved and the standards have been set.

C. Group Norms and Behavior

Over time, a group tends to develop a life, history, and culture of its own. Concurrently, the group members tend either to develop roughly the same attitudes and values or to leave the group. This similarity in attitudes and values is called a norm, or standard, against which the appropriateness of the members' behavior can be judged. Some norms apply only to overt, perceived behavior; some are formal, i.e., written; and others are informal, i.e., they emerge from the interaction of the group members.

A group deviant may be ostracized or even expelled from the group. (The Christian Science Monitor)

Groups or organizations attach differing amounts of importance to various norms.[16] Some norms are *pivotal;* that is, the member of the group or the organization must adhere to these norms. For example, a member of a business organization who does not believe in the value of getting a job done will not long survive in that organization. Similarly, a student who refuses to attend a particular course or to study for it will not long survive if class attendance is mandatory.

Relevant norms, by contrast, are not absolutely essential for a group member to accept as the price of membership to a group, but they are considered as desirable and worthwhile to accept. Frequently, these norms pertain to standards of dress and conduct, such as not being publicly disloyal to the group or the organization. Of course, norms that are pivotal to one group or organization may be only relevant to another group. To belong to a particular club, for example, the norm of wearing a coat and tie may be pivotal. For another group, this norm may be relevant or totally irrelevant.

A group member (whether new or old) thus has several options for behavior. One response is *rebellion;* the individual rejects all of the group's values and norms. A second is *creative individualism;* here, the individual accepts only pivotal norms and rejects some or all of the relevant ones. The third choice is *conformity;* the group member accepts all of the group's values and norms. The second response to socialization (creative individualism) would appear to be the most beneficial for the group. Rebellion results in the individual's either leaving the organization (or being expelled from the group) or turning his or her energies toward defeating group goals. Complete conformity results in a curbing of the individual's creativity, and valuable inputs may be lost to the group.

Knowledge of a group's norms may help an individual decide whether or not to join a particular group. For example, Republicans in a local community tend to associate, at least in their political activities, with other Republicans. Union members tend to associate with other union members. Teenagers tend to associate with other teenagers. The tendency to associate with, pay attention to, and listen to other group members further enhances the commonality of group attitudes and norms.

Group norms can be translated into specific types of behavior resulting from the interrelationships and interdependence of group members. The existence of group norms exerts a pressure on group members to conform to these norms. For example, a college student's behavior may vary greatly, depending on whether she or he is with parents, fellow students at the local bar, or in class. Each of these groups has norms and standards of behavior to which this student is expected to conform.

Unwritten norms may be just as important as formal, written ones. Dalton describes a widespread, unwritten norm that violated established rules in a chain of drug stores.[17] According to the unwritten norm, employees, especially managers, could take free food and confections from the soda fountain, and fountain managers could take food items home. The result of this common practice was that the chain's soda fountains consistently showed only a small profit. In one store, however, the fountain manager adhered rigidly to the published rules, and her profits, of course, were consistently higher. The questioning by higher management, the resentment of other fountain managers, and the unhappiness of the employees in that particular drug store put the store manager under a great deal of pressure. As a result, he continually rechecked her records and withheld the praise she felt she deserved for having the highest profit margin. After two years of increasing frustration and resentment, she quit the firm. Since this particular unwritten norm was in direct violation of established company rules, the store manager was never able to tell her why he was unhappy with her.

This illustration points up the necessity for a group to periodically examine its norms to determine whether or not they should be changed and, indeed, whether or not all of the group members know what the norms are. Norms may be classified into four dimensions: *affective relationships*, which deal with the personality or impersonality of the relationships; *control, decision-making, and authority relationships*, which deal with the equality or inequality of power; *status-acceptance relationships*, which deal with the uniqueness or the position of the individuals; and *achievement-success relationships*, which deal with the matter of prestige and rank.[18]

It is clear that the longer a group's history, the more the group may be "frozen" into a set of norms, some of which may be highly functional and others highly dysfunctional to the effective performance of the group. As a result, effective groups periodically set aside time to examine their norms and to systematically change those which are impeding the progress of the group. Otherwise, for example, a group may become too concerned about having peaceful, harmonious relationships, not recognizing that some conflict and tension would actually be very helpful and productive.

D. Group Cohesion

The term "cohesion" simply means "solidarity." Generally, the greater the *status* of a group, the greater its cohesion. In a high school or college, for example, there are always one or two high-status groups to which many people want to belong. The more cohesive the group, the more likely it is to have common values, attitudes, and standards of behavior. Cohesion has profound implications in industrial settings. The degree of a work group's cohesiveness affects the degree to which that group is helpful or harmful to the organization as a total system.

Solidarity, or cohesion, is also affected by the *homogeneity* of the group. If the group's members have widely differing values or statuses, they will find it difficult to become a cohesive unit. For example, it may be very difficult to foster cohesion in a group that includes both the president and the janitor of the organization.

The more a group is *isolated* from other groups, the more it tends to be cohesive. Similarly, members of an isolated group are more likely to share common values and standards of behavior. Thus a small work group isolated from the rest of the organization may become highly cohesive and demand a great deal of conformity from its members.

Reacting to *outside pressure* is one of the fastest ways a group can develop strong solidarity. In industrial work groups, outside pressure may take many forms: union-management conflict, competition between groups, mistrust between line and staff personnel, or reaction against a dictatorial supervisor.

The *size* of a group affects its cohesion. If a group is too small, e.g., two or three people, there may not be enough skill within the group to perform the task, particularly if it is a problem-solving one. Conversely, if the group is too large, communications within the group may break down, and group members may not find enough opportunity to satisfy their own needs. However, there is some evidence that as a group increases its membership, different effects occur when the group membership is more than seven.[19]

Another major variable affecting group cohesion is the atmosphere, or *climate*, both within and external to the group. (Climate is discussed more fully in Chapter 9.) If the internal climate is open and accepting, cohesion increases.[20] Cohesion also increases if the external climate is negative or hostile, but in addition this type of climate reduces output.[21]

E. The Importance of Group Cohesion and Solidarity

Cohesiveness has direct bearing on a group's behavior. The more cohesive the group, the greater the likelihood that its members will have similar attitudes, values, and behavior patterns. The fact that a group is highly cohesive also increases the chance that members can influence other members to *change* their behavior. If, for example, influence is exerted on members to conform to group norms, changes thereby accomplished should in turn increase the group's cohesiveness. In other words, the more cohesive a group is, the greater the number of members who conform to its norms.

Thus group cohesiveness and conformity to norms are mutually reinforcing factors. The fact that there is cohesiveness means that a member can change the norms to which other members conform. One member's desire to bring about change within the group is of value, particularly if others find those feelings and attitudes worthwhile, thus reinforcing the member's feelings. This leads to a relatively stable situation, which Homans identifies as a basic sort of equilibrium, i.e., the basic variables of group operation (the rate of interaction, who speaks to whom, etc.) remain stable over time. This stability, Homans argues, is reflected in the paradigm: profit = reward — cost, and can be described as "distributive justice."[22] For example, a bright student may feel even more superior (profit) if he or she takes the time (cost) to tutor poor students, an enjoyable activity (reward). In short, by using the reinforcement paradigm, one can predict and account for much of a group's behavior. Homans has helped focus on reinforcement as the basis for group operation. Taking an extreme position, it is virtually certain that if there were no reinforcement for staying in a group, members' needs could not be met, and the group would dissolve.

Although membership in a group provides a number of rewards, the member must accept the group's behavioral demands in order to receive the rewards. Individuals remain or drop out of a group to the extent that they accept these behavioral demands and perceive the rewards to be greater than the "cost" of the demands.

However, when group membership is not highly relevant for achieving the individual's goals, group pressure can still have a profound effect on that person's judgment. For example, Asch conducted a series of experiments in which all but one of the members of a group were "stooges" who had been instructed to publicly state wrong judgments when asked to compare the length of a given line with one of three unequal lines.[23] In a large majority of the cases, the naive (uninstructed) subject conformed to the group judgment of the line length, even when he knew that the consensus was wrong. In other words, he denied the evidence of his senses in order to conform to the group's judgment. However, it must be pointed out that this occurred when the subject was the last person to estimate the line length.

Given that the members of a cohesive group have similar attitudes and behaviors, behavior in work situations is greatly affected by the dynamics of work groups. However, it is important to realize that a cohesive work group is, as far as the organization is concerned, essentially neutral. Conformity to group norms is neither good nor bad; it is merely a fact.

Although there is a pressure toward conformity in a work group, this tells us little about the content of these norms, since they may vary from creativity, originality, and high productivity in one group to rigidity, qualification, and restricted output in another group. In order to deal with the effects of group cohesion and solidarity, therefore, we need to distinguish between group norms or objectives that are helpful to the organization and those that are harmful to the organization.

Even at the national level, group conformity and cohesiveness can lead to either fiascoes or resounding successes, as Janis points out in his book *Group-think*.[24] Janis examined four fiascoes, each of which occurred under a different president: the Bay of Pigs invasion of Cuba, under Kennedy; the attack on Pearl Harbor, under Roosevelt; the invasion of North Korea and the war with the People's Republic of China, under Truman; and the escalation of the Vietnam war, under Johnson. In each instance, profound errors and mistakes of judgment were made by a small, cohesive group that did not allow conflict or deviation—that did not accept, believe, or pass on information that clearly identified the decisions being made as mistakes, and that clearly underestimated the strengths of the other side.

As counterpoint to these fiascoes, Janis selected two cases that avoided groupthink: the Cuban-Russian missile crises in 1962, under Kennedy, and the Marshall plan of 1948, under Truman. In the Cuban crisis, Kennedy and his small group of advisers was able to avoid groupthink, establishing an advisory group that accepted conflict and deviant thinking as the norm. This group accepted information from all sources, considered a wide variety of alternative plans and their possible results, and developed contingency plans that utilized all possible information, including predictions of *how the other nations might act*.

V. GROUP TASK, BUILDING, AND MAINTENANCE ACTIVITIES

From an organizational point of view, the purpose of a group is to perform a task—to accomplish specific objectives. But each individual within the group has a different degree of commitment to the task, as well as unique personal, idiosyncratic needs. Accordingly, a group has no one single objective, but rather a multiplicity of them. Some of these objectives are explicit and discussed; others are implicit and may not be recognized directly.

In this section, we focus on the systems relationships that exist among a group's members. First, however, we need to define the terms "content" and "process." "Content" refers to the subject-matter discussion or to the actual tasks being performed; "process," to the way in which the content is handled or discussed by the group. Process thus includes the methods used by the leader, the degree and quality of participation by the members, the communication methods used, and the like.

A number of different approaches have been developed to describe group process, but one of the most widely used is that developed by Benne and Sheats.[25]

1. *Group task activities*—initiating, clarifying, coordinating, or orienting the group to its goals, giving and seeking information, and establishing contact with the "outside world"—help the group attain its primary goals and objectives. Examples of group task roles are: orientation ("It's getting late, and we need to move along"); information-seeking ("John, don't you have some information that may be of help here?"); clarifying ("Isn't Jim trying to say that . . ."); and information-giving ("The latest report shows that . . ."). All of these statements are attempts by a member of the group to help move it toward the accomplishment of its goals and objectives.

2. *Group-building activities* allow the group to build and maintain itself by helping to satisfy members' needs and by fostering trust and cooperation among group members. Any group can be made more effective by the application of such principles as harmonizing ("You two really aren't as far apart as you think"); using humor to reduce tensions ("That reminds me of the story about . . ."); and encouraging people to participate and compromise ("Mary, we know this is the first time you have attended our group's meetings, but we feel you have a great deal to contribute" or "Let's see if we can work out something that is agreeable to both sides"). All of these activities are attempts to build better relationships within the group so that the group can maintain itself.

3. *Self-serving activities*—attention-getting, dominating, aggression, and withdrawal—help each member of a group to meet his or her own set of unique needs, values, and goals. Although such activities may satisfy the individual's particular needs, they contribute little to the overall success of the group in attaining its formal or primary objectives. Examples of self-serving statements are: "I don't care how you explain it, you're dead wrong" (aggression); "We're not getting anywhere, why don't we each work on the problem by ourselves?" (withdrawal); "I know more about the subject than anyone else, and *I* think . . ." (dominance). An individual who engages in these kinds of activities may be more interested in serving personal interests than in performing either group task or group-maintenance roles.

An understanding of these dimensions is crucial in comprehending the behavior of a group, in diagnosing problems, and in improving the operations of a group.[26] If a group engages in too much task activity and not enough maintenance, its effectiveness may be reduced. On the other hand, too much maintenance activity may also reduce the group's effectiveness, in that the group's focus is on "sweetness and light" rather than on its task. When self-serving roles appear, the group may want to try to understand these behaviors and deal constructively with them, since they may be symptoms of nonconstructive satisfaction of valid personal needs.

Different people should and do play different roles at different times, which means that *each* member may be a leader at various times. Frequently, a group will have a task leader and a maintenance leader, since people are likely to feel more comfortable in different roles.

Although the list of group task, maintenance, and self-serving roles can be considered one of the internal characteristics of groups, these activities have been handled separately, since these are some of the areas a process consultant observes when working with a group to help improve its operation. For a group to be effective, it must address itself to the task *content*, but do

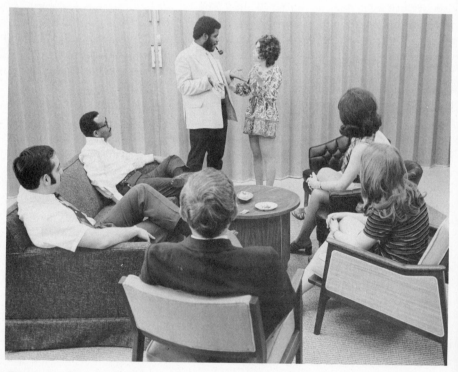

Group members may take on new roles at various times. (H. Armstrong Roberts/ E. P. Jones)

so constructively, by paying adequate attention to group *process*. In a committee meeting, for example, the group must coordinate and merge the efforts of its members so that all are working toward the goals for which the committee was established. At the same time, the emotional and personal-welfare needs of the members cannot be sacrificed without reducing the likelihood of accomplishing the committee's goals and possibly endangering the survival of the group.

This difference between content and process is important because people are not only rational and cognitive beings, but also emotional. Formerly, researchers assumed that in committee meetings, the most important thing was the task at hand and that somehow, people could separate their problem-solving, rational selves from their emotional selves. A sure sign that a group is in trouble occurs when someone suggests, "Let's leave emotions out of this and stick with the facts." Indeed, emotions *are* facts. This neglect of group-maintenance roles is probably one of the most important factors in reducing the effectiveness of many groups and committee meetings.

Attempts to ignore the personal, emotional, and affective components of group meetings impede the progress of the meeting. For example, an analysis was conducted of the tapes of a three-hour staff meeting that had been called to reply to a letter from the corporate office. Early in the meeting, one member of the group brought up an idea which was quickly rejected by the chairman. Several times in the next two hours, he again brought up the same idea, and each time it was quickly rejected by the chairman. Each time his idea was rejected, he became more negative toward the ideas of others. Only toward the end of the meeting was his idea thoroughly discussed by the group. When the idea was once more rejected, the group had done so for what appeared to be good reasons. This time, the individual accepted the rejection, recognizing the logic behind it, and then became one of the most creative members of the group, submitting a number of other ideas which were accepted by the group. If the chairman had been sensitive to group-maintenance needs and had allowed the idea to be discussed earlier, much time would have been saved, and the individual would have become a much more positive contributor earlier in the meeting.

Neither the man who offered the idea nor the chairman was aware of his own behavior and how it contributed to the situation. Both had "blind spots." One way of conceptualizing areas of "openness" and "blind spots" is through use of the Johari Window, which was developed by psychologists Joseph Luft and Harry Ingham.[27] See Fig. 5.2.

Quadrant I of the Johari Window contains information that is known by both the individual and others. Quadrant II contains the blind spot. Here, as in the meeting just described, is information that is known to others, but not

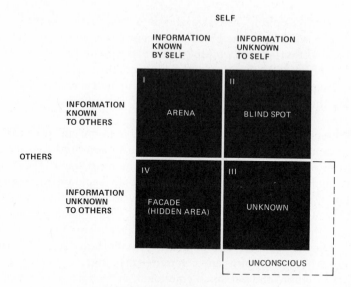

Fig. 5.2 The Johari Window.

to the individual. Quadrant III contains information that is unkown both to the individual and others. Quadrant IV contains information that an individual keeps concealed from others. This information, like that in Quadrant I and II, will vary from group to group, depending on the circumstances, the level of trust and openness, and the like.

Attention to group process is a major way of improving behavior by increasing the size of Quadrant I while reducing the number of blind spots and the need to preserve the façade. As the size of Quadrant I increases, that of Quadrants II and IV is correspondingly reduced.

VI. OBSERVING GROUP PROCESS

The group process is concerned not with the task itself, but with how the task is being accomplished—what is happening between and to group members while the group is working. Here, we will consider two basic areas of process: what to look for in groups, and criteria for effective feedback to groups about group process.

A. What to Look for in Groups[28]

1. Participation Who are the high and low participators? Does participation shift? Do high participators become quiet and vice versa? Why do such shifts occur? How are nonparticipants treated? How is their silence regarded? Who talks to whom? What may be the reason for the communications pattern?

2. Influence   There is a difference between influence and participation, or amount of "air time." Who is influential? Who is not? Is there any rivalry in the group? A struggle for leadership? Who is listened to? Who is not?

3. Styles of influence   Just as there is a difference between participation and influence, so there is a difference between styles of influence. Is anyone *autocratic* in attempting to impose his or her ideas or values on others? Is there a *peacemaker* who supports other members' decisions? Does someone consistently try to avoid conflict by "pouring oil on troubled waters"? Is a group member deferential toward others? Is a member getting attention by being *laissez faire* or by apparently lacking involvement in the group? Does a member seem to go along with decisions without making a commitment one way or the other? Is someone withdrawn and uninvolved? Does anyone try to be *democratic* by including everyone in a group discussion or decision? Who expresses opinions and feelings directly and openly without evaluating or judging others? Who appears to be open to feedback from others? Which members attempt to deal with conflict in a problem-solving way?

4. Decision-making procedures   Frequently a decision is made without the members' considering its impact on others. Does someone want to make a decision without checking with others (self-authorized)? Does the topic of conversation drift? Who changes the topic? Who supports the suggestions and decisions of others? Does such support result in two members deciding for the entire group (handclasp)? How does this affect others? Is there evidence of a majority vote pushing through a decision over others' objections? Is there an attempt to get all members to participate in a decision (consensus)? Which member(s) make contributions that do not receive a response or recognition (plop)? What effect does this have?

5. Task functions   These are behaviors that focus on accomplishing the job or task. Does someone ask for or suggest the best way to proceed? Does anyone summarize ideas that have been covered? Who gives or asks for facts, ideas, opinions, feelings, and feedback? Who keeps the group from going off on tangents? Who keeps the group on target?

6. Maintenance functions   These functions insure smooth and effective teamwork within the group, by creating a group atmosphere that enables each member to contribute maximally. Who helps others get into the discussion (gate openers)? Does anyone cut off other members or interrupt them (gate closers)? How are ideas accepted? Rejected? Are there attempts to help others clarify their ideas?

6. Membership This is the degree of a person's acceptance or inclusion in the group. Does any subgrouping occur? Do some members consistently agree or disagree with one another? Do there seem to be "in" groups? "Out" groups? How are "outsiders" treated? Do some members move in or out of the group, e.g., lean backward or forward in their chairs or physically move their chairs? What are the circumstances under which this occurs?

7. Feelings Feelings, frequently generated by group discussions, are only infrequently talked about. Rather, they must be inferred from nonverbal cues, such as tone of voice, facial expressions, and gestures. Are feelings such as warmth, affection, anger, irritation, frustration, excitement, boredom, or defensiveness seen? Do group members attempt to block the expression of feelings, particularly negative ones? How is this done? Is it done consistently?

8. Norms Norms, standards, or ground rules control the behavior of a group. Are certain areas avoided in the group, e.g., discussing behavior, talking about present feelings, etc.? How is the avoidance reinforced? How is it done? Are group members overly polite or nice to one another? Do members agree with one another too readily? Are only positive feelings expressed?

B. Criteria for Effective Feedback[29]

Since all behavior conveys a message and is thus a form of communication, feedback is one way of helping another person to consider changing his or her (verbal or nonverbal) behavior. Feedback is the process of communicating to an individual information about how that person affects others. As in a guided missile system, the feedback process helps the individual to keep behavior "on target" and thus to better achieve the individual's goals.

Effective feedback has the following characteristics:

1. Rather than being evaluative, it is *descriptive*. The use of descriptive feedback permits the other individual to decide whether or not to use the feedback. Nonevaluative feedback reduces the need for the other person to react defensively.

2. It is *specific*, not general, in nature. Telling a man that he is "domineering" will not be as useful as saying, "When we were discussing the topic, you did not listen to what others said, and I felt that I was forced to either accept your arguments or be attacked by you."

3. It must take into account the needs of *both the receiver and giver* of feedback. Feedback that serves the needs of only the sender can be destructive.

4. It is focused on *behavior that can be controlled* by the receiver. It is frustrating to the individual to be told of some shortcoming over which she or he has no control.

5. It is *asked for* rather than imposed. Feedback is most useful when the receiver can ask the kinds of questions that are personally meaningful.

6. *Timing* is important. Feedback should be given as soon as possible after a specific behavior has occurred. This depends, of course, on the individual's readiness to hear it, the norms of the group, support available from others, and so on.

7. Feedback should be checked to ensure that *communications are clear.* One way of doing this is to have the receiver repeat the information to make sure that it corresponds to what the sender meant to say.

8. When feedback is given in a group situation, both the giver and the receiver should have the opportunity to *check the accuracy* of the feedback with others in the group. Did others observe the behavior or get the same feelings and impressions?

In summary, feedback is a way of giving help to those who desire it. It is opportunity for the individual to learn more about the impact of his or her personal behavior on others. Feedback thus can be used to expand Quadrant I of the Johari Window, at least by reducing the size of Quadrant II. If the norms of the group are to use feedback as a way of increasing interpersonal trust and confidence among group members, Quadrant IV will also be reduced as the indivdual becomes more willing to "share" some of his or her hidden area with others.

VII. TEMPORARY GROUPS

Some authors have suggested that almost all organizations of the future will be free-form, highly participative, and organized around problems to be solved, and that the more traditional hierarchical structure of work will essentially disappear. We disagree. Much of the work done by organizations is routine and repetitive, e.g., a manufacturing plant making a known product, a registrar's office processing grades and issuing transcripts, or an insurance company making up its payroll. In each case, the problems are relatively routine and can be solved within the group itself.

However, some problems cannot be handled in such a manner. Perhaps a particular work group does not have the expertise to solve highly complex problems, those that cut across organizational lines, those involving the interface of more than one group or long-range planning and change, or ones that

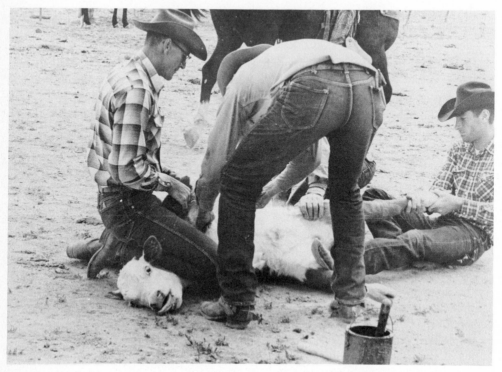

A temporary task group. (H. Armstrong Roberts/E. P. Jones)

have not yet been identified because each work group is concerned with and involved in its own work and problem-solving activities. This is particularly true when the pace of change is rapid and problems are not well defined. In such situations, finding solutions may require a different organizational structure (to be discussed in Chapters 10, 11, and 12). Here, however, we will just introduce the idea of *temporary groups,* which may be used to solve complex, diffuse, or poorly defined problems. The temporary task group is formed to solve a particular problem; after it has performed its task, it is disbanded.

In our discussion, we use three terms somewhat interchangeably: matrix organization, task force, and collateral organization. Although there are subtle differences of meaning among the three, they all include the concept of cross-functional, cross-disciplinary temporary groups identifying or working on poorly defined problems. The matrix organization consists primarily of project teams created to solve a specific problem. The project team has representatives from the different groups that are involved with the problem. The team members are expected to work together as a cohesive unit, sharing responsibility and power for problem solving.

A task force, or project team, is highly relevant if organizations have *unresolved problems* that need to be worked through and if the human resources in the organization are to be continuously fully utilized.[30] The task force brings together people of different backgrounds, knowledge, specializations, and functions. To be effective, the task force must have approval from not only each member's immediate manager, but also those higher in the management hierarchy who can, therefore, exercise more authority than could individual managers or a more permanent group, such as a standing committee. In addition to solving problems, a task force may also lead to job enrichment, learning experiences for those involved, and management development. Despite its benefits, however, relatively little use has been made of the task force. Indeed, a recent survey of small and medium-size organizations showed that fewer than 20 percent had ever used the project-team approach. One reason for its limited use is that managers do not think in these terms, and few managers know how to go about setting up task forces effectively.

A related approach, *collateral organization*, has been described as a "parallel, continuously coexisting organization which a manager can use to supplement his or her existing formal organization. Collateral organizations have norms differing from those usually in force, are used to identify and solve apparently intractable problems, and are carefully linked to the 'regular' organization."[31] The collateral organization focuses on knowledge problems, whereas the more formal organization focuses on authority-production problems, which are more repetitive and more structured. There is evidence that hierarchical groups solve problems more quickly when working on structured problems, whereas ill-defined, knowledge-type problems are solved more quickly by the collateral organization.

A collateral organization can be characterized as follows:

1. All information channels are open, so that managers and others can communicate directly, without using formal communications channels.

2. Exchange of relevant information is complete and rapid.

3. Its norms encourage careful analysis and questioning of assumptions, methods, alternatives, and goals.

4. Individual managers can get problem-solving assistance from anyone in the organization.

5. It operates in parallel with the formal organization, and the formal organization remains intact.

6. The inputs to the formal organization consist of the outputs from the collateral organization. The final decisions are made within the formal organization.

There has been little applied research on the effect of temporary task forces on their members, particularly at the management level. In one study of maintenance workers in a large oil refinery, one set of groups was stable, with membership constant, and the other groups were unstable.[32] Team membership varied according to the needs of the particular job. Members of the stable groups saw themselves as emphasizing teamwork and exercising more influence on lower-level supervisors. The unstable work teams perceived themselves as having more influence on upper management and being better able to use their skills and competence, with less emphasis on teamwork.

There is extensive evidence that the use of temporary work teams can be effective, especially with problems involving more than one subsystem or group in an organization. If *one* group comes up with a solution to such a problem, the *other* groups or subsystems are likely to be opposed. In one study, when representatives of several groups were brought together to study problems and develop joint solutions, the quality of the product was improved by more than 69%.[33]

But not all project or matrix teams succeed. Another study reports one success and one failure.[34] The failure was in the manufacturing operation, where some project team members did not have sufficient authority delegated to them by their immediate supervisors and therefore could never really become part of the matrix organization. A later attempt, involving new-product development and introduction, was a success, probably because of the wholehearted enthusiasm and cooperation of the facility manager. A series of task forces consisted of representatives from R&D, marketing, purchasing, and production departments. Each task force met to integrate the work of the different departments as a particular new product moved through the developmental and manufacturing stages. At each step of the way, the task force met to identify and solve problems.

In a thoughtful article, Argyris has suggested some reasons for failures of matrix organizations.[35] He sees the matrix or project team organization as being one of the most promising new strategies for the future. In doing research in nine large organizations using a matrix of project team approach, he found that when properly used, the project team reduced interdepartmental warfare and win-lose competition. Although management felt the approach made sense, they found it very difficult to put into actual practice. The reason, perhaps, "lies in the everyday *behavior styles that managers have developed, in the past, to survive and to succeed within the traditional pyramidal organi-*

zation."[36] The behavioral styles necessary for the matrix organization and the usual group are different. Management is unaware that their behavioral styles need to change. As a result, Argyris suggests careful training of both matrix members and matrix managers.

A second problem is that managers are overly concerned with making people "happy" and do not understand the difference between crippling and constructive tension. Prior to writing the article, Argyris reviewed his notes from 32 major organizations in which he had done consulting and research. Not one was fully using the matrix approach, sometimes as long as three years after the changeover had been announced. As a remedy, he suggests that rather than *increasing* the forces for change, the forces against change be *reduced* by involving management employees at all levels in the change process. This points up the necessity for doing a better job of team building, examining both the content and the process.

Indeed, even to suggest using a matrix organization can be threatening. In one instance, after analyzing the structure of a school of management in a large university, an internal committee proposed reorganization around the matrix concept. The idea was so threatening that it never went beyond the proposal stage.

VIII. GROUP OUTPUTS—PRODUCTIVITY AND SATISFACTION

From a systems point of view, the outputs of a group can be classified into two areas: its productivity and the satisfaction of its members. A group's productivity is measured by the quality and quantity of its decisions. Decisions may be about something very tangible, such as the number of pieces manufactured or checks handled in a given period of time. At the other extreme are intangible and abstract concepts, such as ideas generated in a research group or the psychiatric treatment given in a mental hospital. Group members' satisfaction is reflected in the cohesion of the group, in the extent to which individual members both satisfy their own needs and believe that the group goals and productivity are satisfactory.

Although no one-to-one relationship between productivity and satisfaction exists as such, there is some indication that high performance leads to high satisfaction rather than the reverse; high performance leads to extrinsic rewards which in turn lead to satisfaction. Yet if work is intrinsically fulfilling, the process also works the other way around; that is, satisfaction leads to performance.[37]

Other important factors are group cohesion and the degree to which individuals' needs are met. Although these factors are normally present in high-producing groups, they may also be present in nonproductive groups.

As this chapter has indicated, both productivity and satisfaction depend on a number of complex, interacting variables—leadership, climate, group membership, size, communications, characteristics of the members, type of group, and the like. In some instances task forces or other forms of temporary groups may make better decisions than already formed work groups, depending on the type of decision that needs to be made. Certainly, a group decision arrived at by consensus and full participation may result in a greater sense of commitment in its members than one arrived at by fiat or majority vote.

Although we have, directly or indirectly, been discussing group outputs throughout this chapter, we would now like to take a closer look at two elements, group size and the kind of group formed. Exploration in detail of every aspect of groups is certainly beyond the scope of this book.

Group Size

Group size affects the degree of participation, consensus, quality of ideas, satisfaction, and the need for a leader. As group size increases, the opportunity for participation decreases. The quality of decisions and the number of individual ideas offered increase up to about a group membership of 12 and decrease when the number is about 15 or more. Larger groups show more internal disorder and conflict and are likely to take more radical positions than are smaller ones.

To obtain the maximum amount of member *satisfaction*, the group should number no more than five or six, although *conflict* seems to be reduced in an odd-numbered group. To strive for *consensus* among the group members, therefore, the best evidence is that the group should be small and odd-numbered. In addition, there is indication that people sitting across the table from each other tend to get into more conflict than do those who are sitting side by side.[38]

Kind of Group

Although we have been discussing primarily interacting groups, those whose members work together on a face-to-face basis, we will also discuss two other kinds of "groups"—nominal and delphi. In the nominal group, members are together, but do not directly interact, and the format is more structured. After the problem has been presented, each member generates ideas independently, silently, and in writing. Then each member presents, in turn, one idea at a time to the entire group. The ideas are summarized and written on the blackboard or large pieces of paper, without discussion. This procedure allows members to "piggy-back" on the ideas of others, amplifying their own ideas after they have heard those of the others. In the third phase, all of the ideas presented are discussed for clarification and evaluation purposes. The meeting is concluded with independent, silent voting on the ideas. The final decision of the group is the summed outcome of the individual votes.

The delphi technique follows a different sequence. The "group" participants are not physically present; rather, a questionnaire is distributed to obtain information on a particular topic. The individuals taking part complete the questionnaire by independently generating their own ideas on the subject and then return it. The responses are summarized and put into a feedback report which, together with a more advanced, second-stage questionnaire, is sent back to the respondents. The members of this "group" then independently evaluate the feedback report, vote on priority ideas contained in it, and generate new ideas based on the feedback and second-stage reports. After the responses have been mailed to a central location, a final summary-feedback report is developed and mailed back to the group members.

The evidence suggests that there is little difference between the nominal and delphi groups on the quantity of ideas generated and that both types generate significantly more ideas than do conventional interacting groups. There appears to be no significant difference in satisfaction between the interacting and delphi groups, but the members of a nominal group expressed significantly more satisfaction than did members of the other two types of groups. In other words, nominal groups are both more productive and more satisfied than interacting groups.[39]

When the size of nominal and interacting groups is varied from four- to seven-person groups, there is little effect on performance of interacting groups, as measured by quantity of ideas.[40] It would be interesting to continue to increase the size of nominal groups to determine if there is an optimal size of such groups for such variables as quantity of ideas and member satisfaction.

In other words, some tradeoffs are necessary. If one wants consensus, one may have to sacrifice the quality and quantity of ideas. On the other hand, if one wants quality of ideas, one may have to use a smaller group. The satisfaction of group members may be obtained at the cost of reducing the number of individual ideas.

IX. IMPLICATIONS FOR THE MANAGER

It is impossible to establish hard and fast rules for improving group performance. However, some general guidelines may be useful.

1. Training Group performance should increase when the members have some understanding of the difference between content and process. An understanding of process variables is of material assistance in achieving a proper balance among group task, maintenance, and self-serving activities. Training is most effective, in descending order, in live situations, in those using experiential materials, and in lecture or similar approaches.

2. Conflict Many groups avoid conflict or let it become dysfunctional. The more effective groups can use conflict in a constructive way without either burying it or allowing it to get out of hand.

3. Type of group In some situations, the normal work group may be the most effective for problem solving, especially for relatively routine problems. Vague, diffuse, poorly structured problems, or those that cut across organizational lines may be solved most effectively by task forces, collateral organizations, or similar approaches.

4. Kind of group Interacting groups are the most widely used and recognized. However, when quantity of ideas is needed, the nominal group may be called for.

5. Quality of ideas When the quality of ideas is extremely important, it may be useful to have a group numbering between seven and twelve, so that more input information is available to the group.

6. Group norms The norms, or standards of behavior, of this group should be periodically examined. Are they clear to the members of the group? Should the norms be changed? Are they currently functional or dysfunctional?

7. Group cohesiveness Cohesiveness should also be periodically examined. Is the group sufficiently cohesive to get the job done? Is cohesiveness stressed so much that productivity is reduced? Is there constructive tension in the group? Are the members too homogeneous to be able to come up with a variety of ideas?

8. Consensus If consensus is desired more than quality or quantity of ideas, the group should consist of about three to five members.

9. Member satisfaction Member satisfaction appears to be related to consensus and smaller group size.

10. Leader As group size increases, there is greater need for a leader who can assist the group with its functioning. Different members may take on the leadership position at various times. Groups also frequently have maintenance leaders and task leaders. The task leader should sit at the head of the table.

11. Process observation A process observer can help a group improve its overall functioning by observing what is happening in the group and feeding back the results to the entire group and/or to the leader.

12. Counterproductive norms Norms against productivity are developed in a variety of ways. For example, the manager can consistently: (a) violate social contracts; (b) violate members' expectations; (c) provide inaccurate task information; (d) deny job-related or needed resources; (e) reinforce nonproductive behavior; (f) emphasize negative reinforcement; and (g) break promises. In effect, these "consistent" actions amount to declarations of war against subordinates, who counter with counterproductive norms. To the degree that group members are successful in enforcing counterproductive norms as a result of the manager's action, their success increases the cohesiveness of the group.

In summary, there is no one best way to establish a group. There are always tradeoffs. The astute manager should be skilled at applying the concepts of group dynamics, so that she or he can decide which tradeoffs are best in a given set of circumstances, e.g., nominal versus interacting groups, quantity of ideas versus consensus.

X. CONCLUSION

In this section we looked at internal group operation. The group can be described as a social system or as a subsystem operating within the larger social organization. We examined some of the reasons and methods of group formation, including their use in the service of the three perspectives of the structural flow, and human systems. Our discussion of the internal structure of groups included group activities, leadership, norms and standards of behavior, and group solidarity. Finally, we suggested various managerial tools for more accurate observation and diagnosis of group dynamics.

Throughout this chapter, we stressed that in addition to accomplishing their objectives or tasks, groups must also satisfy their members' needs. In return, a group makes certain demands of its members; it asks for a certain amount of loyalty and conformity to group norms and standards of behavior. Although interpersonal behavior is always a social exchange, an individual need not lose his or her individuality in a group. In some groups, the norm is for a high degree of individuality and creativity.

In discussing the impact of groups on the organization as a total system, we noted that a group's productivity may be either high or low, depending on what the group wants it to be. As we shall see later, there are ways of helping a group simultaneously meet both its own goals and needs and those of the organization.

REVIEW

1. Attend a meeting (school committee, city council, fraternity), preferably one at which *Roberts' Rules of Order* is not used. What kinds of interaction do you observe? What inferences can you draw?

2. Find two groups that are interdependent. Describe the relationship between them and give recommendations for improving their working arrangements.

3. We have described a number of different types of groups. Give an example of each from your personal experience.

4. How does the behavior of a group affect the way management treats the group?

5. Analyze and describe the impact of an "informal" group on the "formal" organization.

6. Think about a group that you have belonged to. How effective was the group? What factors were involved in its effectiveness or ineffectiveness?

REFERENCES

1. D. Cartwright and D. Lippitt, "Group Dynamics and the Individual," in *Organizational Psychology: A Book of Readings,* ed. D. A. Kolb, I. M. Rubin, and J. McIntyre, Englewood Cliffs, N.J.: Prentice-Hall, 1971.

2. R. Likert, *The Human Organization: Its Management and Value,* New York: McGraw-Hill, 1967.

3. M. Knowles and H. Knowles, *Introduction to Group Dynamics,* rev. ed., New York: Association Press, 1972, p. 8.

4. J. Zenger and D. Miller, "Building Effective Teams," *Personnel* **52,** 2 (March–April 1974): 20–29.

5. W. F. Whyte, *Organization and Behavior,* Homewood, Ill.: Richard D. Irwin and The Dorsey Press, 1969.

6. R. E. Walton, J. M. Dutton, and H. G. Fitch, "A Study of Conflict in the Process, Structure and Attitudes of Lateral Relationships," in *Some Theories of Organization,* rev. ed., ed. A. W. Rubenstein and C. G. Haberstroh, Homewood, Ill.: Richard D. Irwin and The Dorsey Press, 1966.

7. G. Farris, "Organizing your Informal Organization," *Innovation* **25** (Oct. 1971): 2–11.

8. A. Rice, "Individual, Group and Intergroup Processes," *Human Relations* **22,** 6 (Dec. 1969): 565–584.

9. M. Bucklow, "A New Role for the Work Group," *Administrative Science Quarterly* **11,** 1 (March 1966): 59–78.

10. J. Taylor, "Some Effects of Technology in Organizational Changes," *Human Relations* **24,** 2 (April 1971): 105–123.

11. D. Roy, "Efficiency and 'The Fix': Informal Intergroup Relations in a Piecework Machine Shop," in *Sociology: The Progress of a Decade,* ed. S. M. Lipset and N. J. Smelser, Englewood Cliffs, N.J.: Prentice-Hall, 1961, pp. 378–390.

12. G. C. Homans, "Social Behavior as Exchange," *American Journal of Sociology* **63,** 6 (May 1958): 597–606.

13. S. A. Stouffer *et al., The American Soldier: Combat and Its Aftermath*, Princeton, N.J.: Princeton University Press, 1949.

14. D. Ford, Jr., P. Nemiroff, and W. Pasmore, "Group Decision Making Performance as Influenced By Group Tradition," *Small Group Behavior*, (in press).

15. B. Tuckman, "Developmental Sequence in Small Groups," *Psychological Bulletin* **63,** 6 (June 1965): 384–399.

16. E. Schein, "Organizational Socialization and the Profession of Management," in Kolb, Rubin, and McIntyre, *op. cit.*, rev. ed., 1974, pp. 1–15.

17. M. Dalton, *Men Who Manage*, New York: Wiley, 1959.

18. R. Napier and M. Gershenfeld, *Groups: Theory and Experience*, Boston: Houghton Mifflin, 1974.

19. P. Turquet, "Leadership: The Individual and the Group," in G. Gibnard, J. Hartman, and R. Mann, eds., *Analysis of Groups*, San Francisco: Jossey-Bass, 1974, 349–386.

20. R. Likert, *New Patterns of Management*, New York: McGraw-Hill, 1961.

21. D. Hickson, "Motives of Workpeople Who Restrict Their Output," *Occupational Psychology* **35,** 1 (Jan.–Feb. 1961): 111–121.

22. G. C. Homans, *Social Behavior: Its Elementary Forms* New York: Harcourt, Brace & World, 1961.

23. S. E. Asch, *Social Psychology*, Englewood Cliffs, N.J.: Prentice-Hall, 1952.

24. I. Janis, *Groupthink*, Boston: Houghton Mifflin, 1972.

25. K. Benne and P. Sheats, "Functional Roles of Group Members," *Journal of Social Issues* **4,** 2 (Spring 1948): 41–49.

26. Knowles and Knowles, *op. cit.*

27. J. Pfeiffer and J. Jones, eds., *The 1973 Annual Handbook for Group Facilitators*, La Jolla, Calif.: University Associates, pp. 114–119.

28. J. Pfeiffer and J. Jones, eds., *The 1972 Annual Handbook for Group Facilitators*, La Jolla, Calif.: University Associates, 1972, pp. 21–24.

29. Kolb, Rubin, and McIntyre, *op. cit.*, p. 231.

30. T. Quick, "The Many Uses of a Task Force," *Personnel* **51,** 1 (Jan.–Feb. 1974): 53–61.

31. D. Zand, "Collateral Organization: A New Change Strategy," *Journal of Applied Behavioral Science* **10,** 1 (Jan./Feb./Mar. 1974): 63.

32. B. Fine, "Comparison of Work Groups with Stable and Unstable Membership," *Journal of Applied Psychology* **55,** 2 (April 1971): 170–174.

33. E. Huse, "The Behavioral Scientist in the Shop," *Personnel* **42,** 3 (May–June 1965): 50–57.

34. E. Huse and M. Beer, "Eclectic Approach to Organizational Development," *Harvard Business Review* **49,** 5 (Sept.–Oct. 1971): 103–112.

35. C. Argyris, "Today's Problems with Tomorrow's Organizations," *Journal of Management Studies* **4,** 1 (Feb. 1967): 31–55.

36. *Ibid.,* p. 55.

37. E. E. Lawler, *Motivation in Work Organizations,* Belmont, Calif.: Wadsworth, 1973, pp. 83–84.

38. L. Cummings, G. Huber, and E. Arendt, "Effects of Size and Spatial Arrangements on Group Decision Making," *Academy of Management Journal* **17,** 3 (Sept. 1974): 460–475.

39. A. Van DeVen and A. Delbecq, "The Effectiveness of Delphi, and Interacting Group Decision Making Processes," *Academy of Management Journal* **17,** 4 (Dec. 1974): 605–621.

40. T. Bouchard, Jr., J. Barsalous, and G. Drauden, "Brainstorming Procedure, Group Size and Sex as Determinants of the Problem-Solving Effectiveness of Groups and Individuals," *Journal of Applied Psychology* **59,** 2 (April 1974): 135–138.

GROUPS IN INTERACTION

Once again to the breach, dear friends, or fill we the
wall up with our English dead.

SHAKESPEARE

LEARNING OBJECTIVES

When you have finished reading and studying this chapter, you should be able to:

1. Identify the usual causes for intergroup cooperation and conflict.
2. Differentiate between helpful and dysfunctional instances of intergroup cooperation and conflict.
3. Provide suggestions for reducing intergroup conflict and competition when this is appropriate.

You will be expected to define and use the following concepts:

Linking pin	Win-lose
Pooled interdependence	Competition
Sequential interdependence	Status incongruity
Reciprocal interdependence	Perceptual differences
Cooperation	Differentiation
Conflict	Reducing intergroup conflict

THOUGHT STARTERS

1. When is conflict between groups helpful? When is it dysfunctional? (Do not include sports events.)
2. From your own experience, what happens when a group you belong to gets into a conflict with another group? To the other group? To the organization of which both groups are a part (when the groups are subsystems in a larger system)?
3. How do you behave when a group you belong to is in conflict with another group?

I. INTRODUCTION

Especially in organizations, groups can be considered as subsystems in continuous contact with other subsystems throughout the entire system. There are a number of different ways in which groups come into contact and interact. For example, the manager of one group may attend a committee or staff meeting with the managers or representatives of other groups; or he or she may meet formally or informally with other managers or representatives of other groups. Indeed, it is not uncommon for a manager to maintain contact and negotiate with as many as 30 different groups! Group members may interact with members of other groups on either a formal or informal basis. Finally, entire groups may meet with other entire groups, although this type of exchange occurs less frequently. Many meetings are relatively free of conflict; a meeting occurs, decisions get made, and people go back to their other tasks. This is an example of intergroup cooperation to achieve common goals. However, since groups also have their own unique goals, intergroup cooperation may be lessened by conflicting group goals and competition for resources (budgets, personnel, etc.). Thus there exists a range, or continuum, of cooperation and competition. Often, groups cooperate on one issue and simultaneously compete on another issue.

The primary causes for intergroup cooperation stem from a mutual desire to get the job done or to band together against a common enemy. The main causes of intergroup conflict, on the other hand, stem from attempts to reach mutually exclusive goals or competition for limited resources, status, and power. For example, university departments may compete for the better students as "majors," more tenured positions, or more staff.

One focus of this chapter is groups in conflict, because the results of group conflict can be either instrumental in bringing about needed change and innovation in organizations or highly dysfunctional. Furthermore, group conflict occurs more frequently than complete cooperation.

We will examine the functions and types of conflict and competition between groups. We will then consider the group processes that occur when groups are in conflict, as well as the properties of winning and losing groups. Finally, we will suggest ways of reducing intergroup conflict, when greater cooperation seems to be necessary and desirable.

II. INTERGROUP RELATIONSHIPS

The interrelationships among organizational groups can be portrayed in two different ways. According to Likert, for example, the organization is a series of overlapping groups.[1] Each group is linked to the rest of the organization by persons who hold membership in more than one group (see Fig. 1.2, p. 27). The people are called "linking pins," since they form the link between different groups. At each linking-pin level, interaction and decision making rely heavily on group processes, as described in Chapter 5. Of course, interaction also occurs at all levels—among peers, supervisors, and subordinates. Nevertheless, the most important function is that performed by the linking pins. When a good group process of decision making and supervision exists, there is a great deal of intergroup confidence and trust; problem-solving ability is good, productivity and quality are high, responsibilities are clear-cut, and the job is done effectively and well.

Although Likert's approach is both well known and popular, the linking-pin concept assumes (without being specific) that there is equal interdependency among the different groups. The specificity is provided by Thompson, who suggests that there are three different kinds of interdependence among groups: pooled, sequential, and reciprocal.[2]

1. *Pooled interdependence* occurs when the two groups do not need to have any interaction at all except through the total organization which supports them both. For example, workers at a McDonald's restaurant in one state may have no interaction with their counterparts in a different state. However, the two restaurants are interdependent in the sense that they must both show adequate performance if the total organization is to succeed. Failure of one can threaten the whole as well as the other parts. Under this type of interdependence, each part of the organization contributes to the whole organization, and each is supported by the entire organization.

Since pooled interdependence does not require interaction between groups, conflict is not likely to occur. Thus the coordination of the groups can be accomplished through standardization and rules established by the "home office."

2. *Sequential interdependence* occurs when one group must do something before another group can accomplish its tasks. The outputs from group A become inputs for group B. Both groups contribute to and are sustained by the entire organization; thus the interdependence is both pooled and serial. The order of the interdependence can be clearly specified. For example, the dietary department of a hospital must prepare the meals before the people on the nursing floors can serve them. The production department must make the widget parts before they can be assembled by another group.

Sequential interdependence must be coordinated by planning, and it requires more effort than pooled interdependence does. Further, conflict between groups is more likely to occur because of the kind of interdependence.

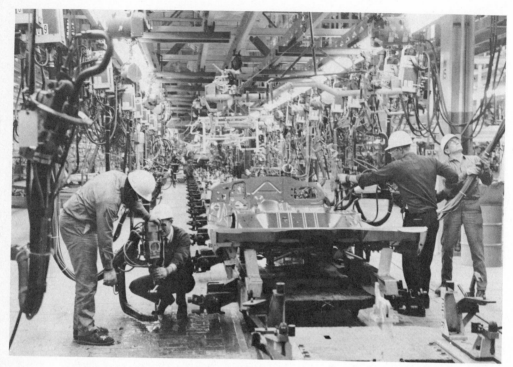

An assembly line is a good example of sequential interdependence. (Photograph courtesy the *Warren Tribune Chronicle*)

3. *Reciprocal interdependence* takes place when the outputs of each group became inputs for the others. The distinguishing aspect of reciprocal interdependence is that each group involved is penetrated by the other, with each group posing contingencies for the other. For example, an airline has both maintenance and operations groups. The maintenance group's output is an input for operations, i.e., a usable aircraft. After the plane has been flown, the maintenance group receives an input—an airplane needing maintenance. Similarly, medical personnel in a hospital send prescriptions (inputs) to the pharmacy. The pharmacists, in turn, send completed prescriptions to the nursing unit (inputs).

Reciprocal interdependence must be coordinated by mutual adjustment between the two (or more) groups. It is the most demanding of communication and decision effort, and it entails the greatest likelihood of conflict.

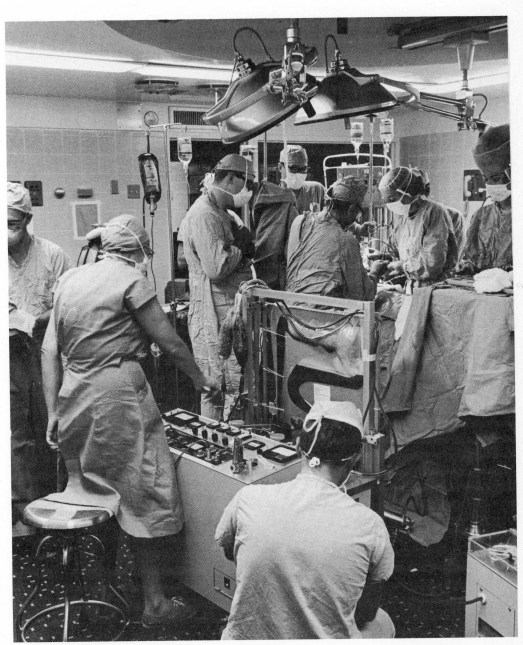

An operating-room team represents a high degree of reciprocal interdependence.
(Marc St. Gil/Black Star)

All groups within an organization have pooled interdependence; more complex organizations have groups that are sequential as well as pooled; and the most complex organizations have pooled, sequential, and reciprocal groups.

III. THE FUNCTIONS AND TYPES OF CONFLICT

Some people feel that conflict between groups is generally good, i.e., "it keeps the workers on their toes." Others, especially classical organizational theorists, feel that conflict should not arise since it is *always* undesirable. To eliminate conflict, these theorists assert, simply establish an elaborate bureaucracy, specify job descriptions, carefully select people to fill specific positions, and establish a complete set of rules to meet every contingency. One of these very specific rules allows subordinates from different groups to talk together about common problems, but as soon as disagreement occurs, they *must* forward the problem up the hierarchy until it reaches someone with the authority necessary to "end the conflict" by unilaterial decision, one that will be accepted without question by everybody.

It used to be that management's strong desire to eliminate conflict stemmed in part from the belief that any sort of tension or conflict was dys-

Infighting.

functional in both individuals and groups. This belief no longer holds. Rather, today a certain amount of tension is seen as being healthy and useful. Organizations change *only* through felt tension. Without tension, no felt need for change and innovation exists. The felt need for change calls attention to problem areas, and the organization, as an open system, searches for solutions or improvements.

Nevertheless, too much conflict and tension are obviously undesirable. Little knowledge exists as to the optimum amount of tension that should exist within individuals and groups and between groups. We can only say that some tension is helpful and that too much is not.

Conflict can be described as *"a type of behavior which occurs* when two or more parties are in opposition or in battle *as a result* of a perceived relative deprivation from the activities of or interacting with another person or group."[3] This definition is from an *organizational point of view*; personality conflicts and internal conflicts are deliberately excluded from this definition. Four major sources of organizational conflict have been identified: win-lose situations, competition over means utilization, status incongruity, and perceptual differences.[4]

A. Win-Lose Situations

Frequently, two groups have goals that cannot be attained simultaneously. To an amazing extent, organizations establish such situations all too frequently. For example, the inspection foreman may firmly believe that the manufacturing people are "trying to slip bad parts through" (a sequential relationship). Conversely, the manufacturing foreman may firmly believe that the inspectors, aided and abetted by their foreman, are out to reject even good parts, just to prove that they are on the job. Indeed, when an inspector in a large manufacturing plant was asked, "What would happen if a day or a week went past and you didn't reject any parts?" he replied, "Oh, I couldn't do that. My boss would think I wasn't doing my job."

Another type of win-lose conflict can occur between the credit and sales groups (a reciprocal interdependency). In order to optimize his or her job and win a bonus, the sales manager encourages the sales people to sell to as many customers as possible. The credit manager, on the other hand, wants a zero loss through bad debts, which will ensure a merit increase and other rewards.

Win-lose conditions occur when the reward systems are tied to individual performance rather than to total organizational success. Frequently, performance is treated as an independent variable, when the performance is in fact highly interdependent.

A football game is a win-lose situation. (H. Armstrong Roberts/E. P. Jones)

B. Competition over Means Utilization

Here, the conflict arises from different ideas about how the goals of the organization will be accomplished. There is evidence that conflicts over means to goal achievement are more conflict-loaded than are conflicts over differing goals.[5] Conflict becomes particularly intense when groups are struggling for a larger share of the budget or other scarce resources.

For example, both the sales and manufacturing groups want to increase the overall profits of the company. But the people in the sales group want to have a variety of products to sell and a continually shifting product mix, whereas the manufacturing group would prefer to build fewer products in larger quantity.

Sometimes, this type of conflict can be potentially harmful to a third party. In the competition for the better students, for example, academic departments may ignore the students' career goals.

In a large hospital, the conflict between overall patient care and meeting the teaching needs of interns and residents may have a deleterious effect upon the patient. In one situation, a patient was hospitalized because of a severe, adverse reaction to a tuberculosis test. Her arm had developed a running sore that had not cured for months. An individual conducting research on tuberculosis gave her a test on her other arm without checking the records to see why she had been hospitalized. Although the outcome is unknown, it could have had a serious, negative impact on the patient.

C. Status Incongruency

For many people, status is highly important; they want to know where they stand in relationship to others. Part of the problem here is that many different standards are operating rather than a single, absolute one. Many different status hierarchies exist, and they are continually changing. A nonhuman example of the problem that status difficulties bring about occurs in studies on chickens. Hens have a well-defined "pecking order." The highest-status hen has first crack at the food dish, but also can peck any other hen in the coop. The lowest-status hen cannot peck any other hen. But when the hens are given an injection that changes their status in the pecking order, e.g., the lowest becomes the highest, egg production falls off markedly.

On a more serious note, one of the difficulties many organizations face is the common assumption held by some men that women are inferior. As a result, until recently women were seldom moved to supervisory or managerial positions until a number of companies were given fines for noncompliance with the Civil Rights Act.

Higher-status people find it difficult to take orders from those they perceive to be of lower status. Whyte's studies in the restaurant industry have clearly shown the reciprocal-interdependence problems that arise when waitresses (lower status) give orders to chefs (high status).[6] Status differences also create problems in hospitals. Frequently, the nurse on the floor is closer to the patient than the physician, who may look in on the patient once or twice a day. But because of status differences, the nurse may find it difficult to make a suggestion to the physician, who is of higher status.

In another situation, newly hired college and MBA graduates were placed in a financial-training program, and their jobs were systematically rotated from one relatively low-level supervisor to another. Prior to employment, the students had been given a number of tests, which were unscored as a part of a program to improve selection. Follow-up supervisory ratings of the trainees were to be used as the criterion against which the tests were to be validated. When the tests were compared with the criterion, intelligence and college grades were *negatively* related. The brighter and more capable the trainee, the poorer the supervisor's rating. Follow-up studies disclosed that the relatively low-level supervisors felt threatened by the trainees. The more ideas and suggestions the trainee had, the greater the threat.

D. Perceptual Differences

Each of us sees the world differently and acts on those perceptions in ways that make sense to us. Perceptual differences are accentuated by group memberships. Marketing groups, for example, perceive marketing problems; manufacturing groups are concerned with manufacturing problems. Perceptual differences are further increased by group interaction. Purchasing agents deal with vendors; salespeople deal with customers; engineers interact with other engineers. Some groups have a great deal of interaction with groups outside the organization; other groups interact primarily with other groups within the organization. For example, Thompson suggests that the technical core of the organization, e.g., the manufacturing group, should be buffered or protected from the outside world.[7]

These different linkages may result in large-scale perceptual differences. For example, the purchasing agent may be highly concerned about the cost of a given part, whereas the engineer may be concerned about the utility of that part.

As we will see in Chapter 10, sometimes it may be important for each group to be *differentiated*—to maintain its own viewpoint and goals—but also develop mediating mechanisms so that conflict is productive. This occurs when there is open discussion and confrontation about ideas about tasks and projects; conflict is regarded as a problem to be worked through rather than as a factor to be eliminated through shared perceptions.

Differentiation arises because each group or unit, e.g., research, sales, or production, performs a different type of task and must cope with a different segment of the environment. Task variety brings about significant group differences. Groups may differ in the time span needed for each to perform its task, the interpersonal relationships among their members (marketing people may be more interpersonally oriented than research scientists, for example), formality of structure, and goal orientation (new scientific knowledge versus customer problems, market opportunities versus costs of raw materials and processing, for example).

E. Conflict Because of the Need for Change

If an organization is to survive and prosper, it must change and adapt. Organizations that do not stimulate conflict are likely to be hindered by inadequate decisions and stagnant thinking.[8] For example, the bankruptcy of the

Penn Central Railroad has been attributed to the failure of the board of directors to question operations mismanagement.[9] Although the board met monthly, few of its members questioned decisions made by operating management, although they were uncomfortable with many major management decisions. The board's desire to avoid conflict and friction allowed poor decisions to remain unchallenged.

A more positive approach is that conflict is absolutely necessary; accordingly, opposition to ideas should be explicitly encouraged; both the stimulation and resolution of conflict should be encouraged, and the proper management of conflict should be considered a major responsibility of all administrators. In other words, conflict is a two-sided coin. The level of conflict between or within groups may be too high and may therefore require a reduction. On the other hand, the level of conflict is frequently too low, and increased intensity is needed.

Change develops from the desire for improvement—from dissatisfaction —and from the creative development of alternatives. As we discussed in Chapter 2, organizations need deviance-reducing and deviance-amplifying feedback loops in order to survive and be successful. As Robbins puts it, "Change does not just happen. It requires a seed—the seed of conflict!"[10]

IV. EFFECTS OF INTERGROUP CONFLICT

A. Consequences of Conflict

When two groups are in conflict, they begin to distrust each other. Second, perceptual distortion increases, and each group begins to build two kinds of stereotypes. The other group is no longer seen as neutral; rather, it becomes a "bad guy." Concurrently, each group tends to see only the best of itself, denying that it has any faults or that the other group has any virtues. In manufacturing plants, for example, it is common to hear the product-development group say (and believe), "We gave those guys (a manufacturing group) a good design and they loused it up." Meanwhile, manufacturing is saying, "We've got all the know-how to build a good product, but we can't do it with the lousy designs that we get."

Third, as conflict increases, each group becomes more cohesive, allowing less deviation from group norms. (For example, can you imagine what would happen if an Army cadet cheered for the Navy during the annual Army-Navy game?) Consequently, the group will accept much more authoritarian, rigid, and dogmatic leadership than under more normal conditions, as can be seen in the extraordinary powers given to the President or the leader of a democratic nation during war.

When two conflicting groups begin to perceive each other as "the enemy," their cooperation with each other drops off markedly, as does communication. As a result, the two groups cannot work together to solve common problems, and neither group gets accurate feedback from the other. Instead, their communication is likely to be hostile and be received defensively. As the distorted perceptions increase, neither group really believes what the other has to say, and the norm is rejection rather than acceptance of the communication. When this occurs within an organization, and it frequently does, effort is spent not in problem solving, but in fault finding, buck passing, and in placing blame on others.

Yet the mutual problems remain and must be solved. Thus the two groups may be forced to interact with each other, e.g., listening to representatives of the two groups present their solutions or positions with reference to a common task. Under these circumstances, "each group is likely to listen more closely to their own representative and not to listen to the representative of the other group, except to find fault with his presentation; in other words, group members tend to listen only for that which supports their own position and stereotype."[11]

The consequences are predictable. They occur not only in organizations, but also in college classrooms and adult training programs using demonstration exercises.

B. Intragroup Consequences of Winning or Losing

Frequently, intergroup competition results in one group's winning and another's losing. This can occur when one group obtains a larger share of the budget than another, when a problem is bucked up the hierarchy for a higher-level supervisor to decide, in interfraternity competition, in labor-management disputes, or when two groups disagree on the proper design of a new product. These are only examples of possible situations, and illustrations can be multiplied many times over. However, the reactions *within* the conflicting groups can be predicted just as closely and accurately as they can between the two groups. The illustrations we use will be of competition between two groups of managers attending a training session.

Eight groups of managers had been meeting for almost a week. Each group was asked to select one of its members, the one most objective, to act as a judge. The eight "judges" then left the group to receive their own briefing. The groups were then paired and given one hour in which to develop a proposal for a problem. Each group then selected a representative to present its solution to the problem.

Although there were four pairs of groups, we will concentrate on only one of the pairs—Groups A and B. When the time came to make the proposal, three judges were selected to determine which group made the best presentation. Two of the judges were from Groups A and B. During the presentations the representatives first gave their solutions and then were allowed to discuss the proposed solution with the representative from the other groups. The members of each group could talk with their own representatives, but not with the other members of their own group. Group members spent little time actually listening to the representative from the other group; rather, they whispered and wrote notes to their own representatives to bolster his arguments.

Then the results were announced. The "objective" member/judge from Group A voted for his group; the "objective" member/judge from Group B voted for his group. The time was broken by the third judge, who voted for Group A, which thus became the "winner." (As could have been predicted, the eight judges voted for *their* team, nonetheless believing that they were completely objective. In all cases, it was the "outside" judge who actually made the decision to break the tie.) For example, one judge said, "When the other group presented first, I was really worried because they had a damn good presentation. However, when you guys made yours, my worries were over. Your's was so much better."

What happened to Group A, the "winners"? It became a more cohesive, playful, and casual group. Its members lost their fighting spirit and became more complacent. Their positive stereotypes of themselves were reinforced, as were their distorted perception of the "loser" group. There was little introspection as to how their own group performance could be improved.

Several stages could be seen in Group B, the "loser." At first, the group members denied the fact that they had lost; the judges were unfair, the rules were not explained well, etc. (This frequently occurs at baseball and football games, as well as in organizations. The boss is prejudiced and does not understand.)

When Group B finally accepted its loss, the group began to splinter. Recriminations arose because of conflicts that had remained unresolved during the work of preparing the presentation. Group members began to blame one another, trying to find a cause for the group's loss. The group became more tense, and intragroup cooperation was reduced. At the same time, the group members began to feel the need to work harder, to reevaluate what the group had done correctly and incorrectly. Thus Group B began to learn more about itself as a group and set out to establish new procedures for becoming more cooperative. (An excellent example of this phenomenon occurred when President Kennedy's group of advisors was much more effective in the Cuban missile crisis than it had been in the Bay of Pigs disaster.)

This exercise took place in a laboratory setting. In such simulations, the dynamics emerge faster and more clearly than in real-life organizational forms. Nonetheless, the dynamics are the same in both contexts.

V. REDUCING INTERGROUP CONFLICT AND COMPETITION

The proper management of conflict can bring about positive, badly needed changes in the organization. The three most common approaches to conflict resolution are smoothing, edicting, and confrontation.

Under the *smoothing* mode, conflict is denied. Basically, the two or more groups in conflict ignore the conflict by "sweeping it under the rug." They pretend that the conflict does not exist.

Under the *edicting* mode, the conflicting groups are told, usually by a higher-level administrator, to cease the conflict and to "get along with each other." Frequently, this does not really resolve the conflict, but only drives it underground so that the administrator does not see the more open conflict that had been visible before.

Under the *confrontation* mode, the conflict is perceived and recognized as such. The opposing parties openly debate the issue, bringing together all of the relevant facts until a decision is reached. Opposition and conflicting viewpoints are encouraged. (This approach is discussed further in Chapter 10.)

In addition, there are other ways of reducing conflict. Methods do exist for minimizing conflict within the existing organizational framework.

A. Insure that Data for Problem-Solving are Generated in Common

Although many organizational problems involve more than one subsystem or group, only one group will develop a solution to the problem. Because the other group may have additional data (thus making the first group look bad), it may reject the solution. For example, in one study of group conflict, there was a high degree of defensiveness between the groups, and numerous efforts to improve the quality of a particular product had been unsuccessful.[12] However, when representatives of the different groups were brought together to study each rejected product lot and to develop *joint* solutions, the quality of the product was improved by more than 60%.

Another study reports on the success of having a task force consisting of representatives from R & D, purchasing, marketing, and production departments meet to integrate the work of the various units and departments as new products moved through the various developmental and manufacturing stages. At each step of the way, the task force met to identify and solve problems.[13]

This illustrates the use by more modern and advanced organizations of "task forces" to solve problems that cut across group and the organization. To be successful, the task force generally has to have representatives from all the groups involved, as well as outside experts.

B. Rotate People Among the Different Groups

This solution is more difficult to accomplish than setting up a task force is, since many groups in social organizations are highly specialized and management does not find it practical to transfer people from one group to another. However, there are many, many groups in which this can, and indeed should, be done. Too often, however, this solution is not even considered or recognized as a possibility.

C. Recognize the Interdependence of the Groups and Establish Methods to Bring Them into Closer Contact

As the old army major said, "What I'm not up on, I'm down on." Frequently, intergroup defensiveness and conflict can be reduced by bringing the groups together for mutual problem-solving meetings or by sending representatives to work with the other group on a temporary basis. One successful technique is to bring the two opposing groups together to share their perceptions of each other, to clear up misunderstandings, and to ensure that each group has a better understanding of the role, purpose, and objectives of the other group. One such meeting can do much to "clear the air" and may be followed by additional meetings to iron out persistent differences between the groups. Blake, Shepherd, and Mouton have shown, in excellent detail, how union-management conflict can be considerably reduced through a more formalized, but highly effective, use of this basic technique.[14] They have the opposing groups write down their perceptions of themselves and of the other group and then discuss these perceptions. (This technique will be discussed more fully in a later chapter on organizational improvement.)

D. Locate a Common Enemy

A recurrent theme in science fiction is an invasion from outer space. In such a situation, the opposing great powers of Earth quickly resolve their differences, pool their technologies, and work together to repel the invader. In the same fashion, groups in conflict can quickly resolve their differences to join forces against a common enemy—a competing company, a governmental agency, or a third group in the organization. For example, a management consultant was sitting in on a meeting at which two managers, each the head of an opposing group, were having a rather heated discussion. When a third manager came in and interrupted them, the two closed ranks against him in a defensive action. After the "intruder" had left, the two managers resumed their conflict. The observer pointed out that only a moment before, they had closed ranks against the intruder. The discussion of why this had happened and its significance marked a real turning point for both managers, and in the next several weeks, cooperation between the two managers and their respective groups improved markedly.

E. Develop a Common Set of Goals and Objectives

In a sense, this is the more positive side of "locating a common enemy." Much of the conflict between groups in any social organization arises because the subsystems have different goals. Currently, most managers are rewarded (pay increases, promotions, etc.) to the extent that they accomplish the goals and objectives of their particular subsystem. This almost automatically breeds conflict, since each subsystem is concerned about making itself look good and is less concerned about working with other subsystems toward common goals and objectives.

Beckhard has developed an approach, called the "organizational confrontation meeting," to encourage organizational subsystems to work toward establishing and striving for common goals.[15] The procedures include the following steps:

1. The two groups agree to work directly on improving their relationships.

2. Each group writes down its perceptions of both itself and the other group.

3. The two groups are then formally brought together, and a representative from each group presents the written perceptions obtained in the previous step. Only the two representatives may speak, since the primary objective is to make certain that the perceptions and attitudes are presented as accurately as possible and to avoid the defensiveness and hostility that might arise if the two groups were permitted to speak directly to each other.

4. The two groups separate, each armed with four sets of documents—two representing their own group's perceptions of itself and the other group, and two representing the other group's perceptions of itself and the other. At this point, a great number of discrepancies, misperceptions, and misunderstandings between the two show up.

5. The task of the group (almost always with the help of a process observer) is to analyze and review the reasons for the discrepancies. In other words, the process observer works hard at getting the group to work at understanding *how* the other group could possibly have arrived at the perceptions it has,

e.g., "What actions on your part may have contributed to that set of perceptions? How did they get that way?" The emphasis is on problem solving rather than on defensiveness.

6. The two groups are again brought together to share both the discrepancies they have identified and their problem-solving analysis of the reasons for the discrepancies. Again, the focus is primarily on the behavior underlying the perceptions. At this point, either the formal representatives may be used or the groups can talk directly to each other.

7. If formal representatives are used, the next step is to allow more open discussion between the two groups, with the goal of reducing misperceptions and increasing intergroup harmony.

A more complete version of this approach is described by Blake *et al.*, who report, for example, excellent results in getting such mutually antagonistic groups as union and management to become more cooperative with each other, thus considerably reducing industrial strife.[16]

VI. SUMMARY

In this chapter, we have been concerned with groups in interaction. Rather than viewing conflict as always undesirable, as did the classical theorists, we have stressed that tension and conflict can be productive when the conflict is not too great. Tension can help to identify problems that need solutions; tension can bring about innovation and change. Of the myriad of possible sources of conflict, we described only five task-related sources: win-lose situations, competition over means utilization, status incongruency, perceptual differences, and conflict because of the need for change.

Conflict does have consequences. We described the ways in which a group in conflict begins to change its behavior and its perceptions, showing that the behavior and perceptions are clearly predictable. We then described the intragroup consequences of winning or losing, showing that there are clearly predictable differences between winning and losing groups. Finally, we made some suggestions for reducing intergroup conflict and competition.

REVIEW

1. Find and describe groups with pooled, sequential, and reciprocal interdependence. How much cooperation and/or conflict do they have?

2. Give illustrations from your personal experience of cases when conflict

was: (a) helpful and (b) harmful to two groups. What made the difference?

3. Find two groups that are reciprocally interdependent. Describe the relationship between them, and give recommendations for improving the effectiveness of both groups. (This might include increasing or decreasing the degree of conflict.)

4. Is conflict necessary to bring about change? Discuss.

5. Describe some situations in which you have seen conflict between two groups reduced. How was it handled? Could you suggest a better approach?

6. Some people feel that conflict is always wrong. Discuss.

7. Assume that you have just watched (or participated in) a sports event in which there was a decisive victory. What are the group characteristics of the: (a) winning and (b) losing teams?

REFERENCES

1. R. Likert, *The Human Organization: Its Management and Value,* New York: McGraw-Hill, 1967.

2. J. Thompson, *Organizations in Action,* New York: McGraw-Hill, 1967.

3. J. Litterer, "Conflict in Organizations: A Re-Examination," in H. Tosi and W. Hamner eds., *Organizational Behavior and Management: A Contingency Approach,* Chicago: St. Clair Press, 1974, pp. 320–328.

4. *Ibid.,* pp. 322–324.

5. *Ibid.,* p. 323.

6. W. Whyte, *Human Relations in the Restaurant Industry,* New York: Harper & Brothers, 1948.

7. Thompson, *op. cit.*

8. S. Robbins, *Managing Organizational Conflict: A Nontraditional Approach,* Englewood Cliffs, N.J.: Prentice-Hall, 1974.

9. P. Binxen and J. Daughen, *Wreck of the Penn Central,* Boston: Little, Brown, 1971.

10. Robbins, *op. cit.,* p. 16.

11. E. Schein, *Organizational Psychology,* 2d ed., Englewood Cliffs, N.J.: Prentice-Hall, 1972, p, 97.

12. E. Huse, "The Behavioral Scientist in the Shop," *Personnel* **42,** 3 (May–June 1965): 50–57.

13. E. Huse, and M. Beer, "Eclectic Approach to Organizational Development," *Harvard Business Review* **49,** 5 (Sept.–Oct. 1971): 103–112.

14. R. Blake, H. Shepard, and J. Mouton, *Managing Intergroup Conflict in Industry,* Houston: Gulf, 1964.

15. R. Beckhard, *Organization Development: Strategies and Models,* Reading, Mass.: Addison-Wesley, 1969.

16. Blake *et al., op. cit.*

7

INFLUENCE, POWER, AND LEADERSHIP

Power tends to corrupt
And absolute power corrupts absolutely.

LORD ACTON

LEARNING
OBJECTIVES

When you have finished reading and studying this chapter, you should be able to:

1. Identify at least four or five different types of power one person exerts over another in organizational situations.

2. Name and then compare and contrast various leadership theories.

3. Define the phenomenon of leadership in terms of process, influence, activities, people, goal achievement, and the situation.

4. Identify the major theorists in the field.

5. Specify the major leadership styles and the several organizational situations calling for leadership; match styles to situations.

You will be expected to define and use the following concepts:

Legitimate power	Interpersonal consideration
Expert power	Theory X
Referent power	Theory Y
Coercive power	Likert's "systems"
Reward power	Contingency theory
"Initiating structure"	Path-goal

THOUGHT STARTERS

1. What differences are there between a "leader" and a "manager"?
2. Describe a situation in which you made leadership attempts to influence others. To what extent were you successful? What type of "power" did you try to use? Why?
3. What kinds of attempts by others to influence you have been most successful? Least successful? What role does the situation play in determining the kind of attempt made?

I. INTRODUCTION

If the chairman of the board of a major oil company in the United States persuades the President of the United States that a certain governmental policy toward Middle Eastern nations is desired by oil interests, and if the President agrees to implement it, is this power or influence? In this chapter, we discuss the nature of influence, the bases, or sources, of power, and the types of leadership styles. Additionally, we examine research that specifies the conditions under which one particular leadership style is more effective than another.

If we were not using the systems approach, we would not need to separate the concepts of influence, power, and leadership from that of management. Influence, power, and leadership may be derived from many sources inside and/or outside the formal or informal organization. The systems approach enables us to examine all three concepts as systems variables and to determine their origin and proper place in the organization. For example, Ralph Nader's book *Unsafe at Any Speed*, which describes certain defects in the Corvair, is an example of an outside influence that helped bring about the demise of this car.[1] Here, Ralph Nader was an outside "input" to the General Motors "system."

II. INFLUENCE AND POWER

Power can be studied in terms of its systemic effects on leadership. Indeed, power is the only thing leaders have. In their thought-provoking monograph, French and Raven identify five different bases of power and influence. One person can influence another, using legitimate power, expert power, reference power, reward power, and coercive power.[2] Only legitimate power is positional; the other types depend on the individual rather than on the position.

A. Legitimate power   Legitimate, or position, power derives from either the culture or the organization, but only if the organization is accepted as legitimate. This is especially true in organizations having a hierarchy of authority. Those at lower levels in the hierarchy accept the power and influence of those higher in the organization. For example, a judge has the "right" to levy fines; the Congress has the "right" to pass laws; the president of an organization has the "right" to make certain management decisions. In a formal organization, legitimate power is exerted primarily on positions or "offices" rather than on individuals.

However, legitimate power depends on the individual's acceptance of the organization or culture and the person exerting the influence. For example, during Prohibition there was widespread violation of the laws because people did not accept the laws as legitimate. Today, many people disregard the laws

A conductor has legitimate power. (H. Armstrong Roberts/E. P. Jones)

about the use of drugs, for similar reasons. The result of widespread rejection of "legitimate power" is a severe reduction in the power potential of the authority figure.

B. Expert power Expert power, based on the authority of knowledge, is particularly important in the flow process. Physicians and lawyers, for example, have a great deal of expert power. Within an organization, people with expert power can wield a great deal of influence; in a meeting with peers and those higher in the hierarchy, the computer expert may in fact have the greatest amount of power simply because he or she is the only one with detailed knowledge of the computer's operation and potential. Similarly, expert knowledge gives the market research analyst a great deal of influence in determining the future direction of the organization.

C. Referent power Referent power, which can be described as the power of "identification," or "charismatic" power, is based on the attractiveness of a particular person or group to others. Mahatma Ghandi and Martin Luther King had little legitimate power, but to their many followers they did have a high degree of referent power. Any currently popular musical group may, at

A doctor has expert power. (H. Armstrong Roberts/E. P. Jones)

any given moment, exercise a tremendous amount of referent power over many people in this country. Similarly one person may be able to exercise much more influence than someone else in a business enterprise simply because people want to believe in that person and his or her ideas.

There appear to be two major ways in which a person obtains referent power. One is to effectively develop and use an issue about which many people feel very strongly. In the early presidential primaries in 1976, for example, most of the candidates went about slamming "big government in Washington" in order to develop that issue. The other way is to be a popular folk hero, usually in sports or entertainment. Think of how many athletes, astronauts, and movie stars advertise various products. Clearly, many marketing people believe that a celebrity's endorsement is more effective than that of a "nobody."

D. Reward power This type of power is based on the leader's ability to reward a follower. In some situations reward power may be closely linked to referent power. In an industrial organization, reward power is closely linked

To those who believe that the future can be foretold, this man holds referent power.
(Harold M. Lambert/E. P. Jones)

to the manager's legitimate power in awarding pay increases or promotions. In a peer group it may be the leader's power to admit a new member. The nature of work-flow relationships is such that an individual manager may have a great deal of reward power simply by his or her place in the work flow. Thus, a purchasing agent can "reward" a cooperative manager by expediting his orders, or a maintenance manager may "reward" another manager by giving her requests higher priority.

E. Coercive power   Coercive power, the opposite of reward power, is the power to punish, whether by firing an employee for insubordination or arresting someone for violating a law. Yet coercive power is not necessarily absolute —the individual may choose to quit or enter a new profession or appeal the case to a higher court.

These five types of power are interrelated and indeed may rest with the same person. Since this interrelationship does exist, the use (or misuse) of one kind of power affects the exercise of the other types of power. For example, a manager who uses coercive power may therefore have less referent power. Conversely, the extensive use of reward power will, over time, increase a manager's referent power.

In other words, each type of power has "costs" associated with it. Certainly a leader who uses power inappropriately will soon exhaust any reserves of power. Thus President Ford's pardon of Richard Nixon lessened his referent power for many people, but increased it for others. Similarly, people may question the judgment of a movie star who pushes a questionable product, thereby reducing that person's referent power. Or, a prison head who uses coercive power inappropriately in a democratic society may be forced from office by public pressure. Thus power begets power if it is *perceived* to be used appropriately. If not, the person's supply of power diminishes.

III. LEADERSHIP

In this section we briefly describe personality-attribute studies of leadership, behavioral theories, some of the newer contingency theories, and path-goal theories. In each category there has been recent organizational research. No one approach seems to exclude the others, although in recent times relatively more research interest has focused on the contingency and path-goal theories.

Historical studies have noted that most great leaders appear to have certain physical differences from the rest of the population. In addition to greater intelligence, leaders have been taller, braver, slightly heavier, and "better looking" than others. Although leaders do not meet all of these criteria, e.g., Napoleon was quite short, the theory nonetheless appears to have some validity in some situations.

It is clear that leadership in various situations call for various talents. Although it is probably unimportant for a university president to be taller and brighter than his or her faculty, it may be more important for an army general to be taller and brighter than his subordinate officers. Furthermore, the mix of skills and traits demanded for a corporation president is certainly different from that for a foreman, yet each is a leader within his or her own milieu.[3]

One major problem with most of the leadership and trait studies is that measurement techniques may not be adequate to truly discriminate between relevant and irrelevant traits and factors. Even carefully defined words and phrases have multiple meanings to people; thus questionnaire research (one of the major research methodologies for trait studies) may not be very accurate.

Finally, the contingency studies have demonstrated that leadership is a complex process. Adding to the confusion is the fact that two persons can be effective leaders in the same role even though their personal styles and the traits they bring to the situation differ.

A. Personality-Attribute Theories

Perhaps the oldest attempts to distinguish effective from ineffective leaders are those that label the personality attributes of successful leaders. Some of the research in this area is nothing more than armchair theorizing, but more recent research has become fairly sophisticated in its methodological approach. Generally, one of the outputs of such research is a list of traits or personality attributes characteristic of effective and ineffective leaders. One recent study found that the most frequently mentioned attributes of an effective leader are "intelligent," "fair," "understanding," "knowledgeable in general," "knowledgeable about the particular job," "perceptive," "having high integrity," being a "leader" and being a "delegator." The traits most frequently attributed to an ineffective leader are "indecisive," "poor communicator," "using poor decision-making process," "lacking in leadership," "uncommunicative," "self-centered," "unaggressive," and being a "nondelegator."[4]

Another study derives personality scores from psychological tests of leaders. The results suggest a smaller, slightly different set of characteristics found more often in leaders than in others.[5]

Yet another study, using two well-known personality inventories in conjunction with the Ohio State University Leadership Opinion Questionnaire (LOQ), found that managerial effectiveness was not related to personality characteristics as derived from the personality inventories. Moreover, managerial effectiveness was not related to subordinate-report results on the LOQ on any combination of leader-initiating structure or on leader consideration, the two reported dimensions of the LOQ.[6]

Thus the research on leadership traits leaves us with the feeling that although much has been accomplished, this area is still a fruitful one for further research. Although personality-attribute research is generally out of vogue at the present time, traits should be included in a composite picture of leadership, for leadership is not simply a function of the situation.

B. Behavioral-Pattern Theories

The behavioral-leadership theories originated with two classic studies that demonstrated the value of participation in decision making.[7] These initial studies provided the impetus for a large number of studies at the University of Michigan and Ohio State University, as well as for several major leadership theories.

Kahn and Katz provide a comprehensive review of an important group of studies conducted at the University of Michigan.[8] One of the key findings of these surveys of a large insurance company, a tractor factory, and section gangs on a railroad was that supervisors of sections with good production records appeared to emphasize the interpersonal functions of their leadership role, i.e., they were employee-oriented. Supervisors of low-producing sections, by contrast, tended to spend more time on their actual task or on the paper-work portion of the job, i.e., they were more production-oriented.

Another dimension that appeared to be related to productivity was closeness of supervision. In all three Michigan studies, *general* supervision was found to be more clearly related to high productivity than was *close* supervision. (A later series of studies, however, indicated that general supervision is effective primarily when the supervisor has a fair amount of influence with his or her own boss.) Since close supervision is likely to go hand in hand with the use of coercive power, it is no surprise that supervisors of low-producing sections of railroad gangs tended to use coercive power, whereas foremen of high-producing sections in the tractor factory appeared to take a great deal of interest in their workers and to use reward rather than coercive power.

Similar studies were conducted at Ohio State University. Fleishman, Harris, and Burtt, who conducted the primary study, developed a "leadership description questionnaire" which was then factor-analyzed (a statistical method for categorizing the individual responses).[9] The factor analysis resulted in two major categories: (1) initiating structure, that is, the degree of structure the supervisor initiated in performing the leadership role, and (2) interpersonal effectiveness. The researchers used grievance rate as a criterion for measuring the supervisor's interpersonal consideration. They found that increasing consideration was highly correlated with a lower grievance rate. Similarly, the higher the initiating structure, the higher the grievance rate.

In a later study, Fleishman and Harris found that the grievance rate was lowest when there was both high structure and high consideration; when low consideration was coupled with low structure, the grievance rate was high.[10] With medium consideration, a high grievance rate was found in conjunction with high structure, and a low grievance rate was found with low structure. Turnover rate showed the same trend.

The initial series of Ohio State University studies was the basis for several questionnaires designed to measure leader behavior. The Leadership Opinion Questionnaire (LOQ) was designed to be completed by the leader; the Supervisory Behavior Description Questionnaire (SBDQ), by the subordinate or follower. Both questionnaires measure initiating structure and consideration. As measured by the SBDQ, initiating structure and consideration remained stable over 20 years in one study, and recent results in West Germany were similar to those in the United States in the mid-1950s. With the concern that questionnaires be restudied from time to time to make sure that they still measure what was originally intended, it is remarkable that this particular questionnaire remained stable over so long a time and across cultures.[11]

In comparing the Michigan and Ohio studies, one might conclude that general supervision is beneficial and that initiating structure is dysfunctional. Furthermore, recent reviews of the research in this area have had the effect of improving research designs and methodologies. Consequently, current work in this area meets rigorous behavioral research standards.[12]

One recent paper suggests a contingency theory of leadership based on the two dimensions of initiating structure and consideration. Some of the suggested contingency factors on which a particular style of leadership should depend for effectiveness are: subordinates' need for information, job level, subordinates' expectations of the leader's behavior, task characteristics, and the leader's influence.[13] The important thing about the contingency approach is the fact that no one leadership style is universally appropriate; rather, leadership style must depend on the situation.

Using production techniques as the contingency factor, Woodward classified 100 firms in England according to their production techniques.[14] She was able to distinguish three different types of production: (1) unit, or one-of-a-kind production (special-purpose electronics equipment or custom-tailored suits); (2) large batch-and-mass production (standard gasoline engines); and (3) continuous-process production (chemical production or gasoline refining).

The manufacture of peanut butter exemplifies continuous-process production. (The Christian Science Monitor)

She found that in continuous-process production, there are: (1) more levels of authority than in mass production and even more than in unit production, (2) a smaller span of control and hence closer supervision, and (3) companies that did not conform to the particular organizational structure appropriate to their technologies tended not to survive.

With these findings in mind, we should now reexamine the Michigan and Ohio State studies, which involved either unit or mass-production techniques. When Fleishman and Peters collected similar data on a detergent factory, a continuous-production industry, they could find no relationship between the leaders' attitudes and effectiveness, and no combination of initiating structure and consideration was predictive of management effectiveness.[15]

These findings, together with the Woodward conclusions, suggest that general supervision is not appropriate in continuous-process production. In more recent research, Lawrence and Lorsch placed successful and unsuccessful organizations on a continuum ranging from highly stable environments (e.g., the container industry) to highly unstable, changing environments (e.g., the plastics industry) and found that the type, nature, and span of successful supervision must vary with the organization and its environment.[16] (This research is discussed more fully in Chapter 10.)

One of the factors affecting organizational environment is the subordinate's perceptions of the supervisor's leadership style. Graen et al. studied "initiating structure" and "consideration" in a large organization in a basic industry by asking 600 managers and supervisors (ranging from first-line supervisors to the president and his immediate staff) to complete a lengthy questionnaire.[17] The researchers found that the leader's "structuring" behavior greatly influenced the relationship between his "consideration" behavior and the performance of his subordinates. This was caused in large part by the subordinates' perceptions of the leader's evaluation of them and by the amount and degree of feedback they received. Subordinates' understanding of their bosses' evaluations was much more accurate if the leader was at either end of the "structuring" continuum than if he had an intermediate position. In other words, the more consistent (either high or low) the leader was in performing his *bureaucratic* role of structuring, the more accurately the subordinate could describe his boss's behavior in his *interpersonal* role of consideration. The researchers conclude that leadership style is important in organizations, but that the difference "may not be so much in terms of what the leader does but may be in terms of how it is *interpreted* by his members."

These landmark studies have stressed the importance of a leader's effectiveness by the type of industry she or he is in, as well as by personal style of leadership.[18] In other words, these studies form the basis for a contingency theory of leadership and organizational design; one cannot be studied without taking into account the other, a failing in most of the early studies on leadership behavior.

Leadership can also be analyzed according to the amount of participative decision making the leader encourages in subordinates. An indirect outgrowth of the pajama factory study, which found that worker participation in decision making is effective in terms of productivity, was increased interest in the study of shared leadership. One theorist has made a typology of the various points of intervention (in goal setting, decision making, problem solving, and organizational change) for participative activities.[19]

The effects of various types of participation have not yet been clearly delineated. One of these effects is an increase in performance effectiveness, resulting from a greater volume of information. This effect usually manifests itself in the improved quality of the output, however "quality" is measured. Other effects are increased effectiveness arising from the increased commitments of the participants or from their increased learning.

In addition, the different methods of participation have not been well catalogued (individual, group, two-person, etc.), even though each method meets different needs and in general operates differently. Similarly, the situational factors relating to when various approaches are appropriate have been ignored. Clearly, the method of participation should be determined in part by the goal that is sought, and to date it has not been.

There have been many recent studies of participation. Some have been laboratory studies; others have dealt with industrial and nonprofit organizations. An appreciable amount of the research has been either cross-cultural or completed abroad.

In a recent laboratory study using college students, three-person groups helped develop and decide on attitude statements to be used in a campus survey of student attitudes. The researchers found that subjects felt they had more influence and satisfaction with the task when they had full participation.[20]

Among studies of participation in an industrial setting, participation in Yugoslavia was highly related to worker motivation, involvement, and identification.[21] In New Zealand, a study of manufacturing organizations found that job satisfaction and positive feelings toward supervisors were related to participation.[22]

The effectiveness of participation has clearly changed over time. For example, the original Coch and French Harwood Pajama Factory study was partially replicated in Norway in the middle 1950s and the participative approach failed.[23] In the late 1960s, however, many Norwegian organizations were successfully using participation, including autonomous work groups.

In Great Britain, in a study of national park workers, participation was strongly valued because of the influence it brought. In this case participation was by action-planning groups of from 6 to 14 persons. These action-planning groups met informally on a monthly basis and generally dealt with issues of information and problems on a local level. For participation in policy formation, many persons desired interaction through union stewards or works council members. For intermediate-level policy formation, the workers wanted personal contact with the relevant middle managers.[24]

Studies published recently in the United States and Canada appear to have been focused more on nonprofit organizations such as hospitals and prisons than on profit-making industrial organizations. One reason for this could be that the industrial executives surveyed in one study felt that participation in decision making reduced "management prerogatives," an undesirable occurrence. This study generally confirmed an earlier study cited in the *Harvard Business Review*.[25]

Of the studies done in hospitals and prisons, participative decision making appeared to have major benefits. In one hospital study, employees' attitudes improved, absences declined, and productivity rose.[26] In a study conducted in a psychiatric unit of a general hospital, lack of participation had little effect on attitudes except that respondents wished to have more influence. Those surveyed were health-care workers, but were not physicians (nurses, psychologists, etc.). Apparently, data were not available from physicians, who were the team leaders, an interesting finding in itself. In a study of 13 health departments, it was found that high participativeness resulted in high effectiveness. This sample did include physicians and dentists, as well as all others in the organization, including janitors and file clerks.[27]

Except for a few publicized instances, participative management has not made the large inroads in the United States that it has in some other countries. For example, in some countries, e.g., West Germany, Sweden, and Norway, the law requires that a few workers belong to the boards of directors of companies over a certain size. Particularly in the Scandanavian countries, autonomous work groups are highly popular. The autonomous group does not have supervision in the authoritarian sense used in the United States. Rather, the group is asked to make many of its own decisions, and the supervisor acts as more of a resource person than as a more direct leader. Contrary to the pattern in the United States, both the unions and top management appear to be stressing "industrial democracy" for its own sake, whether or not the participation results in either increased productivity or satisfaction, although there is evidence that the autonomous work groups are more productive and have higher satisfaction. One attempt to implement such a program in the United States was successful in the initial stages. However, the program was implemented in one division of a large company and eventually failed because corporate management was unable to determine an "appropriate" pay plan, although the program itself was supported by both the local union and local management.

C. One-Best-Way Theories

Certain researchers and theorists have been instrumental in shaping the currently popular theories about supervision and effective leadership styles. Although each of these theorists stresses somewhat different variables, their combined influence is at the root of the current theories and concepts of managerial behavior and organization development and improvement.

1. Douglas McGregor One of the most influential behavioral scientists is Douglas McGregor, who classifies managers according to two basic leadership styles: (1) an authoritarian style, which he calls "Theory X," and (2) a more egalitarian style, which he calls "Theory Y."[28]

According to McGregor, the Theory X style of management, which originated in the Roman Catholic Church and military institutions, is based on the coercive and economic models of human motivation. The typical Theory X manager believes that people are inherently lazy, dislike work, and will therefore avoid work whenever possible. As a result, the Theory X leader must use strong measures to control the behavior of subordinates to ensure that they work toward organizational goals. Subordinates are controlled through the use of coercion and the threat of punishment should they not put forth adequate effort. The use of these external controls is necessitated by the "fact" that most human beings are incapable of self-direction and control; they prefer to respond to direct orders rather than to accept responsibility for their own actions. Implicit in this assumption, of course, is the notion that there are two basic classes of people—those who want to lead and to take responsibility (the manager or leader) and those who want to be directed and who will duck responsibility whenever possible. According to Theory X, the manager's watchword is "you gotta watch 'em all the time."

The assumptions of a Theory Y leader, by contrast, are based on Maslow's concept of self-actualization, i.e., work can be enjoyable, and people will work hard and assume responsibility if they have the opportunity to satisfy their personal needs while at the same time achieving organizational goals. Thus there is no sharp division between elites (leaders) and the masses (followers). Rather, the Theory X leader underutilizes subordinates; they have a great deal more ability and potential for imagination and creativity than he or she gives them credit for. Given the proper conditions, individuals really do want to do a good job and will work hard to do so; their performance will be based on internal rather than external controls.

In his discussion of these two contrasting theories of management, McGregor points out that assumptions about human nature and behavior color and influence every managerial decision or action; the leader will act and behave according to his or her own assumptions and beliefs. He stresses that many managers really do assume that people are inherently lazy and must be coerced in order to work. But these Theory X assumptions are outdated, he declares. Today, Western peoples live in democratic societies with a rising standard of living and an increasing level of education. In fact, by basing their motivational techniques on outdated methods based on false assumptions, Theory X organizations are not motivating their employees toward fulfillment of either organizational or their individual goals. (It should be noted, however, that these assumptions are not necessarily valid for non-Western cultures.)

Managers who believe in Theory Y assumptions about people, on the other hand, structure the work situation so that subordinates can assume self-control and responsibility for the outcome of their efforts, thus helping them to satisfy their needs for relatedness (affiliation) and growth (esteem and self-actualization). The goal of the Theory Y approach is to make the work inherently satisfying to the employee. This means that the manager must work toward fostering an environment conducive to the growth of both the organization and the subordinates. Otherwise, people will look elsewhere for satisfaction, e.g., sabotage or other acts harmful to the organization.[29]

Although McGregor's suggestion was highly thought-provoking, his original conception was overly simplistic, i.e., the one best way approach and the good guys versus the bad guys. McGregor was an original thinker whose ideas were powerful in shaping later thinking and research. His name and the concepts of Theory X and Theory Y are so widely quoted that many assume that the reader has a working knowledge of his ideas.

2. Rensis Likert Likert's approach to the problem of leadership differs somewhat from McGregor's, although the two theories do overlap. Likert feels that managing the human component of the organization is the manager's most important task, because everything else depends on how well this task is accomplished.[30]

Unlike McGregor, Likert focuses on the group and organization within which the manager works. Likert organizes organizational styles into four systems, ranging from a purely exploitative, authoritarian, hierarchical approach (System 1), to one that is less exploitative but still authoritarian (System 2), to a more consultative approach (System 3), to a participative approach (System 4). (Likert's use of the word "system" refers to a category, or type of approach, rather than to the overall structure of an organization, as the term is used in this book.)

Likert has developed a scale, or set of questions, to measure the position of an organization or organizational component on the continuum between the exploitative (authoritation) and the fully participative approaches. Figure 7.1 shows some of the items Likert uses to determine an organization's position on the continuum. This short excerpt from Likert's questionnaire identifies some of the differences among his four systems.

The System 1 manager has little confidence or trust in subordinates. Most of the organizational decisions and goals are determined at the top and are then transmitted directly down the chain of command. Fear, threats, and other types of coercive power are used to force subordinates to work. Since the control process is rigid and authoritarian, subordinates can influence methods and goals only through the informal system, which frequently acts to oppose the goals and aims of the formal organization. There is no cooperative teamwork except on a very informal and *sub rosa* level.

At the other end of the continuum, management has almost complete trust and confidence in subordinates. Decision-making activity is widely dispersed throughout the organization, although mechanisms exist to ensure that decisions are well integrated. Information and communication flow occur freely both vertically and horizontally. Workers are motivated by their opportunity to become involved and participate in setting goals, improving methods, and evaluating their own progress toward established goals. There is a great deal of interaction between subordinates and supervisors, with a high degree of mutual confidence and trust. Responsibility for the control process is not centralized, but is widespread, with the lower units of the organization fully involved. This means that the formal and informal segments of the organization are often identical, and all of the social forces within the organization support the efforts to achieve the goals of the organization.

Likert has used this questionnaire to study a number of different organizations. His basic findings show that management systems leaning toward System 4 are more productive (higher output, less waste, and better labor relations), have lower costs, and have more favorable attitudes toward supervision and the organization than do organizations leaning toward System 1. Likert asserts that the overall consistency of his findings indicates that System 4 has widespread applicability and although its application in different organizations may vary, the basic principles of System 4 management can be applied to all types of situations.

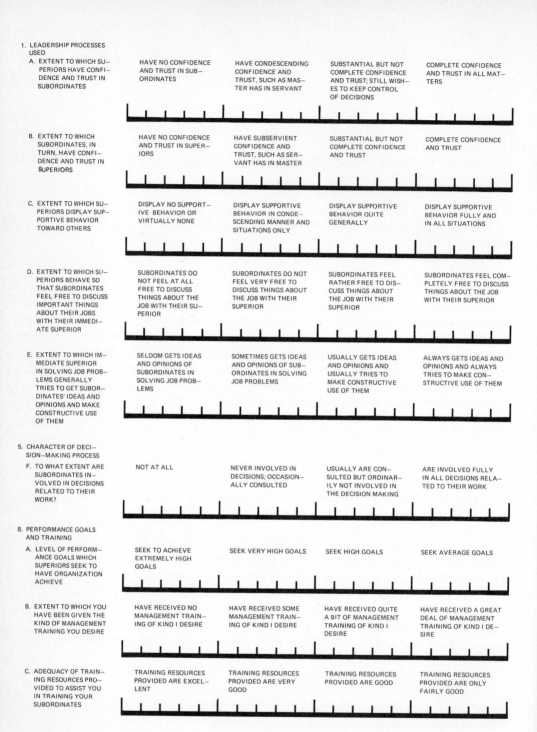

1. LEADERSHIP PROCESSES USED

A. EXTENT TO WHICH SUPERIORS HAVE CONFIDENCE AND TRUST IN SUBORDINATES

HAVE NO CONFIDENCE AND TRUST IN SUBORDINATES | HAVE CONDESCENDING CONFIDENCE AND TRUST, SUCH AS MASTER HAS IN SERVANT | SUBSTANTIAL BUT NOT COMPLETE CONFIDENCE AND TRUST; STILL WISHES TO KEEP CONTROL OF DECISIONS | COMPLETE CONFIDENCE AND TRUST IN ALL MATTERS

B. EXTENT TO WHICH SUBORDINATES, IN TURN, HAVE CONFIDENCE AND TRUST IN SUPERIORS

HAVE NO CONFIDENCE AND TRUST IN SUPERIORS | HAVE SUBSERVIENT CONFIDENCE AND TRUST, SUCH AS SERVANT HAS IN MASTER | SUBSTANTIAL BUT NOT COMPLETE CONFIDENCE AND TRUST | COMPLETE CONFIDENCE AND TRUST

C. EXTENT TO WHICH SUPERIORS DISPLAY SUPPORTIVE BEHAVIOR TOWARD OTHERS

DISPLAY NO SUPPORTIVE BEHAVIOR OR VIRTUALLY NONE | DISPLAY SUPPORTIVE BEHAVIOR IN CONDESCENDING MANNER AND SITUATIONS ONLY | DISPLAY SUPPORTIVE BEHAVIOR QUITE GENERALLY | DISPLAY SUPPORTIVE BEHAVIOR FULLY AND IN ALL SITUATIONS

D. EXTENT TO WHICH SUPERIORS BEHAVE SO THAT SUBORDINATES FEEL FREE TO DISCUSS IMPORTANT THINGS ABOUT THEIR JOBS WITH THEIR IMMEDIATE SUPERIOR

SUBORDINATES DO NOT FEEL AT ALL FREE TO DISCUSS THINGS ABOUT THE JOB WITH THEIR SUPERIOR | SUBORDINATES DO NOT FEEL VERY FREE TO DISCUSS THINGS ABOUT THE JOB WITH THEIR SUPERIOR | SUBORDINATES FEEL RATHER FREE TO DISCUSS THINGS ABOUT THE JOB WITH THEIR SUPERIOR | SUBORDINATES FEEL COMPLETELY FREE TO DISCUSS THINGS ABOUT THE JOB WITH THEIR SUPERIOR

E. EXTENT TO WHICH IMMEDIATE SUPERIOR IN SOLVING JOB PROBLEMS GENERALLY TRIES TO GET SUBORDINATES' IDEAS AND OPINIONS AND MAKE CONSTRUCTIVE USE OF THEM

SELDOM GETS IDEAS AND OPINIONS OF SUBORDINATES IN SOLVING JOB PROBLEMS | SOMETIMES GETS IDEAS AND OPINIONS OF SUBORDINATES IN SOLVING JOB PROBLEMS | USUALLY GETS IDEAS AND OPINIONS AND USUALLY TRIES TO MAKE CONSTRUCTIVE USE OF THEM | ALWAYS GETS IDEAS AND OPINIONS AND ALWAYS TRIES TO MAKE CONSTRUCTIVE USE OF THEM

5. CHARACTER OF DECISION-MAKING PROCESS

F. TO WHAT EXTENT ARE SUBORDINATES INVOLVED IN DECISIONS RELATED TO THEIR WORK?

NOT AT ALL | NEVER INVOLVED IN DECISIONS; OCCASIONALLY CONSULTED | USUALLY ARE CONSULTED BUT ORDINARILY NOT INVOLVED IN THE DECISION MAKING | ARE INVOLVED FULLY IN ALL DECISIONS RELATED TO THEIR WORK

8. PERFORMANCE GOALS AND TRAINING

A. LEVEL OF PERFORMANCE GOALS WHICH SUPERIORS SEEK TO HAVE ORGANIZATION ACHIEVE

SEEK TO ACHIEVE EXTREMELY HIGH GOALS | SEEK VERY HIGH GOALS | SEEK HIGH GOALS | SEEK AVERAGE GOALS

B. EXTENT TO WHICH YOU HAVE BEEN GIVEN THE KIND OF MANAGEMENT TRAINING YOU DESIRE

HAVE RECEIVED NO MANAGEMENT TRAINING OF KIND I DESIRE | HAVE RECEIVED SOME MANAGEMENT TRAINING OF KIND I DESIRE | HAVE RECEIVED QUITE A BIT OF MANAGEMENT TRAINING OF KIND I DESIRE | HAVE RECEIVED A GREAT DEAL OF MANAGEMENT TRAINING OF KIND I DESIRE

C. ADEQUACY OF TRAINING RESOURCES PROVIDED TO ASSIST YOU IN TRAINING YOUR SUBORDINATES

TRAINING RESOURCES PROVIDED ARE EXCELLENT | TRAINING RESOURCES PROVIDED ARE VERY GOOD | TRAINING RESOURCES PROVIDED ARE GOOD | TRAINING RESOURCES PROVIDED ARE ONLY FAIRLY GOOD

Fig. 7.1 Items added to the profile of organizational and performance characteristics. (From *Human Organization* by R. Likert, pp. 120–121. Copyright © 1967 by McGraw-Hill. Used with permission of McGraw-Hill Book Company.)

One of the most useful aspects of Likert's analysis is his stress on management systems. He argues that if a company or other organization wants to apply the results of organizational research, it must shift from one coordinated system to another. Thus if it

wishes to shift its operations from System 1 to System 2 to System 3 or 4, it should plan to modify all of its operating procedures: leadership, decision-making, communications, coordination, evaluation, supervision, compensation, organizational structure, motivation, etc. . . . . A well-integrated system of management should emerge.[31]

However, as we shall see in the chapters on organizational improvement, Likert's statements that System 4 is the best approach in *all* parts of *all* organizations need to be modified.

In a cross-cultural attempt to test Likert's System 4 theory in Brazilian development banks, two researchers found that the Likert organizational profile was not related to objective measures of success such as number of loans made and ratio of loans to total assets, but that it was positively related to employee satisfaction. The researchers concluded that the profile is a useful diagnostic device, but that in this foreign cultural situation, the theory of management systems was supported only partially.[32]

3. Robert Blake and Jane Mouton   These two authors have developed a concept of leadership best described as "the managerial grid," which states that there are several universal characteristics of organizations: (1) purpose—all organizations have some sense of purpose, or goal; (2) people—all social organizations have people who are involved with accomplishing the purpose of the organization; and (3) hierarchy—all organizations have bosses and followers.[33] They also describe the ways in which these universals are interconnected: first, the amount of concern for production; second, the concern for people; third, a manager's set of assumptions in using the hierarchy to achieve production. In other words, different managers have different attitudes about using their hierarchical position.

As shown in Fig. 7.2, the two basic dimensions of leadership are the extent and degree of the manager's concern about (1) people and (2) production. The first dimension, roughly comparable to "consideration" as described earlier in this chapter, is shown on the vertical axis of the diagram. The manager's concern with production, i.e., of getting things done through the subordinates, is roughly comparable to "initiating structure."

Figure 7.2 also shows that concern for both people (vertical axis) and production (horizontal axis) can range from very low (1) to very high (9). It is therefore possible for a manager to have a high degree of concern for produc-

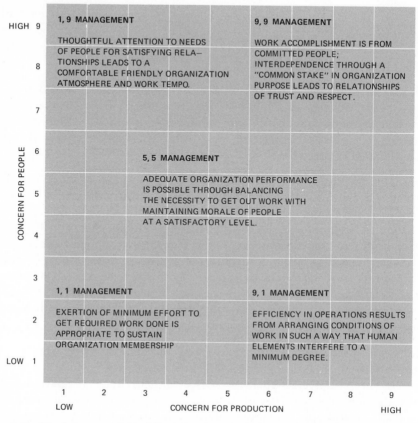

Fig. 7.2 The Managerial Grid.® (Robert R. Blake and Jane S. Mouton, *The Managerial Grid*, Houston: Gulf, 1964, p. 10. Reproduced with permission.)

tion while showing little or no concern for people. Or, a manager may exhibit very little concern for either people or production (1,1). As Blake and Mouton point out, it hardly seems possible that a manager could disregard both dimensions, but some actually do—although they are a part of the business, they do not really function within it.

According to Blake and Mouton, the most desirable is the 9,9 manager, who exhibits a concurrent high concern for both people and production. As does Likert, however, they stress that this 9,9 approach to management cannot be attained without the systematic development and improvement of the entire organization.

Such systematic development generally occurs in six phases.

Phase 1 of the six-phase approach involves studying the managerial grid as a theoretical framework for understanding behavior dynamics of the corporation's culture. In Phase 2, the behavior dynamics of actual organization teamwork is studied and tested in settings of actual work against the Grid model for the perfection of problem-solving methods. The same kind of application is made in Phase 3, but to the interworkings between organized units of the company where cooperation and coordination is vital to success. The top team in Phase 4 engages in a study of the properties of an Ideal Strategic Corporate Model necessary to bring corporate profitability logic to a maximum-thrust condition. Phase 5 involves implementation tactics for converting the corporation from what it has been to what it will become under the Ideal Strategic Corporate Model. Phase 6 measures changes in conditions from pre-Phase 1 to post-Phase 5 for the evaluation and stabilization of achievement and for the setting of new goals and objectives of accomplishment for the future.[34]

In short, although the authors point to the 9,9 manager as the epitome of management style, they also stress that the manager is working within a total system and that the system itself must be changed before the 9,9 style of management can be fully utilized.

Although the managerial grid is one of the most popular approaches to leadership and grid training is worldwide, there seems to be little independent research evidence that this approach, as a "one best way," is effective.

D. Contingency Theories

The major leadership-style theorist to develop a "contingency" ("it depends") theory is Fred E. Fiedler. In marked contrast to the "one best approach to management" stressed by McGregor, Likert, and Blake and Mouton, Fiedler asserts that appropriate management styles depends on the subordinates, the set of conditions in which the manager operates, and the particular situation. Fiedler views management primarily in terms of leadership, which he defines as "a personal relationship in which one person directs, coordinates and supervises others in the performance of a common task."[35]

According to Fiedler, management comprises not only leadership, but also responsibility for results. In brief, a manager can lead in either of two ways: (1) by being highly directive and telling people exactly what to do and how to it, or (2) by involving the group in the planning and execution of the task, thereby sharing the leadership responsibilities. Since these two styles are opposite ends of a continuum, intermediate styles of leadership are also possible. However, the most appropriate style of leadership can be determined only by the circumstances.

Since the most appropriate leadership style varies with the circumstances, the manager must either adapt his or her leadership style to the situation or make the job compatible with that leadership style. Fiedler notes that it is easier to change the situation than leadership style and that part of the job of upper management might be to transfer a particular lower-level manager to a job that better fits his or her individual style.

Fiedler has developed a questionnaire (consisting of a set of adjectives an individual can use to describe one's least preferred co-worker) in order to determine a manager's leadership style. Fiedler's studies have shown that the individual who describes his or her least-preferred co-worker (LPC) in relatively favorable ways tends to be considerate, permissive, and oriented toward human relations; one who describes the LPC in more unfavorable ways (thereby getting a low LPC score) tends to be task-centered, manages closely, and is less concerned with human relations.

In his studies of surveying parties, military combat crews, steel companies, basketball teams, and members of boards of directors, Fiedler found that he could identify three variables that affect the favorability of a situation for the leader.

1. *Leader-member relations*—the degree and extent to which the leader and the members of the group like and trust one another. This conforms to our definition of a charismatic leader; it seems clear that a leader who is trusted and well liked does not have to have a superior rank in order to get the task accomplished.

2. *Task structure*—the way the task is defined. The task can be either spelled out very explicitly so that it can be done "by the numbers" or left rather vague and poorly defined. It is more difficult to exert leadership influence over a poorly defined task, however, because neither the leader nor the followers have a clear idea about the nature of the task or criteria for accomplishing it. If the task is clearly defined, on the other hand, the leader's authority is backed up by the organization, thus making the leadership role easier.

3. *Position power*—the leader's legitimate, as distinct from charismatic or personal, power. Obviously, the leader's job is made easier if he or she has a great deal of position power.

Having defined these three dimensions of the situation, Fiedler proceeds to relate the two basic management styles to the following variables—good versus poor leader-member relationships, structured versus unstructured tasks, and strong versus weak leader position to permissive, considerate leadership versus controlling, active, structuring leadership—which determine the favorableness of the given situation.

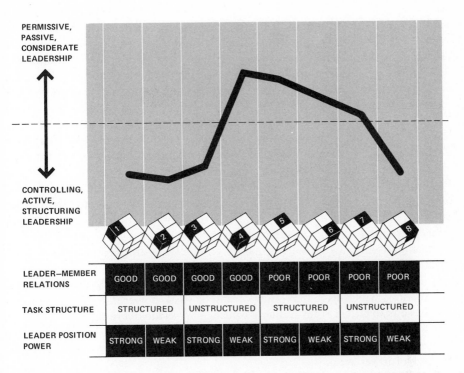

PERMISSIVE, PASSIVE, CONSIDERATE LEADERSHIP

CONTROLLING, ACTIVE, STRUCTURING LEADERSHIP

LEADER—MEMBER RELATIONS	GOOD	GOOD	GOOD	GOOD	POOR	POOR	POOR	POOR
TASK STRUCTURE	STRUCTURED		UNSTRUCTURED		STRUCTURED		UNSTRUCTURED	
LEADER POSITION POWER	STRONG	WEAK	STRONG	WEAK	STRONG	WEAK	STRONG	WEAK

Fig. 7.3 How the style of effective leadership varies with the situation. (F. E. Fiedler, "Engineer the Job to Fit the Manager," *Harvard Business Review* **43**, 5, Sept.-Oct. 1965, p. 118. Reprinted by permission.)

Figure 7.3 shows Fiedler's summary of a number of group studies in which the group were performing well but which used differing styles of leadership according to the situation. The range of leadership styles (as measured by the LPC) is given in the vertical axis; variables of the situations are shown in the horizontal axis. *Fiedler found that either the nondirective and human-relations style of leadership or the managing, directive, task-oriented type of leadership can be effective.* The degree of effectiveness of the leadership style depends on the favorableness of the situation. In other words, there are times when the most effective leadership style is authoritarian; at other times, the most effective leadership style is egalitarian. Fiedler's general conclusion is that task-oriented leaders perform best in very favorable or unfavorable situations and that human-relations oriented, egalitarian leaders perform best in situations of intermediate-favorableness.

Fiedler identifies three approaches to getting the job done. First, position power can be changed by giving the leader more or less power, depending on the leader's style. Second, the task structure can be altered to fit the style of the leader. Finally, the leader-member relationships can be modified by either bringing in subordinates with similar attitudes and beliefs, thereby increasing the homogeneity of the group, or by decreasing the homogeneity of the group by bringing in subordinates whose culture, language, and background are different from the leader's.

In their application of Fiedler's contingency theory, Shiftlett and Nealey divided 132 male undergraduates at the University of Illinois into three-man laboratory groups to explore Fiedler's suggestion that the leadership situation should be engineered to provide a better match between leadership style and the task to be performed.[36] The leaders were assigned on the basis of their very high or very low LPC scores; group members were students with intermediate LPC scores. In addition, groups were divided into "high" and "low" ability groups based on a verbal ability test. When the groups were checked for compatibility, 12 of the original 44 groups were dropped because of their relatively poor interpersonal relations.

The position power of the leader was established primarily through verbal instructions which gave him either strong or weak power. Group productivity predictions obtained from Fiedler's contingency model were supported only in the low-ability groups. The researchers conclude that "situational engineering still may be a viable idea," but that the specific application of the ideal still requires further work.

One recent laboratory study done with students generally supports the Fiedler model. The students worked on unstructured research problems over a six-week period. With unfavorable conditions, groups with task-oriented leaders were more effective; with mixed conditions, however, groups with a person-oriented leader put forth more effort. One slight departure from the theory is that the quality of the product was better in all cases with the task-oriented leader.[37]

Other studies testing the model have not supported the Fiedler results so strongly. In another laboratory study using college students as subjects, leader-member relations were affected by how much coordination was required for the task and by an interaction of interpersonal compatibility as determined by personality inventory with collaboration on the work task. This finding seriously complicates the model, making its situational use that much more difficult.[38]

In a study concluded with military personnel, leader intelligence was operationally defined to mean "ability to integrate one's experience," thereby providing skills to deal with technical and interpersonal aspects of the situation. Using Fiedler's LPC measure as an indication of motivational style (task- or interpersonal-oriented), the researchers found that the relationship between leader intelligence and performance was affected by motivational style, experience, and leader-member relations.[39] Thus in addition to the other moderating variables, experience is an important factor that apparently cannot be overcome by high intelligence. For researchers, this adds another variable which further complicates the basic Fiedler model.

A later article by Fiedler further confirms the notion that experience is important. He argues that experience affects situational favorability, such that a situation moderately favorable for an experienced leader would be unfavorable for an inexperienced leader. Thus task orientation seems effective for experienced leaders in favorable situations, but person-oriented leadership is more effective for inexperienced leaders in intermediate favorability situations.[40]

Two further pieces of research are cautionary in their approach to the Fiedler model. Stinson and Tracey note that LPC scores have disturbing instabilities over time, particularly with young college students. Even with managers, there is some shifting between high and low LPC categories. Another problem is that the meaning of LPC has shifted over time. LPC is an attitude scale, but some researchers use it to make behavioral inferences on leadership styles. Stinson and Tracey conclude that it seems unwise to alter the work situation to accommodate a manager's style when that style is likely to change within a very short time.[41]

Fiedler's work has also been criticized on methodological grounds. For example, Shiftlett is troubled by Fiedler's inclusion of statistically nonsignificant findings in interpreting his model. In addition, he has conceptual difficulty with the collapse of the three original dimensions into a unidimensional concept of favorability. Unlike Stinson and Tracey, however, Shiftlett feels that Fiedler's model does still hold promise, so long as traditional research safeguards are rigorously imposed.[42]

Perhaps because of its commonsense appeal, a large amount of research has been done and continues to be done on Fiedler's contingency model of leadership. Most of the recent work has had the effect of either complicating or calling into question the basic model. Nonetheless, initial research commenced in the mid-1950s and still continues. Thus the Fiedler approach has withstood the test of time better than any other leadership research has.

E. Path-Goal Theories

Because of some confusing and seemingly contradictory findings in the research on leader consideration and initiating structure, House returned to the VIE model of motivation (discussed in Chapter 3) to attempt to develop a predictive model of leadership behavior that would accommodate the previously disparate findings.[43] Path-goal theory is similar to VIE theory in that both are based on situational factors and thus do not come under the "one best way" category.

One of the concepts underlying path-goal theory is that the leader "motivates" subordinates by increasing the personal benefits of work-goal attainment (increasing the valence, or importance, of the goal) while clarifying the path to the benefits by reducing ambiguities or negative aspects of the path. In this way, the subjective probability (instrumentality in VIE theory) that a path will lead to a positive goal will be made more certain.

Second, by clarifying the path-goal relationships, the leader reduces job-role ambiguity in the subordinate, thereby increasing motivation. The motivation is increased because the path to the desired, highly valent outcome is made clear. Since both positive and negative reinforcement are contingent on per-

Clarifying the path-goal relationships. (David W. Corson from A. Devaney/E. P. Jones)

formance, the subordinate has a better "fix" on how to do the job. Third, when the conditions of the job are clear or unambiguous—the path-to-goal relationship is obvious—any leader-imposed structure or clarification will be regarded as redundant or "overkill," and the result will be decreased satisfaction. Finally, leader behavior aimed at reducing subordinates' needs will increase performance to the extent that the needs reduction is related to the valence associated with goal-directed effort.

Put in a less formal way, consider your situation as a student. Perhaps you eventually want additional education beyond your current level. Almost certainly you want a better job than you would get without your present schooling. Your instructor can increase the payoff of work-goal attainment, i.e., finishing the course satisfactorily, by offering to write letters of recommendation or putting in a good word for you with a colleague. This potential payoff increases the "worth," or valence, of finishing the course in a satisfactory manner. Second, the instructor may give you tips on how to study; this clarifies the goal path which you appreciate. However, if you already have good study habits, any additional tips will be redundant, and you are unlikely to appreciate them. However, if the instructor gives you career-planning advice such that you do not need to take as many courses as you thought you had to, you will be more likely to work harder because your goals will be closer.

Some of the recent research on path-goal, or expectancy, theory in leadership suggests that it can have predictive power. Indeed, one objective of such research has been to predict leader's behavior, using leadership as a dependent (end-result) variable and expected value of the leadership behavior as the independent (causal) variable. When leadership is a dependent variable, leadership style depends on the values of particular outcomes of that style to the leader. On the other hand, when leadership is an independent variable, *subordinates' behavior* and *attitudes* are looked on as depending on the particular styles of leadership which allow subordinates to optimal satisfaction of their needs.

An example of the first type of research is a two-part study of naval aviation maintenance crews and public works maintenance shop supervisors. In this research, leaders' actual behavior was predicted, provided that certain facts were known, namely, the leaders' expectation that a particular behavior was related to a particular outcome and the leaders' evaluation (valence) of the outcome.[44] Because of the low amount of variance accounted for, the authors caution that measurement error could be a problem, or that the model only predicts well for certain persons. Still, they see this research as a first step toward relating leadership to the decision processes.

The other major branch of path-goal theory sees leadership as an independent variable and subordinate attitudes and behavior as the dependent variable. One such study included project engineers, military officers, and civil service personnel. Leader consideration was positively related to subordinates' satisfaction in highly structured, unambiguous tasks, but less positively related to satisfaction in conditions of greater uncertainty. This finding is consistent with path-goal predictions. However, the relationship between leader initiating structure and subordinate satisfaction was *more positive* under conditions of high task structure than under conditions of low task structure. This contradicts the basic path-goal theory.[45]

In both of the two preceding studies, the authors suggest that perhaps path-goal theory does not predict well for all persons in all organizations. Interestingly, they suggest that such moderating variables as education, need for achievement, and independence, might explain their actual as opposed to their predicted results.

However, a study in a health-care setting found that initiating structure was more important for satisfaction for associate directors than for the lower-status head nurse, a finding consistent with the original path-goal theory.[46] Perhaps one way to reconcile these results would be to take an in-depth look at the job expectations for each position to see whether job-role ambiguity is more easily clarified in this fashion than by job level.

Another health-care study by these authors found that initiating structure was negatively related to performance of administrative and service personnel (at the high and low ends of the occupational continuum) and unrelated to the professional and technical personnel.[47] These findings are contrary to the path-goal prediction that leader initiating structure clarifies subordinate performance goals. With these findings, the authors conclude that: (1) perhaps the path-goal theory of leadership might be more applicable in industrial than in nonindustrial settings; (2) this part of the theory is weak; (3) measures of performance were not sufficiently valid; or (4) there were measurement problems.

Finally, a study was done in a specialty steel plant, using managers and machine operators as subjects.[48] The researchers found, as in the second health-care study, that although the relationship between consideration and performance and consideration and satisfaction agreed with the original path-goal theory, the relationship between initiating structure and performance and satisfaction were contrary to the theory under conditions of increasing job ambiguity.

These recent path-goal theory findings suggest that the part of the theory integrating initiating structure and performance satisfaction is not predictive across multiple environments. Rather, it may suggest that underlying variables other than role ambiguity moderate the relationship between leader initiating structure and subordinate performance and satisfaction, although such variables have not yet been clearly identified. Perhaps, too, a path-goal theory will be developed that utilizes measures of leader behavior other than consideration and initiating structure. Recent research on one measure of consideration and initiating structure, the Leadership Opinion Questionnaire, found that this device could not separate effective from ineffective managers on *any* combination of initiating structure and consideration, thus casting some doubt on the worth of any of the related questionnaires.[49]

IV. SUMMARY AND CONCLUSION

In this chapter, we have looked at some of the determinants of leadership. Of the five different types of power, one depends on position and the others on access to others or on knowledge. We also made distinctions between successful leadership attempts.

There are several distinct approaches to leadership styles, most of which come from studies describing authoritarian, democratic, or *laissez faire* (literally, "to leave alone") approaches. McGregor, Likert, and Blake and Mouton feel that the one-best-way approach is appropriate; Fiedler believes that a contingency approach is necessary, i.e., the "one best way" varies according to the manager, his or her followers, and the situation; and House feels that a path-goal approach is most viable.

In the first edition of this book, we stated that current thinking favored a contingency, or situational, approach toward leadership. Although we still believe that, recent research has attempted to find the moderating variables on which various leadership styles are contingent. It is around this point that much of the current difficulty arises. It is apparent that Fiedler's contingency model, as first stated, is too simplistic, and it is also apparent that at the present time the path-goal leadership theory can only partially predict leadership behavior. For this second edition, we reiterate that a contingency or path-goal theory may account for the most variation in leadership behavior. However, research has not yet progressed far enough to specify when a particular style of leadership is going to be most effective.

REVIEW

1. Compare Likert's systems theory, Blake and Mouton's managerial grid, Fiedler's contingency theory, and path-goal theory.
2. Look at leaders within your organization or university. Identify some formal and informal positions and specify the kinds of power the leaders are using.

3. What real-life situations might serve to illustrate Fiedler's contingency theory?

4. If you were a consultant on leadership style, what would you advise a pharmaceutical company to do about an appropriate style for top management or for subordinate supervisors?

5. Under what circumstances do you think a Theory X approach to management might be appropriate?

6. Compare what this chapter tells you about leadership of a work team in contrast to leadership of a large corporation.

7. Observe a group in interaction. Can you pick out a task leader and a social leader? How do their behaviors differ?

REFERENCES

1. R. Nader, *Unsafe at Any Speed,* New York: Grossman, 1965.

2. J. French and B. Raven, "The Basis of Social Power," *In Group Dynamics: Research and Theory,* 3rd ed., ed. D. Cartwright and A. Zander, New York: Harper & Row, 1967.

3. H. Leavitt, *Managerial Psychology,* Chicago: University of Chicago Press, 1964.

4. L. Sank, "Effective and Ineffective Managerial Traits Obtained as Naturalistic Descriptions from Executive Members from a Super-Corporation," *Personnel Psychology* **27,** 3 (Autumn 1974): 423–434.

5. E. Ghiselli, "The Validity of Management Traits Related to Occupational Level," *Personnel Psychology* **16,** 1 (Spring 1963): 109–113.

6. W. J. Palmer, "Management Effectiveness as a Function of Personality Traits of the Manager," *Personnel Psychology* **27,** 2 (Summer 1974): 283–295.

7. R. Lippitt and R. K. White, "An Experimental Study of Leadership and Group Life," in *Readings in Social Psychology,* ed., T. M. Newcomb and E. L. Hartley, New York: Holt, Rinehart and Winston, 1974; L. Coch and J. R. P. French, "Overcoming Resistance to Change," *Human Relations* **1** (1948): 512–532.

8. R. Kahn and D. Katz, "Leadership Practices in Relation to Productivity and Morale," in *Group Dynamics: Research and Theory,* 2d ed., ed. D. Cartwright and A. Zander, Elmsford, N.Y.: Row, Peterson, 1960.

9. E. Fleishman, E. F. Harris, and R. D. Burtt, *Leadership and Supervision in Industry,* Columbus: Ohio State University Press, 1955.

10. E. Fleishman and E. F. Harris, "Patterns of Leadership Behavior Related to Employee Grievances and Turnover," *Personnel Psychology* **15,** 1 (Spring 1962): 45–53.

11. D. Tscheulin, "Leader Behavior Measurement in German Industry," *Journal of Applied Psychology* **57,** 1 (Feb. 1973): 28–31.

12. A. K. Korman, "Consideration, 'Initiating Structure,' and Organizational Criteria—A Review," *Personnel Psychology* **19,** 3 (Autumn 1966): 349–361; S. Kerr and C. Schriesheim, "Consideration, Initiating Structure and Organizational Criteria—An Update of Korman's 1966 Review," *Personnel Psychology* **27,** 4 (Winter 1974): 555–568.

13. S. Kerr, C. A. Schriesheim, C. J. Murphy, and R. M. Stogdill, "Toward a Contingency Theory of Leadership Based upon the Consideration and Initiating Structure Literature," *Organizational Behavior and Human Performance* **12,** 1 (1974): 62–82.

14. J. Woodward, *Management and Technology,* London: Her Majesty's Stationery Office, 1958.

15. E. Fleishman and R. Peters, "Interpersonal Values, Leadership Attitudes and Managerial Success," *Personnel Psychology* **15,** 1 (Spring 1962): 127–143.

16. P. Lawrence and J. Lorsch, *Organization and Environment: Managing Integration and Differentiation,* Boston: Harvard University School of Business Administration, Division of Research, 1967.

17. G. Graen, F. Dansereau, Jr., and T. Minami, "Dysfunctional Leadership Styles," *Organizational Behavior and Human Performance* **7,** 1 (April 1972): 216–236.

18. J. Lorsch and P. Lawrence, eds., *Studies in Organization Design,* Homewood, Ill.: Richard D. Irwin and The Dorsey Press, 1970.

19. M. Sashkin, "Participation in Organizations: A Contingency Analysis." Paper presented at the Michigan Psychological Association, April 5, 1974.

20. M. R. Cooper and M. T. Wood, "Effects of Member Participation and Commitment in Group Decision Making on Influence, Satisfaction and Decision Riskness," *Journal of Applied Psychology* **59,** 2 (April 1974): 127–134.

21. B. Kavcic, V. Rus, and A. S. Tannebaum, "Control, Participation, and Effectiveness in Four Yugoslav Industrial Organizations," *Administrative Science Quarterly* **16,** 1 (March 1971): 74–86.

22. G. H. Hines "Sociocultural Influences on Employee Expectancy and Participation Management," *Academy of Management Journal* **17,** 2 (June 1974): 334–339.

23. J. R. P. French, J. Israel, D. Ås, "An Experiment on Participation in a Norwegian Factory," *Human Relations* **13,** 1 (1960): 3–19.

24. J. Lischeron and T. Wall, "Worker Participation Works," *Municipal and Public Service Journal* (May 10, 1974): 563–565.

25. R. Krishnan, "Democratic Participation in Decision Making by Employees in American Corporations," *Academy of Management Journal* **17,** 2 (June 1974): 339–347; D. W. Ewing, "Who Wants Corporate Democracy?" *Harvard Business Review* **49,** 5 (Sept.–Oct. 1971): 12–28, 146–149.

26. J. E. Bragg and I. R. Andrews, "Participative Decision Making: An Experimental Study in a Hospital," *Journal of Applied Behavioral Science* **9,** 6 (Nov.–Dec. 1973): 727–735.

27. L. B. Mohr, "Organizational Technology and Organizational Structure," *Administrative Science Quarterly* **16**, 4 (Dec. 1971): 444–459.

28. D. McGregor, *The Human Side of Enterprise*, New York: McGraw-Hill, 1960.

29. D. McGregor, *The Professional Manager*, ed. D. McGregor and W. Bennis, New York: McGraw-Hill, 1967.

30. R. Likert, *New Patterns of Management*, New York: McGraw-Hill, 1961.

31. R. Likert, *The Human Organization*, New York: McGraw-Hill, 1967, p. 124.

32. D. A. Butterfield and G. F. Farris, "The Likert Organizational Profile: Methodological Analysis and Test of System 4 Theory in Brazil," *Journal of Applied Psychology* **59**, 1 (Feb. 1974): 15–23.

33. R. Blake and J. Mouton, *The Managerial Grid*, Houston: Gulf 1964.

34. R. Blake and J. Mouton, *Building a Dynamic Corporation Through Grid Organization Development*, Reading, Mass.: Addison-Wesley, 1969, p. 16. Reprinted by permission.

35. F. Fiedler, "Engineer the Job to Fit the Manager," *Harvard Business Review* **43**, 5 (Sept.–Oct. 1965): 118.

36. S. Shiftlett and S. Nealey, "The Effects of Changing Leadership Power: A Test of 'Situational' Engineering," *Organizational Behavior and Human Performance* **7**, 3 (June 1972): 371–382.

37. D. D. Hovey, "The Low-Powered Leader Confronts a Messy Problem: A Test of Fiedler's Theory," *Academy of Management Journal* **17**, 2 (June 1974): 358–362.

38. D. Ilgen and G. O'Brien, "Leader-Member Relations in Small Groups," *Organizational Behavior and Human Performance* **12**, 3 (1974): 335–350.

39. L. S. Csoka, "A Relationship Between Leader Intelligence and Leader Rated Effectiveness," *Journal of Applied Psychology* **59**, 1 (Feb. 1974): 43–47.

40. F. E. Fiedler, "Predicting the Effects of Leadership Training and Experience from the Contingency Model: A Clarification," *Journal of Applied Psychology* **57**, 2 (April 1973): 110–113.

41. J. E. Stinson and L. Tracey, "Some Disturbing Characteristics of the LPC Score," *Personnel Psychology* **27**, 3 (Autumn 1974): 477–485.

42. S. C. Shiflett, "The Contingency Model of Leadership Effectiveness: Some Implications of its Statistical and Methodological Properties," *Behavioral Science* **18**, 6 (Nov. 1973): 429–440.

43. R. J. House, "A Path-Goal Theory of Leadership Effectiveness," *Administrative Science Quarterly* **16**, 3 (Sept. 1971): 321–338.

44. D. Debeker and T. Mitchell, "Leader Behavior: An Expectancy Theory Approach," *Organizational Behavior and Human Performance* **11**, 3 (1974): 355–367.

45. J. E. Stinson and T. W. Johnson, "The Path-Goal Theory of Leadership: A

Partial Test and Suggested Refinement," *Academy of Management Journal* **18,** 2 (June 1975): 242–252.

46. H. P. Sims, Jr., and A. D. Szilagyi, "Leader Structure and Subordinate Satisfaction for Two Hospital Administrative Levels: A Path Analysis Approach," *Journal of Applied Psychology* **60,** 2 (April 1975): 194–197.

47. A. D. Szilagyi and H. P. Sims, Jr., "An Exploration of the Path-Goal Theory of Leadership in a Health Care Environment," *Academy of Management Journal* **17,** 4 (Dec. 1974): 622–634.

48. H. K. Downey, J. E. Sheridan, and J. W. Slocum, "Analysis of Relationships Among Leader Behavior, Subordinate Job Performance and Satisfaction: A Path-Goal Approach," *Academy of Management Journal* **18,** 2 (June 1975): 253–262.

49. Palmer, *op. cit.*

8

THE MANAGER
IN THE
ORGANIZATION

I have nothing to offer but blood, toil, tears and sweat.

WINSTON CHURCHILL

LEARNING
OBJECTIVES

When you have finished reading and studying this chapter, you should be able to:

1. Identify the role of the manager within the systems concept.
2. Define and use the concept of "manager."
3. Specify the functions of a manager.
4. Compare and contrast the role of a "manager" and a "leader."
5. Distinguish between fact and myth regarding the managerial job.
6. Identify and use Management by Objectives (MBO).
7. Describe the three steps in establishing an MBO program.

You will be expected to define and use the following concepts:

Boundary-spanning activities	Reactions to role, conflict, and ambiguity
Linking mechanism	Functions of a manager
Role	Exploded myths of management
Role conflict	Management by Objectives
Role ambiguity	Use and misuse of MBO

THOUGHT STARTERS

1. How do you define a manager's job?
2. On the average, how much time does a manager spend with subordinates?
3. Is a symphony conductor a manager? Is a college instructor?

I. INTRODUCTION

It is clear that the role of the manager in today's society is becoming more important and complex. As our society has become increasingly urban, there has been a corresponding growth of social organizations—hospitals, universities, governmental units, insurance companies, industrial establishments, and a myriad of other organizations—which all need to be managed. At the same time, there have been several major corresponding shifts in the structure and composition of these organizations. First, the number of "unskilled," blue-collar workers has decreased while the number of technical, professional, and clerical personnel has increased. These "white-collar" workers now outnumber the "blue-collar" employees. Second, organizations are becoming more complex, with a steadily increasing number of component subsystems to be managed. Finally, there has been a trend away from the owner/entrepreneurial manager to the administrative manager within an existing organization. The "owners" of the enterprise are farther and farther removed from the actual operation of the social organization, e.g., the stockholders of a large industrial organization have relatively little to say about the day-to-day management of the organization.

As a result of these and other forces, the job of the manager has become increasingly more important and complex. The practice of management is becoming less an art and more a science, a profession. Someone must establish the goals and directions for the social organization; someone must shape a productive enterprise out of human and material resources; someone must coordinate the various subsystems of the organization; someone must solve, or cause to get solved, the myriad problems facing any organization; someone must make certain that the total work of the organization and each of its subparts is accomplished.

This does not mean, of course, that the "top manager" does all this alone. Obviously, in a formal organization there are managers at all levels. Higher-level managers may have to be more conceptually and entrepreneurially oriented while those at the lower levels make the technical, "how to" decisions.

II. WHAT IS A MANAGER?

A "manager" may be defined as the person within a formal organization who has at least one subordinate. As noted in Chapter 7, a leader may not necessarily be a manager, but a manager is, by definition, a leader.

This preliminary definition of a manager, however, focuses almost exclusively on manager-subordinate relationships. Many well-known texts suggest that the tasks of a manager are essentially the same at all levels in the organization (from president to foreman) and consist of: planning, organizing, staffing, directing, and controlling. These functions are primarily formally organized supervisor-subordinate relationships. Most managerial job descriptions detail relationships with subordinates and/or the immediate supervisor. Relationships with others in the organization may frequently be covered in a concluding phrase, "and shall conduct such other relationships as are necessary to perform the job."

There is increasing criticism of this approach as being overly simplified and dealing with a closed- rather than an open-system model. Recent research indicates that the term "manager" cannot apply to a single, homogeneous occupational group. Rather, the job of a manager varies considerably, depending on such variables as company ownership (e.g., family versus public), organizational structure, organizational size, type of organization, and hierarchical level.[1] For example, almost all managerial jobs require activities that go beyond the boundaries of the individual work group or subsystem. The higher up the managerial hierarchy, the greater the chance that these boundary-spanning activities will include activities with other organizations or systems in the external environment. There is also evidence that such activities involving other organizations are satisfying at higher managerial levels but create job dissatisfaction for first-level supervisors.

Boundary-spanning activities include not only managers, but also entry-level college graduates, who report that their most frequent activity is selling ideas to others (not their boss). Recent college graduates noted that the most important skill for them was how to "comfortably relate to the variety of people with whom they must interact."[2] Thus the traditional focus on a manager's relationships with subordinates is highly restrictive, since many managerial activities do not involve subordinates at all or only indirectly.

This is one of the reasons why we treated leadership as a separate variable in the previous chapter. The entry-level college graduate is a leader (attempting to influence people) but frequently has no subordinates. It is also one of the reasons why some of the research on leadership *appears* to be contradictory. The research, while focusing on leadership, has not yet been able to control for a sufficient number of variables. The complexity of managerial behavior can be illustrated by reviewing some studies of what managers *actually* do on the job, as opposed to what some people think they *should* do.

In his study of a manager's activities, Ponder found that 12 highly rated and 12 lower-rated supervisors in an electrical equipment manufacturing plant had an average of 457 interpersonal contacts during each eight-hour day, although most of these contacts lasted for only one or two minutes.[3] Thus each supervisor spent about 13% of his time with his subordinates, including group leaders, 3% of his time with his immediate boss, and more than 30% of his time with peer-level individuals or groups. Moreover, Ponder found that the more effective supervisors spent a higher percentage of their time with representatives of such lateral groups, whereas the poorer supervisors tended to focus their efforts and time with their subordinates.

In a similar study, conducted in an automobile manufacturing company, Walker and his associates found that the manager had a high daily number of interpersonal contacts (387) and that the managers in the automobile assembly plants spent a large percentage of their time dealing with people in lateral, peer-level contacts.[4]

Strauss examined the behavior of purchasing agents (functional managers in charge of purchasing departments) and found that their management function could be better analyzed in terms of *work flow* than by either the hierarchical boss-subordinate relationship or the typical concepts of staff-line relationships, even though the purchasing agent is technically a staff-line member.[5] Normally, one assumes that the work flow goes in only one direction. Sales

Interaction in the work-flow process. (Photograph courtesy Boeing Company)

receives an order; engineering designs the product and develops blueprints; production-scheduling establishes the manufacturing schedule; and the purchasing department places orders for the parts and other raw materials needed. Accordingly, the purchasing agent has two basic functions in the hierarchy: (1) to negotiate and place orders; and (2) to expedite orders if they are late. Most purchasing agents, however, are highly dissatisfied with this arrangement. They believe that if they could be involved with engineering at an earlier date, they could suggest specifications or types of parts which would reduce costs substantially. Furthermore, they feel that the production schedule does not allow sufficient time to buy the necessary parts, thus reducing their pool of suppliers or forcing them to pay premium prices. As a result, the purchasing agents strive to reverse the "normal" work flow and to exercise influence much earlier in the work-flow cycle.

The results of the Strauss study were paralleled in a case study of a new department manager, Melvin Moss, who successfully engaged in a power struggle with his boss, Katz, to extend his sphere of influence.[6] Moss used four tactics to expand his influence: (1) neutralizing supporters of Katz to obtain their cooperation; (2) replacing subordinates whose assistance he did not need; (3) ensuring commitment to himself rather than to Katz; and (4) obtaining support from those higher in the organization. Moss, like the successful purchasing agents, used a variety of techniques for exerting influence.

These studies show that the common definition of a manager (planning, organizing, staffing, directing, and controlling the work of subordinates) is not adequate. Rather, the concept and definition of a manager need to be expanded. For example, we have found that managers spend more than 50% of their time with people either within or outside the boundaries of the organization other than their subordinates. Sayles's research shows that 25% or less of a manager's time is spent interacting with subordinates, 75% with other levels of management or associated staff or service groups, primarily at the lateral level. Sayles studied a group of engineering managers in a large corporation and found that they had to maintain contacts with as many as 30 different groups, each of which had its own manager.[7]

Other research findings confirm this diversity of managerial efforts and allocation of time. For example, a study of 160 British managers found that they spent 45% of their time with peers at a lateral work level, 41% of their time with people outside their unit, and only about 12% of their time with their own boss.[8] According to one review of studies on what managers *actually* do, important managerial skills involve developing lateral-level peer relationships. Managers carry out negotiations with a variety of people within and outside the organization, establishing information networks and subsequently disseminating the information, resolving conflicts, making decisions under ambiguous circumstances, allocating resources, and motivating subordinates. "It is time to strip away the folklore about managerial work, and time to study it realistically so that we can begin the difficult task of making significant improvements in its performance."[9] In other words, the empirical studies demonstrate that what managers actually *do* in organizations is quite different from what they are *supposed* to be engaged in, according to the definition, i.e., oversee the activities of subordinates.

What causes this discrepancy? The more traditional definition resulted from failing to consider the organization as a network of interdependent and interrelated subsystems. However, if we take a systems approach and consider our three perspectives—structural-design, flow, and human—of a social organization simultaneously, we can begin to understand why the manager's activities cut across all of the perspectives. In other words, the manager's true function is to serve as the linking mechanism whereby balance among subsystems is maintained. For example, Kahn *et al.* propose that the formal job in an organization be considered as an office and that a manager's expected behavior be defined as a "role."[10] We can then ask, "What other people are linked to this manager within the operating organization?" and "Who does this manager associate with in performing his or her organizational role?"

The manager's work relationships with supervisors, subordinates, peers, vendors, and customers constitute a "role set" (Fig. 8.1.). And by extending this concept, the organizational system becomes a set of overlapping and interlocking role sets both inside and outside the boundaries of the organization. A "role" is thus the sum total of expectations placed on the individual manager by supervisors, peers, customers, vendors, and others, depending on the particular job. For as we mentioned earlier, the manager can have contact with 30 or more other groups in a month.

Since the average manager has contact with so many different groups and people, each with a different set of expectations, he or she must be able to integrate these, as well as personal, expectations into a coherent psychological contract in order to perform successfully. However, "role ambiguity" arises if the manager does not clearly understand what others' expectations are. But if the manager understands these expectations and they conflict with one another and/or his or her own expectations, the result is "role conflict," and the manager will be unable to satisfy some of the expectations.

Table 8.1, which shows the areas of agreement and disagreement between supervisor-subordinate pairs, gives one illustration of role ambiguity. There is moderate agreement of job duties, but the amount of disagreement (and ambiguity) increase when job requirements and obstacles are included. The table shows that supervisor-subordinate pairs have only 8.1% agreement on more

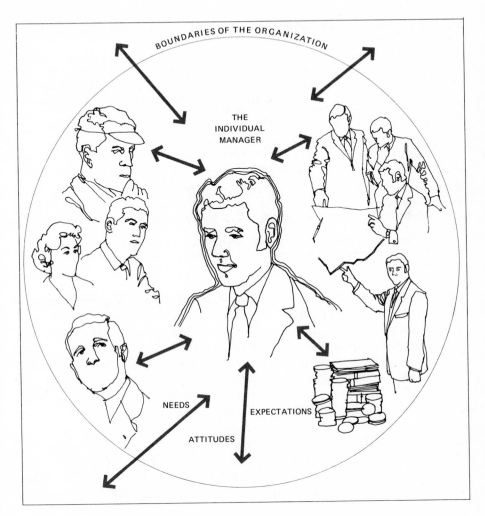

Fig. 8.1 Role expectations placed on the manager.

than half of the topics about obstacles that the subordinate faces in accomplishing the job.

There have been a number of studies of role conflict and ambiguity. Most have shown that role conflict and ambiguity reduce job satisfaction and increase the possibility of sickness, voluntary turnover, and decreased job performance. One study, for example, concluded that role conflict and role ambiguity have a high degree of influence on perceptions, attitudes, and behavior.

Table 8.1 Perceptual agreements and differences between supervisor-subordinate pairs on basic areas of the subordinate's job

	Agreement on less than half of the topics	Agreement on about half of the topics	Agreement on more than half of the topics
Job duties	15.0%	39.1%	45.9%
Job requirements— subordinate's qualifications	36.3%	40.9%	22.8%
Obstacles in the way of subordinate's performance	68.2%	23.6%	8.1%

Adapted from N. R. F. Maier, L. R. Hoffman, J. J. Hoover, and W. H. Read, *Superior-Subordinate Communication in Management*, New York: American Management Association, 1961.

However future studies on behavior in organizations should place more emphasis on role ambiguity. The researchers found that role ambiguity links formal organizational practices and leadership behavior with such factors as organizational effectiveness, job satisfaction, anxiety, and resignations. Therefore, organizational stability and personal satisfaction can be enhanced by working actively to reduce role ambiguity.[11]

Another researcher suggests that stress resulting from role conflict and ambiguity accounted for a loss of 36 million workdays in Britain in 1971.[12] Showing evidence that some managerial roles cause greater stress than others, Pettigrew recommends that organizations identify the jobs with high stress potential to analyze both the job and the incumbent. Then, either the job can be redesigned to suit the manager, or a new manager can be selected; in either case, the goal is to ensure a better fit between the individual and organizational role.

However, as role conflict and role ambiguity are studied in greater depth, it is becoming clear that not everyone reacts negatively to role conflict and ambiguity. Further, as indicated above, role ambiguity and role conflict may have different consequences.

The early study by Kahn *et al.* suggested that role conflict caused tension for introverts but not for extraverts. Further, individuals with a high need for thoughtful reflection had more job tension as role ambiguity increased, whereas individuals with a low need for reflection about job issues were not affected by role ambiguity.[13] A study done with nurses found that the greater the individual's *need* for job clarity, the more the nurse was affected by role ambiguity.[14] There was a clear relationship in that those with a high need for clarity tended to quit when the job became ambiguous. Similarly, role ambiguity and conflict generally result in greater stress, dissatisfaction, and tenseness in individuals with a high need for achievement than in those with a low need for achievement. Those with high need for independence are more affected by role conflict than are those with a low need for independence.[15]

Whatever the reason, role conflict and ambiguity appear to be most harmful to performance at the lower levels of the organization. Employees at higher levels seem to be better able to cope with role conflict and ambiguity. Probably neither has beneficial results.[16]

Particularly for higher-level managers, role ambiguity arising from boundary-spanning activities increases opportunity for action and discretion and

Increasing role conflict. (Ewing Galloway/E. P. Jones)

therefore greater satisfaction. Perhaps the opportunity to interact with others outside the organization gives the manager more knowledge and information, which in turn may allow him or her to gain additional power within the organization.[17] However, role ambiguity particularly affects hard-driving, persistent, work-involved people, who react with anxiety, depression, and increased heart rate.[18]

The evidence also suggests that the effect of role conflict and ambiguity on job satisfaction is multidimensional. Dissatisfaction resulting from role conflict appears to be related to such *extrinsic* factors as supervision, pay, and opportunities for promotion. Dissatisfaction resulting from role ambiguity appears to be related to more *intrinsic* factors involved in the job itself and satisfaction in doing the job well.[19] Faced with role ambiguity, people tend to become dissatisfied with the job itself, whereas in a situation of role conflict, people become dissatisfied with the extrinsic factors.

A manager who reacts negatively to role conflict and ambiguity and the resulting stress may choose several approaches, all of which reduce managerial effectiveness. The manager may become overly aggressive and make "too many waves," impatient to get the job done. Or, he or she may try to resolve the conflict by withdrawing into isolation from the conflicting demands, e.g., taking longer lunch hours. Similarly, a college student who is doing poorly may respond by cutting classes and avoiding his or her professor. One extreme of withdrawal is quitting the job or dropping the class. Unfortunately, however, the existing structure in most organizations provides little in the way of mechanisms for resolving either role conflict or role ambiguity.

Nevertheless, the general implications of role conflict and ambiguity are clear. Some job tension is healthy, but the tension should be directed rather than diffuse. In addition, managers at all levels are much more satisfied with their jobs when expectations for their performance are clear and nonconflicting, depending, of course, on the intrinsic value of the job and the extrinsic rewards. Therefore, managers should be provided with clear and unconflicting role expectations. The manager should know what specific job behaviors are needed to obtain both extrinsic rewards, such as salary increases and promotions, and intrinsic rewards. We will address ourselves to this concept later in this chapter, but first we will examine more carefully the general roles of a manager.

III. MANAGERIAL FUNCTIONS

Although a generalized model of the manager cannot be spelled out precisely, Sayles has suggested that the manager's job can be separated into three distinct roles, or functions.[20]

A. Participant in External Work Flow

A manager can have hundreds of contacts with different people inside and outside the organization, frequently at the lateral, or peer, level. It is at this lateral level of interaction that the manager spends most of his or her time. In these relationships with peers and with people outside the organization, the manager is providing the "connective tissue" that helps to coordinate the organization's activities. The first-line supervisor, for example, works with people in the scheduling, production control, quality assurance, and engineering departments. The purchasing agent works closely with vendors, customers, and the engineering and production control groups. The head of the industrial engineering department works with such internal groups as design, production, and marketing and such external groups as equipment manufacturers.

In these lateral relationships, the manager mainly negotiates with other work groups, which in turn must make adjustments before the manager can tend to something else. The result is a continuously shifting process whereby any one manager's demands must be brought into line with those of other managers; in turn, each manager makes compensating moves and adjustments. This never-ending cycle of securing new agreements, commitments, and assurances in response to the demands made by others results in a decision-making process that can be characterized as a "continuous and *intricate process* of brokerage" within the open system.[21]

For example, a manufacturing manager is simultaneously: (1) trying to get the research and development group to improve the design of a new model so that it is easier to manufacture; (2) pushing the industrial engineering department to provide better equipment; (3) attempting to negotiate with the maintenance group to make quicker repairs; (4) attempting to make certain that the purchasing people expedite order for the parts that have been holding up the production schedule; (5) working with the quality assurance group to ensure higher quality; (6) fighting with the finance people to get a bigger budget for training and employment; (7) attempting to accommodate the requests of salespeople for more samples to be used in the field; and (8) working with the union steward to settle labor grievances. Each decision or negotiation affects other decisions and work groups—priorities change as a result of the ongoing process of decision making.

If we consider the manager as an open subsystem, engaged in a series of role relationships and role expectations with other subsystems, all of which are also open, changing, and dynamic, it is easy to see why more than half of a manager's time is spent in negotiations in lateral-level relationships. Figure 8.2 shows the managerial process in the work flow. Decisions are determined

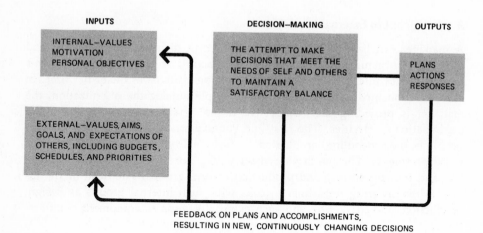

INPUTS

INTERNAL—VALUES
MOTIVATION
PERSONAL OBJECTIVES

EXTERNAL—VALUES, AIMS,
GOALS, AND EXPECTATIONS OF
OTHERS, INCLUDING BUDGETS,
SCHEDULES, AND PRIORITIES

DECISION—MAKING

THE ATTEMPT TO MAKE
DECISIONS THAT MEET THE
NEEDS OF SELF AND OTHERS
TO MAINTAIN A
SATISFACTORY BALANCE

OUTPUTS

PLANS
ACTIONS
RESPONSES

FEEDBACK ON PLANS AND ACCOMPLISHMENTS,
RESULTING IN NEW, CONTINUOUSLY CHANGING DECISIONS

Fig. 8.2 The manager's activities.

by both internal and external inputs. The results, or outputs, of the manager's decision-making process affect other subsystems; as a result, both the manager and other subsystems may be forced to negotiate new plans and decisions. Since the manager must always strive to maintain some sort of balance among these shifting, changing inputs, his or her decision-making activities may be geared toward satisfying as many people as possible rather than trying to find an optimal solution.

B. Leader

The typical manager spends about 25% to 35% of his or her time working with subordinates. The designation "manager" automatically places an individual in the power structure of the formal system and gives that person formal authority over people who may or may not themselves be managers. However, since the manager is an open system, the interaction with subordinates is varied and reflects not only managerial interactions and negotiations at the lateral level, but also those of subordinates. Therefore, we can discern at least three different types of behavior that the manager engages in with subordinates.

1. Leadership as direction This portion of the manager's job is described in the classic definition of a manager, i.e., getting subordinates to respond to the manager's initiative, actions, and directions. Through his or her position in the formal structure of the organization, the manager is truly directing, motivating, controlling, and coordinating subordinates' activities in attempting to meet organizational goals. However, if we consider the manager within a broader systems point of view, at least two other leadership activities are required.

2. Leadership as response to subordinates Decisions are influenced by the inputs the manager receives as a result of interaction with subordinates. A manager not only tells people what to do, but also must respond to their needs and expectations. Subordinates are not merely passive individuals; they have requests that they make of their own boss or supervisor. Students may ask their college professor to explain a particular part of a text or to postpone a scheduled paper. A department chairman may need to respond to a faculty member who asserts that one of his classes is too large for the style of teaching he is using. A first-line supervisor must respond to a subordinate's demand for additional parts. An engineering manager must respond to a subordinate who complains of difficulty in getting drafting help from another part of the engineering department.

3. The manager as a representative A manager/leader who is unable to handle a matter brought up by a subordinae must act on behalf of that subordinate, and this may require the manager to negotiate with his or her peers and/or superiors. Thus the manager as a representative is dealing at both the vertical and lateral levels in response to initiation and inputs from subordinates. For example, a manager must recommend subordinates' increases to his or her own boss. A sales manager may respond to complaints from the sales force about slow delivery time by negotiating with manufacturing for faster delivery. A first-line supervisor may try to get the parts shortage reduced by having purchasing expedite orders. A department chairman may convince the dean that more faculty members are needed to handle an influx of new students.

C. Monitor

In a sense, this function overlaps considerably with the other two functions: participating in external work flow and overseeing the activities of subordinates. Here, however, the manager must set up either formal or informal monitoring subsystems to determine "how things are going." The manager must be sensitive to possible sources of trouble and decide whether to intervene personally or ask others to do so. The manufacturing manager cannot wait until the day a new product arrives on the manufacturing floor to determine whether research and development has come up with a workable design. The retailing manager must monitor sales of certain items to determine how they are selling, in order to know when to reorder and in what quantity. In short, the manager must develop methods for detecting possible disturbances in the work system, as well as criteria for signaling when these disturbances are significant. The manager must then develop corrective actions and be able to assess their effect. This recurring cycle of detection, assessment, and correction (i.e., feedback) is used to predict what new approaches or changes will occur to which the organization or the subsystem will have to adapt.

IV. MANAGEMENT BY OBJECTIVES

Management by Objectives (MBO) embodies both a technique and a philosophy of management. As a managerial approach, MBO reduces managerial or subordinate stress by increasing the communication and shared perceptions between the two. MBO can also be used with subordinates who are not themselves managers.

One of the difficulties with MBO is that it has become a very popular term and therefore has many meanings. A study involving 87 organizations showed that the percentage of respondents defining MBO similarly was as follows:[22]

1. Linking evaluation and performance   35%
2. Helping the manager to plan   25%
3. Motivating subordinates   23%
4. Increasing the interactive and feedback between subordinate and boss   23%
5. Linking departmental and organizational objectives   17%
6. Developing management potential   17%
7. Improving job understanding   13%
8. Helping upper management know what is going on at lower levels   8%
9. Serving as management "club" for higher performance   6%
10. No mention   15%

MBO has two historical roots, or stems. The organizational stem focused primarily on the benefit to the organization; the second, or developmental, stem focused on both the organization and the benefit to the individual. The organizational stem of MBO was originally developed by Drucker, who stressed that organizations need to establish specific objectives in the eight key areas of "(1) market standing; (2) innovation; (3) productivity; (4) physical and financial resources; (5) profitability; (6) manager performance and development; (7) worker performance and attitude; (8) public responsibility."[23] Expanding on Drucker's work, Odiorne stressed the need for quantitative measurement.[24]

The second stem of MBO derives from McGregor, who focused on the more qualitative aspect of MBO in growth and development on the job.[25] Pointing up the reluctance of managers to "play God," McGregor asserted that instead of identifying a subordinate's weaknesses, performance analysis should define strengths and potential for growth. He recommended that the subordinate and boss should agree on major job responsibilities, leaving the subordinate free to develop short-term performance goals, action plans, and criteria for self-appraisal. The subordinate would then discuss his or her self-appraisal with the supervisor, and they would then develop a new set of performance goals and plans. Emphasizing mutual understanding and job performance, the supervisor could act not as a judge, but as a helper, facilitating the work of the subordinate. This is accomplished primarily by focusing more on the *future*, in terms of performance goals and plans, than on the *past*, as used in most other approaches, including performance appraisal.

Although he did not say so explicitly, it seems clear that McGregor's recommendations would also reduce role conflict and ambiguity. This reduction would come about by the mutual superior-subordinate agreement on future performance goals and measures while still allowing the subordinate to develop specific action plans.

This separation between the supervisor as a judge and as a facilitator also ties in to the path-goal theory of leader effectiveness.[26] According to the basic theory, the initiation of structure by the supervisor will increase the subordinate's motivation if the action helps to clarify previously ambiguous paths to the accomplishment of work goals (but only if work goal accomplishment is seen as intrinsically desirable or as a means to extrinsic rewards). In a properly administered MBO program, the path itself is given clear direction and meaning. Further, the intrinsic rewards are increased by the subordinate's participation in the goal-setting process and comparative freedom in developing specific action plans.

In short, an MBO program can be defined as consisting of periodic manager-subordinate meetings that are "oriented toward the daily work and result in mutual planning of the work, a review of progress and mutual solving of problems which arise in the course of getting the job done."[27] The basic steps in this process are as follows:

1. The manager and the subordinate determine the subordinate's specific areas of responsibility for the end results desired. This step is necessary to ensure that both agree on the specifics of the task to be accomplished.

2. The manager and the subordinate must agree on the standard of performance for each area of responsibility.

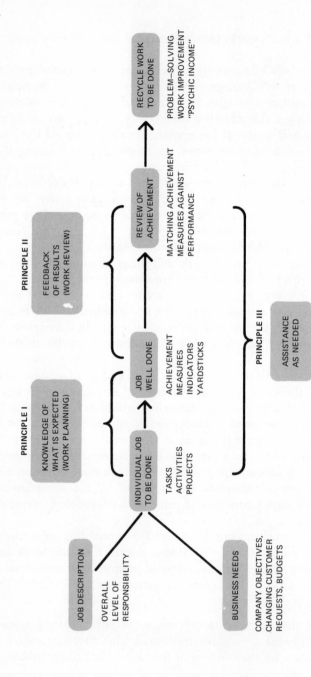

Fig. 8.3 Work planning and review ("psychic income"). (Reprinted by permission from E. Huse and E. Kay, "Improving Employee Productivity Through Work Planning," in *The Personnel Job in a Changing World,* ed. J. Blood, New York: American Management Association, 1964, p. 305.)

3. The manager and the subordinate must agree on a work plan for achieving the desired results in each area of responsibility, always in accordance with the overall objectives of the company.

The cyclical nature of this process is predicated on three basic psychological principles, as shown in Fig. 8.3. Subordinates can improve their job performance only if they

1. *know what is expected of them.* The process provides better information about priorities, expected results, the methods by which results will be measured, and the resources available.
2. *receive feedback about how they are doing.* This is the most basic of the three principles, since knowledge of results, or feedback, is essential for improving job performance.
3. *can obtain coaching and assistance when and as needed.* This means that the climate must be changed from management by crisis, so that the manager can act as a helper rather than as a judge.

The proper utilization of MBO can have considerable effect on management development. Research by Huse and Kay has shown that as a result of proper installation of an MBO approach, subordinates report (at a statistically significant level) greater goal involvement, as well as greater agreement with the boss about the job to be done and ways of improving their current job performance.[28]

Other research has added weight to these findings. Reporting on the results of two studies that implemented a goal-setting and self-control program in a large firm, Raia found that the program had a number of positive results: shifting from a more personal to a more job-centered evaluation of performance, increased productivity, better identification of problem areas, better mutual understanding between supervisors and subordinates, and improved communications.[29]

Tosi and Carroll used a questionnaire to follow up on a Management by Objectives program in an organization manufacturing tools.[30] Their results were similar to those of Huse and Kay and Raia in that the managers reported such advantages as better planning, better identification of problem areas, more objective performance measures, and improved communications. In other word, MBO tends to result in higher motivation, improved performance, and greater identification of individual and organizational goals.

However, Management by Objectives is not a panacea. Thoughtful and realistic critics have pointed out that an incorrectly applied MBO program can have highly negative and unintended results. If, as Levinson points out, a Management by Objectives program based on a power-backed reward-punishment psychology is used to both attain company objectives and appraise subordinates' performance, the results can be psychologically damaging.[31] If subordinates' goals are designed to make the manager or unit look good rather than to contribute to the company's overall objectives, the effectiveness of MBO will be reduced. Similarly, techniques must not be allowed to overshadow the concept, as has happened in a number of organizations. Finally, objectives must not be made overly tangible and specific, thereby reducing effort on less tangible objectives. For example, although managers may be rewarded for meeting immediate, short-term results, few receive credit for an outstanding job of developing the potential of their subordinates.

Ridgway cites a number of cases in which overuse of tangible measurements led to serious dysfunctional consequences.[32] He concludes that the stress on quantitative performance measurements can have highly undesirable consequences for overall organizational performance. For example, there may be high productivity at the end of the accounting period, even though defective parts are allowed to be packed and shipped. As one foreman remarked, "Just tell me what you want my boss to look good on, and I'll make it happen, even if something else goes by the board."

To summarize, a number of longitudinal studies have shown that an MBO program can be beneficial for both the organization and the individual *if* the program is properly designed and implemented.[33] For example, MBO was introduced into two of six plants of a manufacturing company, and a third plant was used as a control.[34] Over a three-year period, the performance of approximately 2500 subordinates of 181 MBO-involved supervisors in the production and marketing departments was studied. The control plant (Plant A) received no treatment. In plant B, MBO was instituted as a matter of policy. In Plant C, MBO was introduced as a matter of policy, as well as a number of additional supporting approaches. These included a letter from the corporate president saying that MBO would be continued in the future, memos from the personnel department to supervisors who were resource persons for MBO, letters from high executives to supervisors thanking them for carrying out the worthwhile MBO program, and a group meeting in which managers discussed their support of MBO.

The results were quite different for the three plants. Plant A, the control plant, showed no changes in any of the performance indices, including three marketing indices and four production indices (quantity, quality, grievance rate, and absenteeism). Plant B, which had introduced MBO as a matter of policy, showed early improvement in the production department, which then died away. The only significant change was that the grievance rate went up significantly. The marketing department showed small but significant changes in marketing potential, sales per visit, and sales performance. Plant C (MBO plus support) showed large, significant, and favorable improvements in all four production indices and all three marketing indices. This improvement was maintained for the full three-year period of the study.

Through MBO, the subordinate has greater opportunity for participation, should this be desired. In addition, individual and organizational goals are more congruent and subordinates have greater opportunity for personal growth on the job. However, MBO may lead to overemphasis on measurement, insufficient emphasis on the discretionary opportunities open to the individual, lack of participation by subordinates (with the manager imposing goals), the tendency to use a win/lose or reward-punishment psychology, and overemphasis on paperwork and red tape. These and other problems will cause many MBO programs to slowly die away. Byrd and Cowan have summarized some of these criticisms by noting that a successful MBO program must meet four criteria: (1) the program cannot be "canned," but must be tailor-made to fit the needs of the specific organization; (2) destructive competitiveness must be avoided; (3) training processes are as important as training content; and (4) all departments must be involved.[35]

V. EXPLODED MYTHS OF MANAGEMENT

In describing the manager's role, we said that the manager participates in external work flow, leads subordinates, and monitors work by developing both positive and negative feedback approaches. Since recent research shows that more than half of a manager's time is spent in work-flow relationships, some of the concepts in more traditional approaches to the manager's job need to be revised.

A. "The parameters of a manager's job can be bounded and compartmentalized into a job description" The inaccuracy of this belief has been amply demonstrated; in actuality, the multitude of the manager's role relationships and the need to trade and negotiate make it impossible to compartmentalize the manager's job. The manager is a subsystem interacting and relating with a large variety of other subsystems. In any given month a manager may have literally hundreds of contacts with a variety of different groups and individuals in an ever-changing set of relationships.

B. "A manager takes orders from one boss" In the traditional structural-design perspective, a manager has only one immediate supervisor. However, by describing the organization in systems terms, we recognize that the manager is an open subsystem interacting with other subsystems both within and outside the boundaries of the system and that each of these subsystems influences the behavior of the individual manager. Thus in a sense any one manager is "bossed" by each of the other people or groups with whom she or he comes in contact. The manager's role is to adjust to and balance these mulitudes of role expectations and demands.

C. "The manager's authority must be equal to responsibility" This is one of the most cherished concepts of the classical management theorists. However, the manager's job, or responsibility, as a subsystem is to get a particular job done, and this requires continuous negotiations with other subsystems over which he or she has no formal authority. Therefore, it is obvious that the manager's effectiveness depends on his or her skill in negotiating, adjusting, and persuading others.

D. "Staff people have no real responsibility or authority" Traditionally, most of the writers on management have been concerned primarily with the concept of hierarchical organizations, which tend to be stable. As a result, they developed a series of concepts postulating that the "staff" serves only an advisory function. The systems approach to work flow, however, may make the entire concept of line and staff obsolete: thus the finance manager in today's organization may well have more power and authority than a manufacturing manager; marketing research, and research and development groups exert a tremendous power and authority over the manufacturing department which must, in essence, manufacture the products determined by these two groups. As Fisch points out, it no longer makes any sense to consider research and development departments as "staff departments."[36] By using a systems approach, however, we can see that each of the groups, or subsystems, within an organization has a tremendous impact on all the other subsystems.

E. "The manager spends most of his or her time with subordinates" The traditional definition of a manager emphasizes the managerial functions of planning, organizing, controlling, motivating, and directing relationships with subordinates. But in actuality, the manager spends most of his or her working time in both internal and external lateral, work-flow relationships.

F. "Formal leadership is closely related to experience" In his summary of both laboratory experiments and field studies of the Post Office, shop craftsmen, meat markets, grocery departments, heavy machinery production, and research chemists, Fiedler used data on 385 managers to test the relationship between length of supervisory experience and leadership effectiveness as measured by the group's "performance of its major assigned task."[37] Fiedler was unable to find any relationship between leadership experience (in years) and group effectiveness (productivity); the "median correlation" across the different samples was −.12.

Anticipating criticism of the notion that time and leadership experience should have a high positive correlation (some organizations even specify the number of years a manager must hold a particular job before being promoted), Fiedler reworked his data in several different ways. All the variations, however, cast profound doubts on the earlier assumptions and raised questions about the traditional criteria for managerial selection and development.

In a related study, Wheatley set up four different types of employer-employee problem-solving groups based on leadership style: (1) participatory, in which the leader encouraged group members to take an active role; (2) supervisory, in which the leader established procedures and an agenda but did not otherwise contribute to the group's efforts; (3) silent, in which the leader merely provides instructions to the group; and (4) leaderless, in which the leader left the room after giving instructions for solving the problem.[38] These various leadership styles provided no measure of effectiveness of problem solving; however, the level of interaction within the group rose significantly when the leader was either silent or absent. Wheatley thus concluded that group effectiveness "might be improved when no leader from management is present."

Although there is widespread belief in these six concepts, they are at best only half-truths, and their acceptance has led to a genuine misunderstanding of the manager's job. Managers have felt extremely uncomfortable with the traditional definition of their job, for it implied that they were not doing their job, because they were spending too much time with lateral, work-flow relationships. As one very competent manager expressed it: "I got nothing done yesterday because I was all tied up in meetings. However, I feel great today. I had a staff meeting with my subordinates and got five letters written, in between meetings." In other words, although this manager was regarded as highly effective by others in the organization, he felt uncomfortable because he was operating under several obsolete concepts, particularly that which says that "the manager spends most of his or her time with subordinates." Although this is always an unwritten dictum, it has had an overly strong influence on the way manager have perceived their job.

VI. SUMMARY

Some management theorists suggest that a managerial job is defined primarily by the job description and the time spent with subordinates. However, research indicates otherwise. Managers have a large number of interpersonal contacts per day and spend much of their time with lateral rather than vertical contacts. Indeed, the better managers spend more of their time in the lateral, work-flow process than do less successful managers. These findings verify our description of a manager as: (1) a participant in external work flow, (2) a leader, and (3) a monitor of work flow. Accordingly, some commonly held myths about a manager's role need to be explored. In actuality, a manager takes orders from (is influenced by) many persons and usually cannot have authority equal to responsibility. Similarly, the line-staff separation is frequently blurred.

The most valid concept of management depicts the manager's role as a complex, shifting set of relationships whereby decisions must continually be renegotiated. In our culture the manager has multiple roles which require a great deal of interaction with many people at a variety of levels inside and outside the organization. However, this leads to both role conflict and role ambiguity. Moderate amounts of role problems may create a positive tension, but role difficulties may also cause undue stress. As a result, Management by Objectives (MBO) may be useful in reducing role stress. When improperly installed or administered, however, MBO may *create* stress rather than reduce it.

REVIEW

1. Give an example of both role conflict and role ambiguity. Show how each affects behavior.

2. Interview a manager and get his or her definition of a manager's job. Does this agree with the definition given in the text? If not, what do you think makes the difference?

3. We have distinguished between a "leader" and a "manager." Is this distinction valid? Explain.

4. If a manager spends a great deal of time interacting with peers and others in the work flow, what implication does this have for managerial development?

5. In Chapter 7 we described various types of power and influence. Under what circumstances may a manager use one type of power rather than another?

6. Does the concept of "Management by Objectives" fit in with the earlier concept of the "psychological contract"? Elaborate.

REFERENCES

1. J. Child and T. Ellis, "Predictors of Variation in Managerial Roles," *Human Relations* **26**, 2 (1974): 227–250.

2. J. Huegli and H. Tschirgi, "The Entry-Level Job—A Neglected Target for our Business Schools?" *Collegiate News and Views* **28**, 2 (Winter 1974–1975): 23.

3. O. Ponder, "Supervisory Practices of Effective and Ineffective Foremen," Ph.D. diss., Columbia University, 1968.

4. C. Walker, R. Guest, and A. Turner, *The Foreman on the Assembly Line*, Cambridge, Mass.: Harvard University Press, 1956.

5. G. Strauss, "Tactics of Lateral Relationships: The Purchasing Agent," *Administrative Science Quarterly* **7**, 2 (Sept. 1962): 161–186.

6. D. Izraeli, "The Middle Manager and Tactics of Power Expansion: A Case Study," *Sloan Management Review* **16**, 2 (Winter 1975): 57–70.

7. L. Sayles, *Managerial Behavior*, New York: McGraw-Hill, 1964.

8. R. Stewart, *Managers and Their Jobs*, London: MacMillan, 1967.

9. H. Mintzberg, "The Manager's Job: Folklore and Fact," *Harvard Business Review* **53**, 4 (July–August 1975): 61.

10. R. Kahn, E. Wolfe, R. Quinn, and J. Sneck, *Organizational Stress: Studies in Role Conflict and Ambiguity*, New York: Wiley, 1964.

11. R. House and J. Rizzo, "Role Conflict and Ambiguity as Critical Variables in a Model of Organizational Behavior," *Organizational Behavior and Human Performance* **7**, 3 (June 1972): 467–505.

12. A. Pettigrew, "Managing Under Stress," *Management Today* (April 1972): 99–102.

13. Kahn *et al.*, *op. cit.*

14. T. Lyons, "Role Clarity, Need for Clarity, Satisfaction, Tension, and Withdrawal," *Organizational Behavior and Human Performance* **6**, 1 (Jan. 1971): 99–110.

15. T. Johnson and J. Stinson, "Role Ambiguity, Role Conflict and Satisfaction: Moderating Effects of Individual Differences," *Journal of Applied Psychology* **60**, 3 (June 1975): 329–333.

16. R. Caplan and K. Jones, "Effects of Work Load, Role Ambiguity, and Type A Personality on Anxiety, Depression, and Heart Rate," *Journal of Applied Psychology* **60**, 6 (Dec. 1975): 713–719.

17. R. Keller, A. Szilagyi, Jr., and W. Holland, "Boundary Spanning Activity and Employee Reactions: An Empirical Study." Paper presented to the 35th Annual Meeting of the Academy of Management, New Orleans, Louisiana, August 10–13, 1975.

18. R. Schuler, "Role Perceptions, Satisfaction, and Performance: A Partial Reconciliation," *Journal of Applied Psychology* **60**, 6 (Dec. 1975): 683–687.

19. R. Keller, "Role Conflict and Ambiguity: Correlates with Job Satisfaction and Values," *Personnel Psychology* **28**, 1 (Jan.–Feb. 1975): 57–64.

20. Sayles, *op. cit.*, p. 28.

The manager in the organization

21. *Ibid.*

22. S. Carroll and W. Tosi, Jr., *Management by Objectives,* New York: Macmillan, 1973, p. 23.

23. P. Drucker, *The Practice of Management,* New York: Harper and Brothers, 1954, p. 63.

24. G. Odiorne, *Management by Objectives,* New York: Pittman, 1956.

25. D. McGregor, "An Uneasy Look at Performance Appraisal," *Harvard Business Review* **35,** 3 (May–June 1957): 410–425.

26. R. House, "A Path Goal Theory of Leader Effectiveness," *Administrative Science Quarterly* **16,** 3 (Sept. 1971): 321–328.

27. E. Huse and E. Kay, "Improving Employee Productivity Through Work Planning," in *The Personnel Job in a Changing World,* ed. J. Blood, New York: American Management Association, 1964, pp. 301–302.

28. *Ibid.*

29. A. Raia, "Goal Setting and Self-Control," *Journal of Management Studies* **2,** 1 (Feb. 1965): 34–58.

30. H. Tosi and S. Carroll, "Management Reaction to Management by Objectives," *Academy of Management Journal* **11,** 4 (Dec. 1968): 415–426.

31. H. Levinson, "Management by Whose Objectives?" *Harvard Business Review* **48,** 4 (July–August 1970): 125–134.

32. V. Ridgway, "Dysfunctional Consequences of Performance Measurements," *Administrative Science Quarterly* **1,** 2 (June 1956): 240–247.

33. Carroll and Tosi, Jr., *op. cit.;* J. Ivancevich, "A Longitudinal Assessment of Management by Objectives," *Administrative Science Quarterly* **17,** 1 (March 1972): 126–138; A. Raia, "A Second Look At Management Goals and Controls," *California Management Review* **8,** 1 (1966): 34–53.

34. J. Ivancevich, "Changes in Performance in a Management by Objectives Program," *Administrative Science Quarterly* **19,** 4 (Dec. 1974): 563–574.

35. R. Byrd and J. Cowan, "MBO: A Behavioral Science Approach," *Personnel* **51,** 2 (March–April 1974): 42–50.

36. G. Fisch, "Line-Staff Is Obsolete," *Harvard Business Review* **39,** 5 (Sept.–Oct. 1961): 67–79.

37. F. Fiedler, "Leadership Experience and Leader Performance—Another Hypothesis Shot to Hell," *Organizational Behavior and Human Performance* **55,** 1 (Jan. 1970): 1–14.

38. B. Wheatley, "Leadership and Anxiety: Implications for Small-Group Meetings," *Personnel Journal* **51,** 1 (Jan. 1972): 17–21.

ORGANIZATIONAL BEHAVIOR: THE MACRO VIEW

Managers are always trying to improve the operation of their organization, whether it be a local service station, a government bureau, a church, a motel, or General Motors. First, however, we need to distinguish, as Etzioni has done, between organizational *effectiveness* and organizational *efficiency*.[1] Organizational effectiveness is the degree to which a particular organization realizes its goals and objectives. Organizational efficiency, on the other hand, refers to the amount of resources an organization must use in order to produce a unit of output. In other words, although the two concepts are interrelated, they are not interdependent. An organization may be very effective in meeting its goals and highly inefficient because it uses up far too many resources in meeting its goals. Conversely, a plant may be highly efficient in its operation but not be very effective, as evidenced by its declining sales and decreasing profit margin. In part, of course, an organization's effectiveness depends on its objectives, their relevance to the environment, and conditions in the environment. In discussing organizational improvement and development, therefore, we must include both terms, since it is important that an organization be both effective in meeting its goals and efficient in using its resources wisely. The "competent" organization is both effective and efficient.

Elements of all three perspectives are needed for an organization to maximize its competency. The structural-design approach looks *downward* in the organization and is concerned with organizational design and structure, including such subsystems as marketing, production, and finance. The work-flow approach looks *across* the organization and emphasizes the flow of material and information. The human approach focuses on the human process of managing, i.e., individual behavior and motivation, group dynamics, managerial and leadership style, and organizational design. This difference in emphasis has led practitioners and theorists to substitute "development" for "improvement" in describing organizational change.

Each of these three viewpoints of the organizational system is legitimate, and it is important to keep these three differing (and overlapping) sets of perspectives in mind, because an organization's work is performed by managers and subordinates through a series of interrelated and interdependent subsystems connected by work flow. Thus the organization must be considered from a number of points of view in assessing its effectiveness and efficiency.

Analyzing an organization from only one perspective leads to the definition of only one set of problems and particular approaches to improvement of the organization. Analysis of the organization from a different point of view leads to a second set of problem definitions, a different set of solutions, and a different design based on a different set of assumptions. *Optimal* problem definition, *optimal* solutions, and *optimal* organizational designs are reached only when all perspectives and all of the assumptions are considered simultaneously, with emphasis placed on differing points of view at appropriate points in time.

CURRENT CONFUSION IN MANAGEMENT THOUGHT

As one surveys the literature in the field, however, one is reminded of the old story about the six blind persons of Indostan who went to "see" the elephant. One felt the trunk and reported that the elephant was much like a snake. Another, feeling the tusk, said that the elephant was similar to a spear. A third, touching the ear, concluded that the elephant was very like a fan, and so forth. Similarly, it is apparent that many of those who write about organizations and organizational improvement and effectiveness have a strong tendency to take a specialized point of view, to the exclusion of others equally valid. Koontz suggests that the welter and variety of differing approaches to management and organizational theory have led to a "kind of confused and destructive warfare" in which it seems to be the style of management theorists to "downgrade, and sometimes misrepresent, what anyone else has said, or thought, or done."[2]

Perhaps this is to some measure inevitable, since the scientific study of management is still very young. In addition, the plethora of books and articles in this field makes it impossible for any individual to really keep up with what is going on. Consequently, both the student and the business person are confused, and legitimately so.

ORGANIZATIONAL IMPROVEMENT—A DEFINITION

There are many definitions of organizational improvement—probably as many definitions as there are theorists in the field. However, an eminently practical one is that offered by Lawrence and Lorsch, who say that when we talk about improving organizational effectiveness and efficiency, "we are implying that we want to change the organization from its current state to a better-developed state."[3]

Before discussing the varying approaches to improving organizations, however, we need to examine the dimensions of the environment within which the organization exists, as well as the effect of the organization and the environment on each other. Prior to any determination of what may be appropriate steps in organizational improvement, an environmental analysis must be performed. Such an analysis must lead to specific goal statements and action plans.

We want to stress again that our three perspectives for analyzing the organization are really "artificial" divisions. Any organization, large or small, exists as an entity and must be managed as such. Indeed, our three approaches overlap considerably and must therefore be considered simultaneously so as to arrive at *optimal* organizational competency. The vast majority of managers are concerned with improving information and work flow; all too few are concerned with improving the productivity and personal growth of their subordinates.

CLIMATE, ENVIRONMENT, AND ORGANIZATIONAL PLANNING (CHAPTER 9)

This chapter starts with a look at internal organizational climate, how climate is measured, and whether it is perceived as affecting or being affected by other factors of organizational life. Research that sheds light on internal climate as it relates to job alienation and job satisfaction is considered. The external environment is treated as both a global, macro concept and as a more precise micro concept, and then the differences in these approaches to studying the environment are compared. We discuss the accelerating pace of change in our culture today, including a brief examination of a new concern—organizational social responsibility. The final part of this discussion focuses on the increasing internationalization of business, a phenomenon that has occurred in the last 25 years. Micro and macro issues of organization-environment interface are discussed, ending with recent environmental research.

With this background, the chapter treats organizational planning and objective setting. Since planning without consideration of the environment is likely to lead to ill-conceived plans, this factor must be incorporated into a planning model. The chapter ends with a brief discussion of deviation-amplifying and deviation-reducing approaches to organizational planning.

ORGANIZATIONAL IMPROVEMENT—STRUCTURAL-DESIGN PERSPECTIVE (CHAPTER 10)

This chapter focuses on current research, theory, and application of organizational improvement from the structural-design approach. After a very brief review of the history of traditional organizational theory, we take up an individual organizational approach. We discuss single organizations, without regard for the environment or other organizations in the same field, focusing instead on how they might be structured differently, e.g., around a product or a function.

Instead of treating organization structure as an independent variable, we review those antecedent conditions and research which help determine the most effective way to organize a company. Thus we treat structure as a dependent variable. What emerges is a contingency approach for the design of organizations, dependent on the environment and rate of technological change. The concepts of differentiation and integration of organizational subsystems are amplified, and the most recent contingency-theory research is discussed and criticized.

ORGANIZATIONAL IMPROVEMENT—WORK-FLOW PERSPECTIVE (CHAPTER 11)

This chapter first describes current efforts to improve the flow processes through the organization by the use of such techniques as mathematical models, operations research, and computers. Some of the benefits and liabilities of these approaches are viewed in the context of the organization as a total system. The second part of the chapter is about integrating technological and cultural systems so that a work-flow system takes account of cultural norms or understandings. This part of the chapter contains an international focus, since much of the work on sociotechnical systems has been done in Europe. Of particular note is the work done with Swedish automobile companies.

ORGANIZATION DEVELOPMENT—HUMAN PERSPECTIVE (CHAPTER 12)

Focusing on the human side of the organization, this chapter describes organization development, the term preferred over "organizational improvement" by practitioners in this area. Chapter 12 stresses the necessity for proper diagnosis before action can be taken on organization development. Following a description of some currently popular approaches to organization development, we examine several criticisms of this area and point out some of the myths about this topic that have developed within the past few years.

TOWARD AN INTEGRATED SYSTEMS THEORY OF ORGANIZATION DEVELOPMENT (CHAPTER 13)

This chapter integrates the approaches to organization development described in the three preceding chapters. After illustrating some of the ways in which the three different perspectives can be combined to improve organizational competence, we conclude with two case studies that use these overall principles.

AN INTEGRATED STUDY OF ORGANIZATION DEVELOPMENT (CHAPTER 14)

The presentation of the case history provides further amplification of the principles of organization development. In this case, several different approaches to organization development were used at varying times. By describing both the successes and failures encountered in this study, we hope that you will get a better understanding of the application of principles for organization development.

REFERENCES

1. A. Etzioni, *Modern Organizations,* Englewood Cliffs, N.J.: Prentice-Hall, 1964, p. 8.

2. H. Koontz, "The Management Theory Jungle," *Journal of the Academy of Management* **4,** 3 (1961): 174–178.

3. P. Lawrence and J. Lorsch, *Developing Organizations: Diagnosis and Action,* Reading, Mass.: Addison-Wesley, 1969, p. 4.

9

CLIMATE, ENVIRONMENT, AND ORGANIZATIONAL PLANNING

*Once to every man and nation comes
the moment to decide.*

JAMES RUSSELL LOWELL

LEARNING
OBJECTIVES

When you have finished reading and studying this chapter, you should be able to:

1. Define "climate" and distinguish between "climate" and "job satisfaction."
2. Distinguish among independent, intervening, and dependent variables.
3. Outline the research on climate.
4. Show how the contingency approach relates to climate.
5. Differentiate between "alienation" and "job satisfaction."
6. Distinguish between a macro and micro approach to environment.
7. Outline what is meant by the accelerated pace of change.
8. Distinguish between internal and external environments.
9. Carry out an environmental analysis of an organization you are in.
10. Relate social responsibility to social power.
11. Discuss how you would measure social responsibility.
12. Develop organizational plans for an organization you currently belong to.
13. Relate organizational plans to internal and external environments and climate.
14. Distinguish between proactive and reactive approaches to planning.

You will be expected to define and use the following concepts:

Climate	Organic system
Job satisfaction	Macro/Micro
Alienation	Social responsibility
Independent variable	Organizational planning
Intervening variable	Social accounting
Dependent variable	Environmental turbulence
Environment	Psychosocial contract
Legitimization	Categories of organizational goals
Static-dynamic dimension	Proactive versus reactive approaches to objectives
Simple-complex dimension	
Mechanistic system	Official versus actual goals

THOUGHT
STARTERS

1. What differentiates climate from culture?
2. What kinds of cultural changes have occurred in the past five years?
3. What are the important dimensions of the environment you are presently in?
4. What kinds of socially responsible acts has industry in your home town accomplished in the past year?
5. When you are planning for a vacation, what general issues need decisions?

I. INTRODUCTION

The congregation was restless, and the new pastor was unhappy. After seven years of uninterrupted growth, the church underwent a change in leadership. Gone was the well-known, kindly, authoritarian clergyman. Gone too was the old service that everyone had felt comfortable with. In its place were a new worship service, which was difficult to follow, and a new pastor, whose leadership style was egalitarian; the parishioners were expected to share in the leadership and managerial functions of the church. The new building had been erected just six years earlier, and now there was nothing to do except face the late 1960s and early 1970s with uncertainty. Building the church structure had provided a concrete and symbolic goal; now all that had to be done was to nourish the congregation and help people grow in their faith—a tall order in the face of ambiguity. The members of the congregation could not agree on where their church should be heading. The country was then in the middle of a protracted war in Southeast Asia, and some factions in the church thought that the church should speak out on one or the other side of the war issue. The national church body had directed that trial worship services be used, and the people were confused. Gone was the familiar service, the singleness of purpose. Clearly, the changes had brought difficulties. The external environment had changed; the internal climate had changed. Concrete goals had been displaced by some rather vague platitudes. The once-flourishing parish was truly in trouble.

This chapter is about some of the dimensions of that trouble. First, we take up the internal organizational issues—the climate. We then examine the organization in its environmental milieu, focusing particularly on the issue of social responsibility. Finally, we look at the development of objectives. We study climate, environment, and objectives in this order because before an organization can make sound objectives, it must (simultaneously) examine its internal and external situations.

Twenty years ago, a major area for research was the relationship between job satisfaction and productivity. But a review of the major studies in the area concluded that there is no consistent relationship between satisfaction and productivity. The earlier assumption that satisfaction in the work situation causes high productivity was not borne out.[1] To make matters more confusing, later research showed some indication that causality went in the opposite direction.[2] The newer argument went like this: High productivity produces rewards, and these rewards produce satisfaction; therefore, high productivity produces satisfaction.

More recently, the issue of job satisfaction has broadened into a more encompassing concern, that of organizational climate. Sociology and journalism have contributed to this by studying worker alienation. Management researchers, however, have focused on organizational climate. The thinking has gone from the economic motivation–Protestant ethic premise that the individual is responsible for his or her own work satisfaction to the realization that external factors, i.e., the organization and its environment, play a significant part in an individual's perception of the work situation.

"Organizational climate" has a number of definitions. Indeed, some theorists have argued that splitting the concept into individual-focused and organizational-focused concepts would be helpful.[3] "Organizational climate" refers to an organizational attribute; "psychological climate," to an individual's attribute. Hellreigel and Slocum, by contrast, treat climate as a more unitary phenomenon, defining it as ". . . a set of attributes which can be perceived about a particular organization and/or its subsystems, and that may be induced from the way that organization and/or its subsystems deal with their members and environment."[4]

However it is defined, "climate" refers to a systemic phenomenon that pervades an organization and its parts. In addition, climate is a perceived phenomenon, knowledge of which is usually gained by administering and scoring a questionnaire. Just as people perceive their world differently, so too do they have various perceptions of the climate of their organizations. All the members of that church discussed earlier could describe the shift in climate from positive and supportive to negative and self-destructive, but each person in the church would undoubtedly characterize the climate in slightly different ways.

Since the interest in climate emerged from interest in job satisfaction, it is appropriate to distinguish between the two. One study of the relationship between climate and satisfaction defines climate as "a global (multidimensional) impression of what the organization is."[5] This definition highlights the perceptual and descriptive nature of climate. The same study describes job satisfaction as "a personalistic *evaluation* of conditions existing on the job."[6] The main difference, then, is that climate is couched in neutral, descriptive terms, whereas job satisfaction is much more subjectively evaluative.

Generally, there appears to be a fairly clear, positive relationship between climate and satisfaction. Perhaps because climate is less evaluative than satisfaction, agreement within organizations about climate is more likely than about satisfaction.

For example, think about why you are taking class for which this book has been assigned. Perhaps you are taking the course to fulfill a requirement; perhaps you are taking it for the fun of it. We have noticed that students are less satisfied in required courses than they are in their electives. Going further, we might say that the climate is generally described by the students as open and fostering discussion. Thus there may be general agreement about climate, but those taking the course as an elective might be more satisfied than those taking it as a required course. This finding would conform to research results of the relationship between climate and satisfaction. In completing the classroom situation, let us say that your satisfaction with the class and the climate have little to do with the grade you will get. Again, this confirms what researchers have found about the relationship of climate and satisfaction to productivity.

The distinction between climate and satisfaction does seem to be useful. Soon, perhaps, research efforts will focus on determining the variables that actually cause productivity, climate, and satisfaction.

The measuring devices commonly used do not help to alleviate the criticisms of overlap between climate and satisfaction. Measurement of climate is usually done by perceptual questionnaires, and individuals, whatever their variations, still have to respond to them. Thus it may be difficult, if not impossible, to keep an individual's satisfaction from intruding into the concept of organizational climate.

What is contained in measures of organizational climate? One source mentions a common core of dimensions: autonomy, structure, reward, consideration, warmth, and support.[7] Most questionnaires, however, also contain other dimensions, but these seem to be the ones found most commonly.

II. RESEARCH FINDINGS ON CLIMATE

In organizational research, climate is conceptualized in one of three ways: as an independent variable, as an intervening variable, or as a dependent variable. The *independent variable* is the one manipulated in an experiment or is the first variable examined to which other variables are related. In a study of food deprivation, for example, some animals might be deprived of food for 6 hours, some for 12 hours, and some for 24 hours. Since we are varying the time, length of food deprivation is the independent variable. If particular climates are "manufactured" for particular organizational settings to see what happens, the independent variable is climate.

The *dependent variable* is the one measured as a result of some prior manipulation. For instance, climate might be measured after the manipulation of organizational structure or leadership style. In this case, organizational structure is the independent variable, and climate is the dependent, or end-result, variable.

The *intervening variable* is inferred from manipulating an independent variable and measuring a dependent variable. In a study on length of food deprivation, one might infer that the experimenters were nipped by the animals "because they were hungry." Hunger is the intervening variable. We cannot ask an animal if it is hungry; we can only observe behavior that is displayed and that is similar to human behavior. Most precisely, we would say that the animal "acts as though it were hungry." Similarly, we might infer the existence of a particular type of climate as a result of a manipulation of an organizational structure. However, the factor measured would be something only tangentially related to climate, e.g., absenteeism or turnover. If absenteeism decreases after an organizational change, one might infer that the climate was improved by that change.

Let us now examine in more detail climate as an independent variable, with other factors dependent on climate. One review of the research found that in terms of interpersonal relations, group cohesion, task involvement, etc., climate was generally related to job satisfaction.[8] Climate has also been found to be related to performance. In other words, if workers perceive the work environment to be supportive, they are more likely to feel satisfied by their jobs. Similarly, if the work environment is supportive, performance is likely to be higher, but that relationship is generally weaker than the preceding one. Other research reported that inconsistent perceptions of climate in the same organization seemed related to lower performance.[9] Even though this article did not review studies from the mid-1950s, the findings are consistent with the 1955 review of studies on satisfaction and performance, which suggested a rather weak, inconsistent relationship between satisfaction and performance and did not really consider which was the causal, or independent, variable.[10]

Climate as an intervening variable is usually found when human relations training or leadership have been used as the independent variables.[11] In one study, a president's leadership style in a business game was varied, and three climates were introduced: authoritarian, friendly, and achieving. As one might expect, the "achieving" condition produced the highest performance level, but the "democratic-friendly" condition resulted in the greatest satisfaction; the authoritarian climate produced low satisfaction and low innovation and productivity.[12] Although climate was not identified as such 25 years ago, the results of this study resemble those of one done with adult leaders of children's clubs in an authoritarian, democratic, or *laissez faire* leadership style.[13] These results also conform to the Blake-Mouton approach.[14] The authoritarian climate seems parallel to the task-oriented management style; the friendly climate, to the people-oriented "country club" style; and the achieving climate has elements of both, much like the Blake and Mouton 9,9 optimal managerial style.

More recently, a study conducted with real-life directors and scientists in research and development organizations examined the relationship between organizational structure and process, climate, and performance and job satisfaction.[15] This correlational study found a moderately strong relationship between organizational processes and climate, but a very slight one between structure and climate (see Fig. 9.1). Climate, in turn, was relatively strongly related to job satisfaction, but less so to organizational performance. Figure 9.1 shows a hint of causality (i.e., process causes climate, which in turn causes satisfaction), but because of the nature of the methodology, the causality issue must await further research confirmation.

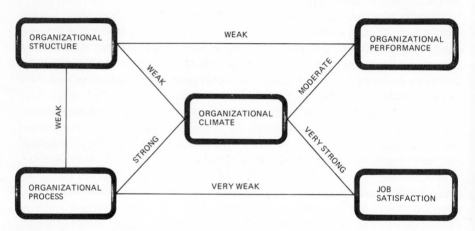

Fig. 9.1 Relationships between variables. (Adapted from E. E. Lawler, III, D. T. Hall, and G. R. Oldham, "Organizational Climate: Relationship to Organizational Structure, Process and Performance," *Organizational Behavior and Human Performance* **11**, 1, Feb. 1974, p. 151.)

Other researchers look at climate as a dependent, or measurable end-result, variable. Hellriegel and Slocum review a number of studies that illustrate this point of view.[16] One aggregate finding is that one's perception of climate varies according to the position held. A common example occurs in the academic setting. A dean may perceive the climate in a vastly different fashion from students or faculty members. An administrator may be poorly regarded because of different perspectives on climate. A dean may think that everything is going well, but students may be unhappy and the faculty frustrated. Those above the dean may be unaware of the local climate until some event gives them evidence of it.

Sensitivity-training programs can also be responsible for changes in climate. Such programs allow persons to try new behavior and see themselves as others see them. In one representative piece of research, sensitivity training was initiated to move the organization toward Likert's System 4 approach.[17] The sensitivity-training program induced and maintained changes in climate over an 18-month period interlude.

One of the major thrusts in recent organizational behavior literature has been the contingency approach, not only for leadership, but also for climate. Thus climate and performance and their relationship to each other are probably affected by certain other variables—technology, production processes, or organizational structure. To date, there appear to be no clear contingency patterns.[18] However, one Norwegian study did find a contingent relationship between technological process and perception of climate.[19] In this study, the researcher categorized industrial firms by their type of production technology (small batch, mass, and continuous process). There was clear evidence that technological process was related to organizational climate; respondents' perceptions of climate were less positive in mass-production organizations than in small-batch or continuous-process firms.

The Norwegian finding appears to offer deeper insight into job enrichment, a topic discussed later in this book. In some traditionally mass-production industries, such as the automobile and fine-glassware industries, job enrichment may occur as a subdividing and grouping of activities to more closely resemble the "small-batch" style of production technology. Such changes reflect a recognition that climate and/or job satisfaction are keyed to the production technology.

Although ther are no clear contingency factors related to climate in a universal way, more and more research on climate is being carried out. Variables that are important in other contingency situations, such as leadership and organizational structure, are beginning to find their way into the research on climate.

A. Alienation: Lack of Job Satisfaction?

The term "alienation" has its roots in sociology and journalism (where it is also called "blue-collar blues"). Defining alienation as lack of job satisfaction is probably too narrow. At one time the term was attributed to Marx's description of the feelings of the worker.[20] According to Marx, alienation resulted from the worker's lack of ownership of the equipment and means of production, as well as the lack of opportunity to enjoy the benefits of work.

More recently, theorists cite three factors likely to cause alienation and/or reflect powerlessness, normlessness, and meaninglessness.[21] Powerlessness refers to a person's feeling that he or she is an object almost completely under the control of other persons or a system. Normlessness is that state of ambiguity about the behavior necessary for attaining organizational rewards. Such ambiguity occurs when the psychological contract has broken down and there is little agreement between management and the worker on those issues confronting them both. A worker who does not comprehend the purpose or the coordinated activity surrounding his or her work experiences meaninglessness. The resultant expressions of alienation are *isolation*, whereby the worker feels unable to identify with organizational goals, and *self-estrangement*, whereby the worker regards work simply as a means to an end rather than as an end in and of itself.[22]

The meanings of the terms "alienation" and "job satisfaction" reveal their roots. "Alienation" is a systemwide phenomenon, whereas "job satisfaction" is tied to the particular set of tasks a worker is called on to perform. Like climate, alienation has a macro focus, whereas job satisfaction relates to a micro emphasis.

B. Summary

Both job satisfaction and alienation are related to climate. There has been a recent explosion in the number of articles on climate. Management may be starting to be aware of the differences between the global issue of climate and the individual, evaluative issue of job satisfaction. Although climate, job satisfaction, and performance all tend to be interrelated, there are many instances when they are not or are connected only weakly. The search for contingency variables in the study of climate has yet to turn up any universals, but has instead started a trend for cataloguing particulars. Although this cataloguing process may appear to be confusing at the present time, time will bring order in the process. Another issue yet to be resolved is whether climate is a cause or a result of high productivity, or whether it is a cyclical phenomenon. The answers to these questions will not be forthcoming until stronger methodologies for research are available. The concept of alienation is rich in meaning, but is not as widely considered in today's management thought as climate is. More research on this topic will undoubtedly appear from both academicians and journalists.

III. THE ENVIRONMENT

"Climate" deals with a person's perceptions about what's going on inside the organization. "Environment" refers to the people and conditions external to the organization which affect and are affected by the organization. In terms of the ailing parish church cited earlier, its environment includes any current external event, process, person, group, or condition which affects it. The state of the nation, the region, and the town affect the church's environment. What is going on in the national church body and other church bodies affect it. The economy and the prevailing popular philosophies affect it.

All of the factors external to an organization constitute its environment. Thus not only people and terrain, but also such abstract concepts as people's feelings about what is going on are part of the environment. Environment is a broad, inclusive term. As such, it exemplifies the "macro" approach to the study of organizational behavior.

There is a "trade off" in micro and macro approaches. The methodologies for studying micro organizational behavior are tighter and more variables can be controlled, but the situation is a little artificial. In the study of the organization as a whole, researchers are forced to rely more on description and anecdotes; there is less attempt to control variables and a greater emphasis on trying to observe what is going on. The result is that the findings from the macro organizational studies conform more to what one might describe as "common sense." However, one also loses predictive power as to what might be appropriate organizational design to meet particular environmental constraints. Accordingly, we should try to look at the organization in the environment from both the micro and macro perspectives; each has something unique to offer. Nonetheless, we conclude that developing an organization to fit the environment is by necessity situational. There is no one best way to approach the problem of designing the organization to fit the environment; rather, it must be done recognizing the contingencies within the environment.

A. Accelerated Pace of Change

One important aspect of an organization's environment is the rate of change. Change is occurring in many areas of life. Some of the areas of environmentally induced areas of change are the knowledge explosion, technological development, the composition of the labor force, environmental and social issues, and the internationalization of business. Although these areas are interrelated, we will deal with them separately.

1. The knowledge explosion More than 90 percent of all the scientists who have ever lived are still living. This has resulted in a tremendous acceleration in the development of knowledge—the "knowledge explosion." For example, for literally thousands of years, the wheel remained one of the most advanced inventions in transportation and, indeed, was reinvented at various times by different peoples. The American Indian had not yet even invented the wheel when Columbus landed in this country less than 500 years ago. The Tasaday tribe in the Philippines, discovered in 1971, is still in the Bronze Age and has not yet invented the wheel. In the thousands of years that the wheel has been used, only minor improvements have been made, e.g., rubber tires. Yet in about 80 years, transportation has progressed to the invention of motor cars, jet airplanes, and rockets to outer space. Indeed, the *first* commercial passenger flight across the North Atlantic occurred less than 40 years ago.

The relatively recent development of the modern vacuum tube was superseded by the development of transistors and microminiature circuitry, which in turn led to the development of solid-state circuits. The recent discovery of DNA makes it possible for geneticists to "design" human beings *in advance*, by altering the sperm or the egg prior to conception.[23]

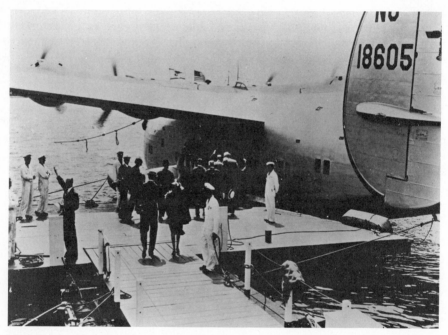

The first transatlantic flight left Port Washington, New York, on June 28, 1939, for Marseilles, France. (Photograph courtesy Pan American World Airways)

The result of the knowledge explosion is that an individual's knowledge can quickly become obsolete. In other words, it is almost impossible to keep up with new knowledge. Information learned in college courses may well be outdated before the student has an opportunity to put that knowledge into practice. In the field of psychology alone, it is estimated that some 21,000

This highly sophisticated microminiature circuit is so small that an ant appears to be quite large by comparison. (Photograph courtesy Jet Propulsion Laboratory)

books, articles, and monographs are written each year, and it has been estimated that the rate of new information is doubling every ten years.

2. Rapid technological development New products are invented, developed, and quickly become obsolete, just as the transistor became relatively obsolete with the development of microminiature circuitry.

Each year, on the average, a higher percentage of the gross national product goes into research and development than ever before. An industrial company develops, for example, a new, complex medical instrument only to find that within a few short months, a competing company has brought out a better instrument at a lower cost. And as more money is poured into research, the rate at which new products are developed increases. This is far different from the manufacturing of the horseshoe, the design of which remained essentially unchanged for hundreds of years.

Product obsolescence is growing at a rapidly accelerating pace. Meanwhile, products are becoming more and more complex. Even as they become more complex, however, their cost may decline. Two good examples are pocket calculators, which have come down in price and size while increasing in complexity, and digital watches.

3. The changing composition of the labor force The urbanization of the United States has resulted in a dramatic shift in population. In 1825 only 10 percent of the American population lived in towns and cities. By 1960, however, 70 percent of the population lived on 1 percent of the land area. It is estimated that in the year 2000, 90 percent of the population will live on 2 percent of the land area. A recent response to such demographic trends has been the planned development of new cities. One such new city is Columbia,

Many people fear that increasing urbanization will be accompanied by greater uniformity and population density. (The Christian Science Monitor)

Maryland, where General Electric built a new distribution facility to serve the Northeast, in which 30 percent of the nation's current population is concentrated on 7 percent of the land.[24]

Paralleling the increasing urbanization is the rising educational level of the population. When Frederick Taylor did his pioneering work in 1900, most industrial workers were immigrants who did not know English. This work force, then, had little education and was accustomed to obeying orders without question. Today, however, it is estimated that 60 percent or more of the urban population is obtaining some form of higher education beyond high school. In fact, today's college diploma is roughly equivalent in value to a high school education of only a few years ago. The same shift is occurring at the graduate level. The United States Office of Education expects the nation to have 1.6 million resident graduate students in 1979, or nearly double the 889,000 in 1969, and almost five times the 331,000 in 1959.

Therefore, the employee of tomorrow will be considerably better educated than the employee of today, regardless of the type of organization in which he or she is employed. In practical terms, this shift in educational background means that the employee of tomorrow will not accept outmoded styles of management. For example, 33 military officers, among the brightest and most capable of those teaching at West Point, recently left the service.[25] A spokesman for the academy indicated that the resignations were disastrous, since these men "are the brightest—they are outstanding officers." All of the officers who resigned had been promoted faster than normal, but all felt that life outside the army would give them greater personal satisfaction. As one officer explained, "you have to play it safe for so long before you can become a general—and by that time you're a different person."

Another major change in the composition of the labor force is the decrease in the median age of the population, a direct result of the baby boom following World War II. In a few short years, the number of births in this country rose by about 50 percent. As a result, the median age of the work force is decreasing, and managers will have to become increasingly aware of the needs and concerns of their younger workers.

The fourth major change is the shift from "blue-collar" workers (laborers and semiskilled workers) to "white-collar" workers (managerial, professional, technical, sales, and clerical personnel). The year 1956 marked a watershed; for the first time, "white-collar" workers outnumbered "blue-collar" workers. The best guess is that the ratio will continue to increase.

4. Social responsibility of organizations   "Profit maximization" and "doing for others" are contradictory values and are the crux of the issue of "corporate social responsibility." There are several value-laden conceptual issues involved in the meaning of this phrase. How does one measure how well a corporation is doing in meeting its corporate social responsibilities? How does a corporation assess the social worth of its programs? How does a health-care delivery program measure its results versus its costs?

Corporate social responsibility is closely linked to environmental issues. (Ewing Galloway/E. P. Jones)

Nicolaou-Smokovitis defined the term "psychosocial contract" as those "mutual interdependencies, obligations between the individual and organization [and] a similar set of mutual interdependencies, obligations and expectations [between society and] both the individual and the organization."[26] The individual and the organization have unwritten assumptions about each other, as do society and the individual and the organization. Here, "society" refers to both the consumer of goods and services and external segments in the organization's environment.

Davis outlines five basic aspects of social responsibility.[27] (1) Social responsibility is derived from social power. Those who use power in ways that society considers irresponsible will lose that power. We have all seen what governmental and popular awareness of automobile pollution and the finiteness of oil reserves have done to encourage legislation to take some of the "power" away from the automobile industry. (2) Business and society operate as reciprocal open systems. Corporate managers have become more concerned about what the consumers and the government think. (3) Social costs and benefits of activities will be calculated in the process of deciding how to measure the results of social-responsibility programs. As is noted below, there is a current emphasis on how to *measure* social costs, benefits, and awareness, as well as on the nature of those costs, benefits, and awareness. (4) Social costs will be priced into a produce or service; thus the users pay for the effects on society of consuming that produce or service. For example, several states have either initiated or are considering initiating "returnable bottle" laws or have forbidden the discharge of untreated waste water into streams. These laws ultimately add costs to the consumer through the prices of goods. (5) "Beyond social costs, business institutions as citizens have responsibilities for social involvement in areas of their competence where major social needs exist."[28]

Another factor in the social-responsibility issue is what managers think. In 1973, 200 executives from the 1000 largest corporations in the United States provided several interesting answers to a questionnaire.[29] First, most executives regard shareholders as investors rather than as co-owners of the concern. This perception (or rationalization) makes it easier for managers to operate without being the shareholders' alter egos. Second, corporate charitable contributions not sanctioned by shareholders are not regarded by executives as a misuse of funds. Thus social-responsibility programs may be set up without the explicit assent of the shareholders. Third, about half of the executives responding did not feel that profit maximization is the best means of serving society as a whole.

These findings reflect how managers feel about corporate social responsibility. Yet one wonders how much social desirability has seeped into those responses. It could be that managers felt obliged to select a socially desirable response, even though it was not an accurate reflection of their own organizations.

Bauer, a major contributor to the area of measuring social responsibility, notes that most social audits, or measurements of social responsibility, are ill-defined.[30] One issue is that subordinates do not know what the superior is thinking. Additionally, a job is invariably bigger than the budget and manpower set aside for it. Frequently, the social audit steps on the toes of the key executives, and there is philosophical disagreement about what should be included in the audit.

Bauer outlines the purposes of a social audit as (1) "satisfying the corporate conscience, (2) staying out of trouble, (3) solving social problems, and (4) improving the financial wisdom of social programs."[31] A fifth motive, reinforcement of corporate social policies, may be the most important one involved in corporate social responsibility. Think about the advertisements comparing American coal reserves with Middle Eastern oil reserves. The ads imply that the United States should develop its own resources, because the coal industry is fairly labor-intensive and to do so would bring more jobs to the coal region. Many of these ads were developed for American Electric Power Corporation, which has extensive facilities in some of the coal-bearing areas of the United States.

One of Bauer's main points is that organizations have difficulties deciding what should be included in their social audits.[32] The research literature points up a corollary. There is disagreement about not only *what* should be included, but also *how* a social audit should be conducted. The three articles summarized below show the magnitude of this problem.

The first article, by Churchill, explores two approaches for social accounting.[33] One method is simply to convert economic-based accounting principles to measure the value of social-responsibility programs. Churchill argues that this narrow approach, however, has several disadvantages. In one example he notes that economic benefits are recognized year after year as a kind of continuous variable, but that social benefits, e.g., instituting pollution control in a facility, are discrete occurrences and are recognized only when they are instituted. A second major weakness is the concept of entity; a business enterprise is considered to be a multidimensional system, but open only to its suppliers, customers, and stockholders, whereas the benefits of a social-responsibility program impact many others. Churchill asserts that the concepts of both entity and cost-to-benefit matching must be broadened in order to take into account *all* of the results produced by particular socially conscious activities. Only then will there be a step toward a better sense of social measurement.

This "expanded concept of entity" is taken into account in two other studies, cited in the second article.[34] The data for these studies included all of the possible constituencies, whether they were directly related in a traditional accounting sense, or indirectly affected in the social sense. However, no attempt was made to account for the costs of the programs and to match them up with benefits—a gargantuan task.

The basic question asked in these two studies was: "What do people inside and outside the facility think about the company?" In one of the studies, customers, workers, suppliers, managers, creditors, and parallel units of a regional sanitation department were asked to fill out questionnaires about how well the department served individual and community needs. In the other, methodologically similar, study, people affected by a power company were asked the same sort of question.

The profiles from these two studies show the relative perceived strengths and weaknesses the two organizations had in fulfilling their social responsibilities. The sanitation department was perceived as doing a much better job for its creditors and managers than for the community, its employees, or society in general. The power company was perceived as doing a better job by management and the stockholders than by the community it served and the people in its wider environment.

The third paper suggests examining the motivation of an organization to start social-responsibility programs.[35] Along with some of the recent work in motivation, this proposal incorporates expectancy theory into the social audit. Thus in addition to having ways of measuring the benefits of social-responsibility programs, one can now map out the decisions that could be made in terms of their valences, instrumentalities, and expectancies. Although using expectancy theory is an interesting proposal, one must view it with some caution, inasmuch as no data have yet been collected to determine its full utility.

5. Increasing internationalization of business This aspect of the changing environment can be seen in the growth of the European Common Market. According to Bass, "60 percent of all the world's business will eventually be done by international firms."[36] He predicts that the concept of the common market will vastly expand and that the typical manager of the future will be involved in a world of mixed economies. Thus, for example, capitalist and socialist ideologies will be closer together, and the organization of the future will be doing business in many different countries, as can be seen in the expanding trade between the United States and Russia.

Table 9.1 shows the income receipts and payments resulting from international trade. In the nine years from 1965 to 1974, the amount increased nearly fivefold for the United States and fourfold for the rest of the world. This increase is in sharp contrast to the doubling that occurred between 1955 and 1965. Even when one takes account of inflation, the 1965–1974 increase is huge. Not only is the United States investing more heavily abroad (to the concern of the Canadian government), but also other countries are investing more heavily in the United States. The oil-rich Middle East countries have capital to

Table 9.1 Imports and exports in world trade (value in billions, U.S. dollars)

	Imports	Exports
International trade		
1955	98.4	93.7
1965	198.6	187.6
1974	843.9	805.6
U.S. trade		
1955	12.5	15.6
1965	23.2	27.5
1974	108.0	98.5

Source: Adapted from *International Economic Report of the President*, Washington, D.C.: U.S. Government Printing Office, March 1975, Tables 17 and 18, p. 131.

invest, and it is small wonder that many of them look toward United States real estate as a relatively safe, economically stable haven for their investments.

In his discussion of cultural barriers, Stone stresses the need to adapt interpersonal and intercultural communications so as to bridge the cultural barriers in international management.[37] One such bridge might take the form of

As business firms become international, they must also become multilingual. (Photograph by Edgar F. Huse)

consciously building a worldwide culture in which international well-being and cooperation can be achieved. Goodman and Moore, however, urge caution in undertaking such an approach.[38] They state that the generally low quality of cross-cultural managerial studies has occurred because the theoretical delineation and operational specification of the culture (and subcultures) were neglected as moderating variables and that data analysis was inadequate.

B. Macro Issues of Environment-Organization Interface

Perhaps the key environmental issue to face an organization is that of legitimacy. In order to survive, an organization must be considered legitimate by its various constituents and publics. For example, an automobile manufacturer cannot survive unless the banks, consumers, suppliers, environmentalists, as well as state and federal agencies, consider this enterprise desirable. This process is called *legitimization*.[39]

In late 1975 a young American businessman with a dream had trouble with his recently formed automobile company. Because of certain labor, tax, and other considerations, Malcolm Bricklin chose to produce his car in the Canadian province of New Brunswick. The car, designed as a fast, high-powered, extremely safe, sports car, however uneconomical, was originally slated to be sold for $7500, but the costs pushed the price up to about $10,000. One of the production problems was that the quality control was not very good. In addition, the general public did not immediately accept the Bricklin. In short, what might have been seen as a legitimate venture a couple of years earlier (before the oil crisis) was not, in 1975, seen by the various constituents as being legitimate. By the end of 1975, Mr. Bricklin estimated that there was only a 50–50 chance that he could stay in production. By early 1976, it was clear that no more Bricklins would be produced.

Similarly, about 15 years ago an organization existed to find a cure for polio. It had legitimate standing at the time, but had to change its goals when researchers Salk and Sabin developed their treatments for polio. How many of you hear of the March of Dimes these days? This organization, which achieved legitimacy in its search for cures for polio, has achieved less legitimacy and visibility in its new venture, combating birth defects. Does the same fate await the Cancer Society and the Heart Fund? Only time will tell.

Perrow notes that there can be a reverse twist on legitimacy.[40] This occurs when an organization recognized and accepted for its output tries to do away with that output. The forced demise of passenger service by most railroads prior to the establishment of Amtrak is an example. This service was unprofitable to the railroads. In order to survive, they had to end the unprofitable segment of their operations, no matter how legitimate it might be to their constituents.

Every organization interacts with the environment, which provides both opportunities and problems. For instance, the oil-producing nations apparently need to fine-tune their demands on the environment so that they can sell their oil at the highest "practical" price. Should they go for short-term riches, the nations buying oil will step up their research on alternative energy sources. Should they set the price of oil so low that they are not getting the returns possible, they are short-changing their own constituents. When representatives of the oil-producing countries met in late 1975, they could not agree on the amount to increase oil prices. Saudi Arabia was quoted as stating that there should be no more than a 5% rise in prices. Most other nations thought that this was far too small. In order to placate Saudi Arabia, there had to be some kind of accommodation, since all of the nations knew that they were far better off presenting a united front.

Since the work force is part of both the organization and the environment, it is fair to say that the environment and the organization each have an effect on each other. For instance, it appeared some years ago that there were more strikes in industries in which the workers were relatively isolated than in those in which the workers came from urban settings.[41] Similarly, a decade ago workers coming from rural settings appeared to desire more autonomy than did those coming from urban settings.[42] However, more recent work has examined the work preferences of urban dwellers, rural dwellers, and rural-to-urban transitionals in continuous-process industries and found that either the earlier study was not well-enough controlled or that its findings are not generalizable from one time period to another. This later work did not support the hypothesis that rurals are more likely than urbans to react favorably to increased job responsibility.[43]

Clearly, time and the world or national economy must be considered in any examination of environment. One of the findings just cited is based on research about 20 years old; the other, about three years old. One might wonder what difference in the more recent findings might result from the current widespread impact of TV and having just had the worst recession since the Great Depression. We suspect that if current research repeated some of the methodology of the classic studies, the results would be startlingly different, reflecting differences in culture, time, and economic conditions.

International guidebooks point up cultural differences very vividly. One does not install participative management techniques if it would be considered culturally inappropriate to do so. For example, Volvo in Sweden uses a job-enriched assembly technique that downplays the importance of the assembly line. However, in Volvo's new assembly facility in Virginia, the company is reportedly undecided about which assembly method to use.

One final example of the organization's impact on the environment is the way in which large companies can control smaller companies, frequently their suppliers. Usually, a supplier for a large corporation has most of its business tied up in that corporation. Thus the buyer can threaten to take the business elsewhere, thus killing the supplier. This is referred to as *"monopsony,* dominance of the market by the buyer."[44]

C. Micro Issues of Environment-Organization Interface

One of the major difficulties in studying the environment is gaining agreement as to what actually constitutes the environment. Table 9.2 shows one particularly clear breakdown of the environment into internal and external components.

In particular, two environmental dimensions have attracted research interest. One is the *simple-complex dimension,* which refers to the number of factors that are operational in the organization's environment. In a lower-level part of an organization, very few factors may be important; in a higher-level part, many. For example, Duncan notes that a lower-level production facility may be concerned only with parts and materials, but that a programing and planning department would have to concern itself with virtually all of the factors found in Table 9.2.

The second major dimension is the *static-dynamic dimension,* which refers to the stability of the organization's internal and external environments over time. The important external component here is the rate of technological change, and success is the degree to which the internal component of the organization adapts to the external conditions. Thus what is appropriate in the rapidly changing technology of the plastics industry is inappropriate for the slowly changing technology of the container industry.[45] In addition, dynamic environmental change is more significant than the number of variables considered along the simple-complex dimension.[46]

How to cope with environmental turbulence, then, is a major issue. Management systems cope with the two extremes of environmental conditions in different ways.[47] On one hand, the stable environment is best confronted with a *mechanistic* management system, which is characterized by highly specialized work. Operations and responsibilities are precisely defined and there is a hierarchy of command. By implication, all knowledge about the total operation is known primarily by the chief executive. In short, this type of approach has most of the characteristics of a stable bureaucracy.

On the other hand, a turbulent environment is most effectively confronted by an *organic* management system, which is characterized by an acknowledgement that problems and requirements for action cannot always be anticipated and distributed among the specialists. Interpersonal interaction occurs laterally and is characterized by a democratic rather than an authoritarian approach. An organic management system is "flat," with little distinction between differ-

Table 9.2 Factors and components comprising the organization's internal and external environments

Internal environment	External environment
Organizational personnel component	*Customer component*
1. Educational and technological background and skills	1. Distributors of product or service
2. Previous technological and managerial skill	2. Actual users of product or service
3. Individual member's involvement and commitment to attaining system's goals	*Suppliers component*
4. Interpersonal behavior styles	1. New materials suppliers
5. Availability of manpower for utilization within the system	2. Equipment suppliers
	3. Product parts suppliers
Organizational functional and staff units' component	4. Labor supply
	Competitor component
1. Technological characteristics of organizational units	1. Competitors for suppliers
2. Interdependence of organizational units in carrying out their objectives	2. Competitors for customers
3. Intraunit conflict among organizational functional and staff units	*Sociopolitical component*
4. Interunit conflict among organizational functional and staff units	1. Government regulatory control over the industry
	2. Public political attitude toward industry and its particular product
Organizational-level component	3. Relationship with trade unions with jurisdiction in the organization
1. Organizational objectives and goals	*Technological component*
2. Integrative process integrating individuals and groups into contributing maximally to attaining organizational goals	1. Meeting new technological requirements of own industry and related industries in production of product or service
3. Nature of the organization's product service	2. Improving and developing new products by implementing new technological advances in the industry

Reprinted by permission from R. D. Duncan "Characteristics of Organizational Environments and Perceived Environmental Uncertainty," *Administrative Science Quarterly* **17**, 3 (1972): 313–327.

ent ranks. Expertise occurs throughout the organization; thus expertise is more important than position or rank.

Expanding on these findings, Lynton describes how to coordinate a subsystem operating within a turbulent environment with the rest of a stable organization.[48] One example is a relatively free-wheeling research and development unit of a stable organization. A balance must be found between the creativity of this unit and maintaining morale on the assembly line.

Lynton notes that subsystems of an organization can be appropriately differentiated along the three dimensions of *technology, territory,* and *time.* That is, subunits can have different technologies, hence different rates of technological change. The territories the subsystems occupy or are responsible for may or may not be similar, and the time focus can be long or short term. According to Lynton, the problem is how to integrate a subsystem having a relatively high rate of technological change, different territory, and a long-term time focus into an overall organization that has a slow rate of technological change, an established work territory, and a short-term time focus. For example, a company might build both power plants (stable technology) and nuclear-power plants (uncertain technology). Integration, or linking, of the two subsystems will fail if the need for systemic change is regarded as negligible or highly specific. His review of research suggests that only if the need for change is regarded to be a continuous process will there be effective mechanisms for linking the subsystem into the overall system. The critical issue is how integration takes place between the organization and its environment or between the organization and a subsystem.

Effective linkage mechanisms have several characteristics in terms of the relationship between the innovative and operating subsystems. First, they must be equidistant between the two subsystems. Therefore, a person in an integrative role must be "intermediate" in terms of the "orientations (of) goals, time, interpersonal relations and the structure of the linkage mechanisms."[49] Additionally, the integrator must have a great deal of knowledge about the specific problems. Finally, the rewards for the linker, or integrator, depend on the success of the linkage effected. In brief, then, effective coping with environment-interacting subsystems relies on the permanent establishment of appropriate linkage mechanisms between the subsystems.

D. Recent Organization-Environment Research

The very fact that research is being conducted is significant; it suggests that whatever the findings, one must consider the surroundings in order to make sense of organizational behavior. Indeed, of all of the factors that impinge on the organization, the environment has the most impact.

Earlier, we discussed the importance of time focus. A closer look at this issue suggests that an intensive knowledge about the immediate environment has very positive short-term effects. However, if the long-term environment is not congruent with the short-term environment, long-term ineffectiveness may result. There may be a positive tradeoff by lessening the knowledge of immediate environmental information and increasing the time horizon to search for long-term environmental information.[50]

For example, many of today's students in higher education are part of the World War II baby boom. Although there have been some environmental changes in terms of research monies, teaching technology, etc., the environment is realtively stable. Let us say that 15 years from now, in order to stay in business, colleges will have to undergo vast changes in order to meet the needs of their students, who may be older, and who perhaps will not even be high school graduates. In other words, the university with five-year plans may do a brilliant job in the short term, but be overtaken by the university that is able to make more accurate plans for the long-term future.

Closely related to the issue of time horizon is that stability or turbulence of the environment. The rate of change of organizational design and structure is contingent on the rate of environmental change. In one study in India, this generalization is partially questioned.[51] Instead, decentralized manufacturing firms were found to be more effective in all types of environments than were centralized manufacturing firms. What makes these data interesting is that decentralization is generally regarded as functional for turbulent environments, but not for stable environments. With the increase of multinational corporations, this finding is just another signal that what may be appropriate in the West needs careful review before it is applied in the East.

Other recent findings continue to cloud this particular point. When routine versus nonroutine decision making was related to environmental uncertainty in manufacturing and research and development organizations, researchers found support for the premise that different sorts of organizational structures were appropriate for different conditions.[52] This finding supports the research conducted in Western cultures.

One final study is of interest because it suggests that management style be considered as a dependent variable (one that is examined as a result of observing or manipulating some prior variables) instead of as an independent (prior) variable.[53] According to this view, management style depends in part on the nature of the environment. This Israeli study found that external influences do have an impact on managerial attitudes toward subordinates. A fruitful area of research would be to replicate this and similar studies in our own culture.

In brief, the environment is an important focal point for research and theorizing about organizational behavior. Frequently the environmental factor is assumed and not considered directly. More recently, however, environmental variables have been taken much more seriously. Theorists realize that they can no longer blindly transfer findings of studies across culture. Nor do they say that there is one best way of organizing industrial firms with similar technological bases. Researchers are also realizing that environmental changes may mean that studies done some time ago may no longer be applicable. In the years to come there will undoubtedly be a great deal more emphasis on this topic, and the findings will add to predictive and interpretive validity in the field of organizational behavior.

IV. ORGANIZATIONAL PLANNING AND OBJECTIVES

Every system needs objectives, or goals. Nearly 30 years ago, Gulick noted that "a clear statement of purpose universally understood is the outstanding guarantee of effective administration."[54] Some 16 years later, Etzioni modified this statement only slightly by pointing out that "an organizational goal is a desired state of affairs which the organization attempts to realize." [55]

The key words in Etzioni's definition are "a *desired* state" that the organization "*attempts* to realize." The organization may not reach the goals or desired state, but it does have plans and purpose. Of course, the objectives will vary with the nature and type of organization. An industrial organization may well have a different set of goals and objectives from a hospital or a social-welfare organization.

Setting objectives organization is a complex task, and no organization has a single set of objectives. Figure 9.2 shows that organizational plans result from a complex interaction of external, internal, and historical forces. Although most industrial managers assert that the objective of their organization is to make a profit, such an oversimplification ignores the influence of both the external environment and the internal subsystems within the organization.

Laws and regulations have a tremendous influence on the objectives of an organization, as do the demands and expectations of the consumer, as witness the untimely death of the Edsel, a car on which Ford lavished a great deal of time and money. More recently, the refusal of the Congress to fund the SST (supersonic transport) caused a tremendous change in the objectives of a number of different organizations. Similarly, the work of Nader and his "Raiders" has caused many organizations to change some of their stated objectives.

Furthermore, there is wide variation between what managers *say* and what they *do* within the organization, as is demonstrated in "Exercise Objectives" developed by Bass.[56] First, managers are asked to make decisions about several organizational problems; then, they are asked, as a group, to give percentage

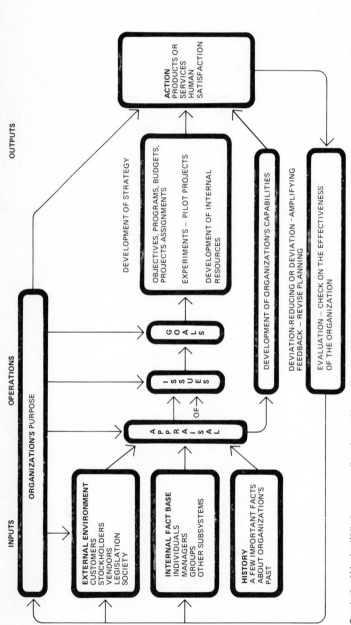

Fig. 9.2 An organizational planning sequence. (Adapted from Charles R. Wilson, *Supervisors and Leaders Training: Planning/Organization Workbook: A System of Management for the Nonprofit Membership Organizations, 1971, 1972.*)

Organizational Identity: While there are many dimensions, problems, and opportunities, the business we are in will help determine the issues which are of particular concern to us.

Environment or external fact base — basic information of importance to the organization about the domain in which it has a mission. This may be demographic data, financial data, cultural, flow data, etc.

Internal Fact Base: Information about the capabilities and resources of the organization.

Appraisal/Issues: Considering the capabilities of the system and the situation posed by the environment.

Goals: What are the medium- and long-range goals we are after?

Strategy: What short-range objectives, programs, and budgets are required to move toward the goals? Perhaps it will be desirable to "pilot" or do something on a small scale, or study the experience of others. At the same time a plan for resource development and utilization and a plan for building the capabilities of the organization are necessary.

Action: People and resources are assigned to domains for putting goals into action within a certain time frame.

Evaluation: The whole process should be kept under review, controls so that the action is what was intended, and is having the intended effect. The environment and organization or system must be monitored so that important changes there can be noted and appropriate modification of goals and program can be quickly instituted.

Table 9.3 Response of managers to "Exercise Objectives"

Objective	Percentage of weight given
Profits	35
Growth	11
Community welfare	21
Improve operations	22
Meet competition	11

Adapted from B. M. Bass, "Exercise Objectives," in *A Program of Exercises for Management and Organizational Psychology*, Pittsburgh: Management Development Associates, 1966.

weights to six possible company objectives. Table 9.3 shows the results of a modified version of the exercise administered by one of the authors. These data were obtained from 60 managers in two industrial organizations. Although profits received the greatest weight, community welfare and improving operations also ranked high. Women executives of a telephone company gave much higher weight to employee welfare and service to the community than to profits; male executives of transit companies gave the highest weight to community welfare and improving operations.

In other words, although people may *say* that profits are the main objective of an organization, they do not *act* that way, either in exercises such as the one described here or as demonstrated by their actions in the organization. Furthermore, the objectives shift, depending on the type of organization in which the person is working.

A. Organizations Have Multiple Objectives

The results of the Bass exercise and the fact that the organization is an open system with interrelated and interdependent subsystems which receive inputs from the outside environment to produce a changing, uneasy balance demonstrate that an organization has multiple objectives. As mentioned in Chapter 8, Drucker notes that industrial organizations must develop objectives in eight key areas: "market standing; innovation; productivity; physical and financial resources; profitability; manager performance and development; worker performance and attitude; and public responsibility."[57] Although the areas cited by Drucker are for a profit-making, or utilitarian, organization, *any* organization needs objectives in every area that affects its survival and effectiveness. It is also clear that since the social system is composed of interrelated subsystems, its objectives will also be interrelated. Thus, for example, market standing and innovation are highly related, as are profitability and worker performance, even though the short-term objectives in one area may contradict those in another area.

Perrow, taking a much broader, sociological approach than Drucker, identifies five categories of organizational goals.[58]

1. Societal goals—refer to society in general and large classes of organizations rather than to single organizations, i.e., the generating and maintaining of cultural values, maintaining order, as well as producing goods and services.

2. Output goals—such consumer functions as business services, consumer goods, education, and health care. For example, some industrial organizations have undertaken "contract education" for school systems. As Perrow points out, however, one societal norm is that an organization not take on too many diverse functions, e.g., a "company town" in which housing, recreation, and retail stores are controlled by the organization. Similarly, the Tennessee Valley Authority, which generates electric power and manufactures fertilizer, has been criticized on the grounds that it represents governmental intervention in the "private sector" of the economy.

Ford Motor Company found it difficult to shift its output goals from automobiles to small appliances when it purchased Philco; most of the top executives at Philco left, and there was a massive transfusion of Ford executives into Philco. But since these executives had no experience in the appliance field, Ford had to bring in someone with the necessary experience. Similarly, organizations accustomed to working under government contracts have had difficulty in making consumer goods and have found it necessary to diversify through purchase of existing consumer-oriented companies rather than use their own people to start such organizations. The parent companies have discovered that the rigid rules and fixed procedures applicable to work on government defense contracts hinder successful operation in a consumer-oriented environment.

3. System goals—the organization's design and operation methods. Some organizations emphasize rapid growth; others, stability and a high rate of profit. Some organizations are loosely controlled; others are tightly controlled. An organization that places a premium on being "the first" with rapid product changes has as its system goal the desire to be an industry leader. Another organization may place little emphasis on research and development, preferring to imitate designs developed by other organizations.

Perrow uses two utility companies to illustrate differing concepts of system goals and strategies for dealing with the environment. Consolidated Edison of New York, the largest gas and electric utility in the nation, relies on its political influence in New York City and Albany. Consequently, "Con Ed has the worst earnings record, service record and general public relations of the utility industry."[59] By contrast, American Electric Power Company, located in depressed Appalachia with only four cities of more than 100,000 people, relies on advanced technology and marketing techniques. Because of aggressive promotion of all-electric homes and the introduction of such innovations as high-voltage transmission and heat pumps, it now generates more electric power than any other utility in the world and has steadily increased the quality of its service and lowered its rates, which "run from 25 to 38 percent below the nation's average." [60]

System goals need to change with the times, but this is sometimes quite difficult to do, as illustrated by Perrow's history of Eastern Airlines. The World War I flying ace Eddie Rickenbacker controlled and managed Eastern from 1935 to 1959. Unlike most other airlines, Eastern showed profits for 25 consecutive years as a result of Rickenbacker's system goal of economy. He managed to keep costs under control by stressing the importance of saving even mills (one-tenth of one cent). This was a desirable system goal in the early years, since Eastern had a near monopoly on its most profitable routes, especially the run from New York to Miami. However, cutting costs could be achieved only by reducing services. Eastern delayed introducing new and better aircraft; scheduling and maintenance were tight and done at the convenience of the company rather than of the customers; seating on its planes was more cramped than on other airlines; coffee and cookies rather than breakfast were served; and overbooking flights was more extensive than the usual industry practice. While Rickenbacker was concentrating on saving money, other airlines were spending money for pretty stewardesses, better food, more convenient schedules, nonstop service, and bigger, faster, and more comfortable planes.

When the Civil Aeronautics Board decided to strengthen smaller lines and increase competition by allowing them to operate on the busier and more profitable routes, Eastern was hard hit. From 1960 to 1963, Eastern lost increasing amounts of money. Although Rickenbacker had retired from active management in 1959, he stayed on as chairman of the board until 1963. When Floyd Hall took over in 1963, he made sweeping changes which stemmed the pattern of revenue losses. In 1964 Eastern lost $5.6 million; in 1965 the company's profit was $29.7 million. As Perrow points out, Rickenbacker's system goal of cost reduction and little innovation was an excellent one in the early years, but it became disastrous when changes in the environment required a system goal of growth and innovation.

4. Product goals—such "product-characteristic goals" as quantity, quality, styling, cost, type, and availability. Some clothing manufacturers specialize in

"one-of-a-kind" dresses; others specialize in mass production. Some steel companies produce only high-quality steel; others manufacture steel in a wide range of quality.

Sometimes product and system goals conflict. For example, Perrow cites the case of a textile company that continued to turn out high-quality material on 500 looms when the market could support production of that material from only 50 looms. The company was taken over by another organization whose primary system goal was to make a profit. The conflict was quickly resolved by converting a product goal (manufacture of high-quality material) to a system goal (profit). However, it is not always easy to shift from one type of goal to another. Management may object ("We're in the woolen business"), or workers may object ("We're making high-quality products"). Gar Wood, for example, specialized in making custom-built, high-quality boats. When they decided to make cheaper, mass-produced boats in order to compete with Chris-Craft, the workers could not make the required transition; finally Gar Wood had to build a new plant staffed with new people to turn out the lower-quality boat.

5. Derived goals—the ways in which the organization uses its power to pursue other goals. Organizations, especially large ones, have a great deal of power which they can use to influence either their own members or the environment, as the controversy generated in the spring of 1972 over International Telephone and Telegraph's proposed takeover of Hartford Insurance illustrates so well.

Perrow points out that this categorization of goals is not as clear-cut as could be desired and that some goals could just as easily be placed in one category as another. His chief message is that organizations pursue a variety of goals and that some system of classification is helpful for categorizing goals.

The fact that organizations do pursue several types of goals is also stressed by Mohr, who after an exhaustive review of the literature concluded that the goals of organizations need to be "viewed as multiple rather than unitary, empirical rather than imputed and to be dichotomized into outwardly and inwardly oriented categories."[61] Mohr calls the outwardly-oriented categories "transitive" and the inwardly-oriented categories "reflexive." Although most people and organizations have both transitive and reflexive goals, they may not give equal emphasis to both. For example, an organization with transitive goals may be highly oriented toward providing a product or service to its environment, whereas a reflexive organization, such as a recreational club or fraternity, exists primarily for the "mutual benefit of its members." This category also includes groups that have had extreme influence in developing both organizational and political theory. Such organizations include labor unions, marketing associations, professional societies, trade organizations, and political interest groups. One of Mohr's chief points is that clear distinctions need to be made between the two, since studies made on reflexive organizations may not be applicable to transitive organizations or to the mix within organizations. For example, a company president may have ambivalent feelings about taking on a risky new product (transitive goal) and maintaining his or her job security (reflexive goal).

B. "Official" versus "Actual" Objectives

An organization's multiple objectives may include both "official" objectives (drawn up for public consumption by a specially selected blue-ribbon committee, signed by the president or the chairman of the board of directors, and then framed and hung on the walls of executive offices and in the lobby) and "actual" objectives (those toward which the organization is actually directing its energies). Perrow describes "official goals" as the organization's "general purposes" as stated in annual reports, the official charter of the organization, and other authoritative pronouncements; "operating" goals, on the other hand, guide the organization's activities, "regardless of what the official goals say are the aims."[62]

An interesting illustration of this distinction occurred when the president of an organization employing about 1500 people was asked to be a member of a panel on employment of the disadvantaged. When he stated that "our organization is not interested in your educational background, your race, color, or creed. We are interested in what you can do!" a member of the audience asked the president if he really meant that statement. The president said yes, whereupon, the questioner remarked, "I wish you would tell that to your employment manager. Last week, I filled out an application blank for your company and when the employment manager looked at it, he said, 'I see you haven't finished high school. We hire only high school graduates.' I didn't even get an interview." Frequently, once the "official" objectives have been established, they are seldom referred to again.

Whatever criteria are used to categorize an organization's goals, however, it must be kept in mind that in and of themselves, *organizations* do not have objectives; rather, *people* have objectives, stemming from their own views and motivations. Thus so-called "organizational objectives" are really uneasy and shifting compromises among the individuals within the organization and the demands made by the outside environment. As Katz says:

Every *strategic action must strike a balance among so many conflicting values, objectives and criteria that it will* always *be suboptimal from any single view-*

point. Every *decision or choice affecting the whole enterprise has negative consequences for some of the parts.*[63]

This contradicts the point made implicitly, if not explicitly, by advocates of the formal, structural-design approach. They stress that objectives are developed at the top and then passed down and accepted unquestioningly through the chain of command to the lowest-level subordinate. However, such a viewpoint is erroneous, for even within the formal perspective there are many conflicting points of view. The research and development department may prefer excellent, elegant, "state of the art" designs; marketing may want a large variety of products in the catalog; manufacturing may wish to concentrate on a few, high-volume products in order to reduce costs; the president of the firm may want to minimize risks, whereas the research director wants to increase the rate of new product development and introduction.

The same types of conflicts occur in nonindustrial organizations. The university administrators may want to reduce costs by having each faculty member carry a full teaching load; individual faculty members, however, may prefer to spend more time on their own research or writing projects. And in one large state mental institution, there continues to be serious conflict between those who favor admitting patients to facilitate the training of psychiatric residents and those who prefer admitting less curable patients requiring long-range custodial care.

Even within two organizations ostensibly having identical purposes and objectives, vast differences can occur. Blau describes two different employment agencies which had the same official objectives.[64] But because of the differing nature of the directors and the work force in the two organizations, one agency emphasized cooperation among employees and service to the "customer," whereas the other agency fostered competition and secrecy among employees and emphasized individual rather than total organizational performance, to the detriment of the "customer."

An organization's multiple objectives emerge from continuous renegotiations among the organization's personnel. Cyert and March point out that such mutual bargaining and perpetual conflict cause the members of the organization to be dissatisfied (a satisfied need is not a motivator); each member has a list (which may not be particularly well organized) of demands which pop up at different times. As a result, most organizations have goals that are highly contradictory but are not really recognized as such because they are rarely considered simultaneously. Such realization occurs only if there is a well-established ordering of priorities, which is rare because attention is given only to the goals relevant at the moment. Thus, for example, they raise the philosophical question about the entire concept of objectives: "To what extent is it arbitrary that we call wage payments costs and dividend payments profits rather than the other way around?"[65]

C. Deviation-Reducing versus Deviation-Amplifying Approaches to Objectives

Koontz and O'Donnell relate the story of a corporate president who decided not to embark on an expansion program, even though there was good potential for a great deal of profit to the company.[66] His rationale was that if he continued making only moderate profits, the stockholders would remain satisfied; if, on the other hand, taking this conservative route resulted in lower profits, he could then blame external political or business conditions, whereas if the expansion proved successful, the stockholders would merely assume that he was doing his normal job and therefore would not reward him properly for his effort and risk. However, if the expansion program failed, the stockholders might fire him. Since his primary goal was to remain as president of the company, he decided to maintain the status quo, thereby forfeiting the almost certain profits resulting from the expansion program.

Two points can be made from this story. First, profit is not always the manager's chief motive in making decisions about the goals and objectives of the organization. Second, and more important, this story illustrates the distinction between proactive and reactive approaches to objectives.

The behavior of individuals and social organizations has multiple causes, and the seeking for balance is a dynamic process. The internal balance of a particular subsystem is threatened by pressures from both other subsystems within the organization and external forces. Feedback, the flow of information back to the subsystem about its performance, is necessary for maintaining a dynamic balance within the individual subsystems and the total system. A social organization strives for *balance* rather than *optimal balance*.

While organizations strive to maintain the balance of the organization and the subsystems within it, there appear to be two necessary but conflicting forces at work in establishing and maintaining objectives. One is the force that resists change and works toward preserving the status quo—deviation-reducing force. The other is the force that works toward change in the system —deviation-amplifying force. These seemingly contradictory forces actually complement each other; an organization needs to grow and change, but it also needs a stabilizing force to keep it from "going off the deep end" by too sudden and rapid change. Thus the organization is always struggling to maintain the proper balance between stability (reactive forces) and growth and improvement (proactive forces).

These forces are analogous to deviation-reducing and amplifying feedback loops. Objectives are affected by inputs from both external and internal sources. One series of feedback loops is directed toward maintaining the organization's direction, i.e., toward maintaining the status quo. Another series of feedback loops is directed toward fostering change, modifying organizational objectives, and thereby changing the organization's direction. For example, a salesman's report that a customer is unhappy with a certain product may have little or no influence on the organization; if, however, many salesmen make similar reports and sales of the product fall off drastically, this input may well represent positive feedback and result in change in organizational objectives.

In his discussion of reactive forces in social organizations, Leavitt describes the tendency of the railroad companies to consider themselves in the *railroad* rather than the *transportation* business.[67] When trucks and airplanes began to be used to transport goods, therefore, the railroads resisted change and lost customers because they refused to shift their objectives—they were oriented toward railroads rather than toward transportation and customer needs. Leavitt also cites the movie business, which initially regarded TV as a competitor for the movie business rather than as another component of the entertainment business. Leavitt criticizes the oil companies for considering themselves part of the oil rather than the "energy" business. As a result, most of the work on fuel cells is conducted not by either oil companies or utilities, but by other organizations.

In other words, some reactive forces cause organizations to cling to objectives or procedures that are actually harmful to the organization. Another type of reactive force is the variety of "control systems" within organizations. One such control system is the accounting approach used in most organizations. For its purposes, the accounting subsystem insists that the books be closed on a monthly or other regular basis so that profit and loss can be computed at short-term intervals. However, this is dysfunctional for the manufacturing subsystem. For example, in a firm with a four-week accounting cycle, great stress is placed toward the end of the period on meeting the established production schedule. Thus on a regularly predictable basis, department managers and first-line supervisors reschedule their work in order to meet the "quota." They "rob the line," that is, do work in the most rapid rather than the most effective sequence, in order to meet production goals. They will, at times, knowingly pack defective products, just to meet the quota for the period. Similarly it is not uncommon for the inspection subsystem to get 50% or more of its work in the last week of the accounting period.

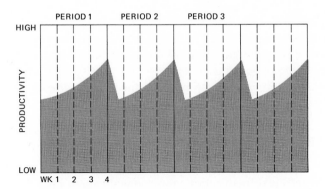

Fig. 9.3 Productivity during accounting periods.

As Fig. 9.3 shows, there is relatively little productivity in the first week of the next production period as first-line supervisors and workers repair the damage done in the last week of the previous accounting period, and this cycle is repeated with each new accounting period. This cycle is recognizable by almost every manufacturing manager and first-line foreman; almost all of them disagree with this pattern and believe that a better method should be used. However, the feedback for positive change is not sufficiently strong to overcome the status quo; most managers accept the use of the accounting period as a "given" condition of the control system and feel there is little they can do about it.

Unfortunately, in most social organizations the control systems for negative feedback are more carefully developed than those for positive feedback. Most control systems are established to ensure that predetermined objectives are met in timely, appropriate fashion, albeit with dysfunctional results. Few "control systems" exist to ensure planned change, improvement, and optimal balance in the system. Leavitt points out that although the marketing department of an organization should perform part of this function, too frequently it suffers from the same myopia that affects the rest of the organization.

Most organizations are now beginning to recognize the need for establishing better methods of positive feedback. For example, it used to be almost unheard of for people on the manufacturing floor to get any feedback about what the customer thought of the product; now, more and more organizations are posting salesmen's reports on the bulletin boards for all to see, including those on the manufacturing floor. Much of the proactive change will come about through planned interaction among the three perspectives. The development of improved lateral information flow will have a positive influence, as will the deliberate design of organizations to better fit their environment.

Much of the change will come about through greater attention to the human perspective. For example, when Tannenbaum surveyed organizational control in about 200 different organizational units, he found that employees at all levels wanted more opportunity to exercise self-control over their own work.[68] As to be expected, the largest gap between the amount and degree of external control and self-control is at the rank-and-file level.

V. SUMMARY

Both climate and environment are critical components of organizational planning and goal setting. Organization improvement cannot be done in a vacuum. It must be conducted with as much information as possible about relevant external and internal conditions. Only then will the plans and improvements be realistic.

Recently many businesses have failed and many others are in turmoil. The W. T. Grant Company went into bankruptcy proceedings because it misjudged the environment and because its organizational objectives were not thought out on the basis of a comprehensive plan. Instead, the company's abrupt shifts of policy left the firm unable to attract customers on a sustained basis.

In many companies the internal climate is a mirror of the external environment. If the environment is turbulent and the organization is not set up to cope with the turbulence, people become unhappy. Every change made within an organization will be reactive, trying to keep up with the leaders in the field. Workers become alienated because they do not understand the changes that take place, and they have little confidence in the decision-making process.

In short, climate, environment, and organizational planning are interrelated. In order to be successful, planning must take into account the organization's environment and climate.

REVIEW

1. How would you distinguish between climate and job satisfaction in an organization for which you have worked?

2. Design a study identifying the independent, intervening, and dependent variables.

3. Is it ever functional to have a restrictive climate? Explain.

4. What are the external and internal parts of the environment of your home?

5. What are the major arguments surrounding the measurement of social responsibility?

6. How would you make long-range plans for the school you are attending?

7. What kinds of long-range plans are currently being made at your school?

8. What is the psychosocial contract your school has with you and its various other constituencies?

9. Give examples of the five types of goals cited by Perrow.

10. From your own experience, elaborate and give examples of the differences between "official" and "operational" ("actual") objectives.

REFERENCES

1. A. Brayfield and W. Crockett, "Employee Attitudes and Employee Performance," *Psychological Bulletin* **52,** 5 (Nov. 1955): 396–424.

2. E. E. Lawler, III, and L. W. Porter, "The Effect of Performance on Job Satisfaction," *Industrial Relations* **7,** 1 (Feb. 1967): 20–28.

3. L. James and A. Jones, "Organizational Climate: A Review of Theory and Research," *Psychological Bulletin* **81** (Dec. 1974): 1096–1112.

4. D. Hellriegel and J. W. Slocum, Jr., "Organizational Climate: Measures, Research and Contingencies," *Academy of Management Journal* **17,** 2 (June 1974): 256.

5. B. Schneider and R. A. Snyder, "Some Relationships Between Job Satisfaction and Organizational Climate," *Journal of Applied Psychology* **60,** 3 (June 1975): 318.

6. *Ibid.,* p. 319.

7. J. P. Campbell, M. Dunnette, E. E. Lawler, III, and K. E. Weick, *Managerial Behavior: Performance and Effectiveness,* New York: McGraw-Hill, 1970.

8. Hellriegel and Slocum, *op, cit.,* p. 263.

9. N. Frederickson, "Some Effects of Organizational Climates on Administrative Performance," Educational Testing Service, Research Memorandum RM-66-21, 1966.

10. Brayfield and Crockett, *op. cit.*

11. Hellriegel and Slocum, *op. cit.,* p. 272.

12. G. Litwin and R. Stringer, *Motivation and Organizational Climate,* Cambridge, Mass.: Harvard University Press, 1968.

13. R. Lippitt and R. K. White, "An Experimental Study of Leadership and Group Life," in *Readings in Social Psychology,* ed. T. M. Newcomb and E. L. Hartley (New York: Holt, Rinehart and Winston, 1947).

14. R. R. Blake and J. S. Mouton, *The Managerial Grid,* Houston: Gulf, 1964.

15. E. E. Lawler, III, D. T. Hall, and G. R. Oldham, "Organizational Climate: Relationship to Organizational Structure, Process and Performance," *Organizational Behavior and Human Performance* **11,** 1 (Feb. 1974): 139–155.

16. Hellriegel and Slocum, *op. cit.*, p. 274.

17. R. Golembiewski and S. Carrigan, "The Persistence of Laboratory Changes in Climate Over an 18 Month Period," *Administrative Science Quarterly* **15**, 3 (Sept. 1970): 330–340.

18. Hellriegel and Slocum, *op. cit.*, p. 272.

19. R. B. Peterson, "The Interaction of Technological Process and Perceived Organizational Climate in Norwegian Firms," *Academy of Management Journal* **18**, 2 (June 1975): 288–299.

20. K. Marx, "Economic and Philosophical Manuscripts," in E. Fromm, ed., *Marx's Concept of Man*, New York: Unger, 1961.

21. C. J. Browning, M. F. Farmer, H. D. Kirk, and G. D. Mitchell, "On the Meaning of Alienation," *American Sociological Review* **26**, 5 (Oct. 1961: 780.

22. *Ibid.*

23. "Altering the Cell—The Vistas are Breathtaking," *New York Times*, October 31, 1971.

24. J. Rosenthal, "Columbia, Maryland—A Tale of One City," *New York Times Magazine*, December 26, 1971.

25. "Thirty-three Teachers at West Point Leave Army in 18 Months," *New York Times*, June 25, 1972.

26. L. Nicolaou-Smokovitis, "The Psychosocial Contract: Its Nature and Effects for Greek Industry," *Review of Social Research*, No. 26/1976, Athens: National Center of Social Research (EKKE).

27. K. Davis, "Five Propositions for Social Responsibility," *Business Horizons* **17**, 3 (June 1975): 19–24.

28. *Ibid.*, p. 23.

29. H. C. VanOver, and S. Barone, "An Empirical Study of Responses of Executive Officers of Large Corporations Regarding Corporate Social Responsibility." Paper presented at the Academy of Management annual meeting, New Orleans, August 1975.

30. R. Bauer, "The Corporate Social Audit: Getting on the Learning Curve," *California Management Review* **16**, 1 (Fall 1973): 5–10.

31. *Ibid.*, p. 7.

32. *Ibid.*

33. N. Churchill, "Toward a Theory for Social Accounting," *Sloan Management Review* **15**, 3 (Spring 1974): 1–18.

34. R. D. Hay, "The Measurement of Social Responsibility by a Social Audit: an Experimental Approach." Paper presented at the Academy of Management annual meeting, New Orleans, August 10–13, 1975; R. D. Hay, and E. Frary, "An Experimental Audit of Social Responsibility: The Pennsylvania Company." Paper presented at the Academy of Management annual meeting, New Orleans, August 10–13, 1975.

35. F. Fry, "Incorporating Expectancy Theory into Social Investment Decisions." Paper presented at the annual meeting of the Academy of Management, New Orleans, August 10–13, 1975.

36. B. Bass, "Panel: Implications of the Behavioral Sciences on Management Practices in the Year 2000," in *Management 2000*, New York: American Foundation for Management Research, American Management Association, 1969, p. 160.

37. D. Stone, "Bridging Cultural Barriers in International Management," *Advanced Management Journal* **34** (Jan. 1969): 56–62.

38. P. S. Goodman and B. E. Moore, "Cross-Cultural Management Research," *Human Organization* **31,** 1 (Spring 1972): 39–45.

39. C. Perrow, *Organizational Analysis: A Sociological View*, Belmont, Calif.: Wadsworth, 1970, Chapter 4.

40. *Ibid.*, p. 114.

41. C. Kerr and A. Siegel, "The Interindustry Propensity to Strike—An International Comparison," in A. Kornhauser, R. Dubin, and A. M. Ross, eds., *Industrial Conflict*, New York: McGraw-Hill, 1954.

42. A. Turner and P. Lawrence, *Industrial Jobs and the Worker*, Cambridge, Mass.: Harvard University Press, 1965.

43. G. Susman, "Job Enlargement: Effects of Culture on Worker Responses," *Industrial Relations* **12,** 1 (Feb. 1973): 1–15.

44. Perrow, *op. cit.*, p. 123.

45. P. R. Lawrence, and J. W. Lorsch, *Organization and Environment: Managing Differentiation and Integration*, Boston: Harvard University Graduate School of Business Administration, 1967.

46. R. B. Duncan, "Multiple Decision-Making Structure in Adapting to Environmental Uncertainty: The Impact on Organizational Effectiveness," *Human Relations* **26,** 3 (June 1973): 273–291.

47. T. Burns and G. M. Stalker, *The Management of Innovation*, London: Tavistock, 1961.

48. R. P. Lynton, "Linking an Innovative Subsystem into the System," *Administrative Science Quarterly* **14,** 3 (Sept. 1969): 398–414.

49. *Ibid.*, p. 410.

50. R. A. Goodman, "Environmental Knowledge and Organizational Time Horizon: Some Functions and Dysfunctions," *Human Relations* **26,** 2 (April 1973): 202–226.

51. A. R. Negandhi and B. C. Reimann, "Task Environment, Decentralization and Organization Effectiveness," *Human Relations* **26,** 2 (April 1973): 203–214.

52. Duncan, *op. cit.*

53. J. Pfeffer, "Canonical Analysis of the Relationship Between an Organization's Environment and Managerial Attitudes toward Subordinates and Workers," *Human Relations* **26,** 3 (June 1973): 325–357.

54. L. Gulick, *Administrative Reflections from World War II,* Tuscaloosa: University of Alabama Press, 1948, p. 77.

55. A. Etzioni, *Modern Organizations,* Englewood Cliffs, N.J.: Prentice-Hall, 1964, p. 6.

56. B. M. Bass, *A Program of Exercises for Management and Organizational Psychology,* Pittsburgh: Management Development Associates, 1966.

57. P. Drucker, *The Practice of Management,* New York: Harper and Brothers, 1954, p. 62.

58. Perrow, *op. cit.*

59. *Ibid.,* p. 155.

60. *Ibid.,* p. 156.

61. L. Mohr, "The Concept of Organizational Goal," *American Political Science Review* **67,** 2 (1973): 470.

62. C. Perrow, "The Analysis of Goals in Complex Organizations," *American Sociological Review* **26, 6** (Dec. 1961): 855.

63. R. L. Katz, *Management of the Total Enterprise,* Englewood Cliffs, N.J.: Prentice-Hall, 1970, p. 13.

64. P. Blau, *The Dynamics of Bureaucracy,* Chicago: University of Chicago Press, 1955.

65. R. M. Cyert and J. G. March, "A Behavioral Theory of Organizational Objectives," in *Modern Organizational Theory,* ed. M. Haire, New York: Wiley, 1959, p. 80.

66. H. Koontz and C. O'Donnell, *Principles of Management,* New York: McGraw-Hill, 1968.

67. T. Leavitt, *Innovation in Marketing,* New York: McGraw-Hill, 1962.

68. A. S. Tannenbaum, *Control in Organizations,* New York: McGraw-Hill, 1968.

10

ORGANIZATIONAL IMPROVEMENT – STRUCTURAL - DESIGN PERSPECTIVE

All nature's structuring, associating, and patterning must be based on triangles because there is no structural validity otherwise.

R. BUCKMINSTER FULLER

LEARNING
OBJECTIVES

When you have finished reading and studying this chapter, you should be able to:

1. Identify the structural design of an organization as one perspective of a total system.
2. Trace the evolution of management thought about the design of organizations.
3. Differentiate between the several principal approaches to organizational design.
4. Name and compare the several principal schools of thought about organizational design.
5. Differentiate between organizational design as an independent and dependent variable.
6. Identify and compare the contingency and the "one best way" approaches.

You will be expected to define and use the following concepts:

"One best way"	Design and dependent variable
Traditional theory	Effect of organizational size
Division of work	Effect of technology
Coordination	Effect of environment
Historical functions of management	Mechanistic
Line and staff	Organic
Bureaucracy	Contingency theory
Individual organization approach	Differentiation
Product	Integration
Function	Integrative devices

THOUGHT STARTERS

1. What is an organization?
2. Name at least five different organizations to which you currently belong.
3. What difference does it make how organizations are designed?
4. Does the design of an organization influence behavior? If so, how?

I. INTRODUCTION

The development of thought about organizational structure, design, and improvement has occurred gradually and inevitably. At the same time, organizations have evolved. Some are fairly simple and stable organizations; others have become complex organizations operating in rapidly changing, international, and uncertain environments. Originally, it was believed that there was "one best way" to organize a social system. This concept has been modified to a "contingency" theory of organizational structure and design, which recognizes the fact that not all types of organizations should have the same type of structure and design.

This chapter briefly traces the evolution of management thought, discusses current contingency approaches, and ends by elaborating on a particular contingency theory. Throughout, our concept of organizational improvement is the enhancing of organizational effectiveness and efficiency. Although

Not all organizations are large. (Harold M. Lambert/E. P. Jones)

such aspects of organizational life as better budgeting or cost-accounting techniques and improved machine design are important considerations in organizational improvement, our discussion is restricted to the structural design of the organization.

The main thrust and concern of early writers in this field reflected their knowledge of organizations as they existed in history and in the first part of the twentieth century. Thus many of the "classical principles" of management were derived from the Roman and Prussian military models and from early industrial organizations. But, of course, organizations have changed considerably since then, with the rise of the conglomerate and the multinational organization.

Further, theorists have tended to either ignore or satirize one another; indeed, in the 1950s and 1960s some writers seemed to "throw out the baby with the bath water." Early management theorists seemed to describe "organizations without people," whereas some of the later theorists tended to focus on "people without organizations." This characterization, although overdrawn, illustrates the fact that many of the early organizational-design theorists were concerned with something akin to the machine-economic model of motivation, to the almost total exclusion of the social or growth models. Similarly, modern behavioral theories were, until relatively recently, concerned with human self-actualizing, to the almost total exclusion of the effect of the organization on human behavior.

Written material on formal organizations has proliferated since the turn of the century. Three major approaches to the topic can be identified. The first two are "final answers"; these recommendations for organizational design are final and definitive, applying to all organizations. The third, a contingency approach, focuses on research to determine what organizational characteristics *should* be like.

The first "final answer," traditional organization theory, describes the one best way to manage. The second, federal decentralization, resulted from the reorganization of General Motors in the early 1920s. When this approach failed to work in all situations, individual organizational approaches were used. The third major approach, contingency theory, is a middle ground between the universal principles ("final answers") approach and the concept that each organization is unique and must be studied separately. All three approaches exist today, although not in their original forms. All three have their adherents. However, it appears that the contingency approach is rapidly gaining ground in comparison to the other two.

Before moving further into the chapter, we need to make two final points. The first is that organizational design and structure is a *powerful way* to change and influence people's behavior. The second is that organizational structure is the result of human thought. It is a product of human hands. *People* build organizations. Organizations are not a given, although they are frequently regarded as such. Typically, once an organization has been "designed," its members accept the design as immutable. This simply isn't so. Organizational structure can and indeed should be changed when and where necessary.

II. TRADITIONAL ORGANIZATIONAL THEORY

Traditional theory (or classical theory, as it is sometimes called) was described in Chapter 1, but will be briefly reviewed here. The theory, with modifications, still has more influence on management practice than almost any other approach. It is concerned with two basic issues—the division of work (specialization and functionalization) and the coordination of the activities resulting from that division. Work should be divided so that each employee, especially at the lower ranks, has a clearly specified job. Coordination is handled through the bureaucratic structure, which is concerned with two subissues—control through a hierarchy of authority (centralization) and control through rules and procedures (formalization). In their search for the proper way to handle the division and coordination of work, the traditional theorists were concerned with the "final answer," with developing *universal* principles that could be applied to *all* organizations.

One of the most influential of the early theorists was Henri Fayol. Around 1910 he developed several principles of management to deal with the division and coordination of work.[1] These principles are listed in Table 1.1 (p. 11) and include structure, division of labor, the coordinative principle, the scalar principle, and the functional principle.

Fayol also described five functions of management: planning, organizing, commanding, coordinating, and controlling. These five functions are widely quoted today, even though many of them cannot fit all organizations under every circumstance. However, Fayol developed his principles from organizations as he knew them. His primary experience was with a coal mining company that had a number of low-level jobs. He also had experience with one-product manufacturing companies.

Urwick, another early theorist, stressed the difference between line and staff functions, probably resulting from his service in the British army.[2] The function of the line is to command; of the staff, to advise. Although this differentiation worked well for the British army in simpler times, it has been a very difficult concept to define and utilize in complex modern organizations. Indeed, the concept almost defies definition, especially when a systems approach, which postulates that the subsystems are highly interrelated and inter-dependent, is used.

Men such as Fayol and Urwick sought to prescribe what an organization design should be. The German social historian Max Weber used a slightly different approach in developing the structural school.[3] The classical approach used *deductive reasoning* to determine how organizations *should* behave. After observing a number of organizations, the structuralists, primarily Weber, used inductive reasoning to describe how organizations *actually are* designed. Nevertheless, the results were quite similar. Both approaches attempted to develop a "one best way" to organizing, developing general rules that could be applied to organizations of any type.

Weber stressed the utility of bureaucracy, which involves a hierarchical structure, rules, and authority to solve the recurring problems of organizations. For Weber, bureaucracy was management by rules, without regard for human emotion. The rules were necessary to control human emotion, to protect the subordinate from favoritism as well as to ensure performance. In the bureaucratic approach, jobs and authority are defined clearly. Appointments to jobs are made primarily on technical efficiency and knowledge rather than on political or familial connections. Behavior is closely regulated through carefully spelled-out rules and by superiors.

Since Weber first coined the term, "bureaucracy" has come to have a bad connotation in the minds of many people. In the free-form days of the 1960s, some authors decried the use of the term. They forgot that Weber had seen bureaucracy as not only contributing to success of the enterprise, but also protecting the individual members. As a result, some more "modern" theorists have tended to overkill, suggesting that bureaucracy is dead and stressing the need for a democratic, participative approach in which decision making is pushed down from the top in all organizations.[4] To suggest that bureaucracy is always dysfunctional and that a participative approach is always better sounds just as prescriptive as the traditional theory.

A more recent one-best-way approach has been developed by Likert.[5] Likert suggests that high-performing organizations can be identified by a questionnaire measuring such dimensions as leadership processes, motivational forces, communications, and decision-making and goal-setting processes. For example, the "best" approach to goal setting is through group participation. Although he does not make the point specifically (nor do Fayol or Weber), Likert strongly suggests that there is one best way to manage—the participative, open way.

Some modern theorists are just as prescriptive in denying the value of bureaucracy as the classical theorists were in promoting its value. Perhaps the biggest difference between the two groups of theorists is that the classical theorists stress *function* in their approach to organizational design, whereas the later theorists stress such *processes* as leadership style and communications.

III. THE INDIVIDUAL ORGANIZATION APPROACH

The "principles" of the individual organization approach resulted primarily from examining what individual organizations were doing and then applying those techniques to other organizations. This approach first emerged a generation after Fayol had given "the answer" for a company manufacturing a single product. Alfred Sloan, president of General Motors, found "the answer" for organizing a complex manufacturing company that was too large to handle according to the functional approach alone. Sloan's solution was "federal decentralization," or centralized control with decentralized responsibility.[6] In the 1920s General Motors' automotive division was basically a single-product concern. Although GM manufactured a number of different automobiles, many of the parts were interchangeable, and much of the engineering technology and know-how was identical. Nevertheless, the company was becoming too large to manage. GM was reorganized, with each operating division (Chevrolet, Buick, Cadillac, etc.) a profit center. Although the names and designs are somewhat different, the Chevrolet Division of General Motors is essentially the same as the Cadillac Division, and their organization charts are very similar. The concept of function was maintained within the individual divisions. Thus those performing the same functional specialties were grouped together, e.g., engineering in one group, assembly workers in another, etc. Nevertheless, overall coordination was obtained through the concept of federal decentralization and central committees for each important central function. Overall policy was still centralized in the parent corporation.

This concept worked well from the 1920 until after World War II, since most organizations essentially had a single product. But then things began to change. Many organizations began developing several product lines, which might require different technologies. This development gave rise to a tendency to design organizations around the concept of product. In a hospital, for instance, the various departments are organized according to medical specialty, e.g., surgery, medical, psychiatry, obstetrics. Nurses are then attached to a "product" specialty, not to a functional specialty, i.e., nursing in general.

One of the most widely known cases of product organization occurred in General Electric shortly after the end of World War II. General Electric had a number of ongoing operating problems. Further, good ideas were not being implemented. Appliances were being designed by engineers, who did not take into account customer wants or more inexpensive manufacturing methods. Under GE's centralized, functional management, specific products were fragmented among several departments, and no one had full responsibility for a particular product.

In 1950 a new president was named, and he soon introduced some very important and drastic changes in GE.[7] Abandoning the functional approach, GE established approximately 100 operating product departments, each relatively independent from the central offices in New York. A manager was in charge of a specific product line in an operating department. Each manager had full responsibility and accountability for results in that department, including decisions about product design, pricing, marketing, and manufacturing of the product. This allowed concentration on relatively independent areas, but still made available to the individual product division the resources of the corporate group.

The decision to organize by product or function was made on a case-by-case basis. Very few guiding principles were available, other than managerial hunch or "Company A is doing it that way and is successful. Why don't we do it that way too?" These individual organization approaches, while modifying classical theory, also maintained many of the principles of classical theory, including the division of labor, span of control, unity of command, etc.

Meanwhile, it was not clear whether it was best for a company to be organized around product or function. In the late 1960s a report suggested that one of the thorniest management questions is: "Should all specialists in a given function be grouped under a common base, regardless of differences in products they are involved in, or should the various functional specialists working on a single product be grouped together under the same superior?"[8] The general conclusion was that a functional organizational design appeared most appropriate for routine, predictable tasks; a product organizational design appeared to be most appropriate for tasks of a more uncertain, problem-solving nature. However, this dichotomy between product and function is overly simplified. The underlying issue is still a major concern of managers.

IV. ORGANIZATIONAL DESIGN AS A DEPENDENT VARIABLE

The classical theorists viewed organizations as a "given"; they believed that design came first. Once the organization was properly designed, the behavior of the members would be properly controlled through the division of labor, hierarchy, and formal rules. With proper design, organizational goals would be met. In other words, design was an independent variable, with all else dependent on the structure. However, the classical theorists were essentially dealing with single-product organizations.

Each year after World War II, a greater percentage of the annual budget has gone into research-and-development activities. Many organizations began to diversify their product lines. The number of service and nonprofit organizations increased. As organizations became multinational, managers had to worry not only about product versus function, but also about the problems of territory. The development of the computer made it possible to handle large volumes of data. Finally, specific studies suggested that some of the cherished tenets of classical theory, such as the span of control, did not hold up under all circumstances.

As a result of such changes, more emphasis was placed on doing empirical research on organizations. In the 1940s and 1950s organizational design came to be regarded as a dependent variable, one that resulted from other factors. One important reason for this attempt to understand how an organization develops its form from its function was the emergence of the individual organization approach.

The study of organizational design has developed several schools, or approaches. The three major approaches overlap, but their major focal points can be summarized as: *size* versus structure, *technology* versus structure, and *environment* versus structure.[9] The first two contingency schools—those emphasizing size and technology—will be described only briefly. Because it appears to both have a greater impact and examine organizational effectiveness, we will spend considerably more time describing contingency theory arising from the relationship of organizational structure and environment.

A. Size versus Structure

Extensive literature reviews stemming from this approach have suggested that the structure of an organization involves three main dependent variables: *centralization,* or the hierarchy of authority; *division of labor,* or specialization; and *formalization,* or rules and procedures.[10] This definition of organizational structure is quite similar to our earlier description of bureaucracy, and indeed it has been called a bureaucratic strategy of organizational control. These three variables appear to be interrelated. Specialization and formalization of activities have a positive relationship; the greater the specialization, the greater the number of rules and procedures. Both are negatively related to centralization.

A number of authors have suggested that size is one of the most important factors related to varying strategies of organizational structure and control.[11] The problem of size is a difficult one to identify, as Drucker has noted.[12] He suggests that size is frequently measured by the number of employees. However, size is relative. Thus a worldwide accounting firm with 4000–5000 employees and offices in 30 countries is indeed big, but a manufacturing firm with that number of employees would be considered small. According to this standard, American Motors would be considered big, but not so in relation to its competitors in the United States.

Most of the research in this area has been concerned with structure only and has not considered such other variables as organizational effectiveness and the degree to which the needs of organizational members are met. In one representative study, Pugh *et al.* collected data on 52 work organizations in order to develop a stratified random sample by size and product or purpose of 46 organizations.[13] There were three dependent structural variables: (1) the *structuring of activities*—the extent to which employee behavior is defined by task specialization, standardized routines, and formal paperwork; (2) *concentration of authority*—the extent to which decision-making authority lies with controlling units outside the particular plant and how centralized the authority is at higher hierarchical levels; and (3) *line control of work flow*—the degree to which control comes from line personnel rather than through more impersonal procedures. Among the environmental, or contextual, variables used were the organization's origin and history, size, charter, technology, location, and dependence. Each of these variables was further broken down. For instance, "origin and history" was further classified into impersonality of origin, age, and historical changes. "Size" was broken down into the size of both the organization studied and the parent organization and included such subvariables as number of employees, net assets, and number of employees in the parent organization.

Detailed statistical analysis generally showed that: (1) structuring of activities was best predicted by size and work integration; (2) concentration of authority was best predicted by dependence and the number of operating sites; (3) line control of work flow was best predicted by operating variability. Although size did not emerge as the best predictor for concentration of authority and line control of work flow, it was highly related to both. The research suggests that the procedure used assesses only the power of the contextual variables to predict the structure of the organization and not their relative importance.

B. Technology versus Structure

The original study on the influence of technology on structure was done by Woodward and her associates.[14] She studied a large number of firms in a relatively small geographic area in England, using a sample of 100 firms which varied considerably in size and type. The purpose of the research was to explore whether or not firms using the principles of classical management were more successful than those that did not. The preliminary results indicated no relationship between business success and "sound organizational structure" as derived from classical theory.

However, in reworking her data, Woodward made an important discovery. Rather than examining organizational effectiveness along the lines of classical theory, she classified organizations into three major manufacturing areas— unit and small batch, large batch and mass production, and continuous process. This classification scheme provided a scale of increasing technological complexity. The new results showed that there was a great deal of variation in organizational characteristics within each of these categories. In general, firms with above-average commercial success tended to be different in design from less-successful firms in the same industry. For example, most successful firms and industries using unit- or batch-production technology had considerably wider spans of supervisory control with fewer levels of hierarchy than did successful firms with more stable, continuous-process technologies.

Building on the work of Woodward and others, as well as on his own extensive work in the field, Perrow has extended the concept of technology as the major variable determining structure. According to Perrow, the *form* of the organization must follow its *function*, i.e., the form of the organization must reflect the "state of the art in each function and the changes required by the environments."[15] Any organization, he notes, is designed to produce something. He therefore raises the question of how one can think about technology (in broad terms) as a method for transforming raw materials (which may be human, symbolic, or material) into some sort of desirable goods and services. The technology of the organization thus determines its form, or structure. Successful complex organizations must adapt their structures to fit their current technology. Rather than using the simple environmental continuum of Lawrence and Lorsch, which ranges from stable to unstable, Perrow's typology uses two variables—"search" and the "number of exceptions," which can be examined independently or concurrently to construct a fourfold table, as shown in Fig. 10.1.

To Perrow, "search" can be either highly analyzable and routine or nonroutine and unanalyzable (few specific and well-established rules and guidelines). A craftsman blowing a unique piece of Steuben glass has a different search problem from one who makes ordinary glass bottles, for which the rules and procedures are well established.

Perrow's second category is the number of exceptions that an organization may have. An automobile factory producing many different models, styles, and colors may have many exceptions. (But after the model has been designed, the rules and procedures (search) may become highly routinized.) Even though a research-and-development firm might have many exceptions, it could

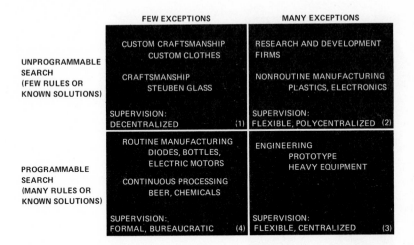

Fig. 10.1 Technology, task, and organizational structure. (Adapted from C. Perrow, *Organizational Analysis: A Sociological View*, Belmont, Calif.: Wadsworth, 1970, p. 83.)

nevertheless fall in the category for which the rules and procedures are unknown (the unprogrammable search).

Perrow demonstrates that there is a close relationship between the type of supervision required and the placement of an organization in a particular cell. For example, supervision in cell 1 needs to be decentralized; cell 2 requires flexible, polycentralized supervision; cell 3 requires formal, centralized, highly bureaucratic supervision; and cell 4 calls for flexible and centralized supervision.

Perrow asserts that an organization's essential nature must be determined before its problems can be solved. The way the organization is designed determines the appropriateness of its approaches to problem solving. In practical terms, this means that techniques for solving organizational problems must be used selectively, since an approach or technique helpful for Organization A may be dysfunctional for Organization B.

In developing a relatively complex conceptual scheme for showing the influence of technology on structural design, Perrow has considerably extended Woodward's work. However, although Woodward's research showed a tie of technology to structure to effectiveness, Perrow's work has not yet done so. We turn now to another approach that has closely tied organizational structure, as a dependent variable, into an independent variable that can then be related to such new dependent variables as profitability and satisfaction of members' needs.

Creating a unique piece of Steuben glass is a nonroutine, unanalyzable task. (Photograph courtesy Corning Glass Works)

The process of removing impurities from petroleum cracking catalysts in the final filter area is a highly routinized procedure with many rules and known solutions. (Photograph courtesy W. R. Grace & Co.)

Assembling a new model is a relatively nonroutine task for which there are few rules or known solutions. (Photograph courtesy Corning Glass Works)

Prototype engineering is a programmable search procedure with many rules and exceptions. (Photograph courtesy Boeing Company)

C. Environment versus Structure

A number of studies have examined organizational effectiveness and efficiency as a function of the structure. First, however, we will describe the historical antecedents of this modern contingency theory of organizational design.

As briefly mentioned in Chapter 9, Burns and Stalker closely examined some 20 different organizations covering a wide variety of products and applications. They found two basic types of organizational structures—"mechanistic" and "organic."[16] The mechanistic system, used in organizations operating under relatively stable external conditions, emphasizes the bureaucratic approach of well-defined rules, procedures, and functional roles. Since only the highest-level managers have access to the overall knowledge and since the command hierarchy is well defined, interaction within the organization is vertical rather than horizontal. The "organic" system, on the other hand, operates in uncertain and changing environments, e.g., the electronics industry. Jobs are less clearly defined, and interaction tends to be lateral, "work flow," rather than vertical. Much more knowledge and decision-making power are contained at lower levels in the management hierarchy.

These two types of systems form a continuum, with the mechanistic system being most suited for organizations when technology and markets are well established, with little change over time. The organic system, at the other end of the continuum, is best suited when the technology is changing quickly in response to changes in the environment.

Using a conceptual rather than an empirical, research-based approach, Thompson has stressed the importance of environment.[17] He suggests that organizations are neither completely rational nor completely irrational, but that as open systems, they are faced with uncertainty and are subject to criteria of rationality and therefore need determinateness and certainty. Thus the most important problem is coping properly with uncertainty. This occurs when the organization protects its core technologies so that they can operate under conditions approximating certainty. In order to do this, other parts of the organization are designed to act as buffers to the core technology. These boundary-spanning buffer units protect the inner core from its outside environment.

In other words, organizational structure is a response to environmental uncertainty and complexity. The number and types of boundary-spanning units reflect the complexity of the environment.

When the task environment is stable, the number of boundary-spanning components, or functional divisions, corresponds to the number of relatively homogeneous segments in the environment. Since changes occur slowly in a stable environment, adaptation to the environment can be accomplished by appropriate modifications in the roles that are established and followed. In a situation of frequent changes (environmental turbulence), decentralization is needed in order for the organization to adapt in a dynamic environment.

Stemming in part from the work of Burns and Stalker, Thompson, and Woodward, an empirically based contingency model of organizations has been developed. This model uses the environment as one of the prime determinants of structure and also examines the relationship of organizational design to organizational effectiveness, including profitability and the effect on members' need satisfaction.

V. A CONTINGENCY THEORY OF ORGANIZATIONAL IMPROVEMENT

Perhaps the most exciting recent line of research to improve organizational effectiveness and efficiency through organizational design has been founded by Lawrence and Lorsch, who used a *comparative, research-based* approach in their study of more and less successful companies.[18] Three general conclusions emerge from their findings:

1. There is no "one best way" to design an organization.
2. The more successful organization and/or its subsystems "fit" environmental demands.
3. When the organization is properly designed, the needs of individual organization members are better satisfied.

After a pilot study to determine the basic variables, Lawrence and Lorsch examined ten organizations. Two organizations were manufacturing identical containers; two were in the consumer-foods industry; and six developed, produced, and marketed plastics. These organizations were selected because they provided a continuum of environmental stability. At one end of the continuum is the plastics industry, which exists in a highly unstable, quickly changing external environment. At the other end of the continuum is the container industry, which exists in a stable, unchanging environment. Organizations in the food industry fall approximately in the middle of this continuum. The study obtained external performance data as well as more subjective interview and questionnaire data to obtain information from top and middle managers about the structure of the companies and their relative success when compared with similar organizations.

The study has been called "D&I," since two of the most basic terms in the work are *differentiation* and *integration*. Thus the study is concerned about specialization of work (differentiation) and the coordination of work (integration), and it provides general guides about the meaning of these terms.

A. Differentiation

Differentiation is the "difference in cognitive and emotional orientation among managers in different functional departments."[19] It occurs in four dimensions.

1. Formality of structure How do the organization's subunits differ in the formality of their rules, procedures, and other controlling processes? Formality tends to be greater in such departments as finance and manufacturing than in long-range planning or research-and-development units, which tend to have less rigid procedures and rules. Similarly, a hospital emergency room has fewer rigid rules than the housekeeping department.

2. Interpersonal orientation This refers to the extent of concern for people rather than for the task. Members of subunits having either highly uncertain or highly certain tasks tend to be less concerned with personal relationships than with tasks. Subunits having moderately uncertain tasks are more concerned with establishing positive social relationships. Interpersonal orientation is more important to sales and marketing personnel than to manufacturing people.

3. Time orientation Subunits differ in the immediacy of feedback. Sales and production subunits have much faster feedback and have a shorter time orientation than do subunits such as research and development, where feedback may occur over a much longer time span. Manufacturing may be concerned with daily schedules; product development, by contrast, may be interested primarily in long-range planning.

4. Goal orientation Subsystems may differ in their goal orientations. Marketing may want to have a wide variety of products so as to increase the level of overall sales, whereas manufacturing may press for a small number of high-volume products so as to reduce manufacturing costs.

Figure 10.2 shows the relative amount of differentiation for three major units of the container, food, and plastics industries. Because both the plastics and food industries exist in uncertain and quickly changing environments, innovation is a major issue for them both. For the container industry, however, the major issues are quality control, price, and delivery; the technology remains unchanged. As a result, the certainty of the container environment is greater than for either the food or plastics industries. Production is the key aspect of the container industry. Once the process has been established, knowledge about it is highly predictable, with few new problems arising.

Further, in the container industry, market information is much more certain than is the technoeconomic knowledge required for production. Just the

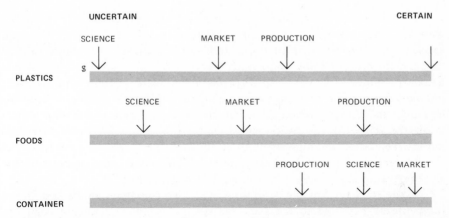

Fig. 10.2 Relative environmental certainty of three industries (Adapted from P. Lawrence and J. Lorsch, *Organization and Environment: Managing Differentiation and Integration,* Boston: Harvard University Graduate School of Business Administration, Division of Research, 1967.)

reverse is true for plastics, since customer demands keep changing. For example, a company manufacturing beer cans has few "model" changes, since breweries have a great deal of money tied up in high-speed filling equipment and do not want to change the specifications of the cans. Sudden change in the plastics industry appears to be the rule rather than the exception. In this respect, the plastics industry is much like the pocket electronic calculator industry. Last year's model is already obsolete.

Two other areas of differentiation are the importance of the market and the time span of feedback to the organization and its subunits. Lawrence and Lorsch found greater differentiation in both areas in the food and plastics industries, but not in the container industry. Time span of feedback for the container industry ranged from a week to a month and was fairly similar for the production, science and market subunits. In the plastics industry the time span ranged from a month in the production subunit to approximately a year in science. In other words, the food and plastics organizations required more differentiation of the organizational subsystems than did the container organizations.

B. Integration

Integration is "the quality of the state of collaboration that exists among departments that are required to achieve unity of effort by the demands of the environment."[20] Integration refers to interdepartmental relationships, as well as to the process by which it is achieved and the organizational devices used to attain it. Thus integration refers to both description and action.

Next, the researchers obtained performance data in each of the three industries and determined whether there was a relationship between the way each organization "fit" its environment in terms of its differentiation and integration and the economic success of each organization. Six plastics organizations had been studied. Two were top performers, two were medium, and two were low performers. The two top performers had the highest degree of both integration and differentiation. The two medium performers were not simultaneously achieving the necessary differentiation and integration. One had low differentiation and high integration; the other had high differentiation and low integration. The two low performers did not have as much differentiation and integration as did any of the other four organizations.

At the stable end of the continuum were two container companies. Direct competitors, they sold to the same markets. The high-performing company was clearly higher in both profits and sales than was the lower performer. Both had about the same degree of differentiation, but the high-performing company had a much better degree of integration because integration could be carried out through the managerial hierarchy. In other words, this company approached the prototype of the *classical* organizational model, in which all decisions are made through the formal hierarchy. Serious attempts in the less-successful container organization to push decision making down into the organization had caused problems because this approach was inappropriate.

The food companies, in the middle of the continuum, did not show the same clear differences. The higher performer had more differentiation and integration, but not higher performance (in part because the lower performer had recently introduced a dramatically successful new product). On other indicators, such as market share, return on investment, and number of new products introduced in the last five years, the low performer was significantly lower.

The states of differentiation and integration in effective organizations will differ, depending upon the demands of the particular environment. In a more diverse and dynamic field, such as the plastics industry, effective organizations have to be highly differentiated and highly integrated. In a more stable and less diverse environment, like the container industry, effective organizations have to be less differentiated, but they must still achieve a high degree of integration.[21]

C. Achieving Integration

Successful organizations in a stable environment have more traditional integrative devices than do organizations in an unpredictable, unstable environment. Table 10.1 shows the integrative devices from the unstable to the stable

Table 10.1 Comparison of integrative devices in three high-performing organizations

	Plastics	Food	Container
Degree of differentiation*	10.7	8.0	5.7
Major integrative devices	(1) Integrative department	(1) Individual integrators	(1) Direct managerial contact
	(2) Permanent cross-functional teams at three levels of management	(2) Temporary cross-functional teams	(2) Managerial hierarchy
	(3) Direct managerial contact	(3) Direct managerial contact	(3) Paper system
	(4) Managerial hierarchy	(4) Managerial hierarchy	
	(5) Paper system	(5) Paper system	

* High score means greater actual differentiation.

Reprinted by permission from P. Lawrence and J. Lorsch, *Organization and Environment: Managing Differentiation and Integration* (Boston: Harvard University Graduate School of Business Administration, Division of Research, 1967), p. 138.

ends of the continuum. Direct contact by the manager is the primary integrative mechanism used by the more successful container organization. Since little differentiation is required, both the plant manager and the research scientist have similar kinds of goals, time, and interpersonal orientations. Both want to get the problem solved as quickly as possible by finding immediate, applied solutions, since both are rewarded for specific, short-term accomplishments.

In the plastics organization, direct contact by the manager is not effective as an integrating mechanism. Here, the time, interpersonal, and goal orientations of the members differ, especially in successful organizations. The research scientist is concerned about whether a new project offers a scientific challenge. The scientist who completes a project successfully may be able to prepare and deliver a paper to a learned society. The production manager, on the other hand, is concerned about immediate, short-run problems and could care less about learned societies.

For example, let us assume that the scientist and the sales manager are discussing a problem. The sales manager may be concerned with establishing warm, friendly relationships (interpersonal orientation). The scientist, on the other hand, may appear rather distant, being more interested in talking about research problems than in engaging in idle chitchat. In addition, the scientist may have more personal freedom to pick and choose projects than the sales manager thinks appropriate (goal orientation). Even worse, the scientist may be frequently late for appointments, whereas the sales manager feels that tardiness is a cardinal sin in business. The sales manager's desire for immediate answers to a technical problem may make the scientist feel uncomfortable, since complex problems take more time to investigate than the sales manager realizes.

As a result, the plastics industry requires many more integrative devices at all levels in the organization to accomplish the necessary integration, since it is the most differentiated of the three industries. These results illustrate the need for a new management function (the integrator or integrative department) in highly differentiated organizations so that high differentiation and high integration *across* the organization may be achieved simultaneously.

In their focus on the role of the integrator, Lawrence and Lorsch note that the integrator needs to have a balanced view of the differing time, goal, interpersonal, and formal orientations of various organization members in different subunits, e.g., the long-range time goals of the scientist versus the short-range time goals of the manufacturing manager. In short, the integrator needs to have the following behavioral characteristics:

1. Integrators need to be seen as contributing to important decisions on the basis of their competence and knowledge, rather than on their positional authority.

2. Integrators must have balanced orientations and behavior patterns.

3. Integrators need to feel that they are being rewarded for their total product responsibility, not solely on the basis of their performance as individuals.

4. Integrators must have a capacity for resolving interdepartmental conflicts and disputes.[22]

In order to resolve conflict and bring about integration, integrators need to use both expert and referent power rather than rely on their position, or "legitimate," power. Lawrence and Lorsch cite three basic ways of resolving interdepartmental conflict: *smoothing*—ignoring the problem in hopes that it will go away; *edicting*—using positional power to force a decision; and *confronting*—dealing with the conflict in open terms until a solution agreeable to all is reached. This is perhaps the most effective method for integration and conflict resolution, although forcing may be needed as a back-up method.

Lawrence and Lorsch have built on the work of theorists preceding them. They are interested in the division of labor, rules, and the hierarchy of authority, but they have operationalized these three areas and found out that they need to be used differentially. Technology, one of the important variables contributing to the certainty or uncertainty of the environment, has been taken into consideration. In other words, the classical theorists may well have been correct in their approaches to unity of command, since they were dealing with organizations in a stable environment; relatively little differentiation was required, and the necessary integration could be done through rules and the management hierarchy. However, the current contingency theory demonstrates very clearly that there is *no one best way* to organize and design an enterprise; rather, there may be several "best ways," depending on environment and technology. The empirical findings of a link between organizational success and structure considerably amplify and extend the work of Burns and Stalker in terms of "mechanistic" versus "organic" systems, as well as the work cited earlier by Woodward.

D. Contingency Theory—Additional Research

The development of contingency theory has sparked a large number of follow-on studies. Research has been conducted in industrial organizations, universities, health-care organizations, high schools, and junior high schools and in such countries as Germany, Australia, and the United States.

One of the best-documented studies in terms of research design took place over about a two-year period.[23] The original diagnostic and proposal stage took about six months, and the change program lasted about 18 months. The general manager of a division had asked for help with a problem he had identified as poor intergroup relationships. Extensive diagnosis suggested that the real problem was poor organizational design. While existing in a highly uncertain and unstable technological environment, the organization was trying to use the management hierarchy to handle all of the integration processes, especially product development. In other words, poor intergroup relationships were not a cause, but a symptom, of the real problem.

After this diagnosis, the division was reorganized so as to better "fit" its environment. Integrators were identified and trained, and four project teams were established for new-product development. Team members were selected partially on the "certainty" of the organizational subunit from which team members came. The less certain areas of research and/or development were represented by someone lower in the hierarchy, e.g., an engineer or scientist. More certain functions, such as manufacturing and finance, were represented by members higher in the hierarchy. In addition, three-day workshops were planned, and a number of intergroup meetings were held to assist with the development of intergroup cooperation.

A problem then arose. Although top management had consented to push down decision making in accordance with the contingency model, they were uncomfortable about not being in the middle of the action and about not receiving the detailed, frequent reports to which they were accustomed. To relieve their anxieties, they were given a 10- to 15-minute thumbnail summary of the status of the projects at the monthly business review meetings. This approach was so successful that management created an additional problem; they wanted to create project teams to solve every organization problem. To avoid such proliferation, it became necessary to establish ground rules to govern the number of additional project teams.

The follow-up data showed that the division had improved markedly. Before the change, only five new products had been introduced in the previous five years. After the change, nine new products were introduced in one year. Further, decision making shifted downward, there was greater commitment to the decisions made, and organizational members reported greater professional and interpersonal competence.

Dow Corning has recently reorganized from a conventional, product-line, divisional organization into a matrix organization, following contingency theory.[24] The company's products—including semiconductor, chemical, and medical products—are on the unstable end of the continuum. Cross-functional matrix teams were formed, decision making was pushed down, and the communications flow was redesigned so that relevant data were available at the lowest-level decision point. It took about four years to complete the reorganization, but "judging from employees' reactions to the new pattern, as well as from the impressive gains in sales, profits, productivity, and exports, the multidimensional organization is a striking success."[25]

There is also evidence that individuals' competence is enhanced when there is a proper "fit" between the organization and its environment.[26] Six research laboratories and four manufacturing plants were studied. Five matched pairs were established, with one unit in each pair a highly effective performer and the other unit a less successful performer, although all pairs were relatively successful. In both types of environments (stable and unstable) organization members working in the more successful units felt an increased sense of competence and mastery. Several possible reasons were explored, including personality differences. Although the evidence was somewhat mixed, it appeared that none of the alternatives explored "is as useful as the fit argument from the practical perspective of improving organizational effectiveness and enhancing the individual's feelings about himself at work."[27]

However, although the contingency theory appears useful in a variety of types of organizations, it does have some weaknesses. First, the model has been used primarily to analyze existing organizations to determine their effectiveness. Not enough work has yet been done on (1) *changing* organizations to better fit the model and to then systematically examine the effect of such changes or (2) *designing* organizations from scratch and then validating effectiveness. Second, some research has raised doubt about the validity of the scales used to measure environmental uncertainty.

One study used different measures of uncertainty and found relatively little relationship between the "objective" measures of environmental volatility and "subjective" measures resulting from a questionnaire completed by managers in the same organizations.[28] Lawrence and Lorsch take sharp issue with this research, showing that the researchers had added to their uncertainty scale by three other methods: selecting industries with sharply contrasting environmental uncertainty, developing "hard" economic indicators, and relying on highly structured interviews.[29] Lawrence and Lorsch also question the "volatility" measures as an equivalent of uncertainty and note that the uncertainty scale has been used in numerous follow-up studies, all of which upheld the validity of the scale.

Since the criticism contrasted "hard," or "objective," measures of volatility and "soft," or "subjective," ones, an interesting note is added by a totally unrelated, but nonetheless significant, piece of research that may shed some light on the controversy.[30] The study reviewed the findings of the size-versus-structure school and noted that the research used both subjective and objective measures. Both types of studies included measurement of such variables as hierarchy, rules and procedures, and division of labor. When little relationship was found between subjective and objective measures of the same variables, the author concluded that the two sets of measures cannot be viewed as interchangeable. (You will remember that the original criticism of the uncertainty subscale was based on subjective and objective measures of volatility.)

A final, broader criticism of contingency approaches has also been raised.[31] The criticism suggests that the fact that contingency questions are being raised shows that organizational theory is maturing as a social science discipline. However, contingency approaches may be moving too far and too fast by overstating the similarity among existing findings and by understating the problems and costs of applying them.

Nevertheless, despite the weaknesses in the contingency approach to organizational design, it appears to be the approach with the greatest potential. Undoubtedly, the contingency model will be subjected to more rigorous research, but it has already had a strong impact on current thinking about organizational design.

VI. CONCLUSIONS

In this chapter we discussed the problem of organizational improvement primarily in terms of organizational structure and design. The early "one-best-way" concepts and the "final answers" have been gradually modified through the years to the contingency theories, which suggest that there is no "one best way." Rather, the structure and design of a successful organization depend heavily on its technology and environment. An organization in a stable environment will generally be successful when its structure follows the classical bureaucratic pattern. An organization in a highly unknown, unstable, and changing technology and environment, however, needs to be designed and structured differently, taking into account its unique problems of differentiation and integration. In other words, it is essential to take a comparative, situational approach to organizational improvement when the variables used are organizational structure and design.

REVIEW

1. What were the two basic issues of traditional, or classical, theory? Are they still issues today?

2. How do the five functions of management described in this chapter compare and contrast with the activities of a manager as described in Chapter 8?

3. Why did federal decentralization appear to be "the answer" in the 1920s?

4. Much modern research treats organizational design as a dependent variable rather than as an independent variable. Historically, how has this come about?

5. Describe the degree of differentiation and integration (high, medium, or low) that would probably characterize the following organizations: chemical plant, hospital, high school, department-store chain, corner grocery store, automobile dealership. What environment does each exist in?

6. Can the Lawrence and Lorsch concepts be applied to a university? Elaborate.

7. List the information you would need to place an organization on the Lawrence and Lorsch continuum.

8. Is the Lawrence and Lorsch discussion of conflict resolution related to group task, maintenance, and self-serving activities?

9. Select an organization (club, fraternity, business) and observe how conflict is handled (smoothing, edicting, or confronting). What are the consequences?

10. Based on your knowledge of using coercive force, explain why the successful integrator uses confrontation before coercion. Can these two forces be applied in reverse order successfully? Why is "smoothing" used last?

REFERENCES

1. H. Fayol, *General and Industrial Management*, trans. C. Storrs, London: Pitman, 1949.

2. L. Gulick and L. Urwick, eds., *Papers on the Science of Administration*, New York: Institute of Public Administration, 1937.

3. M. Weber, *The Theory of Social and Economic Organization*, trans. A. Henderson and T. Parsons, ed. T. Parsons, New York: Oxford University Press, 1947.

4. W. Bennis, *Changing Organizations*, New York: McGraw-Hill, 1966.

5. R. Likert, *The Human Organization*, New York: McGraw-Hill, 1967.

6. D. Brown, *Centralized Control with Decentralized Responsibility*, New York: American Management Association, Annual Convention Series No. 57, 1927.

7. W. Harris, "The Overhaul of General Electric," *Fortune* **52**, 6 (Dec. 1955): 112–130.

8. A. Walker and J. Lorsch, "Organizational Choice: Product vs. Function," *Harvard Business Review* **46**, 6 (Nov.–Dec. 1968): 129–139.

9. V. Sathe, "Contingency Theories of Organizational Structure," in J. Livingstone, ed., *Managerial Accounting: The Behavioral Foundations*, Columbus, Ohio: Grid, 1975, pp. 51–63.

10. V. Sathe, "Measures of Organizational Structure: A Conceptual Distinction between Two Major Approaches." Paper presented at the annual meeting of the Academy of Management, New Orleans, August 10–13, 1975; J. Child, "Strategies of Control and Organizational Behavior," *Administrative Science Quarterly* **18**, 1 (Jan.–Feb.–March 1973): 1–17.

11. M. Meyer, *Bureaucratic Structure and Authority*, New York: Harper & Row, 1972; J. Child, "Predicting and Understanding Organizational Structures," *Administrative Science Quarterly* **18**, 2 (April–May–June 1973): 168–185.

12. P. Drucker, *Management: Tasks, Responsibilities, Practices*, New York: Harper & Row, 1974.

13. D. Pugh, D. Hickson, C. Hinings, and C. Turner, "The Context of Organization Structures," *Administrative Science Quarterly* **14**, 1 (March 1969): 91–114.

14. J. Woodward, *Industrial Organization: Theory and Practice*, London: Oxford University Press, 1965.

15. C. Perrow, *Organizational Analysis: A Sociological View*, Belmont, Calif.: Wadsworth, 1970.

16. T. Burns and G. Stalker, *The Management of Innovation,* New York: Barnes and Noble Social Science Paperbacks, 1961.

17. J. Thompson, *Organizations in Action,* New York: McGraw-Hill, 1967.

18. P. Lawrence and J. Lorsch, *Organization and Environment: Managing Differentiation and Integration,* Boston: Harvard University Graduate School of Business Administration, Division of Research, 1967.

19. *Ibid.,* p. 11.

20. *Ibid.*

21. *Ibid.,* p. 108. Reprinted by permission.

22. P. Lawrence and J. Lorsch, "New Management Job: The Integrator," *Harvard Business Review* **45,** 6 (Nov.–Dec. 1967): 146. Reprinted by permission.

23. M. Beer, "Organizational Diagnosis: An Anatomy of Poor Integration"; G. Pieters, "Changing Organizational Structures, Roles and Processes to Enhance Integration: The Implementation of a Change Program"; A. Hundert, "Problems and Prospects for Project Teams in a Large Bureaucracy"; S. Marcus, "Findings: The Effects of Structural, Cultural and Role Changes on Integration"; and P. Lawrence, "Comments." Papers presented at the Symposium on Improving Integration Between Functional Groups—A Case in Organization Change and Implications for Theory and Practice, Division of Industrial and Organizational Psychology of the American Psychological Association, Washington, D.C., Sept. 3, 1971.

24. W. Goggin, "How the Multidimensional Structure Works at Dow Corning," *Harvard Business Review* **52,** 1 (Jan.–Feb. 1974): 54–65.

25. Ibid., p. 54.

26. J. Lorsch and J. Morse, *Organizations and Their Members: A Contingency Approach,* New York: Harper & Row, 1974.

27. *Ibid.,* p. 58.

28. H. Tosi, R. Aldag, and R. Storey, "On the Measurement of the Environment: An Assessment of the Lawrence and Lorsch Environment Uncertainty Subscale," *Administrative Science Quarterly* **18,** 1 (Jan.–Feb.–Mar. 1973): 27–36.

29. P. Lawrence and J. Lorsch, "A Reply to Tosi, Aldag, and Storey," *Administrative Science Quarterly* **18,** 3 (Sept. 1973): 397–398.

30. Sathe, "Measures of Organizational Structure," *op. cit.*

31. D. Moberg and J. Koch, "A Critical Appraisal of Integrated Treatments of Contingency Findings," *Academy of Management Journal* **18,** 1 (March 1975): 109–123; A. Korman and R. Tanofsky, "Statistical Problems of Contingency Models in Organizational Behavior," *Academy of Management Journal* **18,** 2 (June 1975): 393–397.

11

ORGANIZATIONAL IMPROVEMENT— WORK-FLOW PERSPECTIVE

This new development (automation) has unbounded possibilities for good and for evil.

NORBERT WIENER

LEARNING
OBJECTIVES

When you have finished reading and studying this chapter, you should be able to:

1. Name and then differentiate among three major thrusts in organizational improvement from the flow perspective.
2. Name and compare different forms of model building.
3. Discuss criticisms and limitations of model building.
4. Distinguish between input-based and output-based forms of model building.
5. List the advantages and disadvantages of management information systems and defend the proposition that such approaches are not yet feasible.
6. Demonstrate the importance of the informal organization, giving both examples and general principles.
7. Demonstrate the impact of sociotechnical systems on work, information, and related flows.
8. Defend the relative importance of the three major thrusts described in this chapter.

You will be expected to define and use the following concepts:

Model	Sociotechnical systems
System dynamics	Tavistock Institute
Operations research	Autonomous work groups
Uses of operations research	Production group
Problems with operations research	Development group
Management information systems	Work-area redesign
Informal organization	

THOUGHT STARTERS

1. What does the term "model" mean to you? In how many ways can the term be used?
2. In what ways is the "flow" of students in a university different from the "flow" of paperwork in a bank?
3. What arguments can you give on the issue of designing versus selecting people to fit specific jobs?

I. INTRODUCTION

This chapter discusses three major current thrusts in organizational improvement from the flow perspective. The first is model building, which includes the work of the operations researchers and the more recent work of Forrester. The second is the attempt to improve the flow of communications, materials, and information through the use of computerized management information systems. The third describes the development of sociotechnical systems, which integrate work and information flow with human needs, both through autonomous work groups and through the redesign of the work place. However, the concept of sociotechnical systems has had much more impact on the Continent and Great Britain than in the United States.

II. MODELS AND MODEL BUILDING

The term "model" has many meanings. To some, it connotes a beautiful woman; to others, it represents a small-scale version of an airplane, car, etc. And to yet others, the term "model" represents something less concrete and tangible. For example, as Forrester explains, each of us carries with us a mental image, or model, of the world.[1] This abstract model makes use of particular concepts or relationships to represent "the real thing." However, this type of model is fuzzy and incomplete and differs for each individual.

Here, we use the term "model" as an abstract representation of a system that attempts to give "reality" a mathematical rather than a verbal expression in English or some other language. For example, Einstein's formula $E = MC^2$ is an abstract mathematical model, not a verbal one. A model is a representation of a system and according to Emshoff, its primary purpose is to "integrate data about the system's behavior in a way that provides information about characteristics of that behavior."[2]

Many authors have pointed out that the attempt to build models at the level of the human and social system is very difficult. A clear example of this problem is given by Forrester, who notes that one can construct a computer model that ostensibly reproduces all the assumptions held by a particular person. When the model is used, however, it does *not* usually act in the way that the person acts; each individual has internal contradictions that lead to unanticipated behaviors. Indeed, Boulding, whose levels of systems were discussed in Chapter 2, seriously doubts that our present knowledge is sufficient to build more than the rudiments of theoretical systems, or models, much beyond Level 4 (a self-perpetuating open system, e.g., a cell).[3] For Boulding, human and social systems are at Levels 7 and 8. Despite the inherent difficulties of model building, however, several of the current approaches to organizational improvement do deliberately attempt to build models.

A. System Dynamics

Forrester made extensive use of models in order to describe the behavior of organizations resulting from the interaction of the organization with the outside environment.[4] He used a mathematical model comprising six interconnected networks, or subsystems—orders, materials, money, personnel, and capital equipment—all of which are interconnected by information flow. Using a systems approach to integrate the different functional departments within an organization (marketing, production, finance, and research and development), Forrester stresses that the interconnections and the interactions occurring among the components of the system are the most important factors, not the separate components.

Forrester believes that managing involves the primary tasks of designing and controlling an industrial system. Thus industrial dynamics is an approach for management of systems analysis. There are four basic components of his model, as follows.

1. Information-feedback theory   This term is similar to "deviation-amplifying feedback," i.e., such a system exists whenever information from the environment causes a decision to be made that results in action. This action affects the environment and in turn influences future decisions. In later articles, Forrester emphasizes the need for models in this area, because social organizations are involved in "multi-loop non-linear feedback systems" which the individual mind is not able to understand directly.[5] In other words, the policies and procedures people follow are the very ones that get the organization into trouble, because the human mind is unable to adequately conceptualize "multi-loop, non-linear feedback systems." (See Fig. 2.10, p. 62.)

2. Decision-making processes   This basic premise follows logically from information-feedback theory in that a model can be developed to provide formal rules for short-term tactical decisions. Forrester states that these formal rules are superior to those made by human judgment under the pressure of time, the absence of complete data, or in the rigidity of a large organization. (This may be true only in a self-contained system, however.)

3. An experimental approach to systems analysis   Since mathematical techniques are not as yet adequate for developing general analytical solutions, the experimental approach is needed so that a simulation model can be used to try out different market assumptions and management policies not requiring more sophisticated mathematical approaches.

4. Use of computers   Without the speed and capability of the modern computer, it would be impossible to use simulation models or to cope with a large number of variables.

Perhaps the most important aspect of Forrester's industrial dynamics approach is the utility of his theories. He graphically illustrates that the use of intuitive judgment and "common sense" rather than the model may result in totally unnecessary cyclic swings in production. Small changes in retail sales, for example, may lead to totally unwarranted and wild swings in factory production. Thus a factory manager may at all times be able to produce more goods than are being sold to consumers, yet be unable to fill the orders coming from the sales department. Using the model would reduce or eliminate the cyclic production swings resulting in hiring, overtime, and then layoffs.

Forrester has recently expanded and revised his concepts. He first substituted "system dynamics" for "industrial dynamics" and is now using the term "world dynamics," which reflects his belief that use of his model can have a marked effect on urban and world systems. Concurrently, the Club of Rome (an informal international organization) sponsored its first book, in which a global computer model was used to investigate five "major trends of global concern—accelerating industrialization, rapid population growth, widespread malnutrition, depletion of non-renewable resources, and a deteriorating environment."[6] Although this model is oversimplified and unfinished, data on the five strategic factors were computerized to determine the effectiveness of the model in assessing various alternatives for the future. The resulting predictions demonstrated that humanity is in serious trouble unless quick action is taken to achieve a state of nongrowth (global equilibrium) in which production and population are maintained in a careful balance.

This work, as well as that of Forrester, has been strongly challenged by Passell, Roberts, and Ross, who believe that the models rely on too many unproved assumptions, are overly simplified, and lead to unjustified conclusions.[7] For example, although the work done by the Club of Rome stipulated that the model was incomplete, the review by Passell et al. makes the criticism that " 'limits' pretends to a degree of certainty so exaggerated as to obscure the few modest [and unoriginal] insights that it genuinely contains." Nevertheless, we believe that this work has made an important contribution to the field, and work is continuing in this area.

B. Operations Research

Operations research, or management science, is an attempt to build mathematical models and use mathematical techniques to improve the welfare of the *entire* organization rather than merely certain of its components. As Hillier and Lieberman state, operations research attempts to "resolve the conflicts of interest *among the components* of the organization in a way that is best for the organization as a whole" (italics added).[8]

Proponents of operations research stress that the method can be used in any type of an organization—hospitals, government, military, business, and industry. If one has a computer simulation of an oil refinery, for instance, it is far easier to use the mathematical model to try out different ways of operating the refinery to get different blends and mixes of gasolines and oils than it is to experiment with the refinery itself. The results obtained from using the computerized mathematical model can then be used in the real-life operation of the refinery.

Operations research began about 1940, when the British army asked Nobel Prize winner Professor Blackett to assemble a team of scientists to work on operational problems. Their first problem was to determine what information should be collected from radar equipment in order to decide which gun sites would be most effective in preventing German attacks on the British mainland. The success of this effort prompted the United States military to undertake similar efforts. Since then, the usefulness of operations research has continued to increase; currently, most American universities have courses in OR, although they may be part of the engineering, management, statistics, or mathematics curriculum.

In a survey of the top manufacturing executives of 500 companies, approximately half of the organizations used some form of OR.[9] These organizations tended to be larger, manufacture more complex products, and have executives who had college degrees or better. Indeed, the larger the Amercian business organization, the more likely it is to make active use of an operations research team. Such teams are heavily oriented toward the use of mathematics and models. Typically, the approach of an OR team is as follows:

1. Analyze, study, and observe the real-life system or structure that needs to be understood and explained. Identify both the controllable and uncontrollable variables.

2. Structure the real-life situation so that a mathematical model (a generalized framework) can be developed which fits the observations and data obtained in the first step. This, of course, necessitates looking at the problem in the context of the entire system, including the objectives to be attained.

3. Check the model to find out how it will behave under conditions which have not yet been observed, but which could be observed if the changes were actually made.

4. Modify the model to develop optimum approaches to reach the defined and desired objectives.

5. Test the model by developing experiments or changes in the actual system to determine whether or not the model actually *predicts*, i.e., determine

whether or not the effects of the changes that are predicted by the model actually occur when the changes are made.

6. Refine and change the model as necessary.

7. Use the model as a guide to action in real life, i.e., use it to predict optimum solutions.

Ackoff and Rivett have noted nine organizationwide flow problems which they believe can be solved through operations research.[10]

1. *Inventory.* By defining inventory as idle resources, we can then define "resources" as anything that can be used to obtain something of value. People, material, machines, and money are all inventory resources.

2. *Allocation.* The allocation subsystem is concerned with organizing the resources so as to maximize the overall efficiency of the total system.

3. *Queueing.* The proper mix between the tasks to be performed and the facilities available to perform them must be obtained. For example, a bank needs to consider the optimum number of tellers' windows, which in turn depends on the number of customers expected. Costly waste results from having too many windows, but having too few windows increases the customers' waiting time.

4. *Sequencing.* The order in which operations occur depends on the queue discipline that has been selected. For example, if each of several products requires operations on two machines, the material flow can be sequenced so that maximum utilization of the machines is made. In other types of sequencing problems, priorities need to be considered.

5. *Routing.* In order to attain maximum efficiency of operations, the organization must determine how to best route its products through the manufacturing process, reach its customers, etc.

6. *Replacement.* Since parts break down or wear out over time, people leave, and equipment becomes obsolete, some organized plan of replacing these elements must be determined and ready if the need arises.

7. *Competition.* Within the organization, there may be competition for scarce resources; in the marketplace there is competition for customers. Competition occurs from the effect on one decision maker of decisions made by others. It may arise when the decision maker's action is known in advance; it may involve choices when the competitor's decision can be predicted; or it can result when decisions have been unanticipated.

8. *Search.* This category involves the search for alternative actions or items to produce.

9. *Mixed problems.* An organization's problems can rarely be considered independently of one another; rather, since its subsystems are interdependent, its problems are interdependent.

Terms and techniques used by operations researchers are usually highly mathematical—"linear programming," "Markov chains," "queueing theory," "game theory," etc. This heavy reliance on mathematics and mathematical models is based on the precision, self-containment, logical structure, and convenience of the language of mathematics.

C. Criticisms and Limitations of Mathematical Modeling

One of the biggest problems inherent in the "model" approach to the flow system is that the modern organization is constructed and organized along vertical rather than lateral lines. Thus much of the effectiveness of operations research and similar "modeling" research methodology occurs within, rather than across, individual departments of the organization. For example, the use of linear programming as a tool in production and advertising cannot be readily applied to a consideration of the organization as a total system.

A much more serious criticism is that mathematical models, especially those used by operations researchers, depend primarily on mechanistic "output" models and not with more organic "input" models. An output model assumes known inputs and uses them to provide predictions of outputs. The extent to which the model makes accurate predictions is a measure of its usefulness. However, since the validity of the "known" inputs cannot always be assumed, the predictions of the model may reflect unwarranted or incorrect assumptions.

A related criticism is that the use of models makes too many assumptions about human behavior. For example, Gruber and Niles criticize OR for inadequate attention to human factors, which are difficult to model mathematically.[11] Yet obviously, human factors are perhaps the most important element in organizational life.

Simon criticizes what he calls "normative microeconomics" as being too mechanistic. He points out that although this work is conducted under such labels as "operations research" or "management science," the normative microeconomist acts as though a theory of human behavior is not really needed.[12] The focus is on how people *ought* to behave rather than how they actually *do* behave. In other words, the normative microeconomist makes the false assumption that one can ignore the human system while focusing on the model.

Emshoff extends this criticism by showing that the original work in operations research used mechanistic models, i.e., the input was known in advance (the rate of gunfire, the input from radar, etc.).[13] The problem was to combine

The high priest of the computer room.

these known inputs and to provide a better output from variables that were already known.

As operations research expanded into other fields, the model remained mechanistic; the inputs were generally known or could be easily identified. Therefore, analysis was concerned primarily with how to handle the interaction among the input variables in the model so that the output of the model would be as realistic as possible. However, as operations researchers began working on less mechanistic, more behavioral problems, their models became less successful as predictors. Solving mechanistic problems required only a general knowledge of the behavioral factors, whereas solving behavioral problems required an intimate understanding of human behavior. For example, the premium for a given amount of life insurance is generally governed by the person's age. This relationship is a statistical, actuarial, predictive model; it is known that the life expectancy of a person 75 years old is considerably less than that of one who is 25 years old. This output-based model does not require an understanding of the individual, only a knowledge of the behavioral factors involved, e.g., older people tend to die sooner than younger people.

However, in trying to apply their work to behavioral areas, operations researchers and other model builders have tended to use the output rather than the input model. Emshoff explains that this is inappropriate, since "behavioral problems have fundamentally different characteristics from mechanistic problems and because of this, systems models for behavioral problems must be developed using an input-oriented research focus rather than the traditional output-oriented one."[14] For example, psychiatrists are well aware that some women become pregnant not because they lack knowledge of birth-control techniques, but because they want revenge on parents, something (a baby) of their own, to get married, or to escape from an unpleasant job. A model stressing control of pregnancies among women by means of better dissemination of birth-control knowledge is an output model. An input-based model would focus more heavily on the reasons why unmarried females become pregnant in the first place.

Emshoff insists that it is not sufficient to merely *describe* human behavior; one must also strive to understand human behavior and the reasons for it. Emshoff uses the goal of reducing traffic accidents to illustrate the operation of an input-based model. Insurance companies know that drivers under 25 have the highest accident rate. Psychologists know that the strongest influence on behavior for those under 25 is peer groups. Emshoff therefore postulates that increasing the penalties for traffic violations (output model) has little effect, since the influence of penalties is less than that of peer groups. Emshoff suggests that the accident rate for this age group might be reduced by using the force of peer influence. A probationary license would be issued to the applicant under 25, and it would have to be countersigned by two or more of the applicant's friends, each of whom also had a license and belonged to the same age group (input model). If one of the group lost his or her license due to a traffic violation, all of the cosigners would also lose their licenses. Emshoff theorizes that this might increase peer pressure to drive safely. Although the courts might find such a solution illegal, it does have the advantage of distinguishing between an output-based model—increasing the penalties for traffic violation, which treats everybody equally—and an input-based model—removing the drivers' licenses of peers, which takes into account peer pressure.

Another criticism leveled at the model builders, particularly the OR practitioners, is that OR models are usually structured to seek the optimum solution. Many organizations, however, seek something less, since an "optimum" solution for a particular problem might conflict with other goals and objectives of the organization. Earlier, for example, we cited the case of the executive who refused to take a risk that would have benefited the organization, but not necessarily the executive. An input-based model would take these factors into consideration.

Most models, and operations research in particular, have been successful *within* individual departments of a firm, but have generally been unsuccessful in resolving *interdepartmental* conflict. In fairness to the model builders, however, it needs to be pointed out that behavior models, too, have limitations of both theory and data, although Emshoff does give some suggestions for overcoming some of these "lacks."

Although *ideally*, OR is a systemswide approach, in actuality its use is much narrower. Operations research is most widely used in production planning and control, followed by project planning and control, inventory analysis and control, quality control and analyzing capital investment projects, and last, maintenance planning.[15]

Very few organizations use more than four of the myriad OR techniques. The three main reasons are: "(1) production personnel are inadequately trained, (2) competent personnel with quantitative training are scarce, and (3) staff personnel don't sell these solutions and approaches."[16]

Despite its limited use, operations researchers are continuing to develop computer-simulation models of organizations. In one such study, work flow was used as the basic input variable, and the hierarchical structure of the organization was considered to be the basic output of the model.[17] The simulation was conducted in a small manufacturing firm of about 200 employees. The model was considerably simplified by examining *only* the manufacturing day shift (the technical core). Nonproduction services, such as marketing and other functions, were not included in the model, nor were productivity, motivation, interpersonal stress, and similar variables.

Working on the assumption that work-flow relationships are crucial, the researchers carefully gathered manufacturing work-flow data by conducting interviews, preparing production-flow diagrams, and giving guided tours of the plant. The administrative rules to convert the input (work flow) into the output (simulated organization structure) were developed from Thompson's formal propositions for structuring the technical core (manufacturing).[18] After several revisions of the computer model, the simulation, or *predicted* structure, closely resembled the actual structure of the manufacturing process.

However, the use of the model to reproduce the existing structure does not mean that simulation is yet ready to be used in a normative or prescriptive sense to suggest where the actual structure should conform to the model. There are several reasons for this. First, the model is a very simple one, dealing only with the manufacturing core technology of a noncomplex organization. Second, the model assumes that the actual work flow simulated is appropriate and correct. In many instances, however, it may be better to redesign both structure *and* work flow. Further, the complexity of many modern organizations is such that attempting multivariate simulation of the entire organization is impossible. Nevertheless, the simulation model can be very useful in testing propositions about organizations, refining those propositions, and in developing better operational approaches for designing organizations.

III. MANAGEMENT INFORMATION SYSTEMS

Another main thrust of organizational improvement on the lateral, or flow, level is the integrated management information system, which uses the computer to provide information flow *through* the organization. With the advent of the computer in the late 1950s and its coming of age in the 1960s, the literature was filled with optimistic predictions that the computer would become the basic tool for developing management information systems which would in turn cut across the organization and provide managers at all levels with the knowledge and data necessary to make decisions about their jobs.

For example, one organization made a serious attempt to install a computerized, integrated, management system.[19] The integrated system would take customer orders and, through a series of major computer programs, provide assembly and fabrication schedules, man-machine loadings, and other information through the factory. The system would then provide the purchasing department with requirements for orders from outside vendors. It was hoped that this system would replace or integrate a multitude of manual or partially mechanized systems already existing in the organization. Savings from the installation of the integrated management information system were expected to exceed $1,000,000 annually, since approximately nine work years were required to make the 2,400,000 hand calculations needed to develop a single production planning schedule throughout the factory, and the frequent schedule changes required 40 working days to complete. The new system was expected to reduce the time necessary for a schedule change to about four or five days, including reviews for accuracy, and to require less than 100 hand calculations, with a corresponding increase in accuracy.

Management information systems rely on computer facilities to provide information flow through the organization. (Photograph courtesy IBM)

However, after several years and several million dollars, the program just "faded away," although it was never officially abandoned. One reason for the program's failure was that the company was organized on a classical, vertical basis, and the management information system was designed to cut across vertical lines and break down the departmental walls. However, as shown in Fig. 11.1, blockage occurred each time the program cut across departmental boundaries. Managers in one department refused to trust inputs from other departments and insisted on controlling their own data base. As a result, the resistance by middle managers blocked the installation of the program and caused it to fail.

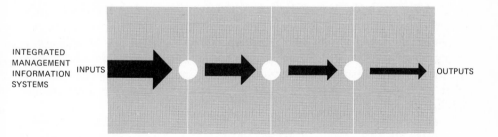

Fig. 11.1 The traditional departmentalized structure and the use of an integrated management information system.

Many writers are becoming disenchanted with attempts to develop a total systems approach without first rethinking concepts about organizations. Kaufman has even suggested that the approach be given up as unsound and that attention be concentrated on more limited, but probably more manageable, approaches.[20]

Although the computer has been of great value within individual departments and sections of an organization, its ultimate value in providing information flow across departmental lines is still far from being realized. Thus the computer is an excellent tool for handling the payroll or conducting scientific research, but such uses are restricted to intradepartmental needs. As a subsystem in its own right, the computer will not be truly successful in the lateral, flow system unless or until the present compartmentalized, vertical form of organizational structure is somehow modified and changed. For as Diebold has stated, "The new technology makes it imperative that we build information systems which break through the compartmentalized structure of the traditional business organization."[21]

IV. INTEGRATION THROUGH THE INFORMAL ORGANIZATION

In our previous discussions of the informal organization, we said that such groups and activities form a network of personal and social relationships which are not established or prescribed by the formal organization. Davis says that the informal organization "arises from the social interaction of people, which means that it develops spontaneously as people associate with each other."[22] And Bakke adds, "As factors influencing human behavior, the formal and informal systems are not separable."[23]

Informal organizations or groups arise from people's needs for relatedness, affiliation, friendship, and security. Argyris contends that "the informal organization helps to decrease the basic causes of conflict, frustration and failure."[24] For example, Van Zelst found that carpenters and bricklayers who formed work groups voluntarily had higher productivity, lower costs, and considerably lower absenteeism; one worker said, "Seems as though everything flows a lot smoother . . . the work's a lot more interesting, too."[25] One of the possible reasons for this preference for informal work groups may be that emotionally stable persons prefer to work with persons from similar backgrounds.[26]

As a method of improving work performance, the informal organization operates without an "official" set of rules or a formal manager. As a result, the members of the informal group work out among themselves approaches to accomplishing their tasks. Need an emergency repair on a machine? "Go see Jim and see if he can work it in between his scheduled jobs." Out of typing paper? "Rather than wait for a requisition to go through, borrow some from Mary." Stuck on a technical detail in R&D? "Drop over to see the mathematician in Section X—she may be able to give you some quick help." Want to get something done by a committee? "Drop in on Felix—he is the power behind the throne on the committee. If you get his O.K., he'll bring the rest of the committee around." Need an order expedited? "Call Bill, he will know how to get it done without having to wait for all the red tape."

Of course, the informal organization does not *always* work for the good of the organization. There are many well-documented cases of restriction in output and other dysfunctional approaches used by the informal organization. Perhaps one of the clearest examples of a dysfunctional approach by the informal organization occurred with a group of subordinates whose boss was highly disliked. One day at lunch, they decided to "get him" by *not* following their usual practice of getting the job done by some of the means just described. Instead, they decided to follow his orders to the letter. For two months, they did just that. From the official, formal organizational point of view, their behavior was impeccable. They did exactly what they were told to do, quickly and accurately. They followed the rules to the letter. Meanwhile, things in their section got worse and worse. Work backed up, and the manager found himself involved in crisis after crisis and in more and more trouble with upper management. He knew what was happening to him, but there was nothing he could do about it, since his subordinates were doing exactly what they were told to do, even though they knew that many of their "correct" actions would get their boss into even deeper trouble. At the end of two months, the boss decided to quit rather than to get fired.

Figure 11.2 shows that the importance of the informal organization in getting work done increases in direct proportion to the instability of the organization. In the nonroutine firm with unprogrammable search procedures and the need to deal with many exceptions, coordination among groups comes

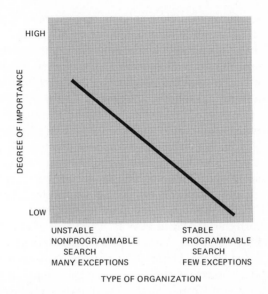

Fig. 11.2 Relative importance of the informal organization in accomplishing work.

about through mutual adjustment as the need arises, and the interdependence of groups in the work-flow process is high. At the other end of the continuum, there is less need for the informal organization, because decisions can be programmed at the top, and there are few exceptions. Here, the informal organization serves social, safety, and affiliation needs rather than work-flow needs. This continuum is, of course, *relative*, since even in stable organizations, organizational members do not always "follow the rules" or, as in the example earlier, do so to the detriment of the organization (or the boss).

V. MORE FORMALIZED INTEGRATIVE APPROACHES— SOCIOTECHNICAL SYSTEMS

Although the informal group can be of material assistance to the organization, its help or hindrance is fortuitous, or accidental. It is becoming increasingly clear that the flow of work and information within the organzation needs to be studied systematically, since these are two of the most important variables within the organization. As a result, there have been numerous attempts to use formalized, nonmathematical approaches to integration. One is the *sociotechnical* approach, which is concerned with organizing both the technology (work- and information-flow processes) and people to obtain an acceptable match.

The discussion of sociotechnical systems in this chapter highlights the interdependence of the three perspectives of organizations. The sociotechnical approach involves the redesign of the organization's structure, and therefore we might have put it in the chapter on organizational structure (Chapter 10). Because the work also involves people, the description of sociotechnical systems could also have logically been placed in Chapter 12, which concentrates on the human perspective. However, since the sociotechnical approach also includes and stresses the basic aspects of work and information flow, we decided to include it in this chapter, on the flow perspective. Nevertheless, you should be clearly aware that sociotechnical systems *include* portions of the other two perspectives and, indeed, clearly overlap them.

Much of the early work on the sociotechnical approach was done at the Tavistock Institute in London, and the name "sociotechnical systems" was coined there shortly after World War II. The work of the Tavistock Institute continues in many countries. For example, the Norwegian Confederation of Employers and the Trade Union Congress of Norway established a joint committee on the subject at the University of Trondheim in Norway. The research was later transferred to the Work Research Institute in Oslo. Although there are other major centers working on sociotechnical systems, these two (the Tavistock Institute and the Work Research Institute) have been prominent.[27] Because of the geographic location of the two institutes, the sociotechnical approach has had much more influence in the United Kingdom and on the Continent than in the United States.

Two early examples of this approach involve coal mining and weaving. Just after World War II, the technology of coal mining changed in Great Britain, with the development of greater mechanization. There are three basic operations in coal mining: (1) the coal must be removed from the seam; (2) the coal must be loaded and removed from the mine; and (3) support work, such as maintenance and the building and installing of roof supports, must be done. The early technology was based on teams of six workers, two teams per shift. Each team was responsible for its own production and was paid according to the group's performance. Team interaction and cohesiveness were high.

The development of new equipment (technology) changed the process, however. Specialization among 40 men replaced the teams, and each specialty had a different pay rate. This new organization ignored several basic facts. First, the change did not take into account the hazardous conditions in mining, such that miners need to feel that they can depend on one another in small, cohesive groups. Second, the miners themselves much preferred doing a whole job rather than part of one. Finally, the older men were resentful when new hirees got higher-paying jobs than those who had more seniority. The result was that productivity went down and absenteeism went up.

The new approach developed by the Tavistock researchers capitalized on the new technology, but also maintained the benefits of the old system. In the new sociotechnical approach, each of three shifts performed the total job. Members of the newly formed work teams had the necessary ability and resources to do the total job. Each member of the team did not have to know every task, but the team itself had all the resources to do the total job. The team was now able to provide its own coordination. The results were significant. Unnecessary absenteeism dropped from 4.3% to 0.4%, and productivity rose from 78% to 95%.[28]

In 1953 another Tavistock researcher examined the interaction between work flow and group performance in a company with two textile plants in Ahmedabad, India.[29] Automatic looms had been introduced to increase productivity, but productivity did not rise. The change in technology was accompanied by a change in job structure. Jobs were set up according to American and British standards regarding the division and specialization of work. Now there were 12 different occupational roles for the 29 men responsible for the operation of the looms in the research area. The workers' interdependence was not recognized, and the fractionalization of jobs did not allow a group structure to develop.

The organization was seriously considering policing the operation more rigidly, but instead modified the sociotechnical system to allow an interdependent group structure to emerge. With the reorganization, a group of workers became responsible for a given group of looms. The workers were enthusiastic. Seven-man groups were formed, with each group responsible for the total operation, including such ancillary services as oiling the machines and removing the bobbins, of several looms. After an initial period of fluctuating productivity, it stabilized at 95%, some 15% higher than it had been under the industrial engineering approach. The amount of damaged cloth fell from 32% to about 15% in the last six months of the experiment. The approach was so successful that it was expanded to the rest of the plant, including nonautomatic looms, with similar results.

A follow-up study was conducted 16 years later to determine what had happened in the interim. Although there had been some regression, the general conclusion was that in at least one area—the nonautomatic loom shed—the levels of performance and work organization had remained constant over 16 years.

The effective persistence of the "group system" in at least one area implies that the assumptions in Rice's original experiment were substantially confirmed. Regression in the two automatic loom-sheds is explained in terms of failure to maintain the necessary boundary conditions for group working in the face of progressive changes in the market and other environmental factors. In conclusion it is suggested that Rice's innovations were more radical than was recognized at the time.[30]

The results of these and other studies have made the idea of autonomous work groups very popular throughout Europe, particularly in the Netherlands, Scandinavia, and Great Britain. The report of the Norwegian Work Research Institutes (Arbeidspsykologisk Institutt) on projects from 1964 to 1972 describes projects in manufacturing organizations, banks, hotels, and shipyards.[31]

The early work on sociotechnical systems focused on developing interdependent production groups. A second stage has been the formation of production groups, with development groups coordinating the work of the production groups. The production groups consist of the operators; the development group, of elected workers working with the foreman and technical specialists, as shown in Fig. 11.3.

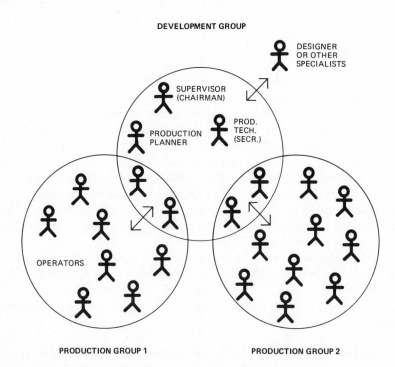

Fig. 11.3 Interlocking production and development groups. (Adapted from "Work Research Institutes: Projects 1964–1972," Oslo: Work Research Institutes (Arbeidspsykologisk Institutt), mimeo., n.d.)

The production group is formed on the basis of several criteria: (1) the spelling out of the joint production effort in clear, simple terms; (2) the attempt to determine a "natural" demarcation of the group from other production centers, so that the group can operate with relative independence; and (3) the grouping of persons whose work is interdependent. This process gives supervisors more opportunity to delegate authority, so that they can work with overall planning and development.

For example, a 600-man plant in Norway manufacturing a variety of electrical heating equipment operates completely on the basis of autonomous work groups. An elected representative receives planning and related information from the reference group, and the group itself schedules production. Individuals within the groups are free to switch jobs as necessary. Elected representatives from each group meet twice a week to discuss operating problems, change production schedules, and the like. Three industrial engineers

A development group in operation. (Photograph courtesy Volvo)

"supervise" about 600 production workers. Productivity appears to be high and absenteeism and turnover are low.

Saab began the first such autonomous work group in one of its plants in 1969. By 1973 there were about 130 production groups and approximately 60 development groups. Approximately 1500 employees were in production groups in late 1973, and the number is still growing.[32] In the meantime, unplanned stoppage time on the production line has been reduced from 6% to about 2%, and turnover dropped from over 70% on the chassis line in 1969 to less than 20% in 1972.

In the first two stages of the development of sociotechnical systems, the technology of the work flow was accepted as a given, and the work group was fitted to it. For example, in the Ahmedabad program, the automatic looms had been installed prior to the work of the Tavistock group. Now, in the 1970s, the technology and work flow are being fitted to current knowledge about workers.

Two of the better-known such programs are the redesign of work at Saab and Volvo in Sweden. In both organizations factory work is being adapted to people, rather than people being adapted to machines. For example, Volvo opened a body-assembly plant at Kalmar, with the first car being produced in July 1974. The new plant was designed so that several work teams are responsible for a particular installation on the car, e.g., the electrical system, controls, instrumentation, etc. The team members work at their own pace and become specialists within their own particular trade. Each work team has 15–25 people, and the members themselves can agree on the distribution of work and decide when and how interchange of work should take place. The work teams are responsible for ordering their own materials. One foreman and one industrial engineer or technician supervise two to four teams. Since the team itself decides on the assembly process, the foreman does not know who is doing what. Supervision focuses on overall quality, ensuring that the team has the necessary equipment, parts, and the like.

Car bodies are conveyed between and within the work teams on self-propelled trolleys. Work on the body can be carried out with the trolley either moving or stationary; a tilting device turns the body 90° so as to facilitate work on the underside.

The space between teams' working areas can be used for "stocking" a number of body trolleys, thereby permitting variation of the working rhythm and providing a "buffer" stock to allow for rest periods, which the employees can schedule for themselves.

The architecture of the Kalmar factory promotes versatility. The outer walls form a star-shaped pattern, ensuring plenty of daylight in the factory. The angular construction of the outer walls also solves the problem of how to

The new Volvo plant at Kalmar, Sweden. (Photograph courtesy Volvo)

conserve the atmosphere of a small workshop in a large factory. The teams work in clearly defined areas with their own entrances, changing rooms, and rest areas. The car assembly itself takes place along the outer walls, and the material stores are in the central part of the building.

Since the factory opened in July 1974, it is yet too early to determine its overall effectiveness. However, in May 1975, the plant had been working at 100% efficiency for two and a half weeks, an accomplishment seldom achieved in an automobile factory, where normal "high" productivity is 80% efficiency. Here, efficiency is defined as the number of work hours required to build a car (calculated by the engineering department) as contrasted with the number of work hours actually expended.

A Saab engine-assembly factory has also experimented with work re-design. This plant was built around a different set of concepts. Some of the primary considerations were to: (1) reduce the extent to which workers were tied to the job; (2) allow individuals to influence the distribution of work; and (3) provide greater flexibility in handling disruptions, simplified line balancing, and easier training.

A number of approaches were considered before it was finally decided to have teams of three or four workers do the complete assembly of an entire engine. Team members decide among themselves how the engine will be assembled and who will take on what tasks. When the engine is assembled, the team tests the engine for performance, doing rework or adjustments as necessary.

However, a number of engineering problems had to be solved before the team approach could be used. Buffer stocks were necessary, and there had to be a way to move the completed engine out of the area. These problems cause little difficulty in a "regular" assembly line, since employees are stationed on both sides of the line. Eventually the layout shown in Fig. 11.4 was adopted. A large conveyor loop adjacent to the work area brings in preassembled parts and takes out the completed engines. Each group is furnished with a U-shaped guide track in the floor. Trucks are allowed free passage to replenish the necessary parts without disturbing the assembly group.

There have been some criticisms of this approach, however. For example, when several American auto workers visited the Saab engine plant, they found the pace of work too fast and the lunch breaks too short.[33] However, immediately after the visit, one Saab executive commented that the training time necessary for complete assembly did not allow the American workers to become completely proficient, one reason they felt that the pace was too fast.

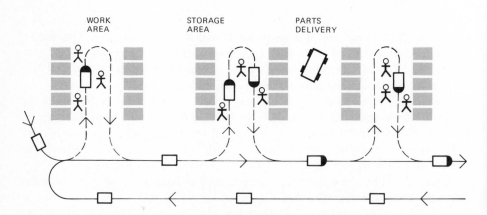

Fig. 11.4 Redesigned work area for engine assembly. (Adapted from J. Norsted and S. Aguren, *The Saab-Scania Report,* Stockholm: Swedish Employers Confederation.)

A different approach has proved successful at the Sickla Works, near Stockholm, of Atlas Copco Mining and Construction Technique.[34] Department 698 of the Sickla Works manufactures about 40 models of rock drills. In this work-redesign project, workers' jobs were expanded from specific tasks at a fixed position. Now, teams of two to four men take a drill lot through the entire production process, moving from one work station to another as necessary for equipment usage and other purposes. The workers have also taken on added responsibilities. Rather than just following orders, they study drawings of the drill, make certain that all the parts are available and correct, and then decide when to begin each operation. Since there are so many different drill models, the workers can switch to another model should parts shortages or other problems develop with one model. Thus the workers do much more problem solving than they did in the past.

Much more work has been done in Europe and Great Britain on sociotechnical systems than in the United States. However, a recent report describes the gains in productivity and job satisfaction at the Gaines pet food plant in Topeka, Kansas, that occurred when autonomous work groups were used.[35] Another study in an organization making complex electronic instruments showed that when autonomous work groups were introduced, productivity rose 17%, absenteeism was reduced by 50%, and quality increased 50%, with a corresponding increase in employee satisfaction and morale.[36]

Despite its advantages, the sociotechnical approach is not always feasible. For example, one division of a large American company attempted to establish autonomous work groups operating numerically controlled lathes. Although the union was in favor of the change and both productivity and quality went up, the approach slowly died. No single reason can be pinpointed for the demise of the program, which lasted for several years. One of the reasons given by those involved is that management did not really want to have leaderless work groups, even though productivity was up. Another reason given was that corporate headquarters was unable to decide how to pay workers who were doing their own scheduling, supervising, and problem solving.

Indeed, the sociotechnical approach can cause additional tensions at a higher level. In one organization in Norway, autonomous work groups have been used since 1965. Productivity is up and absenteeism is down. The plant manager is firmly convinced that he would not return to the old system of managing, noting that this would be "O.K. for people with their heads cut off." However, interviews in 1975 with union members who have worked under the new approach for ten years revealed discontent. They have no desire to go back to the old way. But they would welcome the opportunity to take on even more responsibility and challenge. They feel that they can't make as many decisions as they need to about production scheduling, designing new equipment, and the like because they do not have enough advance, in-depth, information from the corporate headquarters. The union members stressed the need for more marketing, design, and economic information so that they could do their own jobs better. Mistrust was building, since they felt that management was deliberately withholding information they needed to do a better job.

The rising use of autonomous work groups in Sweden has led to warnings that supervisors and managers' jobs must be enriched if they are to support the sociotechnical approach.

In this connection, one should pay an appropriate amount of attention to the situation of supervisors and middle managers. These categories should be given a fair chance even in the new organization to get stimulating and challenging tasks and responsibilities. It might be disastrous to the whole organization, if these categories find their possibilities of performing good and qualified contributions seriously limited.[37]

The sociotechnical approach to work and information flow appears to be extremely powerful. However, little applied research is available to tell us when autonomous work groups and similar techniques should be used. Further, the introduction of sociotechnical systems has frequently been made in conjunction with larger organization-development efforts, such as those described in the next chapter.

VI. CONCLUSION

One modern approach to organizational improvement through the flow perspective is model building, including system dynamics and operations research. Attempts to improve lateral information flow with computerized management information systems may be hampered by the vertical structure of the organization, which reduces the effectiveness of such information flow. However, information flow may be facilitated by informal groups within the organization. Such informal groups may be formalized through the sociotechnical approach. Sociotechnical systems address themselves directly to work and information flow, although in more qualitative ways than the formalized mathematical-modeling approaches.

These are all ways of improving the flow of information, materials, and resources across an organization, but as we have stressed throughout the text, these approaches cannot be considered in isolation. Rather, they must be considered in the context of both the structural design and human perspectives.

In the next chapter, we discuss organization development primarily from the human perspective, and in Chapter 13 we propose a unified theory of organization development that integrates the approaches of the three perspectives.

REVIEW

1. Models of various "systems" are commonly observed in our complex modern world. Give examples of two such models and explain why they are beneficial to us. Do these models contradict Boulding's statement (see Chapter 2) on the ultimate complexity of models or theoretical systems?

2. The computer is just a "black box" in which inputs lead to outputs that a human being would be able to determine, given sufficient time. How can the results of a black box *not* be able to determine behavior and in fact cause interdepartmental conflict? Explain.

3. Give an example from your own experience that shows the difference between an input- and an output-based model.

4. We have given some reasons for the failure of completely computerized information systems. Do you agree or disagree with these reasons? Elaborate.

5. From your own experience, give an example showing how the informal organization has (a) helped and (b) hindered the organization. What caused the difference?

6. What is the value of considering the work-flow process? Give some examples of circumstances helping or hindering the flow process.

7. How does the idea of sociotechnical systems relate to the structural-design and human perspectives?

8. What do you see as the utility of sociotechnical systems? Give illustrations of circumstances when such an approach might be used in an organization with which you are familiar.

REFERENCES

1. J. W. Forrester, "Counterintuitive Behavior of Social Systems," *Technology Review*, Alumni Association, Massachusetts Institute of Technology **73**, 3 (Jan. 1971): 52–68.

2. J. R. Emshoff, *Analysis of Behavioral Systems*, New York: Macmillan, 1971.

3. K. Boulding, "General Systems Theory: The Skeleton of Science," *Management Science* **2**, 3 (April 1956): 197–208.

4. J. W. Forrester, *Industrial Dynamics*, Cambridge, Mass.: M.I.T. Press, 1961.

5. Forrester, "Counterintuitive Behavior of Social Systems," *op. cit.*; "Systems Analysis as a Tool for Urban Planning," paper presented at the Symposium on the Engineer and the City, National Academy of Engineering, Washington, D.C., October 22–23, 1969.

6. D. H. Meadows, D. L. Meadows, J. Ronders, and W. Behrens, III, *The Limits to Growth*, New York: Universe Books, 1972, p. 21.

7. P. Passell, M. Roberts, and L. Ross, "*The Limits to Growth*, World Dynamics, and Urban Dynamics," *New York Times Book Review*, April 2, 1972.

8. F. Hillier and G. Lieberman, *Introduction to Operations Research*, San Francisco: Holden-Day, 1969, p. 5.

9. N. Gaither, "Operations Research Techniques in Manufacturing: What Variables Are Related to Their Use?" Paper presented at the thirty-fifth annual meeting of the Academy of Management, New Orleans, August 10–13, 1975.

10. R. Ackoff and P. Rivett, *A Manager's Guide to Operations Research*, New York: Wiley, 1963.

11. W. H. Gruber and J. S. Niles, "Problems in the Utilization of Management Science/Operations Research: A State of the Art Survey," *Bulletin of the Institute of Management Sciences* **4**, 2 (Jan. 1971): 12–19.

12. H. Simon, "Thories of Decision-Making in Economics and Behavioral Science," in *Managerial Economics*, ed. G. Clarkson, Baltimore: Penguin, 1968, pp. 13–49.

13. Emshoff, *op. cit.*

14. *Ibid.*, p. 25.

15. Gaither, *op. cit.*

16. *Ibid.*, p. 25.

17. D. Gerwin and W. Christoffel, "Organizational Structure and Technology: A Computer Model Approach," *Management Science* **20**, 11 (August 1974): 1531–1542.

18. J. Thompson, *Organizations in Action*, New York: McGraw-Hill, 1967.

19. E. Huse, "The Impact of Computer Programs on Managers and Organizations: A Case Study," in *The Impact of Computers on Management*, ed. C. Myers, Cambridge, Mass.: M.I.T. Press, 1967.

20. F. Kaufman, "Data Systems that Cross Company Boundaries," *Harvard Business Review* **44**, 1 (Jan.–Feb. 1966): 141–155.

21. J. Diebold, "ADP—The Still-Sleeping Giant," *Harvard Business Review* **42**, 5 (Sept.–Oct. 1964): 60–65.

22. K. Davis, *Human Relations at Work*, New York: McGraw-Hill, 1962, p. 236.

23. E. Bakke, *Bonds of Organization*, New York: Harper and Brothers, 1950, p. 194.

24. C. Argyris, *Personality and Organization*, New York: Harper & Row, 1957, p. 230.

25. R. Van Zelst, "Sociometrically Selected Work Teams Increase Production," *Personnel Psychology* **5** (Autumn 1952): 175–185.

26. J. Bowditch and D. King, "The Relationship Between Biographical Similarity and Interpersonal Choice," *Proceedings of the 78th Annual Convention*, American Psychological Association (1970): 381–382.

27. L. Klein, *New Forms of Work Organization*, London: Tavistock Institute of Human Relations, 1974.

28. E. Trist and K. Bamforth, "Some Social and Psychological Consequences of the Long Wall of Goal Setting," *Human Relations* **4**, 1 (Jan. 1951): 1–8; E. Trist, "On Socio-Technical Systems," in W. Bennis, K. Benne, and R. Chin, eds., *The Planning of Change*, 2d ed., New York: Holt, Rinehart and Winston, 1969, pp. 269–282.

29. A. Rice, *Productivity and Social Organization: The Ahmedabad Experiment*, London: Tavistock Publications, 1958.

30. E. Miller, "Socio-Technical Systems in Weaving, 1953–1970: A Follow-Up Study," *Human Relations* **28**, 4 (August 1975): 349. Reprinted by permission.

31. "Work Research Institutes: Projects 1964–1972," Olso: Work Research Institutes (Arbeidspsykologisk Institutt), mimeo., n.d.

32. J. Norsted and S. Aguren, *The Saab-Scania Report*, Stockholm: Swedish Employers' Confederation, 1973.

33. "Doubting Sweden's Way," *Time*, March 10, 1975, p. 40.

34. L. Bjork, "An Experiment in Work Satisfaction," *Scientific American* **232**, 3 (March 1975): 17–23.

35. R. Walton, "How to Counter Alienation in the Plant," *Harvard Business Review* **50**, 6 (Nov.–Dec. 1972): 70–81.

36. E. Huse and M. Beer, "Eclectic Approach to Satisfaction and Morale: Organizational Development," *Harvard Business Review* **49**, 5 (Sept.–Oct. 1971): 103–112.

37. S. Rubenowitz, *Motivational Factors Affecting Managers' Attitudes Toward Industrial Democracy*, Goteborgs: Goteborgs Universitet, 1974, p. 10.

12

ORGANIZATION DEVELOPMENT– HUMAN PERSPECTIVE

The time has come," the Walrus said, "to talk of
many things . . ."

LEWIS CARROLL

LEARNING
OBJECTIVES

When you have finished reading and studying this chapter, you should be able to:

1. Define and use the concept of organization development (OD) within the context of a total system.
2. Describe the assumptions underlying OD.
3. Define and then differentiate between "planned change" and "action research."
4. Name and then differentiate levels of intervention in OD.
5. Identify and demonstrate the use of at least five specific OD tools.
6. Name at least six problems encountered in trying to do OD.
7. State and then criticize each of Sperling's six "myths" about OD.

You will be expected to define and use the following concepts:

OD objectives

OD assumptions

Planned change

Problems with planned change

Action research

Diagnosis

Classification of OD interventions

Operations analysis

Evaluating and controlling individual performance

Job enrichment

Core job dimensions

Evaluating and controlling individual performance

Concern with personal work style

Team building

Improving interdepartmental or intergroup relationships

Intrapersonal relationships

Laboratory training

Change agents

Problems with OD

Ethics and values

Myths about OD

THOUGHT STARTERS

1. Think of some organizations you have belonged to (social, fraternal, industrial, other). What problems has each of them faced that reveal they are less than perfect?
2. In what ways are the needs of a formal organization, such as a bank, insurance company, or manufacturing organization, and the individual employee incompatible?
3. How much influence might you be able to exert over an organization in which you have a job?
4. What did Maslow have in mind when he said, "If the only tool you have is a hammer, you tend to treat everything else as a nail"?

I. INTRODUCTION

The term "organization development" (OD) reflects a behavioral-science orientation. However, both "organizational improvement" and "organization development" have the same objective—to enhance the organization's effectiveness and efficiency.

Organization development is a rapidly expanding field which is continually changing with new knowledge. Essentially, OD is a long-range attempt to improve an organization's ability to both cope with changes in its external environment and improve its internal problem-solving capabilities. However, unlike approaches in the other two perspectives, OD is directed toward integrating the needs, goals, and objectives of the organization with the needs of the individual for involvement, growth, and development on the job. This concern was evidenced in recent Congressional hearings. "One of the central themes of the hearings was the new concern for job satisfaction as an important factor in achieving greater productivity . . . The stakes are high . . . in the final analysis it is people and not machines which produce."[1]

An *explicit* part of the OD approach to improving organizational effectiveness is the deliberate and conscious effort to help human beings grow and develop in the organizational setting (see Fig. 12.1). This assumes that organizational effectiveness and efficiency can both be improved if certain conditions, as stated below, are met in the organizational setting.

1. Most people both need and desire growth and self-realization.

2. When their basic needs have been satisfied, most individuals do not want or seek a soft, secure environment; rather, if given the opportunity, they become more concerned with work, challenge, and responsibility.

3. Organizational effectiveness and efficiency are increased when work is organized to meet the individual's needs for challenge, responsibility, and growth.

4. Increasing the openness of communication facilitates personal growth.

5. Shifting the emphasis of conflict resolution from "edicting" or "smoothing" to open confrontation facilitates both personal growth and the accomplishment of organizational goals.

6. As people working in groups become more open and honest with one another in a "caring" fashion, the group becomes increasingly able to handle problems in a constructive rather than disruptive fashion.

7. Organizatioinal structure and the design of jobs can be modified to more

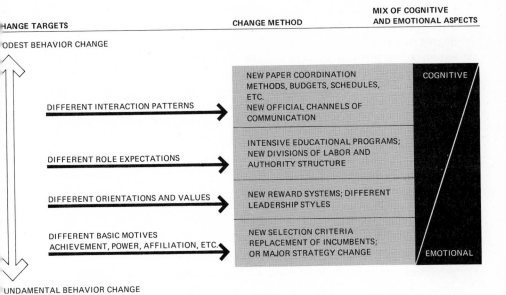

Fig. 12.1 Elements of an organization development program. (Reprinted by special permission from *Developing Organizations: Diagnosis and Action* by Paul Lawrence and Jay Lorsch, Addison-Wesley Publishing Co., Reading, Massachusetts. Copyright © 1969. All rights reserved.)

effectively meet the needs of the individual, the group, and the organization.

8. Many "personality clashes" in organizations result from problems of organizational design.

II. CHANGE, PLANNED CHANGE, AND ACTION RESEARCH

Change in organizations is inevitable. Sometimes change is forced on an organization because of external pressures, such as new laws, regulations, competition, or innovation; at other times, because of perceived problems or opportunities within the organization. In either eventuality, change needs to be *managed* if the goals of OD are to be met.

Change *can* be managed to bring about improvements in the human perspective through the application of behavioral science knowledge. Various models of the change process have been described.[2] We will focus on only two—planned change and action research, the two models most widely used in organization development. These two OD approaches differ in the amount and degree of collaboration between the change agent and the client system they entail. Also, planned change utilizes behavioral science principles, whereas action research places more emphasis on collaborative diagnosis and on the generation of new behavioral science knowledge. Both approaches have their strengths and weaknesses. Both usually require the use of a change agent, who may be external to the total system or internal (but usually external to the particular subsystem involved in the change process).

A. Planned Change

An early model for planned change was developed by Lewin—the father of both planned change and action research—who saw change as consisting of three basic stages: unfreezing, changing, and refreezing.[3]

1. *Unfreezing* refers to a decrease in the strength of old values, attitudes, or behaviors resulting from new or different information or experiences which disconfirm one's perception of self, others, and/or events. Unfreezing is a disturbance of current equilibrium.

2. *Changing* is the bringing about of specific changes through the development of new values, attitudes, and/or behaviors by either identification or internalization.

3. *Refreezing* is the stabilization of change at a new state of equilibrium. For Lewin, the use of this term refers to the attainment and continuation of specific changes in the norms of the reference group, the organizational culture, or organizational policy and structure.

Lewin postulated that organizations exist in a state of "quasi-stationary equilibrium." He developed the concept of "force-field analysis" as a method by which organizations could be moved from one state of quasi-stationary equilibrium to another.

The strategy for planned change developed by Lewin has been further expanded and modified. One group introduced the notion of planned change as a "dynamic, seven-step process: scouting, entry, diagnosis, planning, action, evaluation and termination."[4] Figure 12.2 shows how the original Lewinian model of unfreezing, change, and refreezing may be superimposed on the more refined seven-step model.

1. *Scouting*—neither the change agent (external or internal) nor the client system is committed to a particular project. Rather, both are exploring; the client system with regard to its need for help, and the change agent for an

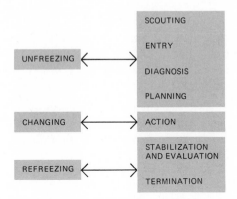

Fig. 12.2 Planned change and Lewin's typology of change. (Adapted from E. Huse, *Organization Development and Change*, St. Paul: West, 1975, p. 98.)

entry point to the system or subsystem and the extent and degree of change effort.

2. *Entry*—the change agent and the client define and establish the helping relationship in terms of how the following stages will be carried out.

3. *Diagnosis*—the change agent begins with the perceived problems of the client to identify more clearly the specific improvement goals to be reached. The most common methods in diagnosis are previous performance data, interviews, questionnaires, and personal observation. Frequently, this phase is not actually followed under conditions of planned change. The change agent may use a particular, specific technique in almost every situation. For example, some OD practitioners use the highly structured Managerial Grid, with little deviation, in almost any organization or situation. Other practitioners tend to rely heavily on MBO, job enrichment/team building, or sensitivity training as *the* basic approach to OD. Instead, however, the OD approach should be varied to fit the situation, the problem, and the client.

4. *Planning*—the goals to be achieved are identified, as are the specific action steps needed to meet those goals. Planning should be done in cooperation with the client to ensure that the plans are consonant with the climate, needs, and expectations of the client system and to ensure commitment to the plans.

5. *Action*—the action steps identified in step 4 are implemented. If the preceding work has been done well, the implementation should go smoothly. However, many "failures" in OD result from improper diagnosis or failure to involve a key group or individual or to properly anticipate the consequences of a proposed action(s).

6. *Stabilization*—the results of the change are evaluated. Frequently, however, evaluation is bypassed or given only lip service through such methods as anecdotal reports or what is known as "testimonial" evidence. Thus, for example, most people will report that a training program they just completed was successful, even though their actual behavior did not change at all.

7. *Termination*—the external change agent takes on a different project or begins the cycle again, initiating the scouting phase. If the change agent is "external," termination may mean working with a different client.

Planned change is not without its weaknesses, however. One criticism is that although Lewin's model has been widely quoted, there has seldom been any clear indication of how the formulation determines the design of the change or of research. Further, Lewin's concept of force-field analysis has never been systematically conceptualized, and the two sets of opposing forces have never been systematically identified or measured.[5]

Planned change programs are more "popular," since "certain 'prepackaged' OD programs such as Grid OD, recent variants of MBO, and laboratory training programs have attained particular prominence and use for at least four reasons."[6] The four reasons are as follows.

1. Many OD practitioners have a favorite technique or approach and do not consider using other strategies. One consultant's past experience may have indicated that all organization members need to develop openness, examine their values and assumptions, and learn how to give and receive feedback. This consultant may consistently use or prescribe sensitivity training to help the organization improve. Other consultants may "specialize" in MBO, job enrichment, the Managerial Grid, etc.

2. Some OD consultants specialize in specific OD activities. Thus a team-building expert may use this approach even when there is no need for such a program.

3. Complete diagnosis is time-consuming, and the client may not be willing to wait so long. Thus a consultant may be called in, accept the client's own diagnosis, and provide immediate recommendations for problem solution. However, in this situation the felt need may not be the real problem or may be only a symptom of a deeper problem.

4. Similarly, the client may feel that its own diagnosis is correct and that additional investment of money, time, and personnel for diagnostic research is unnecessary. Under such circumstances, a consultant's options may be limited to accepting the client's diagnosis or not working with the client system at all.

As a result of these and other factors, the client and consultant may agree on a prepackaged program, and it may achieve satisfactory results. However, there are several negative consequences to the "planned" approach to OD. One is that many users see OD in a very limited fashion. OD is frequently perceived as a one-week Grid program or as a weekend sensitivity session. As a result, the OD approach may not be systematic or systems-based, and the results quickly fade away.[7]

Another negative consequence of prepackaged OD is the tendency to be overly concerned with the *content* or *structure* of the organizational change and neglectful of the *processes* that are involved. As an illustration, people may be "enthralled by the Managerial Grid diagram and consequently ignore the important inter-personal and task behaviors being subject to the change activity."[8]

Third, many OD programs have not been adaptive. Frequently, a commitment is made to a specific OD program or technique (such as MBO), and the program is retained even though its effects may be negative. Only continuing diagnosis and evaluation can ensure that the proper tools for OD are selected.

Perhaps the most fundamental objection to planned change is that it's not systemic, that it emphasizes content at the expense of flexibility. Criticisms to the "canned" approach to OD are growing. For example, one author even asks, "Can management survive OD"?[9] He points out that many aspects of more traditional OD efforts have been dysfunctional to managers and that OD is frequently *imposed* on an organization rather than being made *compatible* with it. He suggests that "if OD is to let management survive, it must take into account the characteristics of the management processes mentioned here, as well as the realities of industrial order."[10]

B. Action Research

Although on the surface, planned change and action research appear to be quite similar, there are some major differences.[11] First, whereas planned change frequently involves the use of a "preplanned package" of OD techniques, action research generally focuses on developing specific actions to solve specific problems. Second, although planned change may use data-based diagnosis of organizational problems, action research emphasizes the diagnostic stage. Third, planned change may or may not include evaluation of the results of interventions; action research emphasizes the evaluation of results as a basis for further diagnosis, further action planning, and further interventions in a cyclic process. Finally, planned change utilizes behavioral science knowledge; one of the aims and goals of action research, however, is to develop and identify *new* behavioral science knowledge.

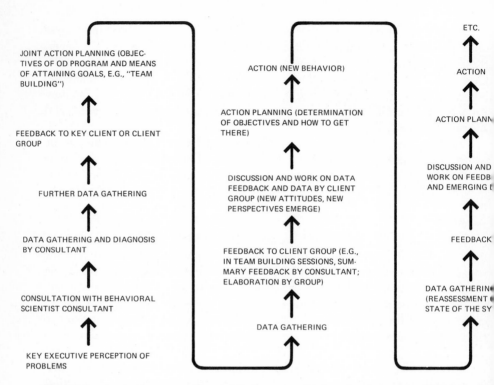

Fig. 12.3 An action-research model for organization development. (W. French, "Organization Development: Objectives, Assumptions and Strategies." © 1969 by the Regents of the University of California. Reprinted from *California Management Review* **XII**, 2, p. 26 (Fig. 12.2), by permission of the Regents.)

The cyclic nature of action research is demonstrated in French's model, shown in Fig. 12.3.[12] The key aspects are data gathering, preliminary action planning, action, and rediagnosis. The diagnostic stage is tremendously important, for a consultant who is not highly sensitive to the prevailing culture of the organization, its state of readiness for change, its technology, and the expectations of the client system, may seek to impose his or her own value system on the client system.

Bennis documents three cases of OD programs that failed because the consultant did an incomplete and inadequate job of diagnosing the current client culture and readiness for change.[13] In one instance, an attempt was made to introduce laboratory training (sensitivity training) in an organization that was not ready for it. The president of the company summarily put a stop to the training, insisting that the training department revert to more traditional methods.

Diagnosis is highly important for another reason. Since organizational subsystems are interrelated, changes in one subsystem will have an impact on the other subsystems. The negative impact a change in one subsystem can have on other subsystems is illustrated in the "Hovey and Beard Company" case.[14] The Hovey and Beard Company manufactured wooden toys—animals, pull toys, etc. After the toys were cut, sanded, and partially assembled in the wood room, they were dipped in shellac and painted. The partially assembled toys were spray painted in the paint room, an operation staffed entirely by women. Although the toys were predominantly two-colored, only one color was applied as the toy went through the paint room. Therefore, this process had to be repeated for each additional color. Most toys required at least two trips through the paint room.

For a number of years, these toys had been produced entirely by hand. However, in order to meet the tremendously increased demand, the painting

Reprinted by permission of Chicago Tribune-New York News Syndicate, Inc. Copyright © 1971 by Chicago Tribune.

operation was reengineered so that the eight women painters sat in a line by an endless chain of continuous-motion hooks that went into a long, horizontal oven. Each worker sat at her own painting booth, which was designed to carry away fumes and to backstop excess paint. The worker would take a toy from the tray beside her, position it in a jig inside the painting cubicle, spray on the color according to a pattern, then release the toy and hang it on the hook passing by. The rate at which the hooks moved had been calculated by the engineers so that each person, when fully trained, would be able to hang a painted toy on each hook before it passed beyond her reach.

The paint-room workers were on a group-bonus plan. Since the operation was new to them, they also received a learning bonus, which decreased by regular amounts each month. After six months, the learning bonus would vanish, for it was expected that by then the group would be able to meet the standard and to earn a group bonus by exceeding the quota.

Over a period of time, the workers were given the authority to regulate the speed of the assembly line. Their participation was high, and productivity soared. Because they were on both the learning bonus and incentive pay, their pay was equal to or above that of the more highly paid workers in the organization, e.g., tool and die makers. However, the rest of the organization was not prepared for the change. As a result, the manufacturing manager took summary action; he restored the slower assembly-line speed originally set by the industrial engineer. Soon the foreman and most of the paint-room personnel quit for jobs elsewhere.

The importance of sensitivity to the client organization's culture, technology, and readiness to change has caused some OD practitioners to stress that the change process must start from the top down. Indeed, Beckhard defines OD as "an effort (1) *planned*, (2) *organization wide*, and (3) *managed from the top*, to (4) increase *organization effectiveness* and *health* through (5) *planned interventions* in the organization's 'processes,' using *behavioral-science* knowledge."[15]

Other OD practitioners, however, disagree that OD must *always* be managed from the top down. "People problems" can seriously hurt, if not destroy, an organization if not properly handled; the task of OD is to identify, diagnose, and treat such problems.[16] To Ferguson, the crucial elements of OD are sensing, mutual coaching, and organizational display. He defines "sensing" as the attempt to use representative subgroups of the various units in the work force to ensure that managers "hear and understand the social dynamics of their employees" (which is similar to our use of the term "diagnosing"). "Mutual coaching" is the help individuals give one another to get the job done better, and "organizational display" is the attempt to bring organizational problems out into the open so that they can be clearly perceived and worked on, i.e., it is the "job of organizational development to search for and display organizational *'worms,'* since if they cannot be seen they cannot be treated."[17]

A slightly more conservative note is sounded by Kegan, who found the results of OD to be ambivalent.[18] Although a "proper" OD program increased trust toward peers inside and outside the work group while simultaneously keeping individuals task-oriented, other data indicated that traditional bureaucratic norms conflicted with the program's development of norms of confrontation, choice, and collaboration. Kegan notes that participants in an OD program must be aware of organizational hostility toward it and that this must be reflected in OD strategy.

The cyclical process of diagnosis, planning, action, and rediagnosis requires that the change agent, as a consultant, operate differently from most other consultants. In the more traditional mode, a consultant comes in, looks at a problem, makes a diagnosis, makes recommendations, and then leaves. In the OD process, the change agent generally does not write reports, but instead usually prefers to work on ongoing problems, acting as a resource person helping the organization to grow and develop and stand on its own rather than acting as either an internal or external consultant giving advice on specific problems. Thus, for example, the OD consultant and the management staff may work jointly in diagnosing the organization's problems and working out solutions. As Brown notes, this "mutual exchange of information between investigator and respondents is critical to both increased understanding (research) and constructive change ('action')."[19] Furthermore, action and research may be incompatible in some situations, but in others action and research may be difficult to separate.

III. APPROACHES TO OD INTERVENTIONS

More and more, OD practitioners are becoming aware that *any* involvement in a client system involves an intervention and may cause changes in the client system. Even preliminary data gathering may cause changes to occur. For example, an American college professor visited a shipyard in Sweden to learn more about how the yard operated. Also present were the manager of the shipyard, the personnel director, and the heads of three unions. The visitor soon realized that a great deal of misunderstanding, tension, and friction existed between two of the union chiefs. The shipyard manager and the personnel manager had not been previously aware of the tension. Thus a plant visit to learn about the operation of a Swedish shipyard may have led to other changes and ramifications.

Bennis describes nine different interventions according to themes.[20]

1. *Discrepancy*—calling attention to contradictions in either attitudes or actions, which then leads to further exploration. This intervention is especially useful in keeping the organization on a new course, so that it does not drift back to an older, less satisfactory pattern.

2. *Theory*—using behavioral science knowledge to show the connection between present behavior and the underlying assumptions influencing the behavior.

3. *Procedure*—critiquing an action to determine whether or not organization development activities are an aid to problem solving and related behavior.

4. *Relationship*—focusing the participants' attention on issues arising between people as they work together, so that interpersonal friction can be reduced or eliminated.

5. *Experimenting*—testing two or more different action plans to determine which is the best before finally selecting a particular plan.

6. *Dilemma*—searching for alternatives other than those under consideration. Such an intervention can aid in accurately identifying a choice point in managerial actions and can help members to reexamine outworn assumptions.

7. *Perspective*—providing a broader historical background to determine whether or not present actions are still "on target." Frequently, people get wrapped up in the day-to-day problems, losing sight of the larger issues. A perspective intervention fosters an evaluation of these larger issues.

8. *Organization structure*—determining whether or not an organization's design is appropriate. Unfortunately, many OD efforts overlook this factor. Often, the roots of organizational ineffectiveness lie not in interpersonal interaction, but in the very structure of the organization itself.

9. *Cultural*—focusing on the precedents, traditions, and practices comprising the organizational fabric. It is difficult to challenge the appropriateness of an organization's culture (or climate), yet it is critically important to do so.

Another classification scheme, given by French and Bell, is directed toward the nature of the *target groups*.[21]

1. *Individuals*—focusing on improving the effectiveness of individuals through coaching and counseling, role analysis, life- and career-planning activities, and sensitivity training. The Grid Phase 1 (described in Chapter 7) can also be included here.

2. *Dyads/triads*—improving the effectiveness of dyads and triads through third-party peacemaking, process consultation, and using Grid Phases 1 and 2.

3. *Teams and groups*—enhancing the effectiveness of teams and groups through task- or process-directed team building, survey feedback, role analysis, group goal setting, and family T-groups.

4. *Intergroup relations*—undertaking process- or task-directed intergroup activities, sociotechnical structuring, survey feedback, process consultation, and Grid Phase 3.

5. *Total organization*—examining the structure of the organization, using sociotechnical approaches, planning confrontation meetings, and using survey feedback and Grid Phases 4, 5, and 6.

A third typology, or classification scheme, has been developed by Harrison.[22] He has classified intervention strategies along the *dimension of "depth,"* which he defines as the extent of overt emotional involvement of the individual in the change process. These four levels can be used for a systems approach to organization development, as shown in Table 12.1.

Table 12.1 A typology of change according to depth of intervention

---

Operations analysis
Contingency theories of organizational design
Survey feedback
Grid organization development (The six-phase Grid OD program covers almost every level, but it is placed here for the sake of convenience and clarity, since it does involve a total, systemwide effort.)

Evaluating and controlling individual performance and behavior
Job enrichment
Decision centers (sociotechnical systems)
Role analysis
Management by Objectives

Concern with personal work style
Process consultation
Third-party intervention
Team building
Family group diagnostic meeting
Improving interdepartmental or intergroup relationships

Intrapersonal relationships
Laboratory training
Encounter groups
Life- and career-planning interventions
Personal consultation

Adapted from E. Huse, *Organization Development and Change,* St. Paul: West, 1975, p. 79.

1. *Operations analysis.* This level is concerned with the roles and functions that are to be performed in the organization rather than with individual values and motivation. This strategy for change focuses on specifying tasks, resources, and power and also defining jobs for individuals and groups in the organization.

This first level of organization development depends on the structural design of the organization and can be applied by any organization to ensure that its structure fits its environment. If the organization is properly designed to fit its environment, individuals are more likely to get a great deal of job satisfaction and sense of competence from performing the job. As Morse and Lorsch indicate, individuals can be highly motivated and have a feeling of competence and achievement when there is a good organization-task "fit," even though the organization may be highly bureaucratic in nature.[23]

2. *Evaluating and controlling individual performance and behavior.* This second level deals with the selection, placement, training, counseling, and appraisal of individual employees. Here, the focus is on observable performance rather than on the individual's personal characteristics. Attempts to bring about change at this level can include use of such external rewards and punishments as salary increases, promotions, or organizational transfers. Management by Objectives is an example of a frequently used change strategy at this level.

This strategy of intervention and organization development is probably applicable to all types of organizations. However, it is generally most useful in stable organizations in which external rewards are of major importance. This strategy may be "wasted" on research-and-development organizations, for example, in which the scientists already have a high degree of freedom and autonomy.

3. *Concern with work style.* At this "depth" the concern is with work performance and the method, style, and processes by which it is achieved. This level includes such "human" factors as how the individual does or does not delegate authority, the extent of one's competition or collaboration with others on work-related issues, and how and if the individual communicates information to others.

Intervention at this level involves attempts to change work behavior and working relationships among individuals and/or groups. This includes the satisfaction or dissatisfaction that organizational members derive from others' work behavior. Such intervention frequently requires intergroup or interpersonal bargaining and negotiating. It is likely to result in changes in formal or informal group norms about communication, collaboration, and methods for resolving present and future conflicts. Such intervention is probably less effective in the more rigid, bureaucratic structures than in less stable environments. There rules, procedures, and policies are not rigidly defined. Intervention is less effective when the informal organization plays a major part in the processes of integration and work flow.

4. *Interpersonal relationships.* Harrison's fourth level of overt emotional involvement focuses on organization members' attitudes, feelings, and perceptions about one another. Their warmth or coldness toward one another and their awareness and expression of such feelings as trust, suspicion, rejection, and acceptance are included. This is the first intervention level at which personal feelings are a direct focus of the intervention strategy. It is at this level that laboratory training and similar approaches can be used to bring these feelings out into the open and work on them. Alternatively, the consultant works with individuals on their deeper values and concerns about their own identities, experiences, and competence, helping them to increase the range of experience they can bring into awareness and begin to cope with. Thus the intervention strategy may be on either a one-to-one or group basis, e.g., marathon laboratory sessions or task-group therapy. This strategy of intervention occurs when the individual is not dependent on economic and bureaucratic pressures, but instead seeks more internal and self-determined rewards to increase his or her sense of autonomy, competence, and worth.

In concluding his analysis of depth strategies, Harrison suggests two criteria for choosing the most appropriate interventional depth: (1) to intervene only at the level necessary to produce lasting solutions to the problems facing the individual and/or the organization; and (2) to use a level of intervention strategy at which the resources and the energy of the organization can be directed most appropriately to change and problem solving.

Figure 12.4 shows Harrison's intervention strategies superimposed on our own typology of system design according to environment, structure, and task. An organization or its subsystems at the right-hand side of the continuum is highly stable and bureaucratic, and therefore the depth of intervention strategy may remain relatively superficial. Thus laboratory training and similar approaches might not be appropriate at this stage. As one moves across the continuum, deeper levels of intervention may become more appropriate, including such approaches as job enrichment and team building. Similarly, for organizations at the far left-hand side of the continuum, such approaches as tighter rules and more bureaucratization may well be dysfunctional, just as "pushing decision making down" and laboratory training may be dysfunctional at the far right side of the continuum.

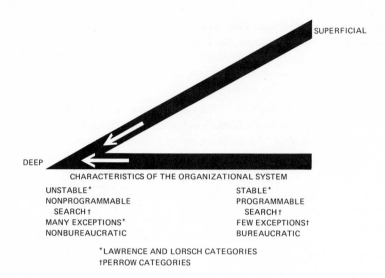

SUPERFICIAL

DEEP

CHARACTERISTICS OF THE ORGANIZATIONAL SYSTEM

UNSTABLE*	STABLE*
NONPROGRAMMABLE	PROGRAMMABLE
SEARCH†	SEARCH†
MANY EXCEPTIONS*	FEW EXCEPTIONS†
NONBUREAUCRATIC	BUREAUCRATIC

*LAWRENCE AND LORSCH CATEGORIES
†PERROW CATEGORIES

Fig. 12.4   Depth of intervention and change strategy.

IV. SELECTED ORGANIZATION DEVELOPMENT INTERVENTIONS

Various approaches are currently being used in OD, and the techniques are becoming more numerous and sophisticated. Table 12.2 lists a number of different interventions in order of popularity.

In describing some of these interventions, we will follow Harrison's typology of interventions by depth. It is important to stress that for any of these approaches to be successful, they be selected not for their popularity, but on the basis of careful diagnosis to determine the most appropriate "tool" or variety of "tools." (As Maslow once said, "When your only tool is a hammer, you tend to treat everything like a nail.") It is also important to stress that efforts must be made to work with the organization (or selected subsystems) as a total system and to help it develop its capacity to handle its own development in the future.

A. Operations Analysis

We have already touched on some of the interventions at this depth, such as contingency theories of organization design and the Managerial Grid. Here, we will describe one other intervention of this type—confrontation meetings.

Developed by Beckhard, the confrontation-meeting intervention is designed to mobilize the resources of the entire organization to identify prob-

Table 12.2 Interventions used in OD programs

Technique	Number reporting use
Team building	33
MBO	30
Systems analysis	20
Job enrichment/enlargement	20
Seminars	20
Mechanization/automation	17
Survey-feedback	13
Confrontation meetings	13
Lectures	12
Career planning	12
Grid training	8
Sensitivity training	5
Other	3

W. Heisler, "Patterns of OD in Practice," *Business Horizons* **17**, 1 (Feb. 1975): 82. Copyright, 1975 by the Foundation for the School of Business at Indiana University. Reprinted by permission.

lems, set priorities and action targets, and to begin working toward them. Beckhard says that confrontation meetings are

particularly appropriate in situations where an organization is in stress; where, for example, there is a new top management, where there has been a loss of a major customer, or where the organization is going into a new product or new area of business. Organizationally, this [meeting] is most appropriate where the top group is relatively cohesive but there is a gap between the top and the rest of the organization.[24]

The model described by Beckhard involves only the managerial and professional people in the organization. Technicians, clerical personnel, and assembly workers can also benefit from this approach, which includes the following steps:

1. A group meeting of all those involved is scheduled and held in an appropriate place. The reason for the meeting is discussed, and the task is assigned. Usually, the task is to identify problems about both the organization's effectiveness and the work environment it provides.

2. Groups consisting of members representing all different parts of the organization are appointed. Thus each group might have one or more members

from manufacturing, quality assurance, finance, purchasing, and sales. However, for obvious reasons, except for top management a subordinate should not be in the same group as his or her boss, and top management should form its own group. Groups can vary from 5 to 15 members, depending on the circumstances, available meeting places, size of the organization, etc.

3. The groups are told, and the point is stressed, that they are to be honest and open and to work hard at identifying the problems they see in the organization. It is also emphasized that no one will be criticized for bringing up problems and that the groups will be judged on their ability to do so.

4. The groups are given an hour or two to identify the problems facing the organization. Generally, an OD practitioner goes from group to group, encouraging them, again stressing that they are to be open about problem identification and, in general, assisting the groups with their task.

5. When the groups reconvene in a central meeting place, each group reports the problems that it has identified and sometimes offers solutions. Since each group hears the reports of all the others, a maximum amount of information is shared.

6. Either then or later, the master list of problems is broken down into categories by those present, by the individual leading the session, or by the manager and his or her staff. This process eliminates overlap and duplication and separates the problems according to functional or other appropriate areas.

7. Once the problems have been categorized, they are divided up and given to problem-solving groups whose composition differs from that of the original problem-identification groups. For example, all manufacturing problems may be handled by people in manufacturing. Or, since the systems approach emphasizes the interrelatedness of organization problems, task forces representing appropriate cross-sections of the organization may be used. Depending on circumstances in the organization, either team leaders are assigned or the task force selects its own leader.

8. Each group is asked to establish priorities among its problems, to develop a tactical plan of action for solving the problems, and to determine an approximate timetable for completing this phase of the process.

9. Each group then periodically reports its list of priorities and tactical plan of action to the larger group, which may in turn make suggestions about priorities, timetables, etc.

10. Schedules for periodic (usually monthly) follow-up meetings are established. At these sessions, the team leaders report to either the other team leaders or the group as a whole their groups' progress and plans for future action.

The formal establishment of such follow-up meetings ensures both continuing action and the modification of priorities and timetables as needed.

Although the first nine steps can be accomplished within a very short period of time, e.g., one day, it may be preferable to spread the process out, e.g., steps 1 through 5 in one afternoon; steps 5, 6, and 7 several days later; and steps 8 and 9 the next week. This allows the problem-solving groups more time for problem categorization, decisions about group composition, and development of action plans. Despite the many variations possible with this approach, in almost every case the results appear to be quite dramatic in mobilizing the total resources of the organization for problem identification and solution.

B. Evaluating and Controlling Individual Performance and Behavior

Several of the interventions at this level have already been described, such as Management by Objectives (MBO) and sociotechnical systems. One other popular approach, job enrichment, will be discussed here.

Job enrichment is directed primarily toward increasing job meaningfulness by allowing the worker to have a greater share in the "ownership" of the job. The term "job enrichment" has become increasingly popular, and it has been described not only in the scholarly journals, but also in such publications as *Atlantic Monthly, Time, Newsweek, Wall Street Journal,* and the *Christian Science Monitor.* In addition, there have been a number of books on the subject, including those by Ford, and Davis and Taylor.[25]

Job enrichment is the redesign of jobs to provide the worker with more opportunity to assume responsibility, autonomy, and closure (doing a complete job), as well as with more timely feedback about performance.

Most tasks have three elements: *planning* (deciding how something is to be done), *doing* (the actual work), and *evaluating* (feedback about the planning and doing steps and taking the necessary corrective action). Many jobs, particularly at the clerical and "blue-collar" levels, are designed so that the worker is not involved in the planning and evaluating stages. Indeed, the specialization of "doing" has progressed so far that as one industrial engineer said recently, "If an assembly-line job takes more than three minutes to complete, the job should be given to two different people, each of whom has a minute-and-a-half cycle."

Myers uses a bowling analogy to explain these three elements.[26] The bowler plans her or his own work—deciding whether to throw a straight or a curve ball, throwing the ball, and observing (evaluating) the results. If the throw results in a "split," the bowler replans the work and tries to knock down the remaining pins with the second ball. Bowling is interesting, it is work, and people *pay* to compete with themselves (improving one's score) and with others.

However, if this model is applied in an industrial setting, the elements change radically. First, an industrial engineeer might decide that right-handed bowling is the "one best way." Next, the foreman would decide exactly how and when the worker would throw the ball. A screen placed between the bowler and the pins at the end of the alley would ensure that only the inspectors in the quality assurance department could evaluate the worker's performance. Occasionally, the bowler would get some feedback, usually negative, e.g., "You've done a lousy job and have to improve."

In this industrial model, the planning and evaluating functions have been separated from the doing, thereby greatly simplifying the job. Therefore, people must be *paid* to bowl, and the *doing* becomes uninteresting and unchallenging; it's no wonder that people "aren't motivated." Actually, following practices developed by Frederick Taylor at the turn of the century in the scientific management movement, many jobs in industry, especially those on production lines, have been "simplified" to such a high degree that workers find them repetitive and unchallenging.[27] Although work specialization has contributed much to industrialization, it is clear that in many ways the process has been carried to an extreme. Job enrichment, as Herzberg notes, is an attempt to reverse this oversimplification by providing workers with greater opportunities for achievement, responsibility, and personal growth through the redesign of the job itself.[28]

For a time, the terms "job enrichment" and "job enlargement" were used almost interchangeably. Today, however, job enlargement refers to rotating jobs and adding horizontal-level duties, e.g., soldering three connections instead of one, putting on both the front and rear wheels of a car rather than just one. However, recent research indicates that this approach can have a negative effect.[29]

Action on job enrichment has developed on two overlapping but different fronts. The first, and most widely known, has been to use Herzberg's two-factor theory to redesign jobs in order to provide opportunities for achievement, recognition, responsibility, and the like. The second approach has focused on the attributes of the job itself. In 1965 an index of job attributes was developed to measure such variables as object variety, motor variety, autonomy, required interaction, knowledge and skill, responsibility, and task identity.[30]

Considerable follow-on research has been devoted to refining and further developing the index of job attributes. Figure 12.5 summarizes the most recent research. Five "core" dimensions of work create three critical psychological states, which in turn have personal and work outcomes, such as internal work

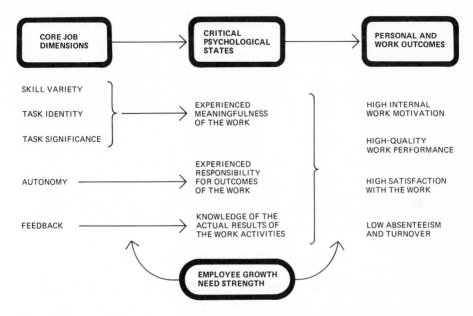

Fig. 12.5 The relationships among the core job dimensions, the critical psychological states, and on-the-job outcomes. (J. Hackman and G. Oldham, "Development of the Job Diagnostic Survey," *Journal of Applied Psychology* **60**, 2, April 1975, p. 161. Reprinted by permission.)

motivation, high-quality work performance, satisfaction with the work, and low absenteeism and turnover. The core dimensions of work are:

1. *Skill variety*—the potential for a meaningful job is increased to the extent that more and different skills are involved.

2. *Task identity*—the degree to which the job allows completion of an identifiable, "whole" piece of work.

3. *Task significance*—having a perceivable impact on others. A nurse who works in an intensive care unit is more likely to perceive the impact on others than is a worker who does nothing but solder relays.

4. *Autonomy*—the degree to which the job gives the worker independence, freedom, and discretion in scheduling and carrying out the task. The greater the autonomy, the greater the sense of personal responsibility.

5. *Feedback*—a measurement of the information a worker receives about the effectiveness, quality, and quantity of his or her work. The most feedback comes directly from the work itself rather than from some other sources,

such as the supervisor. For instance, a worker who both assembles an entire instrument and tests it gets prompt, immediate feedback. On many jobs, however, there is little or no feedback.

The "experienced meaningfulness of the work" is influenced by the first three core dimensions. It is better if all three dimensions can be high, but one that is significantly higher can partially make up for deficiencies in the other two dimensions.

Hackman and Oldham have developed the Job Diagnostic Survey (JDS) to measure whether jobs are high or low on the core dimensions.[31] The instrument also measures individuals' personal reactions to their work and the broader work setting, as well as the readiness of individuals to take on "enriched jobs." The research indicates that individuals with strong growth needs respond more positively to enriched jobs than do those with weaker growth needs.

Two basic uses of the JDS are to diagnose how existing jobs fall on the core dimensions and to determine the effect of job changes on employees. Further, the JDS provides a reliable diagnostic tool for job enrichment by determining how individual jobs score on the five basic core dimensions. The research indicates that a job must be high on all five for a worker to be motivated by the job itself.

The development of the JDS is an excellent example of action research resulting in new behavioral science knowledge. Further, it should help reduce one of the problems with job enrichment, namely, that it has taken on a "quasi-religious flavor and fervor" for some practitioners. They see it as being the panacea to most of an organization's ills and have developed highly prescribed and ritualized procedures for installing job-enrichment programs, despite the evidence that a variety of approaches may be suitable.

The published results on job enrichment are voluminous and positive. Many of the positive cases are reported in *Work in America*.[32] It should be noted, however, that programs that are unsuccessful tend not to be published. A number of other authors have described the increased morale, motivation, commitment, and productivity resulting from various approaches to job enrichment. For example, productivity increased 84% when a multistation assembly line was abandoned in favor of having each worker assemble the complete product, and rejects dropped from 23% to 1%.[33] Similarly positive results of job enrichment are documented by the report on five studies of British technicians, design engineers, and sales representatives.[34] In his study of 18 experiments involving clerical and other personnel in the telephone company, Ford reports that the results of 17 were positive and one was neutral.[35] Ford also outlines a complete training program for managers installing job-enrichment programs.

The increasing importance of job enrichment is documented in a magazine article that describes the growing alienation of assembly-line workers and the corresponding concern about this problem.[36] As the president of one UAW local commented, "Job monotony? Five years ago the union didn't even discuss it." Now, however, it is an important issue, especially since in some plants, absenteeism is as high as 13%, as compared to 3% a few years ago.

Not all workers respond positively to job enrichment, however. For example, Ford reports that although 90% of the workers in his experiments responded positively, some 10–15% did not.[37] As he notes, this small percentage of workers should be allowed to continue working at "nonenriched" jobs.

Job enrichment need not always result in expanded job content. For example, Roche and MacKinnon show that more extensive use of meetings, greater worker participation in overall departmental improvement, etc., can also have powerful effects similar to those of expanding job content.[38] Here, however, the focus is on involving the "doers" in the planning and evaluating aspects.

However, most job-enrichment approaches have lacked methodological rigor and meaningful controls, as Hulin and Blood point out.[39] This deficiency has led some people to regard job enrichment as either a fad or a management tool for manipulation. Many union officials, for example, believe that job enrichment is only another device for "speeding up production" and that it has little impact on increased job satisfaction or motivation. One critic contends that the theory of job enrichment is completely erroneous, that workers do not want increased variety and challenge at work, that job enrichment reduces the number of jobs, and that "the error of job enrichment is that it tries to talk workers into involvement and concern for the nature of their work when their memories and experiences have taught them that increased productivity only results in layoffs."[40] One very sticky problem is that of pay. Many job-evaluation programs do not take into account or properly measure the increased responsibility and other factors involved in "enriched" jobs. As a result, although productivity may increase substantially, pay is frequently not commensurately increased.

C. Concern with Personal Work Style

Interventions at this level involve attempts to change work behavior and working relationships among individuals and/or groups. One such intervention is team building.

Much of a manager's time is spent working in groups or teams which can be either *vertical*, e.g., a boss and subordinates, or *horizontal*, e.g., a task force working on a particular project. However, frequently groups are not as productive as they could be. Managers are often frustrated (and rightly so) because they waste so much time in meetings, which could be made more productive through the use of process observation and consultation, here defined as sitting in and observing a group and helping it to become more productive.

To review briefly, there are two basic assumptions underlying team building and process observation. First, in order for teams to be more effective and productive, the members of the group must coordinate and merge their efforts toward the accomplishment of mutually acceptable work goals (*group task*). Second, the personal welfare and emotional needs of group members must be met (*group maintenance*). If the emotional needs of the individuals are not met—if they are neglected or sacrificed—the group's effectiveness is considerably diminished and, indeed, the group itself may not survive.

In any team or group, events have two dimensions. One is *content*—the topic of conversation, the agenda, etc. The other is *process*—what is happening in the group, e.g., who is talking to whom, how the members feel about the group and one another, and the kinds of subgroups, coalitions, and alliances that have formed.

All of the approaches to team building require the help of a skilled process observer in increasing the effectiveness of the group's task and maintenance roles. One approach is for the consultant to interview each member of the team in advance about his or her feelings, attitudes, and perceptions of the team's effectiveness. A meeting is then scheduled, frequently away from the organization, where the consultant feeds back the information, and the group spends its time in working through the data, agreeing on basic problems, and setting priorities and action plans toward resolving the problems.

Another approach is for the team to come together and for each member to discuss his or her perceived role (or job), with each other member of the team feeling free to make contributions, suggestions, or comments. This form of role identification and clarification can frequently be very helpful in clearing up misunderstandings and in making certain that each team member knows and accepts both his or her own role and that of the other team members. For example, one top boss held a three-day meeting with his subordinates. The first item on the agenda was the mutual establishment of organization goals; the second item was to review the role of each member of the staff, including the top manager. This portion of the meeting required about three hours of discussion for each job before mutual agreement was reached. Following this, the objectives of the organization were redefined. The last item on the agenda was to list problems facing the organization, assign priorities to them, and to agree on which subteams would work on each problem.

Another method of team building, often used in conjunction with that just described, is for the consultant to attend regular staff meetings. Here, the consultant is a process observer who watches and observes how the team goes

about accomplishing its group task and maintenance roles. Paying less attention to the *content* of the meeting, the consultant focuses on the *process*, considering such variables as group atmosphere and the degree of trust and
openness; task effectiveness, including the degree to which the group is working or "goofing off" and whether full use is being made of the talents and
resources of the group; and the amount, degree, and nature of participation,
e.g., whether only a few members participate, the extent and degree to which
people interrupt one another, etc. In other words, the process observer looks
at the ways in which the group goes about accomplishing both its *task* and
maintenance roles, for both need to be accomplished if the group is to be
effective.

Either during or following the meeting, the observer can give feedback
or encourage the group to give its own feedback. For example, Schein describes
a feedback technique whereby group members are asked to respond anony-
mously to a questionnaire about their feelings toward the group, its openness,
and the degree to which group goals were accomplished.[41] After the questions
have been scored and discussed within the group, it may become apparent that
the questionnaire was inadequate, and new questions may be added. Such a
process allows the group to change its direction and agenda somewhat and to
become more productive.

Feedback, whether given directly to the entire group or to individual members, must be supportive and nonthreatening. The purpose of the feedback is
to help increase the effectiveness of both the group and its individual members.
Therefore, it must be positive in tone and given in such a fashion that individuals and groups can use it, e.g., suggesting to an individual that he or she is
continually interrupting and cutting off another person (behavior) is quite
different from telling that person to "get along better with people" (attitude).

D. Intrapersonal Relationships

At Harrison's deepest level of intervention, the consultant works to help individuals and groups regarding their deeper values and concerns about identity, experience, and competence. Here, we will discuss only one intervention
strategy at this level—laboratory training.

Laboratory training, sometimes called sensitivity, or T-group training, is
probably the most popular yet misunderstood technique used in OD. Indeed,
to some people, laboratory training is synonomous with OD. As Bennis explains, "Most organization development cases that finally reach print focus
almost exclusively on the T-Group as the basic strategy of intervention."[42]
However, it is extremely difficult to define laboratory training, as is described
by Schein and Bennis.

1. *Laboratories* vary tremendously *in goals, training design, delegate population, length and setting . . .*

2. *Laboratories attempt to provide a* total *and* integrated *learning experience for the participants, making it difficult to communicate . . . what actually occurs.*

3. *Laboratories are an attempt to provide a learning experience which is, in part,* emotional *and to provide the opportunity for the participants to explore the interdependence of emotional and intellectual learning.*[43]

Laboratory training first came into use in the late 1940s, largely because of the growing realization that the types of human relations training in vogue concentrated far more on the lecture method than on the more vital issues— the feelings and concerns of individuals—and that dealing with the latter was a more powerful form of education. The objectives of laboratory training are of three types:

1. To increase interpersonal competence by helping the individual become more aware of his or her own feelings and emotions and those of others;

2. To instill a greater awareness of one's own and others' role within the organization, to increase a person's willingness to deal with and achieve collaborative relationships with others, and to help increase one's organizational interpersonal competence; and

3. To assist the organization in doing a better job of diagnosing, defining, and working on organizational problems and to help the organization improve itself through the process of working on the training of *groups rather than individuals.*

Laboratory training usually involves a trainer and group of people who form "stranger," "cousins," or "family" groups. In "stranger" laboratories, the participants do not know one another at the beginning. "Cousins" laboratories consist of people from the same organization who may be acquainted with one another, but who do not usually work together. "Family" laboratories consist of people who have direct working relationships with one another, e.g., a boss and a group of subordinates. Obviously, the approach must differ considerably with the type of laboratory used.

A typical laboratory training session for "strangers" consists of four or five T-groups of 10–15 members gathered together under the auspices of an organization such as the National Training Laboratories. The T-group sessions may, at times, be interspersed with general-theory sessions, designed exercises, or management games.

At the beginning of the training session, the trainer first announces that she or he is to serve as a resource to the group and then, after a brief intro-

Getting at emotional responses.

duction, lapses into silence. With this dilemma of leadership and agenda, it is then up to the group to work out its own way of proceeding. What goes on in the group becomes the basic data for the learning experience. The trainer will, as appropriate, intervene, but the nature and type of interventions vary greatly, depending on the trainer and the nature and purpose of the laboratory. Most commonly, however, the trainer encourages individuals to focus on and to understand their own feelings and to "level" with one another about what is going on in the group at the time. The emphasis is on the "here and now" experience rather than on anecdotes or "back home" experiences. It is through the emphasis on openness and leveling in a supportive and caring environment that the participants gain more insight into their own and others' feelings and the mechanics of group dynamics and can thereby begin to be more productive.

Most participants react positively to laboratory training sessions. Frequently, participants express a heightened awareness of self and others, increased ability to listen more intently, to accept feedback about themselves and provide it to other group members, and to feel less constrained by cultural norms about expressing and accepting a fuller range of emotions. Although laboratory sessions are brief, some participants are successful in achieving what Lewin calls unfreezing, experimentation, and refreezing of behavior patterns in rather significant ways.[44] Although participants are occasionally threatened or otherwise overwhelmed to such an extent that they do not benefit from the T-group experience, the causes frequently lie with their deep, unresolved psychological problems.

There are, of course, many variations in T-group training. Some laboratories extend for two weeks or longer. Others, "micro" or "marathon" labs, may last only a weekend or a day.[45]

The effectiveness of laboratory training appears to be mixed. House concludes that although such training has potentially powerful effects on both the individual and the organization, the effects vary widely with individuals and situations.[46] On the other hand, Campbell and Dunnette feel that such training may well have positive value for the individual, but that "the assumption that T-group training has positive utility for organizations must necessarily rest on shaky ground . . . the authors wish to emphasize . . . that utility for the organization is not necessarily the same as utility for the individual."[47]

More recently, Golembiewski et al. have described the success of such laboratory-style organization development work initiated at a small plant and then expanded to a larger, more complex organization.[48] The program was started with divisional managers and during a 245-day period was extended to regional managers through to the top of the organization. The program design was a modified time series with six periods of observations following laboratory work. One of the important features of this work was that like the Blake and Mouton approach, organization development was accomplished over time, starting with a subpart of the organization.

Although it appears that sensitivity training can be a powerful tool for influencing behavior, there is also abundant evidence that the transfer of laboratory learning to daily organizational life is sometimes difficult to achieve, if it can be achieved at all. It is clear that laboratories alone are an inadequate OD strategy and that other interventions are needed both prior to and following the laboratory training.

There has also been a great deal of discussion as to whether or not laboratory training and its variations might be harmful to some individuals. The research has been inconclusive; some studies indicate that the "casualty rate" of trainees is higher than it should be, but other studies suggest that this is not the case. Concerned about unqualified trainers and possible psychological damage, the Swedish government has recently decided not to pay for sensitivity training for any state employees until a task force has evaluated the overall results of laboratory training.[49]

One of the more recent studies reviews the literature, both pro and con, and concludes that "there is some evidence that it may be less stressful than university examinations or perceptual isolation experiments, or indeed, that it may enable participants to cope better with sexual and aggressive stimuli and stressful periods in their life."[50] The study does suggest that T-group participants be systematically screened before participating.

E. Introducing Internal Growth and Change Ability*

Because OD is a new field of applied behavioral science, much of the technology is being brought into organizations by external consultants, many of whom are university-based. Most consultants both try to help their client systems respond more effectively to current problems and also transmit their knowledge and skills to key members of the organization.

One of the OD practitioner's underlying values is to help organizations become more self-sufficient. Although the organization may be momentarily relieved by the consultant's diagnostic and intervention skills in solving current problems, the organization will either need repeated help in the future or will soon return to its previous, less effective state unless the change agent encourages organizational personnel to acquire the tools and skills needed to sustain the change efforts. For unless the change agent makes a deliberate effort to make his or her services unnecessary, one of the long-term objectives of organization development—self-renewal—will not be met.

Changing the culture, work flow, and dynamics in a large organization requires several years. Blake and Mouton, Likert, and others suggest that five years is a reasonable period of time for implementing a program of planned change in a large organization, and their approaches call for the development of large numbers of internal change-agent resources to sustain OD programs.[51] Since visits to the client system are short and/or infrequent, the change agent cannot undertake a major, long-term development effort without the help of knowledgeable and skilled internal organizational resources.

In a field study of the career development of *internal* OD change agents who were teamed with external change agents, Lewis found that the most succssful consultants had as a central part of their intervention strategy the tutorial development of their internal organizational partners.[52] Change-agent development occurred through processes of joint diagnosis and interventions in the client system, whereby the "trainee" was able to observe and emulate

---

* This section was written by John W. Lewis, III.

the model furnishd by the consultant. The most significant growth occurred within the pair relationship itself, to which OD values, concepts, and behaviors were central to the interaction.

In the most effective internal-external OD pairs, the internal change agent gradually becomes the central figure in the effort toward planned change. Thus the external consultant can devote more time to teaching the internal change agent and other key members of the system how to use him or her as a resource. Increasingly, the external change agent's time and effort are spent more in reviewing OD objectives and strategies which have been developed and implemented within the system and less in making direct interventions.

The achievement of long-term change in organizations is made more difficult by the transiency of people within them and the fluid structures and role relationships within the system. This phenomenon of our time creates stress on the stability of the organization, which must nevertheless be maintained through a long-term change effort. An implication for OD is that conflicts continue to erupt even after they have been ostensibly resolved. A management team that has been developed gains new or replacement members and must be developed again. Problem diagnoses that are valid today may be stale or even obsolete tomorrow. Consequently, organizations must have competent internal change agents to continuously monitor the health of the system, diagnose symptoms and problems accurately and rapidly, and provide the skills and resources needed to sustain effective planned change.

V. PROBLEMS WITH ORGANIZATION DEVELOPMENT

A. OD May Be Overly Prescriptive and Culture-Based

Lee describes modern human resource management (MHRM) as consisting of the overlapping concepts and theories of McGregor, Herzberg, Argyris, Likert, Blake and Mouton, and Maslow.[53] He traces the development of management thought from Machiavelli through Adam Smith, Frederick Taylor, Mary Parker Follett, James Mooney, and others, pointing out that each theorist wrote in a cultural context and that the theorists have followed rather than preceded cultural change. He believes that the large majority of today's behavioral theorists advocating MHRM are professors whose "strong autonomy needs and antiauthoritarian bias govern much of their research approach and ideal model building."[54] Lee lists a number of sources of resistance to MHRM and concludes that resistance to MHRM occurs because the culture changes slowly and unevenly and therefore the uses and applications of MHRM will also change slowly and unevenly. His eight-step approach for managers makes maximum usage of our current knowledge, however meager, of human motivation and behavior.

One of the biggest cultural differences has already been noted—the widespread use of autonomous work groups and the sociotechnical approach in Europe, and especially in Scandinavia, and the relatively little impact such approaches have had in other countries, such as the United States, where the emphasis has been more on the individual than on the group. In other words, the Europeans have concentrated more heavily on the interaction of the work flow and human perspectives, whereas American practitioners have concentrated more heavily on the human perspective.

B. The Problem of Ethics and Values

OD has never satisfactorily resolved several ethical issues, e.g., power. Most OD practitioners have avoided discussing this problem. As Bennis puts it, "Organization development practitioners rely exclusively on two sources of influence: truth and love."[55] He suggests that this reliance (and its correlates —trust, openness, and collaboration) has led the OD practitioner to systematically avoid the problem of power and the policy of change. Although the issue has not been resolved, it must be recognized that organizations are essentially political in nature and that power must be considered from both the philosophical and pragmatic viewpoints. As one author suggests, "The political perspective makes it important for the analyst to understand a range of problems that are currently on the periphery of organizational studies. Of political importance is the analysis of power-relationships and power structures."[56]

Another problem is the question of identifying the client. Most OD practitioners see themselves as being responsible for the total organization, but they are paid as consultants to management. The question can be raised as to where their loyalties lie.

A third problem is the use of data and information. For example, Baritz suggests that most organizations use behavioral scientists to increase managerial control over subordinates, resulting in the manipulation of people without their own awareness.[57] This problem is the core of the classical debate between Skinner and Rogers about "conditioning" versus "growth" psychology and raises issues that cannot be "settled" in this text.[58] However, a further issue in this area is who has access to data and the way that the data are, or should be, used.

After reviewing a number of OD interventions, Walton concluded that ethical issues could arise from five types of inconsistencies between

1. the strategies and goals of the organization and the values and norms of the practitioner;

2. the practitioner's concepts of justification and fairness and the managerial actions the change agent's interventions are associated with;

3. the practitioner's personal value system and the consequences of OD interventions;

4. the professional standards governing the practitioner-client relationship and the practitioner's actual behavior and actions;

5. the values generally attributed to the practice of OD and the actual consequences of the interventions.[59]

C. Some Myths about OD

Sperling has listed six myths that are relevant in concluding our discussion of organization development:[60]

1. OD requires top-management involvement and commitment   This is not necessary, since the OD consultant may become unnecessarily involved in the power struggles and politics of the organization.

2. The OD consultant is manipulative   Sperling feels that this myth arises because it is difficult for the consultant to be articulate and clear about OD. In order to dispel this myth, the OD specialist must be as open and candid about his or her work as possible. Specific ground rules should be established that the OD consultant is working for the organization rather than for a specific boss.

3. There is one best way to manage   The currently popular myth is that the "participative" manager is the only good one. As you now know, successful managers use a wide variety of methods, depending on the situation and their subordinates.

4. OD represents "seduction of artifacts"   According to this myth, some sort of "formal program" must be developed and, preferably, be put into a manual. In fact, however, OD work is too "messy" to be this formalized. Merely listing the managers who have gone through training programs or the percentage utilization of company training facilities is, in essence, emphasizing the *form* rather than the *substance* of OD.

5. OD is a "doctor-patient model"   This myth asserts that the OD consultant is like other consultants; that is, the client presents the problem, and the OD practitioner provides the answers. Rather, the OD practitioner works under the assumption that managers are competent and want to do a good job and that the practitioner is a resource person rather than a prescriber of solutions.

6. Organization development is a panacea OD is *not* the solution to all organizational problems. It is not a substitute for good market research or the development of good new products or sound financial management. Although OD can be of tremendous help to the organization, it is not a panacea. Organization development will have a tremendous impact on the traditional personnel department because of the manager's three basic resources—physical, financial, and human. The proper use of human resources may be the "edge" to make a manager really outstanding.

VI. CONCLUSIONS

In this chapter, we have distinguished between "organizational improvement" and "organization development," the term preferred by behavioral scientists working in this field. In discussing the basic assumptions underlying OD, we stressed that an explicit part of OD is the conscious effort to provide opportunities for growth and development of human beings in the organizational setting.

A diagnostic approach to OD is required, since the OD change agent must develop an action-research model designed to fit the needs, objectives, and present values of the organization. Some of the tools and techniques which have been used successfully in OD are laboratory training, team building, job enrichment, organizational confrontation meetings, improving interdepartmental relationships, and inducing internal growth and change.

Although there are many advantages to using OD, there are also some problems associated with this approach. Some OD practitioners tend to ignore structure and technology; some use one approach for all situations; and OD may be overly prescriptive and culture-based. Finally, several myths about the nature and concepts of organization development need to be dispelled.

REVIEW

1. Should the primary job of OD be to improve the individual or to improve the organization? Are these two aims mutually exclusive?

2. Is an internal change agent or outside consultant of more long-term benefit to an organization? For a short-term problem?

3. The text lists a number of approaches to OD. From your own experience, list some organizations in which each of these approaches might be functional or dysfunctional. Discuss.

4. Under what circumstances may "planned change" be: (a) more effective and (b) less effective than "action research"?

5. Explain why job enrichment may have positive consequences on a person's motivation. What motivational factors might cause job enrichment to fail?

6. Under what conditions would organizational confrontation meetings be an effective device? An ineffective device?

7. From your own experience, describe an instance when an attempt to improve an organization (e.g., Little League, Girl Scouts, or job you have held) failed because of improper diagnosis of the problems.

8. Select an organization with which you are familiar and map out a strategy of organization development to be used by an OD consultant.

9. Read one or two articles in the *Journal of Applied Behavioral Science* and critique them on the basis of your knowledge and learning to date.

REFERENCES

1. Subcommittee on Priorities and Economy in Government, Joint Economic Committee, *American Productivity: Key to Economic Strength and National Survival,* Washington, D.C.: U.S. Government Printing Office, 1972, pp. 7, 9.

2. M. Sashkin, W. Morriss, and L. Horst, "A Comparison of Social and Organizational Change Models: Information Flow and Data Use Processes," *Psychological Review* **80,** 6 (Nov. 1973): 510–526.

3. K. Lewin, *Field Theory in Social Science,* New York: Harper & Row, 1951.

4. R. Lippitt, J. Watson, and B. Westley, *The Dynamics of Planned Change,* New York: Harcourt, Brace and World, 1958.

5. R. Kahn, "Organizational Development: Some Problems and Proposals," *Journal of Applied Behavioral Science* **10,** 4 (Oct.–Nov.–Dec. 1974): 485–502.

6. M. Frohman, M. Sashkin, and M. Kavanagh, "Action-Research as Applied to Organization Development." Paper presented at the Organizational Effectiveness Conference of the Comparative Administration Research Institute, Kent State University, Kent, Ohio (April 5, 1975): p. 1.

7. L. Greiner, D. Leitch, and L. Barnes, "The Simple Complexity of Organizational Climate in a Governmental Agency," in R. Tagiuri and G. Litwin, eds., *Organizational Climate,* Boston: Harvard University Graduate School of Business Administration, Division of Research, 1969; E. Fleishman, "Leadership Climate, Human Relations Training, and Supervisory Behavior, *Personnel Psychology* **6,** 2 (Summer 1953): 205–222.

8. Frohman *et al., op. cit.,* p. 2.

9. G. Rimler, "Can Management Survive OD?" Paper presented at the 35th annual meeting of the Academy of Management, New Orleans, August 1975.

10. *Ibid.,* p. 6.

11. For a more complete description of the differences and similarities between planned change and action research, *see* E. Huse, *Organization Development and Change*, St. Paul: West, 1975.

12. W. French, "Organization Development: Objectives, Assumptions and Strategies," *California Management Review* **12**, 2 (Winter 1969): 23–34.

13. W. G. Bennis, *Organization Development: Its Nature, Origins, and Prospects*, Reading, Mass.: Addison-Wesley, 1969.

14. W. F. Whyte, *Money and Motivation*, New York: Harper & Row, 1955.

15. R. Beckhard, *Organization Development: Strategies and Models*, Reading, Mass.: Addison-Wesley, 1969.

16. C. Ferguson, "Coping with Organizational Conflict," *Innovation* **29**, 3 (March 1972): 36–43.

17. *Ibid.*, p. 42.

18. D. L. Kegan, "Organizational Development: Description, Issues and Some Research Results," *Academy of Management Journal* **14**, 4 (Dec. 1971): 453–464.

19. L. Brown, " 'Research Action': Organizational Feedback, Understanding, and Change," *The Journal of Applied Behavioral Science* **8**, 6 (July/Aug. 1972): 697.

20. Bennis, *op. cit.*, pp. 37–38.

21. W. French and C. Bell, Jr., *Organization Development, Behavioral Science Interventions for Organization Improvement*, Englewood Cliffs, N.J.: Prentice-Hall, 1973, p. 107.

22. R. Harrison, "Choosing the Depth of Organizational Intervention," *Journal of Applied Behavioral Science* **6**, 2 (March–April 1970): 181–202.

23. J. Morse and J. Lorsch, "Beyond Theory Y," *Harvard Business Review* **48**, 3 (May–June 1970): 61–68.

24. Beckhard, *op. cit.*, p. 38. Reprinted by permission.

25. R. Ford, *Motivation Through the Work Itself*, New York: American Management Association, 1969; L. Davis and J. Taylor, eds., *Design of Jobs, Selected Readings*, New York: Penguin, 1973.

26. M. S. Myers, *Every Employee a Manager*, New York: McGraw-Hill, 1970, p. 48.

27. F. W. Taylor, *The Principles of Scientific Management*, New York: Harper & Row, 1911.

28. F. Herzberg, "One More Time: How Do You Motivate Employees?" *Harvard Business Review* **46**, 1 (Jan.–Feb. 1968): 53–62.

29. S. Orelius, University of Gothenburg, Sweden, personal communication.

30. A. Turner and P. Lawrence, *Industrial Jobs and the Worker*, Boston: Harvard University Graduate School of Business Administration, Division of Research, 1965.

31. J. Hackman, G. Oldham, R. Janson, and K. Purdy, *A New Strategy for Job Enrichment*, New Haven: Yale University, Department of Administrative Sciences, May 1974, Technical Report No. 3.

32. *Work in America: The Report of a Special Task Force to the Secretary of Health, Education and Welfare*, Cambridge, Mass.: M.I.T. Press, 1972.

33. E. Huse and M. Beer, "Eclectic Approach to Organizational Development," *Harvard Business Review* **49**, 5 (Sept.–Oct. 1971): 103–112.

34. W. J. Paul, K. B. Robertson, and F. Herzberg, "Job Enrichment Pays Off," *Harvard Business Review* **41**, 2 (March–April 1969): 61–78.

35. Ford, *op. cit.*

36. "Boredom Spells Trouble on the Line," *Life*, September 1, 1972, pp. 31–38.

37. Ford, *op. cit.*

38. W. J. Roche and N. L. MacKinnon, "Motivating People with Meaningful Work," *Harvard Business Review* **48**, 3 (May–June 1970): 97–110.

39. C. Hulin and M. Blood, "Job Enlargement, Individual Differences and Worker Responses," *Psychological Bulletin* **69**, 1 (Jan. 1968): 41–45.

40. M. Fein, "Job Enrichment: A Reevaluation," *Sloan Management Review* **15**, 2 (Winter 1974): 88.

41. E. Schein, *Process Consultation: Its Role in Organization Development*, Reading, Mass.: Addison-Wesley, 1969.

42. W. G. Bennis, "The Case Study—I, Introduction," *Journal of Applied Behavioral Science* **4**, 2 (April/May/June 1968): 228.

43. E. Schein and W. Bennis, *Personal and Organizational Change Through Group Methods: The Laboratory Approach*, New York: Wiley, 1965, p. 10. Reprinted by permission.

44. K. Lewin, "Field Theory in Social Science," in *Group Dynamics*, ed. D. Cartwright, New York: Harper & Row, 1951.

45. Schein and Bennis, *op. cit.*; L. P. Bradford, J. R. Gibb, and K. D. Benne, *T-Group Theory and Laboratory Methods*, New York: Wiley, 1964.

46. R. J. House, "T-Group Education and Leadership Effectiveness: A Review of the Empiric Literature and a Critical Evaluation," *Personnel Psychology* **20**, 1 (Spring 1967): 1–33.

47. J. P. Campbell and M. D. Dunnette, "Effectiveness of T-Group Experiences in Managerial Training and Development," *Psychological Bulletin* **70** (August 1969): 73–104.

48. R. T. Golembiewski, R. Munzenrider, A. Blumberg, S. B. Carrigan, and W. R. Mead, "Changing Climate in a Complex Organization: Interactions between a Learning Design and an Environment," *Academy of Management Journal* **14**, 4 (Dec. 1971): 465–495.

49. S. Rubenowitz, University of Gothenburg, Sweden, personal communication.

50. G. Cooper, "How Psychologically Dangerous are T-Groups and Encounter Groups?" *Human Relations* **28,** 3 (June 1975): 258.

51. R. R. Blake and J. S. Mouton, *The Managerial Grid,* Houston: Gulf, 1964; R. Likert, *The Human Organization,* New York: McGraw-Hill, 1967.

52. J. W. Lewis, III, "Growth of Internal Change Agents in Organizations," Ph.D. diss., Case-Western Reserve University, 1970.

53. J. Lee, "Behavioral Theory vs. Reality," *Harvard Business Review* **49,** 2 (March–April 1971): 20–28.

54. *Ibid.,* p. 28.

55. Bennis, *Organization Development, op. cit.,* p. 77.

56. M. Tushman, "Organizations—A Perspective," n.d., p. 20.

57. L. Baritz, *The Servants of Power,* Middletown, Conn.: Wesleyan University Press, 1960.

58. C. Rogers and B. Skinner, "Some Issues Concerning the Control of Human Behavior: A Symposium," *Science* **124** (Nov. 1956): 1057–1066.

59. R. Walton, "Ethical Issues in the Practice of Organizational Development," Boston: Harvard Graduate School of Business Administration, Working Paper #1840, May 1973.

60. K. Sperling, "Getting OD to Really Work," *Innovation* **26** (Nov. 1971): 39–45.

13

TOWARD
AN INTEGRATED
SYSTEMS THEORY
OF ORGANIZATION
DEVELOPMENT

The true rebel in a society where the only certainty is change itself is the individual who resists change.

EUGENE JENNINGS

LEARNING
OBJECTIVES

When you have finished reading and studying this chapter, you should be able to:

1. Describe the characteristics of a competent organization and use the description to analyze organizations.

2. Define and critique the major steps in successful change efforts and demonstrate their usefulness in bringing about organizational change and improvement.

3. Use systems theory to provide an integrated approach to organization development.

4. Define and demonstrate competence in using more individualized approaches to organization development.

5. Critique the application of the systems approach to organization development in two minicases.

6. Demonstrate competence in integrating the structural-design, work-flow, and human perspectives.

You will be expected to define and use the following concepts:

Competent organization	Diffusion rate
Optimal balance	Decision centers
Equilibrium	Contingency approach to leadership
Adaptive-coping cycle	Perspective integration

THOUGHT STARTERS

1. Can change really be managed?
2. What influence can the individual have on organizational change?
3. Why does the text repeatedly stress that the three different perspectives cannot be considered in isolation?

I. INTRODUCTION

In Chapters 10, 11, and 12, we discussed approaches to organization development from the structural, flow, and human perspectives. Throughout the text, however, we have stressed that the organization is a total system of interrelated and interdependent subsystems and that the three perspectives represent somewhat artificial and arbitrary ways of looking at organizations. We have already pointed out the vital importance of the linkage among organizational subsystems; a change in one subsystem causes changes, stresses, and strains in all of the other subsystems.

In this chapter, we show how the three perspectives fit together and can be used as an integrated theory of organization development. First, we reexamine the concepts of organizational competence and describe some of the characteristics of a competent organization, together with some problems of attaining an optimal balance among the subsections of the system. We then list a number of recommendations for organization development from a systems point of view. Finally, we present two case studies which illustrate how these recommendations have been used in real-life situations.

II. THE COMPETENT ORGANIZATION

The competent organization is both efficient and effective. Organizational efficiency can be defined as the amount of resources an organization must use in order to produce a unit of output. Organizational effectiveness is the degree to which a particular organization actually realizes its goals and objectives. In this section, we consider the characteristics of the competent organization, as well as some of the forces that reduce organizational competence.

A. Characteristics

Schein uses the term "organizational health" to describe organizational competence.[1] We, however, prefer the term "organizational competence," which includes the following elements.

1. Adaptability This refers to the organization's ability to react quickly and to solve problems in the face of both external and internal changes.

2. Sense of identity Organizational members have a clear understanding of the direction of the organization, its goals and purposes, and the extent to which the perceptions of the individual members coincide.

3. Capacity to test reality A number of studies have shown that organizations need to considerably increase their ability to test reality and to sense the changing demands of the organization and the environment. (This topic was discussed in some detail in Chapter 8.)

4. The need for integration   Although the organization needs to be divided into subsystems, some mechanism must exist for ensuring that the subsystems work together.

5. Simultaneous consideration of the three perspectives   Throughout the text, we have repeatedly stressed that the competent organization must always bear in mind the interaction of the structural, flow, and human perspectives. Optimal organizational effectiveness and efficiency can be attained only when all three perspectives are considered concurrently. Similarly, organizational goals and objectives must be integrated with the needs and goals of employees at all levels within the organization.

B. Problems in Attaining and Maintaining Organizational Competence

Perhaps the biggest single obstacle to organizational competence is finding and maintaining an optimal balance for the organization at any particular point in time, as was discussed in Chapter 2. To Clark, the adaptive organization is able to adequately handle the need for balance with the corresponding need for growth and change.[2] For example, the manufacturing department must strive for a stable, relatively unchanging production schedule so that costs can be reduced, and the sales department must be aware of changes in this schedule so that an early delivery to an important customer can be made. In this case, the manufacturing department serves as a deviation-reducing force to protect the status quo—the manufacturing schedule—whereas the sales department is a deviation-amplifying force trying to bring about change in order to please an important customer. Both functions are necessary in a competent organization.

Clark notes that people sometimes confuse these two forces by failing to make the proper distinction between them. He cites the example of a group of women production workers who contributed about 120% profit to the firm through their effectiveness and efficiency. Their productivity had increased about 300% in two years, even though they were not on an incentive system. The openness, freedom, and trust within the group enabled them to solve problems that outside "experts" had been unable to solve.

However, top management and engineers became dissatisfied with the women's freedom to switch around on jobs, design and operate their own test equipment, etc. As a result, their foreman was promoted to another job, and a new foreman was brought in to "really set the place straight."

Clark extensively quotes a new engineering executive who also had just been brought in. The executive couches his language in proactive terms, although it is clear from the interviews that his attitude is highly reactive. In essence, this manager says that since the women have far too much responsibility, he will have to really "take the place over," remove the womens' testing and inspecting responsibilities, and make certain that every operation will be under close surveillance by engineering (despite a 120% increase in profitability and a 300% increase in productivity).

This example illustrates three things. First, Theory X assumptions about people, particularly production workers, are deeply embedded in many managers, who refuse to modify these perceptions and assumptions. Second, this example reinforces the idea that a change in one subsystem causes stresses and strains through the entire system. Third, this case illustrates a reliance on obsolete concepts about the role of the manager. As we discuss in the next chapter, structural and interpersonal changes must go hand in hand; the very climate of an organization must be changed if some of the developmental changes are to work.

Another barrier to organizational competence is the common fallacy that people resist change as such. This is not true; when people clearly recognize that the change is beneficial to them, they welcome it. Few students resist a professor's changing their grade from "B" to "A." Few managers resist a 25% increase in salary. Rather, what people resist is the real or imagined *threat* implicit in change. Thus middle management may resist computerized integrated management information systems, fearing that they will lose control of their own data base and that the information will be used against them in a punitive fashion.

Yet the competent organization must be able to quickly accommodate itself to the rapidly increasing pace of change while still maintaining the status quo where this is necessary. Many feel that organizations that are not adaptive and flexible will quickly become obsolete and, indeed, may go out of business. The validity of this belief is evidenced by the fact that in less than a year, three major corporations (Penn-Central, Rolls-Royce, and Lockheed) either went bankrupt or were on the brink of bankruptcy. More recently, W. T. Grant filed for bankruptcy, and New York City continues to be in financial distress.

III. DEALING WITH ORGANIZATIONAL CHANGE

The organization of today is profoundly affected by the rapidly increasing pace of change, and the organization of the future will be even more profoundly affected. Tomorrow's hospitals, governmental units, and businesses will have to improve and increase their ability to change in modern society in order to survive. The fiscal crises in municipalities such as New York and states such as Massachusetts, the inability of school systems to simultaneously achieve racial integration and improve the quality of education, the failure rate of small colleges—all of these indicate that the need for increased adaptability to changing situations occurs in all types of formal organizations.

In Chapter 2, we discussed the concept of force-field analysis—the tendency of an organization to seek an equilibrium, or balance, and the analysis of deviation-amplifying and deviation-reducing forces to help optimize the balance. However, this process is made difficult because the deviation-reducing (reactive) forces resist change and work to preserve the status quo; the deviation-amplifying (proactive) forces work toward change and the attainment of a more optimal balance in the system. These two sets of forces represent two opposing sets of vectors.

The organization can reach a new balance point if one set of vectors is either increased or decreased. However, the forces exerted on feelings, attitudes, and emotions cannot be easily quantified. For example, a group of high school students were working as dishwashers and general kitchen help in a small college. When a new supervisor was put in charge of the kitchen, he shortened lunch breaks, eliminated coffee breaks, and pushed hard for increased work in an effort to increase productivity. The students, however, slowed down their work, taking even longer to accomplish their tasks than they had in the past. The equilibrium level of productivity actually moved downward as a direct result of the pressure to move productivity upward. Strikes or "sick-outs" by policemen and teachers are other illustrations of what can be considered normal "reactive" pressures. In other words, a simple, mechanistic model cannot be applied to the organization, since increased pressure from one direction may result in increased counterpressure from the other direction.

Organizational equilibrium can be altered by either *increasing* the set of forces in the desired direction or *reducing* the set of opposing vectors, as was suggested in Chapter 2. One noted author, Chris Argyris, believes that the strongest reactive forces lie not only within the managers, but also within the other individuals within the organization.[3] He postulates that most individuals are "systematically blind" to their behavior and are therefore "culturally programmed" to behave in ways that reduce the probability of change. The strength of these reactive forces cannot be lessened simply by increasing the amount and degree of the proactive forces. Rather, a much more effective approach is to reduce the amount and degree of the resistance to change by reducing the strength of the reactive forces.

There are several ways to reduce resistance to change. One alternative is to differentiate between cost-control and value-adding strategies.[4] Cost-control strategies include restricting behavior through the use of budgets, rules, reports, and standards. Value-adding strategies make use of such proactive forces as job enrichment and increased worker participation. Although these two approaches are not necessarily mutually exclusive, the time may have come to emphasize the value-adding approach to increase overall productivity and quality of working life.

One can also distinguish between "structure-maintaining" and "structure-elaborating and changing" features of the system.[5] If it is to survive, grow, and prosper, the modern organization should probably shift its emphasis from structure-maintaining to structure-elaborating behavior.

Resistance to change might also be lessened by modifying and changing the traditional personnel department which, in the opinion of some, has failed.[6] These theorists recommend establishing two separate and distinct personnel departments. One would deal primarily with such factors as pay and working conditions, and the other would establish the opportunity for the satisfaction of growth and related needs. Further, personnel activities would be grouped according to selected classes of workers, e.g., scientific and technical, culturally disadvantaged, and women. There is strong evidence that scientific and research-and-development personnel should be managed differently from blue-collar workers, for example.

Such suggestions stress the need for change and improvement in organizations, not by increasing the forces for change, but rather by reducing the forces against change. One discussion points out the need to improve organizations by designing jobs that provide "pursuit of pleasure" on the job, arguing that since current job designs are not coping with the rising frustration index of people on jobs, they are thereby destroying the "good life."[7] "It is this very asset that is continuously, assiduously plowed under . . . and kicked into sullen submission by 99% of employees today."[8]

The growing importance and concentration on quality of life programs is illustrated by the existence of a national Quality of Working Life program, as well as similar programs in the states. For example, both Massachusetts and California are sponsoring experimental programs concerned with approaching change and change projects on a broad basis, frequently involving both management and the union.

Greiner reviewed 18 studies of organizational change and found that the more successful change attempts involved six major steps.[9]

1. Pressure and arousal At this level, there is a felt need for change, particularly at the top-management level. Such pressure comes from either external forces—competitor breakthroughs or stockholder discontent—or internal events—interdepartmental conflict, decreased productivity, or a union strike.

2. Intervention and reorientation This step usually involves bringing in a newcomer, usually an outside consultant, who has a more objective viewpoint, can appraise organizational needs, and can reorient the thinking of top managers by getting them to reexamine their practices and procedures, thereby helping them define the real problem.

3. Diagnosis and recognition Here, the newcomer, or consultant, helps the organization at all levels to do a better job of "seeking the location and causes of problems." In the more successful attempts at change, this is a shared rather than a unilateral or delegated approach. In the unilateral approach, the top brass make the decisions; in the delegated approach, top management delegates, but remains involved.

4. Invention and commitment Effort is now directed toward developing more effective solutions to problems, using the shared approach to obtain full commitment for the implementation of the new solutions. Greiner stresses that successful change approaches involve intensive searches for new, innovative solutions which depend on the collaboration of many people who provide their own solutions. In his study, Greiner found that none of the less successful attempts at change reached this stage and that rather than commitment, there was serious resistance to the proposed changes. (In other words, the *reactive* forces became stronger than the *proactive* forces.)

5. Experimentation and search The successful change approaches used "reality testing" to determine the usefulness of the solution prior to the introduction of large-scale changes. Greiner stresses that the concept of *shared power* ensures that a number of minor decisions are implemented at all levels of the organization. In short, the decision-making process is tentative rather than final.

6. Reinforcement and acceptance Successful change leads to clear improvements in organizational performance, with corresponding support for change from all levels of the organization. This reinforces the impact of the change, particularly as it involves a sense of experimentation and reward for those who continue with change efforts.

From these studies of successful and less successful change attempts, Greiner concludes that successful organizational change requires four positive actions.

1. The myth that organizational change must consist of a master blueprint designed and executed at the top by an "omniscient consultant or top manager" must be dispelled.

2. Managers too often assume that change is for those lower in the organization, who are seen to be less productive and less intelligent than those who are higher in the hierarchy.

3. Successful change efforts cannot rely on either unilateral or delegated approaches to change.

4. Those involved in the change must develop broader outlooks and become less parochial in their viewpoints toward change.

Greiner's findings, based on study of successful and less successful change efforts, closely parallel what Schein has called the adaptive-coping cycle, which consists of six steps: (1) sensing a need for change in either the external or internal environment; (2) ensuring that appropriate parts of the environment receive the information as soon as possible; (3) bringing about the appropriate change in the appropriate subsystems; (4) stabilizing the change while managing or reducing the undesired changes which have occurred in related subsystems; (5) exporting the new products or services resulting from the change; and (6) obtaining appropriate feedback on the success of the change.[10]

Some authors, however, disagree with Greiner's emphasis on the need for high involvement by top management. In many instances, it is asking too much for top management to be highly involved from the very beginning. Frequently, higher-level management becomes involved only after a lower-level manager has been able to demonstrate success with one or more aspects of OD, e.g., job enrichment, survey feedback, changes in the sociotechnical systems.

Even under optimal conditions, the diffusion rate of expansion and adoption of new ideas may be slow. In one report assessing the diffusion rate of organizational improvement in eight companies in the United States, Canada, and Scandinavia, the author concluded: "I expect relatively little diffusion of potentially significant restructuring in the work place—over the short run. Hopefully, the long run may tell a different story."[11] However, some have criticized his choice of organizations, particularly in Sweden, suggesting that the choice may have been biased.[12]

Perhaps we can put the matter in perspective by examining the diffusion of new ideas in the "hard sciences." The time span from the development of a new idea to its widespread application is, on the average, 19.2 years, as Table 13.1 shows. For example, the time span between the development of the heart pacemaker and its relatively widespread application was 32 years. It

Table 13.1   Rate of diffusion of new ideas

	Year of first development	Year of widespread application	Duration (years)
Hybrid corn	1908	1933	25
Heart pacemaker	1928	1960	32
Magnetic ferrites	1933	1955	22
Organophosphorous insecticides	1934	1947	13
Input-out (economic analysis)	1936	1964	28
Hybrid small grains	1937	1955	19
Electrophotography	1937	1959	22
Video tape recorder	1950	1956	6
Green revolution (wheat)	1950	1966	16
Oral contraceptive	1951	1960	9
Average time lapse			19.2

Adapted from R. Dean, Jr., "The Temporal Mismatch—Innovation's Pace vs. Management's Time Horizon," *Research Management* **17**, 3 (May 1974) : 12–15.

took 22 years for electrophotography to become widely used. However, as Table 13.1 indicates, the time span is decreasing. If the development of new ideas is slow in the hard sciences, the relatively widespread knowledge of such phenomena as job enrichment and contingency theories of organization suggests that the application rate of new concepts in the behavioral sciences may be slow, but possibly not as slow as in the "hard sciences."

IV. USING SYSTEMS THEORY TO PROVIDE AN INTEGRATED APPROACH TO ORGANIZATION DEVELOPMENT

In this section we build on the material in the three preceding chapters to provide you with some guidelines for integrating the three perspectives for a more unified, comprehensive approach to organization development. However, since no firmly established theory of organization change exists, our recommendations must be regarded as tentative, especially since the field of organization development is expanding so rapidly.

A. Broad, Organizational Approaches

Such factors as careful diagnosis, organizational design, information- and work-flow analysis, task forces, and temporary groups are some of the approaches to be considered.

1. Need for careful diagnosis in using tools "If the only tool you have is a hammer, everything else tends to be treated as a nail." The preceding chapters described some tools for increasing organizational competence. However, all of the approaches described in this part of the text must be considered *only as tools to be used after proper diagnosis*. Using job enrichment, Management by Objectives, or other tools may be very appropriate in some situations, but not in others.

2. Use of systems theory in organizational design Any organizational system (industrial, service, nonprofit, or others) must be carefully designed to fit its environment or technology. The work of Perrow and Lawrence and Lorsch has demonstrated there is no "one best way" to design an organization as a total system. Although formal research on organizational design is in its infancy, the evidence is clear that a contingency theory of systems must be applied. An organizational structure and design that "fit" a business making glass bottles (stable environment), for example, must be different from that for a firm manufacturing plastics or hand electronic calculators (unstable environment). The original work in this area, which applied to manufacturing organizations, has been extended to such other types of organizations as municipal governments and educational systems.[13] Further, it is becoming clearer that people's feelings of competence and mastery are increased when the organizational structure and design "fit" the environment. Within the next few years we will know much more than we do now about systems theories of organizational structure and design. We do know now, however, that the pattern of differentiation and integration *within* specific organizations must be modified to fit the internal and external environment of the firm.

We also know that the concept of line and staff may well be obsolete for a systems approach. Indeed, in discussing different types of organizations, Etzioni concludes that in a professional organization, e.g., a university, the traditional line-staff organization is reversed. Here, the real decisions are most frequently made by the faculty, and the traditional "line" organization, e.g., the president and deans, may serve primarily to provide resources to the faculty or "staff."[14]

3. Use of systems theory in information and related flows The use of a systems approach to improve information flow may result in a redesigning of the organization. Major advances in organizational improvement have resulted from the use of models and the computer *within* particular departments. However, the results have generally been disappointing when such approaches have been applied across departments and organizations. Deardon points out, for example, that although every organization has a number of formal and informal information systems, it is impossible to design, develop, and imple-

Plant operations such as gas preparation, synthesis, and other processes can be monitored from this central control panel. (Photograph courtesy W. R. Grace & Co.)

ment an integrated, computerized management information system (MIS).[15] The creation of such a "supersystem" requires the input of too many principles and details, even though such concepts are being advocated in many business schools. The University of Minnesota, for example, has both a Ph.D. program and a research center in MIS.

One of the major difficulties is that organizations rarely make a careful analysis of their information and related flows. Mockler describes a case in which a large mail-order house carefully analyzed its information and paper flow before buying a computer.[16] As a result of its thorough self-analysis, the firm reorganized itself to *fit* the needed information and materials flow. Mockler points out that superficially, at least, the organization looked much the same as it had before, but that in reality there was a strong shift from an "authority-centered" to a "systems," job-centered organization. Reorganization also caused major adjustments to be made in the grouping of functions *within* departments and in the daily arrangements *among* departments.

The benefits of work-flow analysis are illustrated by a consultant's work for the Bureau of Vital Statistics in a large municipality. The organization was designed to accomplish three basic tasks—receive and issue birth certificates, receive and issue death certificates, and report vital statistics to the state government. However, the Bureau was six months late in getting these data to the state and two months tardy in issuing birth certificates.

The director of the Bureau requested three new employees to supplement his twelve-man staff, but his request was denied. In order to help justify his plea for additional people, he then sought the help of a consultant retained by the organization. Subsequently, they decided to use documents published by the U.S. Government Printing Office for studying paperwork flow. The employees (all of whom were under Civil Service) carried out the actual work, with a small amount of pretraining. Within a few weeks, the work load had been considerably reduced so that the average time lag for sending out a birth certificate was only two days. Two employees eventually transferred out of the Bureau (only because better jobs opened up), and it was found that only nine of the ten remaining people were really needed to carry out the Bureau's work. In other words, through proper analysis, the Bureau was able to reduce its work load, which resulted in a 25% reduction in its work force.

4. Use of systems theory to combine the formal and informal organizations
For many years the philosophy originally developed by Taylor and emphasized by the "efficiency experts" of the 1930s and later has dictated the design of jobs. Accordingly, jobs should be specialized, compartmentalized, and clearly specified in terms of rules, regulations, and procedures. There *is* a need for these kinds of jobs in many organizations. However, research on job enrichment and groups following the sociotechnical systems point of view suggests that at times another type of job design may be more appropriate. The rigidly specified job may be more appropriate in highly stable, unchanging, bureaucratic organizations. Such a job design may be less effective in the less stable, nonprogrammable organization. Here, more work and effort may need to be spent in combining the concepts of formal and informal organizations and groups. This modification has been discussed under the concept of "sociotechnical system." For our purposes, the term "decision center," which emphasizes redesigning (where appropriate) the organization to improve the interrelatedness of the structural, flow, and human perspectives, may be more appropriate.

The use of decision centers includes the following steps:

a) Determine "natural" work units. First, the work flow must be analyzed to identify the interrelatedness and interdependence of work tasks and units, irrespective of the existing "formal" organizational structure. Such "natural" work units can be grouped together within the existing formal structure to capitalize on the fact that certain segments of the work are more closely related than others.

A combined participative and statistical procedure has been developed to assist with the design of decision centers. Known as "MAPS" (Multivariate Analysis, Participation, and Structure), this procedure uses multivariate analysis (a statistical technique) for separating the total number of tasks into independent task clusters.[17] Individuals are then assigned to submit structures according to the similarity and interdependence of their tasks, preferences, and viewpoints. A statistical analysis is necessary because it is impossible for a group to reach the optimal solution on an intuitive basis.

b) Develop work team "decision centers." Once natural work units have been identified, the members of those groups should be brought together geographically to form the new, natural work teams. The teams should consist of six to fifteen members, depending on the work unit, the technology, and other situational constraints. In manufacturing, for example, such a decision center might consist of highly interrelated task groups in the manufacture, assembly, and inspection of a particular product. In purchasing, such a work team, or decision center, might consist of those involved with purchasing, scheduling, inventory control, and expediting for a particular product line.

Individual interaction and decision-making responsibility within the decision center should be maximized within the constraints of the situation. For example, although the decision center may not have the option of deciding to make "X" number of widgets and "F" number of gadgets during the month, it can have the opportunity to determine its own daily schedule. Similarly, individuals within the decision center should be given the opportunity to "grow into" as much responsibility, challenge, and discretion as they are capable of handling; at the same time, it is wise to leave room to "back off" if the process moves too rapidly.

c) Provide for rapid communications flow. The flow of communications and information is both internal and external to the decision center. Rapid internal communication facilitates work accomplishment. Work gets done better when: (1) people know what they are doing and why; (2) there is frequent and open interchange of ideas; (3) feedback is nonpunitive; and (4) group members trust one another and the accuracy of their information. For instance, in a manufacturing decision center, the frequent interaction of team members can be maximized by making sure that members working on one stage of fabrication or assembly are close enough, geographically, to others working on other stages of production so that mistakes or errors can be quickly detected and corrected through rapid feedback. Whenever possible, data and solutions to problems should be generated in common so that group conflict can be avoided.

Proper external communication is needed to ensure that the group members get the information they need in the time span, form, and shape in which they need it. Too often, information goes to the wrong person for the wrong reason. Frequently, a higher-level manager receives information that should have been sent to individuals within the decision center. For example, it might be more appropriate for customers' comments about product quality to go directly to the appropriate decision center rather than to management.

5. Greater use of task forces and temporary groups   Formal and informal organizations can be combined through the use of decision centers, which remain relatively stable as a part of the formal organizational design. Industry and business are also making greater use of less stable groups—"task forces" or "temporary groups"—that are formed to handle a specific problem or problems and are then disbanded. The growing use of terms such as "product" or "project manager" illustrates the increasing use of such temporary groups. The use of such groups occurs most frequently in organizations with relatively unstable environments, although their use in stable organizations is increasing.

The accelerating pace of change will require much more extensive use of such temporary groups, frequently under the leadership of a product or program manager. Bennis predicts the growing use of such temporary groups and task forces, especially in enterprises that are in a state of rapid technological change or that exist in an uncertain or unclear environment.[18] His recommendations appear to closely parallel the work of Lawrence and Lorsch in their description of the work and role of the integrator.

The use of temporary groups or task forces has several advantages.

a) Greater use of the human resources of the organization.   If the members of the task force are chosen carefully, they will represent the resources necessary to get the job done. For example, in one organization using such an approach for special projects, there is a chairman ("integrator") for each such project or program. Members of the task force represent key areas of the organization involved with the project. A particular group might consist of engineers, production workers, representatives from purchasing, etc. When the task force meets, the "integrator" reports on the present status of the project and as problems come up and are identified, specific individuals are assigned to begin work on the problem. For example, at one point vendor problems delayed delivery of a vital part to the organization until four days before the product had to be shipped. A key production worker learned of the problem two weeks in advance and began to make plans for ensuring that he could get his job done in time. He therefore requested that a worker from another area of the plant be a consultant for at least half a day after the part arrived, and the production worker was thus able to get his job done on time.

In another organization, $250,000 had been spent in three months in an effort to solve a problem on a product that would be sold for $250,000. It was imperative to ship the product, even at a considerable loss, since the customer also purchased many other products. Yet in all that time, the key people involved had never met as a group to even discuss the problem. As a result, each member of the production effort was able to "cast the blame" on the others, since a mutual problem-solving, task-force approach had not been used.

b) *Greater involvement of the personnel.* The involvement of the individual members of a temporary team is usually extremely high. Their motivation comes from the "authority of the task" rather than from the "authority of the boss." Generally, temporary teams work harder and put in longer hours than they do on their regular jobs.

c) *Greater ability to innovate and consider new approaches.* More stable work groups have a greater need for maintaining the "status quo." By contrast, task forces more readily accept new, innovative approaches than do more stable, permanent groups.

d) *Greater effect on the major, more permanent organization.* By bringing together representatives from various parts of the organization, there is a greater likelihood that the solutions and recommendations arrived at by the temporary group will be accepted by the larger organization, since the proponents of the change or new approach act as "ambassadors" for the change and are more effective in combating the status quo. For example, a committee was assigned to consider a specific problem in a particular university. Representatives were brought together from all parts of the organization, including some who had been the strongest proponents of the status quo. During their deliberations, the committee members consulted with a number of people within the university. After writing down recommendations, the committee held a public hearing for open discussion of the problems involved and the reasons for the recommendations. As a result, changes that had been bitterly resisted by the larger organization for at least ten years now took place within three months.

e) *Increased communication and information flow.* When task forces are properly constituted and used, the lateral flow of information is highly increased. The early identification of problems that must be solved to ensure successful completion of the project is made possible by use of a task force whose members come from every key area of the organization. Although some authors have questioned whether such temporary groups can be successful, Fine has shown that they can be effective and do not require more enduring, long-term work relationships.[19]

B. Individualized Approaches

The two approaches described in this section focus on the individual as an integrative factor in organization development.

1. Use of systems theory in formal leadership style　In Chapter 7, we concluded our discussion of leadership with Fiedler's contingency theory, according to which different types of leadership style are effective, i.e., result in high group performance, under different conditions—the quality of leader-member relationships, the amount and degree of task structure, and the amount of the leader's position power.[20] In general, task-oriented leadership is associated with high performance under extreme conditions, whereas relationship-oriented leadership is more effective under middle-range conditions.

In their study of more and less successful organizations at either end of the continuum, Morse and Lawrence found that task-centered leadership is more effective, but that the leadership style must vary.[21] In the high-producing container industry, for example, top managerial behavior must be directed toward the task and enforcing specific rules and procedures. In the high-producing research laboratory, on the other hand, leadership style must be directed more toward the individual than toward enforcing depersonalized rules and procedures. This leadership style emphasizes coordinating and focusing the group's attention on the overall task to be performed.

Vroom found that people who have weak independence needs really do not want to be, nor are they, influenced by the opportunity to participate in making decisions.[22] By contrast, persons who either have strong needs for independence or are more egalitarian are more highly motivated in their performance by the opportunity to participate. Similarly, a person's personality may influence his or her choice of a job. For example, Vroom found that truck drivers want to be told by the dispatcher where to go on their next trip, whereas package handlers become more involved and more highly motivated when they can participate in the decision-making process.

Perrow believes that the type of leadership required depends on the technology and structure of the organization, as depicted in Fig. 1.2, p. 27.[23] By combining the variables of technology, task, and organizational structure, he concludes that supervision in firms with few rules or known solutions and many exceptions, such as research-and-development firms, must be flexible and polycentralized, whereas supervision in organizations with few exceptions and many rules or known solutions needs to be formal and bureaucratic.

These studies clearly indicate the need for both a systems approach to leadership and a leadership style that varies according to the situation. Fiedler points out that even within particular subsystems of the organization, the situation may vary and therefore require different types of leadership style.[24] He notes, for example, that the manager of a fairly routine operation can prescribe well-defined rules for subordinates to follow. However, when a crisis occurs, the leader is likely to call a staff conference and to become more nondirective and permissive until the crisis has passed. The reverse of this procedure occurs in a research planning group, whose leader under normal conditions is permissive and encourages subordinates to participate, speak up, give suggestions, and offer criticisms. However, when a specific research plan has been developed with the full participation of the subordinates, the manager becomes more directive in accordance with the more highly structured situation. As Fiedler remarks, "Woe be to the assistant who decides to be creative by changing the research instructions."[25]

Fiedler thus stresses that the appropriateness of leadership style depends on the situation, even though a person's preferred style may make him or her a better manager in certain types of operations. Etzioni echoes this point of view by advocating that the situation, rather than people, should be changed.[26] He notes that in 1972, $88,000 was spent per "life saved" in driver training (an attempt to change people), whereas $87 per car was spent on safety devices, such as seat belts, which do a far more effective job of saving lives. In short, "Solving social problems by changing people is apparently less productive than accepting people and changing their circumstances instead."[27] Since, as Hersey and Blanchard note, there is a great deal of mobility if the manager is a "producer," it may be necessary for the organization to make a careful assessment of that person's *styles* as well as *capabilities* before assigning him or her a "permanent" position in an organization.[28]

In conclusion, then, when considered from a systems point of view, leadership style must be varied to fit the situation, the attitudes and feelings of subordinates, and the amount of power that the leader has. As Schein has said:

The most successful manager must be a good diagnostician and value a sense of enquiry . . . He may be highly directive at one time and with one employee but very nondirective at another time. He may use pure engineering criteria in the design of some jobs but let a worker group completely design another set of jobs. In other words, he will be flexible and will be prepared to accept a variety of interpersonal relationships, patterns of authority and psychological contracts.[29]

In other words, it is the formal leader who has direct control over the psychological contract, and the style of leadership must reflect the circumstances, the task, the motivation of subordinates, and the relationships among these variables. Since the manager's role is so critical, it may be appropriate to consider either putting the leader in a job that fits his or her style or reconstructing the job to better fit the person's style.

2. Use of systems theory in management development In Chapter 7, we stated that in many organizations, whether stable or unstable, most of the manager's time is spent in the lateral work-flow process rather than in supervising. Research confirms that the better managers do become more involved in the work-flow process.

However, since most management texts stress the manager's supervisory functions, little has been done to help the manager either understand his or her vital linking function or become fully effective in peer-level relationships. Therefore, the OD practitioner's use of such techniques as sensitivity training and team building is a direct attempt to help managers become more effective with others in the network of lateral relationships. But this is not sufficient. Universities, personnel departments, and outside training agencies need to place much more emphasis on helping the current manager to understand and deal with this linking role. Also, college students in management programs should be given much more understanding about group behavior and how to work and deal more effectively with their peers.

V. APPLICATION OF THE SYSTEMS APPROACH TO ORGANIZATION DEVELOPMENT

A. Review of Concepts

Before describing two brief organization development programs, we should first quickly review some of the concepts discussed previously. A social organization is a complex of interrelated and interdependent subsystems and can be analyzed from three different viewpoints—structural-design, work-flow, and human. These three sets of differing, but overlapping, subsystems are shaped in large measure by the way in which the organization is designed and how it approaches the problems of differentiation and integration. Analysis and design of the organization from one perspective lead to the definition and solution of problems in terms of that perspective. *Optimal* problem definitions, solutions, and designs are most likely to be reached only when all three points of view, and the assumptions underlying these perspectives, are considered concurrently, with shifts in emphasis as appropriate. Such an integrated, or systems, model of organizations is shown in Fig. 13.1.

When this type of systems model is used as the basis for organizational change, the three perspectives form a pattern of inputs, organizational processes, and outputs, as shown in Fig. 13.2. For example, the management

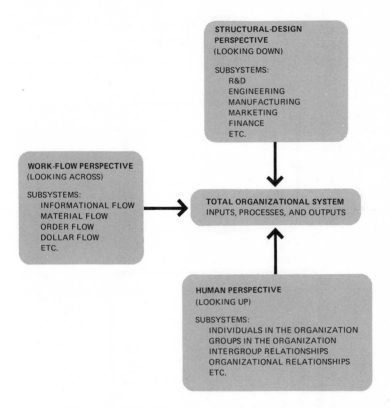

Fig. 13.1 Integrated systems model of an organization.

hierarchy modifies the attitudes and potential brought to the organization in the form of individuals' needs and abilities so that they are compatible with the needs and goals of the organization. Similarly, the flow of information and resources through the organization cannot exist independently of interpersonal variables, which are subject to managerial control.

Within this structural-design system, both interpersonal and flow-process variables are important for effective and permanent organizational change. For example, many studies have shown that managerial control systems over employees may lead to their restricting output, playing the "numbers game," and other dysfunctional practices. Too often, the effect of control systems on human behavior has not been adequately understood.

Since organizational outputs reflect the quantity and quality of both input and processes, it is obvious that organizational outputs can be increased by improving the quality of the input, e.g., selecting people with higher levels of abilities and needs. However, the costs associated with selecting better per-

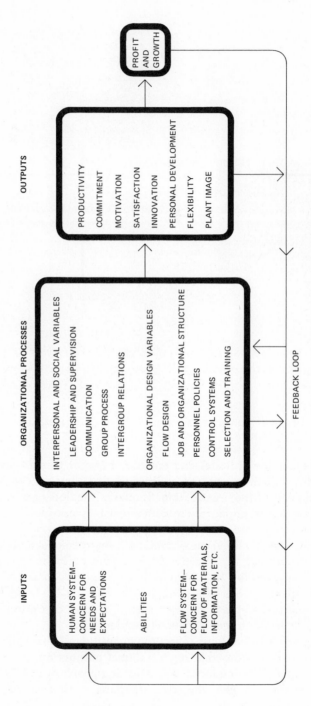

Fig. 13.2 Human- and flow-systems model of an organization.

sonnel do not necessarily lead to greater organizational efficiency. Although the organization may improve its performance, this gain has been obtained only because the quality of people has been improved through better selection, not because there has been a change in the organization's use of its human resources.

Because organizations are open systems, outputs of organizational performance can usually be improved by modifying organizational flow processes so that more of the potential inherent in the human resources can be unleashed. Outputs normally increase because the conversion process has been made more efficient. This can be done, for example, by changing the job structure to allow for greater challenge, better communications, and prompt feedback or by restructuring the formal system to improve materials or information flow. The adjustment of flow processes to more accurately reflect organizational and individual needs is one of the key objectives of organization development.

B. Non-Linear Systems

Note: The following description of Non-Linear Systems, which appeared in the 1973 edition of this text, was based on extensive personal communications with the president of the company, Andrew Kay. These communications took place in 1971 and 1972. Immediately following the original presentation, we will describe some changes that have taken place in the organization between 1972 and late 1975.

Combining the three perspectives

For about eight years, Non-Linear Systems had been a successful manufacturer of digital converters, electronic test equipment, and other complex electronic devices. The company was organized along conventional structural-design lines, with such "line-staff" functions as engineering, manufacturing, and purchasing. However, in the early 1960s, Andrew Kay, president of the company, became dissatisfied with this arrangement because he wanted to "put more meaning into work for the individual employees."

Taking a "systems approach" to organizational design, he brought in several consultants whose backgrounds and approaches were diverse. Using their advantages as well as his own intuition, Kay decided to redesign the company's structure to better fit the firm's unstable, rapidly changing environment.

Choosing an appropriate level of organizational intervention
Use of systems theory in organizational design

Figure 13.3 gives a simplified version of the organization's "before and after" designs. The new design has remained essentially unchanged since the early 1960s.

Before the change, the engineering department was subdivided in the traditional manner into specialities in mechanical design, electrical design, etc. Under the new design, engineering project teams were established, each of which contained all the resources —designers, engineers, machinists, draftsmen, and (when necessary) production workers—needed to design and develop a complete product. In effect, after the management group requested the development of a particular product, the project team was given responsibility for designing it, and the design engineer in charge of the project was allowed to purchase some experimental parts directly, without having to go through the normal purchasing-agent channels.

At the time of the reorganization, there were about 12 such teams, each consisting of 10 to 12 members. Each team worked independently, but was able to draw on the resources of the total organization as necessary. Mr. Kay reports that this was difficult for some members of the organization to accept, since this approach highlighted individual capability and acceptance of responsibility.

The assembly-line operation was broken down into eight or nine teams of six or seven workers. Each team had its own work area—a 12-by-20-foot cubicle.

Use of systems theory in information and related flows

When prototypes were developed by the design team, some were given to the marketing teams for display and sale to customers. The assembly teams were also given a prototype model and in essence told to "make it like this one." Rather than working according to the highly detailed instructions and rigid job descriptions typical of most assembly-line operations, each team was free to decide how the work load would be shared. Individual job enrichment as well as the team concept were encouraged, and the assembly team was allowed to assemble, inspect, sign, and pack its own instruments for distribution to cus-

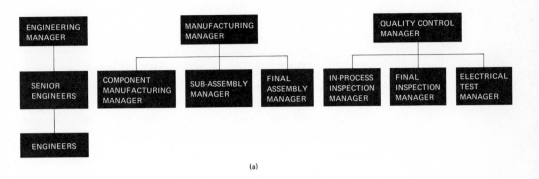

(a)

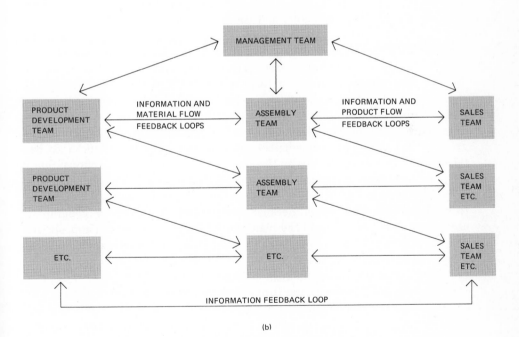

(b)

Fig. 13.3 Non-Linear Systems' organizational design: (a) before, and (b) after the change process.

tomers. Inspection of the product by "outside" inspectors was limited to areas mandated by government requirements.

Sales teams assigned to different regions of the
country were freed from having to write detailed reports. Instead, they were encouraged to use the telephone for direct, personal communication with the
plant, including the assembly teams.

To lessen status differences among employees, all were put on salary, thus
making labor costs fixed and known. Indeed, by reducing the complexity of the
pay system, the organization was able to correspondingly reduce its costs of
preparing the payroll by having it done at the bank.

1. Integration of the three perspectives In terms of the *structural-design
perspective*, the reorganization was undertaken so that the company would
better fit its changing, unstable, and complex environment (electronics). The
new organizational structure was extremely flat, consisting of 12 product development teams. Decision making was pushed downward in the organization,
whereas formerly it had been more centralized at the top.

The new organizational structure resulted in great improvement in *information, material, and related flows*. For example, rather than having specialized groups in engineering, everyone directly involved in the design and
development of a new product was on the same team and in the same geographical location. This immediately reduced communications blockages between such specialized groups as the electrical and mechanical sections. Since
all aspects of the manufacturing process were represented on one team, there
were few communication difficulties between the development and assembly
teams or within each team. Because sales teams (assigned by geographic
area) were encouraged to call the plant directly and could call the appropriate
people, the information flow between sales and the project and assembly
teams was materially improved. Direct communication by telephone increased
the speed, accuracy, and amount of feedback.

The new design merged the formal and informal structure of the organization (*human perspective*). Furthermore individual workers received much
more satisfaction from involvement in their jobs through the use of such
approaches as increased individual responsibility, team building, job enrichment, etc. The nature of the psychological contract clearly changed from
rational/legal to normative. After all personnel had been put on salary, increases were relatively large, but usually occurred only for exceptional performance, promotions, or similar reasons.

The president of the company points out that although this is participative management, it is also "tough" management in that high, difficult goals are established and maintained. Incompetent performers are discharged.

2. Evaluation of results   There were three major areas of change.

a) Managerial time. Because of the increased emphasis on group and individual decision making and responsibility, managerial time was freed for more long-range planning. As the individuals and groups gained proficiency, they were consistently able to expand their ability to assemble a wider variety of products of higher quality in a shorter period of time.

b) Productivity. The design change was made quickly. As a result, although productivity initially dropped, it was back to normal within a few months and continued to climb until it leveled off to about 40% above what it had been prior to the change. Since the production workers were more highly involved in their jobs and got prompt feedback from the field, customer complaints dropped off sharply.

c) Employee morale and commitment. When manufacturing workers were put on salary, they were given the same sick-leave benefits as management people, and their absenteeism rate droppd from about eight percent to about one percent. Avoidable turnover became nearly nonexistent. Marked improvement was seen in employee morale and commitment, as evidenced by not only the turnover and absentee reduction, but also more requests for training and greater involvement in the task. One difficulty has been noted in this area, however. Some of the attempts at individual job enrichment went too far— some workers became discouraged when it took three weeks or longer to assemble an instrument. Therefore, for the more complex instruments, team effort was substituted for individual job enrichment, with the workers themselves deciding how large a segment to handle.

3. Changes since 1971   Several events occurring in the external environment affected Non-Linear Systems. Instruments became less complex, competition increased as more organizations entered the field, and the recession caused a drop in sales. Changes also occurred within the organization. Today, there are fewer development teams, in part because the instruments are less complex. In addition, Mr. Kay states that the change of the engineering department from the more traditional, specialized approach to the "engineering team" approach made it easier to identify incompetent personnel, who were then dismissed. Thus the overall competence level increased, and fewer teams were necessary. Because the instruments are simpler, less team work is required, and individual assemblers have greater opportunity to assemble the entire instrument. Inspection is still carried out by the individual (or team) unless government or other requirements dictate otherwise.

Not all hourly employees are on salary. The longer-term employees feel that some of the newer employees might be taking advantage of the salary program. As a result, they requested that new "blue-collar" employees be paid by the hour until they can demonstrate that they are trustworthy. (Very few other employees are paid on an hourly rate.)

For a time, the president had spent little time within the plant, but instead had concentrated on broader, societal goals. Now, however, he believes that he had spent an undue amount of time on such matters. Today, although he is still interested in broader, societal goals, he feels that he needs to spend more time *within* rather than *outside* the organization.

Productivity and quality are still high, and turnover and absenteeism are still low. Kay suggests that as a result of his experience, an organization cannot remain stable, but must continue to adaptively react to changing conditions. He expects that further changes will be made within the organization over time.

Organizational change and development needs to be an active, continually evolving process. It is not accomplished through a one-shot effort. Rather, the competent organization needs to be adaptive, have a sense of identity, and continually test reality to ensure that it can react positively to the changing demands of its environment.

C. Plant X

This study involved extensive changes in the flow and human perspectives. Plant X had been in existence for three years and had consistently lost money (as is to be expected for a time in most new subsidiaries or plants). However, top management was becoming concerned because the earnings rate was not improving, and a consultant was brought in to diagnose the situation and make recommendations.

Use of systems theory to determine depth of intervention

Within a month, the consultant had recommended that the top-management team spend several days away from the plant to build a management team that could work more effectively together. Their first task at the off-site session was to identify plant objectives. Their second task was to discuss the role expectations that each member of the management group had of each other member. As might be expected, this exercise revealed a large number of differing role expectations. For each job, three to four hours of discussion were needed to iron out the differing and conflicting role expectations to the satisfaction of everyone in the group. Next, the group redefined organizational goals, since the role discussions had indicated that this was now necessary. The redefinition of organizational goals resulted in a much sharper and clearer set of goals than had resulted previously. Finally, the group listed problems facing the organization and developed ways of solving these problems.

Use of systems theory in management development

During the next several months following his arrival in April, the consultant worked with the management staff on establishing leadership styles more appropriate to their particular jobs. It became apparent that although the top-level managers had improved their working relationships, conflicts and misunderstandings still existed at lower levels in the organization, thereby reducing the effectiveness of not only information and other flows, but also the morale of the individuals and work groups. As a result, it was decided to try to improve both the flow and human perspectives simultaneously by building a more cohesive work force.

Use of systems theory in formal leadership style

It was decided to use a modification of the organizational confrontation meeting (described in Chapter 12) to accomplish both of these objectives simultaneously. In August the plant was shut down for an afternoon, and teams were established to identify plant problems. Every member of the organization, excluding top management, was involved. In order to achieve the greatest mix, each team had at least one representative from each department and included all levels of personnel: guards, manufacturing employees, engineers, janitors, clerks, and management personnel. The design ensured that a subordinate was not in the same group with his or her immediate boss. Since this was a union plant, union members were present in each group.

Choosing the level of organizational intervention

Greater use of task forces and temporary groups

The task of each group was to identify problems facing the organization, in terms of either its overall effectiveness or the work environment it provided to employees. At the end of the afternoon, the groups reported their findings and conclusions to the entire organization. There were, of course, overlapping problems, since more than one group identified some of the same problem(s). The problems were then sorted into functional categories. Two weeks later, the plant was shut down for another afternoon, at which time new, cross-functional employee groups were formed to work on specific lists of problems. During the next two months (September and October), the plant shut down every Friday afternoon to allow the groups to work on their lists of problems, which caused a 10% reduction in "productive" time.

The time span in each of the following diagrams is calendar year 1970 and the first period of 1971. The reason for this is that three corporate decisions were made in 60–70 days. Although the decision to close down the plant was made in November 1970, dramatic changes in the plant were already beginning to show up. Therefore, a decision to keep the plant open was made in December (period 13). In period 1 (January 1971), a third corporate decision was made to not only keep the plant open, but also to *add* a research-and-development facility and a sales and marketing group.

Figure 13.4 shows the reduction in manufacturing cost for each four-week accounting period.* (Sales remained relatively constant during this time span.) After the original problem-identification and problem-solving meetings were held during period 8, there was a marked drop in manufacturing costs, amounting to about 45% over the next few periods.

Figure 13.5 shows the increase in productivity dollars per work hour during this time period. It is obvious that productivity increased considerably.

Figure 13.6 depicts the dollar reduction in the scrap rate. The horizontal line represents the budget figure for scrap, an item budgeted by every manufacturing plant. As a result of organizational changes, the amount of scrap decreased considerably.

The percentage of absenteeism during the time shown is given in Fig. 13.7. Absenteeism decreased markedly, although the decrease preceded period 8, when the original organizational confrontation meetings were held.

---

* To protect confidential company information, the figures in these diagrams have been modified by a constant.

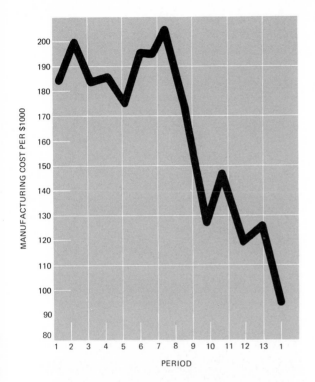

Fig. 13.4 Reduction in manufacturing costs per accounting period.

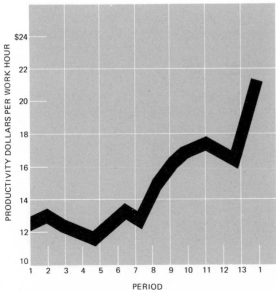

Fig. 13.5 Productivity dollars per work hour.

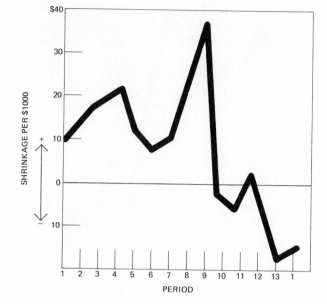

Fig. 13.6 Dollar reduction in the scrap rate.

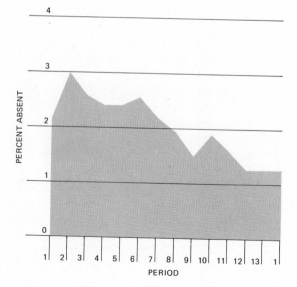

Fig. 13.7 Rate of absenteeism per accounting period.

In this case study, no attempt was made to change the basic organizational structure of the plant. Rather, time and effort were expended to simultaneously improve the flow and human perspectives. The results, we think, speak for themselves. The team building at the upper-management level allowed the organization to be receptive to the concept of problem-identification and problem-solving meetings at all levels. These meetings materially improved both the flow and human perspectives by bringing problems out into the open where they could be acted on.

VI. CONCLUSION

The effective and efficient organization has: the ability to adapt, a sense of identity, the capacity to test reality, and the ability to be well integrated and to simultaneously consider the three different perspectives. In reexamining the concept of proactive and reactive forces affecting organizational balance, we pointed out that both are necessary. A major problem, however, is the inability, at times, to make a proper distinction between the two. Many managers have deeply embedded Theory X assumptions about people, and it is frequently difficult for them to alter their assumptions and perceptions, even in the face of directly contradictory evidence.

Systems theory can be used to restructure organizational design and information and related flows. It can also be used to combine the formal and informal organizations and to determine the most appropriate levels of organizational intervention and change. A final broad, systems approach to organization development is the increased use of task forces and temporary groups.

In addition to these broad approaches, which focus on the organization as a system, other, more individualized systems approaches can be used. Thus systems theory can be used in both formal leadership style and management development to enhance organizational competence.

The two case studies presented in this chapter illustrate how the three perspectives can be integrated to improve organizational efficiency and effectiveness. In each case, the results provide dramatic evidence of the usefulness of an integrated approach to organization development.

The extensive presentation of the case study in the next chapter describes in greater detail how an integrated systems approach to organization development can result in a more adaptable and flexible organization with greater effectiveness and efficiency. Because this was an actual case study conducted under field conditions, it will not exactly parallel the recommendations presented in this chapter. Rather, Chapter 14 stresses the impact of the three different perspectives.

REVIEW

1. Using the same organization for which you devised a strategy for organization development in Chapter 12, redesign the strategy by taking into account structure and the various flow processes.

2. Compare the different perspectives and determine how each views the organization, the effect of one on the others, and give examples of each.

3. Describe how you would enrich the following jobs: a salesman in a hardware store, a cashier in a supermarket, a service station attendant, and a carpenter on a construction project.

4. This chapter lists several "principles" for organization development. Based on your reading and experience to date, make up your own list of principles, which may differ from those given in the text. Explain the reasons for your list.

5. Select an organization to assess for competence. What criteria would you use on each dimension?

7. Choose five organizations you wish to improve. Describe the depth of intervention and the intervention strategy you would use. Where on the Lawrence and Lorsch continuum does each organization appear?

8. Give a critique of one of the two cases presented in this chapter and indicate how you might have approached the problem differently.

REFERENCES

1. E. Schein, *Organizational Psychology*, 2d ed., Englewood Cliffs, N.J.: Prentice-Hall, 1970.

2. J. V. Clark, "A Healthy Organization," *California Management Review* **4**, 4 (Summer 1962): 16–30.

3. C. Argyris, *Management and Organizational Development*, New York: McGraw-Hill, 1971.

4. S. Gellerman, "Behavioral Strategies," *California Management Review* **12**, 2 (1969): 45–51.

5. W. Buckley, "Society as a Complex Adaptive System," in *Modern Systems Research for the Behavioral Scientist*, ed. W. Buckley, Chicago: Aldine, 1968.

6. S. Sokolik, "Reorganize the Personnel Department," *California Management Review* **11**, 3 (Spring 1969): 43–52.

7. J. Lane, "Hedonistic Management," *Advanced Management Journal* **34**, 1 (Jan. 1969): 74–77.

8. *Ibid.*, p. 75.

9. L. Greiner, "Patterns of Organizational Change," *Harvard Business Review* **45,** 3 (May–June 1967): 119–130.

10. Schein, *op. cit.*

11. R. Walton, "The Diffusion of New Work Structures: Explaining Why Success Didn't Take," *Organizational Dynamics* **3,** 3 (Winter 1975): 22.

12. S. Rubenowitz, personal communication.

13. E. Huse, *Organization Development and Change,* St. Paul, Minn.: West, 1975.

14. A. Etzioni, *Modern Organizations,* Englewood Cliffs, N.J.: Prentice-Hall, 1964.

15. J. Deardon, "MIS is a Mirage," *Harvard Business Review* **50,** 1 (Jan.–Feb. 1972): 90–99.

16. R. J. Mockler, "The Systems Approach to Business Organizations and Decision Making," *California Management Review* **11,** 2 (Winter 1968): 53–58.

17. R. Kilmann, "An Organic-Adaptive Organization: The MAPS Method," *Personnel* **51,** 3 (May–June 1974): 35–47.

18. W. G. Bennis, "Beyond Bureaucracy," in *The Temporary Society,* ed. W. G. Bennis and P. E. Slater, New York: Harper & Row, 1968.

19. B. D. Fine, "Comparison of Work Groups with Stable and Unstable Membership," American Psychological Association, Experimental Publication System, December 1970, issue 9, Ms. No. 333–1.

20. F. Fiedler, "Engineer the Job to Fit the Manager," *Harvard Business Review* **43,** 5 (Sept.–Oct. 1965): 115–122.

21. J. Morse and J. Lorsch, "Beyond Theory Y," *Harvard Business Review* **48,** 3 (May–June 1970): 61–68.

22. V. Vroom, *Some Personality Determinants of the Effects of Participation,* Englewood Cliffs, N.J.: Prentice-Hall, 1960.

23. C. Perrow, *Organizational Analysis: A Sociological View,* Belmont, Calif.: Wadsworth, 1970.

24. Fiedler, *op. cit.*

25. *Ibid.,* p. 46.

26. A. Etzioni, "Human Beings Are Not Very Easy to Change After All," *Saturday Review,* June 3, 1972, pp. 45–47.

27. *Ibid.,* p. 46.

28. P. Hersey and K. H. Blanchard, "The Management of Change," *Training and Development Journal* **26,** 3 (March 1971): 28–33.

29. Schein, *op. cit.,* pp. 70, 71. Reprinted by permission.

14

AN
INTEGRATED
STUDY OF
ORGANIZATION
DEVELOPMENT

When there is no wind, row.

OLD POLISH PROVERB

LEARNING OBJECTIVES

When you have finished reading and studying this chapter, you should be able to:

1. Demonstrate the impact of structural-design changes on a total system.
2. Demonstrate the impact of work-flow changes on a total system.
3. Demonstrate the impact of changes in the human perspective on a total system.
4. Demonstrate the necessity for considering the three perspectives in bringing about organizational change.
5. Demonstrate the concept of organization development within the framework of a total system.
6. Use the concept of depth of intervention as an analytical tool for organization diagnosis and change.
7. Apply the textual material to other organizations.

THOUGHT
STARTERS

1. What does OD mean to you now?
2. Have you seen instances of OD in action, even though they might not have been called OD programs?
3. As you look at different organizations, what OD techniques or approaches might be helpful?
4. Would OD be used differently in a church or other voluntary organization on the one hand, and in a profit-making organization on the other?

I. THE APPROACH TO CHANGE

A. Background

The organization development program described in this chapter successfully integrated the three perspectives of the organization as a system. The results were increased plant productivity and profitability, improved product quality, reduced absenteeism and voluntary resignations, greater maturity of attitude and acceptance of responsibility by hourly workers, and fewer layers of supervision. In addition, such other outcomes as the increased satisfaction and motivation of the company's employees verify current research findings that these factors optimize an organization's long-term profitability and growth.

The organization studied is one of a 50-plant corporation with facilities in the United States and overseas. This plant, which interacts with the parent corporation as well as with the outside environment, manufactures a variety of electronic and electrical instruments and related equipment that are used in medical and laboratory products. The products range from relatively simple hot plates to a highly complex instrument (containing more than 500 parts and 12 printed circuit boards) used to perform blood analyses and give a visual, electronic readout.

Prior to its program for development, the plant followed the traditional structural model. There was a plant manager and structural departments, e.g., plant engineering, manufacturing, personnel, quality assurance, and materials control (including purchasing, plant planning, and scheduling). Since its products were primarily electronic, the plant purchased most of the needed components, e.g., transistors and capacitors, and was therefore oriented toward assembling rather than manufacturing parts. One section—the glass shop—of the plant, however, did manufacture parts out of glass tubing for use in electrodes. A machine shop built and repaired equipment.

Because of the fast-moving nature of the electronic instrument business, the plant was continually faced with the problems of introducing and changing new products and modifying and improving existing ones. Some products, of course, did remain stable for a considerable period of time.

Most of the hourly assembly workers were women, most of whom had

This chapter has been modified from E. F. Huse and M. Beer, "Eclectic Approach to Organizational Development," *Harvard Business Review* **49**, 5, Sept.-Oct. 1971, pp. 103–112.

Note: We would like to express our appreciation to the innovative and far-sighted managers and supervisors of the organization described in this chapter: J. Sabin, C. Wheatley, C. Barebo, L. Macarelli, R. Banach, D. Sweyer, and C. Carlozzi.

less than a high school education. The research and development, marketing, and sales groups reported to supervisors whose chain of command differed from that of the plant manager.

B. Assumptions Underlying the Change Program

1. This organization falls on the left of the Lawrence and Lorsch continuum, i.e., it operates in an unstable, rapidly changing environment.

Use of systems theory in organizational design

2. Organizations should improve if they work actively to meet the needs of people (change the psychological contract) and the organization. Under such conditions, individuals at all levels of the organization will grow and mature.

3. Simultaneous attention should be paid to the three basic perspectives; one cannot be stressed to the exclusion of the others. Each approach to change has an appropriate place in a total organization development program, and no single tool or technique should be the paramount vehicle for change. For example, although sensitivity training has been widely used as an instrument for organization development, it was not used at this plant and, indeed, may never be used unless it appears appropriate at a particular time.

Use of action research in organizational intervention and change

4. Most managers want to do a good job and improve their own performance and that of their subordinates. As a result, they will try out, and continue to use, techniques that help them to get their job done better. The individual manager will cease taking what he or she perceives to be nonbeneficial actions. The manager should therefore be more concerned about results than about "theory" as such.

5. The role of the change agent should be directed toward helping the operating manager do a better job. The change agent can do this by acting as a resource person rather than by telling a manager how to do his or her job.

Use of systems theory in

6. The most effective and permanent learning comes after the individual has experimented with new ap-

management
development

proaches. This is consistent with research indicating that behavioral change precedes attitudinal change. By working with a change agent, a manager may experiment with new means of communication, job enrichment, or organizational structural change. Successful experiences begin in a subtle way to change the culture and norms of the plant, thus initiating a continuously evolving cycle of change.

C. The Change Team

The organization development team consisted primarily of three people. There were two "external" change agents—the manager of organizational research and development for the parent corporation and an organization development consultant. In addition, there was an "internal" change agent—the personnel manager of the plant. A fourth person, who visited the plant periodically, was a researcher who conducted interviews and gathered data for use in diagnosis, feedback, and research.

The basic approach of this team was for the two "outside" change agents to establish working relationships with individuals at all management levels within the plant and to present themselves as resource persons available to help solve specific, ongoing problems or to initiate small-scale experiments in management practices. The change team wanted to get someone or some organizational component to begin implementing certain managerial concepts (see Fig. 13.2). With the help of the change team, a few individuals in various parts of the organization began to apply these new concepts. These initial experiments were successful, thereby reinforcing both the individual's and the organization's commitment to the change program, which in turn enhanced their interest and motivation to continue with the change process.

The change team conducted surveys and used survey-feedback techniques throughout the change period, but the initial, continuing, and most important changes were achieved through the consulting-counseling approach, which focused on helping operating managers solve their problems in ways that would have both immediate and long-term effects. In other words, the change team had two objectives—to help the manager with immediate problems and to fit this type of help to an integrated, systems model for OD.

II. RESULTS OF THE PROGRAM

The overall results of the organization development program are given in Fig. 14.1. The figure is largely self-explanatory and will be referred to throughout the remainder of the chapter.

One of the most significant results of this organization development program was that hourly workers developed more mature attitudes and became more willing to accept responsibility on the job. The change in these workers is even more marked when they are compared to hourly workers in conventional organizations which are managed according to Theory X assumptions.[1] The following are typical reactions of workers at all levels to the development program.

Since I've been working here, my husband is a much better supervisor in his plant. I tell him what he should do to make his people more interested in what they are doing, based on what our supervisors do here. (Assembly worker)

I wondered about this organization development approach when I got here and kinda thought it was for the birds. But the thing that convinced me was how those new products go into production. In any other plant I've worked in, it would have been a complete fiasco. (Engineer)

The more I get into this thing, the more I see that it is going to be a way of life for me from here on. Everybody wins. (Plant manager)

A. Changes in the Human Perspective

We discuss the organizational changes that occurred within the framework of three distinct perspectives only for the sake of clarity. In fact, the three perspectives are interdependent, and work on all three proceeded simultaneously.

In order to bring about changes in the human perspective, the change team had to work on organizational processes having to do with interpersonal and social variables—the needs and motivations of individuals within the organization. Therefore, the change agents focused on improving the leadership and supervision potential in the plant, enhancing the vertical and horizontal flow of information, expanding workers' jobs, establishing and developing more effective work groups, and improving intergroup relationships.

Use of systems theory in formal leadership style

1. Communications One of the first tasks of the change agents was to open up better communication channels so that the organization members could develop mutual trust and understanding before new and more profound changes were made. Although the organization already made use of staff meetings and other types of traditional communication channels, the change agents wanted to do more.

a) Departmental meetings. With relatively little training, individual supervisors at all organizational

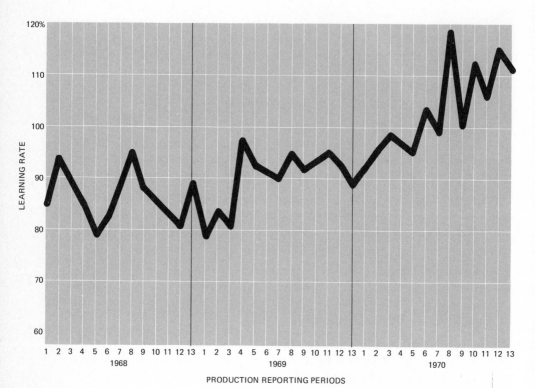

A.   Plant efficiency

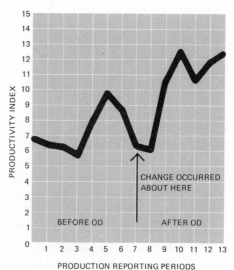

B.   Productivity in the hot-plate department

C. **Other results during 1968–1970 period**

Hot-plate department
Productivity increase 84%
Controllable rejects drop .... 23% to 1%
Absenteeism .... 8% to 1%
Elimination of "weekly" inspector job

Glass shop
Productivity increase 84%

Materials control department
Parts shortage list reduced from 14 IBM pages
to 1 page

Instrument department
Four new products introduced in eight months
with only a slight drop in overall
productivity. New product efficiency*
now never less than 80%
Productivity increase 17%
Quality increase 50%
Absenteeism reduced 50%

Supervision
Elimination of job of manufacturing manager
Elimination of 1/3 of first-line supervisory jobs†

Incremental profit
One of the best among 50 plants
in corporation

* Measured in terms of speed in learning new production
tasks.

† Vacant jobs not filled after promotion of individuals.

E. Huse and M. Beer, "Eclectic Approach to Organizational
Development," *Harvard Business Review* **49,** 5 (Sept.-Oct.
1971). Reprinted by permission.

Fig. 14.1 Economic impact of organization development.

levels began to hold monthly meetings with their subordinates. At first, these meetings consisted only of the supervisor's telling his subordinates what was going on in the plant and in his department. The supervisor stated the organization's monthly objectives and the status of progress toward these goals; he also described the relationship between departmental and organizational goals. The supervisor tried to get feedback in the form of ideas, comments, and suggestions about the things he had discussed and tried to get subordinates' views about what was going on in the plant.

Over a period of several years, these meetings evolved into truly two-way communication sessions; discussion shifted from "minigripes" to "megagripes." The subordinates began to be concerned about such questions as: "What is our product being used for?" "Who is using it?" "What do they think of it?" "Are the quality standards high enough?" "How do the customers feel about it?"

b) *"Coffee with the boss."* Every week a sample group of hourly and weekly employees (on a rotating basis) met with the plant manager in an effort to close the communication gap at the top. Over time, the same shift in concerns emerged as it had in the departmental meetings.

Use of systems theory in information and related flows

c) *Plant tours.* As the content and openness of meetings changed, it became apparent that employees at all levels wanted more information about their jobs, their place in the organization, and how the business was doing. Therefore, plant tours were initiated so that employees could see what was happening in other departments. Significantly, hourly employees began to conduct the tours for both employees and visiting dignitaries.

d) *Use of charts.* At the major traffic point in the plant, charts were put up every month to show actual versus budgeted programs in sales, inventory, plant effectiveness, etc. Although no dollar figures were given, all employees could see where the organization was in relation to its objectives, and this openness contributed to employee morale. As one assembly worker commented, "We're proud of where we are."

e) Mutual goal-setting. Goals for each department were derived from plant objectives, and weekly or monthly goals for individuals or work groups were set after discussion by the boss with his subordinates. This process of mutual goal-setting enabled workers to understand how their own production goals were related to the goals of the plant. As a result, there was less need for close supervision for long periods of time.

2. Group and intergroup relationships These factors were an important aspect of increasing effectiveness, communications, and trust. In order to help managers become more effective, change agents sat in on manager-staff meetings. After the meeting, the change agent could give the manager suggestions for making future meetings with his staff more effective.

The plant routinely used a "Rate the Boss" form on which subordinates rated their immediate superior on a number of variables. Change agents then discussed these forms with the managers, clarifying the meaning of the ratings and making suggestions for increasing the manager's effectiveness.

Use of systems theory in organizational intervention and change

When the organization development program was initiated, professional and supervisory personnel felt that interdepartmental relationships needed to be improved. Therefore, a meeting (attended by the change agents) of department managers was held so that each manager could discuss his perception of his own and others' departments.

This first frank discussion was followed by other meetings at which the format and style were expanded. For example, periodic cross-department meetings were held at which the "monthly" personnel of one department discussed their expectations, perceptions, and their strong and weak points with the "monthly" personnel of another department. Most employees agreed that such meetings were helpful. As one employee explained, "Before we had these meetings, I really wasn't concerned about the people in 'X' department. Now, I'm beginning to understand some of the problems. I'm beginning to listen to them and work with them."

Depth of
intervention

Although T-groups were discussed as a "family group," the plant personnel felt that they really did not need such an approach. The other approaches were accomplishing a level of openness that was sufficient for their purposes.

3. Job enrichment The change agents wanted to create opportunities for employees to satisfy their individual needs on the job. A process of job enrichment was developed to enlarge jobs, to give individuals more opportunity to handle the whole job, and to give them responsibility for the planning, doing, and evaluating of their own work. The change agents felt that people at all levels in the organization should be given interesting and challenging work for which they could assume full responsibility. Since such an approach obviously depends not only on the situation and the individual but also the job, the change agents felt that job enrichment should be determined by circumstances and could be accomplished by using either a team or an individual approach.

Use of action
research and
systems theory
in organizational
change

a) The hot-plate department. An engineer who became excited about this idea wanted to try it out. Both he and his first-line supervisor wanted to do something about the layout of the hot-plate department, which assembled several models of hot plates for laboratory and hospital use.

At the time, this operation was already pretty well streamlined into the normal assembly-line approach, with each worker having a small part in the total assembly process. The line was balanced, and management was generally satisfied with the department's rate of productivity. After considering and discussing several alternatives with others in the organization, the first-line supervisor and the engineer developed a radically different design—they decided to have each person assemble the entire hot plate. The only change in the department was that each worker was expected to do the entire job, and the response was positive, e.g., "Now, it is *my* hot plate."

The results of this job redefinition were dramatic (see Fig. 14.1). First, there was a drop in controllable rejects from 23% to less than 1%. Second, absenteeism dropped from about 8% to about 1%, where it has remained for several years. Third, productivity rose sharply, as Fig. 14.1 shows. A comparison of the average productivity for the first and second halves of the year shows that there was an 84% gain in productivity. (The temporary increase in productivity in periods 5 and 6 was caused by emergency pressure to get the product out to meet a sudden, unexpected increase in sales.)

By all criteria, the development program in the hot-plate department was successful. Having each assembly worker be responsible for the total product had marked effects on productivity, efficiency, quality performance, and morale. In fact, the quality of the workers' performance increased so much that inspectors were no longer needed. Now, each woman does her own inspecting and signs her own name to "brag tags" which go directly to the customer.

b) The glass shop. In this department women work on lathes to form glass for electrodes. Because of the nature of this operation, the supervisor decided to try the team approach to productivity. At the beginning of the change program, team formation and the effectiveness of cohesive work units had been discussed, and the supervisor simply went ahead and divided his people into teams, with minimal discussion with outsiders, although the supervisor's boss and the plant manager had given their approval to the change beforehand.

Each person is responsible for assembling the total product. (Photographs courtesy Corning Glass Works)

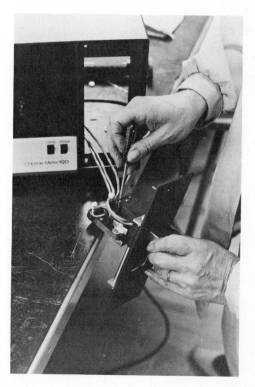

Use of socio-technical approach to combine the formal and informal organizations

The supervisor's approach was very simple. After he had formed the teams, he told the women:

Look, I think we ought to organize around teams, and you four women are responsible for the "X" electrode. You three are responsible for the "Y" electrode. You are going to be responsible for the total task; I want you people who are working on the "X" electrode to know that we're going to need 500 of these by the next accounting period, and you decide who's going to do what, how you're going to do it, and you schedule it.

The women did not all react positively to this sudden change. Some saw it as a tribute to their capability and were enthusiastic. Others, who were not used to working in this kind of climate and with this type of supervisor, were suspicious and thought that the supervisor was abdicating his responsibility. (This kind of suspicion, which emerged from the researcher's interviews, existed in many of the stages of change.)

Despite some workers' apprehension, however, productivity soon showed a 20% increase. In addition, there were immediate and lasting changes in the involvement, commitment, and interest by the women in their work. For example, they sometimes stayed late to discuss manufacturing problems and schedules over a cup of coffee. Furthermore, one person took the schedules home at night to type so that they would be neat, even though she knew that she should not work overtime without pay.

As time went on, the composition of the groups changed, and at one point the concept was almost abandoned when a new supervisor, who had come in from another plant, was dubious about the value of the team approach. However, within a year he had become an enthusiastic supporter of the work-team concept. His conviction was strengthened by the obvious contrast between the department he had managed previously and the glass shop. In the glass shop the teams knew their schedule, pooled their efforts, and swapped jobs as necessary to get the work done. In the other department, however, it was necessary for the supervisor to assign work at the beginning of the work day to each employee.

Inappropriate use of systems theory in organizational intervention and change

c) The instrument department. This department, which makes highly complex and complete systems ranging from relatively standard models to sophisticated electronic equipment, experienced both successes and failures in organization development. To help him assign workers to various production areas, the department supervisor decided to use a sociometric questionnaire (which asks respondents to specify in rank order others with whom they would like to work). However, because the supervisor had neither prepared his people very well for this task nor established sufficient trust to carry out such a plan, the women rebelled, saying that it was his responsibility to make work assignments. Underlying this negative reaction was the womens' feeling that they were not ready for this type of change and that they were unprepared to accept such a role.

Appropriate use of systems theory in organizational intervention and change

Some months later, this supervisor left the plant for a better job, and a new manager took over the instrument department. Unlike his predecessor, the new manager was extremely frank and open with his people in explaining why schedule changes were necessary. Using a team-building approach, he began discussions with his subordinates about how schedules could be met and began involving them in the planning process. In addition, he began working toward what he called the "total job concept," his term for job enrichment. Within a year, individuals were undertaking the complete assembly of complex instrument systems. With yet more complex instruments, he used groups of workers to do the assembly work.

After the job-enrichment program was initiated, four new instruments were introduced into the department. In contrast to the initial low productivity when new products go into the traditional assembly-line process, the introduction of the new instruments caused only a slight reduction in productivity.

Using data for several instruments that had been in production for at least two years prior to the job-enrichment program, the plant accountant was able to show just how effective the change in approach had been. The average productivity for the eight months preceding the change was used as a base. After the job-enrichment program had been implemented, productivity rose by 17%, or approximately $1500 per year per worker. Quality also improved; the number of rejects decreased from an average of 25% to an average of 13%, an increase in quality of about 50%. Absenteeism was reduced from 8.5% per month to 3.4%, a reduction of about 50%.

An engineer associated with the introduction of the new products asked the change agents how they could be certain that job enrichment would be better than the more traditional use of assembly lines, time standards, etc. When asked in return how the introduction of a specific new product would have been handled in a conventional type of plant, the engineer supplied the answer to his own question.

It would have been utter chaos. Under the circumstances, we just couldn't have gotten a normal assembly-line process going for months. At least with the workers making the entire product, they learned about the problem quickly; you had fewer people to talk to and train, and they were so involved that if they had questions, in most cases, they solved the problem by discussing it among themselves. I guess that's the kind of proof I needed.

These are examples of some of the improvements that occurred by initiating changes in the human perspective. Later, we will document the gain in workers' maturity and their increasing acceptance and willingness to take on additional responsibility. Certainly one evidence that workers' needs were being met was the considerably reduced absenteeism and voluntary resignation rate throughout the plant. As one worker said, "It's important to come to work in the morning. I'm interested in the team and what we can do to meet our production goals. Sometimes, when I'm sitting at home, I think about how we can improve our performance and better the goal."

In the next section we discuss how changes in the flow perspective helped improve plant effectiveness. However, it is important to stress that these perspectives are interrelated and that many of the changes in the human perspective had a direct impact on the flow of information and materials throughout the plant.

B. Changes in the Flow Perspective

Here, the change team wanted to improve the lateral flow of information, materials, etc., through the plant in addition to the vertical flow of information discussed in the previous section. Obviously, some of these latter approaches improved the lateral flow as well. For example, the interdepartmental meetings greatly increased the amount of "informal communications flow" across departments, and departmental relationships improved accordingly.

In this section we discuss more direct approaches to improving communications, information, and other flows across the organization. These changes also affected the formal, hierarchical structure of the organization, as will be discussed in the next section.

Use of socio-technical approach to combine the formal and informal organizations

1. The matrix organization This approach, based on the research findings of Lawrence and Lorsch, includes the use of the integrator and the matrix organization. However, before going into detail, a little background is needed. In most industrial organizations, problem-solving, or production, meetings are usually attended by the heads of different functional groups and key production people in the organization. This plant was no different. The daily production meeting was attended by the plant manager and the heads of such departments as engineering, quality assurance, materials control, and the individual first-line supervisors as needed. Prior to the meeting each functional head and first-line supervisor met with subordinates to become up to date in his or her own area. After the meeting, each manager communicated specific courses of action or problems to subordinates. Such meetings served to help unify the plant, disseminate information to the departments, and ensure that production schedules were met.

However, the plant manager felt that this design could be improved and that he and his managers should spend more time in long-range planning. In addition, communication failures, delays, and misunderstandings occurred because the managers served as "communications carriers" to and from their own departments.

Several basic objectives evolved from discussions between the plant manager and department managers.

1. Increase the effectiveness and rapidity of the information flow through the plant to make certain that the right people have the right information at the right time.

2. Move the decision-making and problem-solving processes down to the level of the person responsible for doing the work.

3. Increase the responsibility for the total job and push that responsibility as far down as possible.

Use of socio-technical approach in organizational design

The design that evolved from these discussions was the matrix organization. Each production supervisor would be an "integrator" for a team consisting of representatives from each of the staff departments that serviced his production department. Those from engineering, materials control, and quality assurance, for example, were to be "doers" rather than supervisors or managers. A typical team might thus consist of a technician from quality assurance, a technical engineer from engineering, and one or more representatives from materials control.

The readiness of the plant's management for a major change of this magnitude was evidenced by the relatively short period of time in which the new structure was discussed and a decision reached. It seemed clear to everyone that the matrix structure more accurately combined and represented the informal, most effective communication links. Nevertheless, the change has not been totally successful to date, although there continues to be improvement.

In part, this lack of success was caused by management's failure to effectively train and prepare individuals for the change and their new roles. The matrix structure has worked best when the staff department representatives are competent, motivated, and skilled in working in groups. In addition, since the head of one functional department was not fully committed to the change program, he did not delegate full responsibility to his subordinates on the team. Some integrators lacked clear understanding of their role and the means of influence and control open to them. Finally, neither the plant manager nor the change agents gave proper attention and follow-up to the changes that had been made.

The reasons for these difficulties were discussed with the change agents and the key people involved with designing the matrix. Following a diagnosis of the problems and subsequent discussion of the difficulties, it was agreed that most of the problems could be overcome. A decision was made to continue with the matrix because it fit operational needs, reflected management philosophy, and complemented the culture of the plant.

Use of action research in organizational change

Even though the introduction of this level of matrix organization did not totally meet expectations, it is important in several respects. First, the organization's willingness to undertake such a major change reflects management's adaptability as fairly sophisticated consumers of new managerial methods. Second, the ability to examine and diagnose failure reflects the openness of the plant and management's willingness to invest time in examining the organizational process, even in the face of continuing task pressures. Third, the failure itself supports the thesis that change must be preceded or accompanied by changes in individuals' abilities, motivation, role understanding, interpersonal skills, or other social and behavioral changes. In other words, change depends on the interaction of the formal, flow, and human perspectives.

2. New product introduction Almost all manufacturing companies have difficulty in introducing new products—there are delays, misunderstandings, parts shortages, etc. The resulting conflict may cause the research-and-development group to complain, "We have given you (manufacturing) an excellent product—you loused it up." Manufacturing, in turn, may grumble, "If you gave us a well-designed product, we could build it." Elsewhere, we referred to the tactics of the purchasing agent who tried to ensure that he got as close to the design of the product as possible, even though in the more formal, traditional sense, his job was simply to order parts as cheaply as possible and to expedite their delivery.

When a new product goes into production, cost standards are developed for the product; that is, labor and parts costs are estimated in order to give the organization some idea of the number of people needed to manufacture the product, selling prices, etc. In addition, most companies expect a learning curve, the time needed for the organization to learn how to build the product. Thus the actual costs versus predicted costs in the first month or so of actual production generally result in a 20% efficiency rate. As Fig. 14.1 shows, however, the efficiency rate of new product introduction in this plant never fell below 80%, a very high figure for highly complex products.

How was this efficiency rate achieved? A higher-level, modified matrix approach is now being used to integrate such diverse sectors of the organization as the marketing, research and development, materials control, manufacturing, and sales departments.

Greater use of task forces and temporary groups

This matrix consists of a product team for each new product. The task of the product team, led by an integrator, is to ensure that all the "bugs" are out of the product before it is manufactured. In addition, this team ascertains that the product is well designed and marketable, generates and stabilizes a parts list in order to give purchasing sufficient lead time, and ensures that the product fits the demands and needs of the marketing people. Interviews conducted in the plant in December 1970, as well as information obtained later in 1971, indicate that this approach is succeeding—many of the previous problems have been reduced, if not eliminated.

Although not all changes led to immediate improvement, the organization remained committed to the idea of change and has been willing to experiment. As one engineer put it:

I've never seen new products move so easily, quickly, and smoothly into the plant as they do now. We are taking care of the problems early that used to really plague us in the past. Sure, we have our conflicts, but they are brought out into the open early, and this lets us iron them out and get them solved before it's too late. I think that for the first time, we are really integrated.

C. Changes in the Structural-Design Perspective

Changes in the design perspective are highly dependent on changes in the other two perspectives. For example, the interdepartmental discussions initiated by the change agents improved interdepartmental relations and therefore brought the formal and informal organizations closer together. Although most of the formal, structural changes have already been described in the sections on changes in the human and flow perspectives, there were also others—the redesign of part of the formal organization, changes in leadership and managerial style, reduction in levels of supervision, and changes in the parent organization.

1. Changes in the materials control department This department had responsibility for purchasing, inventory control, scheduling, and expediting, and people were assigned to one of these four specialty areas. However, the plant was being plagued by parts shortages, which caused delays in production. (This was well before the development of the matrix organization or the new-product task forces.)

After experimenting with individual job enrichment, particularly for his secretary, the department supervisor decided that the entire departmental structure should be reorganized through job enrichment. As he said:

I don't think these people who are expediting really like expediting; it's not a very challenging kind of a job. In addition to that, I think my people are having tremendous problems communicating across functional lines.

Use of systems theory to combine the formal and informal organizations

The materials control manager then developed a plan of action. Rather than having each work group specialize in a particular functional area, he decided to formally organize his department around product-line teams. Each group would have total responsibility—expediting, scheduling, purchasing, and inventory control—for a particular product line. The manager felt that this change would reduce the parts-shortage problem, solve communications problems, and make the work more interesting for his people. Since this was a radical change, he moved slowly and discussed with the plant management, the change agents, and his people some alternative ways of implementing the structural change, the impact it would have on his people, and the need to go slowly and to keep the "back door" open in case he needed to retreat from the project-team approach.

When he made the change, people were ready. Within three months, the parts-shortage list was reduced from 14 large computer-printout pages to less than one page (as Fig. 14.1 shows), while the department maintained the same volume of business. Even though the total volume of business increased as more complex instruments were introduced and the absolute number of parts shortages increased correspondingly, the relative number of parts shortages still showed a considerable net decrease. The introduction of the new product teams at a later time also helped to significantly reduce the number of parts shortages.

Departmental personnel reacted positively to the changes brought about by job enrichment:

You no longer operate in a vacuum. I used to schedule with only one point of view—that of getting everything produced for delivery to a customer. I never thought about or was concerned about inventory problems or lead time involved in buying. I wasn't really concerned with other people's point of view. We just didn't communicate, and therefore there was very little cooperation.

Now, we can relate our successes to theirs (the manufacturing area). It gives you a great sense of satisfaction to know that you have coordinated the back-up work for an entire department.

My job is a lot more interesting since the reorganization. I no longer have to do the same things day after day, and things have real meaning for me.

Uses of systems theory in formal leadership style

2. Changes in management and leadership style
There is no doubt that managerial leadership and supervision have an important impact on the motivation, commitment, adaptability, and satisfaction of employees. One of the aims of the change events was to help the plant move toward a management style that emphasized participation, consideration, and support of employees, with proper delegation of responsibility. As changes occurred in group processes, intergroup

relationships, job structure, communications and information flow, and organizational structure, supervision in the plant became less centralized and increasingly participative and supportive. It is clear that
leadership style is not merely reflected in the nature
of communication flow, job structure, and organizational structure; it is in turn affected by them. In
short, leadership cannot be isolated from the other
variables.

a) Search for an appropriate managerial style.   Since the plant's environment
was uncertain, it appeared appropriate to push decision making downward, a
change that reflects the research by Lawrence and Lorsch. Perhaps the most
interesting aspect in the development of participative management was the
early difficulties encountered by the managers in understanding and applying
the concept. After participative and supportive management had been discussed in seminars and with individual managers, the change agents found
that some managers interpreted this to mean a hands-off, be-warm-and-
friendly-to-everyone-regardless-of-the-situation approach, i.e., a *laissez-faire*
style of management. This extreme shift in direction was most often reflected
in increasing managerial uncertainty about how to handle problems and problem employees. For example, should a supervisor discuss lagging performance,
absenteeism, or tardiness with an employee? In short, concern for people was
being emphasized to the exclusion of concern for production. Occasionally,
a manager's confusion led to an abrupt "swing" in style from *laissez-faire* to
highly structured directiveness. When, not surprisingly, *laissez-faire* and warm
friendliness did not work, the manager's frustration exploded in a new, tough,
and (from the subordinate's point of view) quite unexpected approach to a
problem. To the change agents, these swings were not surprising and reflected
a trial-and-error learning process on the part of the managers.

The search for an appropriate managerial style reflects common managerial confusion about participative, or Theory Y, management. Participative
management does not lie on a "hard-soft" continuum; rather, it is an integrated, simultaneous concern for both people and production. Participative
management requires the mutual involvement, at all levels, of boss and subordinate in setting goals and making decisions that affect the employee. Concern for people is expressed by their involvement in making decisions, defining
tasks, and setting objectives. Participative management is a third alternative
which is more difficult to apply than directive leadership, under which the
manager can simply "go by the book."

b) Installation of work-planning.   Counseling and work by the change agents
led to the use of a Management by Objectives, or work-planning, approach at

all levels of the organization. For example, production and other goals were mutually planned and set by the plant manager and the production supervisors. Mutual goal setting was also adopted with production workers. Rather than having an industrial engineer determine standard piece rates, etc., departmental goals are now derived from the plant goals, and weekly or monthly individual and team goals are derived from departmental goals after the boss and his subordinates have discussed them. This process enables workers to clearly understand how their goals fit into the goal structure of the plant, and they can therefore work on their own for long periods of time without close supervision. Performance reviews, held periodically with all employees, including hourly workers, are two-way discussions. In addition, "Rate Your Boss" forms are used.

c) Promotions and dismissals. The concept of participative management has been extended to include the handling of promotions and dismissals. The plant has a relatively high turnover rate for ineffective employees. When termination is deemed necessary, the employee is told frankly the reasons for his or her dismissal. This practice reflects not only the organization's concern for people and their needs for security and understanding what is happening, but also the company's assumption that most people are interested in doing a good job and are mature enough to understand why they are being dismissed.

Performance is the primary criterion for promoting an employee. Again, participative practices are used by management to make sure the employee knows the reasons for the promotion and has a clear understanding of his or her new responsibilities.

The concept of participative management has pervaded the "culture" of the organization. It has encouraged managers and subordinates to take a more realistic look at themselves and to assume individual responsibility for difficult decisions that in more traditional organizational cultures are often postponed or bucked upward.

d) Reduction in the work force. Perhaps one of the best illustrations of this change in the plant's culture is the approach that was used to reduce the size of the work force. During late 1970 and early 1971, sales were declining, and the plant was accumulating an inventory of unsold products. Top management therefore decided that a layoff was necessary. The management staff discussed a number of alternatives and then decided that since this was an "open" plant, these alternatives should be discussed with the production workers. The assembly workers had a major share in the final decision, which was to reduce the number of work weeks for individual employees. (To the best of our knowledge, this is the *only* time that a decision to reduce the work force in *any* organization has been greeted by spontaneous applause by those affected.)

3. Reduction in managerial personnel When the program for change began, the plant hierarchy consisted of a plant manager and staff departments, including a production superintendent and first-line supervisors. As the study progressed and as workers and managers grew in maturity and willingness to accept responsibility, less and less close supervision was needed. As a result, when the original plant manager was promoted, the production superintendent was promoted to take his place. The latter's position was not filled, however, since by this time the first-line supervisors had grown more and more skilled and were able to take on greater responsibilities.

As the plant increased in size, consideration was given to employing an additional first-line supervisor, but it was decided that this was unnecessary. Finally, when one of the first-line supervisors was promoted, the two remaining supervisors felt that they would be able to supervise the entire plant floor, i.e., 80 production workers in several departments.

In other words, as people developed more mature attitudes and were increasingly able to assume responsibility at all levels, one layer of supervision (the production superintendent) and one-third of the first-line supervisory force were eliminated. This major change in the formal system resulted from the improvements that had been made at all levels in the human and flow perspectives.

4. Relationships with the parent corporation So far, we have discussed this plant only as a system in its own right. Since this plant is part of an international corporation with about 50 plants in the United States, we can also consider this particular plant as one subsystem within the larger system, the parent corporation. Accordingly, some of the established policies, procedures, and controls of the parent company affected, and were affected by, this plant as a subsystem.

For example, most large corporations have well-established pay programs for hourly employees which are based on the assumptions that the manager leads and directs and that the hourly workers merely follow directives. What kind of pay system should be devised for hourly workers whose jobs have been enlarged by their taking over the job of inspecting their own work? How can traditional methods of job evaluation take into consideration the fact that hourly assembly workers have grown and matured on the job so that they have taken over many of the calibration and related tasks that previously required the work of technicians who were paid on a weekly basis? Such problems illustrate the fact that a change in one subsystem creates stresses and strains throughout the entire system. In this case, the parent corporation is still considering what action to take with regard to the revision of pay systems.

III. SUMMARY AND CONCLUSION

This case study shows how concepts of organization development were used and applied in a concrete, real-life situation. We have tried to show that organizations *can* improve and that individuals at all levels *can* grow and develop. In other words, the needs of the individual and the needs of the organization can be met through changing the nature of the explicit and the implicit psychological contract.

Perhaps more importantly, we have tried to demonstrate through concrete examples the entire concept of systems. First, the organization is an open system composed of a number of interdependent and interrelated subsystems. Second, optimal problem definitions, solutions, and designs occur only when all three perspectives of systems are considered simultaneously, with emphasis being placed on differing points of view only as appropriate.

REVIEW

1. Compare the company in this case before and after change according to McGregor's Theories X and Y. Should the results that occurred in this case have happened according to theory? Were there other things that should have happened but didn't?

2. "Behavioral change precedes attitude change." How can action precede thought? What is the role of reinforcement in such a process? What is the role of feedback?

3. What was the purpose of the "brag tags" the women signed and sent to the customer? What function did the concept of competition have here? Is this a return to the craft concept of manufacture? Under what circumstances will this solution prove feasible in the hot-plate department?

4. How is the managerial style of leadership related to the total system concept of organizational operations? What is the benefit of participative management in this context? Was it used in this case?

5. What were the primary functions of the change agent in this case? Should the agent solve the client's particular problem? What is the relationship between the outside change agent(s) and the internal agent?

REFERENCE

1. E. Huse and P. Price, "The Relationship Between Maturity and Motivation in Varied Work Groups," *Proceedings of the 70th Annual Convention of the American Psychological Association*, September 1970, pp. 587–588.

15

CONCLUSION

*Man ultimately decides for himself, and in the end,
education must be education toward the
ability to decide.*

VICTOR FRANKL

Perhaps the most important concept presented in this book is that all of us are born, live, work, and die within organizational frameworks, be they formal or informal. The individual can become more effective merely by recognizing this fact and understanding some of the ways in which organizations operate.

I. THE MICRO APPROACH

A. The Importance of the Individual and the Psychological Contract

In Chapter 3, we described several models of motivation. These included both content and expectancy models. Although no model can yet precisely explain human behavior, several points are clear. First, the individual is a subsystem within the organization. Second, every individual is *always* motivated by his or her own particular set of needs. Therefore, no individual can "motivate" another. Since motivation is a process internal to the individual, it can be "tapped" by someone else only by changing the situation. In other words, the clock-watcher who leaves promptly at 5 P.M. is highly motivated—to leave on time. From the organizational point of view, such motivation may be dysfunctional. Rather than directly trying to get the individual to give up the clock-watching habit, an attempt should be made to transfer the "motivation" to more functional outlets by changing the work situation, i.e., by enriching the job. But this does not mean that the individual will now become "happy." A person is a perennially wanting being, and as soon as one set of needs is satisfied, another set emerges. However, there is a vast difference between the "mini-gripe" (the quality of food in the cafeteria) and the "maxigripe" (parts shortages or poor scheduling). The "minigripe" is much easier to handle than the "maxigripe," but the latter signifies a much healthier organization.

One of the most powerful influences on an individual's emotional response to work is the psychological contract. People learn very quickly about the psychological contract and react accordingly. If it is a rational-legal contract, the individual will put in a "fair day's work for a fair day's pay," although the person's concept of a fair day's work may differ from the organization's. If an organization wants loyalty and commitment from an employee, by contrast, it needs to set up normative contract.

In Chapter 4, we discussed the concepts of perception and communication. The perceptual process is an active one. Since the individual is flooded with different sensations, perception is *selective;* not all of the inputs are responded to. Because everyone's background is unique and because motivational needs differ in intensity at various times, each person perceives the world differently. As a result, people behave in ways that make sense to them *as they perceive the world.*

One way to improve the perceptual process is through improving communications. A common fallacy is to describe communications in a judgmental fashion, e.g., "good" or "bad." In actual fact, however, communications are neither good nor bad. Rather, they are effective or ineffective. Frequently, someone will say that two people (or groups) are not communicating with each other; in fact, the communications are very clear, but they are ineffective.

B. The Importance of the Group in the Organization

In Chapter 5, we discussed the ways in which the group affects individual and organizational behavior. We first discussed the group as a system and then considered the group as a subsystem of the total organization. We examined why and how groups are formed. Next, we considered the internal operation of groups, including leadership and the importance of group cohesion and solidarity. Cohesive groups can be helpful to the organization, if helpfulness is one of the group norms or standards of behavior. Group effectiveness can be improved by examining group task, group maintenance, and self-serving activities. We also made specific recommendations for using groups for various purposes and objectives, e.g., interacting, nominal, and delphi groups.

Chapter 6 moved from the group itself to a consideration of intergroup interaction. At times conflict between groups can be helpful, constructive, and productive. At other times it can be dysfunctional to the groups themselves and to the organization as a larger system. By understanding the causes of conflict, one can learn to handle conflict in positive ways.

II. THE MACRO APPROACH

A. The Organization as a Total System

Organizations can be considered as systems with a number of subsystems, each of which acts on and affects the other subsystems. Explicitly recognizing that any organization is a complex of subsystems makes it more difficult to apply what has been called the "one best way," or "'single-cause solution," to organizational problems. Therefore, we have stressed the need to view organizations and their problems from three perspectives. Although such a separation is artificial, it provides a useful framework for understanding the operation of organizations. Only by simultaneously considering the structural-design, work-flow, and human factors can one deal realistically and successfully with the complexities of organizational life. Thus the most successful attempts to improve organizations take into account all three perspectives.

Just as unidimensional approaches are likely to fail, so too are model-building and operations-research approaches which neglect the inputs of human behavior. The failures occur because the output-based models, which work well in *mechanistic* systems, are not valid for use with *social* systems. Similarly, many attempts at computerized, management information systems, which cut across departmental lines, fail. They fail because they concentrate on the flow perspective, neglecting the structural-design and/or work-flow perspectives.

B. The Need for Better Understanding of Deviation-Reducing and Deviation-Amplifying Forces

Organizations exist in a changing environment. Some organizations exist in a more turbulent environment than others do. Yet every organization can be considered as a subsystem within the larger environment, as was discussed in Chapter 9. What occurs in the environment affects the organization. However, organizations and/or their component subsystems seek to find a relatively stable balance, or equilibrium. This process is made more difficult by the action and reaction between forces seeking to bring about change and those seeking to maintain the relative, current status of the organization.

The concept of force-field analysis helps us to understand the interplay between deviation-reducing and deviation-amplifying forces. Change in itself is neither good nor bad. The manager, however, must know and be able to clearly identify the difference between the proactive and reactive forces. In addition, it is important to realize that the organization *requires* the two opposing sets of forces. Proactive forces allow the organization to change and adapt; reactive forces offer a restraint to wild organizational shifts in direction and purpose.

Organizational conflict is inevitable. There are three basic ways of handling conflict: (1) forcing, or edicting; (2) smoothing, or sweeping the problem under the rug; and (3) confrontation, or bringing the facts out on the table and discussing them openly. This last technique is the most useful, because it recognizes the validity of feelings and emotions and asserts that their denial is a type of smoothing. Thus under normal circumstances, the best way of handling conflict and change is through confrontation, which "faces the facts" of feelings and emotions.

C. Techniques for Improving Organizational Competence

Much of Part III of the text dealt with approaches to improving both organizational effectiveness and efficiency. Such approaches are of several forms.

Contingency theory of organizational design represents a major breakthrough. Whereas structure and design were once regarded as "given," in contingency theory they are regarded as dependent on the climate and environment in which the organization finds itself. We are really only beginning to see the implications of this concept. The next few years will bring a great expansion of research and thought in this area. The continuation of an adaptive, competent organization may require a continual review and reexamination of the structure and design of the organization. The review will need to be in terms of the nature, type, and state of the organization's relevant environment and the nature of the continuous interchange between the organization and its environment.

The problem of how best to design an organization has concerned management theorists for decades. This problem, and the research necessary to more clearly define the type of structure that is optimum for an organization at a given time, will receive an increasing amount of attention, and deservedly so. Although attention to organizational structure and design may be a major consideration in the survival of specific organizations, only now are we beginning to develop systematic and applied methods for examining this problem in greater depth.

Sociotechnical approaches are beginning to be more widely considered in the United States. This type of effort involves redesigning work and information flows to more appropriately fit what we know about people and their motivation. Although the term "sociotechnical systems" is not a new one, the application of this approach has been used much more widely in European and other countries than in the United States. Two of the better known of such programs are the redesign of work in Saab and Volvo in Sweden, especially at the Volvo body-assembly plant in Kalmar.

Organization development programs are becoming much more widely accepted and used. OD emphasizes managing change in ways that are helpful not only to the organization, but also to the people involved. Since the first edition of this book, the number of organizations using OD has increased greatly. Quality-of-life programs have been established at federal and state levels. The number of universities offering courses in OD has also greatly increased. Research efforts have also increased, not only in number but also in variety and sophistication. The fact that a number of people are working full time doing OD work in the United States Army is only one indication of the increasing thrust of this approach.

As methods of increasing organizational competency, contingency theories, sociotechnical approaches, and OD approaches are clearly closely related. Indeed, the three approaches represent our three primary perspectives: structural-design, work-flow, and human.

III. THE MANAGER OF THE FUTURE

The manager is the most important link among the subsystems of the organization. The manager has at least three different roles. One is to act as a *participant* in the work-flow process. The second is to act as a *leader* to subordinates, including directing, responding, and representing. The third role is to act as a *monitor*, both horizontally and vertically, both within and outside the individual subsystem. Managers actually spend more time interfacing with others in the lateral work-flow process than they do with their own subordinates. The manager, as leader, can exert several types of power and influence: legitimate, expert, referent, reward, and coercive. According to contingency theory, each of these types of power is appropriate at different times.

Since change is inevitable, the roles, tasks, and characteristics of the successful manager of the future will also undergo modification.

A. Greater Ability to Deal with Conflict and Change

The increasing use of project management and task forces will require that the manager of the future spend even more time in the work-flow process. The manager will probably belong to a variety of groups and interact with a wider variety of people. At the same time, organizational change and redesign will increase through the adaptive-coping cycle. As these changes lead to more and more employee participation at all levels, the manager of the future will have to rely increasingly on social skills. Because of the increased interaction and use of temporary groups, the successful manager of the future will need to be able to move quickly and easily into new groups, develop working arrangements, and be prepared to work with people more quickly. Even now, several studies show that managers rate as most valuable the behavioral science courses taken in college.[1] Since the amount of working with and through people is likely to increase rather than decrease, the manager of the future will not be able to rely as heavily on position power as was done in the past. Thus knowledge of the behavioral sciences will become increasingly important.

B. Greater Tolerance for Ambiguity

According to the bureaucratic model, organizations could operate successfully under set rules. Managers could, essentially, survive by following the rules. Although the bureaucratic model can and should be followed in stable organizations or subsystems, those existing in uncertain, quickly changing environments must be able to respond quickly to change. Therefore, the manager must be able to tolerate ambiguity and to make decisions even when much of the data are unknown or inaccessible. If computers can handle many of the routine, repetitive problems, the manager will be freed to contend with the vague, the general, and the unprogrammable data.

C. Sharply Improved Diagnostic Skills

With the present knowledge, the use of mathematical and other models is still severely limited and will continue to be so in the foreseeable future. In addition, the inevitability of change will force the manager to greatly improve his or her ability to identify and diagnose problems. This is, of course, closely related to greater tolerance for ambiguity. When resistance to change does appear, it should not be considered as something to be overcome, but rather as a signal—a red flag—that something is going wrong. This means better diagnosis and therefore more easily and quickly putting new ideas into effect. For example, the engineering manager who was able to "overlook" a 300% increase in productivity showed no diagnostic or problem-solving skills at all. Rather, he was being highly reactive and resistant to change. In other words, one of the biggest jobs of the manager of the future will be to improve diagnostic and problem-solving skills so as to reduce the forces opposing change.

D. Managing within a Larger Environment

The modern organization is becoming not only larger, more complex, and multinational, but also increasingly involved in social and ecological issues, as we pointed out in Chapter 9. The manager of the future must become more aware of the fact that the organization is part of a much larger system. The boundaries between social systems become blurred when this occurs. The manager will have to develop working relationships with other organizations and the public and governmental sectors of the economy. More and more, public policy is impacting on organizations. This means that the manager will have to walk the fine line between maintaining responsibility for the organization (or a subsystem of the organization) while at the same time carrying out public policy, e.g., employment of minorities.

E. Broader Education and Viewpoint

There is an increasing tendency for managers to become more "professional" and to receive more and broader management training. Such training is especially important for those who have "come up through the ranks" and are suddenly expected to adopt a broader outlook. The "knowledge explosion" creates the obsolescence of current knowledge. Relevant new knowledge *is* being generated at a faster rate. The successful manager will be the one who can do a better job of continuing self-education and do a better and faster job of importing new knowledge into the organization of all levels. This reduces the lag between the generation and the application of knowledge. Managerial personnel must make a determined effort to discard old facts and ideas and replace them with more modern concepts. If not, they will become managerial illiterates—unable to relearn and to assimilate new ideas.

Managers of the future will need to be knowledgeable about the three perspectives we have discussed throughout the text. This is not to imply that each manager must become an expert on computers or on model building or on the behavioral sciences. Nevertheless, the manager will certainly need to be more conversant and knowledgeable about these fields than the average manager is today. Just as "war is too important to leave to the generals," so too "computers are too important to leave to computer people."

To summarize, continuing education is important because:

1. Government and governmental intervention will be more influential, and organizations and the government will become more interdependent.

2. The manager of the future must have greater knowledge about psychology and the behavioral sciences, world affairs, and the humanities.

3. He or she must be a catalyst who can integrate human resources and information technology.

4. With the increasing use of the computer to handle highly routine data analysis, the manager of the future will be freer to consider both the short- and long-range implications of decisions.

5. Organizations need to *manage* change. Organizations will become more flexible in their ability to respond to a rapidly changing environment.

REVIEW

1. This chapter lists some of what we feel to be the book's most important concepts. Develop your own list of the points that have been most important to you.

2. Apply the systems concept of an organization to a university and describe why a particular individual or group within the university has experienced certain successes and failures.

3. List (and be prepared to defend) what you consider to be the five most important questions a manager can ask about any given situation. These questions should also be applicable to a situation that might occur in the year 2000.

4. What is the contingency theory of leadership? Will it work for all types of managerial positions? Could the job of the president of the United States be accomplished according to such a theory?

5. In your present organizational situation, what could be done in the area of "job enrichment"? What kinds of needs are being unfulfilled? Would a normative rather than a psychological contract help to improve your situation?

6. Using the organizational structure of your college or university, outline a management information system that would be adaptable to a change in the organizational environment of your school. Be sure to include feedback loops to allow for modifications necessitated by reactions to output from the external environment.

REFERENCE

1. R. F. Pearse, *Manager to Manager: What Managers Think of Management Development*, New York: American Management Association, 1974; L. Ward, Harvard University, personal communication.

APPENDIX:

CASE STUDIES

CHANGING WORK PROCEDURES

This is a four-part case. It is strongly recommended that you not read beyond any single part until your instructor gives you the signal to begin.

PART 1

The Harwood Manufacturing Company, located in West Virginia, produces pajamas, a process requiring frequent changes in production routine. All operators (mostly female) are on a piece-rate basis, with a standard, or minimum, of 60 units per hour, a rate that had been determined by a time study. (In other words, all work was converted to standard units for each task.) A woman exceeding the standard receives commensurate pay, e.g., a woman doing 25% over the standard rate is paid 25% above her base pay. In addition, the operators receive a special transfer bonus when they are transferred from one set of duties to another to ensure that they do not lose any money.

When task changes occur, however, a number of related events take place simultaneously. First, the workers whose tasks have been changed show evidence of hostility toward both their immediate supervisor and the organization. Second, their work rate decreases and is slow to reach the standard rate again. The recovery rate is so slow, in fact, that a new operator has a faster learning time than an experienced operator. Only about 38% of the operators whose jobs have been altered eventually reach the standard; the other 62% either quit during the relearning period or fail to reach the standard work rate.

PART 2

After analyzing these findings, the company decided to set up a series of experiments. They picked four groups that seemed to be about equal in productivity and capacity. Group 1, the "no participation" control group, followed the usual routine when a factory job was changed, i.e., the job was modified by the production department, and a new piece rate was established. Normal procedures were followed by bringing the group together to explain that competitive conditions necessitated the change, and the new piece rate was thoroughly explained by the time-study expert, who also answered any questions that workers might have.

Adapted from L. Coch and J. R. P. French, Jr., "Overcoming Resistance to Change," *Human Relations* 1 (1948): 512–532.

The members of Group 2 were brought together, the reasons for the change in production methods were explained in a rather dramatic fashion, and the necessity for cost reduction was shared with the group. Then management outlined a plan to eliminate unnecessary frills and fancy work from the garment by studying the present job, eliminating work that was unnecessary, training several operators in the new methods, and establishing piece-work rates by time studies on operators who had been specially trained. The group informally approved the plan and chose the operators who were to receive the special training. Everyone was cooperative and made a number of suggestions. After training, these specially trained operators instructed the other workers in the procedures for doing the new job.

All of the operators in Groups 3 and 4 participated in the change process. Again, the need for a change in methods to reduce costs was made dramatically clear. Since these two groups were smaller than Group 2, all of the operators were involved in planning and designing the new jobs, and they all were studied by the time-study observer. The "total participation" was so effective that the stenographer had difficulty in keeping up with the many suggestions and recommendations. The two groups approved the revised plan informally, although no official or formal decision was made.

PART 3

What were the results on productivity of the three different methods? The nonparticipation, or control, group began with an initial productivity of about 45 units and continued at about this level during the trial period. The usual resistance to the change occurred immediately after the change and continued during the 32 days of the recording period. In addition, there was a great deal of hostility and aggression against management. When grievances about the piece rate were filed, the standard was rechecked and found to be too "loose" rather than too tight. In the first 40 days, 17% of the workers quit, and those remaining never reached the standard production rate of 60 units a hour.

Group 2, with its specially trained "representatives," averaged 61 units per hour at the end of 14 days. Their productivity climbed steadily to a high of about 68 or 69 units at the end of the 40 days. The researchers felt that the figures for the group's learning period and productivity would have been even higher had work been less scarce during the first week of the study. The workers' attitude toward management, the methods engineer, and the supervisor was generally cooperative.

Groups 3 and 4, the total-participation groups, recovered more rapidly, and their productivity was considerably higher than that of either the control group or the representative group. One of the groups reached a temporary high of about 80 units, although the average for the total period was about

70–73 units per hour, an increase in productivity of about 14%. No workers in Groups 3 and 4 quit during the 40 days that records were kept on this variable.

PART 4

After the experiment, the control group was broken up, and individual members of the group were reassigned to jobs scattered throughout the plant. About ten weeks later, the 13 members of the group that still remained were brought together again for a second experiment, which consisted of giving the group members a new job based on the total-participation technique. The approach was much like that already explained for the two participation groups of the first experiment, and the new job was roughly comparable in complexity to the one they had had in the first experiment.

The result of the second experiment with the 13 remaining members of the original control, nonexperimental, group was in startling contrast to the first. Under the total-participation method, the group started at a productivity level of about 55 units per hour (versus about 45 units in the first experiment). The productivity of the second group climbed and at the end of 18 days had reached a level of about 75 units. (In the first experiment, productivity had leveled off after 32 days at about 45 units per hour.) During the second experiment there was no evidence of the hostility and aggression that these same operators had shown previously, and there was no turnover such as had occurred earlier.

Some time later, a similar experiment was conducted in Norway.* In this study, which was fashioned after the original Harwood study, the researchers found *no* significant differences between the productivity of the participative and the nonparticipative management conditions. In other words, an approach effective in the United States did not have the same positive result in Norway.

DISCUSSION QUESTIONS

1. Why was this experiment a success in the United States?

2. Why did it fail in Norway in 1959?

3. Many similar projects in Norway have been successful in the 1970s. What could make the difference?

---

* J. R. P. French, Jr., J. Israel, and D. Ās, "An Experiment on Participation in a Norwegian Factory," *Human Relations* **13**, 1 (1960): 3–19.

CLEANING THE TANK

BACKGROUND

The Acme Company employs about 20 people, including 12 production workers. Because the company works with precious metals, all residue is pumped into a specially designed settling tank before the liquids go into the normal sewage system. Once or twice a year, depending on production, the tank must be drained and the sludge shoveled out into barrels to be taken to another plant for recovery of the precious metals. Unfortunately, because of the chemical process involved, removing the sludge is much like cleaning a septic tank —it is a thoroughly unpleasant, dirty, smelly, distasteful, and filthy process. Because the tank cannot be cleaned during normal working hours, whoever cleans the tank works on an overtime basis.

Because this is a role-playing case, you should not read ahead until your instructor has selected the two people who are to play the two roles.

ROLE FOR CHRIS

According to Acme custom, the person with the lowest seniority has the task of cleaning out the sludge tank. This worked equitably, as far as you can tell, when the company had normal turnover. But since jobs have been hard to find recently, turnover has been low. You have been on the job for three years and have had to clean out the tank five times. Bill, your predecessor, had to clean the tank only once, as did Alice, who preceded Bill. After cleaning the tank, you feel dirty and unclean for several days, no matter how often or for how long you take a shower. Besides, it makes you almost physically ill while you are doing it, and afterwards you fight with your spouse and are unpleasant to the children.

You feel strongly that you have done more than your share and that it is now time to let someone else "do the dirty work." You don't care whether it is a matter of drawing straws or flipping a coin or what, but you've cleaned the tank for the last time, and you're tired of the unnecessary ribbing you take for always getting stuck with the job.

You notice that the tank will need to be cleaned within the next several days, and this time, you are really going to "have it out" with the boss. You are under a union contract, and nothing in the contract says that the person with the least seniority has to clean the tank. Just because it has been done that way in the past doesn't mean it has to stay that way.

ROLE FOR MICKEY, PRODUCTION FOREMAN

You notice that the sludge tank needs cleaning out, and you are about to tell Chris to do it in the next day or so. You have been with the plant ever since it opened 15 years ago, and the person with the lowest seniority has always been given the job; now it is a "normal shop practice." Therefore, you have no hesitation about telling Chris, who has the lowest seniority, to do it. Besides, although a good, productive worker, Chris has an attitude you just don't like. However, you just can't quite put your finger on it. In the past few weeks, this attitude has somehow grown worse, and you don't really know why. Other than Chris, you have a good, loyal, cohesive work force, and most of the people have been with you for a long time.

EXERCISE CAREER VALUES

A. PURPOSE

In order to "motivate" someone else, it is necessary to know something about his or her own individual and unique needs. The purpose of this exercise is to see how well you can estimate some of the attitudes and feelings the members of your study group have toward their career values and also to provide you with feedback about others' perceptions of you.

B. PROCEDURE

First, read the definitions of various types of career values. Then you will be asked to rank both your own career values as you perceive them and those of other members of your study group. Finally, you and the others in your group will announce and discuss the rankings. The discussion is the most important part of the exercise, since it will enable you to give and obtain valuable feedback about how you perceive others in the group and how the others perceive you.

DEFINITIONS OF CAREER VALUES

Step 1: Read Definitions

Career values can be divided into a number of different areas. Listed below are nine such areas that involve a number of varying aims that an individual may have in life.

A. Top management The individual wants to rise to the top in an organization and be a high-level manager, even though disliked by subordinates.

B. Competence The person wants to be a competent specialist rather than a manager, in order to make maximum use of his or her intellectual problem-solving abilities and to see the applied results of this work.

C. Affiliation The person wants to contribute to the satisfaction of others and to be helpful to them.

Adapted from B. Bass, "A Program of Exercises," Pittsburgh: Management Development Associates, 1966.

D. Leisure The individual wants the time and opportunity to really enjoy life, even if this means giving up some income potential with a lower overall rate of earning.

E. Security The person wants a job that is congenial and ensures a stable and secure future.

F. Risk The person wants a career that has growth potential, although there is a correspondingly high possibility of a financial loss.

G. Creativity The individual wants a career that permits him or her to be original, innovative, and creative.

H. Independence The person wants the opportunity to be free from supervision by others.

I. Analysis The person wants to probe deeply and thoroughly into problems; is more concerned with the "why" than with the application of results.

Step 2. Complete Career-Values Ranking

First, rank your own career values. Give a "1" to the value or goal that is most important to your own career satisfaction and write it in the first column of Table 1. For example, if you decide that "risk" is most important, place the number "1" across from the letter "F" in the first column. If, on the other hand, you feel that "leisure" is most important to you, place the "1" opposite the letter "D." Then decide which career value is next most important to you and give it a rank of "2." Continue this process until you have ranked all nine career values.

Alternatively, begin with the most important, giving it a rank of "1," and then rank the least important, giving it a value of "9," thus working toward the middle. Do not tie any ranks. If you have to, guess; usually your first impression is the most accurate.

Now, at the top of the second column, write the name of the person sitting on your immediate right. Without any consultation, rank that person's career values *as you perceive them.* Again, your first impression is generally the most accurate, so work quickly. When you have completed this ranking, use the third column for the next person on your right, etc., until you have completed all the rankings and recorded them in Table 1. Only when your group has ranked every person should you proceed to Step 3.

Step 3: Announce, Record, and Discuss Career-Value Rankings

As soon as everyone in your study group has finished all of the rankings, you should begin announcing the rankings each of you has assigned to yourself and to the others. First, enter in the *parentheses* of Table 1 each person's *self-*

ratings. As each member of the study group reports about you, enter those rankings in Table 2. You should repeat your own self-ranking (Table 1, Column 1) in Table 2, Column 1, to make subsequent comparison easier. To get an idea of how the others see you, you should complete Table 2 by totaling the values assigned to each row (excluding your own self-ranking) and finding the mean value. To do this, divide each total by the number of the members in your study group (excluding yourself). When you have completed this step, proceed to "discussion of rankings."

C. DISCUSSION OF RANKINGS

1. Raters

There are four interrelated reasons why you made the rankings you did:

1. You are accurate in your perception of others, even on short acquaintance;
2. You "project" your own feelings onto others;
3. Your impressions about others are based on a few cues or mannerisms;
4. You are influenced by "social" factors and rank yourself and others in what you think is a socially acceptable way.

2. Ratees

Look at the ranks that others have given you. In many cases, you will find a great deal of "inaccuracy," i.e., their rankings do not agree with yours. Yet this may be the way you "come across" to others. You should then ask yourself, "Why?" Ask the other members of your group to give you feedback about their reasons for their ratings; you will find it helpful and illuminating.

3. Actual Life

One of the frequent comments following this exercise is that there has been insufficient time to get to know one another. In one sense, this is true. You have been together for only a limited period of time. Yet in real life, we are frequently asked to make decisions about others with less data than you currently have. For example, the average campus interview lasts for about 20 minutes. You should ask yourself how this exercise can be applied to real life. For example, if you "projected," that is, if you showed a strong tendency to describe others as you see yourself, this may have a number of implications. You may, as a manager, try to "motivate" others with those factors that motivate you, although these may not apply to others. At meetings and conferences, you may "dance to your own music," that is, you may be insensitive to the needs, motivations, and reactions of others.

Table 1 Career value rankings *by you* of yourself and *by you* of everyone else in your study group

(Do not write anything in the parentheses until directed to do so in Step 3)

	(1) Yourself	(2)	(3)	(4)	(5)	(6)
	Ratee name	Ratee name	Ratee name	Ratee name	Ratee name	Ratee name
A. Top management	——	——(*)——( )	( )	( )	( )	( )
B. Competence	——	__( )__( )	( )	( )	( )	( )
C. Affiliation	——	__( )__( )	( )	( )	( )	( )
D. Leisure	——	__( )__( )	( )	( )	( )	( )
E. Security	——	__( )__( )	( )	( )	( )	( )
F. Risk	——	__( )__( )	( )	( )	( )	( )
G. Creativity	——	__( )__( )	( )	( )	( )	( )
H. Independence	——	__( )__( )	( )	( )	( )	( )
I. Analysis	——	__( )__( )	( )	( )	( )	( )

* Parentheses are for inserting values assigned to you by each other ratee.

Table 2 How other study group members rank you

	(1) Yourself	(2)	(3)	(4)	(5)	(6)
	Rater name	Rater name	Rater name	Rater name	Rater name	Rater name
A. Top management	——	——	——	——	——	——
B. Competence	——	——	——	——	——	——
C. Affiliation	——	——	——	——	——	——
D. Leisure	——	——	——	——	——	——
E. Security	——	——	——	——	——	——
F. Risk	——	——	——	——	——	——
G. Creativity	——	——	——	——	——	——
H. Independence	——	——	——	——	——	——
I. Analysis	——	——	——	——	——	——

Table 1 (cont.)

	(7)	(8)	(9)	(10)	(11)	(12)	
	Ratee name	Ratee name	Ratee name	Ratee name	Ratee name	Ratee name	
A.	___(	)___(	)___(	)___(	)___(	)___(	)
B.	___(	)___(	)___(	)___(	)___(	)___(	)
C.	___(	)___(	)___(	)___(	)___(	)___(	)
D.	___(	)___(	)___(	)___(	)___(	)___(	)
E.	___(	)___(	)___(	)___(	)___(	)___(	)
F.	___(	)___(	)___(	)___(	)___(	)___(	)
G.	___(	)___(	)___(	)___(	)___(	)___(	)
H.	___(	)___(	)___(	)___(	)___(	)___(	)
I.	___(	)___(	)___(	)___(	)___(	)___(	)

Table 2 (cont.)

	(7)	(8)	(9)	(10)	(11)	(12)	Total (row) (Exclude Col. 1)	Mean (row)
	Rater name	Rater name	Rater name	Rater name	Rater name	Rater name		
A.	___	___	___	___	___	___	___	___
B.	___	___	___	___	___	___	___	___
C.	___	___	___	___	___	___	___	___
D.	___	___	___	___	___	___	___	___
E.	___	___	___	___	___	___	___	___
F.	___	___	___	___	___	___	___	___
G.	___	___	___	___	___	___	___	___
H.	___	___	___	___	___	___	___	___
I.	___	___	___	___	___	___	___	___

AN EXERCISE IN
RATING SUPERVISORY BEHAVIOR

Today, we are going to discuss and rate first-line supervisory behavior. You are asked to *work as a group,* to *discuss,* and to *rate* the eight statements given below which might describe a supervisor's behavior.

The group should take about 10–15 minutes for the discussion and rating. You may take longer if you feel it necessary.

Place a "1" in front of the statement the *group* decides is the most important characteristic of the good supervisor, a "2" in front of the statement the group decides is the next most important, etc. Rate all eight behaviors.

You must work as a group—talk together and rate together.

Do not choose a formal discussion leader.

Record the rating as the group decides it.

Now: Read through the statements carefully and then begin discussing and rating *as soon as you are ready.*

_____ The supervisor praises work when it is a job well done.

_____ The supervisor communicates the reasons for important decisions to subordinates.

_____ The supervisor encourages subordinates to make suggestions about his or her policies and practices.

_____ The supervisor consults with subordinates before making changes affecting their work.

_____ The supervisor shows no favoritism.

_____ The supervisor reprimands subordinates in private, not in public.

_____ The supervisor delegates authority to subordinates on matters directly affecting their work.

_____ The supervisor backs up subordinates when they are in trouble.

THE EXPERIMENTAL PROGRAM

BACKGROUND

Over a period of several years, one plant of a large corporation had purchased a number of numerically controlled lathes, each costing about $250,000. Each "numerically controlled" lathe had its own minicomputer to control the operation of the machine and to reproduce the actions of a skilled lathe operator. Despite management's expectations and a great deal of time, trouble, and attention, productivity leveled off at about 28% effectiveness, and the scrap rate was extremely high.

After discussion with the personnel department, an innovative manager made the crucial decision to turn the problem over to the workers, and this decision led to "the experimental program." Scheduled to last one year, the program focused on seven automatic lathes in the middle of the production floor. Twenty-one machinists and three "lead hands" were selected to participate in the program. There was to be no foreman in the work area, intershift communication would be facilitated by a 15-minute paid overtime, and participants would receive a 10% bonus over their normal, straight-time earnings for participating in the study.

The initial months of the program were chaotic. Utilization, productivity, and worker attitudes plummeted to record lows. Many of the workers were confused about their new role expectations, whereas others seemed to be testing management's sincerity. Workers in "support" groups who were not otherwise participating in the program showed hostility to those in the special group. In addition, problems were caused by the extensive training required. Finally, there were problems with the quality of both incoming components and the computer tapes. All of these difficulties resulted in the uneven performance of the experimental group during the first two years of the study.

However, things began to stabilize when the union became a participant in the management of the program. The union's participation resulted from its dispute with management over the selection of a new work leader, which in turn led to the activation of a union-management steering committee for the program. A union counsellor's boastful remark that "too much management"

Adapted from a true case prepared by a manager (Austin deGroat), a union representative (Peter Teel), and personnel representatives (Robert Curry and David Burton).

was inhibiting progress resulted in the program manager's reassignment and the subsequent transferral of the foreman out of the group; thus all immediate supervision was removed from the experimental group. Finally, management recognized the validity of the workers' assertion that *group* rather than the traditional individual measurements were most appropriate for managing this particular group.

Within three months, the group's performance had surpassed management's highest expectations. Machine utilization jumped from 40% to 70%, and scrap rates fell to new lows. Quality soared, and "operators" finally got involved. With no foreman or upper-level manager to "guide" them, the operators in the group soon were stepping forward to take the "role" of production supervisors, methods planners, production control foreman, and process-control engineers to deal successfully with the complex "support" systems around them. To demonstrate what they could do, program members eliminated a "backlog," brought in complex new work with unprecedented ease, and modeled worker-management relationships that quickly brought top-management attention, although not all of the latter was positive.

In 1971, the third year of the study, machine utilization dropped to a fairly consistent rate of about 60%, not because the operators were incapable of achieving higher productivity, but because this was the rate at which new pieces were coming in. Management "support" jobs around the unit had been eliminated, i.e., production planning and control people, methods planners, process engineers, the foreman, and the next higher levels of management.

Because of the program's success, management began to seriously consider extending the process to the rest of the automatic-lathe operators in the building. Management had been given enough data so that they could make a firm decision to institutionalize the experimental program, at least for the original members, by establishing a formal job classification and rate of pay.

ROLE-PLAYING SITUATIONS

With the background information that has been provided, you should be able to assume one of the roles described in the following pages. Now that the experiment has survived the initial chaos and uncertainty, jobs must be defined, fair rates of pay must be determined, and a decision must be reached about expanding the program into other areas of the company.

Management Team

The management team is charged with negotiating a job classification and pay rate for members of the experimental program. As a member of this team, it is clear to you, as it is to the others, that significant advances in worker-management relations have resulted from the program. It is also apparent that management's relationships with the union have improved significantly, and this is especially important in light of the plantwide and companywide strikes that have occurred in recent years. There are, however, several serious problems that must be ironed out with the union. Among these problems are the following:

1. fear that the last seven months of the program have been only a lengthy "up" period for the program and that a "down" period will occur again;
2. genuine concern about the dimensions of change, i.e., it may be possible to extend this type of "management" beyond the lathe operators;
3. uncertainty about whether you can measure a group's progress and provide pay rewards without adopting incentive pay plans, which you do not want to do because of your past experience in the organization;
4. genuine inability to peg the new job into the existing pay structure for hourly workers in the corporation—you cannot use the accepted "skill-care-effort" approach, and you are uncertain how to determine the job's value;
5. a sense of foreboding that "we" may be stepping out too far ahead of the rest of the company, especially since corporate headquarters has been sending "signals" about this;
6. concern that over the long term, the productivity gains may be eroded;
7. concern about how to manage the program, which seems to call for a "new" kind of foreman-manager, but you don't know where to find such a person or what his or her function should be;
8. a lingering gut feeling that "everybody needs a boss," despite the program's success without one.

As you enter negotiations with the union, you feel distressed. Looked to for leadership and an "answer," you are instead unsure and you do not have "the" answer that will put the issue to rest. You can't "cave in." You can't give away the shop. You want to reap the program's gains.

Roles within the Management Team

Employee relations manager This person, in charge of compensation programs for hourly and salaried employees, is a traditionalist who believes in the companywide job-evaluation program that emphasizes skill, care, and effort as guidelines for measuring the value of production workers' jobs. This manager feels utterly frustrated about how to "measure," or evaluate, the worth of work done by the members of the experimental program—some of their activity is "exempt," some is "salaried," and some is "hourly."

Employee relations manager for union relations   A creative innovator, this manager believes that people want to work in a changed environment. This person feels that the union is ready to work in a progressive approach with management to solve the many problems of managing the changed work force of the 1970s and to alleviate the union/management distrust typical of the immediate past. However, the employee relations manager fears that daring and innovation may incur corporate hostility.

Program manager   Creative, willing to take risks, and aggressive, the program manager has lived with the program and watched it mature as "controls" were eased. Committed emotionally to the Theory Y style of management, the program manager will press very hard to have the program implemented on a broader basis throughout the plant.

Plant manager   Unsure about what the experimental program is or why it is working, the plant manager is convinced that it is making very impressive productivity gains. Shop-operations managers in other buildings are asking about the program. The plant manager wants to implement the program on a broader basis, but is concerned about what will happen to displaced management personnel should the program be extended to other areas.

Union Negotiating Brief

The responsibility of the union local's negotiating committee is to work with local company management toward a just settlement of the experimental program. According to the agreement when the program was initiated, the 21 machinists are at job level 19 and receive a bonus of 10%. One operator, the designated tool setter, receives nothing extra. The three lead hands, one per shift, are paid at job level 22 plus 10%. In addition, an overtime factor of 2.5 hours a week allows a 15-minute overlap between shifts, which facilitates communications.

Under the terms of the initial agreement, the experiment would be evaluated after one year, and both the company and the union maintained the right to terminate the experiment at any time by mutual agreement. After the program had been evaluated, the company asked for an extension of the program because there were no meaningful data. The union agreed to an indefinte extension because in its view, the experiment had made some significant gains and was, indeed, a success.

The program's accomplishments have given the union some strong negotiating points:

1. The scrap and rework costs have been reduced from $8000 per month to $3000 per month while productivity has more than doubled.

2. Machine utilization in the first year rose from 28% to 45%. Now, in the second year, utilization is regularly 50–60%, depending on input from other parts of the plant, and you know that machine utilization can go even higher.

3. Operator attitudes have considerably improved, and absenteeism has been reduced. It is obvious that the operators' responsibilities have been considerably increased.

4. Various management levels have openly expressed their belief that the pilot program is an unqualified success.

After job classification and pay rates have been determined, the union must decide how seniority and bumping, upgrading, and other transfers will be handled for the experimental group and for other areas if the program is expanded.

Process Observer's Guide

During the exercise, you are to make notes on the processes operating at various times within the management team, the union committee, and the combined negotiating committee. Be prepared to discuss with all parties the nature and significance of your observations in the negotiations. (You may want to refer to the section in Chapter 5 on observing groups.)

GROUP CONFLICT

Three different groups—marketing, research and development, and manufacturing—were located in the same building, but reported to different bosses in the corporate organizational structure. Animosity and suspicion existed among the three groups, and their managers seldom spoke to one another. Indeed, on one occasion, the manufacturing manager locked the office door while the marketing manager stood outside pounding on the door and demanding to be let in. The research-and-development group felt that marketing was doing a poor job of predicting the market and that manufacturing was systematically lousing up "good designs," e.g., "The people over there in manufacturing don't know what they are doing." In return, the manufacturing group felt that the research-and-development people were arrogant, did not know or realize manufacturing problems, and were providing designs that were almost impossible to manufacture. They also felt that marketing was establishing a selling price for the equipment manufactured that did not include any profit for the plant.

A reorganization took place, and a new manager was put in charge of the three groups. The new manager told them, in no uncertain terms, that from now on, they were to "get along with one another." The three managers merely nodded their heads and left the room.

DISCUSSION QUESTIONS

1. What do you think the results of the new manager's ultimatum will be? In the short term? In the long term?
2. Was this the best approach that could have been used?

THE HOWARD COMPANY

This is a role-playing case with three parts. Do not read past the introduction until your instructor has assigned you the role you are to take, and then read *only* that role.

INTRODUCTION

The Howard Company, a large conglomerate, manufactures a variety of products in about 30 plants scattered across the country. Purchasing has always been done locally by individual plants. However, the company has been steadily growing, and the president of Howard has recently employed an experienced new man as vice-president of purchasing. The president felt that closer coordination of purchasing would result in substantial savings.

After several weeks on the job, the new man, Mr. Leavitt, decided that one of the best ways to bring about substantial economy was to have all contracts or purchases of $10,000 or more coordinated and approved by company headquarters. The idea was presented to the president, who in turn got the approval of the board of directors. Mr. Leavitt then sent out a memo to the plant purchasing agents informing them that from then on they were to notify the vice-president at least a week before any contract exceeding $10,000 was signed.

During the next months almost every plant acknowledged receipt of the memo and promised to cooperate. But although the company was in the beginning of its peak buying season, Mr. Leavitt received no notices that any large contracts were being negotiated.

MR. LEAVITT, VICE-PRESIDENT OF PURCHASING

You are competent in your field, with a Ph.D. in economics, a number of publications (including two books) to your credit, and 15 years of experience in a number of organizations. Since you have always been successful in making substantial savings in purchasing wherever you have worked, you are confident that the new policy will work at Howard, even though you expect a lot of resistance. You know that local managers are usually jealous of their rights and prerogatives and that the new policy will lessen their autonomy.

In addition, although you got polite answers to your memo, you feel certain that it is being disregarded; you have received no notices of contracts or purchases in the six weeks since it went out, and the peak buying season is now here.

You have decided that the best way to implement the new policy is to personally visit each of the plants and discuss the new policy and its implementation with the plant purchasing agents. After all, since the board of directors approved the policy, the purchasing agents report to you, at least indirectly, on all purchases or contracts over $10,000. By coordinating and pooling these purchases, you can realize substantial savings for the company, for you are one of the few persons in the company who sees the "big picture," and you are not going to get sidetracked with minor problems and objections. Today, you have scheduled a meeting with Mr. Jones, chief purchasing agent for the Reading plant, which makes electronic instruments for hospital use.

MR. JONES, CHIEF PURCHASING AGENT

You have an M.A. in business administration and a major in purchasing. During your five years with Howard's Reading plant, you have substantially reduced costs through improved purchasing methods. Prior to coming to Reading, you held purchasing jobs with several other companies.

You feel that the Reading plant's purchasing problems are unique. Your plant builds medical electronics equipment, which requires frequent engineering changes or the introduction of new products. Most of the other plants, by contrast, have more stable product lines. Your special problem, therefore, is to walk a tightrope between buying too soon (with the possibility of the parts becoming obsolete) and waiting too long for the parts lists to become more stabilized (with the risk of parts shortages caused by late delivery times). In the past five years, you have worked hard to select good, reliable vendors who understand your situation and are willing to "give and take" with you.

When you received the memo a few weeks ago, you showed it to your boss, the plant manager, whose only comment was that "they are always trying something new at Corporate. These fads come and go. I've seen a lot of them in my time." However, you don't really feel that the memo applies to you, since a large percentage of the materials you buy are unique to your plant, although you would have no problem with such minor items as office furniture, toilet paper, and paper towels. Indeed, centralizing these purchases makes a lot of sense, but to centralize the purchase of special materials would be a major disaster that would increase delays and paperwork and disrupt the vendor relationships you have worked so hard to build up. Mr. Leavitt is arriving today, and you want to make these points *strongly*. You told your boss about the meeting, and he may drop in. Although he has not said so directly, you know he feels as strongly about it as you do.

MR. BROWN, GENERAL MANAGER, READING PLANT

You are the general manager of one of Howard's largest plants. Since the plant opened ten years ago, you have steadily progressed from foreman in manufacturing, through purchasing and marketing, until you took over as general manager six years ago. Since that time, you have carefully selected and developed an outstanding management team. One of your best decisions was to fire the existing chief purchasing agent and bring in Mr. Jones, who has made a major impact by reducing parts shortages, reducing material costs, and developing excellent vendor relationships. Additional "red tape" and delay in clearing through Corporate would only result in parts shortages or excessively high inventories and parts obsolescence. The other managers now reporting to you have also improved the operation. In fact, when you took over six years ago, the plant was barely breaking even, and last year the plant's profits were the highest in the organization, and you received a company award for your accomplishment.

Your plant makes electronic instruments for hospital and similar uses and is the only one of its kind in the Howard Company. You saw the memo from Leavitt about the $10,000 limitation on purchases and were opposed to it. No plant managers were involved with the decision, and when you checked with some of them, they too saw it as a "power grab" by the new man. If the new policy is fully implemented, Jones will be reporting to Leavitt. This first step toward centralization could result in the loss of power and authority by all the general managers.

You have decided to attend the meeting and to make your views known quickly and definitely. Leavitt's power grab needs to be stopped before it begins. After all, Howard is *not* a chain of grocery stores.

INTERNATIONAL SYSTEMS CORPORATION— AJAX PLANT

You are Robert Bedford, the new plant manager of Ajax Plant, part of the International Systems Corporation. Previously you had been manager for research and development for another of International's plants in a different part of the country. You spent a week at Ajax in Central City getting acquainted with the plant and the people. Then you had to spend a week at your old plant to finish up some business there. You arrived back in Central City late Sunday night. You came to the plant an hour early Monday morning, January 10, to catch up on your work and to review what had happened since you left.

The Ajax plant had been growing steadily under the management of Kenneth Chandler, the previous manager, who left the company for a better job. The plant now has a capital investment in excess of $24,000,000 and produces a variety of electronic and electromechanical testing and analyzing equipment for both military and civilian markets. The plant staff, excluding top management, now includes 55 engineers and 35 technicians; there are approximately 1100 production employees who work in two shifts.

The department manager in charge of production is William Silva. He has been with the company about 15 years, but has been in his current job for less than a year. The department manager in charge of marketing is Joseph Fleming, who has been in the job approximately two years. Before then, he had been a regional sales manager. His present functions include sales promotion, merchandising, market research and development, and sales. Eighty-five employees are under his supervision.

Al Mumford, the section manager in research and development, is an electronics engineer. Prior to his promotion less than a year ago, he headed up the electrical engineering subsection in the engineering department. His functions are shown on the organization chart. He had 38 engineers and 15 technicians and draftsmen working for him. Because of Chandler's strong interest in research and development, close to seven percent of the plant's profits are allocated to this function.

The finance manager is James Cardinal, who has held this job for about three years. His functions include general and cost accounting, accounts receivable and payable, payroll, and the computer unit. He has a staff of about 25 people.

Charles Gray, the employee and community relations manager, has a staff

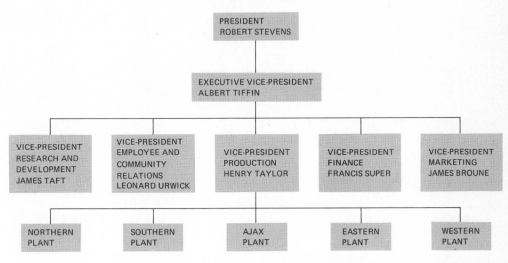

INTERNATIONAL SYSTEMS CORPORATION

of approximately 18 people. He transferred from the corporate staff a little over six months ago.

On the following pages are some memos and other correspondence. On a separate sheet of paper, outline and briefly describe what action you would take on each item. *Everything you decide or do must be in writing.* You might write on the items themselves or make memos to yourself about things you want to do later. Draft letters, if appropriate, for your secretary to type. Outline plans or draw up the agenda of meetings you want to call. Sign papers, if necessary. Actually write out memos to your subordinates or to others or make notes of anything you plan to say to them at some future time. (Do not, however, assume what they may say to you in return.) Enter any planned interviews, confirming letters or memos, telephone calls, meeting agenda, notes to yourself or others, and whatever thoughts you may have in connection with each item on the calendar. *Each time you make a decision, record fully the reasons behind your actions.*

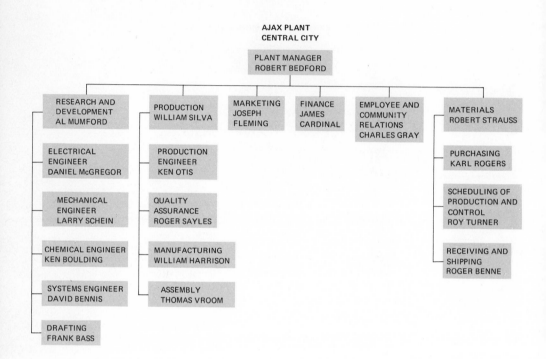

AJAX PLANT
CENTRAL CITY

PLANT MANAGER
ROBERT BEDFORD

RESEARCH AND DEVELOPMENT
AL MUMFORD

PRODUCTION
WILLIAM SILVA

MARKETING
JOSEPH FLEMING

FINANCE
JAMES CARDINAL

EMPLOYEE AND COMMUNITY RELATIONS
CHARLES GRAY

MATERIALS
ROBERT STRAUSS

ELECTRICAL ENGINEER
DANIEL McGREGOR

PRODUCTION ENGINEER
KEN OTIS

PURCHASING
KARL ROGERS

MECHANICAL ENGINEER
LARRY SCHEIN

QUALITY ASSURANCE
ROGER SAYLES

SCHEDULING OF PRODUCTION AND CONTROL
ROY TURNER

CHEMICAL ENGINEER
KEN BOULDING

MANUFACTURING
WILLIAM HARRISON

RECEIVING AND SHIPPING
ROGER BENNE

SYSTEMS ENGINEER
DAVID BENNIS

ASSEMBLY
THOMAS VROOM

DRAFTING
FRANK BASS

Calendar Pad—March 1969

Sunday	Monday	Tuesday	Wednesday	Thursday	Friday	Saturday
						1
2	3	4	5	6	7	8
		Out of plant all week				
9	10	11	12	13	14	15
16	17	18	19	20	21	22
23	24	25	26	27	28	29
30	31					

AJAX PLANT
CENTRAL CITY

OFFICE MEMORANDUM   January 6

TO: Mr. Robert Bedford, Plant Manager
FROM: Charles Gray, E. & C.R.
SUBJECT: Employment of the Disadvantaged

According to information I received at a personnel meeting last night, both the State and
Federal Equal Opportunity people will shortly be
giving a hard look at industrial plants in this
area. Currently, our ratio of disadvantaged to
white employees is extremely low, and we may be
in serious trouble.

    I would recommend that we put on a crash
program to recruit and employ at least 70 - 80
nonwhites, in all areas of the plant. I would
further recommend that we not use our normal
testing program for these new employees, since
the use of our regular intellectual and aptitude
tests can also open us to charges of discrimination. We should continue to use the tests for
our normal employment of whites.

    I realize that a crash program may involve,
for the short-run, increased training and labor
costs, but this is preferable to losing our
defense contracts or the bad publicity coming
from an investigation. Besides, I think that
this is the right thing to do.

BR   XCL   292 RQ - WVX   January 7

NY   NY   4:30 PM

MR. ROBERT BEDFORD, PLANT MANAGER

MR. JOSEPH FLEMING, MARKETING MANAGER

GOOD NEWS STOP HAVE JUST LEARNED THAT ED BAKER
OF BAKER & BAKER READY TO PURCHASE LARGE NUMBER
OF MODEL 80 SYSTEMS AND RELATED ACCESSORIES STOP
CONTRACT APPEARS LIKELY IF WE CAN PROMISE EARLY
DELIVERY ON GUARANTEED BASIS STOP ADVISE ME OF
ACTION STOP

                                            JIM BROUNE

AJAX PLANT
CENTRAL CITY

OFFICE MEMORANDUM   January 5

TO: Bob Bedford
FROM: Robert Strauss
SUBJECT: Increased Materials Costs

As you know, I've been concerned for quite a while about parts shortages, high inventory, and the steadily increasing materials costs. This is particularly true since more than half of our direct costs come from purchased materials, due to the nature of our business.

My people are working hard to reduce costs and establish decent manufacturing schedules, but we can't do it by ourselves. We are continually having to revise our production schedules because of manufacturing problems, particularly with the new models. As a result, my purchasing people don't get the word early enough on what we need to buy, and everything needs to be on rush order and expedited. About the time we get it into the plant, there is another design change, and sometimes the parts we have just rush-ordered are then obsoleted. As a result, our materials costs are skyrocketing.

We need to get designs locked in so that we can establish decent manufacturing and purchasing schedules. For example, the Model 95 is supposed to go into manufacturing shortly, but as yet we have been unable to get a parts listing that we can rely on.

AJAX PLANT
CENTRAL CITY

OFFICE MEMORANDUM   January 6

TO: Plant Manager

FROM: Jim Cardinal, Finance Operation

SUBJECT: Integrated Management Information System

Two months ago, we completed and debugged our
computer-based integrated management information
system at a cost of $80,000. This system is
aimed at providing us with much more timely and
accurate information about sales figures,
production and assembly scheduling, vendor order
status, and the like. I have been particularly
concerned with the fact that the new System
would provide me with considerably better cost-
accounting data.

However, the new system is not working well.
Its effectiveness has been considerably reduced
by the fact that many managers do not use it, but
instead maintain duplicate records and do not
update the computer files regularly. Further,
they appear reluctant to give me the cost-
accounting figures that I need and do not fully
adhere to the new policies and procedures
necessary to make the new system work.

Any and all assistance in this matter would
be greatly appreciated.

INTERNATIONAL SYSTEMS CORPORATION
CHICAGO, ILLINOIS

INTRACOMPANY MEMORANDUM   January 4

TO: Mr. Robert Bedford
FROM: Henry Taylor, Vice-President
SUBJECT: Meeting   Production Division

I plan to come to Central City on March 25 to
meet with you now that you have had a chance to
become acquainted with the plant. In addition
to the routine general review, I would like to
take enough time for us to discuss the problem
of increasing our rate of new product introduction. We need to increase our research and
development emphasis in both personnel and
facilities, especially since the rate of product
obsolescence is being considerably affected by
our competitors. I would like to have you
prepare a special report on this subject for me.
     In addition, the latest budget reports
indicate that the plant is running well above
the projected operating expenses for both the
last quarter and the year to date. Furthermore,
does the current slight decrease in sales
constitute a signal of a downward trend? We
will want to look at this for both near- and
long-term implications.
     You may ask any members of your staff to
meet with us should you feel it is appropriate.

                              Henry Taylor

HT:hs

AJAX PLANT
CENTRAL CITY

OFFICE MEMORANDUM   January 6

TO: Bob Bedford
FROM: William Silva
SUBJECT: Model 80 retrofit

Although we had a discussion about the Model 80
last week, I thought it wise to drop you a note
on the subject. It does not appear possible to
make the schedule for the Model 80 retrofit and
at the same time make the schedule for the new
Model 80s coming out. My production engineering
people are going flat out trying to make the
necessary production design changes and at the
same time help the production people with the
retrofit program. I would recommend stopping
production on both the retrofit and new
production until we get the design problems
cleaned up once and for all.

        The mistake that I made was accepting the
Model 80 for production when I knew that there
were a lot of design bugs in it. I won't make
that mistake again.

        By the way, can you get the finance people
off my back for a while? They are trying to put
in the computer system. It still hasn't been
fully debugged, and I'll be glad to help them
out in a month or so when I've had a chance to
get caught up with production problems.

AJAX PLANT
CENTRAL CITY

OFFICE MEMORANDUM   January 7

TO: Robert Bedford, Plant Manager
FROM: Joseph Fleming, Marketing Manager
SUBJECT: Slippage of the Model 95

The latest word that I have is that the Model 95
will not go into production for another month.
As you know, we have had repeated delays on
introducing this system. Originally, it was
supposed to go into production last August. Our
sales for this year were forecast on the firm
promise from R&D that the Model 95 would be ready
for production by January 1 of this year.
Apparently, the earliest date now is April 15.
    Our sales forecasts are based on the
expectation that new products will come into the
plant and go into production on specific dates.
Any further delays in the introduction of the
Model 95 will seriously reduce sales for the
year, particularly since delays on the 95 will
also affect other models in the series,
especially the 96 and 97.

AJAX PLANT
CENTRAL CITY

OFFICE MEMORANDUM   January 4

TO: Mr. Robert Bedford
FROM: Al Mumford
SUBJECT: Project Status Report

This is a brief status report with some accompanying recommendations.

1. Model 95. Although there have been some slippages, the Model 95 is close to coming into production. We have had one brief hangup due to the failure of the system to pass the packaging tests, but we anticipate no further difficulty, and the project should be ready to hand over completely to production in the next few weeks.

2. Models 96 and 97. As you know, the Model 96 is a simplified and less complex version of the 95. The 97, as an ancillary system, adds considerably to the capability of the 95. Both are progressing and should be ready to be put into production within the next two months.

3. We would like to begin design on a completely new and original system for hospital-laboratory analysis. What we have in mind is a multichannel digital system which can conduct as many as ten different blood analyses almost simultaneously. However, we are having difficulties, since Jim Cardinal tells us that funds cannot be made available within the current year.

Recommendations:

1. We recommend that you seriously consider hiring some really capable people in production engineering. We don't want to repeat the Model 80 problem again. We gave those people a good design, and they were unable to follow it through.

2. We recommend that you talk to Cardinal about considerably increasing funding for the purpose of going into the digital blood system.

NASA MOON SURVIVAL TASK

OBJECTIVES AND INSTRUCTIONS

Contrary to what many people believe, there is nothing inherently good or bad about groups as such. Groups (and this term is meant to include all human assemblies from committees and social clubs to project teams and departments) have certain unique properties, it is true; but from a performance standpoint, groups function as their members make them function.

The objective of this exercise is one of exploring the performance characteristics of the decision-making group—both its pitfalls and potentials—and the significance of member contributions for the quality of group production. Much is known from basic research about the conditions of effective group functioning. The present exercise attempts to incorporate these conditions in such a way that group performance may be approached in a more systematic cause-and-effect fashion, allowing the individual group member to identify those functions which either hinder or facilitate group productivity.

Instructions   As much as possible, the design of this exercise parallels the typical group decision-making situation in which an individual (1) forms one's own private opinions regarding a decision issue, (2) joins with other individuals—each of whom has personal preconceptions on the issue—for purposes of discussion and decision, (3) makes a public commitment to some group position, and (4) reformulates a private individual decision which may or may not coincide fully with the group position. You will be asked to undertake the following decision steps in the order they are presented below:

1. Working alone and unaided, complete the NASA Moon Survival Task. Be sure that all items have been ranked and that your group designation has been given in the space provided.

2. When asked to do so, turn to the "Decision Process Instructions." Read these comments thoroughly; they serve as guidelines to effective group process. Adhere as closely as you can to their provisions.

3. When all have completed their individual decision and read the Decision Process Instructions, you will be asked to join with your group for purposes of reaching a group consensus on the NASA task.

Developed by Jay Hall, Ph.D. and published by Teleometrics International. Copyright 1963; not to be reproduced without express permission of the author.

The guidelines provided on remaining pages are optional; use the forms as you see fit.

DECISION PROCESS INSTRUCTIONS

Research in group dynamics has revealed that the manner in which groups utilize their member resources is a critical determinant of how they perform. In this exercise you are asked to use the technique of *group consensus*. This means that the ranking for each of the 15 survival items must be agreed upon by each member before it becomes a part of the group decision. Consensus is difficult to reach. Therefore, not every ranking will meet with everyone's complete approval. Unanimity, however, is not a goal (although it may be achieved unintentionally), and it is not necessary, for example, that every person be as satisfied as if he or she had complete control over what the group decides.

What should be stressed is the individual's ability to accept a given ranking on the basis of logic—whatever the level of satisfaction—and the willingness to entertain such a judgment as feasible. When the point is reached at which all group members feel this way as a minimal criterion, you may assume that you have reached a consensus as it is defined here and the judgment may be entered as a group decision. This means, in effect, that a single person can block the group if considered necessary; at the same time, it is assumed that this option will be employed in the best sense of reciprocity. Here are some guidelines to use in achieving consensus:

1. Avoid arguing for your own rankings. Present your position as lucidly and logically as possible, but consider seriously the reactions of the group in any subsequent presentations of the same point.

2. Avoid "win-lose" stalemates in the discussion of rankings. Discard the notion that someone must win and someone must lose in the discussion; when impasses occur, look for the next most acceptable alternative for both parties.

3. Avoid changing your mind only in order to avoid conflict and to reach agreement and harmony. Withstand pressures to yield which have no objective or logically sound foundation. Strive for enlightened flexibility; avoid outright capitulation.

4. Avoid conflict-reducing techniques such as the majority vote, averaging, bargaining, coin-flipping, and the like. Treat differences of opinion as indicative of an incomplete sharing of relevant information on someone's part and press for additional sharing, either about task or emotional data, where it seems in order.

5. View differences of opinion as both natural and helpful rather than as a hindrance in decision making. Generally, the more ideas expressed, the greater the likelihood of conflict will be; but the richer the array of resources will be as well.

6. View initial agreement as suspect. Explore the reasons underlying apparent agreements; make sure that people have arrived at similar solutions for either the same basic reasons or for complementary reasons before incorporating such solutions in the group decision.

7. Avoid subtle forms of influence and decision modification; e.g., when a dissenting member finally agrees, don't feel that he must be "rewarded" by having his own way on some later point.

8. Be willing to entertain the possibility that your group can excel at its decision task; avoid doom-saying and negative thinking.

NASA MOON SURVIVAL TASK

Background information Think of yourself as a member of a space crew whose mission is one of rendezvousing with a Mother Ship on the lighted surface of the moon. Due to mechanical difficulties, your ship has crashlanded some 200 miles from the rendezvous site. All equipment, with the exception of 15 items, was destroyed in the crash. Since survival depends upon reaching the Mother Ship, you and your fellow crew members must determine which among the 15 items of equipment left intact are most crucial for survival.

Instructions The 15 items left intact after the crash are listed below. You are asked to rank these in order of their importance for insuring survival. Place the number "1" in the space by the item you feel is most critical; the number "2" by the second most important item; and so on through number "15" by the least important item.

Rank	Items
____	Box of matches
____	Food concentrate
____	50 feet of nylon rope
____	Parachute silk
____	Portable heating unit
____	Two .45 calibre pistols
____	One case dehydrated Pet milk
____	Two hundred-pound tanks of oxygen
____	Stellar map (of the moon's constellation)

——	Life raft
——	Magnetic compass
——	Five gallons of water
——	Signal flares
——	First aid kit containing injection needles
——	Solar-powered FM receiver-transmitter

Group Summary Sheet

You may find it helpful to begin your discussion by recording each member's rank order on the following chart. This will afford each of you an overview of where the group stands on the decision items.

Individual Predictions													
Items	1	2	3	4	5	6	7	8	9	10	11	12	Group Prediction
Box of matches													
Food concentrate													
50 feet of nylon rope													
Parachute silk													
Portable heating unit													
Two .45 calibre pistols													
One case dehydrated Pet milk													
Two hundred-pound tanks of oxygen													
Stellar map (of the moon's constellation)													
Life raft													
Magnetic compass													
Five gallons of water													
Signal flares													
First aid kit containing injection needles													
Solar-powered FM receiver-transmitter													

Note: Once you have completed your group decision, you may want to complete the individual (private) ranking on the next page.

Postdiscussion Ranks

Instructions   Having now had an opportunity to hear what others think, your own thinking may have changed regarding the appropriate ranking of items. On the other hand, you may be more firmly convinced than ever of your initial position. Based on what has transpired in your group (and without referring back to your original ranking of the 15 items) rerank the items *as you now feel they should be evaluated.*

Rerank	*Items*
____	Box of matches
____	Food concentrate
____	50 feet of nylon rope
____	Parachute silk
____	Portable heating unit
____	Two .45 calibre pistols
____	One case dehydrated Pet milk
____	Two hundred-pound tanks of oxygen
____	Stellar map (of the moon's constellation)
____	Life raft
____	Magnetic compass
____	Five gallons of water
____	Signal flares
____	First aid kit containing injection needles
____	Solar-powered FM receiver-transmitter

SCORING YOUR DECISION

Group and NASA Comparisons

On the forms below you may (1) score your individual decision for accuracy by comparing it with the NASA solution, (2) compare your initial decision with that finally produced by your group, and if you made a postdiscussion ranking (3) determine the effect on accuracy of group discussion by comparing preerror scores with posterror scores, and (4) determine the amount your group influenced your thinking by comparing the pre- and postrankings you made with that produced by your group. All these data may serve to enhance discussion of your group's performance and its impact on you and, in turn, your impact on the group.

Degree of Group Influence

A Difference (C−B)	B Pre-rank	C Group Rank	D Post-rank	E Difference (C−D)
	TOTAL		TOTAL	

Influence Score
(A−E)

Changes in Decision Quality

A Error (C−B)	B Pre-rank	C NASA rank	D Post-rank	E Error (C−D)
	TOTAL		TOTAL	

Gain-Loss Index
(A−E)

Group Data Summary

Sample scoring:

NASA rank	Predicted rank	Error score
1	3	2
2	2	0
3	9	6
/	/	/
/	/	/
/	/	/
/	/	/
/	/	/
15	10	5
		13 Total

Group Performance

	BEFORE		AFTER GROUP DISCUSSION				
Group	(a) Average resource	(b) Most accurate resource	(c) Group score	(d) Gain/Loss (a vs. c)	(e) % +/−	(f) No. ind. sup.	(g) Creativity index (b vs. c)
					%	/	
					%	/	
					%	/	
					%	/	
					%	/	
					%	/	
					%	/	
					%	/	
					%	/	
					%	/	
					%	/	
					%	/	

For an in-depth discussion of group effectiveness, see the related material prepared for this exercise: Jay Hall, *The Utilization of Group Resources,* (1970), Houston, Texas: Teleometrics, Inc.

THE NEW PRODUCT MEETING

A product manager (PM) had arranged a meeting with representatives of manufacturing and accounting in order to present certain information and to ask them questions about a new product scheduled to go into a test market in several weeks. The meeting took place in a conference room located in the product department office area. The manufacturing and accounting personnel were already present when the PM came into the room carrying a note pad and a dummy model of the package to be used for the new product.

As he walked toward the head of the table, he tossed the package dummy onto the table and said, "Here's the box." As the package was passed around from person to person, the manufacturing and accounting managers asked about its specifications. The PM answered with precise facts and figures and told how these had been determined.

One of the manufacturing representatives asked about the brand's shelf location. The PM replied that shelf location had also been decided on, adding that an alternative location had been considered, but that: "If we go into that section of the store that is an area our competitors' salesmen visit every day, they will simply throw us into the back room."

The manufacturing man nodded. The group continued by discussing topics on the order in which the PM presented them: schedule, direct mail sample promotion, carton size, etc. In each of these areas the PM presented his plans and the reasons for them. There were no disagreements.

Things began going less smoothly, however, when the PM asked the manufacturing people about quality control. In asking the questions, the PM made reference to his superiors: "I've been asked what we are going to do to ensure the taste. This is crucial on this brand, and I've got to have something specific to say about it. How would you like to answer this?"

The manufacturing representatives replied that taste was important on all brands and that they would, of course, use the same procedures that were always used to ensure quality. A lengthy discussion followed, during which the PM asked the manufacturing representatives to write a special quality-control procedure for the new product, a step the manufacturing managers felt was unnecessary. With minor variations, the parties repeated the following statements.

This case was written by Dalmar Fisher.

PM: I'm expected to know exactly what you are going to do on this product.

Manufacturing: But we *know* how to do quality control. What's the matter, don't you trust us? We will use the same statistical techniques on this product that we do on other products having similar ingredients.

PM: I understand that this is your responsibility, but it's our concern as well. Would it be too much to ask you to send us a note saying that the quality will be what is supposed to be?

Manufacturing: You're going to have to accept that we do the job and have faith that we're going to do the same thing that we do on the other products.

PM: It's a bigger problem on this product.

Manufacturing: Well, I wish we had a little black box that we could put the product into and it would flash a light "good" or "bad." You've got to trust us.

Finally, the PM reluctantly replied: "OK, OK, so I trust you," and changed the subject by saying, "OK, what about costs?" Another lengthy discussion resulted when the PM discovered that the cost estimates for the product were now considerably higher than those the accountants had made a few months earlier. The PM expressed a feeling that perhaps the costs had been overstated, since they seemed to be based on start-up, rather than full-scale production.

PM: Now, the way we're starting producing is not the real-world basis, it it? A lot can happen in six months—cartoning improvements, a lot of things. Can't we stay with the old numbers? See, I'm confronted with a situation where a pricing decision has already been made, so if contribution is less than we thought, I'm faced with having to raise price or reduce marketing expenditures, and I have to have an annual program on Friday on this. If people start seeing a lower contribution, I lose all we've fought for. We'll get drilled.

Accounting: If you stay with the old numbers, you'll defeat our whole structure. As we've said, right *here*, on these sheets, are the costs, and as you can see, there is a solid reason behind each of them. We are being as optimistic as we can. After all, how can you quote costs when you haven't even produced a unit of product yet?

PM: Well, that's just it. So you must be saying you're quoting the most conservative costs you can. What if we produced it at the other plant?

Accounting: Well, that would save you some money, but we can't go all the way back to the beginning on costs. You can see from these sheets how much is involved in putting these figures together.

The issue was not resolved. The PM concluded the meeting by saying that he would arrange another meeting with his superior and the controller present. The accounting managers agreed. As the participants were preparing to leave, the PM noticed his superior walking by the door. The PM went into the corridor and quickly briefed his boss on the cost problem:

PM: Look, these guys are coming in with an increase that affects the pricing structure and the marketing budget, so it's getting to be a top-management problem. They're still in there. How about coming in and letting them expose you to it?

Superior: (Frowning and taking two steps backward, away from the direction of the conference room.) What's the probability their numbers are correct?

PM: I'd say 50–50.

Superior: Now wait. Why don't you lay out the numbers on paper, and we will talk about them in the morning. Meanwhile, I'll talk to the controller and get his feel for the reliability of these numbers. See, the company has a history of coming down from these estimates. That makes them a hero. They've "saved" money.

PM: OK, I'll lay out the numbers and then see you again in the morning.

Superior: OK. See, you have to get tough with these guys. They want to make the estimates very conservative so they will look good later.

PM: Yeah.

DISCUSSION QUESTIONS

1. Why was agreement reached in the meeting about shelf location? Why did the cost problem remain unresolved? Was the quality-control issue resolved? How and why?

2. What did the product manager expect and want from the manufacturing and accounting representatives and from his superior? What did they expect and want from him? Why do you suppose these expectations were what they were?

3. What are the requirements for effective performance in the integrator (in this case, the product manager's) role? How effectively did the product manager in this case perform as an integrator?

4. Do you agree or disagree with the superior's statement that "You have to get tough with these guys"?

PARTICIPATIVE DECISION MAKING

Ned Wicker is the manager of the systems proposal department in the electronics division of a large company. This department was organized a year ago to improve the division's efforts to gain new systems business. The department's specific functions are: (1) to review bid specifications for new electronic systems required by aerospace users of such equipment; (2) to evaluate which bids are attractive and within the technical capability of the company; and (3) to prepare the necessary business proposals to win contracts from potential customers.

Ned had been a senior proposal analyst with another company when he was hired to set up the new department. It was his first managerial position, and he wanted to be successful from the start. He recruited and hired seven highly qualified engineers, most of whom had prior experience with customer requirements in the industry. The division manager was enthusiastic about the new group and Ned's aggressive approach to getting things launched.

Since generating technical proposals is costly and time-consuming, Wicker felt that the key to success would be the careful screening and selection of bids on which proposals were to be prepared by the group. It was largely for this reason that he had developed both an elite group to work with him and a procedure for full participation by the group in the RFP selection (request for proposal) process.

The procedure was for incoming RFPs to be given a preliminary evaluation by the individual analysts in the group, who gave their informal, written recommendations to Ned on Friday each week. Over the weekend, Ned would carefully review all RFPs and recommendations and arrive at his own tentative conclusions and priorities for bid-no bid decisions. Final decisions on proposals were made on Mondays at a full morning review meeting by the entire group. At these sessions Ned explained each RFP in detail, after which the group discussed it. During these discussions Ned was careful not to disclose his own tentative conclusions. After all the RFPs had been reviewed in this way, final selections for making proposals were reached by group consensus. Occasionally, Ned would find it necessary to overrule the group when he felt he had a better understanding of a particular situation. This was not done

---

This case was written by John W. Lewis, III.

high-handedly, however, and usually the group could be led to see the wisdom in his final decision.

The RFP selection procedure seemed to work effectively for the first three or four months, and two proposals submitted by the group resulted in major new contracts for the company. During the next several months, however, the batting average started to decline. Over this period, Ned became disturbed by an apparent change in the Monday morning review meetings. Initially, discussions about the RFPs were lively and included the entire group. Frequently, the sessions ran over into the afternoon. Gradually, however, discussion became more formal, and sometimes Ned and the analyst who had done the preliminary evaluation were the only participants in the discussion. The final blow came one morning when the session lasted merely 45 minutes, and Ned did most of the talking. Since he considered the review meeting to be the heart of the RFP selection process, Ned became alarmed. Although he still had complete confidence in the people he had selected, he felt more and more that they were holding back their ideas and technical judgment, both of which were crucial for arriving at the soundest bid-no bid decisions.

THE PROVINCETOWN ADVOCATE

PROVINCETOWN—By the time he was in his mid-thirties, Dan Boynton was, by all conventional definitions, a success.

Audio Lab, the stereo component business he had started with $500 in a Harvard Square basement, was grossing $2 million annually. He owned a big house in Newton and a chauffeur-driven Packard limousine.

But Dan Boynton was unhappy, and so was his wife Janet. Their problem, Boynton recalls, was that "we had so much money we didn't know what to do with it." They were bored with their success and disturbed by the pressures and style of life that came with it.

So in 1972, Dan Boynton sold Audio Lab. For the next two years he and his wife spent most of their time trying to figure out what to do next. Fifteen months ago, convinced that they had found the answer, they embarked on careers as owners and publishers of the *Provincetown Advocate*, a 105-year-old weekly, they purchased in an attempt, Boynton says simply, "to find work and a lifestyle that really made you feel good."

Now the 40-year-old Boynton can usually be found in the *Advocate* office one block from Commercial street, laboring over a news story on tax assessments, or trying to reach a selectman on the phone, while Janet Boynton, 37, is apt to be standing in front of the Truro post office with a camera around her neck asking passers-by such questions as: "Do you think the Town of Truro should reconsider Civil Service control over police hiring?"

The Boyntons have found their new lifestyle. But, much to their surprise and distress, they're not at all sure they like it.

They came to Provincetown, they admit, full of romantic notions about editors and the leisurely pace of life in a small Cape Cod town. Instead they have found hard work and little free time, as well as resentment and criticism they quickly learned was inherent with owning a newspaper.

The experience has left them more than a little confused but with a much more realistic idea of weekly newspapers, small towns, and the general difficulties involved in starting over again in a period of their lives perilously close to middle age.

This article was written by William B. Hamilton and appeared in the *Boston Globe*, July 9, 1975. Reprinted courtesy of *The Boston Globe*.

"The fantasy is over," says Boynton, a boyish, soft-spoken man, "and whether we can build a real good life out of this or not is yet to be proven."

Neither Boynton is ready to give up on their venture in journalism—at least not yet—but they say that at times they have been as unhappy as they were during their Audio Lab days.

Boynton had started Audio Lab in 1957 when he was 23, after dropping out of Brown and after a brief stint as an engineer for WBZ Radio. A hi-fi buff, he intended the business to be an outlet for his interest and a way "to make a little money to be free and independnt."

The Boyntons, who had both grown up in Bristol, R.I., and who had been married for a year, lived in the back of the Harvard Square basement that served as the Audio Lab store.

The business started slowly. Then, in the early '60s, came that boom in sound equipment. The Boyntons, located in the midst of an affluent university community, turned out to be sitting on a gold mine.

Audio Lab expanded, until it finally became a chain of four stores. The Boyntons began making a lot of money, moved to Brattle Street and then to Newton, and bought the Packard.

While Janet Boynton became a suburban housewife, Dan Boynton, who liked working in the store and talking to customers, became an executive. "It got to the point," he says, "where I was sitting in some upstairs office looking at an IBM computer printout on how many record changers we sold this week. It wasn't music. It was business—just what I was trying to avoid."

At the same time it was acquiring the trappings of a growing business— the time clock and multiple invoices—Audio Lab also began to face more competition in the stereo field. Unhappy at having so little personal involvement in the business and convinced that the future meant only more of the same, Boynton, in 1972, decided to sell.

With the $250,000 and the guaranteed monthly income they received from the sale, the Boyntons decided to start over.

"We went about the occupational change fairly scientifically," said Janet Boynton. With their four children they made lists of what they wanted in the place they lived. Dan Boynton went on a scouting trip to California to look for houses and jobs, and both he and his wife took vocational aptitude tests to find out what they were best qualified to do.

They came to no decision about careers. But they did decide they wanted to live on Cape Cod, which emerged as a compromise between going to California and staying in Boston. In the Spring of 1973, they moved to Orleans with the intention of buying a house and operating some sort of business out of their home.

But they still had problems deciding what that endeavor ought to be. Finally, in December, they took an unusual step—they placed an ad in a local paper, *The Cape Codder*, and asked for ideas.

Beneath a picture of them huddling under a blanket on the beach, and the headline "It's no fun being a tourist in December," was the admission that, "to put it bluntly, we're bored."

"The obvious solution," the ad continued, "is to go back to work, but where on Cape Cod are there challenging opportunities? Our hope is that someone reading this ad can solve our problem."

It was the kind of off-beat approach the Boyntons had used in Audio Lab advertising, and it worked—even before it appeared. It happened that Malcolm Hobbs, editor and publisher of *The Cape Codder*, owned a controlling interest in the *Advocate*, an interest that he wanted to sell.

In fact, an acquaintance had already mentioned to Hobbs that the Boyntons might be the kind of people interested in buying the *Advocate*, a chronic money-loser for a number of years, so a meeting was arranged.

"It seemed perfect in a lot of ways," Janet Boynton recalls. "We had come to Provincetown summers for weekends for years and years. So of all the places on the Cape, we knew it the best."

As for their lack of newspaper experience, the Boyntons were confident that their background in advertising would be enough to carry them through. And, Dan Boynton says, "I figured what the hell. I made a success out of Audio Lab, I'll make a success out of this."

So they bought the paper, and their troubles began.

"It was sort of like when I had my first child and brought her home from the hospital," according to Janet Boynton, "and put her down on the bed and said, 'What do I do now?' "

The first problem was their own staff who, with Hobbs and several others as absentee owners, had been used to running the *Advocate* in a free-wheeling fashion that often offended the more conservative in Provincetown.

They figured that Boynton was going to restrict that freedom, and they resented the fact that they would be taking orders from someone "who couldn't get a job on a paper," as one put it.

As it turned out, the Boyntons did not replace anyone, for they had decided to begin their new careers from the bottom up, while the old staff continued to run the paper.

But the resentment remained, and the Boyntons, who were used to being liked, couldn't understand it.

Their frustration was compounded by their lack of experience and the fact that they had to take orders from their own employees. "To be told that a picture of mine couldn't run," says Janet Boynton, "I felt like stamping my foot and saying, 'It's my paper.' "

And other things weren't going so well either. The Boyntons soon found themselves working seven day weeks, because it took them so long to do things. The commute from Orleans got to be so bad that they rented an apartment in Provincetown, and as a result they hardly ever saw their children.

What they were most unprepared for, however, was the kind of criticism from the community that most small-town editors eventually learn to take in stride. And the cantankerous readers of the *Advocate* were only too glad to tell its new owners what they thought was wrong with the paper, stopping the Boyntons in the street, writing them letters and calling up after every issue with a complaint that something was left out or that something else should never have gotten in.

If a church social or a concert wasn't covered, then the Boyntons heard about it.

"It's funny," Dan Boynton says ruefully. "No one expects a carpenter to work on Sunday night."

In recent weeks, the Boyntons have tried to cut down on the time they spend at the *Advocate*, but on an average day they still arrive at work by 9:30 or 10 and stay until 7 or 8. When there's a night meeting or reception, they work much longer.

As a rule, the Boyntons are home for dinner for only three or four nights a week, and their children, who range from 10 to 17, have had to learn to fend for themselves.

The Boyntons still don't rule out selling all or part of the *Advocate*, especially since it is still losing money, despite their efforts to increase advertising.

But the last months have gone much better, and both Boyntons agree that they are finally becoming comfortable in their new roles, and are experiencing some of the satisfactions they anticipated when they bought the *Advocate*.

THE ROAD TO HELL

John Baker, Chief Engineer of the Caribbean Bauxite Company of Barracania in the West Indies, was making his final preparations to leave the island. His promotion to production manager of Keso Mining Corporation near Winnipeg —one of Continental Ore's fast-expanding Canadian enterprises—had been announced a month before, and now everything had been tidied up except the last vital interview with his successor—the able young Barracanian, Matthew Rennalls. It was vital that this interview be a success and that Rennalls leave his office feeling uplifted and encouraged to face the challenge of his new job. A touch on the bell would have brought Rennalls walking into the room, but Baker delayed the moment and gazed thoughtfully through the window, considering just exactly what he was going to say and, more particularly, how he was going to say it.

John Baker, an English expatriate, was 45 years old and had served his 23 years with Continental Ore in many different places—the Far East, several countries of Africa, Europe, and for the last two years in the West Indies. He hadn't cared much for his previous assignment in Hamburg and was delighted when the West Indian appointment came through. Climate was not the only attraction. Baker had always preferred working overseas (in what were termed the developing countries) because he felt he had an innate knack—better than that shown by other expatriates working for Continental Ore—of knowing just how to get on with regional staff. Twenty-four hours in Barracania, however, soon made him realize that he would need all of this "innate knack" if he was to deal effectively with the problems in this field that now awaited him.

At his first interview with Hutchins, the production manager, the whole problem of Rennalls and his future was discussed. There and then it was made quite clear to Baker that one of his most important tasks would be to "groom" Rennalls as his successor. Hutchins had pointed out that Rennalls was not only one of the brightest Barracanian prospects on the staff of Caribbean Bauxite—at London University he had taken first-class honors in the B.Sc. Engineering Degree—but also the son of the Minister of Finance and Economic Planning, and he thus had no small political pull.

This case was written by Gareth Evans. Used with permission of the author and Shell-BP Petroleum Development Company of Nigeria Ltd.

The company had been particularly pleased when Rennalls decided to work for them rather than for the government in which his father had such a prominent post. They ascribed his action to the effect of their vigorous and liberal regionalization program, which since the Second World War had produced 18 Barracanians at midmanagement level and given Caribbean Bauxite a good lead in this respect over all other international concerns operating in Barracania. The success of this timely regionalization policy had led to excellent relations with the government. This relationship had been given an added importance when Barracania, three years later, became independent—an occasion that encouraged a critical and challenging attitude toward the role foreign interests would have to play in the new Barracania. Hutchins had therefore little difficulty in convincing Baker that the successful career development of Rennalls was of the first importance.

The interview with Hutchins had taken place two years ago. Baker leaned back in his office chair and reviewed just how successful he had been in the "grooming" of Rennalls. What aspect of the latter's character had helped and what had hindered? What about his own personality? How had that helped or hindered? The first item to go on the credit side would without question be Rennalls' ability to master the technical aspects of his job. From the start he had shown keenness and enthusiasm and had often impressed Baker with his ability in tackling new assignments and the constructive comments he invariably made in departmental discussions. He was popular with all ranks of Barracanian staff and had an ease of manner that stood him in good stead when dealing with his expatriate seniors. These were all assets, but what about the debit side?

First and foremost, there was Rennalls' racial consciousness. His four years at London University had accentuated this feeling and had made him sensitive to any sign of condescension on the part of expatriates. It may have been to give expression to this sentiment that as soon as he returned home from London, he threw himself into politics on behalf of the United Action Party, which later won the preindependence elections and provided the country with its first Prime Minister.

The ambitions of Rennalls—and he certainly was ambitious—did not however, lie in politics, for staunch nationalist as he was, he saw that he could serve himself and his country best—for was not bauxite responsible for nearly half the value of Barracania's export trade?—by putting his engineering talent to the best use possible. On this account, Hutchins found that he had an unexpectedly easy task in persuading Rennalls to give up his political work before entering the production department as an assistant engineer.

It was, Baker knew, Rennalls' well-repressed sense of race consciousness that had prevented their relationship from being as close as it should have been. On the surface, nothing could have seemed more agreeable. Formality between the two men was at a minimum. Baker was delighted to find that his assistant shared his own perculiar "shaggy dog" sense of humor, so that jokes were continually being exchanged, and they entertained each other at their houses and often played tennis together. Yet the barrier remained, invisible, indefinable, but ever present. The existence of this "screen" between them was a constant source of frustration to Baker, since it indicated a weakness that he was loath to accept. If successful with all other nationalities, why not with Rennalls?

But at least he had managed to "break through" to Rennalls more successfully than any other expatriate had. In fact, it was the young Barracanian's attitude—sometimes overbearing, sometimes cynical—toward other company expatriates that had been one of the subjects Baker had raised last year when he discussed Rennalls' staff report with him. He knew, too, that he would have to raise the same subject again in the forthcoming interview, because Jackson, the senior draftsman, had complained only yesterday about the rudeness of Rennalls. With this thought in mind, Baker leaned forward and spoke into the intercom. "Would you come in Matt, please? I'd like a word with you," and later, "Do sit down," proffering the box, "and have a cigarette." He paused while he held out his lighter and then went on.

"As you know, Matt, I'll be off to Canada in a few days, and before I go, I thought it would be useful if we could have a final chat together. It is indeed with some deference that I suggest I can be of help. You will shortly be sitting in this chair, doing the job I am now doing, but I, on the other hand, am ten years older, so perhaps you can accept the idea that I may be able to give you the benefit of my longer experience."

Baker saw Rennalls stiffen slightly in his chair as he made this point, so added in explanation, "You and I have attended enough company courses to remember those repeated requests by the personnel manager to tell people how they are getting on as often as the convenient moment arises and not just the automatic 'once a year' when, by regulation, staff reports have to be discussed."

Rennalls nodded his agreement, so Baker went on, "I shall always remember the last job performance discussion I had with my previous boss back in Germany. He used what he called the "plus and minus" technique. His firm belief was that when a senior seeks by discussion to improve the work performance of his staff, his prime objective should be to make sure that the latter leaves the interview encouraged and inspired to improve. Any criticism must therefore be constructive and helpful. He said that one very good way to encourage a person—I fully agree with him—is to tell him about his good points—the plus factors—as well as his weak ones—the minus factors—so I thought, Matt, it would be a good idea to run our discussion along these lines."

Rennalls offered no comment, so Baker continued: "Let me say, therefore, right away, that as far as your own work performance is concerned, the plus far outweighs the minus. I have, for instance, been most impressed with the way you have adapted your considerable theoretical knowledge to master the practical techniques of your job—that ingenious method you used to get air down to the fifth-shaft level is a sufficient case in point—and at departmental meetings I have invariably found your comments well taken and helpful. In fact, you will be interested to know that only last week I reported to Mr. Hutchins that from the technical point of view, he could not wish for a more able man to succeed to the position of chief engineer."

"That's very good indeed of you, John," cut in Rennalls with a smile of thanks. "My only worry now is how to live up to such a high recommendation."

"Of that I am quite sure," returned Baker, "especially if you can overcome the minus factor which I would like now to discuss with you. It is one that I have talked about before, so I'll come straight to the point. I have noticed that you are friendly and get on better with your fellow Barracanians than you do with Europeans. In point of fact, I had a complaint only yesterday from Mr. Jackson, who said you had been rude to him—and not for the first time, either.

"Matt, I am sure, there is no need for me to tell you how necessary it will be for you to get on well with expatriates because until the company has trained sufficient men of your caliber, Europeans are bound to occupy senior positions here in Barracania. All this is vital to your future interests, so can I help you in any way?"

While Baker was speaking on this theme, Rennalls had sat tensed in his chair, and it was some seconds before he replied. "It is quite extraordinary, isn't it, how one can convey an impression to others so at variance with what one intends? I can only assure you once again that my disputes with Jackson —and you may remember also Godson—have had nothing at all to do with the color of their skins. I promise you that if a Barracanian had behaved in an equally peremptory manner, I would have reacted in precisely the same way. And again, if I may say it within these four walls, I am sure I am not the only one who has found Jackson and Godson difficult. I could mention the names of several expatriates who have felt the same. However, I am really sorry to have created this impression of not being able to get on with Europeans—it is an entirely false one—and I quite realize that I must do all I can to correct it as quickly as possible. On your last point, regarding Europeans holding senior positions in the company for some time to come, I quite accept the situation. I know that Caribbean Bauxite—as they have been doing for many years now —will promote Barracanians as soon as their experience warrants it. And finally, I would like to assure you, John—and my father thinks the same too— that I am very happy in my work and hope to stay with the company for many years to come."

Rennalls had spoken earnestly and although not convinced by what he had heard, Baker did not think he could pursue the matter further except to say, "All right, Matt, my impression *may* be wrong, but I would like to remind you about the truth of that old saying, 'What is important is not what is true, but what is believed.' Let it rest at that."

But suddenly Baker knew that he didn't want to "let it rest at that." He was disappointed once again at not being able to "break through" to Rennalls and having yet again to listen to his bland denial that there was any racial predudice in his makeup. Baker, who had intended ending the interview at this point, decided to try another tack.

"To return for a moment to the 'plus and minus technique' I was telling you about just now, there is another plus factor I forgot to mention. I would like to congratulate you not only on the caliber of your work, but also on the ability you have shown in overcoming a challenge which I, as a European, have never had to meet. Continental Ore is, as you know, a typical commercial enterprise—admittedly a big one—which is a product of the economic and social environment of the United States and Western Europe. My ancestors have all been brought up in this environment for the past two or three hundred years, and I have therefore been able to live in a world in which commerce (as we know it today) has been part and parcel of my being. It has not been something revolutionary and new which has suddenly entered my life. In your case," Baker went on, "the situation is different because you and your forebears have only had some 50 or 60 years' experience of this commercial environment. You have had to face the challenge of bridging the gap between 50 and 200 or 300 years. Again, Matt, let me congratulate you—and people like you—once again on having so successfully overcome this particular hurdle. It is for this reason that I think the outlook for Barracania, and particularly for Caribbean Bauxite, is so bright."

Rennalls had listened intently and when Baker finished, replied, "Well, once again, John, I have to thank you for what you have said, and for my part I can only say that it is gratifying to know that my own personal effort has been so much appreciated. I hope that more people will soon come to think as you do."

There was a pause, and for a moment Baker thought hopefully that he was about to achieve his long-awaited "breakthrough," but Rennalls merely smiled back. The barrier remained unbreached. There remained some five minutes' cheerful conversation about the contrast between the Caribbean and Canadian climates and whether the West Indies had any hope of beating England in the Fifth Test before Baker drew the interview to a close. Although he was as far as ever from knowing the real Rennalls, he was nevertheless glad that the interview had run along in this friendly manner and, particularly, that it had ended on such a cheerful note.

This feeling, however, lasted only until the following morning. Baker had some farewells to make, so he arrived at the office considerably later than usual. He had no sooner sat down at his desk than his secretary walked into the room, a worried frown on her face. Her words came fast. "When I arrived this morning, I found Mr. Rennalls already waiting at my door. He seemed very angry and told me in quite a peremptory manner that he had a vital letter to dictate which must be sent off without any delay. He was so worked up that he couldn't keep still and kept pacing about the room, which is most unlike him. He wouldn't even wait to read what he had dictated. Just signed the page where he thought the letter would end. It has been distributed and your copy is in your 'in-tray.'"

Puzzled and feeling vaguely uneasy, Baker opened the envelope marked "Confidential" and read the following letter:

FROM: Assistant Engineer   14th August, 1969

TO: The Chief Engineer, Caribbean Bauxite Limited

ASSESSMENT OF INTERVIEW BETWEEN MESSRS.
BAKER AND RENNALLS

It has always been my practice to respect the advice given me by my seniors, so after our interview, I decided to give careful thought once again to its main points and so make sure that I had understood all that had been said. As I promised you at the time, I had every intention of putting your advice to the best effect.

It was not, therefore, until I had sat down quietly in my home yesterday evening to consider the interview objectively that its main purport became clear. Only then did the full enormity of what you said dawn on me. The more I thought about it, the more convinced I was that I had hit on the real truth—and the more furious I became.

With a facility in the English language which I--a poor
Barracanian--cannot hope to match, you had the audacity to
insult me (and through me every Barracanian worth his salt)
by claiming that our knowledge of modern living is only a
paltry 50 years old whilst yours goes back 200-300 years.
As if your materialistic environment could possibly be
compared with the spiritual values of our culture. I'll
have you know that if much of what I saw in London is
representative of your most boasted culture, I hope
fervently that it will never come to Barracania. By what
right do you have the effrontery to condescend to us? At
heart, all you Europeans think us barbarians, or, as you
say amongst yourselves, we are "just down from the trees."
    Far into the night I discussed this matter with my
father, and he is as disgusted as I. He agrees with me
that any company whose senior staff think as you do is no
place for any Barracanian proud of his culture and race--
so much for all the company "clap-trap" and specious
propaganda about regionalisation and Barracania for the
Barracanians.
    I feel ashamed and betrayed. Please accept this letter
as my resignation, which I wish to become effective
immediately.

c.c.   Production Manager
       Manager Director

STATE OF VERMONT, WELFARE COMMISSION, OLDCITY DISTRICT

Oldcity, Vermont, is a medium-sized city that has recently been going through economic hardship. Its primary industry is granite quarrying, which in recent years has not been doing very well. Fifteen years ago it was a bustling city with a number of textile and tanning factories, but they have departed to the South to take advantage of favorable wage rates so that they can compete with foreign companies. The skilled workers remaining in Oldcity are French, Welsh, and Irish. There has been something of an influx of Canadians and Indians recently. They are largely unskilled.

The granite industry has been getting sicker lately for two major reasons. First, there is a slack in construction; and second, use of granite for foundations is now being phased out, with the widespread changeover to use of cement and cinder blocks.

The population of the area is around 90,000. There are approximately 300 families on Aid for Families with Dependent Children (AFDC), 1000 families on general relief, and 4000 on Supplemental Security Income.

The governor, Francois LaPorte, was known as a liberal Democrat when he was elected, but is currently using welfare as a whipping boy. His frugal, hard-working background is preventing him from sympathizing with welfare recipients.

Georges Champlain, the present Oldcity District Director, is an M.S.W. from Boston College. He is bright, aggressive, and determined to make a name for himself by running a good organization. He has considered going into teaching and has just found out that he has been awarded a grant from the Dansforth Foundation to study welfare systems in Greece. Because he has some unused vacation time, he will be leaving immediately and is not likely to return to this position.

You are Hugh Smithies, and you grew up in the Yankee section of Burlington. Your father was killed in an automobile crash which also injured your mother, and she cannot work. You want to do the best possible job by the welfare clients with whom you empathize, since you were an AFDC child. You are not particularly comfortable about the governor's present stance on welfare.

You went to Dartmouth on scholarship, graduated *cum laude*, and have an M.S.W. from Simmons in Boston. You have ten years of welfare experience —six years as a case worker and four years as Champlain's administrative assistant. This morning, June 3, 1975, you have just learned that you will be taking over for Champlain. You have been invited to attend a state legislature hearing in Burlington at 1 P.M. and because of preparations for that, you have half an hour to empty out your in-basket and make some decisions as to what you should do. You should not expect to return in less than a week.

Below are some thumbnail sketches of key persons with whom you will have to deal in your new job.

Thomas LaFleur, the director of the Welfare Department for the State of Vermont, is 60 and rather conservative. He came up through the ranks, and received a B.A. degree in English from the University of Vermont nearly 40 years ago. He has appointed you Acting District Director and strongly indicated that if you do well, he will appoint you to the permanent position of District Director in one of the districts.

Irene Tomahawk is a politically active woman of 33. Although she has little formal education (the school on the reservation was not very good), she is very bright and has considerable political savvy. She has been on AFDC for three years because of her two small children. Her husband deserted her nearly four years ago.

Randolph Hurt is the very aggressive, conservative "muckraking" publisher of the Oldcity *Sentinel*. His motto is "Eternal Vigilance." Although he was a substantial contributor to LaPorte's Republican opponent, he hedged his bet by also contributing to LaPorte's campaign. Recently he and LaPorte have seemed to have arrived at a meeting of minds about welfare.

Estella Sympatico, a caseworker, has a recent M.S.W. degree from Boston College. She has a strong feeling for the needs of her clients.

Jacques Largesse, 35, was the governor's campaign manager. His mother, Brigitte, is 59, lives in $30,000 house, has a rental income of $4000, and has applied for old age assistance.

FiFi Tousignang, Georges Champlain's secretary, is 50ish and knows the ropes. She has been good at covering for Mr. Champlain during his absences, and she knows many of the caseworkers personally.

John Smith is an experienced caseworker with some administrative experience. He is 45 and conservative.

David Johnston, a legislator, is chairman of the welfare committee in the Vermont House of Representatives. He has been supportive of the types of reforms which the Welfare Department has been instituting.

Ginger Rogers is a caseworker who is a friend of yours. She is liberal, but has only two years of experience.

Remember: You are Hugh Smithies, Acting District Director of the Oldcity District. In 30 minutes you will leave for about a week to attend hearings on welfare reform bills presently in committee in the Vermont House of Representatives. Write out the action you decide to take on each item.

MEMORANDUM

FROM: Thomas LaFleur

TO: Hugh Smithies

SUBJECT: Appointment as Acting District Director

You are hereby appointed Acting District Director of the
Oldcity Welfare office. This appointment is to take effect
on June 3, 1975. Congratulations, you deserve the chance.

Action you would take:

Phone call from Jacques Largesse about his mother's asking whether
we couldn't "bend" the rules a bit and allow her to be eligible for
old age assistance.

Action you would take:

MEMORANDUM

TO: Hugh Smithies   Date: June 3, 1975

FROM: FiFi Tousignang

SUBJECT: Vacation

When we were planning this year's schedule, Mr. Champlain
agreed that I could have two weeks off, from June 4th to
June 18.   I have bought tickets on the Linblad "Majorca
Tour," and they are nontransferable and nonrefundable.
To date, I have been unable to find someone to cover your
office while I'm gone.

Action you would take:

MEMORANDUM

TO: Georges Champlain   Date: June 2, 1975

FROM: Thomas LaFleur

SUBJECT: HEW Compliance Review

HEW should be at Oldcity on June 9th for an office practices audit. They are looking for instances of fraud and
poor management practice as part of a statewide survey.
Please have things shipshape.

Action you would take:

MEMORANDUM

TO: Georges Champlain

FROM: Ginger Rogers

SUBJECT: Attendance at Summer   June 1, 1975
         Training Institute

This is just a reminder to tell you that I am scheduled
to go to the Social Work Training Institute at Brandeis
University on June 9th for a week. I will need someone
to look after my clients.

Action you would take:

Irene Tomahawk
11 Alcott Street
Oldcity, VT

Dear Mr. Champlain:

The newly established organization, Mothers Adamant Against
Discrimination, would like to have a meeting with you on
the week of June 2nd. You have tried to be helpful to us,
but before we go to Mr. LaFleur about the disgraceful
pittance we have been receiving from AFDC payments, we
thought we would talk with you about it.

Sincerely yours,

Irene Tomahawk

Action you would take:

Juanita Hernadez
12 Story Street
Oldcity, VT 05793

Dear Mr. Champlain,

I live next to Mr. Henrique Rodriquez, who is currently on welfare because he allegedly cannot find a job. A social worker, Estella Sympatico, has been spending nights there, and the neighborhood is scandalized.

I think this welfare nonsense has gone too far. Rodriquez was never any good, and now he is shacking up with the social worker and getting paid for it. I thought you would like to know.

Yours truly,

Juanita Hernadez

cc: Randolph Hurt
    Oldcity Sentinel

Action you would take:

STATE OF VERMONT

HOUSE OF REPRESENTATIVES

David Johnston

Mr. Hugh Smithies   May 30, 1975
Oldcity District Office
55 Joy Street
Oldcity, VT

Dear Hugh,

You have been very helpful in your suggestions for the new
flat grant proposal bill (HB 76-75). In case the bill runs
into problems in committee, we need you and a caseworker to
come up and explain how the bill would affect administration
and the actual recipients. We figure that the hearings will
take a week--two days in front of the committee, three days
in front of the House. Passage is pretty much ensured out
of the committee, but should things go sour later, we will
want to consider alternatives.

Cordially,

Dave

David Johnston

Action you would take:

MEMORANDUM

TO: Georges Champlain

FROM: John Smith

SUBJECT: Resignation June 3, 1975

For personal reasons I am submitting my resignation, effective June 5, 1975. I am sorry to do this with such short notice, but my wife is undergoing treatment for cancer, and I have accepted a position which allows me to spend more time at home.

Action you would take:

HERBERT ANGST
Director, Family & Children
Service Association
27 Adamson Road
Oldcity, Vermont

Mr. Georges Champlain   June 1, 1975
Department of Welfare
District Director, Oldcity Office
55 Joy Street
Oldcity, Vermont

Dear Georges:

At last we are getting under way with our regional health
and welfare council. We are planning to have a kickoff
luncheon at 1 p.m. on June 4th at the Holiday Inn to get
the council launched. Because you have been so identified
with the progressive elements in this county, it is imperative that you be there.

                    Cordially,

                    Herbert Angst

                    Herbert Angst

Action you would take:

MEMORANDUM

TO: All District Directors   May 29, 1975

FROM: Thomas LaFleur

SUBJECT: Data processing equipment down time

This is to alert you that the data processing unit will be down on June 2nd and 3rd for purpose of installing new core storage equipment. This means that on those days you will not be able to access any information on your terminals.

Action you would take:

SURVIVAL TRAINING

A bomber crew, in the last stages of their training, had generally worked well together. One of the reasons for this was that the pilot, the leader of the crew, was liked and respected both personally and professionally. Another reason was that all but one of the crew members came from the New York City area and had much in common. During off-duty hours, they sometimes went to local bars, had a few beers, and interacted well as a social group. However, one of the crew members, an enlisted man, was a social isolate. He came from the mountains of West Virginia, was unacquainted with urban life, and was prevented by his religious training from participating in such social activities as playing cards, dancing, and drinking. When the crew got together socially, therefore, this man was usually absent. He spent much of his off-duty time writing letters to his girl and to his parents and reading the Bible.

As part of their training, the crew had to go on survival training, which consisted of being dropped by helicopter into a remote area of the American Rockies with a minimum of equipment and being asked to find their way back to "civilization." In this situation, the mountaineer was in his element. The weather was cold and rainy, and he was the only person who could find dry moss and bark with which to start fires. He knew how to wade in mountain streams and reach down to feel for trout with his bare hands and flop trout out onto the bank of the stream. Gradually, he became the "leader" of the group. The other crew members followed his suggestions and as a result, passed their survival test with flying colors.

DISCUSSION QUESTIONS

1. Why did the mountaineer become the "leader"?
2. What does this tell us about leadership?
3. What effect might this have on his future relations with the rest of the crew?

TECHNOLOGY-INCORPORATED

ENGINEERING MANAGER (FRANK DOWNEY)

You are the engineering manager for a small technology company which you helped John Upton, the president, build from scratch. Most years have been good ones, but several months ago sales began to dip sharply, and the picture is now grim. You have already cut departmental expenses substantially, but unless business picks up shortly, you will have to lay off Mary Bright, your youngest, but most promising, engineer.

Several weeks ago, a potential customer in Chicago expressed interest in buying some new equipment from your company. The prospect is especially attractive to you because: (1) there is substantial engineering involved in the product, and (2) gaining the business will make it possible to retain Mary, whose special talents will be needed on the project. After concluding that this could be a breakthrough for the company, you got Upton's agreement to go ahead, but he stipulated that expenses were to be kept as low as possible.

At this point, you have made three trips to the customer's plant in Chicago, two of them in the last ten days. Although progress toward a signed contract has been slower and more painful than you anticipated, you are still optimistic about getting the business. Even though so much traveling is wearing you down and is causing problems here and at home, you have planned one final trip this weekend. You hope that this trip will bring you a firm order.

PRESIDENT (JOHN UPTON)

With the help of Frank Downey, the engineering manager, and a few others, you have built this company from scratch. When business began to turn down sharply a few months ago, the company's picture became bleak, and you fear that the company may not survive unless new production business is brought into the plant soon. Of course, you can't share such a fear, even with Frank. To avert disaster, you have been shaving expenses to the bone in all areas.

A few months ago, Frank made an enthusiastic pitch about some possible engineering contracts from a potential customer in Chicago. Though you strongly doubt his 80/20 odds on the chances for the business, you have given him the go-ahead to pursue it further with the customer. You are not overly

---

This case was written by John W. Lewis, III.

excited about the project. Although it will provide needed work in the engineering department, it will do little in the short term to increase production volume, which is your major problem.

After three expensive trips to Chicago (averaging $560 per trip) by Frank with little noticeable progress, your "gut" tells you that the effort to go after the business should be stopped. To do so would hurt Frank deeply, and this bothers you, but you would rather spend what little resources you have to cultivate new business in more fruitful areas. You'd like to convince him tactfully, yet forcefully, to give up the project.

YOUNG ENGINEER (MARY BRIGHT)

It is hard to believe this is the same company you joined two years ago. Then the place was humming with work, and because it was small, you have had an unusual opportunity to take on major responsibility for engineering projects. In fact, this prospect was the deciding factor in your accepting this job over the more attractive offers of larger organizations. Now you wonder whether it was the right move.

You boss is trying to get a new order from some outfit in Chicago, and the engineering involved on the product is right up your alley. Frank has said that if and when the contract comes through, you will have full responsibility for the project. After the idling you've been doing lately, almost anything to do would make you feel good.

At first, it looked like a shoo-in for getting the business, but Frank has visited the customer three times already, and nothing seems to be happening. Since the technology is not Frank's specialty, you feel sure he is not using a winning approach. Now he is going out there again tomorrow, and you are convinced you should go along to make the technical pitch and that this would clinch the order. There is a lot riding on that trip for you. If that (or some other) order is not obtained soon, you will not have a job.

ENGINEERING MANAGER'S SON (CHIP DOWNEY)

You are 17 and were just elected captain of the varsity basketball team, an achievement of which you are proud. During basketball season, your dad has been a regular fan at the games except when he had to make an occasional trip or became involved at the plant. Recently, however, things have changed. Two weeks ago, he missed the game and a half-time ceremony in your honor cooked up by the Boosters Club. No big deal, but it would have felt good to have him there. He was also out of town for last week's game, in which you scored 43 points, establishing a new varsity record at the school. This Saturday will be the toughest game of the season, and you were angered and hurt when your mom said he would have to be out of town again.

AUTHOR INDEX

Ackoff, R. L., 19, 20, 360–361
Adams, J. S., 77
Aguren, S., 374
Aldag, R., 349
Alderfer, C. P., 92–93, 99–100
Allen, J., 136
Andrews, I. R., 77, 230
Anthony, R. M., 107
Arendt, E., 188
Argyris, C., 54, 186–187, 367–368, 429
Arnoff, E. L., 19, 20
As, D., 229
Asch, S. E., 175
Athanassiades, J., 131, 152

Bakke, E., 56, 367
Bamforth, K., 88, 370–371
Baritz, L., 415
Barnes, L., 391
Barone, S., 299
Barrett, D., 137
Barsalous, J., 189
Bass, B., 36, 310
Bavelas, A., 137
Baver, R., 299–300
Beatty, R., 87
Beckhard, R., 215, 394, 401–403
Beer, M., 186, 210, 347, 377, 406
Behling, O., 103
Behrens, W., III, 358
Bell, C., Jr., 396–397
Benne, K. D., 177, 412
Bennis, W. G., 331, 392, 395–306, 409–412, 415, 438
Berne, E., 141
Bertalanffy, L., 37, 38
Bevan, R. V., 84
Binxen, P., 206–207
Birdwhistell, R., 132

Bjork, L., 375
Blake, R. R., 211–213, 235–237, 289, 413
Blanchard, K. H., 441
Blau, P., 316
Blood, M., 408
Blumberg, A., 412
Bouchard, T., 189
Boulding, K., 38, 39, 43, 356
Bowditch, J., 368
Bradford, L. P., 412
Bragg, J. F., 230
Brayfield, A., 96, 105, 286
Brown, D., 332
Brown, L., 395
Browning, C. J., 291–292
Bruner, J. S., 122
Buckley, W., 42, 430
Bucklow, M., 165
Burke, H., 135
Burns, T., 26, 305, 340
Burtt, R. D., 24, 226
Butterfield, D. A., 235
Byrd, R., 271

Calero, H., 133
Campbell, J. P., 103, 288, 412
Caplan, R., 261
Capwell, D., 96
Carrigan, S. B., 290–291, 412
Carroll, S., 266, 269, 270
Cartwright, D., 157
Chandler, M., 45
Child, J., 255, 334
Christoffel, W., 43, 364
Churchill, N., 33
Churchman, C. W., 19, 20
Clark, J. U., 427–428
Coch, L., 24, 225
Cooper, G., 413

Cooper, M. R., 229
Coska, L. S., 241
Cowan, J., 271
Crockett, W., 96, 105, 286
Cummings, L., 188
Cyert, R. M., 316–317

Dalton, M., 173
Dana, C., 82
Dansereau, F., 228
Daughen, J., 206–207
Davis, F., 133
Davis, K., 137, 149, 229, 367
Dean, R., 433
Deardon, J., 434–435
Delbecq, A., 189
Dermer, J., 105
Dible, D., 107–108
Dickson, W. J., 22
Diebold, J., 21, 59, 367
Dornbusch, S. M., 125
Downey, H. K., 244
Drauden, G., 189
Drucker, P., 266–267, 311, 334–335
Duncan, R. B., 305–306, 308
Dunnette, M. D., 103, 208, 412
Dutton, J. M., 165

Ellis, T., 255
Emshoff, J. R., 21, 356, 361–364
Etzioni, A., 15, 16, 77, 79, 278, 309, 434,
    441
Ewing, D. W., 230

Farmer, M. F., 291–292
Farris, G. F., 165, 235
Fast, J., 133
Fayol, H., 10, 13, 330
Feeney, E. J., 86
Fein, M., 408
Ferguson, C., 394–395
Fiedler, F., 28, 237–241, 272, 440–441
Fine, B. D., 186, 440
Fisch, G. G., 12, 272
Fitch, H. G., 165
Fleishman, E. A., 24, 226, 228, 391

Ford, D., 170
Ford, R., 403, 406–407
Forrester, J. W., 21, 58, 62, 356, 357–358
Frary, E., 300–301
Fredrickson, N., 289
French, J. R. P., 24, 220–223, 225, 229
French, W., 392, 396–397
Frohman, M., 390–391
Fry, F., 301

Gaddis, P., 61
Gaither, N., 359–360, 364
Gamboa, V. U., 87
Gellerman, S., 430
Gershenfeld, M., 173
Gerwin, D., 43, 364
Ghiselli, E., 225
Gibb, J. R., 138–139, 412
Goggin, W., 348
Golembiewski, R. T., 290–291, 412
Goodman, C. C., 122
Goodman, P., 141
Goodman, P. S., 303
Goodman, R. A., 308
Graen, G., 228
Greiner, L., 391, 430–432
Gruber, W. H., 360–361
Grunes, W. F., 123
Guest, R., 256
Gulick, L., 309, 330–331
Gullet, C. R., 87

Hackman, J., 405
Haire, M., 123
Hall, D. T., 92, 290
Hall, R. H., 19
Harris, E. F., 24, 226
Harris, W., 333
Harrison, R., 397–399
Hastorf, A. H., 125
Hay, R. D., 300–301
Hefferline, R., 141
Heisler, W., 401
Hellriegel, D., 287, 289–291
Henderson, L., 38
Hersey, P., 441

Herzberg, F., 96, 404, 406
Hickson, D., 174, 335
Hillier, F., 358
Hines, G. H., 229
Hinings, C., 335
Hinton, B. L., 97
Hoffman, L. R., 260
Holland, W., 262
Homans, G. C., 76, 167, 175
Hoover, J. J., 260
Horst, L., 387
House, R. J., 103, 242, 260, 267, 412
Hovey, D. D., 240
Huber, G., 188
Huegli, J., 255
Hulin, C., 408
Hulme, R. D., 84
Hundert, A., 347
Huse, E., 61, 186, 208, 210, 267–268,
    365–366, 377, 391, 406, 434, 465

Ilgen, D., 240
Israel, J., 229
Ivancevich, J., 270
Izraeli, D., 257

James, L., 287
James, M., 141–148
Janis, I., 176
Janson, R., 406
Jasinski, F. J., 58
Johnson, T. W., 244
Jones, A., 287
Jones, J., 179, 180–182
Jones, K., 261
Jones, T., 261
Jongeward, D., 141–148

Kahn, R., 42, 43, 225, 258, 260, 390
Kast, F., 43, 44
Katz, D., 42, 43, 56, 225
Katz, R. L., 315–316
Kaufman, F., 367
Kavanagh, M., 390–391
Kavcic, B., 229
Kay, E., 267–268

Kegan, D. L., 395
Keller, R., 262
Kerr, C., 304
Kerr, S., 226–227
Kilman, R., 437
King, D., 368
Kirk, H. D., 291–292
Klein, L., 370
Koch, J., 348
Koivumaki, J., 133
Kolb, D. A., 106, 182–183
Koontz, H., 18, 56, 279, 317
Korman, A. K., 226, 348
Knowles, H., 158, 177
Knowles, M., 158, 177
Krishnan, R., 230
Kukla, A., 95

Lane, J., 430
Latham, G. P., 87
Lawler, E. E., III, 18, 72, 92, 103, 186–
    187, 286, 288, 290
Lawrence, P. R., 28, 62, 228, 279, 304,
    305, 341–347, 349, 387, 404
Lawson, R., 124
Leavitt, H. J., 135, 224
Leavitt, T., 318–319
Lee, J., 414–415
Leitch, D., 391
Levinson, H., 270
Lewin, K., 52, 388–390, 412
Lewis, J. W., III, 413–414
Lieberman, G., 358
Likert, R., 26, 125–126, 157, 174, 198–
    199, 232–235, 331
Linden, E., 133
Lippitt, D., 158
Lippitt, R., 25, 227, 289, 388
Lischeron, J., 229–230
Litterer, J., 203–204
Litwin, G., 289
Locke, E. A., 98
Lorsch, J., 28, 62, 228, 279, 305,
    333, 341–347, 348, 387, 398,
    399, 440

Lundberg, C., 41
Lundgren, D., 188
Lynton, R. P., 307
Lyons, T., 260–261

McClelland, D., 93–95
McCroskey, J., 129
McGregor, D., 231–232, 267
McIntyre, J., 106, 182–183
MacKinnon, N. L., 408
Maier, N. R. F., 260
March, J. G., 24, 118, 316–317
Marcus, S., 347
Maslow, A., 88–91, 93
Mausner, B., 96
Marx, K., 291
Mead, W. R., 412
Meadows, D. H., 358
Meadows, D. L., 358
Meyer, M., 334
Miller, D., 158
Miller, E., 371–372
Miller, G., 135
Minami, T., 228
Mintzberg, H., 258
Mitchell, G. D., 291–292
Mitchell, T. R., 103–104, 243
Moberg, D., 348
Mockler, R. J., 436
Mohr, L. B., 230, 315
Mooney, J. D., 10, 12, 13
Moore, B. E., 303
Morriss, W., 387
Morse, J., 348, 398, 440
Mouton, J. S., 211, 213, 235, 289, 413
Mueller, R. A. H., 135
Mumo, H., 82
Munzenrider, R., 412
Murphy, C. J., 227
Murray, H. A., 124
Muzzy, R. E., 125
Myers, M. S., 97, 404

Nader, R., 220
Napier, R., 173
Nealey, S., 240

Nebeker, D., 243
Negandhi, A. R., 308
Nemiroff, P., 170
Nicolaou-Smokovitis, L., 298–299
Nierenberg, G., 133
Niles, J. S., 360–361
Nord, W. R., 85, 87, 98
Norsted, J., 374
Nougaim, K., 92

O'Brien, G., 240
Odiorne, G., 267
O'Donnell, C., 18, 56, 317
Oldham, G. R., 290, 405
Ondrack, D. A., 100
O'Reilly, A., 127
Orelius, S., 404

Palmer, W. J., 226, 245
Pasmore, W., 170
Passell, P., 358
Paul, W. J., 406
Pearse, R. F., 492
Pedalino, E., 87
Perls, F., 141
Perrow, C., 25, 28, 29, 79, 86, 87, 303–305, 312–314, 336–339, 440
Peters, R., 228
Peterson, R., 96, 291
Pfeiffer, J., 179, 180–182, 308–309
Pieters, G., 347
Poiret, M., 133
Ponder, O., 255–256
Porter, L. M., 91
Porter, L. W., 18, 286
Price, L., 465
Pugh, D., 335
Purdy, K., 406

Quick, T., 185
Quinn, R., 258, 260

Raia, A., 269
Raven, B., 220–223
Read, W. H., 260
Reiley, A. C., 10

Reimann, B. C., 308
Reisen, R., 87
Rice, A., 165, 371
Richardson, S. A., 125
Ridgway, V., 270
Rimler, G., 391
Rivett, P., 360–361
Rizzo, J., 260
Robbins, W., 206–207
Roberts, M., 358
Robertson, K. B., 406
Roche, W. J., 407
Roethlisberger, F. J., 22, 130, 131, 139
Rogers, C. R., 131, 139, 415
Ronders, J., 358
Rosenbaum, W. E., 77
Rosenthal, J., 297
Rosenthal, R., 124–125
Rosenzwieg, J., 43, 44
Ross, L., 358
Roy, E., 166
Rubenowitz, S., 378, 412–413, 432–433
Rubin, I., 95, 106, 182–183
Rus, V., 229

Sank, L., 225
Sashkin, M., 229, 387, 390–391
Sathe, V., 334, 349
Sayles, L., 45, 59, 257, 262–263
Schein, E., 78, 93, 106, 172, 208, 409–
    412, 426–427, 432, 441
Schneider, B., 287
Schneier, C., 87
Schriesheim, C., 226–227
Schuler, R., 262
Scott, R., 79
Scott, W. G., 18
Seiler, J., 55
Serrin, W., 80
Sheats, P., 177
Shepard, H., 211, 213
Sheridan, J. E., 244
Shetty, Y. K., 29
Shiflett, S. C., 240, 241
Siegel, A., 304
Simon, H. A., 24, 118, 360–361

Sims, H. P., Jr., 244
Skinner, B. F., 84–85, 415
Slocum, J. W., Jr., 244, 287, 289–291
Sneck, J., 258, 260
Snyder, R. A., 287
Snyderman, B., 96
Sokolik, S., 430
Sperling, K., 416–417
Stalker, G. M., 26, 305, 340
Starke, F. A., 103
Stinger, R., 289
Storey, R., 349
Stewart, R., 257–258
Stinson, J. E., 241, 244, 261
Stogdill, R. M., 227
Stone, D., 303
Stouffer, S. A., 167
Strauss, G., 256–257
Strayer, J. R., 82
Susman, G., 304
Suttle, J., 92
Szilagyi, A. D., Jr., 244, 262

Tannenbaum, A. S., 229, 320
Tanofsky, R., 348
Taylor, F. W., 17, 83, 404
Thompson, E., 199–202, 207
Thompson, J. D., 29, 40, 340, 364–365
Tosi, H., 269, 270, 349
Tosi, W., Jr., 266
Tracey, L., 241
Trefethen, F. N., 19
Trist, E. L., 88, 370–371
Tscheulin, D., 226
Tschirgi, H., 255
Tuckman, B., 170
Turner, A., 256, 304, 404
Turner, C., 335
Turquet, P., 174
Tushman, M., 416

Urwick, L., 330–331

Valenzi, E. R., 78
Van DeVen, A., 189
VanOver, H. C., 299

Van Zelst, R., 368
Vinake, W. E., 74, 75
Vreeland, R. S., 125
Vroom, V. H., 92, 103, 440

Wahba, M. A., 103
Wainer, H., 95
Walker, A., 333
Walker, C., 256
Wall, T., 229–230
Walton, R. E., 165, 377, 415–416, 432
Wanous, J. P., 105
Watson, J., 388
Weber, M., 16, 84, 331
Weick, K. E., Jr., 41, 43, 44, 103, 288
Weiner, B., 95

Weir, T., 135
Westley, B., 388
Wheatly, B., 273
White, R. K., 25, 227, 289
Whyte, M., 205
Whyte, W. F., 163, 393
Wiener, N., 49
Wolfe, E., 258, 260
Wood, M. T., 229
Woodward, J., 26, 227–228, 335–336
Worthy, J. V., 18

Yukl, G. A., 87

Zand, D., 185–186
Zenger, J., 158

SUBJECT INDEX

Accelerated pace of change, 293–302
Achievement motivation, 93
Action research, 391–395
Adaptive-coping cycle, 432
Affective/affiliation, 87
Alderfer's model, 93–99
  existence, 93–99
  growth, 93
  relatedness, 99
Alienation, 291–292
Allocation, 360
Ameslan, 133
Assembly line, 376
Autonomous work groups, 372–377
Autonomy, 166, 405

Balance, 50, 317
  fixed point, 50
  forces affecting, 50
  optimal, 317
  steady state, 50
Behavior, structuring, 228

Behavioral-modification technique, 87
Behavioral-pattern theories, 225
Boundary, 49–50, 165
Boundary-spanning activities, 255
Building blocks, 7
Bureaucracy, 14–16, 331

Centralization, 334
Change, 29, 386–395, 428, 463
  and action research, 391–395
  approach to an organization, 463
  managed, 386–387
  organizational, 428
  planned, 388–391
  refreezing, 388
  unfreezing, 388
Change agents, 413
Characteristics of competent organiza-
    tion, 426–428
Characteristics of manager of the future,
    492–494
Characteristics of successful change at-
    tempts, 430–432

Classical model, 344
Classification of O.D. interventions, 395
Climate, 138, 139, 287–292
  and alienation, 291–292
  defensive, 138
  defined, 287
  distinction from satisfaction, 287–288
  research finding, 288–292
  supportive, 139
Coercive power, 223, 224
Cohesion, 173
Collateral organization, 185
Communications, 128–150, 465
  effects of climate, 138
  factors affecting, 129–140
  influence of group structure, 136
  interpretation, 128
  physical location, 136
Competent organization, 426–428
  characteristics of, 426–428
  problems in attaining and maintain-
    ing, 427–428
Competition, 264, 360
Complexity of systems, 45
Concern with personal work style, 397,
  407–409
Conflict, 202, 206, 346, 347
  confronting, 347
  edicting, 346
  need for change, 206
  smoothing, 346
Confrontation meeting, 400–403
Confronting, 347
Confusion in management thought, 279
Contingency theory, of leadership, 28,
  237–241
  of organizational improvement,
    341–349
    differentiation, 341–343
    integration, 343–347
  of organizational structure, 28
Contrived systems, 42
Control systems, 318
Cooperation, intergroup, 198
Coordination, 330
Coordinative principle, 13

Core job dimensions, 404–407
Cybernetic approval, 43

Decision centers, 436
Decision-making process, 357
Decoding, 128
Defensive climate, 138
Delphi technique, 188
Dependent variable, 288
Depth, dimensions of, 397
Development group, 372
Deviation-amplifying forces, 50–53, 490
Deviation-reducing forces, 50–53, 490
Diagnosis, 389, 392–394
Different systems perspectives, 55–60
Differentiation, 206, 341–343
Dissatisfiers, 97
Division of labor, 12–13, 330, 334
Dynamic-expectancy models of motiva-
  tional systems, 100

Economic/machine, 82
Edicting, 346
Effect of environment, 340
Effect of organizational size, 334
Effect of technology, 336
Efficiency, 375
Ego state, 141, 142
  Adult, 142
  Child, 141
  Parent, 141
Emery Air Freight, 86
Encoding, 128
Entry, 389
Environment, 29, 60, 292–302
  defined, 292–293
  rate of change, 293–302
Environment-organization interface,
  302–308
  macro issues, 302–305
  micro issues, 305–308
Equilibrium, 45, 50, 55, 429
  dynamic, 45
  optimal, 55
  status, 45

ERG theory, 93
Ethics and values, 415
Evaluating and controlling individual
    performance, 398
Evaluation of management thought, 328
Exchange, 76–80
Expectancy, 100, 121
Expert power, 220
Exploded myths of management,
    271–273
Extrinsic rewards, 101

Feedback, 49, 135, 182, 405
Filters, 128
Flow perspective, changes in, 477
Force and coercion model, 81–82
Force-field analysis, 52–63, 429
Formal group, 161
Formal organizations, major approaches
    to, 329
Formalization, 334
Functional principle, 13
Functions of a manager, 253, 262–266

Game, 146
General systems theory, 37–38
Goals, categories of, 312–315
    derived, 314
    output, 312
    societal, 312
    system, 312
Group, 159–191
    ad hoc, 169
    autonomous, 230
    cohesion, 173–176
    conformity, 172
    creative individualism, 172
    decision-making, 181
    definition, 160
    established, 170
    feelings, 182
    formal, 161
    formation of, 161–168
    forming, 170
    history, 169–170
    influence, 181

informal, 161
internal structure, 168
leadership, 168–169
maintenance functions, 181
membership, 182
norming, 170
norms, 171–173, 182
observation, 180–183
operation, 168–176
outputs, 187
participation, 180
performing, 170
process, 180
rebellion, 172
as a system, 159–160
self-serving activities, 177
storming, 170
structural-design viewpoint, 163
task activities, 177
task functions, 181
temporary, 163
work-flow perspective, 163
Group-building activities, 177
Group leader, official, 168
Growth/hygiene, 97
Growth-open system model, 88
Growth seekers, 97–98

Halo effect, 123
Hawthorne studies, 22–24
Historical functions of management, 329
Hovey and Beard company, 393
Human organizations, characteristics of,
    44
Human perspectives, 22–25, 59, 60
    changes in, 465
    environment, 60
    group, 60
    individual, 59
    organization, 60
Human relations school, 22

Income, financial, 84
    psychological, 84
Independent variable, 288
Individual goals, 74

Individual organizational approach, 332
Influence, 220–224
Informal organization, 367–369
Information-feedback theory, 357
Initiating structure, 228
Input, 47
Input models, 21
Instrumentality, 106
Integrated approach to O.D., 433–442
Integrated perspective of management, 25
Integration, 341, 343–346
  of approaches, 60
  of the three perspectives, 443
Integrative devices, 344
Interacting group, 189
Interaction: individual and organization, 76–80
Interdependence, 199
  pooled, 199
  reciprocal, 199
  sequential, 199
Intergroup, 198, 203–207
  competition over means, 204–205
  conflict, 207–210
    confrontation mode, 210
    edicting mode, 210
    effects of, 207–210
    reducing of, 210–213
    smoothing mode, 210
  need for change, 206–207
  relationships, 198
  status incongruity, 205–206
  win-lose, 203
Intervening variable, 288
Intrapersonal relationships, 397, 409–413
Intrinsic rewards, 101
Introducing internal growth and change ability, 413–415
Inventory, 360
Isolation, 292

Job-centered organization, 435
Job diagnostic survey, 406
Job enlargement, 404
Job enrichment, 403–407, 470

Job satisfaction, 291
Job tension, 262
Johari Window, 179

Kalmar, 374–375
Knowledge explosion, 293

Labor force, changing composition of, 296
Laboratory training, 409–413
Leader-member relations, 238
Leadership, 168, 224–245
  contingency theory, 237–241
  path-goal theories, 241–245
  style, 24–25, 235, 482
    authoritarian, 24
    changes in, 482
    democratic, 25
    dimensions, 235
    laissez-faire, 25
Legitimate power, 220
Legitimization, 302
Levels of systems, 38–39
Line and staff, 10, 11, 18, 330
Linkage mechanisms, 307
Linking pin, 27, 199

Macro approach, 29, 488–491
  to organizational behavior, 29
Macro issues in environment, 302–305
Maintenance seekers, 98
Management by objectives, 266–271
Management development, using systems theory, 442
Management information systems, 365–367
Management style, 28–29, 482
Manager, 254, 262–266, 271–273, 492–494
  activities, 264
  defined, 254
  functions of, 262–266
  myths of, 271–273
  of the future, 492–494
Managerial Grid, 235–237
Manifest versus latent content, 130

Maslow's theory, 89–90
Mathematical models, 356–365
  limitations, 361–365
Matrix organization, 186
Mechanistic structure, 26, 340
Mechanistic system, 305
Micro approach to organizational be-
  havior, 7, 488–489
Micro issues in environment, 305–308
Model, 21, 28
  input, 21
  output, 21
  reality, 80
Modern human resource management,
  414
Motivation, 74, 80, 95, 106
  implications for the manager, 106
Motivational models, 81–99, 100–105
  affective affiliation, 87–88
  economic machine, 82–87
  force and coercion, 81–82
  growth-open system, 88–89
  VIE theory, 100–105
Motivational systems, static-content
  models, 80
Motivation-hygiene model, 95
Multiplicity of purposes, functions, objectives, 53–55
Mutual goal-setting, 469
Myths about O.D., 416–417

Need for achievement, 93
Need hierarchy, 88
Noise, 129
Nominal group, 188
Non-Linear Systems, 445–450
Nonverbal communication, 132
Normative rewards, 78
Normlessness, 291
Norms, 172
  pivotal, 172
  relevant, 172

Objectives, 309–320, 315–317
  as compromise, 315–316

deviation-amplifying, 317
deviation-reducing, 317
multiple, 311–320
"official" versus "actual," 315–317
organizational, 309–320
Observing group process, 180–183
Open versus closed systems, 38–40, 49
Operant conditioning model, 84
Operations analysis, 397, 400–403
Operations research, 19–20, 358–361
Optimal balance, 429
Organic structure, 26
Organic system, 305
Organization, 29, 55, 297, 489–490
  definition as a social system, 55
  social responsibilities, 299
  theory and practice, 29
  total system, 489–490
Organization development, 25, 394–417,
  450, 491
  approaches to, 395–400
  assumptions, 387
  concern with personal work style, 397,
    407–409
  defined, 394
  diagnosis in, 392–394
  evaluating and controlling individual
    performance and behavior, 397,
    403–407
  individualized approaches, 440
  interpersonal relationship, 397, 409–
    413
  levels of intervention, 397, 400
  myths about, 416–417
  objectives, 386
  operations analysis, 397, 400–
    403
  problem in, 414–416
  results in Plant X, 450
  school, 25
  team building, 407–409
  using systems theory, 433
Organizational behavior, 293
  macro, 293
  micro, 293
Organizational change, 428, 430

Organizational competence, 490
Organizational design, 333, 434
  dependent variable, 333
  using systems theory, 434
Organizational effectiveness, 278
Organizational efficiency, 278
Organizational-environment research,
  308
Organizational improvement, defined,
  279–280
Organizational planning and objectives,
  309–320
Organizational structure, 335–337, 340–
  341
  environment, 340–341
  mechanistic, 340
  organic, 340
  size, 334–335
  technology, 335–337
Organizations, multiple objectives, 311–
  320
Output, 47
Output models, 21
Overload, 135

Path-goal theory, 241–245
Perception, 119–129, 206
  perceptual bases, 127
  perceptual data, manipulation, 122–
    123
  perceptual differences, 206
  perceptual set, 129
  perceptual variation, 122
Performance, 74
Personality-attribute theories, 224
Physical versus social systems, 42–43
Planned change, 387, 388–391
Planning, organizational, 309–320
Pooled interdependence, 199
Position power, 238
Power, 15, 220–223
  coercive, 223
  expert, 221
  illegitimate, 15
  legitimate, 15, 220

referent, 221
reward, 223
Powerlessness, 291
Problems in O.D., 414–416
Problems with operations research, 363
Problems with planned change, 391
Process, 42, 176
Process observatory, 408
Production group, 372
Productivity, 18–19, 187
Projection, 123
Psychological climate, 289
Psychological contract, 76–77, 488
Psychosocial contract, 298

Quality of working life, 430
Queuing, 360

Rate of diffusion of new ideas, 432–433
Reactions to role conflict, and ambiguity,
  259
Reciprocal interdependence, 200
Reducing intergroup conflict, 210–213
Referent power, 221
Replacement, 360
Reward power, 223
Role, 258
  ambiguity, 258
  conflict, 258
Routing, 360

Saab, 80, 374–376
Satisfaction, 18, 189
  and productivity, 105
Satisfiers, 97
Scaler chain, 13
Scaler principle, 13
Scientific management school, 16–17
Scouting, 388
Search, 336, 360
Selective perception, 125
Self-actualizing model, 88
Self-estrangement, 292
Sensation, 119–123
Sentiments, 130
Sequencing, 360

Sequential interdependence, 199
Sickla works, 377
Simple-complex dimension, 305
Situational model of motivation, 106
Skill variety, 405
Smoothing, 346
Social audit, 300
Social group, 159
Social responsibility, 297–301
Social systems, 45
Sociotechnical approaches, 491
Sociotechnical systems, 165, 369–378
Span of control, 18
Stabilization, 390
Static-dynamic dimension, 305
Static equilibrium, 45
Status incongruity, 205
Stereotyping, 123
Stroking, 145
Structural-design perspective, 6, 57, 480
    changes in, 480
Structuralist school, 14–16
Structure, 11, 26, 42
    mechanistic, 26
    organic, 26
Structuring behavior, 228
Styles of leadership, 28–29
    authoritarian, 28
    democratic, 28–29
Subsystem, 41
Successful change attempts, character-
    istics of, 430–432
Supersystem, 435
Supportive climate, 139
System, 37–46, 159–160
    closed, 39–40
    group as a, 159–160
    open, 40
    precise terminology, 43
System dynamics, 21, 357–358
Systems approach, 7, 9, 39–43
    advantages of, 39–40
    difficulties in measurement, 43
    disadvantages of, 42
    organizational improvement, 9
Systems level of analysis, 41–42

Systems theory, an integrated approach
    to O.D., 433–442

Task forces, 186, 438
Task identity, 405
Task significance, 405
Task structure, 238
Task system, 165
Tavistock Institute, 370–372
Team building, 407–409
Temporary groups, 183, 438
Termination, 390
T-groups, 25
Theory X, 231
    assumptions, 428
Theory Y, 231
Time-and-motion studies, 17
Time structuring, 146
Total organizational system, 443
Traditional theory, 330
Transactional analysis, 141–148
Transformation, 47

Universal principles of management
    school, 10–13
Use of systems theory in Plant X, 450–
    454
Uses of operations research, 359

Valence, 100
VIE theory, 101–105
    limitations, 103–104
Volatility, 349
Volvo, 80, 374–375

Win-lose, 203
Work-area redesign, 374–375
Work-flow analysis, benefits, 435
Work-flow perspective, 6, 19–21, 58–59
    capital equipment, 59
    information flow, 58
    material flow, 58
    money flow, 59
    order flow, 59
Work-planning, 483